THE OXFORD

Essential Guide to
Ideas & Issues
of the Bible

Oxford Titles Available
from Berkley Books

THE OXFORD

Essential Guide to
Ideas & Issues
of the Bible

Edited by

BRUCE M. METZGER
MICHAEL D. COOGAN

BERKLEY BOOKS, NEW YORK

Advisers
Jo Ann Hackett
Barbara Geller Nathanson   William H. Propp
Philip Sellew

THE OXFORD ESSENTIAL GUIDE TO
IDEAS & ISSUES OF THE BIBLE

A Berkley Book / published by arrangement with
Oxford University Press, Inc.

PRINTING HISTORY
Oxford University Press, Inc., hardcover edition / November 2001
Berkley mass-market edition / July 2002

Visit our website at
www.penguinputnam.com

ISBN: 0-425-18661-X

BERKLEY®
Berkley Books are published by The Berkley Publishing Group,
a division of Penguin Putnam Inc.,
375 Hudson Street, New York, New York 10014.
BERKLEY and the "B" design
are trademarks belonging to Penguin Putnam Inc.

PRINTED IN THE UNITED STATES OF AMERICA

10 9 8 7 6 5 4 3 2 1

CONTENTS

The Oxford Essential Guide to Ideas & Issues of the Bible

INTRODUCTION

For nearly two millennia, the Bible has been the cardinal text for Judaism and Christianity. Its stories and characters are part of both the repertoire of Western literature and the vocabulary of educated women and men. It is, however, more than a collection of ancient tales. Even before a canonical list of books considered sacred scripture or holy writ was established, the writings we now call the Bible were considered normative: they laid down the essential principles of how human beings should deal with God and with each other. The practice of quoting from, and alluding to, earlier texts as authoritative is found within the Bible itself and has continued unabated in subsequent Jewish and Christian writings. At the same time, the Bible has also been formative; subsequent generations of believers have seen themselves as descended from, and in continuity with, those to whom God had spoken and for whom he had acted definitively in the past, and the recital of those words and events has been instrumental in shaping the religious communities of succeeding generations. The Bible has thus had an immeasurable influence on Judaism and Christianity, on the cultures of which they have formed a part, and on all those traditions in some ways derived from them, such as Islam.

Although the word Bible means "book," and the Bible has been treated as a single book for much of its history,

it is in fact many books, an anthology of the literatures of ancient Israel, and, for Christians, also of earliest Christianity. The Bible thus speaks with many voices, and, from the time of its emergence as an authoritative sacred text, readers and interpreters have noted its many repetitions, inconsistencies, and contradictions. Since the Enlightenment especially, critical consideration of the Bible—that is, study of it insofar as possible without presuppositions—has irreversibly affected what may be called the "precritical" understanding of the Bible as simply a unified text, God's eternal, infallible, and complete word. Discoveries of ancient manuscripts (such as the Dead Sea Scrolls) and of literatures contemporaneous with, or earlier than, those preserved in the Bible (such as stories of creation and the Flood from ancient Babylonia and the gospels of Thomas and Philip from Nag Hammadi in Egypt), as well as innumerable archaeological finds, have deepened our understanding of the Bible and the historical and cultural contexts in which its constituent parts were written. This new understanding of the Bible has resulted in continuous scholarly attention and popular interest.

The Oxford Essential Guide to Ideas & Issues of the Bible is derived from *The Oxford Companion to the Bible* (1993). For this book we have selected entries from the original work, without duplicating those found in *The Oxford Essential Guide to People & Places of the Bible* (2001), under a number of headings:

- Concepts and institutions found in the Bible, including afterlife and immortality, faith, hope, and love, circumcision, the Sabbath, and the second coming of Christ;
- Key events and realities of daily life in biblical times, such as the Exodus, the Flood, feasts and festivals, and animals and plants;
- Issues of contemporary attention and controversy, including abortion, homosexuality, marriage, nature and ecology, and feminism;
- Important ancient sources that shed light on the Bible, such as the Dead Sea Scrolls;
- The history, theory, and practice of the interpretation of the Bible, in entries such as the history of interpretation, quotations of the Jewish scriptures in the New Testament, fundamentalism, computers and the Bible, and archaeology;
- The influence of the Bible in Jewish, Christian, and Muslim traditions, in entries on topics such as African American traditions, art, literature, music, and popular culture;
- The fascinating story of how the Bible was produced and how it continues to be disseminated, found in entries such as writing in antiquity, translations, printing and publishing, and illustrated Bibles.

The *Guide* provides up-to-date discussions of these topics by modern scholars, bringing to bear the most recent findings of archaeologists and current research methods from such disciplines as anthropology, sociology, and literary criticism. Like the *Companion*, the *Guide* is consciously pluralistic, and its contributors encompass a wide spectrum of intellectual and creedal perspectives. They represent the international community of scholars, coming from some dozen countries, on five continents. No attempt has been made by the editors to produce any dogmatic unanimity; readers should not be surprised to find differing interpretations in different entries. Contributors have been urged to present their own scholarly views while noting diverse perspectives. In general, the articles aim to present the consensus of interpretation, or its lack, attained by the most recent scholarship, and to avoid partisanship and polemic.

The *Guide* does not aim to be an encyclopedia or encyclopedic dictionary, and is not intended as a substitute either for the Bible itself or for a concordance to the Bible. Quotations from the Bible have deliberately been kept to a minimum, and biblical references are illustrative, not exhaustive.

Within the scope of one volume, then, the *Guide* is a reliable resource for what the Bible says and how scholars have interpreted biblical traditions. The *Guide* is an authoritative and comprehensive reference for a wide audience, including general readers; students and teachers in high schools, colleges, seminaries, and divinity schools; rabbis, ministers, and religious educators; participants in religious education and Bible study programs; and scholars in the variety of disciplines for which the Bible is in some way pertinent.

Use of the Guide

Cross-references. The *Guide* is arranged alphabetically. Extensive cross-references direct the reader to related entries; these cross-references are of three types:

1. Within an entry, the first occurrence of a name, word, or phrase that has its own entry is marked with an asterisk (*).

2. When a topic treated in an entry or a related topic is discussed elsewhere in the volume, the italicized words *see* or *see also* refer the reader to the appropriate entry term(s).

3. "Blind entries," that is, entry terms that have no accompanying text but are terms that the reader might expect to find discussed, appear alphabetically in the volume and refer to the entries where the topics are actually treated. Thus, the blind entry **Decalogue** refers reader to **Ten Commandments.**

Index. Further investigation of particular topics is made possible by a detailed index, which provides page references for pertinent subjects and for ancient and modern proper names.

Bibliography. At the end of the volume, there is an extensive annotated bibliography, which will enable readers to explore in more detail topics covered in the *Guide*. The bibliography is divided into categories for easier use, such as the history, geography, and archaeology of biblical times; anthologies of nonbiblical texts; critical and popular introductions to the Bible; reference works; surveys of the history of interpretation; and methodologies used in biblical scholarship.

The translation used in the *Guide* is *The New Revised Standard Version* (NRSV), the most recent authoritative translation of the Bible into English, produced by an interfaith committee of scholars and published in 1990. The renderings of the NRSV are the basis for entry titles. Within individual entries, contributors have on occasion used other published translations or their own; in these cases, differences from the NRSV are noted. Following increasingly frequent practice, the term "Hebrew Bible" is used in preference to "Old Testament," and the abbreviations BCE (Before the Common Era) and CE (Common Era) are used in place of BC and AD.

Acknowledgments

In preparing this *Guide* we have had indispensable assistance from the staff of the trade reference department at Oxford University Press. We especially thank Catherine Carter, who guided the *Guide* from idea through production. We are most grateful, of course, to the contributors, whose expert contributions are the essence of the volume; their names are listed after this introduction.

Bruce M. Metzger
Michael D. Coogan
June 2001

DIRECTORY OF CONTRIBUTORS

ELIZABETH ACHTEMEIER, Adjunct Professor of Bible and Homiletics, Union Theological Seminary, Richmond, Virginia

SUSAN ACKERMAN, Assistant Professor of Religion, Dartmouth College, Hanover, New Hampshire

PHILIP S. ALEXANDER, Nathan Laski Professor of Post-Biblical Jewish Literature, University of Manchester, England

BERNHARD W. ANDERSON, Adjunct Professor of Old Testament Theology, Boston University, Massachusetts

HECTOR IGNACIO AVALOS, Carolina Postdoctoral Fellow, Departments of Religious Studies and Anthropology, University of North Carolina at Chapel Hill

E. BADIAN, John Moors Cabot Professor of History, Harvard University, Cambridge, Massachusetts

KENNETH E. BAILEY, Research Professor of Middle Eastern New Testament Studies, The Ecumenical Institute, Jerusalem, Israel

PHILIP L. BARLOW, Assistant Professor of Theological Studies, Hanover College, Indiana

WILLIAM H. BARNES, Associate Professor of Biblical Studies, Southeastern College

of the Assemblies of God, Lakeland, Florida

JAMES BARR, Professor of Hebrew Bible, Vanderbilt University, Nashville, Tennessee; Regius Professor of Hebrew, Emeritus, University of Oxford, England

JUDITH R. BASKIN, Chair, Department of Judaic Studies, State University of New York at Albany

WILLIAM A. BEARDSLEE, Charles Howard Chandler Professor of Religion, Emeritus, Emory University, Atlanta, Georgia

CHRISTOPHER T. BEGG, Assistant Professor of Theology, Catholic University of America, Washington, D.C.

G. E. BENTLEY, Jr., Professor of English, University of Toronto, Ontario, Canada

JERRY H. BENTLEY, Professor of History, University of Hawai'i at Manoa

ADELE BERLIN, Professor of Hebrew, University of Maryland at College Park

OTTO BETZ, Professor and Lecturer of New Testament and Jewish Studies, Retired, Eberhard-Karls-Universität, Tübingen, Germany

M. H. BLACK, Fellow, Clare Hall, University of Cambridge; Former Publisher of Cambridge University Press, England

ROBERT G. BRATCHER, Translation Consultant, United Bible Societies, New York, New York

PAUL L. BREMER, Professor of Biblical Studies, Reformed Bible College, Grand Rapids, Michigan

S. P. BROCK, Reader in Syriac Studies, University of Oxford, England

BERNADETTE J. BROOTEN, Kraft-Hiatt Chair of Christian Studies, Near Eastern and Judaic Studies Department, Brandeis University, Waltham, Massachusetts

GEORGE WESLEY BUCHANAN, Professor of New Testament, Emeritus, Wesley Theological Seminary, Washington, D.C.

EDWARD F. CAMPBELL, Francis A. McGaw Professor of Old Testament, McCormick Theological Seminary, Chicago, Illinois

BRUCE D. CHILTON, Barnard Iddings Bell Professor of Religion, Bard College, Annandale-on-Hudson, New York

DAVID J. A. CLINES, Professor of Biblical Studies, University of Sheffield, England

DONALD COGGAN, Archbishop of Canterbury, England, 1974–1980

H. J. BERNARD COMBRINK, Professor of New Testament, University of Stellenbosch, South Africa

EDGAR W. CONRAD, Reader in Studies in Religion, University of Queensland, Australia

DEMETRIOS J. CONSTANTELOS, Charles Cooper Townsend Sr. Distinguished Professor of History and Religious Studies, Richard Stockton State College of New Jersey, Pomona

MICHAEL D. COOGAN, Professor of Religious Studies, Stonehill College, North Easton, Massachusetts

JAMES I. COOK, Anton Biemolt Professor of New Testament, Western Theological Seminary, Holland, Michigan

ROBIN C. COVER, Dallas, Texas

JAMES L. CRENSHAW, Professor of Old Testament, Duke University, Durham, North Carolina

ROBERT C. DENTAN, Professor of Old Testament, Emeritus, General Theological Seminary, New York, New York

J. DUNCAN M. DERRETT, Professor of Oriental Laws, Emeritus, University of London, England

T. KEITH DIX, Assistant Professor, Department of Classical Studies, University of North Carolina at Greensboro

CARL S. EHRLICH, Professor, Hochschule für Jüdische Studien, Heidelberg, Germany

BARRY L. EICHLER, Associate Professor of Assyriology, University of Pennsylvania, Philadelphia

J. A. EMERTON, Regius Professor of Hebrew, and Fellow, St. John's College, University of Cambridge, England

DAVID EWERT, President, Mennonite Brethren Bible College, Winnipeg, Manitoba, Canada

GILLIAN FEELEY-HARNIK, Professor of Anthropology, The Johns Hopkins University, Baltimore, Maryland

JOSEPH A. FITZMYER, S.J., Professor of Biblical Studies, Emeritus, Catholic University of America, Washington, D.C.

DANIEL E. FLEMING, Assistant Professor, New York University, New York

PAULA FREDRIKSEN, Professor, Department of Religion, Boston University, Massachusetts

EDWIN D. FREED, Professor of Biblical Literature and Religion, Emeritus, Gettysburg College, Pennsylvania

ERNEST S. FRERICHS, Professor of Judaic Studies, Brown University, Providence, Rhode Island

KARLFRIED FROEHLICH, Benjamin W. Warfield Professor of Ecclesiastical History, Emeritus, Princeton Theological Seminary, New Jersey

REGINALD H. FULLER, Professor Emeritus, Virginia Theological Seminary, Alexandria, Virginia

RUSSELL FULLER, Assistant Professor of Theological and Religious Studies, University of San Diego, California

FRANCIS T. GIGNAC, S.J., Professor of Biblical Greek, Catholic University of America, Washington, D.C.

THOMAS FRANCIS GLASSON, Lecturer in New Testament Studies, Retired, University of London, England

ANDRÉ L. GODDU, Director, Program in the History and Philosophy of Science, Stonehill College, North Easton, Massachusetts

EDWIN M. GOOD, Professor of Religious Studies, Emeritus, Stanford University, California

CYRUS H. GORDON, Joseph and Esther Foster Professor of Mediterranean Studies, Emeritus, Brandeis University, Waltham, Massachusetts; Director, Center for Ebla Research, New York University, New York

ROBERT P. GORDON, Lecturer in New Testament, University of Cambridge, England

JOSEPH A. GREENE, Curator of Publications, Semitic Museum, Harvard University, Cambridge, Massachusetts

ROBERT A. GUELICH, Professor of Theology, Fuller Theological Seminary, Pasadena, California, *deceased*

JO ANN HACKETT, Professor, Department of Near Eastern Languages and Civilizations, Harvard University, Cambridge, Massachusetts

WILLIAM W. HALLO, The William W. Laffan Professor of Assyriology and Babylonian Literature, and Curator, Babylonian Collection, Yale University, New Haven, Connecticut

BARUCH HALPERN, Professor of History, Pennsylvania State University, University Park

RAYMOND HAMMER, Professor of Theology, Emeritus, Rikkyō University, Tokyo, Japan; Former Director, Bible Reading Fellowship, London, England

ANTHONY TYRRELL HANSON, Professor of Theology, Emeritus, University of Hull, England, *deceased*

DOUGLAS R. A. HARE, William F. Orr Professor of New Testament, Pittsburgh Theological Seminary, Pennsylvania

WALTER HARRELSON, Distinguished Professor of Hebrew Bible, Emeritus, Vanderbilt University, Nashville, Tennessee

GERALD F. HAWTHORNE, Professor of Greek, Wheaton College, Illinois

JOHN H. HAYES, Professor of Old Testament, Candler School of Theology, Emory University, Atlanta, Georgia

PETER D. HEINEGG, Professor of English, Union College, Schenectady, New York

GEORGE S. HENDRY, Professor of Systematic Theology, Emeritus, Princeton Theological Seminary, New Jersey

THEODORE HIEBERT, Associate Professor of Hebrew Bible/Old Testament, Harvard Divinity School, Cambridge, Massachusetts

DAVID HILL, Reader in Biblical Studies, Retired, University of Sheffield, England

LATON E. HOLMGREN, General Secretary, Retired, American Bible Society, New York, New York

J. L. HOULDEN, Professor of Theology, King's College, University of London, England

J. KEIR HOWARD, Diocese of Wellington Institute of Theology, New Zealand

EDWARD HULMES, Spalding Professorial Fellow, World Religions, Department of Theology, University of Durham, England

ALAN JACOBS, Associate Professor of English, Wheaton College, Illinois

JOHN FREDERICK JANSEN, Professor of New Testament, Emeritus, Austin Presbyterian Theological Seminary, Texas, *deceased*

DAVID LYLE JEFFREY, Professor of English Language and Literature, University of Ottawa, Ontario, Canada

HOWARD CLARK KEE, Aurelio Professor of Biblical Studies, Emeritus, Boston University, Massachusetts; Senior Research Fellow, Religious Studies, University of Pennsylvania, Philadelphia

DOUGLAS A. KNIGHT, Professor of Hebrew Bible, Vanderbilt University, Nashville, Tennessee

GEORGE A. F. KNIGHT, Professor of Old Testament Studies and Semitic Languages, Emeritus, and former Principal, Pacific Theological College, Fiji

DONALD KRAUS, Senior Editor, Oxford University Press, New York, New York

WILLIAM SANFORD LASOR, Professor, Fuller Theological Seminary, Pasadena, California, *deceased*

SOPHIE LAWS, Fellow, Religion and History, Regent's College, London, England

A. R. C. LEANEY, Professor of Christian Theology, Emeritus, Nottingham University, England

MARY JOAN WINN LEITH, Lecturer, Department of Literature, Massachusetts Institute of Technology, Cambridge

BARUCH A. LEVINE, Professor of Hebrew and Judaic Studies, New York University, New York

THEODORE J. LEWIS, Associate Professor of Hebrew Bible and Semitic Languages, University of Georgia, Athens

I-JIN LOH, Coordinator of Asia Opportunity Program and Translation Consultant, United Bible Societies, Asia Pacific Region, Taipei, Taiwan

JOHANNES P. LOUW, Professor of Greek, University of Pretoria, South Africa

FRANCIS LYALL, Dean of Faculty and Professor of Public Law, University of Aberdeen, Scotland

GIORA MANOR, Editor, *Israel Dance Quarterly;* Adviser, *Israel Dance Library*, Jerusalem, Israel

STEPHEN A. MARINI, Professor of Religion, Wellesley College, Massachusetts

I. HOWARD MARSHALL, Professor of New Testament Exegesis, University of Aberdeen, Scotland

RALPH P. MARTIN, Professor of Biblical Studies, University of Sheffield, England

GENE MCAFEE, Harvard Divinity School, Cambridge, Massachusetts

SAMUEL A. MEIER, Associate Professor of Hebrew and Comparative Semitics, Ohio State University, Columbus

WILLIAM W. MEISSNER, S.J., University Professor of Psychoanalysis, Boston College; Training and Supervising Analyst, Boston Psychoanalytic Institute, Massachusetts

BRUCE M. METZGER, George L. Collard Professor of New Testament Language and Literature, Emeritus, Princeton Theological Seminary, New Jersey

CAROL L. MEYERS, Professor of Biblical Studies and Archaeology, Duke University, Durham, North Carolina

ERIC M. MEYERS, Professor of Bible and Judaic Studies, Duke University, Durham, North Carolina

ALAN MILLARD, Rankin Professor of Hebrew and Ancient Semitic Languages, University of Liverpool, England

PAUL S. MINEAR, Winkley Professor of Biblical Theology, Emeritus, Yale University, New Haven, Connecticut

LEON MORRIS, Former Principal, Ridley College, Melbourne, Australia

PAUL G. MOSCA, Professor, Department of Religious Studies, University of British Columbia, Vancouver, Canada

LUCETTA MOWRY, Professor Emerita, Department of Religion, Wellesley College, Massachusetts

JOHN MUDDIMAN, Fellow, New Testament Studies, Mansfield College, University of Oxford, England

MOGENS MÜLLER, Professor of New Testament Exegesis, Københavns Universitet, Denmark

BARBARA GELLER NATHANSON, Professor, Department of Religion, Wellesley College, Massachusetts

FRANS NEIRYNCK, Professor of New Testament, Katholieke Universiteit, Leuven, Belgium

WILLIAM B. NELSON, Jr., Professor, Department of Religious Studies, Westmont College, Santa Barbara, California

EUGENE A. NIDA, Translations Consultant, American Bible Society, New York, New York

MARK A. NOLL, Professor of History, Wheaton College, Illinois

ROBERT NORTH, S.J., Editor, *Elenchus* of *Biblica;* Professor of Archaeology, Emeritus, Pontificio Istituto Biblico, Rome, Italy

ANDREW J. OVERMAN, Professor, Department of Religion and Classics, University of Rochester, New York

JOSEPH PATHRAPANKAL, C.M.I., Professor of New Testament and Theology, Dharmaran College, Bangalore, India

WAYNE T. PITARD, Associate Professor, Program for Study of Religion, University of Illinois at Urbana-Champaign

JAMES H. PLATT, Denver, Colorado

J. R. PORTER, Professor of Theology, Emeritus, University of Exeter, England

SCOTT F. PRELLER, Christian Science Practitioner, Andover, Massachusetts

WILLIAM H. PROPP, Associate Professor of Near Eastern Languages and History, University of California at San Diego

BO REICKE, Universität Basel, Switzerland, *deceased*

ERROLL F. RHODES, Editorial and Non-English Manager, Department of Translations and Scripture Resources, American Bible Society, New York, New York

HARALD RIESENFELD, Professor of Biblical Exegesis, Emeritus, Uppsala Universitet, Sweden

J. W. ROGERSON, Professor and Head, Department of Biblical Studies, University of Sheffield, England

DAVID T. RUNIA, C. J. de Vogel Professor Extraordinarius in Ancient Philosophy, Rijksuniversiteit Utrecht, the Netherlands

D. S. RUSSEL, Baptist Union of Great Britain, Bristol

LELAND RYKEN, Professor of English, Wheaton College, Illinois

BRUCE E. RYSKAMP, Corporate Vice-President, Zondervan Corporation, Grand Rapids, Michigan

LEOPOLD SABOURIN, S.J., Professor of Sacred Scripture, Emeritus, Pontificio Istituto Orientale, Rome, Italy

KATHARINE DOOB SAKENFELD, William Albright Eisenberger Professor of Old Testament Literature, Princeton Theological Seminary, New Jersey

JAMES A. SANDERS, Professor of Biblical Studies, School of Theology at Claremont, California

NAHUM M. SARNA, Dora Golding Professor of Biblical Studies, Emeritus, Brandeis University, Waltham Massachusetts; General Editor, Jewish Publication Society Torah Commentary

DANIEL N. SCHOWALTER, Associate Professor, Department of Religion, Carthage College, Kenosha, Wisconsin

EILEEN SCHULLER, Professor, Department of Religious Studies, McMaster University, Hamilton, Ontario, Canada

PHILIP SELLEW, Associate Professor, Department of Classical and Near Eastern Studies, University of Minnesota, Minneapolis

C. L. SEOW, Associate Professor of Old Testament, Princeton Theological Seminary, New Jersey

DRORAH O'DONNELL SETEL, Seattle, Washington

GREGORY SHAW, Professor, Department of Religious Studies, Stonehill College, North Easton, Massachusetts

MICHAL SHEKEL, Rabbi, Jewish Center of Sussex County, New Jersey

DANIEL J. SIMUNDSON, Professor of Old Testament, and Dean of Academic Affairs, Luther Northwestern Theological Seminary, St. Paul, Minnesota

J. A. SOGGIN, Professor of Hebrew Language and Literature, Università di Roma, Italy

WALTER F. SPECHT, Chair, Department of Religion, Retired, Loma Linda University, California

HENDRIK C. SPYKERBOER, Professor of Old Testament Studies, Trinity Theological College, Brisbane, Australia

LYNN STANLEY, Manufacturing Controller, Oxford University Press, New York, New York

ROBERT H. STEIN, Professor of New Testament, Bethel Theological Seminary, St. Paul, Minnesota

KRISTER STENDAHL, Professor of Christian Studies, Brandeis University, Waltham, Massachusetts

PHILIP STERN, White Plains, New York

ROBERT STOOPS, Associate Professor, Department of Liberal Studies, Western Washington University, Bellingham

JOHN N. SUGGIT, Professor Emeritus, Rhodes University, Grahamstown, South Africa

SARAH J. TANZER, Professor, McCormick Theological Seminary, Chicago, Illinois

ANTHONY C. THISELTON, Professor of Christian Theology, and Head, Department of Christian Theology, University of Nottingham, England

DEREK J. TIDBALL, Secretary for Mission and Evangelism, Baptist Union of Great Britain, Marcham, England

JOHN TINSLEY, Professor of Theology, University of Leeds, 1962–1976; Bishop of Bristol, 1976–1985, England, *deceased*

EMANUEL TOV, Hebrew University, Jerusalem, Israel

STEPHEN H. TRAVIS, Vice-Principal and Lecturer in New Testament, St. John's College, Nottingham, England

ALLISON A. TRITES, John Payzant Distinguished Professor of Biblical Studies, Acadia University, Wolfville, Nova Scotia, Canada

ETIENNE TROCMÉ, Professor of New Testament, Université des Sciences Humaines de Strasbourg, France

DAVID H. VAN DAALEN, Minister, United Reformed Church, Huntingdon, England

GERRIT E. VAN DER MERWE, General Secretary, Emeritus, Bible Society of South Africa, Cape Town

ALLEN D. VERHEY, Director, Institute of Religion, Texas Medical Center, Houston, Texas

BEN ZION WACHOLDER, Solomon B. Freehof Professor of Jewish Law and Practice, Hebrew Union College, Cincinnati, Ohio

GEOFFREY WAINWRIGHT, Robert E. Cushman Professor of Christian Theology, Duke University, Durham, North Carolina

GORDON J. WENHAM, Senior Lecturer in Religious Studies, Cheltenham and Gloucester College of Higher Education, England

CLAUS WESTERMANN, Professor Emeritus, Universität Heidelberg, Germany

RICHARD E. WHITAKER, Information Research Specialist, Speer Library, Princeton Theological Seminary, New Jersey

JOHN L. WHITE, Professor of New Testament and Christian Origins, Loyola University of Chicago, Illinois

SIDNIE ANN WHITE, Assistant Professor of Religion, Albright College, Reading, Pennsylvania

TIMOTHY M. WILLIS, Professor, Religion Division, Pepperdine University, Malibu, California

ROBERT McL. WILSON, Professor of Biblical Criticism, Emeritus, University of St. Andrews, Scotland

VINCENT L. WIMBUSH, Professor of New Testament and Christian Origins, Union Theological Seminary, New York, New York

DAVID F. WRIGHT, Senior Lecturer in Ecclesiastical History, and former Dean of Faculty of Divinity, University of Edinburgh, Scotland

EDWIN M. YAMAUCHI, Professor of History, Miami University, Oxford, Ohio

JOHN ZIESLER, Reader in Theology, University of Bristol, England

ABBREVIATIONS

Biblical Citations

Chapter (chap.) and verse (v.) are separated by a period, and when a verse is subdivided, letters are used following the verse number; thus, Gen. 3.4a = the book of Genesis, chap. 3 v. 4, the first part. Biblical books are abbreviated in parenthetical references as follows:

Acts	Acts of the Apostles	Josh.	Joshua
Amos	Amos	Jude	Jude
Bar.	Baruch	Judg.	Judges
Bel and the Dragon	Bel and the Dragon	Jth.	Judith
1 Chron.	1 Chronicles	1 Kings	1 Kings
2 Chron.	2 Chronicles	2 Kings	2 Kings
Col.	Colossians	Lam.	Lamentations
1 Cor.	1 Corinthians	Lev.	Leviticus
2 Cor.	2 Corinthians	Luke	Luke
Dan.	Daniel	1 Macc.	1 Maccabees
Deut.	Deuteronomy	2 Macc.	2 Maccabees
Eccles.	Ecclesiastes	3 Macc.	3 Maccabees
Eph.	Ephesians	4 Macc.	4 Maccabees
1 Esd.	1 Esdras	Mal.	Malachi
2 Esd.	2 Esdras	Mark	Mark
Esther	Esther	Matt.	Mathew
Exod.	Exodus	Mic.	Micah
Ezek.	Ezekiel	Nah.	Nahum
Ezra	Ezra	Neh.	Nehemiah
Gal.	Galatians	Num.	Numbers
Hab.	Habakkuk	Obad.	Obadiah
Hag.	Haggai	1 Pet.	1 Peter
Heb.	Hebrews	2 Pet.	2 Peter
Hos.	Hosea	Phil.	Philippians
Isa.	Isaiah	Philem.	Philemon
James	James	Pr. of Man.	Prayer of Manasseh
Jer.	Jeremiah	Prov.	Proverbs
Job	Job	Ps(s).	Psalm(s)
Joel	Joel	Rev.	Revelation
John	Gospel of John	Rom.	Romans
1 John	1 John	Ruth	Ruth
2 John	2 John	1 Sam.	1 Samuel
3 John	3 John	2 Sam.	2 Samuel
Jon.	Jonah	Sir.	Sirach

Song of Sol.	Song of Solomon	Titus	Titus
Sus.	Susanna	Tob.	Tobit
1 Thess.	1 Thessalonians	Wisd. of Solomon	Wisdom of Solomon
2 Thess.	2 Thessalonians	Zech.	Zechariah
1 Tim.	1 Timothy	Zeph.	Zephaniah
2 Tim.	2 Timothy		

Rabbinic Literature

To distinguish tractates with the same name, the letters *m.* (Mishnah), *t.* (Tosepta), *b.* (Babylonian Talmud), and *y.* (Jerusalem Talmud) are used before the name of the tractate.

'Abod. Zar.	'Aboda Zara	Nez.	Neziqin
'Abot R. Nat.	'Abot de Rabbi Nathan	Nid.	Niddah
B. Bat.	Baba Batra	Pesah.	Pesahim
Ber.	Berakot	Qoh. Rab.	Qohelet Rabbah
'Erub	'Erubin	Šabb.	Šabbat
Gen. Rab.	Genesis Rabbah	Sanh.	Sanhedrin
Ḥag.	Hagiga	Sukk.	Sukkot
Ketub.	Ketubot	Ta'an.	Ta'anit
Mek.	Mekilta	Yad.	Yadayim
Mid.	Middot	Zebah.	Zebahim
Midr.	Midrash		

Other Ancient Literature

Adv. haer.	Irenaeus, *Adversus haereses*	1QIsaᵇ	Qumran Cave 1, Isaiah, second copy
Ag. Ap.	Josephus, *Against Apion*		
Ant.	Josephus, *Antiquities*	1QM	Qumran Cave 1, *Milḥāmāh (War Scroll)*
Apol.	Justin, *Apology*		
Bapt.	Tertullian, *De baptismo*	1QpHab	Qumran Cave 1, *Pesher on Habakkuk*
CD	Cairo Geniza, Damascus Document	1QS	Qumran Cave 1, *Serek hayyahad (Rule of the Community, Manual of Discipline*
1 Clem.	1 Clement		
De Dec.	Philo, *De Decalogo*		
De spec. leg.	Philo, *De specialibus legibus*	4Q246	Qumran Cave 4, No. 246
Did.	Didache	4Q503–509	Qumran Cave 4, Nos. 503–509
Ep.	Cyprian, *Epistles*	4QDeutᵃ	Qumran Cave 4, Deuteronomy, first copy
Exhort. Chast.	Tertullian, *De exhortatione castitatis*	4QMMT	Qumran Cave 4, *Miqsat Ma'aseh Torah*
Geog.	Strabo, *Geographica*		
GT	Gospel of Thomas	4QpNah	Qumran Cave 4, *Pesher on Nahum*
Haer.	Epiphanius, *Haereses*		
Hist.	Polybius, *Histories*	11QMelch	Qumran Cave 11, Melchizedek text
Hist. eccl.	Eusebius, *Historia ecclesiastica*		
Instit. Rhetor.	Quintilian, *Institution of Rhetoric*	11QTemple	Qumran Cave 11, *Temple Scroll*
Jov.	Jerome, *Against Jovianum*	Praescr.	Tertullian, *De praescriptione haereticorum*
Leg. ad Gaiiem	Philo, *Legatio ad Gaium*	T. Naph.	*Testament of Naphtali*
1Q34	Qumran Cave 1, No. 34	War	Josephus, *Jewish War*
1QH	Qumran Cave 1, *Hôdāyôt (Thanksgiving Hymns)*		

Other Abbreviations

ABS	American Bible Society	M	Special Matthean material
AV	Authorized Version	MB	Middle Bronze
BCE	Before the Common Era (the equivalent of BC)	MSS	Manuscripts
		MT	Masoretic Text
BCP	Book of Common Prayer	NBSS	National Bible Society of Scotland
BFPS	British and Foreign Bible Society	NEB	New English Bible
ca.	circa	NJV	New Jewish Version
CE	Common Era (the equivalent of AD)	NRSV	New Revised Standard Version
chap(s).	chapter(s)	P	Priestly source in the Pentateuch
D	Deuteronomist source in the Pentateuch	par.	parallel(s), used when two or more passages have essentially the same material, especially in the synoptic Gospels
E	Elohist source in the Pentateuch		
EB	Early Bronze		
GNB	Good News Bible	Q	from German *Quelle,* "source," designating the hypothetical common source used by Matthew and Luke
Grk.	Greek		
H	Holiness Code		
Hebr.	Hebrew		
J	Yahwist source in the Pentateuch	REB	Revised English Bible
KJV	King James Version	RSV	Revised Standard Version
L	Special Lucan material	RV	Revised Version
Lat.	Latin	TDH	Two Document Hypothesis
LB	Late Bronze	UBS	United Bible Societies
LXX	Septuagint	v(v).	verse(s)

TRANSLITERATIONS

HEBREW AND ARAMAIC

Transliteration	Pronunciation		Letter
Consonants			
ʾ	(now generally not pronounced; originally a glottal stop)		א
b	b (also sometimes v)		ב
g	g		ג
d	d		ד
h	h		ה
w	v (originally w)		ו
z	z		ז
ḥ	(not found in English; approximately like German -ch)		ח
ṭ	t (originally an emphatic t)		ט
y	y		י
k	k (also sometimes like German -ch)		כ,ך
l	l		ל
m	m		מ,ם
n	n		נ,ן
s	s		ס
ʿ	(now generally not pronounced; originally a voiced guttural)		ע
p	p (also sometimes f)		פ,ף
ṣ	ts		צ,ץ
q	k (originally an emphatic k)		ק
r	r		ר
ś	s		שׂ
š	sh		שׁ
t	t		ת

Transliteration	Pronunciation	Hebrew Name	Symbol
Vowels			
ă	father	ḥāṭēp pataḥ	־ֲ
a	father	pataḥ	־ַ
ā	father	qāmeṣ	־ָ

Transliteration	Pronunciation	Hebrew Name	Symbol
â	father	qāmeṣ followed by hē	◌ָ
ĕ	petition	šĕwā, or ḥāṭēp sĕgôl	◌ְ ◌ֱ
e	bet	sĕgôl	◌ֶ
ē	they	ṣērê	◌ֵ
ê	they	ṣērê or sĕgôl followed by yôd	◌ֵי ◌ֶי
i, ī	machine	ḥîreq	◌ִ
î	machine	ḥîreq followed by yôd	◌ִי
ŏ	hope	ḥāṭēp qāmeṣ	◌ֳ
o	hope	qāmeṣ ḥāṭûp	◌ָ
o, ō	hope	ḥōlem	◌ֹ
ô	hope	ḥōlem with wāw	וֹ
u, ū	sure	qibbûṣ	◌ֻ
û	sure	šûreq	וּ

Other Semitic

ḥ	(not found in English; approximately like German -ch)

GREEK

Transliteration	Pronunciation	Letter
a	a (father)	α
b	b	β
g	g	γ
d	d	δ
e	e (bet)	ε
z	z	ζ
ē	e (they)	η
th	th (thing)	θ
i	i (bit or machine)	ι
k	k	κ
l	l	λ
m	m	μ
n	n	ν
x	ks	ξ
o	o (off)	ο
p	p	π
r	r	ρ
s	s	σ, ς
t	t	τ
y, u	u (like German ü), or part of a diphthong	υ
ph	ph (phase)	φ
ch	ch (like German -ch)	χ
ps	ps	ψ
ō	o (hope)	ω
h	h (hope): rough breathing	ʽ

A

ABBA. The word for "my father" or "the father." This *Aramaic word appears three times in the New Testament, followed by a translation into Greek: once in Jesus' prayer in Gethsemane (Mark 14.36) and twice in the letters of Paul, where it is an ecstatic cry of believers in *prayer (Rom. 8.15; Gal. 4.6).

The prayers of Jesus in the Gospels regularly address God as "Father"; probably the Aramaic word ʾabbāʾ lies behind the Greek word for father in these prayers. Christian liturgical usage, which drew on reflection about the relation between the "Son" and the "Father," may have shaped the language of some or even all of these passages.

Originally, *abba* was probably a child's word, but it had become an accepted way of speaking to or about one's father. It expresses a close relation to God on the part of Jesus, a relation that is also expected of the disciples, who were told by Jesus to pray, "Our Father . . ." (Matt. 6.9; *see* Lord's Prayer). Some scholars have held that the relation between God and Jesus as father and child, which this language expresses, was highly distinctive and original with Jesus, but others point to similar language in Jewish prayers of the period.

In early Christianity, this Aramaic word was retained as an address to God in prayer even after Greek had become the language of worship. It expressed the newly found relation to God as father, a relationship assured by the presence of the Spirit. The original setting for this exclamation may have been *baptism, but it probably also functioned as a response to preaching.

The word also underlies the English word "abbot" (cf. French *abbé*), a monastic title originating in Syriac Christian usage.   *William A. Beardslee*

ABORTION. Abortion as such is not discussed in the Bible, so any explanation of why it is not legislated or commented on is speculative. One possibility is that the cultural preoccupation with procreation evident in the Hebrew Bible ruled out consideration of terminating pregnancy. Archaeological evidence indicates that in ancient Israel the infant mortality rate was as high as fifty percent. It is also possible that, given the diet and living conditions at the time, female fertility was low. Male control of reproduction and a belief that numerous descendants are a sign of divine blessing are also found in the Bible. These factors support the view that abortion would not have been common.

Alternatively, it can be argued that abortion was practiced without censure. Many women died in childbirth, a strong incentive to avoid carrying a pregnancy to term. Biblical legislation, as in Leviticus 27.3–7, indicates that the lives of children as well as women were not valued as highly as those of adult men, while no value whatsoever was given to a child under the age of one month. There is no indication that a fetus had any status.

A key text for examining ancient Israelite attitudes is Exodus 21.22–25: "When people who are fighting injure a pregnant woman so that there is a miscarriage, and yet no further harm follows, the one responsible shall be fined what the woman's husband demands, paying as much as the judges determine. If any harm follows, then you shall give life for life, eye for eye, tooth for tooth, hand for hand, foot for foot, burn for burn, wound for wound, stripe for stripe." Several observations can be made about this passage.

The Hebrew text at v. 22 literally reads "and there is no harm," implying that contrary to current sensibilities, the miscarriage itself was not considered serious injury. The monetary judgment given to the woman's husband indicates that the woman's experience of the miscarriage is not of significance, and that the damage is considered one to property rather than to human life. This latter observation is further supported by the contrast with the penalties for harm to the woman herself.

Several texts have been influential in late discussions of abortion. Both Jewish and Christian traditions have regarded the divine command "Be fruitful and multiply" (Gen. 1.28) as demanding a high rate of procreation incompatible with abortion in a non-life-threatening situation. Like Leviticus 27, later rabbinic teachings differentiated between life under and over the age of one month, while relying on biblical injunctions to respect and choose life in determining that abortions could be performed to preserve the life of the mother. Christians opposed to abortion have referred to Luke 1.41–44 as evidence that a child is cognizant in the uterus.   *Drorah O'Donnell Setel*

ABYSS. The abyss, or bottomless depth, appears in biblical tradition in several related senses. In the Hebrew Bible, *tĕhôm* (NRSV: "the deep") usually refers to the primordial waters upon which the ordered world of God's creation floats. Related terms are used to describe the depth of springs, the sea, or the earth. The abyss can also stand for the depth of the underworld understood as the realm of the dead. Because of its associations with *chaos and death, the abyss is identified in postbiblical Jewish literature as the realm, or more often prison, of rebellious spirits. This usage appears in the New Testament in Luke 8.31 and throughout the book of Revelation (NRSV: "bottomless pit").

See also Hell.   *Robert Stoops*

ADULTERY. Adultery is voluntary sexual intercourse by either a married man or a married woman with someone other than his or her spouse. In ancient Israel, both the man and the woman would be considered guilty. It was prohibited by both versions of the *Ten Commandments as well as by the Holiness Code of Leviticus. According to Leviticus 20.10, which prohibits adultery with the wife of one's *neighbor, the penalty for this crime was death. The mode of execution was probably the same as that specified in Deuteronomy 22.23–24, which deals with the case of a young woman, a virgin, who was engaged to be married but met and had sexual intercourse with another man in the city. Both were guilty of adultery and were to be taken to the gate and stoned to death. This punishment is also assumed in the New Testament story of Jesus and the young woman accused of adultery, where Jesus says, "Let anyone among you who is without sin be the first to throw a stone at her" (John 8.7).

Adultery was probably considered sufficient grounds for *divorce in ancient Israel. This is implied in Deuteronomy 24.1, an introduction to the law concerned with remarriage, where one interpretation of the phrase "something objectionable" has been that it refers to adultery on the part of the woman and that only this behavior justified a divorce. If a man suspected his wife of adultery but did not have any evidence, he could require her to submit to trial by ordeal, which would both determine her guilt or innocence and incorporate a physical punishment in the case of her guilt. In the Gospels, adultery is the only acceptable reason for divorce, although some scholars think that the phrase "except on the ground of unchastity" (Matt. 5.32) is an addition to earlier tradition.

See also Marriage; Sex.

Russell Fuller

AFRICAN AMERICAN TRADITIONS AND THE BIBLE.

Introduction: Reading the Bible = Reading the Self and the World. African Americans' engagement of the Bible is complex and dynamic. It is a fascinating historical drama, beginning with the Africans' involuntary arrival in the New World. But as sign of the creativity and adaptability of the Africans and of the evocative power of the Bible, the drama continues to the present day, notwithstanding the complexity and controversies of intervening periods. Thus, there is in African Americans' engagement of the Bible potential not only for an interpretive history of their readings as a history of their collective self-understandings, visions, hopes, challenges, and agenda, but also—because of their singular experience at least in the United States—for significant, even singular challenges for critical biblical interpretation.

First Reading: Awe and Fear— Initial Negotiation of the Bible and the New World. From the beginning of their captive experience in what became the United States, Africans were confronted with the missionizing efforts of whites to convert slaves to the religions of the slavers. These religions or denominations—especially Anglicanism—were for the most part the establishment religions of the landed gentry; they did not appeal much to the slaves. Numerous testimonies from clerics, teachers, and missionaries of the eighteenth century register frustration and shock over the Africans' lack of understanding of and uneasy socialization into their religious cultures. The formality and the literacy presupposed by these cultures—in catechetical training and Bible study, for example—clearly frustrated the easy or enthusiastic "conversion" of the African masses. Not only were the Africans, on the whole, according to custom and law, deemed (and made) incapable of meeting the presupposed literacy requirements, but they did not seem emotionally or psychically disposed toward the customary sensibilities and orientations of the establishment religions. These missionary efforts were not very successful.

The Bible did have a place in these initial missionary efforts. But that place was not primary: its presence was indirect, embedded within catechetical materials, or muted and domesticated within doctrinaire or catechetical, and mostly formal, preaching. But it needs to be stressed that the Africans' introduction to "the Bible," or "the scriptures," by whatever agency, would have been difficult, according to available evidence. Cultures steeped in oral traditions at first generally find frightful and absurd the concept of a religion and religious power circumscribed by a book, then certainly difficult to accept and fathom; later, perhaps, they may find it awesome and fascinating.

Second Reading: Critique and Accommodation. It was not until the late eighteenth century, with the growth of nonestablishment, evangelical, and free-church and camp-meeting revivalistic movements in the North and South, that African Americans began to encounter and engage the Bible on a large scale and on a more intimate basis, minus the bewilderment. Finding themselves directly appealed to by the new evangelicals and revivalists in vivid, emotional biblical language, and noting that nearly the entire white world explained its power and authority by appeal to the Bible, the Africans could hardly fail to be drawn closer to it. They embraced the Bible, transforming it from the Book of the religion of the whites—whether aristocratic slavers or lower-class exhorters—into a source of psychic-spiritual power and of hope, a source of inspiration for learning and affirmation, and into a language capable of articulating strong hopes and veiling stinging critique. The narratives of the Hebrew Bible and the stories of Jesus, the New Testament's persecuted but victorious one, captured the collective African imagination. This was the beginning of the African American historical encounter with the Bible, and the foundation for the cultivation of the phenomenological, sociopolitical, and cultural presupposition(s) for its different, even conflicting historical readings of the Bible to come.

From the late eighteenth century through the end of slavery, the period of Reconstruction, and into the modern Civil Rights era of the 1950s and 1960s, African Americans continued their engagement with or readings of the Bible.

These readings reflected major dynamics in the self-understandings and orientations of a major segment of African American culture, if not the majority. The founding of the independent churches and denominations beginning in the late eighteenth century historically postdates and logically presupposes the cultivation of certain identifiable African diaspora religious worldviews and orientations. The Bible played a fundamental role in the cultivation and articulation of such worldviews and orientations. It was discovered as a type of language world full of drama and proclamation such that the slave or freed person could be provided with certain powerful rhetorics and visions that fired the imagination.

The most popular reading of the Bible was one in which the Protestant *canon provided the rhetorics and visions of prophetic critique, the blueprints for "racial uplift," and social and political peace (integration) as the ultimate goal, in addition to steps toward personal salvation. This reading of the Bible reflected the dominant sociopolitical views and orientations among African Americans in this period. The "reading"—both of the Bible and of American culture—expressed considerable ambivalence: it was both critical and accommodationist. On the one hand, its respect for the Protestant canon reflected its desire to accommodate and be included within the American (socioeconomic, political, and religious) mainstream; on the other hand, its interpretation of the Bible was on the whole from a social and ideological location "from below," as it were, and reflected a blistering critique of Bible-believing, slave-holding, racist America. Important personalities—from Frederick Douglass to Martin Luther King, Jr.— are among the powerful articulators of the reading. But the popular sources, some anonymous, some by not-very-well-known individuals—the songs, conversion narratives, poetry, prayers, diaries, and the like—are a truer, more powerful reflection of history.

That this reading reflected considerable ambivalence about being in America on the part of a considerable segment of African Americans over a long period of history is indisputable. That it reflects class-specific leanings within the African American population is also indisputable. Those who continued to "read" the Bible and America in this way continued to hope that some accommodation should and could be made. Those most ardent in this hope on the whole saw themselves as close enough to the mainstream to make accommodation (integration) always seem feasible.

The great interest in the dramatic narratives of the Hebrew Bible notwithstanding, it was the motifs of a certain cluster of passages from the New Testament, especially Galatians 3.26–28 and Acts 2 and 10.34–36, that provided the hermeneutic foundation for this dominant "mainstream" African American reading of the Bible—and American culture. These passages were important because of their emphasis on the themes centering around the hope for the realization of the universality of salvation and the kinship of humanity. The passages were quoted and/or paraphrased in efforts to relate them to the racial situation in the United States by generations of African Americans—from the famous to those known only in statistics, stereotypes, and generalizations, in settings ranging from pulpits and lecture halls to nightclubs and street corners, in the rhetoric of the sermon and in the music of the streets.

That this reading continues to reflect the ethos and orientation of a considerable number, perhaps the majority, of African Americans, can be seen in its institutionalization in most African American institutions and associations—from the churches to civil rights organizations. Further, some of the most powerful and influential voices among African Americans continue to accept the ethos reflected by the reading. This suggests the continuing power of the ethos, even if it be argued that it is no longer the singular dominant ethos.

Third Reading: Critique from the Margins. Another reading was cultivated in the early decades of the twentieth century, primarily in the urban centers of the North and South. It reflected the sentiments of displaced and disoriented rural and small-town residents who moved to the big cities in search of better job opportunities. These individuals formed new religious communities that gave them a sense of belonging and solidarity missing in the established "mainline" churches and communities. A very different reading of the Bible is in evidence among such groups, one that was also reflective of a different attitude about society and culture. It was a more critical, even radical attitude about America; there was little hope of full integration into the mainstream. America was seen as racist and arrogant; its "mainstream" religious groups—including the African American groups—were seen as worldly and perfidious.

The engagement of the Bible and of religious texts in general more clearly reflects and articulates this attitude. The latter was not held by one single group; it was held by a number of groups—the Garvey Movement, Father Divine and the Peace Mission Movement, the Black Jews, the Nation of Islam, the Spiritual churches, the Pentecostal movement, among the most prominent. What they had in common were sensibilities, attitudes about the world, which were reflected not only in their more radical (Afrocentric or racialist) interpretation of the (Protestant-defined and -delimited) Bible, but also in their acceptance of other esoteric authoritative texts that, of course, justified their sensibilities and agenda. Whether through the radical reading of the (Protestant) Bible, the rejection or manipulation of its canonical delimitations, or through acceptance of other esoteric authoritative texts, these groups expressed their rejection of the racist and worldly religious ways of America and of the accommodationist and integrationist agenda of the African American religious mainstream. Many of them focused, to degrees far beyond anything on record among the African American establishment churches, on the utter perfidy and hopelessness of whites (e.g., Nation of Islam, Garvey Movement) as well as the destiny and salvation of African peoples (esp. Black Jews).

Fourth Reading: Leaving Race Behind. Another African American reading of the Bible and American culture emerged as a dominant one in the late twentieth century. It is in many respects a reaction to both the integrationist/accommodationist and the separatist readings discussed above. Its use of the Bible is a sharp departure from the traditional African American engagement of the Bible. To be sure, African Americans have historically been evangelical in their religious sensibilities, including the attachment of primary importance to the Bible as guide. But there has heretofore generally been a looseness, a kind of playfulness with the Bible. The letters of the Bible and its literal sense were less important than the evocative power of the stories, poetry, and prophetic proclamations. What generally mattered most was the power of the Bible to function as a language, even a language world, into which African American visionaries, prophets, rhetors, and politicians could retreat in order to find the materials needed for the articulation of their own and their communities' views. Now there are many African Americans whose engagement to the Bible is more doctrinaire and literal, even fundamentalist. And the hermeneutic foundation or presupposition, too, has shifted from historical and cultural experience, from being race-specific (as with the mainstream groups) or radical (as with the "sects" and "cults"), to being (as it is claimed) "Bible-based," that is, focused upon true doctrine in the letters of the Bible, relativizing racial identity and experience.

In this reading of the (Protestant) Bible, which is considered the deracialized and depoliticized quest for the truth and salvation, the most radical criticism of African American religious communities and culture is expressed. Insofar as the Protestant canon is not questioned, and insofar as the foundation or presupposition for reading the canon is claimed to be other than historical experience, then a total rejection of African American existence is expressed. In much the same way that the rise of fundamentalism among whites in the early decades of the twentieth century represented a rejection of modernism, so within the world of African Americans a turn toward fundamentalism represents a rejection of African Americans' special historical experiences and claims. That in religious matters African American religious communities are being abandoned or are being transformed into fundamentalist camps on the order of white fundamentalist camps, that religious truth can now be claimed to be unrelated to experience, is a most significant development. The proliferation of new fundamentalist churches and denominational groups among African Americans, as well as the new alliances with white fundamentalist groups, is astounding.

The phenomenon begs further comprehensive investigation. But it is very clear that it represents a most significant turn in African American religious and cultural history.

Women's Reading. In evidence throughout this history of African American "readings" of the Bible are the special readings of African American women. From Phyllis Wheatley to modern "womanist" and other interpreters, women are part of each of the "readings" distinguished above. But across each of these readings, differences in historical periods, locations, classes, and other factors notwithstanding, collectively women have for the most part added special emphases. Especially poignant among them is the radical challenge of consistency in prophetic communal self-judgment as African American religious communities apply the moral imperative to define the universality of God's economy of salvation.

See also Slavery and the Bible.

Vincent L. Wimbush

AFTERLIFE AND IMMORTALITY. *This entry consists of two articles on views of life after death within the historical communities of* Ancient Israel *and* Second Temple Judaism and Early Christianity. *For related discussion, see* Death; Israel, Religion of.

Ancient Israel

Israelite views of the afterlife underwent substantial changes during the first millennium BCE, as concepts popular during the preexilic period eventually came to be rejected by the religious leadership of the exilic and postexilic communities, and new theological stances replaced them. Because many elements of preex-

ilic beliefs and practices concerning the dead were eventually repudiated, the Hebrew Bible hardly discusses preexilic concepts at all; only scant and disconnected references to afterlife and the condition of the dead appear in the texts. A few passages from late-eighth through sixth-century sources are illuminating, however, because they attack various aspects of the popular notions about the dead during that period. With these data, a general though sketchy picture of Israelite views can be proposed.

Like all cultures in the ancient Near East, the Israelites believed that persons continued to exist after *death. It was thought that following death, one's spirit went down to a land below the earth, most often called Sheol, but sometimes merely "Earth," or "the Pit" (*see* Hell). In the preexilic period, there was no notion of a judgment of the dead based on their actions during life, nor is there any evidence for a belief that the righteous dead go to live in God's presence. The two persons in the Hebrew Bible who are taken to heaven to live with God, Enoch and Elijah, do not die. All who die, righteous or wicked, go to Sheol.

The exact relationship between the body of a dead person and the spirit that lived on in Sheol is unclear, since the Bible does not discuss this issue. Many scholars assume that the Israelites did not fully distinguish between the body and the spirit, and thus believed that the deceased continued to have many of the same basic needs they had when they were alive, especially for food and drink. Unless these needs were met, the dead would find existence in Sheol to be unending misery. Such a close connection between feeding the dead through funerary offerings and their happiness in the afterlife is well attested in Mesopotamia and Egypt. It is assumed that Israelite funerary practices were similar and included long-term, regular provision of food and drink offerings for the dead.

Other scholars have pointed out the lack of evidence in the Bible for such funerary offerings. Two passages often quoted in reference to such offerings, Deuteronomy 26.14 and Psalm 106.28, are ambiguous and can be interpreted in different ways. Archaeological evidence from Iron Age tombs suggests that food and drink were provided at the tomb only when the *burial took place. There is no evidence for regular post-funeral offerings of food at tombs in Israel. It is possible that the Israelites assumed that Sheol had its own food supply, and that the food placed in the tomb was conceived as provisions for the journey of the deceased to Sheol, but this is speculative.

Virtually no discussion of what existence in Sheol was thought to be like is preserved in preexilic literature. The few datable texts in the Bible that describe Sheol tend to be late and belong to authors who opposed important aspects of the popular view. They present Sheol in negative terms, as a place of darkness and gloom, where the dead exist without thought, strength, or even consciousness.

These texts appear to be reactions against a considerably more positive view of existence in Sheol that was held in the preexilic period. There is evidence that many Israelites thought that the dead continued to play an active role in the world of the living, possessing the power to grant blessings to their relatives and to reveal the future. This was done through the process of necromancy, the consultation of the dead by a medium, and related practices, which appear to have been quite popular in Israel. Evidence for this is found in the substantial number of vehement denunciations of necromancy in the prophetic and legal

literature of the eighth through sixth centuries BCE. Only one narrative account of a necromantic session has been preserved in the Bible—the story of Samuel's ghostly consultation with Saul at Endor (1 Sam. 28), and Saul is roundly criticized by the seventh-century editor of the books of Samuel for having resorted to this practice.

Necromancy was particularly opposed by the religious group that supported the worship of Yahweh alone. This group argued that blessings and the telling of the future were prerogatives of Yahweh, not of the dead, and that consultation with the dead for such purposes was an abomination against Yahweh. The popular views of afterlife and the dead came under increasing attack during the late eighth and seventh centuries. The laws against necromancy date to this period, and a number of outright attacks and satires on the older ideas about the nature of existence in Sheol appear in the literature of the time. It is interesting to note, however, that the laws against necromancy in Deuteronomy and Leviticus still assume not that it was impossible to summon the dead from Sheol but that it was inappropriate.

These laws apparently did not have the desired effect on the Judean population. During the exile, when the "Yahweh alone" party finally came to control the religious leadership of Judah, a further step was taken. Several texts appearing to date from the exilic and postexilic periods suggest that it is not only improper to consult the dead but actually impossible to do so. A new theology developed arguing that there is no conscious existence in Sheol at all. At death all contact with the world, and even with God, comes to an end. This notion explicitly appears in several late Psalms, Job, and Ecclesiastes. This startling idea was not new in the Near East. Skepticism about the afterlife is found in some Egyptian texts as early as the Middle Kingdom (ca. 2000–1750 BCE), but such notions were never adopted as an official doctrine there. In postexilic Judah, however, this became the authoritative stance of the religious leadership, though it was probably not widely held by most Judeans.   *Wayne T. Pitard*

Second Temple Judaism and Early Christianity

In the postexilic period, and particularly in the Hellenistic period following the conquest of Alexander the Great in 332 BCE, Jewish thought concerning *death and afterlife underwent a major change, owing to the widespread influence of the Platonic idea of the immortality of the soul (*see* Human Person). Whereas prior to the period of the Hellenistic empires the official religious stance of Israel acknowledged some form of shadowy existence in Sheol for the person after death (*see* Hell; *also the previous article in this entry*), beginning in the third century we find a flowering of literature describing the fate of the human soul after death, often in vivid and moving terms. This change is best illustrated by two passages from the wisdom literature. The book of Ecclesiastes (ca. third century BCE) illustrates the dominant view at the end of the *exile: "Whoever is joined with all the living has hope, for a living dog is better than a dead lion. The living know that they will die, but the dead know nothing; they have no more reward, and even the memory of them is lost. . . . Whatever your hand finds to do, do with your might; for there is no work or thought or knowledge or wisdom in Sheol, to which you are going" (Eccles. 9.4–5, 10). The Wisdom of Solomon, written during the Hellenistic period, shows strong influence of Greek, especially Stoic, thought: "God created

us for incorruption, and made us in the image of his own eternity, but through the devil's envy death entered the world, and those who belong to his company experience it. But the souls of the righteous are in the hand of God, and no torment will ever touch them. In the sight of the foolish they seemed to have died, and their departure was thought to be a disaster, and their going from us to be their destruction; but they are at peace. For though in the sight of others they were punished, their hope is full of immortality" (Wisd. of Sol. 2.23–3.4).

Two ideas concerning the fate of the soul after death were held in tension during the Hellenistic and Roman periods. The first was that of resurrection, that is, that at the end of time the soul would be rejoined with the body and each person would then receive reward or punishment. The concept is found in the Hebrew Bible only at Daniel 12.2: "And many of those who sleep in the dust of the earth shall awake, some to everlasting life, and some to shame and everlasting contempt." A modification of this idea was that only the righteous dead would be resurrected to share in the messianic age.

The second idea was that the immortal soul lived on after the death of the body, and immediately received its reward or punishment. This idea is vividly illustrated in the Testament of Abraham (ca.. 100 CE), which depicts the judgment of souls after death. Each soul is brought before Abel, son of Adam, for judgment. The deeds of the soul are weighed in the balance; the righteous receive salvation, but the wicked are given over to fiery torments.

The tension between these two ideas continued in rabbinic Judaism and early Christianity. References to the rabbis' views of the afterlife are scattered, but may be summarized thus: at death, the soul leaves the body, but may return from time to time until the body disintegrates. The righteous souls go to *paradise, but the wicked to hell. Finally, in the messianic age there will be a bodily resurrection.

In early Christianity, the tension of the "already" of immortality and the "not yet" of resurrection continued to exist, but was transformed by the death and *resurrection of Jesus. This is best illustrated by the teaching of Paul: "But if Christ is in you, though the body is dead because of sin, the spirit is life because of righteousness. If the Spirit of him who raised Jesus from the dead dwells in you, he who raised Christ from the dead will give life to your mortal bodies also through his Spirit that dwells in you" (Rom. 8.10–12). In certain groups, such as the community of John, the notion of the bodily resurrection was overridden by the spiritual life of the believer in Christ: "Very truly, I tell you, anyone who hears my word and believes him who sent me has eternal life, and does not come under judgment, but has passed from death to life" (John 5.24). Neither view has become dominant, and both continue to exist in tension in Judaism and Christianity until the present.

See also Heaven.   Sidnie Ann White

AGRAPHA (EXTRACANONICAL SAYINGS OF JESUS).

Since the publication of J. G. Körner's De sermonibus Christi "agraphois" (1778), "agrapha" (literally "unwritten things") has become the name for sayings attributed to Jesus, but not found (i.e., "not written") in the canonical *Gospels. Interest in collecting such sayings started in the sixteenth century, but Alfred Resch was the first to present the results of a systematic research in 1889. His extensive collection of more than three hundred extracanonical sayings were substantially enriched in the twentieth century by new manuscript discoveries.

Sources. Within the New Testament, but outside the Gospels, there are a few sayings attributed to Jesus. Some sayings, though transmitted in some manuscripts of the Gospels, have not been adopted into the *canon, and have been relegated to the critical apparatus of the various editions of the Greek New Testament. The fragmentary papyri (especially those from Oxyrhynchus in Egypt) discovered since the end of the nineteenth century, and the more extensive apocryphal gospels (especially the *gnostic gospels discovered in 1945 at *Nag Hammadi), contain a rich collection of "logia." The most important is the Gospel of Thomas; other gnostic writings containing revelations and hymns also provide a large range of peculiar sayings. Numerous church fathers, from the second century on, quote words of Jesus that are only partially present in the Gospels, if at all. A few words have been found in ancient liturgies and church orders. The Talmud preserves two unparalleled sayings of Jesus (ᶜAbod. Zar. 16b, 17a; Šabb.116 a–b). The *Qurʾān and later Islamic writings also refer to several unknown sayings.

Origin. Oral tradition preceded and even for some time accompanied the written tradition of the Gospels. Therefore, in principle at least, some ancient sayings may have survived in oral form even after the Gospels were written, and later authors may have integrated them into their works. But it is also likely that an important figure like Jesus himself became the center of a creative tradition. Others' statements were attributed to him, and new sayings were created.

Evaluation. Taking into account the plurality of sources, spread over several centuries, there is naturally a great variety among the agrapha. They vary from possibly authentic sayings, through adaptations and combinations of sayings from the Gospels, to pure fantasy and tendentious creations. Several of them have been forged for a particular situation, for example, to support with Jesus' own authority a later (orthodox or heretical) concept or practice.

Each saying is in some way a witness to a certain concept and a particular setting. Certain collections, especially the gnostic logia, provide valuable information about various tendencies in early Christianity. In most cases, differences from the form and content of the canonical sayings, together with some evident peculiarity, clearly exclude authenticity. Among the several hundred agrapha, only a few have some chance of being really ancient and perhaps authentic. This complex documentation, therefore, adds little to a better knowledge of the historical Jesus or the earliest Christian tradition.

Examples of agrapha that have often been thought to be authentic sayings of Jesus are

"Be approved money changers."

"The one who is near me is near the fire; the one who is far from me is far from the kingdom."

"No one can obtain the kingdom of heaven who has not passed through temptation."

"There shall be divisions and heresies."   *Joel Delobel*

ALLEGORIZING. See Interpretation, History of, *article on* Early Christian Interpretation; Typology.

ALMS. There is no word for "alms" or "almsgiving" in the Hebrew Bible, and there are almost no specific references to the practice of giving alms as such. Generosity to the poor and needy was, however, required and praised. There are many commands to show benevolence to the poor, a group that included Levites, foreigners living among Israelites, widows, and orphans, for whom there was also a special *tithe. Those who gave to the poor were thought to be blessed or happy.

The Greek word for alms is *eleēmosynē*, which comes from the basic verb *eleeō*, meaning "to pity" or "have mercy on" someone. In the Septuagint *eleēmosynē* frequently translates the Hebrew words for "loving kindness" (*hesed*) and "*righteousness" (*ṣĕdāqâ*). It is used of both God and humans having mercy toward others. Almsgiving came to be regarded as a particular form of righteousness and could gain merit and forgiveness of sins for the giver.

In the New Testament *eleēmosynē* is always used in the sense of giving alms. In the *Sermon on the Mount, piety and almsgiving are synonymous (Matt. 6.1–4). Elsewhere *eleēmosynē* occurs in the New Testament only in Luke and Acts, where it refers either to the gift or to the process of giving. In Luke 11.41 and 12.33, the expression "give alms" corresponds to the rabbinic "give righteousness" (ʾ*Abot* 5.15). Paul exhorted his communities to make special efforts to remember the poor.   *Edwin D. Freed*

ALPHA AND OMEGA. The first and last letters of the Greek alphabet, spoken in the book of Revelation to John as the self-disclosure of God and also of Jesus Christ. Letters of the Greek alphabet could have numerical value, though in Revelation the focus is on the full scope of divine concern and control. "Alpha and Omega" refers to God's place at the beginning of the world, as its creator, and at the end, as its judge. John the Seer's use of these terms evokes the language of the prophets, like Isaiah

44.6: "Thus says the Lord . . . I am the first and the last; besides me there is no god." Other New Testament writers discuss Jesus' role in the world's origin, alluding to the *creation account in Genesis, and at its final judgment.

Philip Sellew

AMARNA LETTERS. Discovered in 1887, the archive of El-Amarna in Egypt has yielded 379 cuneiform tablets that are among the most precious finds of Near Eastern archaeology. Tell el-Amarna, located about 310 mi (500 km) up the Nile from the Mediterranean, is the modern name of ancient Akhetaten, King Akhnaton's capital. The letters constitute diplomatic correspondence from the reigns of Amenophis III and Akhnaton in the first half of the fourteenth century BCE. Except for two in Hittite and one in Hurrian, their language is Babylonian. Some are from the rulers of the other great powers of the day—Babylonia, Assyria, Mitanni, and Hatti—but most are written by Egyptian vassals in Canaan and Syria. The former group largely concerns exchanges of ambassadors and expensive gifts, but the letters from Canaanite vassals bespeak a period of unrest, as the vassal kings, caught in the power struggles of the great kingdoms, form short-lived coalitions against one another. The texts frequently refer to a disruptive group called the *hapiru* (pronounced ᶜ*apiru*), a word equated by many with the Hebrew ᶜ*ibrî*, "Hebrew." Although the name may be the same, the nature of the ᶜ*apiru* precludes a simple identification with the Israelites. Scholars are divided on whether the term refers properly to a specific people or to a social class; most see them as militant outcasts, that is, as brigands or mercenaries. We also read of the depredations of the Syrian kingdom of Amurru, later to give its name to the

Amorites of the Bible. The Amarna letters describe the vicissitudes of cities such as Hazor, Akko, Megiddo, Taanach, Shechem, Gezer, Ashkelon, Gaza, Lachish, and Jerusalem in the pre-Israelite period. Because the Canaanite scribes had an imperfect command of Babylonian, their lapses have also taught scholars much about their native dialects, and thus about the prehistory of the closely related *Hebrew language.

Although they do not mention the still inchoate Israelites, the Amarna letters are an invaluable window on the world from which Israel was to emerge in the following century.

William H. Propp

AMEN. A Hebrew word meaning "certainly" or "may it be so." In the Hebrew Bible *amen* appears as a response to someone else's statement. Sometimes it appears in a liturgical setting as a response of the people, sometimes as a solemn response to another person's statement (1 Kings 1.36; Jer. 28.6 [an ironic response]), sometimes as a response to God's word. The doubled form, *amen, amen* also occurs; compare "*amen* and *amen*" (Ps. 41.13). *Amen* may be used as a substantive: "the God of *amen*" = "the God of faithfulness" (Isa. 65.16); this meaning is reflected in the New Testament.

The Hebrew *amen* was retained among early Greek-speaking Christians as a confirmatory response to prayer, whether one's own or someone else's. This continues in Christian liturgical usage.

In the speech of Jesus in the Gospels, *amen* often appears not as a closing response but as an opening affirmation of the validity and seriousness of what follows: "*Amen* ('Truly') I tell you . . ." (Matt. 5.18). In the Gospel of John, the *amen* that frequently introduces Jesus' speech is doubled: "*Amen, amen* ('Truly, truly' [NRSV: 'Very truly']) I say to you . . ." (John 1.51; etc.). The opening *amen* indicates the solemn claim of the speaker to authority. Many scholars see in this introductory *amen* a clear reflection of Jesus' sense of his own authority. The introductory *amen* was not completely new in the words of Jesus, however; there are a few instances of similar speech in contemporary sources. It is possible, however, that the language of early Christian worship influenced these passages.   *William A. Beardslee*

AMERICAN LITERATURE. *See* Literature and the Bible, *article on* North American Literature.

ANATHEMA. A Greek word corresponding to Hebr. *ḥērem* and designating an object dedicated or devoted to a deity either for consecration or to be cursed (devoted to destruction). In the former sense, objects were devoted to God and belonged to him; offerings were given to God to adorn the Temple. Most occurrences of the term, however, describe something or someone accursed or given to God for destruction. According to Leviticus 27.29, no one who had been devoted to God for destruction could be ransomed, nor could devoted things be used by human beings. According to Paul, if someone preaches a gospel contrary to the one that he preached, that person is anathema (NRSV: "cursed").

In Romans 9.3, Paul affirms his strong ties to the Jewish people and asserts that he is prepared to be "anathema from Christ" (NRSV: "accursed and cut off from Christ"), if that would benefit them—a statement similar in thought to that of Moses being willing to have his name blotted out of God's book for the sake of the Israelites.

Individuals also invoked anathema on themselves to ensure that they would keep an oath (see Acts 23.12, 14, 21, where the Greek verb is a form of *anathema*). Such individuals called on God to curse them if they did not perform the oath they had made.

In later usage, anathema becomes virtually synonymous with excommunication.

See also Curse.   *Paul L. Bremer*

ANCIENT VERSIONS. *See* Translations, *article on* Ancient Languages.

ANIMALS. As a modern general designation for all living creatures other than plants, "animal" does not always have a simple equivalent in the Bible. The closest equivalents in the Hebrew Bible include *ḥayyâ,* ("living [creature]," Lev. 11.2) and *běhēmâ,* which usually refers to all quadrupeds, or more specifically to domesticated animals. Yet even these Hebrew terms do not usually include birds or fish. The Septuagint and the New Testament frequently use *tetrapous* ("quadruped") or *thērion* to translate both Hebrew terms.

Classification Systems. Aside from problems in basic terminology, the differences between biblical and modern Linnaean systems of animal classification sometimes create uncertainties in translation. For example, the Hebrew *dîšōn* (Deut. 14.5) has been translated by different versions or scholars as "ibex," "white-rumped deer," "pygarg," or "Arabian oryx," all representing completely different genera in most modern classifications. More than one species of predatory birds (e.g., eagles and vultures) may be subsumed under the Hebrew term *nešer.*

Dietary laws in Leviticus 11 and Deuteronomy 14.3–20, as well as the sacrificial system, depended on a system of classification that distinguished clean and unclean animals. In general, a clean land animal had cloven hoofs and chewed its cud (a ruminant artiodactyl in modern zoology), thus eliminating reptiles, amphibians, rodents, and carnivorous animals from the diet. Animals that only chewed their cud (e.g., the hare) or only had cloven hoofs (e.g., the pig) also were eliminated. Most insects are unclean (the locust being one exception), and only those aquatic animals with fins and scales are fit to eat. The logic underlying the clean/unclean dichotomy in Leviticus remains unclear. Other ancient Near Eastern cultures had views similar to those found in Leviticus and Deuteronomy regarding unclean animals, including the pig. Not surprisingly, for the Jewish sect that became known as Christianity, Levitical animal classification was a major issue in the debate about observance of dietary laws. (*See* Purity, Ritual.)

Origin, Use, and Relationship with Humans. Biblical views concerning animals are linked closely with the two principal myths of *creation. In the first account, generally ascribed to P, all the animals were created before both man and woman (Gen. 1.20–30). In the other account (Gen. 2.7–22), usually ascribed to J, the creation of all the animals follows that of the first man, and God creates the first woman only after none of the animals was found helpful to the man. In both accounts animals were created to serve the needs of human beings, though Genesis 9.3 indicates that humans were not expected to use animals for food before the *Flood. Psalm 104.10–30 depicts Yahweh, not human beings, as responsible for the general welfare of the animal kingdom.

Sheep, goats, cattle, and pigs are the most extensively attested domestic animals from the Neolithic period onward in ancient Palestine. The camel may have been domesticated by the early third millennium BCE in some portions of Asia, but the geographical extent of domestication by the second millennium remains undetermined.

Aside from providing a ready reserve of fresh meat and milk, most domestic animals could provide hides, bone implements, transportation, and other commodities. Wealth and status were often measured by the number of animals that a person owned. The raising and trading of horses played an important role in achieving and maintaining military power in the Near East.

Although offering animals to appease a deity has a strong magico-religious basis, animal *sacrifice formed an important part of the economy in ancient Israel. Ordinances that required that only the best of the flock be brought to the Temple for sacrifice in effect demanded the allocation of the best animal resources (especially cattle, sheep, and goats) for the priesthood. Smaller animals such as pigeons were acceptable if the worshiper was too poor to offer larger animals. Christian writers argued that Jesus' death nullified the need for animal sacrifice altogether.

The Bible also mentions various animals that were considered harmful. Some of the *plagues sent upon Egypt included the uncontrolled multiplication of frogs, gnats, flies, and locusts. Locusts were particularly feared because they could destroy agriculture and so cause a famine. Rituals sometimes were devised for protection from poisonous animals (e.g., snakes in Num. 21.1–4).

Animal Imagery. Biblical authors often use animal imagery to express aspects of their culture. Sheep imagery is used to depict a future messianic utopia, as well as the Israelite community. In the

New Testament Jesus was portrayed as a *lamb, and he warned his disciples about wolves dressed in sheep's clothing.

Lions and other ferocious animals are often used to speak of hostile armies or personal enemies, though lions may also symbolize positive figures (e.g., Judah in Gen. 49.9). Certain birds are associated with desolation. Dogs usually are represented negatively in the Bible, though a recently discovered dog cemetery from the Persian period at Ashkelon may suggest the existence of non-Israelite cults that viewed the dog positively.

The Bible is also stocked with a variety of mythological creatures such as the cherubim and seraphim, which combine human and animal traits. Leviathan and Rahab are primordial beasts that were believed to threaten God's creation. As was the case with El, Baal, and other Canaanite deities, Yahweh may have been depicted as a bull (*see* Golden Calf). Bull figurines from the second and first millennia BCE have been found at, among other places, Hazor and Ashkelon, though it is difficult to determine which deity, if any, is represented by the figurines.

Aside from biblical scholars and archaeologists, ecologists and ethicists have recently become interested in the extent to which the biblical view of animals has influenced the relationship of modern civilizations with *nature.

Hector Ignacio Avalos

ANOINT. To touch, smear, or rub an object or person with oil. The use of scented oils on the body was enjoyed as a cosmetic luxury in Near Eastern and Hellenistic societies (and sometimes condemned as such). It was especially used on festive occasions and, conversely, refrained from in times of mourning or *fasting. The soothing qualities of oil

made anointing part of medical practice, but as most *medicine involved an invoking of divine power, anointing in that context might have the character of a religious rite. Similarly, the anointing of corpses for *burial might be viewed both as a last gesture of affection toward the dead and as part of the religious ritual of burial. The woman who anointed Jesus with precious scented oil probably did so as an extravagant gesture of joy at his presence, and he receives it as such in Luke 7.36–50, while in Mark 14.8 and John 12.7 he sees it as an anticipation of his death.

Anointing has a firm place in religious practice. Objects are anointed as a sign of their dedication to the deity, such as Jacob's pillar at Bethel. The book of Exodus prescribes the anointing of the *tabernacle and its furnishings, especially the altar. With the institution of *kingship in Israel, anointing rather than coronation was the ceremony in which the king took office. This rite was widely practiced in the ancient Near East; the *Amarna letters suggest that anointing was a rite of kingship in Syria-Palestine in the fourteenth century BCE, and Jotham's parable assumes its familiarity (Judg. 9.8, 15). Once kingship was established, the anointing was probably performed by a priest, as Zadok anointed Solomon. Samuel, a prophet and probably also a priest, is said to have anointed Saul and David, though according to 2 Sam. 2.4; 5.3, David was anointed by the people of Judah and Israel respectively. According to 1 Kings 19.15–16, Elijah the prophet is instructed to anoint Hazael as king of Damascus and Jehu as king of Israel; Elisha carries out the latter task by proxy. The king's anointing symbolized his special relationship with God and was seen as the occasion when he received God's spirit; it therefore made his person sacrosanct, so that David, with Saul in his power, will not touch "the Lord's anointed" (1 Sam. 24.6, 10; 26.9–11, 16, 23).

The anointing of priests is prescribed only in the later, Priestly strata of the Pentateuch. The anointing of the high priest probably began in the postexilic period, when the high priest assumed many of the leadership functions that had belonged to the king. It was only perhaps later still extended to other priests. The ritual was not practiced in the Roman period in Herod's Temple, where the high priest's institution was by investiture.

As anointing symbolized the special responsibility and relationship to God of king and priest, so the language might be used metaphorically of anyone thought to stand in a similar position. Thus, the prophet of Isaiah 60.1 is said to be anointed (though for the possibility that prophets were actually anointed, see 1 Kings 19.16; Ps. 105.15). King Cyrus of Persia is God's anointed in Isaiah 45.1, as is the whole people of Israel in Habakkuk 3.13. Jesus is described as "anointed with the Holy Spirit and with power" in Acts 10.38.

By the Roman period, some Jews had come to hope that God would restore them a king, and because anointing was remembered primarily as the sign of kingship, this hope was expressed as hope for the "anointed one," Hebr. *māšîaḥ* (English "messiah"), Grk. *christos* (John 1.41). The Qumran community looked for two "anointed ones," priest and king, the Messiahs of Aaron and Israel. A more generalized hope for a future leader whose precise functions were unclear might still be expressed as hope for a "Messiah," but the primary association of the title with kingship would inevitably suggest political aspirations, and it may be for this reason that Jesus

appears reluctant to accept the title for himself.

Anointing remains an essential part of the English coronation ritual, in direct dependence on the Bible.   *Sophie Laws*

ANTHROPOLOGY AND THE BIBLE. *See* Social Sciences and the Bible.

ANTI-JUDAISM. *See* Anti-Semitism.

ANTI-SEMITISM.   Anti-Semitism has become the term commonly used for attitudes and actions against Jews. It was coined in the 1870s by the German agitator Wilhelm Marr in the campaign to eradicate Jewish influences in German culture. Sometimes the valid distinction is made between anti-Semitism as a secular term built on racial and cultural thinking out of the Enlightenment, and anti-Judaism as the earlier theologically grounded forms of contempt for Jews and things Jewish. Not least with the contemporary Arab-Israeli conflict, the term anti-Semitism is a sign of the narrow Western perspective in which the term was coined—both Jews and Muslims being Semites. Yet for the victims of anti-Semitism, such distinctions, though valid, carry little weight.

The record of pre-Christian anti-Semitism in the Greco-Roman world is mixed. The Jews were seen as a people of philosophers and the wisdom of Moses was highly respected. But there was also criticism of their rituals and their keeping to themselves, and the *Sabbath was seen as laziness. The Roman satirists especially ridiculed *circumcision. Yet on balance it seems that Cicero's reference to Judaism as a "barbarous superstition" (*Pro Flacco* 28[67]) has been wrongly taken as representative of attitudes toward the Jews. In the history of anti-Semitism, the continuity between Christian and Greco-Roman anti-Semitism is often stressed in order to minimize Christian responsibility.

While at times making use of themes found in Greco-Roman writers, Christian anti-Semitism differs in one fundamental respect: Christianity claims to be the fulfillment of the prophecies and aspirations of Israel as they are expressed in Israel's own scriptures, which became the Old Testament of the church, now interpreted in the light of the life, death, and resurrection of Jesus Christ.

The Jesus-movement was a totally Jewish event—the Gospels know of few contacts of Jesus with gentiles. Christianity begins as a Jewish reform movement, and the formative conflicts by which the Christian identity is formed are conflicts within Judaism. The very Jewishness of Jesus and the apostles gives anti-Semitism its intensity. The scars of the intra-Jewish conflicts with Pharisees in Galilee and the chief priests and elders of Jerusalem, and with synagogue leaders in the Jewish diaspora, are clearly visible in the New Testament, now from the perspective of churches where the "no" of the Jewish majority to the Christian claims is often contrasted with the "yes" of gentiles.

Jesus—and John the Baptist—speak the harsh language of the prophets, ridiculing or condemning the foibles of their contemporaries, cursing their unwillingness to listen and to repent. Woes are uttered and the listeners are called. The rhetoric is heavy: "brood of vipers" (Matt. 3.7; 12.34; 23.33; Luke 3.7), and so forth. When such words are spoken by a Jewish prophet for a Jewish people, Jesus identifies with his people; it has been said that a true prophet of doom prays intensely that his prophecy be proven wrong, that it be a warning toward repentance.

Such discourse from within the Jew-ish communities fell into the hands of increasingly gentile churches when the vast majority of Jews did not accept Christian claims for Jesus of Nazareth. The gentile churches began to hurl the words of Jesus at the Jewish communities. What Jesus had said with prophetic pathos, identifying with his people, was now spoken by gentiles against "the Jews," gentiles who felt that the fall of the Jerusalem Temple (70 CE) had proven them right and the Jewish people wrong. In that shift of setting lie the roots of Christian and New Testament anti-Semitism. For the Jewish disciples there was the sadness, the disappointment, perhaps the frustration over the "no" of the majority of their fellow Jews; hence the need for a new identity, as the Jewish communities sometimes treated them harshly. The gospel of John already lives in that perception, sharpened into a literal demonizing of "the Jews" as having the devil for a father (John 8.44). Jewish Christianity—by any account the nucleus of Christianity—is marginalized and declared unacceptable by both synagogue and church. The "we and they" dichotomy does not allow such complications.

The first to have discerned the specter of gentile Christian contempt for the Jews was Paul, the Jew who understood himself to be the apostle to the gentiles. In his final reflection on how his mission fits into God's total plan, he warns his gentile converts against their haughty attitude toward Israel by affirming that all Israel shall be saved. He does so not by affirming that they will become Christians but rather refers to God's *mystery. Perhaps Paul's sensitivity was due to his personal history: it was religious zeal that had made him a persecutor of Christians.

In spite of Paul's warning, anti-Semitism follows Christianity as its dark shadow. This anti-Semitism remains basically rhetorical until the church becomes wedded to the political power of empires and governments. About a century after the emperor Constantine's conversion to Christianity (312 CE), Augustine lays down the principles on which Jews are allowed to exist in the Christian empire, yet with inferior status. His interpretation of Psalm 59.11 ("Do not slay them, lest my people forget; scatter them . . .") established the status of the Jews as both protected and suppressed—a pattern that makes the Jews a necessary negative witness to the truth of Christianity. Within this pattern of Christian anti-Semitism, two motifs become prominent, both argued on biblical grounds: the Jews are guilty of deicide, of being godkillers (of having killed God), and Judaism is the wrong way to relate to God (by law rather than by faith). While the former charge is more prominent in Catholic and Orthodox lands, the latter dominates in Protestant cultures.

How can Christians read the Bible in a manner that guards against anti-Semitism? Perhaps the majority of Christians have read and do read the New Testament's critique of Jews and things Jewish as directed to themselves: it is my hypocrisy, my boasting, my self-righteousness that is attacked; it is my sin and lack of faith that swings from "Hosanna" to "Crucify, crucify." Yet history shows that when calamities and frustrations call for scapegoats, these very texts have preconditioned Christian cultures toward anti-Semitism.

To counteract such an effect of the Christian Bible—not least after the *Holocaust—different strategies have been devised. A renewed study of the passion narratives makes it clear that Jesus was crucified by the Roman authorities. *Crucifixion was a Roman means of ex-

ecution. Also in the accounts of the Gospels it is the Jerusalem establishment, not "the Jews," who collaborate. This agrees with *Josephus's notes about the execution of James in 62 CE that the Sadducees are the harsh judges, while the Pharisees plead mercy. As the story is told in the Gospels, the responsibility of the Jewish leadership is stressed and that of Pontius Pilate minimized, as he washes his hands and the crowd accepts the responsibility: "His blood be on us and on our children" (Matt. 27.25). And Judas usually looks more Jewish than do Jesus and the other disciples in the history of Christian art; one may ask: Why? The shift of emphasis from the Romans to the Jews is often explained by the need of Christianity to present itself as acceptable to the Roman authorities. A deeper reason may well be the theological need for understanding the passion as a fulfillment of the scriptures of the Jews and thus as an inner Jewish event. Yet there can be no historical doubt that Jesus was crucified under and by Pontius Pilate as a Jewish threat to Roman law and order.

When the New Testament and especially the gospel of John gives the impression that "the Jews" are the constant enemies and opponents, we must remember that both believers and unbelievers in the Jesus story are Jews. In order to make that more clear some translators choose to use words like "Judeans" or "the Jewish leaders." One could even think of "the establishment," for there is really nothing especially Jewish in the attitudes of those leaders. While such moves help to correct the historical understanding of the events and put them into perspective, it still remains a fact that the Gospels did perceive the controversies as part of Israel's refusal to accept God's offer of redemption in Jesus Christ. Judaism, on its part, understands the Christian claim for Jesus as false, while sometimes willing to recognize Jesus as a teacher among teachers in Judaism.

But Christians burdened by the horrendous history of anti-Semitism have urgent reasons to recognize how the rhetoric of a fledgling and beleaguered minority turned into the aiding and abetting of lethal hatred when endowed with the power of being in the majority. Anti-Semitism could be branded the most persistent heresy of Christian theology and practice. To unmask it is the first step. And the second is to complete and further develop the work begun in the Second Vatican Council: a vigilant audit of Christian preaching, teaching, Bible study, and liturgy as to what perpetuates and engenders contempt for Jews and Judaism. In such a task, dialogue with Jews is indispensable. In dialogue it becomes impossible for Christians to treat Jews and Judaism as obsolete or as a nonentity after the coming of the church. Yet such patterns of so-called supersessionism have functioned as a major factor in the history of Christian anti-Semitism.

Krister Stendahl

APOCALYPTIC LITERATURE.

The words "apocalyptic" and "apocalypse" (from a Greek root meaning "to uncover, reveal") are terms that came to be used from the second century CE onward to indicate a type of Jewish and Christian literature akin to the New Testament Apocalypse (an alternative title of the book of Revelation), which gave its name to this style of writing.

The term "apocalyptic literature" is taken to refer to a body of revelatory writing produced in Jewish circles between 250 BCE and 200 CE and subsequently taken up and perpetuated by Christianity. It includes not only the genre "apocalypse" but may also include other related types of literature, such as testaments, hymns, and *prayers, which share some of its more important characteristics and motifs; that is, it does not have a common literary form but is diverse and even hybrid in its literary expression. The apocalypse type of writing, which forms the core of this literature, is a record of divine disclosures made known through the agency of angels, *dreams, and visions. These may take different forms: an otherworldly journey in which the "secrets" of the cosmos are made known (the so-called vertical apocalypses), or a survey of history often leading to an eschatological crisis in which the cosmic powers of evil are destroyed, the cosmos is restored, and Israel (or "the righteous") is redeemed (the so-called horizontal or historical apocalypses).

Biblical Apocalypses. The scholarly consensus sees a strong link between the apocalypse and biblical prophecy, and regards such writings as Ezekiel 38–39, Isaiah 24–27, Zechariah 12–14, and Joel 3 if not as apocalypses per se then as forerunners of them. The wisdom tradition undoubtedly also influenced the apocalyptic in its growth and development, but arguments that its origins lie there rather than in prophecy remain unconvincing. However closely related prophecy and apocalyptic may be, they are to be distinguished from each other in at least two respects: whereas the prophets for the most part declare God's word to his or her own generation, the apocalyptists record revelations said to have been made known by God to some great hero in earlier times and now to be revealed in a "secret" book at the end of the days; and whereas the prophets see the realization of God's purpose within the historical process, the apocalyptists see that purpose reaching its culmination not just within history but above and beyond history in that supramundane realm where God dwells.

Within the Bible itself there are two great apocalypses: Daniel and Revelation. In the first of these, five stories are told of a wise man, Daniel, who remained faithful to his Jewish religion during the Babylonian *exile in the sixth century BCE, and was enabled by God to interpret dreams and visions. In the second half of the book, four of Daniel's visions are recorded, along with their interpretations, which give a survey of history from the exile (when the writer is reckoned to have lived) to its denouement in the second century BCE in the time of Antiochus IV, when the book in its present form was actually written. In this sense, the book of Daniel is addressed to the writer's own contemporaries, but the method and approach are altogether different from those of the prophets. So too with his hope for the coming kingdom: in keeping with the prophets, he sees it established here on earth as the climax of history, but in no way is it to be separated from that transcendent, heavenly realm where God dwells with his holy angels.

The book of Revelation follows a somewhat similar form, for it too reveals the future course of events by means of visions and declares the triumph of God's purpose. In the course of time other Christian apocalypses appeared, some as independent works, such as the Apocalypses of Peter and Paul, and others as interpolations in or additions to existing Jewish apocalyptic books.

Extrabiblical Apocalyptic Books. A number of extrabiblical Jewish apocalypses appeared during the Greco-Roman period which, for the most part, have survived only in translation, having been preserved within the Christian tradition. They are of considerable value for the light they throw on the four hundred and fifty or so years between 250 BCE and 200 CE and not least on our understanding of the background of the New Testament. There is no agreed list of such books, but the following works are generally so regarded: 1 Enoch (Ethiopic Apocalypse of Enoch), third century BCE to first century CE Apocalypse of Zephaniah, first century BCE to first century CE; Apocalypse of Abraham, first to second century CE; 2 Enoch (Slavonic Apocalypse of Enoch), late first century CE; 2 Esdras (= 4 Ezra) 3–14, ca. 100 CE; 2 Baruch (Syriac Apocalypse of Baruch), early second century CE; and 3 Baruch (Greek Apocalypse of Baruch), first to third century CE.

Besides these, there are from this period certain other Jewish writings that, though not themselves apocalypses, belong to the same milieu and are generally recognized as part of the apocalyptic literature. They are as follows: Jubilees, second century BCE; Testaments of the Twelve Patriarchs, second century BCE; Jewish Sibylline Oracles, second century BCE to seventh century CE; Treatise of Shem, first century BCE; Testament (Assumption) of Moses, first century CE; and Testament of Abraham, first to second century CE.

To this list may be added material found among the *Dead Sea Scrolls: fragments of a Testament of Levi (related to a late and redacted Greek Testament of that name) and a Testament of Naphtali, and likewise fragments of the (composite) first book of Enoch and the book of Jubilees. Other writings and fragments belonging to the Qumran community indicate a close relationship between the religious outlook of the apocalyptic writers and that expressed in the scrolls, such as certain passages in the Manual of Discipline, the War Scroll, the Hymns, and such works as the book of Mysteries, the Genesis Apocryphon, and the Description of the New Jerusalem.

Literary Features. The apocalypse is recognized by many scholars as a distinct literary genre expressing itself, as we have seen, in terms of divine disclosure, transcendent reality, and final redemption. As such, it shares with other related apocalyptic books certain literary features that are worthy of note:

Revelation through visionary experience. This is a stock-in-trade of these writings, though visions may be replaced by dreams, trances, auditions, and visual/physical transference to the ends of the earth or to heaven itself. The ancient seer (in whose name the author writes) is confronted with the heavenly mysteries, either directly or as mediated by an angel, and is bidden to record what he has seen and heard.

In so doing, the writer often makes use of two literary devices that, though not confined to the apocalyptic writings, are a common feature. The first is that of secret books, in which the seer is bidden to conceal these mysteries until the end time, when he will reveal them to the wise as a sign that the end is now at hand. The second is that of pseudonymity, whereby the author writes in the name of some honored person of antiquity, such as Adam, Enoch, Abraham, Moses, or Ezra. The intention is not to deceive but rather to strengthen the conviction that the apocalyptist is transmitting a long and authoritative tradition. The same device is followed in Christian apocalypses, such as those of Peter and Paul, but not in the book of Revelation, where it is enough that the writer should declare in his own name the revelations he himself has received directly from his risen Lord.

Symbolic imagery. Symbolism, it has

been said, is the language of the apocalyptic style of writing, a code language rich in imagery culled both from biblical and from Canaanite and Babylonian traditions. Generally speaking, the code is fairly easily recognizable: wild beasts represent the gentile nations, animal horns are gentile rulers, people are angels, and so on. Elsewhere it is less easily broken, particularly where vestiges of early myths have no obvious relation to the content of the book itself.

Tracts for the times. The apocalyptic books, particularly those "historical" apocalypses of Palestinian origin, were in many cases the product of their age and its political and economic climate. As tracts for the times, they were written to encourage those who were oppressed and saw little or no hope in terms of either politics or armed might. Their message was that God himself would intervene and reverse the situation in which they found themselves, delivering the godly from the hands of the wicked and establishing his rule for all to see. Sometimes such encouragement is given in the form of discourse in which the revelation of God's sovereignty is disclosed; at other times, as in the book of Daniel, it takes the form of a story or legend concerning the ancient worthy in whose name the book is written.

Such features are not peculiar to the apocalyptic books, but their form of presentation, together with their recurring theme of revealed secrets and divine intervention, indicates an identifiable and distinct body of literature within Judaism that, though sharing the ideals of prophecy, is nevertheless markedly different from it.

Common Themes. Certain well-marked themes run through the apocalyptic writings:

History and "the end." The whole of history is a unity under the overarching purpose of God. It is divided, however, into great epochs that must run their predetermined course; only then will the end come, and with it the dawning of the messianic kingdom and the age to come when evil will be routed and righteousness established forever.

Present troubles are in fact birth pangs heralding the end. Calculations, involving the use of numerology (*see* Number Symbolism), demonstrate that soon, very soon, earth's invincible empires will disappear and be replaced by God's eternal rule: "The coming of the times is very near. . . . The pitcher is near the well and the ship to the harbor, and the journey to the city, and life to its end" (2 Bar. 85.10). The writer of Daniel tries to be more precise, interpreting Jeremiah's seventy years' captivity as seventy weeks of years, ending in the writer's own day. The Christian expectation is no less eager, though less precise: " 'Surely, I am coming soon.' Amen. Come, Lord Jesus!" (Rev. 22.20; *see* Second Coming of Christ).

Cosmic cataclysm. The coming end will be "a time of anguish, such as has never occurred since nations first came into existence" (Dan. 12.1). Sometimes this is described in terms of political action and military struggle; at other times the conflict assumes cosmic proportions involving mysterious happenings on earth and in the heavens—earthquakes, famine, fearful celestial portents, and destruction by fire. Such things find an echo in the New Testament, where it is said that in the last days there will be an eclipse of the sun, and the stars will fall from heaven.

This cosmic upheaval is closely related to the concept of cosmic powers in the form of angels and demons. The angel hosts are drawn up in battle array against the demon hosts under the command of Satan. In the final battle the

powers of evil, together with the evil nations they represent, will be utterly destroyed.

The consummation. The coming kingdom is, generally speaking, to be established here on this earth; in some instances it has a temporary duration, and is followed by the age to come for, as 2 Esdras puts it, "The Most High has made not one world but two" (7.50). In this new divine order, the end will be as the beginning and *paradise will be restored. "Dualism" is sometimes used to describe the discontinuity between this age and the age to come, but continuity remains: generally speaking, this earth (albeit renewed or restored) is the scene of God's deliverance.

In some of these writings, the figures of Messiah and *Son of man, among others, are introduced as agents of the coming kingdom. These probably represent two originally distinct strands of eschatological expectation, which, in the course of time, became intertwined.

One significant development is the prevailing belief in a resurrection, a coming judgment, and the life to come (see Dan. 12.2 for an early reference). It is by this means that the gap, as it were, between the eschatology of the nation and the eschatology of the individual is finally bridged. Both together find their fulfillment in God's final redemption when all wrongs are to be righted and justice and peace are established forever.

D. S. Russell

APOCRYPHA. *This entry consists of two articles dealing with books or parts of books not considered canonical by every community of faith,* Jewish Apocrypha *and* Christian Apocrypha. *The first article,* Jewish Apocrypha, *surveys Jewish religious writings not recognized as part of the Bible in Jewish tradition nor by some Christian churches (see Canon). Among the latter these* *are commonly referred to as the Apocrypha of the Old Testament; those churches that do include some or all of these writings in their canon frequently refer to them as "deuterocanonical." See also Apocalyptic Literature and Pseudepigrapha. The second article, Christian Apocrypha, deals with early Christian writings not included in the canon of the New Testament but which contain similar types of literature often attributed to figures of the apostolic age.*

Jewish Apocrypha

The word *apocrypha*, a Greek neuter plural (singular, *apocryphon*), is used to designate a group of important religious writings from antiquity that are not universally regarded as belonging to the authentic *canon of Scripture, though many of them have been so regarded by particular communities. The word is applied primarily to the fifteen (or fourteen) books that are included in many editions of the English Bible as a supplement, usually printed between the Hebrew scriptures and the New Testament. The name, which means "things hidden away," is inappropriate, since none of these books (with the possible exception of 2 Esdras) was ever regarded as hidden or secret. For the most part, they are simply those books found only in manuscripts of the Septuagint (LXX), the ancient Greek translation of the Hebrew scriptures, and therefore possibly regarded as "canonical" by Greek-speaking Alexandrian Jews, though ultimately rejected by the Jewish community of Palestine and rabbinic authorities of later times (2 Esdras and the Prayer of Manasseh are not covered by this definition). Their preservation is largely due to the Christian community, which, for most of the first four centuries CE, accepted the Greek Old Testament as normative for its life and thought. In modern times the term "apocrypha" has

been extended more loosely to other books from the later Hellenistic and early Roman periods but which, so far as we know, never attained even quasicanonical status (these books are more commonly designated as *pseudepigrapha), and has also been extended by analogy to a large group of early Christian writings excluded from the New Testament canon in its final form. In this article we shall be concerned principally with the fifteen books described at the beginning of the paragraph. *(For the analogous early Christian writings, see the second article in this entry.)*

Canonical Status. Until recently it was commonly assumed that Jews of the period immediately before and after the beginning of the common era had two canons, one that was current in Palestine and another in Alexandria, the greatest center of Jewish life in the Hellenistic world. But newer evidence, including that from Qumran, suggests a more complex reconstruction, and indeed the use of the word "canon" may be somewhat inappropriate, since the list of included books was not explicitly fixed until the second century CE. The contents of the first two parts (Law and Prophets) of what would ultimately be called the canon had been accepted as sacred and authoritative since at least 200 BCE, but the works that constitute the third part of the Hebrew Bible (the Writings) have a less authoritative status and have been individually evaluated in quite different ways. It is to this last class that the books of the Apocrypha belong. Their one common denominator is the fact that all are contained, in Greek, in some manuscript of the Septuagint (with the exception, once again, of 2 Esdras and Prayer of Manasseh, to which we shall return).

The definition and final closing of the Jewish canon was in large measure due to the inner restructuring of Jewish society and the tightening of standards that resulted both from the destruction of the Temple in 70 CE and from the need for self-definition in the face of the threat presented by the rise of an aggressive Christian church. Christians, increasingly of gentile origin, naturally accepted the scriptures in the form most accessible to them, the Greek Septuagint. Jews, quite as naturally, reacted by emphatically rejecting the Septuagint and insisting that only those ancient books that were written in Hebrew could be regarded as authoritative. Even such books as Sirach and 1 Maccabees, which had clearly been written originally in Hebrew, were rejected, since internal evidence showed that they had been composed long after the time of Ezra, when, it was believed, prophecy had ceased.

Among Christians, the Old Testament continued for a long time to be tacitly accepted in its Greek form, even though objections were occasionally voiced by theologians and other scholars who were familiar with the Jewish position. The question of the canonicity of the "extra books" became acute only with Pope Damasus's choice of Jerome, in 382 CE, to make an authoritative translation of the Bible into Latin. As he worked on the Old Testament, Jerome became convinced that the Hebrew text alone was definitive and he therefore felt obliged to reject those books found only in Greek; these books he called "apocrypha." Whatever precise meaning he attached to that word, it was certainly intended to be pejorative. Strangely, his views were not accepted, and to the present the books he designated as "apocryphal" are incorporated in the canon of the Roman Catholic Church and distributed, according to their type, among the other books of the Old Testament. The formal designation for these books among Roman Catholics is "deuterocanonical," meaning books that belong to a second layer of the canon, but with no implication that they are of less worth than the others. The view of the Orthodox churches, for most of which the Septuagint continues to be the authoritative form of scripture, is substantially the same, though the list of books they regard as at least liturgically useful tends to be somewhat longer and can include such works as 1 Esdras, 3 and 4 Maccabees, and Psalm 151. (*See* Eastern Orthodoxy and the Bible.)

It was only with the Reformation and its emphasis upon the sole authority of scripture that Jerome's view came into its own. Protestants were unanimous in accepting the Jewish definition of the Old Testament canon. They were agreed that the extra books of the Greek canon, which was also that of the Latin Vulgate, should be gathered together and removed from among the books of the Hebrew canon; if included in the Bible at all, they should be placed in a separate section between the Testaments clearly labeled "Apocrypha." But they were not of one opinion with regard to the value of these books. Calvinists took the most extreme view, asserting in the Westminster Confession that they were of no more value than any other human writings, and their use was discouraged. Lutherans were inclined to value them more highly and to encourage their study, though not with any sense that they were of equal value with the authoritative books of the Hebrew canon. The Church of England requires the books of the Apocrypha to be included in any edition of the Bible authorized for use in public worship, and provides for considerable use of them in its lectionary while also insisting (in Art. 3 of the Thirty-Nine Articles) that they cannot be used to prove any point of doctrine.

In the early seventeenth century some Protestant editions of the Bible were published without the Apocrypha and, since 1827, when the British and Foreign Bible Society, followed shortly by the American Bible Society, under pressure from the Calvinist (Presbyterian) churches, decided to omit the apocryphal books from all its editions, omitting them has become the common practice. In the middle of the twentieth century, however, there began a considerable revival of interest in these books among both Protestants and Jews, based partly upon a more relaxed view of the nature of the canon, but even more upon a realization of the importance of the apocryphal literature for biblical research and interpretation. As a result, numerous editions of the Apocrypha have become available and a number of significant new commentaries on the apocryphal books have been published. Newer translations (e.g., GNB, NRSV) often include them in at least some editions.

Contents. Briefly described, the books of the standard Apocrypha are as follows: 1 Esdras is an alternative version of the Hebrew book of Ezra that includes a short extract from 2 Chronicles at the beginning and from Nehemiah at the end. It is found in manuscripts of the Septuagint, but is not considered one of the deuterocanonical books by the Latin church; in the Vulgate it is called 3 Esdras and is printed, for purely historical reasons, in an appendix after the New Testament. The *apocalyptic work traditionally called 2 Esdras is of Jewish origin, with some Christian additions, and was never part of the Septuagint. Except for a tiny fragment, the Greek text is lost, so it is best known in the Latin version that (like 1 Esdras) is printed in an appendix to the Vulgate, where it is called 4 Esdras; it is not considered deuterocanonical. Tobit is a romantic oriental tale,

best known for its very human characters, its high ethical teaching, and its use of magic and demonology. Judith is the fictitious story of a heroic Jewish woman who delivers her people by using feminine wiles to accomplish the assassination of the general of a pagan army that was besieging them. The Additions to the Book of Esther consists of a series of discontinuous passages that appear only in the Greek version of that book, apparently added, for the most part, to give a religious tone to that embarrassingly secular work. Two of the apocryphal books fall into the category of wisdom literature: there is, first of all, the Wisdom of Solomon, a patently pseudonymous work that deals with such basic themes as immortality and the nature of divine wisdom in language that is a mixture of Jewish theology and Greek philosophy; and, second, Sirach (or Ecclesiasticus), a much more traditional work, originally composed in Hebrew, that has its closest analogue in the book of Proverbs. The second part of the confused composition called Baruch (3.9–4.4) also belongs to wisdom literature, being a poem in praise of wisdom as God's special gift to Israel, while the preceding prose section consists of a brief narrative introducing a lengthy confession of Israel's sins as the cause of the Babylonian exile; the concluding poem (4.5–5.9) deals with the theme of Israel's restoration. If the Letter of Jeremiah is counted as chap. 6 of Baruch, as is often done, there are fourteen rather than fifteen apocryphal books, but it is clearly a separate work having for its theme the foolishness of idolatry. The Prayer of Azariah and the Song of the Three Young Men, Susanna, and Bel and the Dragon are additions that appear in the Greek version of Daniel, the first containing two widely used liturgical hymns, while the other two are popular tales in which Daniel is the hero. A

Greek form of the Prayer of Manasseh exists, but was not part of the original Septuagint, and it is deuterocanonical for only some eastern churches. The books called 1 and 2 Maccabees are two entirely independent and disparate historical narratives that record the heroic struggles that led to a brief period of independence for Jews in the second and first centuries BCE.

The importance of these books arises first of all from the fact that they were composed later than the canonical books of the Hebrew Bible and, apart from 2 Esdras, before the books of the New Testament. They therefore shed a welcome light on political, religious, and cultural developments in the later Hellenistic and early Roman periods and thus on the background of the New Testament. Furthermore, when regarded for their own sake, the Wisdom of Solomon is an important theological treatise, representing the first attempt to fuse two different intellectual strains, the Israelite and the Greek; and, for most readers, Sirach is at least as interesting as Proverbs and perhaps more accessible; Tobit, Judith, and Susanna are splendid examples of narrative art; and 1 Maccabees is a fine specimen of sober historical writing.

Among other ancient works sometimes classified as "apocrypha" are 3 and 4 Maccabees, the Psalms of Solomon, the several books of Enoch, the Baruch apocalypse (2 Baruch), the Book of Jubilees, and the Testaments of the Twelve Patriarchs.   *Robert C. Dentan*

Christian Apocrypha

Beyond the twenty-seven books collected in the New Testament canon, many other examples were produced of each of the four types of New Testament literature: gospels, acts, letters, and apocalypses. The intentions of the authors of these books, which are now known as

New Testament Apocrypha, were diverse; some sought to supplement works already in circulation, while others sought to supplant them. In some cases, these books simply served as light entertainment for Christian believers; in others, the authors wanted to promulgate practices and ideas condemned by the church.

Apocryphal Gospels. Of the roughly two dozen gospels produced during the early centuries of Christianity, those concerning on the one hand Jesus' infancy and childhood, and on the other his *descent into hell between his death and his *resurrection, clearly augment the canonical Gospels, which pass over these matters in almost total silence (Luke 2.42–51 relates one incident when Jesus was a boy of twelve). Naturally, however, early Christians were curious about both of these periods; not surprisingly, traditions grew up around each and were recorded. The Protevangelium of James and the Infancy Gospel of Thomas, two second-century infancy gospels, were developed over the following centuries into the History of Joseph the Carpenter and the Arabic Gospel of the Infancy, as well as other similar writings describing Jesus' early years and the miracles surrounding contact with the infant, his clothing, and even his bathwater.

In these works, the young Jesus is portrayed as possessing miraculous powers. The uses to which such powers are put, however, is often incompatible with the character found in the canonical Gospels. For example, while playing with other children on the Sabbath, Jesus molded twelve clay birds. When an elder reported Jesus' desecration of the Sabbath to Joseph, Jesus clapped his hands and the birds came to life. Another time, when Jesus was walking through a crowd, someone bumped him, whereupon Jesus turned and said, "You will never get to where you are going," and the person fell down dead.

Apocryphal accounts of Christ's descent into the underworld and his victory over its powers are more rare. One of the earliest can be found in the fourth-century Gospel of Nicodemus (also called the Acts of Pilate); another, from the next century, is the Gospel of Bartholomew.

With the discovery in 1945 of the *Nag Hammadi library, several previously unknown (or known only by name) gnostic gospels have come to light. These and related works (e.g., the Epistle of the Apostles), commonly present the risen Christ's revelations to the disciples during the period between his resurrection and *ascension (a period that the gnostics expanded from 40 to 550 days). Often these accounts are related as a dialogue in which the disciples question Jesus about subjects that remained obscure in his earlier teaching. Most often, however, the discussion goes beyond the Gospel traditions to speculations about cosmology, gnostic interpretations of the creation accounts of Genesis, and the fate of the different classes of humanity. Notable examples preserved at Nag Hammadi are the Apocryphon of James, the Sophia of Jesus Christ, the Book of Thomas, and the Dialogue of the Savior. Among the most significant of the Nag Hammadi documents, and very different in character, is a Coptic version of the Gospel of Thomas, a collection of 114 sayings *(logia)* of Jesus, many similar to logia in the synoptic Gospels and in a late second-century CE papyrus (*see* Agrapha).

Still other gospels are known only by name or from brief patristic quotations. Some of these originated among early Jewish-Christian sects, as is clear from their titles (Gospel of the Hebrews, Gospel of the Ebionites, Gospel of the Nazarenes).

Apocryphal Acts. Since the canonical Acts of the Apostles record in detail the activities of only a few of the apostles, second- and third-century Christian authors drew up narratives of the other apostles' activities. Even apostles portrayed in Acts had further exploits recounted, sometimes in minute detail. The most notable are five works from the second and third centuries, attributed to Leucius Charinus, alleged to have been a disciple of John; scholars agree, however, that the actual authors of these and all other apocryphal acts remain unknown.

The Acts of Peter (ca. 180–190 CE) describes the rivalry between Simon Peter and Simon Magus. Among Peter's miracles are a speaking dog, a dried fish restored to life, and resurrections from the dead. The comical climax of the contest takes place in the Roman forum, when the magician attempts to fly to heaven. The document closes with an account of Peter's martyrdom by crucifixion.

The Acts of John (ca. 150–180) purports to be an eyewitness account of John's missionary travels in Asia Minor. The sermons attributed to him evince docetic tendencies: Jesus had no proper shape or body, only an appearance, so to one person he appeared in one shape, and to another in a totally different shape; when he walked, he left no footprints. Besides a droll tale about bedbugs, the work has a Hymn of Christ as well as the apostles dancing in a circle.

The Acts of Andrew (early third century?) is known chiefly through a long epitome prepared by Gregory of Tours (sixth century). To judge by the extant portions, the Acts are in essence a narrative of Andrew's journey from Pontus to Achaia, during which he performed many miracles and delivered many lengthy, severely ascetic exhortations. The Martyrdom of St. Andrew, a variant text of part of the work, describes the apostle's death by crucifixion.

The Acts of Thomas (first half of the third century) is the only apocryphal Acts preserved in its entirety, surviving in Greek, Syriac, Ethiopic, Armenian, and Latin versions. It tells of Thomas's missionary work in India, his healing miracles, and his martyrdom. It also contains several fine liturgical hymns; the best-known is the "Hymn of the Soul" (also called the "Hymn of the Pearl"), which has suggestive allegorical overtones.

The Acts of Paul, according to Tertullian, was written by a presbyter of Asia Minor with the purpose of honoring the apostle. Despite ecclesiastical disapproval, his book became quite popular with the laity. Among the surviving episodes is one that tells of Paul and Thecla, a noblewoman and follower of Paul who preached and administered *baptism; in this section we find the famous description of Paul: "little in stature, with a bald head and crooked legs . . . with eyebrows meeting, and a nose somewhat hooked." Another episode, discovered in 1936, gives a detailed account of Paul's encounter in the amphitheater at Ephesus with a lion to which he had earlier preached the gospel and had baptized.

These works are generally sectarian in character, whether orthodox or theologically deviant (Docetic, Gnostic, Manichean). Sectarian influence can especially be seen in emphasis on sexual asceticism and martyrdom. Other legendary Acts dating from the fourth to the sixth century are the Acts of Andrew and Matthias among the Cannibals, Acts of Andrew and Paul, Acts of Barnabas, Acts of James the Great, Acts of John by Pro-chorus, Acts of the Apostles Peter and Andrew, Slavonic Acts of Peter, Acts of Philip, Acts of Pilate, and Acts of Thaddaeus. This type of literature may be seen as paralleling the novels of antiquity.

Apocryphal Letters. The apocryphal epistles are relatively few in number. The spurious Third Letter of Paul to the Corinthians, with an introductory note to Paul from presbyters at Corinth, is part of the Acts of Paul, and came to be highly regarded in the Armenian and Syrian churches. It addresses doctrinal issues such as prophecy, creation, the human nature of Christ, and the resurrection of the body.

In the west, Paul's Letter to the Laodiceans was disseminated widely and is actually included in all of the eighteen printed German Bibles prior to Luther's translation. The Correspondence between Paul and Seneca, consisting of fourteen letters between the Stoic philosopher Seneca and Paul, has come down to us in more than three hundred manuscripts; the banal content and colorless style of the letters show that they cannot come from the hands of either the moralist or the apostle. Other apocryphal letters are the Epistle of Titus and the Epistles of Christ and Abgar.

Apocryphal Apocalypses. In addition to the Revelation of John, there are several apocalypses attributed to other apostles. The earliest is the Apocalypse of Peter (ca. 125–150 CE), preserved in part in Greek and fully in Ethiopic. Making use of beliefs about the afterlife from the *Odyssey* and the *Aeneid,* it tells of the delights of the redeemed in heaven and (at much greater length) the torments of the damned in hell. These ideas were elaborated extensively in the following century by the author of the Apocalypse of Paul, who describes how Paul is caught up to paradise and witnesses the judgment of two souls, one righteous and the other wicked. He is then led through hell, where he sees the tortures of the wicked and intercedes on their behalf, obtaining for them relief every Lord's day. A visit to paradise ensues, during which Paul meets the patriarchs, the major prophets, Enoch, and finally Adam. Some of these themes became part of medieval beliefs given wider dissemination through Dante's *Divine Comedy*. The Nag Hammadi library also provided a number of apocryphal apocalypses, including another Apocalypse of Peter, another of Paul, the First and Second Apocalypses of James, and others.

Modern Apocrypha. The urge to supplement the Bible has continued down through the ages. In modern times, fraudulent productions continue to excite the hopes of naive readers that priceless treasures have been uncovered. Despite repeated claims of authenticity, such productions invariably lack historical or literary value. Among the most often published are The Aquarian Gospel, The Archko Volume, The Letter of Benan, The Description of Christ, The Confessions of Pontius Pilate, The Gospel of Josephus, The Book of Jasher, The Lost Books of the Bible, The Nazarene Gospel, The Letter from Heaven, Cahspe, and The Twenty-ninth Chapter of Acts.   *Bruce M. Metzger*

APPLE OF THE EYE. The translation "apple of the eye" corresponds to several related phrases, all of which mean the pupil of the eye and indicate something near and dear which is to be protected. In Hebrew, these expressions (ʾîšôn ʿayin ["little man of the eye"]: Deut. 32.10; Prov. 7.2; *bat ʿayin* ["daughter of the eye"]: Lam. 2.18; Zech. 2.8; ʾîšôn bat ʿayin [a double reading]: Ps. 17.8) refer to the reflected human image that appears in the pupil of

the eye. The same idiom is found in Sirach 17.22, in classical Greek, and in Latin (*pupilla*, from which the English word "pupil" is derived). The English phrase "apple of the eye" is a periphrastic translation, using a different metaphoric idiom.   *Russell Fuller*

AQEDAH. The Hebrew word for "binding," and the common designation for Genesis 22.1–19, in which God tests Abraham by commanding that he sacrifice his son Isaac. Abraham binds Isaac. When he is about to slaughter him, an angel calls to him to desist, whereupon Abraham offers a ram instead. Although the Aqedah is the climax of the Genesis narratives about Abraham, a final testimony to his faith in, obedience to, and fear of God, it is not mentioned elsewhere in the Hebrew Bible. Isaac's role in Genesis 22 is passive, but postbiblical Jewish interpretations of the first to the eighth centuries CE transform him into an adult, voluntary sacrificial offering. Some texts give reasons for the episode, including Satan's questioning of Abraham's devotion to God and Isaac's and Ishmael's arguments concerning who was the more righteous. During this period, the Aqedah became associated with the Rosh Hashanah liturgy, with the shofar recalling the substituted ram. Mount Moriah, where the Aqedah took place, was identified with the site of the Temple. Isaac emerges both as the paradigm of the martyr and as the perfect sacrifice whose act brings merit to and has redemptive value for his own descendants. Some rabbinic traditions maintain that Isaac, as a sacrificial victim, shed blood, and others conclude that he also died and was resurrected; thus wrote the twelfth-century rabbi Ephraim of Bonn, in the context of the martyrdom of many Rhineland Jews and the destruction of their communities.

The New Testament refers to the Aqedah not as an example of a redemptive sacrificial death but rather as an example of faith. Echoes of the former may however be found in Paul's understanding of the significance of the death and *resurrection of Jesus, and the Septuagint of Genesis 22 may be alluded to in Romans 8.32, Mark 1.11, and Matthew 3.17. Early church fathers such as Clement and Tertullian understood Isaac's sacrifice as a prototype of the sacrifice of Jesus (*see* Typology). The divine testing of Abraham and the subsequent near sacrifice of his son also appear in the *Qurʾān. Early Muslim exegetes disagreed as to whether the son, unnamed in the Qurʾānic passage, is Isaac or Ishmael. Some of the earliest traditions declare him to be Isaac, but by the ninth or tenth century the consensus was that Ishmael, increasingly associated with Mecca and identified as the ancestor of the northern Arabs, was the voluntary sacrificial offering.

From antiquity to the present, the Aqedah has been portrayed in the arts. For example, it appears on a wall painting of the third-century CE synagogue at Dura-Europos and on a floor mosaic of the sixth-century synagogue at Beth Alpha. During the Renaissance, such sculptors and painters as Ghiberti, Donatello, Titian, Caravaggio, and Rembrandt included the Aqedah among their depictions of biblical subjects. Among notable modern literary treatments of the Aqedah is Søren Kierkegaard's *Fear and Trembling* (1843).

See also Suffering.

Barbara Geller Nathanson

ARAMAIC. A Northwest Semitic language related to *Hebrew. It was usually written in the twenty-two letters of the Phoenician alphabet, although originally some letters had to represent more than one Aramaic consonant. The shapes of the letters used for Aramaic developed into the square script, which was adopted for Hebrew too in the Persian period. Aramaic differs from Hebrew in various ways. For example, the vocabulary is different, although some words are similar (e.g., Hebrew šālôm, "peace," but Aramaic šĕlām); Hebrew uses the prefix ha- as the definite article, but Aramaic uses the suffix -ā; some consonants in Hebrew correspond to different ones in Aramaic (e.g., Hebrew hāʾāreṣ, "the land" or "earth," but Aramaic ʾarqāʾ, later ʾarʿāʾ).

A number of Old Aramaic inscriptions are known from the tenth or ninth century BCE onward from Syria and Mesopotamia, and in the latter region it replaced Akkadian (Babylonian and Assyrian) as the language of everyday speech.

According to Deuteronomy 26.5, the Israelites were of Aramean descent, but the Bible nowhere represents Aramaic as their language, and Genesis 31.47–48 tells how Jacob called a pillar Galeed ("heap of witness"), whereas his Aramean father-in-law Laban used the Aramaic equivalent, Jegar-sahadutha. In 2 Kings 18.26 (= Isa. 36.11) officials of Judah plead with an Assyrian official during the siege of Jerusalem in 701 BCE not to speak "in the language of Judah" (i.e., Hebrew) in the hearing of the ordinary people of the city, but to use Aramaic. Aramaic had thus become the language of diplomacy (one understood by Judean leaders), while ordinary people understood only Hebrew; and the Assyrian wanted such ordinary people to understand his call to surrender.

From the sixth century BCE Aramaic continued to spread as the vernacular in the Palestinian region. Jeremiah 10.11 is in Aramaic, as is Ezra 4.8–6.18; 7.12–26. The Aramaic passages in Ezra are primarily official documents, and they reflect the fact that the Persian empire recognized the position of Aramaic by making one form of it an official language—the so-called Imperial or Official Aramaic. A Jewish colony at Elephantine (Yeb) in Upper Egypt has left many Aramaic papyri from the fifth century BCE (including letters about the rebuilding of a Jewish temple there and about the *Passover); other documents in Aramaic from Egypt, Palestine, and other Near Eastern countries of this century and succeeding centuries have been found. Daniel 2.4b–7.28 is in Aramaic, and the book is usually dated around 164 BCE, though the author probably used earlier sources. Some scholars postulate a connection between the story of Nebuchadnezzar's madness in Daniel 4 and the Prayer of Nabonidus, an Aramaic text from Qumran which tells how Nabonidus, the last king of Babylon, was ill in Tema in North Arabia and was healed by the intercession of a Jew. Among other Aramaic texts from Qumran are the Genesis Apocryphon (the story of Abraham, in general dependence on Genesis), parts of 1 Enoch, and a Targum (a free translation) of Job, which differs from the Targum of later times (*see* Translations, *article on* Targums).

By the first century CE, Aramaic was in general use in Palestine, especially in Galilee, although Hebrew was also spoken as a vernacular, especially in Judea. In the New Testament we find *bar*, the Aramaic word for "son," instead of Hebrew *ben*, in several personal names (e.g., Barabbas, Bartholomew, Bartimaeus) and in the patronymic of Simon Peter, Bar-Jona, and Aramaic words are used even in Jerusalem: Golgotha (Mark 14.72, etc.), Gabbatha (John 19.13: "in Hebrew" probably means "in the language of the Hebrews" and can thus denote Aramaic), and Akeldama (Acts 1.19).

Some of the words of Jesus are Aramaic: "Talitha cum" (Mark 5.41) and "Eloi, Eloi, lema sabachthani" (Mark 15.34; cf. Matt. 27.46, but there is a variant reading in Hebrew); but "Ephphatha" (Mark 7.34) and "*Abba" (Mark 14.36; cf. Rom. 8.15) can be explained as either Hebrew or Aramaic. The statement in Matthew 26.73 that Peter's speech showed him to be a Galilean has been illustrated by rabbinic references to the inability of Galileans to pronounce guttural consonants correctly. As a Galilean, Jesus spoke Aramaic, and on the cross he quoted Psalm 22.1 in Aramaic, not in the Hebrew original, but he probably also spoke Hebrew. When Rabban Gamaliel wrote to Jews in Galilee—probably in the late first century CE—he wrote in Aramaic, according to the Babylonian Talmud.

Many Aramaic documents from the early centuries CE have been preserved. The Nabatean Arabs, who lived to the east and south of Palestine, used an Aramaic dialect, as did the inhabitants of Palmyra in the Syrian desert. Some letters and other documents from the Second Jewish Revolt against the Romans in 132–135 CE are written in Aramaic, some in Hebrew, and some in *Greek. They include letters from the leader of the revolt, who has usually been known as Bar Kokhba ("the son of the star" in Aramaic; cf. Num. 24.17), but whose real name was Bar or Ben Kosiba. Texts of the following centuries show differences between western and eastern dialects of Aramaic. The distinction appears, for example, in the Targums: the Jerusalem or Palestinian Targums (on the Pentateuch) are in western Aramaic, whereas the Targums of Onkelos (the Pentateuch) and Jonathan (the Former and Latter Prophets) reached their final form in the east, though they were probably originally composed in Palestine.

Western dialects include Jewish Palestinian Aramaic (e.g., the Jerusalem Talmud) and Samaritan and Christian Palestinian Aramaic; and eastern dialects include Babylonian Aramaic (e.g., the Babylonian Talmud), Syriac, and Mandaic (the language used of the texts of the gnostic Mandean sect).

Syriac reached its present form ca. 200 CE. Although there are earlier, non-Christian inscriptions, most of the Syriac literature is Christian, because it became the standard language of many eastern churches. They carried its use as far as South India and even China.

Aramaic was eventually replaced by Arabic in the Near East as a result of the spread of Islam. A western form survives in a few Syrian villages, and there is still a vernacular form of Syriac.

J. A. Emerton

ARCHAEOLOGY AND THE BIBLE.

History of Archaeology. Archaeology is the study of the remains of ancient civilizations uncovered through excavations. It is a relatively young discipline, for the first excavations in Mesopotamia were those of Paul Emile Botta at Nineveh in 1842 and Austin Henry Layard at Nimrud in 1845, while the first in the Aegean area were conducted by Heinrich Schliemann at Troy in 1870 and at Mycenae in 1876.

Egyptian antiquities had been brought to the attention of Europe by Napoleon's invasion in 1798. Most of the activities in Egypt in the nineteenth century, such as those by Giovanni Belzoni, were treasure hunts and not excavations. At the end of the nineteenth century, William Matthew Flinders Petrie introduced some semblance of order.

Petrie was the first to excavate in Palestine at Tell el-Hesi in 1890. From his prior experiences in Egypt, Petrie recognized the value of pottery for dating the strata. The first American excavations in Palestine were at Samaria in 1908–1910 by George A. Reisner and Clarence S. Fisher, who introduced systematic methods of recording discoveries.

William Foxwell Albright, the dean of American archaeologists in the first half of the twentieth century, established a sound basis for pottery chronology in his excavations at Tell Beit Mirsim in 1926–1932. Nelson Glueck, Albright's student, conducted extensive surface surveys in Transjordan from 1933, and in Israel's Negeb from 1952.

At excavations at Samaria (1931–1935) and Jericho (1952–1958), Kathleen Kenyon introduced more precise methods of analyzing soils and debris. She later excavated in Jerusalem (1961–1967). Significant work was also carried on by many French and German scholars.

Since 1948, Israeli scholars have assumed leading roles in the exploration of their homeland. Yigael Yadin conducted large-scale excavations at Hazor (1956–1958) and Masada (1963–1965). At the latter site, Yadin initiated the practice of using volunteers rather than paid workers. After 1968, Benjamin Mazar, Nahman Avigad, and Yigal Shiloh directed major excavations in Jerusalem.

G. Ernest Wright, in his excavations at Shechem (1956–1964), and William G. Dever, in his work at Gezer (1964–1971), trained scores of young American excavators. It was in the 1966 season at Shechem that a geologist was first added to the staff. Since 1970, influenced by New World archaeology, archaeologists in the Near East have also enlisted the help of numerous scientific specialists such as osteologists, paleobotanists, and paleozoologists to reconstruct ancient ecologies and societies. Specialized laboratories are used for such processes as carbon-14 dating and neutron activation of pottery to determine its place of origin.

Ironically, often the most spectacular discoveries have been made by chance rather than by scientific deduction. At Ras Shamra in Syria, a peasant's plow struck a tomb, which led to the discovery of ancient *Ugaritic. A Bedouin in search of a lost goat discovered the cave at Qumran that contained the *Dead Sea Scrolls. Peasants seeking fertilizer in Egypt discovered the *Amarna tablets in 1887 and the Coptic Gnostic codices at *Nag Hammadi in 1945.

Archaeological Methods. The first important attempt to identify sites in Palestine with biblical cities was made by Edward Robinson and Eli Smith in 1838 on the basis of modern Arabic place names. In a few cases, inscriptions have confirmed the identity of ancient sites, as at Gibeon, Gezer, Arad, Lachish, Dan, and Abila. According to Yohanan Aharoni, out of the approximately 475 place names mentioned in the Bible, only slightly more than half have been identified with any degree of certainty.

Sites of ancient settlements may be discovered by systematic surveys of surface remains. Israeli surveys in 1965 in the Haifa area and the Negeb uncovered two hundred previously unknown sites. Benno Rothenberg discovered two hundred new sites in the Negeb and Arabah and a hundred in the Sinai in 1966–1968. Surveys of the Golan Heights and the West Bank since 1968 have plotted hundreds of other new sites.

Most ancient Near Eastern cities have left their remains behind in stratified mounds called "tells" ("tell" is the transliteration of the Arabic, while the spelling "tel" is from Hebrew; cf. Josh. 11.13). These trapezoidal mounds are to be found in the Near East because settled urban populations have existed there for millennia, with generation after generation rebuilding upon earlier rubble; the debris was kept in a compact shape by the city wall. The height of a tell can be considerable. In Mesopotamia the tells range from 56 ft (17 m) at Kish up to 140 ft (43 m) at Tell Brak. In Palestine, the depth of debris at Jericho is about 60 ft (18 m), and at Beth-shan and Megiddo about 70 ft (21 m).

The excavator's first step is to secure permission from the country's Department of Antiquities. The next step, if the land is privately owned, is either to purchase the area to be excavated, as at Megiddo and Dothan, or more usually to rent it with the understanding that the land will be restored to its former condition after the termination of the excavations. Not only must rent be paid for the use of the land but compensation must be given for the crops destroyed. The cost of excavating areas occupied with houses is prohibitive. Only where generous funding is available, such as for the excavations of the Athenian Agora, is this possible.

The cost of financing excavations has varied greatly. At one extreme was the luxury of the University of Chicago's expedition after World War I at Megiddo with its budget of sixteen million dollars. At the other extreme was the fabled austerity of Petrie's camp in Egypt, where a little more than a dollar per week was spent for provisions. Kenyon's excavations at Jericho cost about twelve thousand dollars per year, and her later work at Jerusalem about thirty thousand dollars per year. On average, the cost of a season's expedition now runs well over 100,000 dollars.

In the nineteenth century, individual subscribers in Britain supported the Palestine Exploration Fund and the Egypt

Exploration Fund, which sponsored surveys, excavations, and publications. Wealthy patrons such as John D. Rockefeller, Charles Marston, Jacob Schiff, and Leon Levy have helped pay for excavations respectively at Megiddo, Lachish, Samaria, and Ashkelon.

Recent excavations have depended upon consortia of schools and other organizations. Funds for Kenyon's work at Jericho came from forty-three universities, societies, and museums. Along with securing the necessary funds, the director must assemble a staff of trained supervisors and a work crew of laborers.

The site to be excavated is surveyed, both horizontally, in a grid marked with pegs, and vertically, in elevations from a benchmark. The supervisor then determines which fields should be excavated, for example, over the probable sites of the gate, the wall, the chief residences. In some recent cases, the use of a magnetometer or aerial/satellite photography has facilitated the location of such structures. Each field is then subdivided, often into a series of 20-ft (ca. 6-m) squares. Each of the square areas is worked by an area supervisor and six or eight workers or volunteers.

The digging season varies from two weeks to six months. Most expeditions take place in the summer for the sake of participating professors and students. The exception would be work at sites such as Jericho or Susa, which are unbearably hot in the summer.

The average workday is a strenuous one, beginning long before sunrise to avoid having to work in the hot afternoon. Workers often rise before five A.M., dig for three hours, have breakfast, and then work for another three hours before lunch. After lunch, pottery is washed and sorted. The director and his staff often work late into the night, recording their finds.

The object of the excavator is to dig stratigraphically, that is, to remove the debris and associated objects layer by layer. Bulldozers have sometimes been used to remove modern remains or ancient fill. But even those who are interested chiefly in earlier levels are obliged to record carefully later occupations, such as those of Byzantine and Islamic periods.

Since successive strata were not deposited at a uniformly level rate over a flat surface, absolute heights are not chronologically meaningful. Added complications arise from intrusions such as pits. The archaeologist often finds "robber trenches," where stones have been removed for reuse.

Picks are used to break up the soil, and large oversized hoes to scoop up the dirt into baskets. For finer work a small pick is used together with a trowel and a brush. Also essential are meter-sticks, levels, strings, tags, and labels for measuring and recording; computers are being used more and more in the field for registering excavated materials, as well as in preparing them for publication after the digging has come to an end. When a special object is found, its exact location and level are recorded. Ordinary sherds are placed in carefully labeled buckets for washing and later examination.

It is often worth sieving the soil to retrieve small objects such as coins. Most bronze coins appear as tiny spots of green in the soil. During the first three years of the Mazar excavation at Jerusalem ten thousand coins were found.

The earlier Fisher-Reisner methods had included the careful recording of objects and of building levels. But between levels their diagrams often showed empty spaces where attribution to a stratum was made according to the absolute height of the deposits. Kenyon introduced improved methods, which involved the careful cutting of balks (unexcavated strips between squares) and the minute analysis of the different types of soils that appeared in the vertical sections created by the balks. Her methods are best suited to small areas where sizable architecture is not present, although attention to stratigraphy is essential in any context.

One of the important problems facing the excavator is the location of the dump for depositing the earth that has been dug up. Care must be taken that nothing of value is thrown away. From the Chicago dump at Megiddo, for example, Israeli shepherds recovered an invaluable fragment of the Babylonian *Gilgamesh Epic.

Special difficulty attends the excavations of sites where buildings are made of stones, which are almost invariably reused. On the other hand, the detection of mud brick walls is also difficult. Tombs present special problems: they have often been reused and may be tightly packed with skeletons and objects that must be removed with special care. Tombs often reward the excavator with whole vessels and even jewelry. Caves are often packed deep with noxious bat droppings.

It is highly desirable that the areas excavated should, if possible, be tested to bedrock or to virgin soil. When, however, the water table is reached, the entire trench turns quickly into a quagmire. This is why Robert Koldewey in his work at Babylon could explore only the later Neo-Babylonian level of Nebuchadrezzar and not the Old Babylonian level of Hammurapi.

The development of underwater archaeology was made possible by the invention in 1942 by Jacques-Yves Cousteau and Emile Gagnan of the aqualung and depth-compensating regulator. The advent of scuba (Self-Contained Underwater Breathing Apparatus) diving made the process much cheaper and simpler. Underwater explorations have clarified the Herodian seaport of Caesarea, and other coastal sites and harbors throughout the Mediterranean.

Archaeological Finds. The most common objects to be found are sherds of broken pottery in enormous quantities. James Pritchard estimated that four seasons at Gibeon produced in excess of 200,000 sherds. All the pieces of pottery are washed and sorted, but often only a fraction are saved and recorded. Of almost 150,000 sherds washed in the first season at Dothan, Joseph Free recorded 6,000 pieces.

A tiny fraction of sherds may have inscriptions on them. Over fifty thousand pieces were washed at Gibeon before an inscribed ostracon appeared. Important inscriptions have been preserved on ostraca from Samaria, Arad, and Lachish.

An ivory from Megiddo depicts nude captives being brought before a king seated on a throne. Hundreds of decorated ivory fragments have been found, fittingly enough, at Samaria in view of the reference to Ahab's "ivory house" (1 Kings 22.39). These illustrate the "beds of ivory" denounced by Amos (6.4). Carved ivories from Arslan Tash and elsewhere depict an alluring goddess or woman peering out of a window.

From the Assyrian siege at Lachish in 701 BCE, excavators found an extraordinary assemblage of fifteen hundred to two thousand skeletons over which animal bones, mostly of pigs, had been scattered. Human skeletons can provide medical information. Three skulls from Lachish had been trephined, that is, holes had been cut into their skulls, perhaps to drain fluids resulting from trauma or disease. Evidence of gold, silver, and even bronze implants have been found in teeth from Egypt, Phoenicia, and Palestine. Measurements of skeletons found in tombs of the Herodian period indicate that the average person of that day was quite short, about 5 ft 3 in (1.6 m) tall.

Highly perishable objects, such as textiles, have been found but rarely in Palestine, and only in the dry Dead Sea region. For example, wooden boxes, coils of flax, basketry, and the oldest preserved toga were found in the caves occupied during the Second Jewish Revolt (ca. 135 CE). Even the tresses of a woman were preserved at Masada.

The many figurines found are generally interpreted as cultic, especially the nude female figurines. Representations of riders and horses found at Jerusalem may have been related to a solar cult; animal figurines from Beth-shan may have emanated from the cult of Nergal/Mekal/Seth.

Many small seals bear not only important inscriptions but also fine artistic representations. The seal of Shema found at Megiddo has a magnificent engraving of a roaring lion, the seal of Jaazaniah from Tell en-Nasbeh depicts a fighting cock, and a seal from Arad bears the outline plan of the citadel.

Metal objects vary greatly in their state of preservation. Gold objects are the best preserved; silver is usually covered with black tarnish, and bronze with a greenish patina. Iron rusts badly—often to a residue of reddish powder. Among the most significant objects in silver ever found are two amulets (ca. 600 BCE) inscribed with the priestly benediction of Numbers 6.24–26—the oldest biblical text discovered to date.

Among the most valuable metal objects are coins, usually made of silver, copper, or bronze. Coinage, which was invented in the seventh century BCE, was introduced into the Levant by the sixth century and was being minted locally by

the fifth. Discoveries of coins in Palestine from the Persian period indicate that references to coins in Ezra 2.69; 8.27; and Nehemiah 7.70–72, whether they are interpreted as Persian darics or Greek drachmas, are not anachronistic. The earliest Greek coins (sixth century BCE) found in Palestine include one from Thasos found at Shechem, one from Athens, and another from Cos found at Jerusalem.

Archaeological Evidence and Biblical Traditions.

Chronological terms. Beginning with the fourth millennium BCE, the following is the usual division of eras for the Levant: Early Bronze Age (EB) = ca. 3300–2000 BCE; Middle Bronze Age (MB) = ca. 2000–1550 BCE; Late Bronze Age (LB) = ca. 1550–1200 BCE; Iron Age = ca. 1200–539 BCE; Persian Period = 539–332 BCE; Hellenistic Period = 332–63 BCE; Roman Period = 63 BCE–324 CE.

Primeval history. Mesopotamian literature provides some parallels to the biblical stories of the *creation and the *Flood. *Enuma Elish,* the "Babylonian creation epic" (ca. 1100 BCE), describes how Marduk, the god of Babylon, created the heavens and the earth from the carcass of Tiamat, the goddess of the deep. The publication by George A. Smith in 1872 of the Babylonian flood story from the Gilgamesh Epic created something of a sensation because of its parallels with the biblical Flood story. In 1965, W. G. Lambert and Alan Millard published another epic, Atrahasis, which contains both a creation and a flood account. The Babylonian gods sent the flood because they could not sleep due to the noisy tumult of human beings.

Leonard Woolley believed that he had found evidence of the flood in a 10-ft (3-m) water-borne layer of sediment at Ur dated to roughly 4000 BCE. But this does not correlate with other flood deposits, such as those at Fara and Kish, dated to about 2700 BCE, and flooding in the Mesopotamian river basin was a frequent occurrence. Thus, while there is general support for a background of catastrophic flooding, there is no certain correlation of a sediment layer with the biblical Flood.

Ancestral age. Although Julius Wellhausen and many later scholars have questioned the historicity of the narratives of the ancestors of Israel as found in Genesis 12–50, evidence from Mesopotamia and Syria tends to support the antiquity and authenticity of at least some of the biblical traditions.

Woolley's excavations revealed the advanced civilization of Ur in the third millennium BCE. Ur-nammu, a king at the end of the third millennium, promulgated the earliest known law code. Ur and Haran, where Abraham and Terah are said to have sojourned, were both centers of the worship of Sin, the moon god.

The MB royal palace at *Mari on the Euphrates has yielded an archive of 25,000 tablets, which provide evidence that names in Abraham's *genealogy were current in the area in the early second millennium BCE. The Mari texts illustrate the system of power alliances prior to the rise of Hammurapi, similar to the alliance related in Genesis 14.

Texts from Alalakh (eighteenth century BCE) and Nuzi (fifteenth century BCE) have been cited to illuminate the social customs of the ancestors. Sarah's provision of her handmaid to Abraham to procure a son was an accepted custom, also attested in the Code of Hammurapi.

Many scholars date Abraham and Isaac to the MB I period (also called EB IV and Intermediate EB/MB). A number of nonwalled villages and hundreds of smaller settlements from this period in the Negeb may illustrate the kind of seminomadic sites implied in Genesis.

The story of Joseph, which contains what may be called "Egyptianisms," can be set in the Hyksos period (seventeenth century BCE) or earlier. A papyrus in the Brooklyn Museum dated to the eighteenth century BCE contains a list of Semites sold as slaves to Egypt; a Ugaritic text tells of a man who was sold by his companions to some passing Egyptians. Many scholars, however, date the Joseph narrative to the first millennium.

The Exodus. The sojourn of the Israelites in Egypt is not recorded in Egyptian documents. The sole reference to Israel comes from the stele of Merneptah (late thirteenth century BCE), which refers to them in the land of Canaan. The storehouse of Ramesses has been identified with Qantir.

Canaanite parallels have led many scholars to argue for the antiquity of the Song of the Sea. Literary comparisons between the Mosaic *covenant and second-millennium treaties, especially those of the Hittites, support arguments for its antiquity.

The date of the *Exodus is disputed; some scholars have proposed an early date, in the sixteenth or fifteenth century BCE, but a majority prefer a date in the thirteenth century. No archaeological evidence confirms the traditional southern route through the Sinai peninsula or the location of Mount Sinai.

The Israelites are reported to have passed from the Sinai through the Transjordanian kingdoms of Edom and Moab. A glistening bronze snake found at Timnah illustrates the episode recorded in Numbers 21.9. The account concerning the prophet Balaam, called by the king of Moab to curse the Israelites, is remarkably paralleled by an Aramaic inscription from Deir ᶜAlla in Transjordan, dating from the late eighth century BCE.

One of the arguments for the late date of the Exodus was Nelson Glueck's conclusion from his surveys of Transjordan that there were no settled populations in Edom and Moab in the Middle and Late Bronze Ages. More recently, evidence of settlement in these periods has been found.

The conquest. Palestine before its conquest by the Israelites was occupied by the Canaanites, whose culture has been illuminated by texts from the Syrian coastal site of Ugarit, destroyed around 1200 BCE. Ugaritic literary texts feature such Canaanite deities as Baal, El, and Astarte. Canaanite temples have been uncovered at many sites, including several at Hazor, the greatest city in ancient Palestine.

The date of the conquest of Canaan hinges on the date of the Exodus. The fourteenth-century BCE Amarna letters discovered in Egypt include correspondence from Palestinian kings, asking for Egyptian aid against the Habiru. Although it is not possible to equate the Hebrews with the Habiru, the former may have been a part of the larger movement of the Habiru.

Archaeological evidence for the conquest is problematic. Evidence for LB settlements at Jericho, Gibeon, and Ai are nonexistent, scanty, eroded, or not yet discovered. The destruction in the thirteenth and twelfth centuries of strong Canaanite cities such as Hazor, Bethel, and Tell Beit Mirsim has been attributed to the Israelites. Some of the destructions of western cities at this time may have been caused by the Egyptians or invading Philistines. The evidence of early Iron Age newcomers in Upper Galilee and in the Negeb may indicate a peaceful infiltration of Israelites in those areas. Since Shechem shows no evidence of destruction in this period, it may have passed peacefully into Israelite hands.

The judges. The archaeological record of random destructions correlates with the picture of political chaos that prevailed in the era of the judges. The miraculous victory over Canaanite chariots celebrated in the archaic Song of Deborah may be the explanation of the destructions around 1125 BCE of the sites of Taanach and Tel Qedesh in the Jezreel Valley. A twelfth-century ostracon with an abecedary from Izbet Sartah demonstrates the partial literacy of the day. The late twelfth-century destruction at Shechem may come from the violent episode of Abimelech. Micah's household shrine may be compared to a shrine found at Tel Qiri. The destruction of the Canaanite city of Laish (Dan) may be attributed to the migration of the tribe of Dan.

Much of Judges and 1 Samuel are occupied with the conflict between the coastal Philistines and the Israelites over the Shephelah territory between them. The plan of the Philistine temple that Samson overthrew has been illuminated by the discovery of such a temple with two column bases at Tell el-Qasile. Philistine pottery from Ashdod and elsewhere, which resembles Mycenean prototypes, betrays their Aegean origins.

The united monarchy. The twelve Israelite tribes were united briefly under three kings, Saul, David, and Solomon. Saul won renown by his triumphs over the Philistines, who had dominated the Israelites by their monopoly of metallurgical technology. An iron plow point was discovered in the excavations of Saul's fortress at Gibeah.

David succeeded in capturing the Jebusite city of Jerusalem. Kenyon's excavations at the base of Ophel, the city of David, uncovered a corner of the wall of the Jebusite city. A sloping, stepped structure on Ophel attributed to David by Shiloh is now thought to have been constructed earlier. The "filling" (Hebr. *millô*) built by both David and Solomon was identified by Kenyon as the series of terraces on the slope of Ophel.

Although Solomon built a splendid Temple and palace in Jerusalem, no remains of these have been found. Solomonic palaces have been uncovered at Megiddo. With brilliant insight, Yadin suggested that similar triple gates at Hazor, Megiddo, and Gezer were built by Solomon, although this is now disputed. Solomon's trading and fame were on an international scale. An ostracon from Tell Qasile speaks of "the gold of Ophir" (1 Kings 10.11), imported by Solomon. A ninth-century South Arabian stamp seal found at Bethel may be evidence of the trade established by the queen of Sheba.

The divided monarchy. Jeroboam I, who led the revolt against Rehoboam, Solomon's son, had taken refuge in Egypt under Shishak. In the fifth year after Solomon's death, Shishak invaded Palestine, as the Bible and his own inscriptions at Karnak attest. A stele of Shishak has been found at Megiddo.

The polytheism that characterized popular religion in both Israel and Judah has been amply attested. A startling example from the eighth century BCE is a painting with an inscription of "Yahweh and his Asherah" found at Kuntillet ʿAjrud near Kadesh-barnea. Images of riders on horses found at Jerusalem may have belonged to a cult of the sun.

Jeroboam's northern city of Dan has yielded impressive structures, including a monumental gate with benches, a pedestal for a throne, and a high place. Excavators found at Samaria magnificent buildings of Ahab and his Phoenician wife Jezebel, including Proto-Aeolic columns and ivory fragments.

From Ahab's reign come also the elaborate underground water system at Hazor and the "stables" at Megiddo.

Ahab's military might is attested outside the Bible by texts of the Assyrian king Shalmaneser III, which credit Ahab with two thousand chariots and ten thousand infantry at the battle of Qarqar (853). One of the rare monumental inscriptions from the area is the Moabite Stone of Ahab's enemy, King Mesha.

The famous Black Obelisk depicts King Jehu (843–816 BCE) of Israel prostrating himself before Shalmaneser III. A stele of Adad-nirari III lists Joash of Samaria as offering tribute to the Assyrians. Menahem of Israel also paid tribute to Tiglath-pileser III.

Sargon II claimed that he captured 27,290 prisoners and "their gods" when Samaria fell in 722 BCE. The exiles were taken to places like Gozan and Calah; ostraca from these places list Israelite names like Menahem, Elisha, and Haggai. Sargon's army later (712) invaded Judah, as a fragment of his stele at Ashdod confirms. The Assyrian presence is evidenced by a fortress at Tell Jemmeh, and a standard found at Tell esh-Shariʿa.

The Assyrian juggernaut of Sennacherib invaded Judah in 701 and overwhelmed city after city, including the key southern fort of Lachish. The assault with battering rams up a ramp is illustrated in detail by reliefs from Sennacherib's palace at Nineveh. Excavations at Lachish have uncovered the siege ramp, a counter ramp, arrowheads, the crest of a helmet, chain mail, and a chain used by the defenders against the ram.

Sennacherib, though he claims to have received tribute, does not claim the capture of Jerusalem. Hezekiah had built the Siloam Tunnel to provide water to the city. His inscription describes how workers dug from both ends to meet in the center. Segments of the "broad wall" (Neh. 3.8), which he probably built to the west of the Temple area to enclose the "Second Quarter" (2 Kings 22.14) have been discovered. A funerary inscription from Silwan may belong to Shebna(yahu), who was rebuked by the prophet Isaiah for building an ostentatious tomb.

Invasions of Judah. The early reign of Nebuchadrezzar, including his attack on Syria and Palestine in his first year in 605 BCE, has been greatly illuminated by the publication in 1956 of the Babylonian Chronicles. These reveal a hitherto unknown battle of 601 BCE that may have misled the Judeans to rely on help from Egypt, against the advice of Jeremiah. The Chronicles also describe the Babylonian attack on Jerusalem in 597, but the portion describing the final attack in 587/586 is missing.

The advance of the Babylonian army is dramatically announced by a Lachish ostracon, which reports "we cannot see Azekah" (see Jer. 34.7). Evidences of the devastation wrought by the Babylonians have been found at numerous Judean sites, including Jerusalem itself.

A number of seals or seal impressions probably belong to personages from this era; these bear names of such biblical figures as Baruch, son of Neriah, Jeremiah's scribe; Jerahmeel, Jehoiakim's son; Jaazaniah; and Gedaliah.

An ostracon from Arad implies an imminent attack from the direction of Edom. The reason Obadiah denounced the Edomites must stem from their taking advantage of Judah during the Babylonian attack. A poignant expression of Yahweh's faithfulness even after the destruction of Jerusalem has been found at Khirbet Beit Lei.

Some of the splendors of the great city of Babylon erected by Nebuchadrezzar, such as the Ishtar Gate, have been recovered. At Babylon tablets dated 595–570 BCE explicitly confirm the biblical account that the exiled Jewish king Jehoiachin received rations from the Babylonian court.

The puzzling role of Belshazzar (instead of his father Nabonidus) in the book of Daniel has been clarified by Babylonian and Aramaic documents that reveal that Nabonidus spent ten years in self-imposed exile in Arabia.

The capture of Babylon by the Persians in 539 BCE resulted in the liberation of the Jews by Cyrus. The magnanimity of the Persian king (Ezra 1) to other religions is fully corroborated by such documents as the Cyrus Cylinder. The Murashu texts, which list about a hundred Jewish names from the reigns of Artaxerxes I and Darius II, document the prosperity of the Jews who chose to remain in Mesopotamia.

The events recounted in Ezra-Nehemiah have been illuminated by the Elephantine papyri from Egypt, by the Xanthos inscription from Lydia, and by tablets from Persepolis. Inscriptions or papyri can be correlated with Nehemiah's opponents—Geshem, Tobiah, and Sanballat. Some seventy bullae acquired in 1970 reveal the names of governors of Judah who preceded Nehemiah. Kenyon's excavations in Jerusalem clarified the line of the wall that was rebuilt and uncovered the tumble that blocked Nehemiah's donkey.

The Hellenistic and Roman periods. The greatest discovery is the cache of Dead Sea Scrolls, which includes our oldest manuscripts of the Hebrew Bible. In addition, Hebrew and Aramaic originals of *apocryphal works such as Sirach and *pseudepigraphical works such as Enoch were found.

The extensive building projects of Herod the Great are found everywhere in Palestine: at Jerusalem, Sebaste, Caesarea, Masada, Machaerus, Jericho, and Herodium. The magnificent ashlars are visible at the Temple platform in Jerusalem. Excavations nearby have uncovered a 210-ft (64-m) wide stairway, a limestone object inscribed qrbn, and debris from Titus's capture of Jerusalem. Work in the Upper City has revealed homes of the wealthy high priests, including an inscription of Bar Kathros, the head of a priestly family accused in the Talmud of exploitation.

The magnificent remains of the synagogue at Capernaum have been dated to the fourth century CE on the basis of coins. Basalt remains of an earlier synagogue are visible. The second/third-century synagogue at Chorazin contains a so-called seat of Moses. Buildings or structures identified as rare first-century CE synagogues have been found at Gamla, Herodium, and Masada. Near the Capernaum synagogue, a first-century CE fisherman's house, later venerated as Peter's house, has been uncovered.

In Jerusalem the twin pools of Bethesda and the pool of Siloam have been identified. Some scholars have placed the site of the praetorium, where Jesus was tried before Pilate, north of the Temple area, where flagstones under the Sisters of Zion building have been identified as the lithostraton of the Fortress Antonia. The more probable site of the trial, however, is near the Jaffa Gate, where remains of Herod's palace have been found in the citadel area. In 1961, an inscription of Pilate was found at Caesarea.

In 1968, Israeli archaeologists discovered the first physical evidence of a victim of *crucifixion. In an ossuary, a limestone box for the redeposition of bones, were discovered a young man's calcanei or heel bones still pierced by an iron nail. His right tibia or shin bone had been fractured into slivers by a blow. A crease in the radius indicates that the victim had been pinioned in the forearms rather than in the palms. Accordingly, the Greek word cheiras in Luke 24.39–40 and John 20.20, 25, 27, usually translated "hands," should perhaps be translated "arms."

Several rolling-stone type tombs may be seen in Jerusalem. Excavations in and around the Church of the Holy Sepulcher suggest that the site was outside the walls in Jesus' day. The Greek "Nazareth" inscription, thought by some to date from the reign of Claudius, warns against tampering with tombs.

Many discoveries have illuminated the far-flung missions of Paul. Excavations at Nea Paphos have uncovered an inscription of Sergius Paulus, the governor of Cyprus converted by Paul. A text dedicated to Zeus and Hermes near Lystra illustrates the episode of Acts 14.12. Inscriptions from Thessalonica confirm the accuracy of Luke's use of the term "politarchs" for rulers of that city (Acts 17.6).

Paul's speech at Athens may have been addressed to the Areopagus council, which met in the royal stoa recently uncovered in the agora. The reference in Paul's speech to the "unknown God" (Acts 17.23) is illustrated by an inscription from Pergamon referring to "unknown gods."

The date of Paul's ministry in Corinth (51 CE) has been fixed by the inscription of Gallio, the governor who tried him (Acts 18.12–17). An inscription of Erastus is probably that of one of the few wealthy members of the Corinthian church. An inscription of a butcher marks the site of the "meat market" (1 Cor. 10.25). At Corinth, the average space available in typical triclinia (dining rooms) and atria not only limited the size of the house churches but could cause divisions when the wealthier Christians would be invited into the triclinium for the *love-feast, leaving the rest of the Christians outside in the atrium.

Athletic facilities have been excavated at Isthmia, east of Corinth, the site of the Pan-Hellenic games probably observed by Paul. A first-century harbor has been traced at Corinth's eastern harbor, Cenchreae, the home of Phoebe.

Magnificent remains have been exposed at Ephesus. The foundation of the temple of Artemis, one of the seven wonders of the ancient world, was discovered after a search of six years by J. T. Wood. In front of the temple a U-shaped altar has been uncovered. Inscriptions speak about the silver images of Artemis, and the garment dedicated to the goddess. Statues of the famed goddess have been found in thirty different places, including Caesarea. One can observe the theater that Luke gives as the scene for the assembly provoked by Paul's preaching. A fresco from a house nearby depicts scenes from Greek dramatists, including Menander, whom Paul cites.

Although most New Testament cities have been excavated, there are still a number of key sites associated with Paul, such as Derbe and Colossae, which have been identified but are as yet unexcavated.   *Edwin M. Yamauchi*

ARK. The English word "ark" translates two Hebrew words that differ from each other in both form and usage, though the Septuagint employs one Greek word *(kibōtos)* for both.

Tebâ means "box" or "chest." Apart from its use to designate the papyrus basket in which Moses, as an infant, was left to float among the bulrushes of the Nile, this word is used in the Bible solely as the designation of the vessel that God commanded Noah to construct of gopher wood, a wood not mentioned elsewhere. It was to be large enough to contain one representative human family along with one pair of every species of animals. Another form of the story speaks of seven pairs of clean animals, sufficient quantity for the sacrifice after the *Flood, and one pair of unclean animals. These would ride out the rainstorm of the wrath of God. The description of Noah's ark is rather hard to understand. Its dimensions, roughly 450 ft (140 m) long, 75 ft (22 m) wide, and 45 ft (12 m) high, make it literally a very large "box." The ark had three decks, and also naturally a door. An opening, about 18 in (.5 m) high, apparently ran all around the ark just below the roof and gave light and air to the vessel. There are certain points of resemblance, but more of dissimilarity, between Noah's ark and Utnapishtim's gigantic boat of the *Gilgamesh flood story.

In 1 Peter 3.20–21, Noah's ark prefigures *baptism.

ʾĀrôn, apart from its use in the sense of "coffin" (Gen. 50.26) and in the sense of "chest" for receiving money offerings (2 Kings 12.9–10; 2 Chron. 24.8, 10–11), is employed as the name of the sacred box that is variously called the ark of God, the ark of the Lord, the ark of the covenant, and so on. Data concerning this ark come from different sources and periods. It was in form a rectangular box or chest, measuring about 45 by 27 by 27 in (1 by .7 by .7 m), and made of acacia or shittim wood.

As the years went by this object became ever-more venerated. It symbolized the presence of the living God at one particular spot on earth; for the God who dwelled "in the high and holy place" was also present at the ark in the midst of his people. As a result, later generations embellished descriptions of it in their traditions, seeing it as overlaid with gold both within and without. The ark was transportable; it could be carried on poles overlaid with gold, which passed through rings on its side. It was considered to be of such sanctity that were an unauthorized person to touch it, even accidentally, this infraction would be punishable by death.

The ark seems at one time to have contained only the two tablets of the *law, but according to other traditions it contained also Aaron's rod that budded and a golden urn holding *manna.

The history of the ark parallels many of the vicissitudes of Israel. It was carried by the sons of Levi on the wilderness wanderings; borne over the Jordan by the priests; captured by the Philistines; and brought to Jerusalem by David. After being kept in a tentlike sanctuary (see Tabernacle), it was finally installed in the holiest chamber of Solomon's Temple.

The ark had a cover or lid. Its name (Hebr. *kappōret*) is actually a theological term (cf. *kippēr*, "to purify, atone"), so we do not know what this cover looked like. Martin Luther described it in his German Bible as the "mercy seat" because the Lord "sat" enthroned over it in mercy, invisibly present where the wingtips of two cherubim met above it, guarding the divine presence. So the ark represented for Israel the localized presence of God in judgment, mercy, forgiveness, and love; and because it contained the *Ten Commandments, it was a visible reminder that their life was to be lived in obedience to the expressed will of God. Since the Ten Commandments were incised on stone so as to last for all time, Israel carried in her midst God's demands for total loyalty and obedience to himself and for social justice and love of neighbor.

The ark is thought to have been captured when Jerusalem fell in 587/586 BCE, and nothing is known of its later history. Later legend reports that Jeremiah rescued it and hid it on Mount Nebo.   *George A. F. Knight*

ART AND THE BIBLE.

Early Art. Stories from the Bible had become the subject of a developed narrative art by the middle of the third century CE in the synagogue discovered at Dura-Europos, where dozens of biblical scenes are depicted in frescoes; the Christian church there from the same period also has paintings representing both Old and New Testament subjects. In the sixth century, mosaics in a number of synagogues also represent biblical subjects, such as at Gerasa (modern Jerash), from the fourth or fifth century, where the procession of animals into Noah's ark is depicted, and from the sixth century, those at Beth Alpha (the sacrifice of Isaac), Naaran (Daniel in the lions' den), and Gaza (David as Orpheus). Other early illustrations of the influence of the Bible on Christian art are the mosaics in churches throughout the Near East and especially the sequence of paintings in the Roman catacombs that extend chiefly from the third to the fourth centuries CE. The purpose of these fresco paintings is not primarily to illustrate biblical material but rather to interpret them. The subjects are those that could be *typologically linked with what "fulfills" them in Christ: Moses striking water from the rock, Noah delivered from the flood, the three men escaping from the fiery furnace, Daniel saved from the lions' den—all are juxtaposed and depicted in such a way as to indicate their anticipation of the saving, healing, releasing power of Christ as exhibited in the healing of the paralytic, the woman with the issue of blood, the Samaritan woman at the well, the miracle of the loaves, or the raising of Lazarus. No attempt is made in this painting at descriptive realism, to represent how the incident looked when it happened. Christ and the other figures are taken from contemporary art; indeed Christ is sometimes presented as a new Orpheus or Hercules, and if he appears as the good shepherd he is depicted in terms of the Hellenistic models of the day. Early Christian art is a symbolic language, and this gives it a certain indirectness; only the Christian initiate would be able to decipher in full its powerful inner meaning.

The move toward a comprehensive theological program by typological juxtapositioning of material from the Old and New Testaments is developed in the relief sculpture that began to appear on the sides of sarcophagi particularly after the Edict of Milan (313 CE). The unifying theme of these works is again salvation through Christ, and again it is treated cryptically and indirectly. On a sarcophagus in Santa Maria Antiqua in the Roman forum (third century CE), Christ appears unobtrusively as the good shepherd and as a young boy being baptized; the key to the whole work (Christianity as the new philosophy of salvation, here being pondered by a seated philosopher figure) is indicated by the extensive treatment of Jonah, reclining like the Greek god Endymion, as a type of the saved soul. This presentation of Christian salvation does not use the *crucifixion. The same kind of typological arrangement, but more substantial and integrated into an artistic whole, is seen on the sarcophagus of Junius Bassus in the Vatican Grottoes (fourth century CE). In two panels, Christ (enthroned or entering Jerusalem) is flanked by the sacrifice of Isaac (see Aqedah), Adam and Eve, the sufferings of Job, and Daniel in the lions' den. The only scene from the passion of Christ is the trial before Pilate; again, there is no crucifixion.

A particularly mature and instructive treatment of the theme of salvation, with

allusions to the crucifixion, is to be seen on a Vatican sarcophagus of the middle of the fifth century CE. In the center a plain Greek equal-armed cross is surmounted by the chi-rho monogram, which is encircled by a laurel victory wreath. There is no body of Christ on the cross, but on either side of it below are sleeping soldiers. To the left of the center panel are the episodes of Simon of Cyrene carrying the cross and the mock crowning of Jesus by the soldiers. To the right a double panel is devoted to the trial of Jesus before Pilate. In this sequence the artist has integrated the themes of crucifixion and *resurrection. This ability to present two themes simultaneously is one of the great strengths of visual art. The crucifixion is present in this sculptural program but only indirectly; in organic relation to the resurrection it comprises the real, though hidden, crowning of Christ in contrast to the vicarious cross-bearing of Simon, the simulated crowning of the soldiers, or the trial before Pilate—where Christ is, despite appearances, the real king who judges.

With the development of church architecture following the Edict of Milan, art soon became an important vehicle linking the Bible and liturgy. This is particularly the case with mosaic decoration that is organically related to its architectural setting. The best example of this is to be found in the cluster of fifth- and sixth-century Christian buildings at Ravenna, particularly the church of Sant'Apollinare Nuovo in Ravenna. In this early Byzantine church, along the north and south sides of the nave, a series of mosaic panels uses episodes from the Gospels in relation to the eucharistic celebration, which would be focused in the apse of this basilica. On the north side are scenes from the life of Jesus (including the parable of the Pharisee and the publican) leading up to the miracle at Cana of Galilee at the edge of the sanctuary. The series on the south side starts with the Last Supper and goes through the story of the passion (omitting the crucifixion) ending with the episode of doubting Thomas. It is likely that the choice of these subjects was determined by the liturgical calendar in use at the time. As in the catacombs and sarcophagi, the unifying theme of the whole program is the salvation brought by Christ, with particular emphasis on martyrdom as the response to this in human life. The historiated panels just described are closely linked with two very lively processions of male and female martyrs making their way to the sanctuary; the mosaics convey a vivid sensation of movement. Martyrdom as the classic expression of following in the way of the cross is also the theme in the two baptisteries in Ravenna (of the Arians and of the Orthodox). The crucifixion is not given as a separable episode, but its meaning is diffused, so to speak, throughout the whole scheme, indicating the source of the life of the Christian martyr-follower. In the apse of the church of Sant'Apollinare in Classe (just outside Ravenna) the crucifixion is again obliquely presented, this time in the context of the transfiguration, implying that it is not an episode only of the past but is reenacted sacramentally in the eucharistic action performed in the body of the church.

Another vivid presentation in mosaic of typological themes in relation to the Eucharist is to be found in the sanctuary of the sixth-century church of San Vitale in Ravenna. On the north side, there is an integrated scene comprising Abraham receiving the three heavenly visitors (to what looks like a eucharistic meal) and the sacrifice of Isaac, a common typological pointer to the sacrifice of Christ.

Above this are Moses receiving the *law and Jeremiah with a martyr's crown and scroll. On the south side the prefigurations of the Eucharist are Abel offering his sacrificial lamb, and Melchizedek. Above are Moses as shepherd and at the burning bush, and Isaiah with martyr's crown and scroll.

The Ravenna mosaics throw light on early Christian attitudes to biblical history. The historical incidents are sketched in such a way as to suggest their permanent significance, and through the liturgy these past events become present realities.

The Middle Ages. During the Middle Ages, two very significant phases took place in the development of art: Romanesque and Gothic.

Romanesque is a term that covers the art and architecture of the eleventh and twelfth centuries, which developed from various and very different sources: classical, Byzantine, Islamic, and Mesopotamian. It thus became an art admirably equipped to express both the narrative and the symbolic requirements of a Christianity based on the Bible. Perhaps the best surviving fully articulated biblical and theological program in the Romanesque tradition is the sculpture on the royal portal of the cathedral at Chartres. The central tympanum has the seated Christ in glory surrounded by the symbols of the evangelists (Matthew: young man; Mark: lion; Luke: ox; John: eagle) and the seated elders. This derives from the visions of the book of Revelation and is very prominent in Romanesque sculpture and painting. The adjacent bays are given over to the *ascension and the *incarnation. The latter is deliberately designed to stress the incarnation as itself God's act of self-sacrifice (the child lies on an altarlike structure and the presentation of Christ in the Temple is over an altar); no doubt this reflects eucharistic preaching of the time. As well as being a divine sacrifice, the incarnation is presented as the crown of human culture and the key to the universal meaning of all time by having the liberal arts and the signs of the zodiac in the archivolts. Somewhat in the manner of Sant'Apollinare Nuovo, a series of historiated capitals giving episodes from the life of Jesus binds the three bays together. The biblical antecedents of the New Testament story are suggested in the pillar figures of kings, queens, priests, and prophets on the columns of all three bays. Other outstanding Romanesque sculptural treatments of biblical themes in France are to be found at Vézelay, Moissac, Arles, and St. Gilles-du-Gard. The tympanum at Vézelay is especially interesting for the way it blends into one scene Christ's mission charge to the apostles with scenes of all kinds of strange and deformed creatures drawn from early medieval fables and bestiaries, thus making a very striking interpretation of the universal Christ. In Spain, the sculptures in the cloister of Santo Domingo de Silos also relate Christ to biblical history and to a strange, somewhat surrealistic, natural world of birds with animal heads. Particularly profound at Silos is a sculptured relief that, in a way reminiscent of the Vatican sarcophagus, works into one artistic whole both crucifixion and resurrection.

The Romanesque period also saw a marked development in the use of biblical themes in painting, both in illuminated manuscripts and in fresco painting in church interiors. Some extensive examples of fresco painting are to be found in France at St. Savin-sur-Gartempe (with an impressive series of scenes from the Hebrew Bible on the ceiling of the nave), at Vicq and St. Chef; in Spain at San Isidoro in Leon; in Italy at Sant'Angelo in Formis; and in Germany on the island of Reichenau.

Extending from the thirteenth to the fifteenth centuries, the Gothic period is the high-water mark in the evolution of medieval art and architecture. In comparison with Romanesque, the tendency now is toward greater realism in representation. This is well illustrated if one compares the Romanesque royal portal at Chartres with the sculpture of the north and south porches. Not that this means that the motive has become solely to illustrate the biblical narrative more strikingly by showing in more detail how the event actually happened. Rather, the typological and allegorical relating of Old and New Testament subjects still predominates, and the aim is to present as a unified whole an encyclopedia of Christian doctrine and ethics. France, where the Gothic style originated, again supplies the best examples. Chartres is the finest remaining example of this attempt to integrate architecture, sculpture, and stained glass into one comprehensive scheme. Bourges and Laon are other notable examples. The typological treatment of subjects from the Hebrew Bible remains basically that of the catacombs: biblical anticipations are juxtaposed with their fulfillment in the birth, passion, and death of Christ. The more realistic treatment of scenes from the Gospels does not indicate an interest in history for its own sake; in fact, the use of material from the Gospels in the Gothic period shows a surprising austerity compared with previous centuries. Healings, hitherto very common (the paralytic, the woman with the issue of blood, the blind man), are conspicuously absent in the Gothic period. Incidents from the life of Jesus prior to the passion story are confined to the baptism, the temptation, the sign at Cana of Galilee, and the transfiguration. This is true of illuminated manuscripts, stained glass, and sculpture. Remarkable, too, is the paucity of parables that appear in the art of this period. The emphasis falls on four parables: the good Samaritan, the ten virgins, the prodigal son, and Dives and Lazarus—all of which were christologically interpreted in patristic and medieval preaching. Artists were not intent on giving a fully illustrated version of the biblical story, but rather on providing an accompaniment to the liturgy and on embodying the teaching of the preachers and theological commentators. The motive is still to make a doctrinal point, but not until the Italian Renaissance do we find anything like a descriptive treatment of the nativity. Throughout the Gothic period, the scene of the nativity is mysterious and troubled: the mother of Christ lies apart from her son who appears not in a manger but on a sacrificial altar.

The Renaissance and Reformation. As far as the influence of the Bible on art is concerned, the Renaissance and the Reformation are best considered together. The early Italian Renaissance led to a fresh development of the classical tradition in art, already discernible in the Gothic sculpture at Chartres, and to a renewed emphasis on humanism and textual studies. As the Reformation proceeded, the *authority of the Bible became more isolated; there was also a revival of the aniconic principle found in the *Ten Commandments, so that the visual arts were regarded at best as unnecessary decoration to the biblical text and at worst as a misleading distraction. The Counter-Reformation saw a deliberate attempt to restore the position of the arts as ancillary to the Bible and subject to the rules laid down by the Council of Trent in 1563.

The great change noticeable in the use of biblical subjects at the Renaissance is the move from a largely two-dimensional hieratic art to something more realistic and more three-dimensional in perspective. Byzantine and medieval art as a whole had presented biblical subjects in their transcendental and theological perspective, especially in the light of the Last Judgment. Renaissance art, while not denying this reference, gave more prominence to the natural and the human. The change of mood is well illustrated by the sequence of biblical scenes by Giotto (1266/1267–1337) in the frescoes of the Arena chapel at Padua. Such scenes as the betrayal or the lamentation have a depth of human feeling and a realism that herald developments to come in Renaissance painting. This new accent affected the treatment of New Testament subjects. One can say that a certain kind of "quest of the historical Jesus" began in art in, for example, a painter like Masaccio (1401–1428?) in his frescoes in the Brancacci chapel of Santa Maria del Carmine in Florence. These, whether the *Expulsion from the Garden of Eden* or *The Tribute Money,* show a new kind of bodily realism and a new interest in the happening for its own sake rather than its symbolic, didactic, or doctrinal significance. A compellingly realistic treatment of the resurrection by Donatello (1386–1466) in San Lorenzo, Florence, has also great religious depth. It succeeds in linking resurrection with crucifixion; the austere Christ who emerges from the slime of the tomb is a risen Christ who has really suffered and really died. This is in great contrast to the crucifixion of Raphael (1483–1520) in the National Gallery, London, where the interest of the artist is more in classical harmony, design, and symmetry. Leonardo da Vinci (1452–

1519) is more successful (e.g., in his *Madonna of the Rocks* and *The Last Supper*) in combining technique of design with religious depth. Michelangelo (1476–1564) shows the late Renaissance exuberance in the human body and composition on the grand scale. His treatment of *creation and Last Judgment in the Sistine chapel in the Vatican contrasts sharply with the handling of these themes in Romanesque art.

Something of Luther's realism in Christology ("You can't drag Christ down too deeply into our human nature") finds its way into the work of an artist who was much influenced by his teaching, Albrecht Dürer (1471–1528), especially his woodcuts and engravings. His series on the passion, in which he sees himself involved in the situation of Christ, is very Lutheran in feel. Equally striking are his woodcuts on the book of Revelation, with their realistic detail and the way Dürer contextualizes the apocalyptic scenes in contemporary society. Dürer's contemporary, Mathias Grünewald (ca. 1470/1480–1528), was also influenced by Luther, and his famous Isenheim altarpiece of the crucifixion in the Unterlinden Museum in Colmar, France, marks a turning point in the iconography of that subject. It is a crucifixion that in its grim detail would not have been possible in the patristic period, when the victory of the crucified Christ was emphasized. While Luther, too, saw the atonement in terms of a great divine victory over death and sin, he felt that such a theology of glory could play down the stark realities of human life in its suffering. Grünewald's Isenheim crucifixion, with its gangrenous-looking flesh and clawlike hands, is a powerful statement of what Luther would have called a theology of the cross. Grünewald's crucifixion is not only a realistic representation but it also retains symbolic elements with its unusual introduction of John the Baptist to the scene (against a background of the text: "He must increase, but I must decrease" [John 3.30]) and the lamb with the vexillum of victory.

The Reformed tradition attained its most considerable expression in art in the work of Rembrandt (1606–1669), who must be classed as one of the great artistic commentators on the Bible. Biblical events and personalities were for Rembrandt more than a source of material for dramatic illustration, as they tended to be for Rubens. Rembrandt came to see in the biblical history his own and everyone's personal story. His painting of subjects from both testaments have a deeply felt interior quality, and his biblical work as a whole embodies a profound sense that the Bible is not only past history, but also present and universal experience. This is particularly true of the paintings and etchings of his later years, for example his crucifixions, where, like Dürer, he sees his own tribulations as a participation in those of Christ. The Hebrew Bible for Rembrandt is important in its own right and not simply as a preface to the New Testament, and no artist had hitherto entered with such intensity into the spirit of such subjects as the sacrifice of Isaac (before this time treated for the most part typologically), Joseph interpreting his dreams, or the relations between Saul and David. Memorable New Testament subjects are Christ healing the sick, the return of the prodigal son, the crucifixion (especially those of his later years), and Christ at Emmaus.

The Modern Period. The eighteenth century did not produce many works of significance for appreciating the use of the Bible in art. The biblical paintings of Tiepolo (1695–1770) are on a rich and dramatic scale but remain primarily decorative. Idiosyncratic as may have been the personal religion of William Blake (1757–1827), his watercolors and etchings of biblical subjects have a sweep and intensity of great power. Especially worthy of mention are his engravings for the book of Job.

The nineteenth century, however, saw a new attempt at authentic realism and feeling in the work of the pre-Raphaelites and the painstaking attempts to reproduce accurately the Palestinian scene in the work of systematic illustrators of the Bible, such as James Tissot (1836–1902).

The twentieth century proved to be a creative period for the use of biblical themes in art, and especially of new interpretations of the crucifixion. Graham Sutherland (1903–1980) has said that no one can conceive of the crucifixion apart from Auschwitz. His crucifixions in St. Matthew, Northampton, and in Coventry Cathedral fuse event and symbol in a way that is reminiscent of Grünewald.

The two most significant artists in the twentieth century influenced by the Bible are Georges Rouault and Marc Chagall. Rouault (1871–1958), in his portraits of Christ and especially in his scenes from the passion, draws on the Byzantine tradition of the icon, and in his "biblical landscapes" he makes an innovative attempt to convey the nature of salvation in terms of landscapes, which, while they appear threatening to human life, nevertheless contain space for human beings to experience the accompanying presence of Christ.

Marc Chagall (1887–1985) is an outstanding commentator in art on biblical subjects. Drawing on both Jewish and Christian traditions and developing, like Blake, his own personal mythology, his work in painting, etching, and stained glass constitutes a uniquely important interpretation of the Bible. No painter since Rembrandt has so entered into the spirit of the Bible. Examples of how he relates, for example, creation and crucifixion are to be found in the series *Message biblique* housed in the Musée National in Nice. Chagall is also a significant figure in the evolution of the iconography of the crucifixion. He combines the suffering and hope in a new and compelling manner by relating the *Torah and the crucifixion of Christ. In a way reminiscent of Rouault's biblical landscapes, Chagall's volcanic and tumultuous scenes yet suggest the possibility of deliverance and hope, in, for instance, *Obsession* (1943), by the insertion of a green crucifix, recalling very effectively the cross as the tree of life in medieval art.

See also Illustrated Bibles.

John Tinsley

ASCENSION OF CHRIST. Despite the great importance and influence of the early church's belief in the ascension of Christ, it is described explicitly in the New Testament only twice. In Acts, after the resurrected Christ reminded his apostles that they will be empowered by the *Holy Spirit, he was "lifted up, and a cloud took him out of their sight" (Acts 1.9). The second-century CE addition to the conclusion of Mark adds that after Christ's ascension he "sat down at the right hand of God" (Mark 16.19).

In the Hellenistic world the ascent of a king, prophet, hero, or holy man to the heavens—the place of the gods—was a well-known motif signifying the divine status of the one who ascended. Heracles was deified through an ascension to heaven, and Ganymede became immortal when Zeus lifted him into heaven to serve as cupbearer to the gods. More generally, under the influence of Platonism, all human souls were believed to be immortal and returned to the heavens when cleansed of their mortal attachments. Christ's ascension similarly demonstrated his divinity, but more importantly, through the church's prophetic *interpretation of the Jewish scriptures, the ascension of Christ also signaled the beginning of a messianic kingdom and the empowerment of Christ's followers by virtue of their identification with him through the rite of *baptism.

Although rare in Jewish tradition, ascent into heaven is recorded in the case of Enoch, who "walked with God; then he was no more, because God took him" (Gen. 5.24), and the prophet Elijah, "who ascended in a whirlwind into heaven" (2 Kings 2.11); noncanonical writings also record the ascensions of Abraham, Moses, Isaiah, and Ezra. The ascension of Christ was unique, however, because of its eschatological significance for early Christianity. The authors of the New Testament believed that Psalm 110, celebrating the king seated at the right hand of God, referred to the ascended and victorious Christ who was exalted over all heavenly powers. The ascension was also seen as an elevated form of priestly sacrifice, for Christ is described as "the great high priest who has passed through the heavens" (Heb. 4.14), the sanctuary made by God.

The earliest kerygma of the church thus proclaimed not only Christ's *resurrection but also his ascension into heaven and enthronement at God's right hand. Christians celebrated the inauguration of this messianic kingdom and the demise of the present eon, for when Christ was given dominion over the demonic powers of this age, so were the members of his church. The letter to the Ephesians speaks of the "immeasurable greatness of God's power for us who believe" (Eph. 1.19), for the members of the church were united with Christ who

is "above all rule and authority and power and dominion" (Eph. 1.21).

The *exorcisms and miraculous cures performed by the apostles in Acts were understood to be manifestations of the Holy Spirit that Christ "poured out" (Acts 2.33) on his apostles after his ascension, sharing his dominion over the demons of this world with all members of his church. Thus, Paul says, "So, if you have been raised with Christ, seek the things that are above, where Christ is, seated at the right hand of God. . . . For you have died, and your life is hidden with Christ in God" (Col. 3.1–3). This "death" and hidden exaltation of Christians was effected through the ritual of baptism, which Paul compared to a burial and rebirth with Christ; baptism thus elevated the members of the church into Christ's heavenly kingdom.

Among gnosticizing Christians, baptism was understood to be a rite of immortalization that deified its initiates. According to the *gnostics, if baptism initiated Christians into the death and resurrection of Christ, as Paul argued, then it also united them with Christ's ascension and enthronement, separating the baptized entirely from the mortal sphere. The gnostics' radically transcendent interpretation of baptism was opposed by Paul, who argued that Christ's exaltation was achieved through his humiliation and suffering on the cross and that the ascension of Christians would not come until the *parousia.

Nevertheless, otherworldly speculations on the ascension and immortalization of the soul developed rapidly among gnostic Christians for whom the ascension of Christ established the pattern for their visionary journeys. The gnostics' elaborate portrayals of the soul's ascent, although influenced by Hellenistic thought, in turn came to influence the understanding of the ascent and deification of the soul in Platonic, Hermetic, and other philosophical circles from the second to the fourth centuries CE.

See also Theophany.   *Gregory Shaw*

ATONEMENT. *See* Day of Atonement.

AUTHORITY OF THE BIBLE.

This terminology is characteristic of Christian theology, and so the following entry appropriately discusses the issue from a Christian perspective. For consideration of the topic in Jewish tradition, see Interpretation, History of, *article on* Jewish Interpretation; Torah. *For related discussion, see* Inspiration and Inerrancy; Revelation.

"Here is Wisdom; this is the royal Law; these are the lively oracles of God": these are the words used when the Bible, described as "the most valuable thing that this world affords," is presented to the British monarch in the course of the coronation ceremony. They illustrate the value ascribed to the Bible and indicate that its authority is ultimately the authority attributed to God. It is therefore not an authority intrinsic to the book but one linked to the conviction that the book somehow or other emanates from God. Because God was held to be holy, the Bible too is described as holy, and terms like "holy scriptures" and "sacred writings" become commonplace.

The Israelites believed that it was possible to receive a divine communication, and so the book of the Law was invested with divine authority. Later rabbinic piety came to think of the *Torah as eternal in the heavens but communicated through angels to Moses, the divinely appointed lawgiver. The sanctity of the communication was associated with the manuscripts as well so that infinite care was demanded in copying the text. The prophets, too, saw themselves as called into the divine council, and

their utterance was consequently regarded as the very utterance of God. They were held to be God's own mouthpieces, inspired by him, and the fulfillment of their message validated its truth.

Because they conveyed God's revelation for Israel, the writings, as collected, were revered as authoritative. As the authors had been "inspired," their writings, in turn, were held to share in the inspiration, and it became customary to speak of them as the *word of God.

The Hebrew Bible was accepted as "holy scripture" by the early Christian communities, for Jesus had set the seal of his authority on these writings. The early church saw them as the preparation for the coming of Jesus. It was not a matter of affirming every detail (although some would argue this) but rather the tenor and ethos of the writings that were seen as authentically indicating God's will and purpose. The early Christians saw in Jesus the climax of all that the Jewish scriptures taught. It was felt that everything had been written down in the light of the critical events associated with Jesus; hence a new interpretation came into being. While *Philo could read his own philosophical understanding and mystical experience into the scriptures, the Pharisaic rabbis see their own rules for life emanating from them, and the Essenes reinterpret them in the light of the fortunes of the founder of their sect and the continuing destinies of their community, the Christians likewise read the scriptures in terms of their own faith and experience. Christ came to be seen as the center of scripture; he was the key to its understanding and its continuing validity. As Martin Luther (1483–1546) was to put it, "Christ is the Lord and King of the scriptures." The writer of 2 Timothy can accordingly speak of "the sacred writings that are able to instruct you for salvation through faith in Christ Jesus" (3.1) and can thus affirm that "all scripture is inspired by God" (3.16).

Gradually the same authority was granted to the New Testament writings, for they were the factual sources for his life and teaching and encapsulated the early apostolic preaching and instruction. Over against views regarded as illegitimate and later condemned as heretical, the New Testament documents were seen as pointing to an authentic faith. Fixing the *canon of the New Testament thus involved discrimination between those books seen as authoritative and so part of the sacred tradition and those that were not. It was felt to be a case not of the church's conveying authority but recognizing an intrinsic authority already present. As Origen (ca. 185–254) put it, "The sacred books were not the works of human beings; they were written by the inspiration of the Holy Spirit at the will of the Father of all through Jesus Christ" (*De principiis* 4.9). Just as the writings bear witness to the acts of God in history, so the church points to the Bible, preaching and teaching from its pages and subjecting itself to its guidance. But it also interprets it, providing the mainstream of tradition. The church recognizes in the scriptures the classical, normative account of Christian origins. So a sense of identity between the present and the church's roots is guaranteed and a measure of stability secured.

Inspiration. The Bible speaks of inspiration or the divine breath as the source of vitality and power. Genesis 2.7 asserts that the Lord God "breathed into his nostrils the breath of life, and the man became a living being." Ezekiel 37.10 says of lifeless bones that "the breath came into them, and they lived, and stood on their feet." So Paul can say, "Our message of the gospel came to you not in word only, but also in power and

in the Holy Spirit" (1 Thess. 1.5). The implication is that, just as divine inspiration had made the prophetic message a living one, so the words of scripture are mere signposts to something that goes beyond words.

Some have linked the notion of verbal inspiration with inerrancy and infallibility, but it is significant that, while Luther can speak of the Bible as "the Holy Spirit's very own book," with "God . . . in every syllable," he can also affirm that mistakes and inconsistencies do not affect the heart of the gospel. "The Holy Spirit," he affirms, "has an eye only to the substance and is not bound by words." We may agree that inspiration is no guarantee against human fallibility, nor does it affirm uniformity in quality and authority. There are levels in the scriptures: the kernel is encased in a shell; the baby lies in a manger.

Approaches to Biblical Authority. In early Christianity, the scriptures were used "for teaching, for reproof, for correction, and for training in righteousness" (2 Tim. 3.16). In the West, during the Dark Ages and the Middle Ages, the documents were viewed as the raw materials of revelation, a veritable mine of doctrinal statements. Isolated verses could be picked at random and used for the authoritative establishment of dogma. The Bible was often used as a sourcebook for the support of ecclesiastical doctrine, but scriptural authority was largely subordinated to the authority of the church. Contradictions in the text were smoothed out by an elaborate and even overly subtle system of allegorical interpretations. (*See also* Interpretation, History of, *article on* Christian Interpretation from the Middle Ages to the Reformation.)

The Reformation saw the overthrow of ecclesiastical power structures, and scripture seemed to be substituted for the church. The revival of learning was instrumental in initiating intensive biblical study. Luther saw the Bible as "the crib in which Christ lay," a sacrament by which the living God addressed the individual soul. "All sound books agree in this, that they witness to Christ," he said. "That which does not preach Christ is not apostolic though it came from St. Peter or St. Paul. Contrariwise that which preaches Christ would be apostolic even though it came from Judas or Annas or Pilate or Herod." Luther also declared that the truth of God's self-revelation through scripture was written "inwardly in our hearts" by the Holy Spirit. This point was subsequently taken up by John Calvin (1509–1564), who wrote of the "inner witness of the Holy Spirit," leading to the conviction that not only was the Bible an authentic, dependable record of God's encounter with humanity in the past but also the means of his contemporary encounter with us. At the same time, his position suggested that it is not possible to prove that God speaks through the scriptures.

It was the post-Reformation period that saw the rise of a kind of *fundamentalism, in which emphasis was laid on the very words of scripture and concerns about infallibility and inerrancy arose. Bibles were now more readily available, and "scripture alone" (sola scriptura) became a clarion call. What was often forgotten was that the principles of interpretation followed created a tradition of their own.

Liberal criticism of the Bible in the nineteenth century seemed to many to undermine the authority that had been attached to scripture. It appeared to turn the Bible into an ordinary collection of Near Eastern documents that had to be placed within their own historical contexts.

A different approach is undertaken by Karl Barth (1886–1968) and "*biblical theology," in which stress is laid on the act of proclamation, within which the Bible becomes the word of God. The Bible is not identified with past revelation but bears witness to a revelation in the past, as it becomes the means of hearing the voice of God today.

Contemporary thought also emphasizes the empirical test and accepts that God does speak through the scriptures and that faith is nourished by it. Charismatic movements hold that the Bible comes alive through the action of the Holy Spirit. The words become a vehicle through which a vivid awareness of the presence and activity of God is developed.

An unwarranted authority would be attributed to the Bible if the words were stressed and the human origins of the documents neglected. Just as in Christology the church rejected a docetic viewpoint that tried to support the assertion of Christ's divinity by denying the full reality of his humanity, so, with the Bible, it is important to reject an equation with the divine word, which neglects the very human character of the words of its authors. If the Bible were precisely the word of God, questions of authority would not arise and one would expect an immediately recognizable meaning within the words of scriptures. The biblical language that speaks of the dynamic character of the word suggests that it is preferable to speak of the Bible as conveying or mediating the word of God. This then points to the experience of the community of faith through the centuries. To treat the Bible simply as a compendium of ancient literature and to limit oneself to a critical, historical analysis of its contents would be a denial of believers' experience that in the Bible they have found the word of God addressing them with "transforming and liberating power," as Thomas Merton put it. The words of scripture take on the character of the preacher who bears witness to the reality of what has been experienced. There is a need, then, for a mediating position between a fundamentalism that almost invites a worship of the Bible instead of the God of the Bible and a purely rationalistic exegesis. A claim to discover God's word and so God's own authority within the Bible must not obscure the truth of the humanity and so the limitations of its authors. Different authors have different styles, interests, and emphases, and express their convictions in different ways; their language and mode of expression are not ageless. And what is true of the writers is also true of the reader. If Christianity is a religion of the spirit rather than of the letter, we should expect a degree of variety in interpretation. There must be a subjective element in interpretation just as there was in the writing. The more one brings of human experience, spiritual sensitivity, and common sense to the Bible, the more one will get from it. And, since life is lived in community, so the experiences and insights of others illuminate the understanding of the individual reader. Finally, the biblical message is addressed to the whole person and not simply to the intellect. Hence, to recognize the authority of the Bible is to respond to the imperatives made by the God of the Bible. For ultimately what is looked for is an encounter not with language but with a person.

See also Eastern Orthodoxy and the Bible; Interpretation, History of.

Raymond Hammer

B

BAPTISM. A term first appearing in the New Testament as a purification ritual used by an unorthodox Jewish figure named John (the Baptist). All four Gospels and the book of Acts describe him "preaching a baptism of repentance for the forgiveness of sins" (Mark 1.4; Luke 3.3).

Scholars have speculated how John's mission might be related to other Jewish separatist groups such as the Qumran community, but exact origins remain unclear. There is abundant evidence that lustral bathing was an important aspect of Greco-Roman religions, especially related to healing divinities such as Asklepius. In the Hebrew Bible, cleansing with *water is an important part of purification rites, especially after sexual activity or contact with a corpse (*see* Purity, Ritual). John the Baptist calls for a more general repentance symbolized by baptism.

The report that Jesus himself was baptized in the Jordan by John raises the possibility that Jesus was a disciple of John who broke off and started his own movement. It is clear that later followers of Jesus were concerned about this perception. Matthew's gospel includes a dialogue in which John recognizes Jesus' spiritual superiority and baptizes him reluctantly only after Jesus insists. Luke goes a step further by excluding John from the account of Jesus' baptism and telling the story of John's imprisonment immediately before the event takes place. Thus, in Luke, Jesus is baptized, but the storyline indicates that the baptism could not have been performed by John.

In the Gospels, John is of interest only as he is related to the ministry of Jesus, but the baptism symbol used by John becomes a central image for the developing churches. Matthew's gospel concludes with the charge to "make disciples of all nations, baptizing them in the name of the Father and of the Son and of the Holy Spirit" (Matt. 28.19). The book of Acts elaborates further when Peter says to the crowd gathered on *Pentecost, "Repent, and be baptized every one of you in the name of Jesus Christ so that your sins may be forgiven" (Acts 2.38).

Baptism in Acts takes place immediately after someone comes to believe in Christ, and it is usually followed by receiving the *Holy Spirit. This two-stage process is founded on the contrast between John's water baptism and "being baptized by the Holy Spirit" (Acts 1.5). It is so important that the leaders of the Jerusalem church send Peter and John to lay hands on believers in Samaria who had "only been baptized in the name of the Lord Jesus," after which they receive the Holy Spirit (Acts 8.14–17; *see* Laying on of Hands). The situation is reversed when the gentiles of Cornelius's house come to believe. They receive the Holy

Spirit and speak in tongues as a sign of God's acceptance of gentile converts (*see* Glossolalia), so Peter asks, "Can anyone withhold the water for baptizing these people who have received the Holy Spirit just as we have?" (Acts 10.44–48).

Paul's letters provide the earliest evidence about baptism among the Jesus followers. It is striking, therefore, that Paul makes no mention of John the Baptist or of baptism and receiving the Holy Spirit as a dual process. Paul sees that the person who has been baptized is "in Christ," no longer subject to the divisions of human society, and part of a unified body. Emphasis is on the state that has been achieved, not the way in which it has been accomplished. In fact, Paul is concerned that the Corinthians are putting too much stake in the person by whom they were baptized, and he is grateful that he baptized only a few of them: "For Christ did not send me to baptize but to proclaim the gospel" (1 Cor. 1.17).

In 1 Corinthians 15, Paul is using every possible argument to convince his readers that a resurrection of the dead will take place. In doing so, he asks why people are baptized on behalf of the dead if there will be no resurrection. This brief allusion indicates that within the early churches it was possible to receive baptism in order to include in the body of Christ a friend or relative who was already dead. Paul does not specifically condemn the practice here, but it did not become an accepted part of Christian ritual.

Paul equates baptism symbolically with the death of Jesus, and he insists that rituals such as baptism are not spiritual guarantees, since God was not pleased with the Hebrews even though they went through a proto-baptism with Moses at the Red Sea. This latter point is also made in the letter to the Hebrews, while 1 Peter contends that the story of Noah's *ark prefigures the saving value of baptism.

The New Testament evidence is used in debating later Christian baptismal practice, but it is rarely definitive. Certainly the majority of people who are baptized in the New Testament are adults who are entering the community. The exception might be children included in some of the households baptized in Acts. The baptism of infants became a more routine practice within the church as the doctrine of original sin became more widely accepted.

Another controversy concerns baptism by immersion or by the sprinkling of water on the participant. The descriptions of specific New Testament baptisms indicate that the person being baptized was dipped under the water. Jesus is said to come out of the water, while Philip and the Ethiopian eunuch go down into the water. Going under the water also fits best with the image of being buried with Christ in baptism. At the same time baptisms in the New Testament are not described in specific terms, so diverse interpretations and practices develop.

Daniel N. Schowalter

BIBLE. The English word "Bible" is derived from the Greek word *biblia* (neuter plural), which means simply "books." As the collections of Jewish and Christian texts came increasingly to be considered as one unit, the same plural term in medieval Latin began to be understood in popular usage as feminine singular, no longer denoting "The Books" but "The Book." By the second century BCE the adjective "holy" had come to be used to designate some of these books, and so now "Holy Bible" means a collection of sacred books.

Contents. The number of these sacred and/or authoritative books varies in different religious traditions. The Samaritans recognize only five books (Genesis, Exodus, Leviticus, Numbers, and Deuteronomy) as their canon. Twenty-four books, classified in three groupings, make up the Hebrew Bible (*see* Canon): the Law (*Torah: Genesis, Exodus, Leviticus, Numbers, Deuteronomy); the Prophets, comprising the Former Prophets (Joshua, Judges, Samuel, Kings) and the Latter Prophets (Isaiah, Jeremiah, Ezekiel, and the Twelve Prophets); and the Writings (Psalms, Proverbs, Job, Song of Songs, Ruth, Lamentations, Ecclesiastes, Esther, Daniel, Ezra-Nehemiah, and Chronicles). Samuel, Kings, the Twelve, Ezra-Nehemiah, and Chronicles are each counted as one book.

Historically, Protestant churches have recognized the Hebrew Bible as their Old Testament, although differently ordered, and with some books divided so that the total number of books is thirty-nine. These books, as arranged in the traditional English Bible, fall into three types of literature: seventeen historical books (Genesis to Esther), five poetical books (Job to Song of Solomon), and seventeen prophetical books. With the addition of another twenty-seven books (the four Gospels, Acts, twenty-one letters, and the book of Revelation), called the New Testament, the Christian scriptures are complete.

The Protestant canon took shape by rejecting a number of books and parts of books that had for centuries been part of the Old Testament in the Greek Septuagint and in the Latin Vulgate, and had gained wide acceptance within the Roman Catholic church. In response to the Protestant Reformation, at the Council of Trent (1546) the Catholic church accepted, as deuterocanonical, Tobit, Judith, the Greek additions to Esther, the Wisdom of Solomon, Sirach, Baruch,

the Letter of Jeremiah, three Greek additions to Daniel (the Prayer of Azariah and the Song of the Three Jews, Susanna, and Bel and the Dragon), and 1 and 2 Maccabees (*see* Apocrypha, *article on* Jewish Apocrypha). These books, together with those in the Hebrew Bible and the New Testament, constitute the total of seventy-three books accepted by the Roman Catholic church.

The Anglican church falls between the Catholic church and many Protestant denominations by accepting only the Hebrew Bible and the New Testament as authoritative, but also by accepting segments of the apocryphal writings in the lectionary and liturgy. At one time all copies of the Authorized or King James Version of 1611 included the Apocrypha between the Old and New Testaments.

The Bible of the Greek Orthodox church comprises all of the books accepted by the Roman Catholic church, plus 1 Esdras, the Prayer of Manasseh, Psalm 151, and 3 Maccabees. The Slavonic canon adds 2 Esdras, but designates 1 and 2 Esdras as 2 and 3 Esdras. Other Eastern churches have 4 Maccabees as well. (*See* Eastern Orthodoxy and the Bible.)

The Ethiopic church has the largest Bible of all, and distinguishes different canons, the "narrower" and the "broader," according to the extent of the New Testament. The Ethiopic Old Testament comprises the books of the Hebrew Bible as well as all of the deuterocanonical books listed above, along with Jubilees, 1 Enoch, and Joseph ben Gorion's (Josippon's) medieval history of the Jews and other nations. The New Testament in what is referred to as the "broader" canon is made up of thirty-five books, joining to the usual twenty-seven books eight additional texts, namely four sections of church order from a compilation called Sinodos, two sections from the Ethiopic Book of the Covenant, Ethiopic Clement, and Ethiopic Didascalia. When the "narrower" New Testament canon is followed, it is made up of only the familiar twenty-seven books, but then the Old Testament books are divided differently so that they make up fifty-four books instead of forty-six. In both the narrower and broader canon, the total number of books comes to eighty-one.

Format. The traditional division of chapters (previously ascribed to Hugh of St. Cher and dated about 1262) is now attributed to Stephen Langton, a lecturer at the University of Paris and subsequently Archbishop of Canterbury (d. 1228). The present method employed for verses was originated by the scholarly printer Robert Stephanus (Estienne), whose Greek New Testament with numbered verses was issued in Geneva in 1551. The first English Bible to employ Stephanus's system of numbering verses was the Geneva version (New Testament 1556; Old Testament 1560). (*See* Chapter and Verse Divisions.)

The English Revised Version of 1881–1885 relinquished the separate verse division of older versions in favor of a format employing paragraphs; verse numbers, however, were still provided in the margin for ease of reference. Before the employment of this modern system the many verses, or texts, of the Bible were the subject of much statistical and even superstitious research. Fortunes were divined or the "will of God" learned by random selection of biblical passages (*see* Sortes Biblicae). Some individuals undertook the daunting task of tallying the verses, words, and even the letters of the words, as though some all-important information was encoded in the result. The example below is a typical compilation, made by Thomas Har-

twell Horne (1780–1862) over a three-year period. According to Horne's computations, the Authorized or King James Version of the Bible is comprised of:

	Old Testament	New Testament	Total
Books	39	27	66
Chapters	929	260	1,189
Verses	33,214	7,959	41,173
Words	593,493	181,253	774,746
Letters	2,728,100	838,380	3,566,480

This type of analysis has also brought to light miscellaneous information such as the following: the word "and" occurs in the Bible 46,227 times; the word "Lord" 1,855 times; "reverend" only once; "girl" also only once; "everlasting fire" twice; also, no words are longer than six syllables. These students of the letter of the Bible (like the Masoretes in ancient times) inform us that the middle book is that of Proverbs; the middle chapter, Job 39; the middle verse, 2 Chronicles 20.17; that the longest verse is Esther 8.9, and the shortest John 11.35 ("Jesus wept").

See also Curious Bibles.

Bruce M. Metzger

BIBLE SOCIETIES. With their concern for the translation, production, and distribution of the scriptures, Bible societies are relatively recent institutions, but the concept underlying their worldwide activity is ancient. The notion that the Bible should be in the language of the people prompted the Hellenistic Jewish community of the third century BCE to produce a Greek translation (Septuagint) of the Hebrew Bible. Inspired by this example, the early eastern Greek-speaking church began to produce translations of the Bible in a variety of languages so as to make sure that the gospel would be known as widely as possible. Likewise, the Roman church produced its own edition of the Bible, in the "vulgar" Latin of the common people, which became the most widely used translation in the western church for a thousand years, the Vulgate.

Although there were some attempts in medieval scriptoria to mass-produce copies of the Bible, the process was slow, and the handwritten copies issued were enormously expensive. With the invention of movable type for *printing (about 1456), the situation changed, and the Bible began to be translated into vernacular languages and commercially produced for general circulation. It was, however, not until the evangelical revival in the eighteenth century and the consequent formation of missionary societies, principally in the United Kingdom, that the importance of scripture translation and publication began to be fully recognized. These missionary societies placed special emphasis on the use of the scriptures in preaching and teaching ministries, and included scripture distribution among their ongoing programs.

The organization of this period which most completely resembled the later Bible societies was a direct outgrowth of the Pietistic movement, the von Canstein Bible Institution of Halle, organized in 1710 to supply inexpensive scriptures to the poor of Germany. Although the von Canstein group confined its efforts to Germany and eastern Europe, by the end of the eighteenth century it had achieved the remarkable record of circulating over three million low-cost Bibles and New Testaments.

Meanwhile, across the English Channel a great awakening had begun, generated in large part by the preaching of John and Charles Wesley and George Whitefield. Missionary societies were formed to spread the gospel, and often their first assignment was to master the local language in order to translate the Bible. Thus William Carey (1761–1843), a shoemaker who had taught himself both Hebrew and Greek, went to India under the auspices of his Baptist Missionary Society and launched a translations program at Serampore; he participated in thirty-five translations. Robert Morrison (1782–1834), sponsored by the London Missionary Society, produced in Canton and Macao the first Chinese translation of the Bible, though he was broken in health and working against incredible odds. A bit later, Robert Moffat (1795–1883), David Livingstone's father-in-law, went to Capetown to begin his distinguished career as a pioneer missionary, his first duty being to produce a translation of the Bible in seTswana. Still others followed, and as their numbers increased and their tasks became more demanding, they and their parent societies at home found themselves, in view of their many other commitments, unable to meet the rapidly growing needs for Bible translation and production. It became clear that a new strategy was required, calling for an organization that would be concerned solely with the translation and production of scriptures for the missions in Asia, Africa, and Latin America.

The British and Foreign Bible Society. The formation of the British and Foreign Bible Society (BFBS) on 7 March 1804 was the answer. Nearly three hundred people met in the London Tavern to discuss the place of Bible distribution in Christian work and witness. Despite their deep doctrinal and ecclesiological differences they agreed to form a society whose single purpose would be to print the scriptures, without note or comment, and to distribute them without financial gain, in the British Isles and throughout the world.

The new Society grew rapidly, and within a decade there were throughout the British Isles over two hundred local groups called auxiliaries that were committed to supporting the cause. Equally important, other Bible societies, patterned after the BFBS, were being formed on the European continent and in North America.

American Bible Society. Meanwhile, in the United States, Bible societies were being organized in several states and in many county seats and principal cities of the fledgling republic. In a period of less than ten years, more than 130 such regional Bible societies were established. There were fifteen "female" Bible societies among them, the first being the Female Bible Society of Geneva, New York (1813). A similar development took place in Canada, where auxiliaries of the British and Foreign Bible Society were established.

The resulting situation was far from satisfactory, for while some communities were well served, others were destitute of scriptures. This was particularly true of the growing West in the United States, where it was reported that not a single Bible could be found in many of the new settlements and where vernacular scriptures were desperately needed in the former French and Spanish territories. The need for some kind of a central organization became increasingly evident, and a call finally went out to create a "General Bible Society." Fifty-six delegates met in New York on 8 May 1816, agreed to establish a new national organization called the American Bible Society (ABS), adopted a constitution modeled on the British one, and issued an "address" to the people of the United States in which they said of the new so-

ciety that "local feelings, party prejudices, sectarian jealousies are excluded by its very nature. Its members are leagued in that, and in that alone, which calls up every hallowed, and puts down every unhallowed, principle—the dissemination of the scriptures in the received versions where they exist, and in the most faithful where they may be required." Many of the provincial societies merged at once with the new national body, but some preferred an "auxiliary" status and a few opted to remain independent, some maintaining separate organizations to the present.

Thus, by the end of the second decade of the nineteenth century, Bible societies were firmly established in Europe and North America, and their distinctive purpose and mission had become widely recognized and generally approved. As they developed, they became noted for the involvement of large numbers of lay men and women, often giving them precedence over their clergy members. They also became widely respected for the ecumenical composition of their boards and staff, for they were careful to maintain close relationships with all Protestant groups; active Roman Catholic participation in their programs did not occur until the middle of the twentieth century. They developed an enviable reputation for careful scholarship both in publishing source texts and in providing quality translations in an incredible number of languages; they also have been (and continue to be) a significant presence in the development of linguistic theory and practice. Similarly, they maintained through the years a policy of strict impartiality in offering their services and productions to all; to that end they remained extremely cautious in avoiding the inclusion of doctrinal notes or comments in their publications.

Throughout they held fast to their founding principle to present to all persons an opportunity to possess the scriptures in their own tongues, with price as no barrier to ownership.

The United Bible Societies. Throughout the nineteenth century, most of the Bible societies confined their activities to work within their national borders. The ABS and BFBS, and to a lesser extent the National Bible Society of Scotland (NBSS) and the Netherlands Bible Society, were conspicuous exceptions. These four "missionary" societies met needs not only in their own countries but also moved out across the world to engage in scripture translation and distribution, largely following the missionaries of their own national churches, with little communication or consultation among themselves. At first there was little friction, but as the overseas outreach of these larger societies continued to expand, areas of duplication and tension began to appear. Some experimental comity arrangements were made in the early years of the twentieth century, preparing the way for a formal consultation in London in 1932 involving three of the principal societies at work in overseas areas, namely, the ABS, BFBS, and NBSS. The London meeting led to innovative cooperative efforts, particularly between the ABS and BFBS in places such as Brazil and Japan, and to a larger conference in 1939 at Amsterdam, when it was proposed to create a kind of world council of Bible societies. The outbreak of war in Europe, however, made it impossible to carry out those plans.

Following the war, in 1946 at a conference held at Haywards Heath in England, sixty-three delegates from twelve European Bible societies and the ABS brought into being the United Bible Societies (UBS), a loose federation of national societies. The UBS has flourished and serves today as a valuable center of coordination, appraisal, and strategic planning.

Working in concert through the UBS, Bible societies and offices in more than 127 countries worldwide have been able to improve their service to churches and missions through greatly improved and accelerated translation techniques, efficiently coordinated production centers, wider interconfessional relationships, and the use of more scientific marketing methods.

See also Circulation of the Bible; Translations.   *Laton E. Holmgren*

BIBLICAL CRITICISM. *See* Interpretation, History of, *article on* Modern Biblical Criticism.

BIBLICAL THEOLOGY. *This entry consists of two articles, one on the Old Testament and one on the New Testament. (The term "Old Testament" is appropriate in this context, since biblical theology has been an almost exclusively Christian enterprise.) For related discussion see* Interpretation, History of, *article on* Modern Biblical Criticism, *and* Israel, Religion of.

Old Testament

Strictly speaking, Old Testament theology is a Christian discipline, for it presupposes the *canon of the Christian Bible, which is divided into two parts, the Old and New Testaments. In this scriptural context, Old Testament theology is part of the larger discipline of biblical theology.

The early Christian community interpreted the life, death, and resurrection of Jesus Christ in the perspective of the scriptures of Israel (Law, Prophets, Writings). In the New Testament, almost without exception, "scripture(s)" refers to these sacred writings. From time to time, beginning with Marcion in the second century CE, questions have been raised as to whether Israel's scriptures belong in the Christian Bible; but the church has steadfastly maintained that the Old Testament as well as the New bears witness to God's *revelation and hence has an indispensable place in Christian life, thought, and worship.

The Nature and Method of Old Testament Theology. The separation of Old Testament theology as an independent discipline occurred fairly late in the history of biblical interpretation, specifically in the period of the Enlightenment when modern views of historical development emerged. The revival of biblical theology in the twentieth century, which began in the 1920s under the leadership of such theologians as Karl Barth (dogmatic theology) and Walter Eichrodt (Old Testament theology), challenged the view of theological liberalism, in which the relation between the Testaments was understood as a unilinear historical development from lower to higher stages of spiritual evolution. Once again theologians in various ways began to address themselves to the overall theological witness of the bipartite canon of Christian scripture. Nevertheless, the earlier separation between Old Testament and New Testament theology has persisted. In part this separation is justified by the vast expansion of knowledge that requires a division of labor among biblical theologians. More important, the Old Testament has a quasi-independent role within the Christian Bible, contributing theological dimensions that supplement, enrich, and at points even qualify the witness of the New Testament. The church considers both testaments to be necessary for a full understanding of God's self-disclosure

and human response to the divine initiative.

Since the Old Testament is a vast and diverse body of literature, the question immediately arises: how should one present a theology of the Old Testament? One way is to organize the material according to a structure or principle derived from the outside. This method was dominant in the late medieval and Protestant scholastic periods, when the task of biblical theology was to provide the proof texts (dicta probantia) for the support of the dogmas of the church. The method is still advocated by theologians who structure Old Testament theology according to the topics of systematic theology (God, humanity, salvation, etc.) or who interpret the Bible according to a modern philosophical perspective (evolutionary development, existentialism, Marxist social philosophy, etc.). Another approach is to try to let the Bible set the issues and determine the method, in which case theology of (subjective genitive) the Old Testament refers to what belongs to, and inheres in, the Old Testament itself.

If the latter way is followed, one immediately faces a methodological problem as to whether Old Testament theology should be presented synchronically (structurally) or diachronically (historically). The debate over method is seen in the works of two leading Old Testament theologians of the twentieth century. The Swiss theologian Walter Eichrodt (*Theologie des Alten Testaments*, issued 1933–1939) attempted to present the "structural unity" of Old Testament belief by using the relational model of *covenant. The German theologian Gerhard von Rad (*Theologie des Alten Testaments*, published 1957–1961) attempted to understand the Old Testament dynamically as a history of traditions, and in this sense a *Heilsge-schichte* ("salvation history"). Probably a combination of both methods is required. On the one hand much of the Old Testament is story/history; indeed it begins with a history that extends from *creation to the *exile of the Israelite people (Genesis–2 Kings). On the other hand, patterns of organization and symbolism are discernible in this historical presentation and elsewhere.

The Relationship between God and People. The starting point in an exposition of Old Testament theology is the self-disclosure of the holy God, who chooses to enter into relationship with a particular people, Israel, called to be the means through whom other peoples may know and glorify God, the creator and redeemer. The term Israel, both in biblical times and today, may be used of a political state, (e.g., the kingdoms of Israel and Judah), but basically it is a sacral term which refers to "the people of God." In its inclusive sense the term is often used in the Old Testament, and in this larger sense Paul could speak of the Christian community as being essentially related to, and indeed part of, Israel, the people of God.

In the scriptures of Israel, primacy is given to the *Torah, traditionally called the "five books of Moses." In the view of the community of faith, God gave torah or instruction to the people, so that they may properly serve (worship) God and live faithfully and obediently in God's presence. This Torah has the form of an overall story or history, which includes within it commandments, or *law in the narrower sense of the term. God's self-disclosure as creator and sovereign established a relation between God and human beings, who are made in the divine image, and particularly a relationship with one people, whose election is portrayed in the calling of Abraham and Sarah to respond in faith to the divine promise and the choice of Jacob, also called Israel, over his twin brother Esau.

The heart of the Torah story, however, is found in the tradition that begins with the book of Exodus. The disclosure of God's name, that is, identity, is associated primarily with fundamental root experiences that constitute the fountainhead of the Mosaic tradition, namely Exodus and Sinai. These core traditions, which signify the inseparably related dimensions of divine initiative and human responsibility, of *salvation and obligation, are paradigmatic for Israel's knowledge of who God is and how the people are to live faithfully in God's presence. The holy God whom Israel knows and worships is characterized as one, jealous (zealous), righteous, gracious, faithful, and trustworthy, whose judgment falls, however, upon those who betray their religious loyalty and turn to iniquity. This knowledge of God is further elaborated in the preaching of prophets, the teaching of priests, and the counsel of sages.

Covenant History. The relationship between God and people, often expressed in the language "your God" and "my people," is understood in the Old Testament as that of a covenant. The significance of covenant is far greater than a statistical count of the occurrences of the term would indicate. Eichrodt took this concept, understood in the broad sense of relationship, as the organizing principle in his theology. In the Reformed tradition there is precedent for this, reaching back at least to the federal (covenantal) theology of the Dutch Calvinist Johannes Cocceius (1603–1669). In the Old Testament, however, covenant is not a univocal term, nor is it a theological umbrella that covers everything. Three major covenantal perspectives or patterns of symbolization are evident. All of these are covenants of *grace, for they rest upon the initiative and superior status of the divine covenant maker, but each nuances the relationship between God and people differently.

The Torah gives primacy to the covenant with Abraham. This covenant is based on God's gracious commitment, unconditioned by human performance. Therefore, it is designated an "everlasting covenant," one that has perpetual validity. Characteristic of this type of covenant is the giving of divine promises, not the imposition of obligations. In the priestly perspective that governs the Torah in its final form, the Abrahamic covenant belongs to a periodized history that is punctuated with three divine covenants, each of which is termed an everlasting covenant. The first period extends from creation to the covenant with Noah after the *flood, a universal, ecological covenant embracing all human beings, animals and birds, and the earth itself. The second extends from Noah to Abra[ha]m, and includes the divine promises of the land of Canaan as an everlasting possession, a numerous posterity, and a special relationship between God and the descendants of Abraham and Sarah ("I will be your/their God"). The third period extends from Abraham to Moses, the mediator of the Sinai covenant, also designated as everlasting. These covenants are accompanied by three signs: the *rainbow, *circumcision, and the *Sabbath, respectively, the latter harking back to God's creation. In this perspective, the Sinai covenant is regarded as the ratification or fulfillment of the ancestral covenant that God "remembers." The special relationship with God, promised in the Abrahamic covenant, finds expression in the disclosure of

the cultic name, Yahweh, and the "tabernacling presence" of God in the midst of the people. The whole cult is regarded as the God-given means of grace that enables a holy people to live faithfully in the presence of the holy God. *Sacrifices are provided (the book of Leviticus) for the expiation of sin and reconciliation to God.

A second covenantal pattern of symbolization, following the sequence of the Hebrew Bible, is associated with Moses. It is set forth classically in the book of Deuteronomy, canonically joined to the priestly Torah discussed above, and provides the dominant theological perspective in the Former Prophets (Joshua through 2 Kings), that is, the Deuteronomic history. In contrast to the Abrahamic covenant, which was based unilaterally on God's gracious commitment and promise, this covenant is more of a two-way affair, and places greater emphasis on human obligation. The covenantal pattern, on the analogy of ancient suzerainty treaties, includes several characteristic elements: the story of the saving deeds of the covenant initiator, the stipulations that are binding on the covenant recipient, and the sanctions of *blessing and *curse in case of obedience or disobedience. Like the Abrahamic covenant, this too is a covenant of grace, but it carries within it "the curse of the law" (cf. Gal. 3.10, 13), for the judgment of God could bring severe punishment upon the people or even annul the relationship if the people fail in their covenant responsibilities.

A third covenantal pattern of symbolization is also found in the Deuteronomic history, where it is introduced as a theme secondary to the Mosaic covenant. This is the royal covenant theology, according to which Yahweh made an everlasting covenant with David, promising perpetual divine grace (*ḥesed*) to the throne, even though particular kings performed badly in office and had to be chastised. This Davidic covenant did not supersede the Mosaic covenant; indeed, the *ark of the covenant—the sacred symbol of Mosaic tradition—was escorted into Jerusalem and eventually was placed in the holy of holies of the Temple. This covenant perspective, however, moves beyond the horizon of Israel's sacred history into the cosmic dimension of God's sovereignty as creator of the universe and ruler of history. As in other religions of the ancient Near East, the two salvific institutions are *kingship and Temple, both of which were alien to the Mosaic tradition. The reigning monarch is Yahweh's anointed ("messiah") and is elected to the special role of *son of God. When the king is gifted with wisdom, divine blessing flows into Israel's society and overflows to other nations. The Temple, in Davidic theology, also has cosmic significance, for it is founded at the cosmic center—the meeting place of heaven and earth, where God is present in the midst of the people. This covenantal perspective is dominant in the books of Chronicles, and is a major factor in the Psalms, which in their final form were issued under the aegis of David, regarded as the type of God's anointed one or messiah.

These three covenants, associated with Abraham, Moses, and David respectively, should not be understood as following one another chronologically but as existing side by side, like overlapping theological circles. In the Torah, the Mosaic covenant fulfills the promissory Abrahamic covenant; the Deuteronomic history emphasizes the Mosaic covenant, but also includes the promissory Davidic covenant; and the Chronicler's history gives priority to the Davidic covenant (this historian bypasses the Mosaic period), but also includes elements of the Priestly tradition and the Mosaic torah understood in its halakic or legal sense. Indeed, to express the relationship between God and human beings all three theological perspectives are required. Each nuances in its own way polarities of the divine-human relationship: God's sovereignty and human freedom, God's transcendence (distance) and immanence (presence), and God's relation to the particular people, Israel, and God's universal sway as cosmic creator and sovereign. All three include promises and obligations, but the Abrahamic and Davidic covenants are primarily promissory, while the Mosaic covenant is primarily one of obligation.

Prophecy and Covenant. The interrelation of these covenant perspectives is evident in the second part of the canon of the Prophets: the so-called Latter Prophets, namely the books of Isaiah, Jeremiah, Ezekiel, and the Twelve. The message of the eighth-century prophet, Isaiah of Jerusalem, was based primarily on royal covenant theology. Virtually ignoring Exodus and Sinai, this prophet proclaimed that Yahweh is the cosmic king, whose rule is manifest on earth through the Davidic monarch and whose dwelling place is on Mount Zion. The imminent *day of the Lord would manifest divine judgment against all presumptuous claims of earthly powers and would purge Zion, the city of God, of corruption, so that it would be the center of a social order that corresponds to the order of God's cosmic rule. Later interpreters enriched Isaiah's message with the *typology of a new exodus and transferred to the people the promises of grace made to David. This synthesis of covenant traditions provided the theological basis for proclaiming the coming of the *kingdom of God—a new age, indeed a new creation, in which Israel and all nations would participate.

Two of the prophets of Israel, Hosea and Jeremiah, stood primarily in the Mosaic covenant tradition. Both opposed the allurements of Canaanite culture, particularly the Baal fertility religion. In the case of Hosea, however, who was active in the northern kingdom just before its fall in 722 BCE, the contact with Canaanite culture served to enrich covenant theology. He poetically portrayed the relationship between God and Israel in terms of a sacred marriage, in which the "wife," after experiencing divine discipline for her infidelity, eventually is reconciled with her "husband" in a new covenant, like the one made in "the days of her youth" (the time of the Exodus). In this restored relationship, the land will become fertile and yield abundant agricultural blessings. Shifting to another family *metaphor, this poet portrayed God's relationship to the people as that of a parent who disciplines and nurtures a child.

Jeremiah, at the time of the collapse of the southern kingdom of Judah, was also an interpreter of the Mosaic covenant. Portrayed as a "prophet like Moses" (Deut. 18.18), he attacked the weaknesses of royal covenant theology, as evident in the exploitative policies of Davidic kings and false confidence in the Temple. Recalling the story of Yahweh's saving action in the Mosaic period, he indicted the people for their violation of the covenant commandments (Jer. 7.1–15, the "Temple sermon") and summoned them, under the threat of divine judgment, to repent, that is, to turn away from false loyalties and to return to loyalty to Yahweh and the demands of the covenant. The book of Jeremiah also includes conditional promises to Davidic kings and messianic hope for a coming Davidic ruler. The new covenant, to supersede the Mosaic covenant, which the people broke, would be based on God's forgiving grace and would introduce an everlasting covenant.

The interaction of theological perspectives is especially evident in the message of Ezekiel. Basically this prophet stood in the priestly tradition that provided the overarching theological perspective of the Torah in its final form. This is evident in Ezekiel's sense of the divine holiness that separates God from mortal human beings, the tabernacling presence of God in the Temple, and the cultic and ethical laws designed to insure the holiness of the people. As in the priestly recension of the Torah, the Exodus tradition is important, but is invoked to demonstrate that from the very first Israel had been a sinful people under the judgment of God. The Mosaic covenant, broken by the people, will be superseded by a new covenant which, because it is based on the faithfulness and forgiveness of God and not on the people's behavior, will be an everlasting covenant. Portrayals of the divine restoration beyond the day of judgment include elements of royal covenant theology: the raising up of a Davidic leader who will be a "good shepherd" of the people.

The Justice of God and the Problem of Evil. Taken together, the Torah and the Prophets (Former and Latter) portray a temporal movement from creation to final consummation under the governance of God, whose providence is evident in nature and history, and whose will is made known to, and through, Israel, the people of God. The covenantal perspectives described above accompanied Israel's sacred history, as evident in the Psalms that contain the hymns, laments, and thanksgivings of the pilgrim people.

The intensification of Israel's sufferings, owing to the fall of the nation and the exile of the people, called into question the adequacy of covenantal theology, which consistently explained *suffering as the deserved consequence of human sin or failure. The third part of the Hebrew canon, the Writings, reflects two major theological shifts of emphasis. One was the movement from torah to wisdom. Wisdom had always been a major ingredient in covenantal theology, as evident in the Mosaic tradition with its appeal to walk in the way that yields blessing, and was especially at home in royal covenant theology, which sought to align the social order with the righteousness and peace of God's cosmic kingdom. In the postexilic period the shift to the halakic dimension of the Mosaic torah, evident in the Chronicler's writing, facilitated the identification of torah and prudential wisdom (as in torah and wisdom psalms, e.g., 1, 37, 119; see the book of Proverbs). Facing the question of theodicy, however, some sages maintained that the divine wisdom hidden in creation is beyond human grasp (Ecclesiastes; Job). Wisdom was even accorded a cosmic role as the agent of God in creation.

The other major development was the movement from prophecy to *apocalyptic, which can be traced within the book of Isaiah. Although human wisdom cannot grasp the divine secret, the mystery of God's kingdom, i.e., the time and manner of its coming, is revealed to a seer (the book of Daniel). In apocalyptic the scene is not restricted to Israel's sacred history but unfolds into a universal drama in which the kingdom of God is triumphant over all powers of evil, including *death itself. Apocalyptic writers eclectically drew upon all of Israel's covenantal traditions, as well as extrabiblical motifs, to portray the final consummation.

The Relation between the Testaments. There is no smooth and easy transition from the Old Testament to the New, as evident from the fact that the very scriptures of Israel that nourished the early Christian community have proved to be problematic. Nevertheless, New Testament writers appropriated Israel's scriptures in various ways to interpret and elaborate the good news about Jesus, who was confessed to be the Messiah or Christ. Viewed in Christian perspective, the sacred history of Israel is part of "the story of our life"; indeed, the whole biblical narrative, extending from creation to consummation, has its center in Jesus Christ.

Accordingly, the early Christian community affirmed that God's covenants with Israel are ratified in Jesus Christ, though preference is usually given to the promissory covenants associated with Abraham and David (cf. "the covenants of promise," Eph. 2.12). To invoke the typology of Calvin, Jesus Christ is prophet, priest, and king—that is, the eschatological "prophet like Moses" of the Mosaic covenant tradition, the "son of God" of the royal or messianic tradition, and the priestly mediator who effects reconciliation with God (Letter to the Hebrews). Furthermore, in him converge the wisdom movement (cf. the *Logos of the prologue to the Fourth Gospel) and the apocalyptic expectation of the heavenly *Son of man. Finally, the Old Testament, functioning as Christian scripture, offers to the Christian community supplementary theological dimensions that are vital for a full understanding of Christian faith, such as creation theology, a healthy this-worldliness, the role of nationhood in God's economy, expostulation with God in times of human distress and perplexity, and the insistence that the command to love God and one another must be informed by God's demand for justice and *mercy in political, social, and economic relations.   *Bernhard W. Anderson*

New Testament

Strictly speaking there is no theology of the New Testament, but as many theologies as there are authors. Theology is systematized reflection, and only Romans has some claim to be that. All the New Testament books are occasional in character, i.e., written for specific situations, not statements of timeless truths. Nevertheless, underlying all the books of the New Testament there is a coherent center, the proclamation (Grk. *kerygma*) of Jesus crucified and risen. This coherent center may itself be expressed in different ways, even in the same author (e.g., in Paul, compare 1 Cor. 15.3–5; Rom. 10.9; 14.9). Sometimes only the *crucifixion is mentioned, sometimes only the *resurrection. But each always implies the other. Sometimes Paul gives brief statements of the kerygma, sometimes extended confessional formulae. The preaching in Acts is similarly focused on Jesus' death and resurrection. The four Gospels are structured so as to bring out the centrality of the cross and resurrection (cf. the three passion predictions in Mark 8.31; 9.31; 10.33–34 par.) and the importance of the "hour" of Jesus' death and glorification throughout the Fourth Gospel.

This death and resurrection of Jesus constitutes the "Christ event," in which God acted definitively for the salvation (or condemnation) first of Israel, then of the human race, and finally of the whole cosmos. It is a proclamation set in the framework of Jewish *apocalyptic hope of a new heaven and a new earth. This consummation has now been inaugurated in the Christ event and will be completed when Christ returns (the *parousia).

The Doctrine of God (Theology). The New Testament offers no new doctrine of God, but simply proclaims that the Old Testament God has now acted definitively. The God of Abraham, Isaac, and Jacob is now the God and Father of Jesus Christ. Even the fatherhood of God is not new. Thus all Old Testament theology is implied in the New Testament: God is the creator and Lord of history, the God who acts, who calls Israel into covenant, who promises the redemption of his people. The New Testament proclaims that these promises have now been fulfilled, or rather are now in the process of being fulfilled.

The Earthly Jesus. Although the coherent center of the New Testament focuses upon the death and resurrection of Jesus, his earthly ministry is an integral part of the Christ event. For the earthly ministry of Jesus gives shape and contours to the cross. There were hundreds of crosses in Palestine in the first-century CE, but only in this cross did God act for the salvation of humankind. That is not an arbitrary claim, but is legitimated by the fact that the earthly Jesus had preached the in-breaking of God's kingdom, i.e., God's definitive salvation. Hence the four Gospels, four versions of the Good News, encapsulate the earthly ministry of Jesus in their proclamation of his death and resurrection. And although Paul seldom alludes to the earthly ministry of Jesus—only a few echoes of his sayings and an occasional reference to his character and lifestyle—nevertheless Paul's frequent use of the human name "Jesus" in significant contexts is testimony to his conviction of the importance of Jesus' earthly history. Moreover, the resurrection does not relegate the earthly Jesus to the archives; rather it perpetuates him, making the salvation that he offered on earth forever available through the preaching of the kerygma.

The Person of Christ (Christology). There is no single Christology in the New Testament but a variety of Christologies. But these Christologies do have a coherent center. Jesus is always interpreted christologically in the New Testament; he is always the one in whom God has decisively acted for us and for our salvation: "In Christ God was reconciling the world to himself" (2 Cor. 5.19). This coherent center of Christology is given contingent application by a variety of christological titles, patterns, and, in the Gospels, portraits. Jesus is the final prophet and servant of Yahweh; he is Messiah (Christ, anointed one), Lord, *Son of God. In later books he is the *incarnation of the preexistent *Logos or Word of God. Some early patterns have two foci, looking back to his first coming and forward to his return. Some patterns depict two stages, his earthly career and his subsequent exaltation. Some patterns are threefold, speaking of his preexistence, incarnate life, and exaltation. Each Gospel has its own portrait of Jesus. Mark emphasizes the *messianic secret; Jesus' messiahship is hidden on earth, and can be confessed only after the cross and resurrection. For Matthew, Jesus is the new Moses; as such, he gives the definitive interpretation of the *Law and founds a church, the true Israel. For Luke, Jesus is the end-time prophet who shows human sympathy and compassion for the poor, for the outcast and the sick, and for women. For John, Jesus is the incarnate revealer whose revelation, when received, confers salvation. These various portraits are directed toward the specific situations for which the respective evangelists wrote. Some Christologies emphasize the death and resurrection (paschal Christologies); others (like the sending formula) are focused upon the beginning and purpose of Jesus' career (God sent his son, plus a statement of saving purpose). The infancy stories at the beginning of Matthew and Luke give narrative expression to this type of Christology, and the incarnation pattern

is a more developed form of it. These Christologies emphasize the divine initiative in the Christ event, of which the virginal conception (see Virgin Birth of Christ) is a powerful symbolic expression.

The Work of Christ (Soteriology). At the outset, it was the total career of Jesus that was interpreted as the saving act of God (so the earliest preaching as recorded in Acts). Very soon the death of Christ was interpreted as the focal point of God's saving act. This was expressed by means of the hyper- (Grk. "for, on behalf of") formula, which was particularly at home in the tradition of the *Lord's Supper, in the bread and cup words, though it also figures in some forms of the kerygma. The hyper-formula does not mean that the death of Jesus was vicarious or substitutionary, as though the human Christ were appeasing the wrath of an angry deity and rendering him propitious toward humankind. Rather, in Christ God was acting to liberate humanity from the bondage of sin.

Often, though not invariably, combined with the hyper-formula is the language of "giving" or "giving up": God gave (up) his son to the death on the cross. Often the verb is in the passive: "he was given up," but this is a so-called divine passive, a phrase implying so that it was God who gave him up. Sometimes too the subject is Jesus himself ("who gave himself for me," Gal. 2.20). These formulae emphasize the cost of Christ's death, both to the Father and to himself. But whether God or Christ is the subject, the cross is primarily an act of God, initiated by him.

Christ's death was interpreted in earliest tradition as a sacrifice like that of the *Day of Atonement or the *Passover lamb. Subsequent references to *blood in connection with the death of Christ echo both of these traditions, and also the cup word in the Supper tradition. Blood denotes not a material substance, but the event of Christ's death in its saving significance.

Most New Testament writers are content simply to repeat or to echo such traditional formulae. Only Paul and the author of Hebrews reflect further upon the meaning of Christ's death and apply their insights to their churches' situations. Paul reflects particularly on the saving benefits of the cross in response to the judaizing (Galatians; Romans; Phil. 3) and gnosticizing (Corinthian correspondence) controversies.

Paul uses many images to describe the saving effects of Christ's death. They include *justification, reconciliation, redemption (see Redeem), and expiation. These metaphors are derived from various sources. Justification originates in the law courts where it means acquittal. It denotes neither making people ethically righteous nor merely treating them as righteous, but bringing them into a right relationship with God. This sets the believer on the road to obedience. Reconciliation comes from international or personal relations. It presupposes that human beings were in a state of enmity with God and affirms that God in Christ has overcome that enmity and brought the believers into a right relationship with God. Redemption is a metaphor from the manumission of slaves. It also occurs in the Hebrew Bible as a metaphor for salvation in connection with the *Exodus and with the powers of evil, including *sin, *death, and the devil. Expiation is a sacrificial term, not developed by Paul but occurring in the hymn whose imagery is derived from the day of atonement. It denotes that the death of Christ covers or wipes away sin.

The letter to the Hebrews is also a contingent application of the central affirmation of the saving death of Christ. It was written to revive the flagging enthusiasm of second- or third-generation Christians and asserts the once-and-for-all quality of Christ's saving death. There is no further sacrifice for sin and no return after apostasy. To make this point the author develops a Christology of Christ as eternal high priest, and his sacrifice as the fulfillment of the Levitical ceremonies of the Day of Atonement with an occasional glance at the daily sacrifice.

The Holy Spirit (Pneumatology). Although only Acts casts the giving of the Holy Spirit into a story, it is the general belief of the New Testament writers that the Spirit came as a result of the Christ event. The Hebrew Bible and Jewish tradition expected an outpouring of the spirit in the last days, and the early Christian community saw in its post-Easter experiences the fulfillment of this promise and a foretaste of the full end-time salvation. Paul expresses this general conviction when he calls the Spirit the "first fruits" (Rom. 8.23) or "down payment" (2 Cor. 1.22 [NRSV: "first installment"]; 5.5 [NRSV: "guarantee"]) of final redemption. In the early community the presence of the Spirit was seen primarily in ecstatic phenomena, such as *miracles and speaking in tongues (see Glossolalia). Paul had problems in this connection at Corinth, where the gifts of the Spirit were allowed to run riot, and he found it necessary to grade the gifts, giving priority to prophecy, and making love (Grk. *agapē*) the gift which must inform all the other gifts. The Fourth Gospel developed the doctrine of the Spirit (called "Paraclete"; NRSV: "Advocate") in a theological rather than ethical direction: the function of the Spirit is to lead the community into truth, not away from the truth revealed in Jesus but to an even deeper apprehension of it.

The Church (Ecclesiology). Jesus' intention was the end-time renewal of God's people. As a result of his saving deed in the cross and resurrection and the subsequent outpouring of the Spirit there came into being a new community that understood itself to be the saints, the elect, and the *ekklēsia* (translating Hebr. *qāhāl*, "assembly"), the church or people of God. Sociologically the church was as yet only a sect within Judaism, but it was conscious of being the true Israel, now definitively renewed. Throughout the apostolic age the word *ekklēsia* was used primarily for the locally gathered community, especially in house-churches, but in the subapostolic period, e.g., in the deutero-Pauline Ephesians, it was used for the universal church. But the universal church was arrived at not by adding the local congregations together; rather, each local congregation was the visible embodiment of the one universal *ekklēsia*.

Paul developed the image of the church as the body of Christ in order to emphasize the mutual responsibility of the members for one another. The image first occurs in connection with the Eucharist—by partaking of the sacramental body the believers become the ecclesial body. The theme is developed in 1 Corinthians 12.12–31, and summarized in Romans 12.4–8. There was no formalized ministry in the apostolic age; members exercised their various gifts ministerially, though under the control of the apostles. A more institutionalized church order first developed in the Jewish-Christian communities, beginning at Jerusalem and in the subapostolic age was taken over in the Pauline churches. At this period (ca. 70–110 CE) the institutional ministry takes over the task of preserving and transmitting the apostolic tradition, encapsulated in creedal forms, together with an incipient *canon of apostolic writings. A reaction occurred in the Johannine community, which saw itself as a loosely gathered society of "friends," and only later accepted a more formal ministry. Prior to this the Johannine circles developed the image of Christ and the church as a vine and branches, characterized by their mutual indwelling ("I in them and they in me"), a parallel to the Pauline image of the body of Christ.

Baptism. The foundation members of the community received a direct baptism of the Spirit at *Pentecost. But all others henceforth became members of the community and participants in the Holy Spirit through water *baptism. The community believed it had been led to this practice by the risen One, and expressed this conviction in story form by the command to baptize. Baptism was performed in the name of Jesus, i.e., under his authority. As a result believers were "added" (a divine passive denoting that baptism is the occasion of an act of God, i.e., in later church language a *sacrament) and became partakers of the Holy Spirit in the already established Spirit-filled community.

In response to new situations in his Hellenistic communities Paul developed the doctrine of baptism further. The believers were now baptized into Christ, made over to his ownership. For Paul this meant being baptized into Christ's death, with the hope of future resurrection. Note too that Paul carefully refrains from saying that they are already participating in his resurrection; that would not come until the end, and was conditional on their walking in newness of life. Paul also speaks of the believers as being baptized into one body. Although the texts are not very clear, it appears from some New Testament writings that the custom arose of marking the connection of baptism with the gift of the Spirit by adding to water baptism the additional act of the *laying on of hands. This was probably not a separate rite, but an attempt to underline part of the rich meaning of water baptism itself.

The Lord's Supper. The earthly Jesus had regularly celebrated *meals with his disciples. These meals were foretastes of the *kingdom of God, which was frequently depicted as a banquet. This table fellowship was renewed after Easter and some of the postresurrectional appearances are associated with meals. Common meals were continued by the early community after the Easter event, and were characterized by exuberant joy, the focus being on the risen One's coming in anticipation of his coming at the end (cf. the acclamation Maranatha ["Our Lord, come!"]; 1 Cor. 16.22). Another strain in the tradition, perhaps originally associated with Passover, stressed the connection between the Supper and Christ's death. This tradition interpreted the act as a proclamation (Grk. *anamnēsis*, "memorial" [NRSV: "remembrance"]) of Christ's death. Its effect was to make the benefits of his death presently operative for the participants (*koinōnia*) in the body and blood of Christ. Paul further develops the ecclesial significance of this act: by partaking of the one loaf the believers become one body. The Johannine tradition emphasizes eternal life already here and now through eating the bread (John 6.35–51a—note the *manna *typology), while John 6.51b–58 speaks of eating the flesh and drinking the blood of the *Son of man, an act that nourishes the mutual indwelling of Christ and the believers.

The Last Things (Eschatology).

Throughout the New Testament there is a tension between the "already" and the "not yet." On the one hand, the end-time kingdom has come as a result of the Christ event, while on the other hand it awaits final consummation. In Jesus' proclamation the kingdom is already breaking through in Jesus' activity; yet his disciples are to pray, "Your kingdom come," and Jesus faces death with the conviction that after it that kingdom will shortly be consummated. The Easter event was in a sense an inauguration of the end-time rule of the kingdom of God (see above), though the final coming of the kingdom and the general resurrection were still outstanding. This expectation was expressed in imaginative language in the hope of Christ's "parousia" or return as judge and savior, which the early Christians believed would take place shortly. It was the sense of what had happened already in the Christ event that enabled the early communities to weather the storm of the delay of the parousia, while maintaining the tension between the already and the not yet, though the weight placed on either side of the balance varied from writer to writer. Thus in Ephesians and John the emphasis is placed on the already; the future hope practically disappears, though never quite. Other writings (such as 2 Thessalonians, Jude, 2 Peter and Revelation) place the primary emphasis on the future coming, though without losing the sense that something of the end has already occurred through the Christ event.

The Normative Character of New Testament Theology. While the pluralism of New Testament theology appears to undermine its normative character, the coherent center, which we have defined as the kerygma of Christ crucified and risen, provides a criterion for the developments of theology through contingent application within the New Testament, a canon within the canon. The way in which writers like Paul move from coherent center to contingent application provides a pattern for a similar movement in contemporary theology, belief, and practice. Furthermore, the pluralism of the New Testament moves forward on certain trajectories to convergences lying beyond the New Testament period. We see that particularly with the varieties of New Testament Christology that eventually converge in the Christologies of Nicea and Chalcedon, in the doctrines of the consubstantiality of the Son with the Father, and of Christ as truly divine and truly human, with two natures and one person. The remaining problem is whether earlier Christologies, e.g., the functional Christologies of Jesus as the end-time prophet, or as the servant who is now enthroned as Christ and Lord, still have any role to play, and whether the later christological definitions represent an impoverishment. Whereas the New Testament Christologies focus upon Jesus' earthly career, his exaltation, and his parousia, and were thus concerned with God's redemptive act in the Christ event, the later definitions concentrated upon the eternal being of the Son of God and the moment of his entry as a human being into the world. The Fourth Gospel perhaps points the way for the solution of the modern dilemma in that it retains earlier christological perspectives, such as the sending of the Son for the purpose of redemption, alongside the later Christologies of preexistence and incarnation.

In short, New Testament theology does not provide a static norm, but a dynamic one, inviting the church and theology to return continually to the coherent center of the New Testament, and to move forward to its contingent application today, using the contingent application within the New Testament as a model. *Reginald H. Fuller*

BLESSING. In most biblical texts, the associated verbs (to bless), adjectives (blessed), and nouns (blessing, blessedness) express a reciprocity pertaining between God and his chosen people. God blesses them as a mark of his *grace and favor; their blessing of God is a recognition of his presence among them. His blessing conveys to his people a share in his own vitality and ageless purpose. Their blessing of him, often in song, dance, and instrumental *music, celebrates their gratitude for his goodness and help. Each movement in this mutual activity elicits the other, so that the words point to the conjunction of two activities, especially in *worship.

This intersection is especially prominent in four types of literature. First are the historical narratives of the *Pentateuch, which describe God's choice and guidance of the ancestors of Israel. Typical is God's promise to Abraham, "I will make of you a great nation, and I will bless you . . . and by you all the families of the earth shall bless themselves" (Gen. 12.2–3; NRSV: "shall be blessed"); the importance of this tradition is made clear in Romans 4.6–9. The intersection is prominent, second, in Deuteronomy, which records the *covenant sealed between God and Moses. Here the command "You shall bless the Lord" (8.10) is linked to the promise "The Lord your God will bless you" (15.10). Third, the hymnbook used in Temple and synagogue shows how dominant this reciprocal action appears in regular worship. We frequently hear the injunction "Bless the Lord, O my soul" (Ps. 103.1), as well as the assurance "The Lord will bless you from Zion" (Ps 128.5). This dual motif may be found in more than a third of the Psalms. Then there is a fourth type of literature, the writings of the prophets and apocalyptists. The visions given to Daniel, for instance, made him bless the name of the Lord, and in response he declares as blessed by God all who persevere until "the end of the days" (Dan. 12.12–13). So too in the Christian apocalypse, the book of Revelation, faithful saints receive beatitudes and join in grateful doxologies addressed to God. Significant in the Christian Eucharist are the word and the cup of blessing. Further, Jesus' followers are enjoined to respond to *curses with blessings as an imitation of generous divine blessing.

In the Bible the idea of blessing forms an important link between theology and liturgy, theology and ethics, theology and a way of looking at all human history and experience. Literary documents are introduced by extensive liturgical preludes that bless God for what he has done. The beatitudes pronounced by Jesus become well-remembered clues to his entire legacy (see Sermon on the Mount); translators of these beatitudes despair of finding equivalents in English (should "blessed" be replaced by "happy" or "fortunate"?). The problem remains: How to do justice to the conjunction of divine and human activity in a language that limits itself to human relationships.   *Paul S. Minear*

BLOOD. Words translated as "blood" occur nearly four hundred times in the Hebrew Bible and nearly a hundred times in the New Testament. Of these occurrences, more than half in the Hebrew Bible and more than a quarter in the New Testament have to do with death by violence, by far the most frequent reference.

There are some passages in which life and blood are connected, principally in connection with the prohibition of eating meat with blood still in it. This as-

sociation has led some scholars to conclude that in the offering of *sacrifice, the death of the victim is unimportant; sacrificial atonement does not depend on an animal dying in place of the worshiper but rather on life set free from the body and offered to God. Similarly, in the New Testament it is not the death of Jesus that is the atonement, but his life.

Such a view scarcely accords with the statistical evidence summarized above, nor with the obvious fact that it is death that occurs when an animal is offered in sacrifice. Leviticus 17.11 and similar passages are to be understood in the sense that it is the life given up in death, rather than the life set free from the flesh, that is the atonement. And in the New Testament, phrases like "the blood of his cross" (Col. 1.20) cannot point to the release of life, for relatively little blood was shed in *crucifixion. Similarly, "justified by his blood" is parallel to "reconciled to God through the death of his son" (Rom. 5.9–10). In the Bible, therefore, blood normally points to the undergoing of death rather than to the release of life.

This association of blood and death partially explains the concept of blood taboo. Just as those who had contact with a corpse became unclean, so contact with the blood of the slain rendered a warrior ritually impure.

See also Purity, Ritual.   *Leon Morris*

BOOK OF LIFE. This symbolic phrase is parallel in meaning to other terms that the Bible associates with the phrase "of life": tree, bread, *water, fountain, river, path, word, crown. In each case, God is the source and giver of this life, which is more than the years between birth and death.

The image of a book suggests a roster of names, the names of those who through grace and obedience become members of God's family and share his life. Conversely, death is the destiny of those who have been erased from this roll call. The book image also indicates the record that God keeps of human debits and credits, in preparation for a final accounting. Finally, the book of life can be visualized as containing the plans of God for his people, all that has happened and will happen to the community and to each of its members.

One reason why this image remained current was that in every service of worship from at least the *exile onward, whether in synagogue or church, the scripture would be read as God's word to his people. The act of opening and closing the scroll carried symbolic force. *See also* Day of Judgment.

Paul S. Minear

BOOKS AND BOOKMAKING IN ANTIQUITY. "This word came to Jeremiah from the Lord: Take a scroll and write on it all the words that I have spoken to you" (Jer. 36.1–2). This passage illustrates the various words in Hebrew, Greek, and Latin translated into English as "book," "scroll," or "roll." In the Hebrew phrase *mĕgillat sēper*, the word *mĕgillâ* designates a roll. While the word *sēper* seems to mean "book" in this and other passages, it can also designate a letter, a legal or private document, or even an inscription. The Septuagint (LXX) renders the Hebrew phrase with the Greek *chartion bibliou*, "roll of a book." The word *chartēs* and its diminutive *chartion* designated paper made from the papyrus plant; both could be used for a piece of paper of any size, including a roll. *Biblos* was the Greek name for the papyrus plant; *biblos* and its diminutive *biblion* acquired the transferred meanings of a roll of paper made from the papyrus plant and the work written on a papyrus roll, that is, a book; the

word "bible" is also derived from *biblos*. The Vulgate uses the Latin phrase *volumen libri*, "roll of a book." *Volumen* comes from the verb *volvo*, "to roll," and so refers originally to the form of the writing material. *Liber* designated the bark or inner rind of a tree; thus, from the supposed use of tree bark as a primitive writing material, *liber* came to be the standard Latin word for "book."

The phrases used in all three languages point to the roll as the standard form of the "book," at least for longer and more formal texts. The reader needed both hands to handle a roll, one to unroll a new section for reading, the other to roll up the section already read. Luke's account of Jesus' visit to the synagogue at Nazareth mentions this procedure: "He stood up to read, and the scroll of the prophet Isaiah was given to him. He unrolled the scroll and found the place where it is written: 'The Spirit of the Lord is upon me . . . ' And he rolled up the scroll, gave it back to the attendant, and sat down" (Luke 4.16–20).

A roll might be made up of sheets either of papyrus or animal skin. Papyrus is a marsh plant *(Cyperus papyrus)* that grew at various spots in Africa and the Near East, including the Sea of Galilee in Israel; but the commercial production of paper from the papyrus plant was probably always the monopoly of the Nile Valley of Egypt. Two layers of strips from the soft interior of the plant, with the upper layer at a right angle to the one below, were pressed together; this pressing released a natural gummy substance which bonded together the strips and layers. Finished dried sheets of paper would then be glued together into a roll. Animal skins (primarily of sheep, goats, and cattle) might be tanned to produce leather, or they might undergo a more complicated process of washing, depilating, soaking in lime, and stretching and drying on a frame, to produce parchment. To form a roll, the sheets of skin would be sewn together.

The Septuagint phrase *chartion bibliou* suggests that the Greeks preferred papyrus as a writing material. In Palestine, however, the preferred material seems to have been animal skin, at least for the writing of the scriptures. The great majority of the *Dead Sea Scrolls, for example, are on skin. The reasons for this preference are unclear; it may simply be that animal skins were available locally, while papyrus had to be imported from Egypt. The Talmud apparently reflects earlier tradition when it directs that the *Torah be written on animal skin, saying this rule was given to Moses at Sinai.

The writing instrument used since early pharaonic Egypt was a reed that had been chewed or frayed to produce a brush. The Greeks preferred a reed pen with a split nib, resembling a modern fountain pen. The simplest form of black ink was made by mixing soot or lampblack with gum.

Other writing materials are mentioned in the Bible or are known from archaeology. Public documents that were to be preserved or displayed might be inscribed on stone (as were the *Ten Commandments) or on bronze plates (as was the decree honoring Simon the high priest). For school lessons, rough drafts, record keeping, and other temporary or personal documents, wood tablets with wax surfaces were used. The tablets consisted of two or more boards hinged to close flat. Wax filled a recess formed by a raised ridge. A stylus made of metal, wood, or bone served as the writing instrument; one end was sharpened to incise the wax, while the other end was blunt or flattened to rub out mistakes and resmooth the surface. The prophets Isaiah and Habakkuk may have recorded

their oracles on such tablets, and the mute Zacharias, father of John the Baptist, asked for a writing tablet to write the name of his son.

These writing tablets with their hinges and multiple leaves resembled a modern book; and the Latin name for a set of wooden writing tablets, *codex* (from *caudex*, "block of wood"), became the name of the modern book form. By the late first century CE, the Romans had devised another type of notebook, consisting of sheets of parchment sewed or fastened together at the spine. The Romans called these notebooks *membranae* ("skins"). Paul seems to refer to such parchment notebooks when he asks Timothy to bring him a cloak left behind at Troas, "also the books, and above all the parchments" (2 Tim 4.13).

Two other writing materials were used in antiquity. Clay tablets were the principal medium for cuneiform, the writing system of wedge-shaped signs that originated in Mesopotamia. A broad-headed stylus was used to impress the signs on wet clay tablets; those tablets with temporary texts, such as letters and receipts, were baked in the sun, while those containing laws, history, or literary works were fired in a kiln to make them more durable. Fragments of broken pottery, called *ostraca* (from their Greek name), were free for the picking in ancient rubbish heaps and provided a cheap and convenient medium for writing notes or receipts.

Christianity brought with it a startling change in ancient bookmaking, namely, the rise of the codex; see Colin H. Roberts and T. C. Skeat, *The Birth of the Codex* (London, 1983). A codex—the form of modern books—is a collection of sheets fastened at the back or spine, usually protected by covers. By the second century CE, the papyrus codex had become the exclusive form for the books of the Christian Bible. For the Jewish scriptures, on the other hand, the roll continued to be the only acceptable form; in the case of Greek literature, the codex achieved parity with the roll about 300 CE and then surpassed it in popularity.

The reasons for the Christian adoption of the codex form remain a matter for speculation. The practical advantages of the codex over the roll seem obvious to the reader accustomed only to the modern book. The codex ought to have been less expensive, since it uses both sides of the writing material, while the roll rarely used both sides; for the same reason, the codex is more compact, therefore easier to store; and its compactness would allow the collection in one volume of previously separate texts. The roll seems cumbersome to read, given the need to unroll and reroll it. Such practical considerations must have played a role in the triumph of the codex in non-Christian as well as in Christian literature; yet they seem insufficient to explain (in the words of Roberts and Skeat) the "instant and universal" adoption of the codex by Christians as early as 100 CE. Pointing to the Jewish custom of committing isolated decisions of the oral law or rabbinic sayings to tablets or small rolls, Roberts and Skeat suggest that papyrus tablets similarly were used to record the oral law as pronounced by Jesus and that these tablets developed into a primitive form of codex. In whatever way the papyrus codex first came into being and came to be used for Christian texts, Christians may have favored the codex because its use differentiated them from Jews and other non-Christians.

See also Writing in Antiquity. *For discussion of the production of Bibles after the invention of printing, see* Printing and Publishing.   *T. Keith Dix*

BURIAL CUSTOMS. A part of the story of Abraham is the record of his concern and care for the burying of Sarah (Gen. 23). He buys a cave for her tomb; this purchase is his first land acquisition in the land of Canaan. The Hittites offered one of their sepulchers, but Abraham preferred to buy and utilize his own cave. For those outside the Promised Land, burial in the ancestral territory continued to be important. For example, the body of Joseph was embalmed in Egypt and returned to Canaan. In like manner, many Jews of the Dispersion of the Roman period preferred to be buried in the Holy Land. The burial customs and practices, as with Abraham, were carried out amid outside cultural influences but yet maintained their own distinctiveness.

Tomb construction saw considerable change and variety. Abraham, as noted above, used a cave. In later periods tombs were cut from the rock. Jesus mentions "whitewashed tombs" (Matt. 23.27), which implies buildings. One of the few monuments from the first century CE still intact in Jerusalem is the so-called Tomb of Absalom, a monument that exhibits both Greek and Nabatean influence. Extended families often had a single connected cluster of underground tombs with niches for the various individuals or families. Often these were re-used. Individual rock-cut tombs were also common. The bodies were generally not enclosed in coffins; after decomposition the remaining bones were then removed to a bone chamber in the floor or at the side of the burial ledge and the space reused. Rock tombs were sealed with a hinged door or a heavy wheel-shaped stone. Criminals were buried under a pile of stones.

With regard to the preparation of the body for burial, neither embalming (an Egyptian custom) nor cremation (called idolatry in *m. ᶜAbod. Zar.* 1.3) was allowed. The body was washed and enclosed, and finally a napkin was placed over the face. The Greek custom of individual coffins was occasionally followed in New Testament times; the earlier period did not use coffins.

Secondary burial, in which the remains, after decomposition, were placed in a small stone or clay box called an ossuary, gradually increased over time. A coffin (sarcophagus) averaged 6 ft (1.8 m) in length, while the ossuary was often only 2.5 ft (.8 m) long. Many tombs had numerous small niches (Hebr. *kôkîm*) into which the ossuaries were placed. Considerable evidence on burial customs has been gleaned from the excavations of the extensive Jewish cemetery at Beth Shearim, where secondary burials dominated. Often the ossuaries were decorated with various geometrical patterns. Roman Jericho has yielded a significant collection of wooden coffins. It seems likely that the biblical phrase "to sleep with [or to be gathered to] one's ancestors" refers to secondary burial in the family tomb.

Burial in the Middle East has always taken place without delay; almost always the person is buried the same day. The warm climate and the lack of embalming has necessitated this practice. In the case of the burial of Jesus, the approaching *Sabbath added to the desire to complete the burial formalities before sundown.

The Middle East has long known the tradition of demonstrative mourning. The walls of ancient Egyptian tombs often depict groups of professional women mourners as a part of the funeral procession. This profession was also known in Israel; Jeremiah explains the purpose of the presence of evocative funeral songs sung by the professionals: "that our eyes may run down with tears" (Jer. 9.18). Instruments used at funerals included the flute; Rabbi Judah (140–165 CE) said, "Even the poorest in Israel should hire not less than two flutes and one wailing woman" (*m. Ketub.* 4.4).

The Bible records a number of poems composed for the deceased, the most famous being David's lament over Saul and Jonathan. The prophets use the funeral lament satirically in speaking of the ruin of nations such as Babylon, Tyre, and Egypt, and the book of Lamentations uses the genre for Jerusalem after its destruction in 587/586 BCE.

In biblical tradition mourning continued for seven days. The places of burial were generally apart from the dwellings of the people; in earlier periods some burials took place within the house. While the Egyptians made elaborate preparations for the dead and placed the surroundings of life in the tomb of the deceased, these customs were kept to a minimum in Palestine. Tombs were comparatively modest and ostentation was criticized. Eighty percent of the tomb inscriptions in the Beth Shearim cemetery are in Greek, yet the inscriptions themselves display a minimum of Greek ideological influence. Resurrection as a concept remains dominant over the idea of the immortality of the soul.

See also Afterlife and Immortality.

Kenneth E. Bailey

C

CALENDAR. *See* Time, Units of.

CANADIAN LITERATURE. *See* Literature and the Bible, *article on* North American Literature.

CANON. *This entry discusses how various writings and collections of writings were officially accepted by various religious authorities and communities as scripture; it consists of three articles:*

Order of Books in the Hebrew Bible
Canon of the Hebrew Bible and the Old Testament
New Testament

The first article deals with the arrangement of books in the sacred text of Judaism, and the second article describes the processes by which those (and other) books were accepted as canonical by both Jewish and Christian communities, in the latter case as the Old Testament. The last article deals with the canonization of the New Testament.

Order of Books in the Hebrew Bible

No traditions have survived concerning the authorities who fixed the canon of Hebrew scriptures, or about the internal order of the books, or about the underlying principles that determined their sequence. It is probable, but not certain, that the three distinct collections known as the *Pentateuch, the Prophets, and the Writings (Hebr. *tôrâ* [*Torah], *nĕbî'îm*, and *kĕtûbîm*, respectively, the initial letters of which form the acronym *tanak*, used in Jewish tradition for the Bible) represent the three successive stages of canonization. Apart from the Pentateuch, the order of whose five books is invariable, the arrangement of the contents of the other two corpora was not uniform in manuscripts and printed editions until fairly recently.

An anonymous tannaitic tradition, no later than ca. 200 CE, lists the order of the books of the Prophets and the Writings. This presents a problem because the codex form was not adopted by Jews before the fifth century CE and because the general and favored scribal practice—with one exception—was to restrict each scroll to a single biblical book. What then is the meaning of term "order" in the rabbinic text? The most likely explanation is that it refers to the manner of storage and the system of classification and cataloguing in vogue in the libraries and schools of Palestine. The library procedures of the Hellenistic world would have required each of the three collections of canonical works to be placed in a separate armarium, with the scrolls arranged in their appropriately assigned order.

The sequence of the Former Prophets following the Pentateuch is Joshua, Judges, Samuel, Kings. This arrangement never varies and presents one long continuous history of Israel from the beginning of the conquest to the fall of the Judean kingdom, the Babylonian *exile, and the release of King Jehoiachin from prison in 561 BCE.

The variations in the order of the books occur in the Latter Prophets and particularly in the Writings. A majority of manuscripts and most printed Bibles feature Isaiah, Jeremiah, and Ezekiel, which is the proper historical order. The above-cited source, however, followed by some manuscripts, lists Isaiah in third place in juxtaposition with its contemporary Hosea. Another tradition has Jeremiah after Kings and before Isaiah and Ezekiel. This is because that prophet was active during the last years of the monarchy, and Jeremiah 39 and 52 largely duplicate 2 Kings 25.

The small prophetic books, generally known as the "Minor Prophets," were habitually transcribed onto a single scroll and were collectively designated "The Twelve" (so already in Sir. 49.10, ca. 180 BCE). Their internal arrangement is Hosea, Joel, Amos, Obadiah, Jonah, Micah, Nahum, Habakkuk, Zephaniah, Haggai, Zechariah, Malachi. This is also the order of a scroll of the second century CE from Wadi Murabba‘at (see Dead Sea Scrolls) containing the Hebrew Minor Prophets, and it apparently reflected traditional views about their historical sequence. The same order, but with Micah following Amos and succeeded by Joel, is given in 2 Esdras 1.39–40. This groups together three prophets of the eighth century BCE.

The order of the Writings in Hebrew-printed Bibles is Psalms, Proverbs, Job, Song of Solomon, Ruth, Lamentations, Ecclesiastes, Esther, Daniel, Ezra, Nehemiah, Chronicles. Passages like 2 Maccabees 2.13–14 and Luke 24.44 seem to attest to the great antiquity of the initial place of Psalms. The aforementioned tannaitic source has

Ruth before Psalms due to the concluding genealogy of David, the reputed author of the Psalter. The Aleppo Codex (end of ninth century CE) and the Leningrad Codex of 1008 CE both open the Writings with Chronicles, probably because that work duplicates the Pentateuchal genealogies and much of the Former Prophets.

The tannaitic practice, also found in manuscripts and ultimately standardized in the printed editions, was to conclude the Hebrew scriptures with Chronicles following Ezra-Nehemiah. This must have been a very early tradition, for it is reflected in Matthew 23.35 and Luke 11.51. The inversion of the chronological order must have arisen out of a desire to close the canon on a note of consolation, and to make the statement that the fulfillment of biblical prophecy involves the return of the Jewish people to its ancestral land. Apart from this messianic exegesis, it also serves to encase the Hebrew scriptures within a framework of historical narrative, for Chronicles begins with Adam and its last sentence contains the same two key Hebrew verbs of redemption with which Genesis concludes (pqd, ‘lh).

Christian editions reverse the order of Prophets-Writings, so that the closing words of Malachi concerning Elijah become transitional to the New Testament, and connect with the role of John the Baptist.

Least stable in respect of order are the small books in the corpus of the Writings. The tannaitic source follows Proverbs with Ecclesiastes and the Song of Solomon because all three are attributed to King Solomon. Most medieval manuscripts preserve this association in one way or another. Lamentations, Daniel, and Esther are grouped together since they all belong to the period of the exile. In medieval times, the Song of Solomon,

Ruth, Lamentations, Ecclesiastes, and Esther were all clustered together in that order, based upon their use as *lectionaries in the cycle of the Jewish religious calendar, commencing with *Passover. This system became the rule in the printed editions. Greek Bibles differ considerably from the Hebrew scriptures in that the books are arranged according to genres of literature. Ignoring the additional *Apocrypha that are interspersed among the canonical works, the following classification emerges. First comes a narrative-historical collection that comprises the Pentateuch and Former Prophets, with Ruth attached to Judges, and Chronicles following Kings. Second is a prophetic collection consisting of Isaiah; Jeremiah, to which is adjoined Lamentations for thematic reasons and traditions of authorship; Ezekiel; Daniel, because he is regarded as a prophet, a contemporary of Ezekiel, and is identified with the personality of that name mentioned in Ezekiel 14.14, 20; 28.3; and the Twelve in a slightly different internal order. The two complete Greek codices, the fourth-century CE Vaticanus and the fifth-century CE Alexandrinus, share these characteristics. However, the latter has Esther and Ezra-Nehemiah immediately after the prophetical collection, while the former places Ezra-Nehemiah after Chronicles. The third part is a poetic-didactic collection. Codex Vaticanus has Psalms, Proverbs, Ecclesiastes, Song of Solomon, Job, and Esther. The order of Codex Alexandrinus is Psalms, Job, Proverbs, Ecclesiastes, and Song of Solomon. Also the sequence of the second and third collections interchanges in the two codices.

Other Greek codices feature different arrangements and there is no uniformity in the traditions of the churches. All extant Greek codices and lists are of Christian origin, and it is uncertain whether or not any represent alternative Jewish conventions about the order of the biblical books.   *Nahum M. Sarna*

Canon of the Hebrew Bible and the Old Testament

Origins. From the fourth century CE, the word "canon" (from a Greek word meaning "a rule") has been used to denote the correct list of the biblical books, and in consequence the collection of books thus listed. It is important to distinguish between the composition of the biblical books and their recognition as scripture. Scholars sometimes envisage a five-stage process of composition, circulation, revision, collection, and recognition as canonical, and such a long process may indeed have been involved for some books. Others of the books may have been much more rapidly acknowledged. But if we may judge from the history of the New Testament canon *(see the next article in this entry)*, some books were probably recognized as having divine authority more slowly than others. It was at one time widely believed that the whole canon had been recognized by the time of Ezra, and this idea is already reflected in 2 Esdras 14.44–48, where Ezra is said to have "made public" twenty-four books (the standard Jewish count of the canonical books). The idea that Ezra knew the canon is probably not entirely without foundation, for most of it had then been written, and an older tradition speaks of Ezra's contemporary Nehemiah, after the calamity of the *exile, gathering together in a library "the books about the kings and prophets, and the writings of David, and letters of kings about votive offerings" (2 Macc. 2.13). In addition, Ezra would have known the books of the *Pentateuch, which must also have been gathered together by this time, so most scholars agree, and which were the basis of his reforming work. A few of the latest books, however, had not yet been written, and they at least would obviously have had to be added to the sacred collection later. Moreover, there is reason to believe that Esther and Daniel were not finally accepted into the canon until the crisis of the second century BCE, related in the following verse of 2 Maccabees, where we are told that "in the same way Judas also collected all the books that had been lost on account of the war that had come upon us" (2 Macc. 2.14). This would have taken place about 164 BCE. The Judas in question is Judas Maccabeus, and the war is the persecuting campaign of the Hellenistic Syrian king Antiochus Epiphanes, who attempted to destroy the scriptures.

Many factors contributed to the recognition of certain books as canonical; among them are the following: the tradition that many of the books came from Moses or one of the other acknowledged prophets; the spiritual authority of the books themselves, as it was experienced in public or private reading, and in exposition; the fact that the books had come to be laid up in the Temple as sacred; the opinions of religious leaders and the common convictions of the people about the books. And for Christians, there was the additional consideration that Jesus himself and his apostles, in the pages of the New Testament, often refer to the Jewish scriptures in general, and to many of the individual books, as having the authority of God.

The division of the Hebrew Bible into three sections (not four or five, as in Greek, Latin, and English translations), known as the Law, the Prophets, and the Writings, can be traced back to the second century BCE, when it is three times referred to in the prologue of Sirach, added by the Greek translator of the book in about 130 BCE. He refers to the

three sections as "the Law and the Prophets and the others that have followed them," "the Law and the Prophets and the other books of our ancestors," "the Law and the Prophecies and the rest of the books." It should be noted that the third section had not yet been given a definite name, though the use of the definite article and the expression "the rest of" suggests that it already had a fixed content. In other early references to the three sections, the third section seems to be called "the Psalms," taking its name from one of the chief books it included. The later Jewish name, the Writings (Hebr. *kĕtûbîm*, translated into Greek as *hagiographa*), is first found in rabbinic literature.

Thematic Arrangement. For the past hundred years it had been commonly believed that the three sections do not really have any distinct identity, but are accidents of history, reflecting the different stages at which books were accepted as canonical: the Law in the fifth century BCE, the Prophets in the third century BCE, and the Hagiographa at the "synod" of Jabneh or Jamnia, about 90 CE (an academic debate that discussed, among other things, the canonicity of Ecclesiastes and the Song of Solomon). The Law, however, clearly does have a distinct identity, consisting of the four books that comprise the life of Moses and the legislation bearing his name (Exodus to Deuteronomy), together with a historical introduction (Genesis) tracing the course of events between creation and his own day. This leads one to suspect that the other two sections may also have a logical rationale, even if it is less obvious; and, especially if one takes the books in traditional order, recorded in an early quotation in the Babylonian Talmud, it is not too difficult to see what this rationale is. Both sections, like the Law, include narrative books (covering the two subsequent periods of history) and books of another kind, not legislative, but in the case of the prophets oracular, and in the case of the Hagiographa lyrical and sapiential (wisdom literature). The four narrative books in the Prophets are Joshua, Judges, Samuel, and Kings, carrying on the history from the death of Moses to the end of the monarchy; these are followed by the four oracular books Jeremiah, Ezekiel, Isaiah, and the Twelve (the Minor Prophets). In the Writings the four narrative books Daniel, Esther, Ezra-Nehemiah, and Chronicles continue Jewish history by covering the period of the exile and return, Chronicles being put last probably because it begins with Adam and ends with the return, thus recapitulating the whole of Israel's history. Preceding these are the six lyrical and sapiential books in the Hagiographa, Psalms, Job, Proverbs, Ecclesiastes, Song of Solomon, and Lamentations, with Ruth prefixed to Psalms (but counted separately) because it ends with the genealogy of the psalmist David. Thus, there is nothing irrational (as has usually been supposed) in the isolation of Chronicles from Samuel and Kings, and of Daniel from the Prophets, in a different section of the canon.

Formation. The belief that the Law was the first complete section to be recognized as canonical is very likely true, given its traditional association with Moses. It is quite possible, however, that some of the earlier books in the other two sections were recognized as canonical alongside the Law; and these may originally have been a single collection of non-Mosaic books, like Nehemiah's "library," which gradually increased and was only organized in two sections after it was complete. The view that the canon of the Samaritans, which consists of the Law alone, shows that when their schism with the Jews took place this was all the Jewish canon consisted of, cannot be sustained. Qumran evidence has now made it probable that the schism did not become final until the destruction of the Samaritan temple on Mount Gerizim by the Jews in about 120 BCE. So the Samaritans of that period must certainly have rejected books which were already canonical among the Jews, probably because many of those books explicitly recognized the Jerusalem Temple.

One of the main reasons for supposing that the Hagiographa were not received into the canon until a late date is that four of them (Proverbs, Ecclesiastes, the Song of Solomon, and Esther) raise serious problems that were debated among the rabbis of the first few centuries CE. We know, however, from rabbinic literature that similar problems were raised by most of the other canonical books, and that it was only because in these books they were particularly intractable that they were taken so seriously. Moreover, there was a fifth book that raised equally serious problems, Ezekiel, which is in the Prophets. If the canonicity of this book could be debated after the first century CE, clearly the question was not one of adding books to the canon but of removing books from it. Needless to say, nothing of the kind was actually done.

Competing Canons. It has been widely supposed that certain schools of thought had divergent canons. Some of the church fathers say that the Sadducees accepted only the Law, like the Samaritans. The Sadducees may have joined up with the Samaritans during the century after the destruction of the Jerusalem Temple (the center of their influence) by the Romans in 70 CE, but prior to that time their canon seems to have been the same as that of the Pharisees. Again, the presence of books of the *Apocrypha in Septuagint manuscripts has led to the suggestion that the Hellenistic Jews of Alexandria had a wider canon than that of the Jews of Palestine. However, the voluminous writings of the first century CE Alexandrian Jew Philo are against this theory. Moreover, the manuscripts in question were produced by Christian scribes, at a date when knowledge of the Jewish canon was becoming somewhat vague in Christian circles; and in any case they are evidence of what Christians regarded as edifying reading rather than as strictly canonical. Finally, the Essenes have been supposed to have included in their canon congenial pseudonymous apocalypses such as 1 Enoch and Jubilees. In fact, they seem rather to have treated these as a sort of interpretive appendix to the canon, on a lower level of inspiration. Jude 14–15, which quotes 1 Enoch, is certainly not saying more than this about it, and in Jude's Christian (not Essene) context is probably saying less, that is, he may be using the quotation as an ad hominem argument.

The New Testament shows Jesus and his apostles endorsing a canon wider than that of the Samaritans and indistinguishable from that of the Pharisees, which now seems to have been the standard (if not, indeed, the only) Jewish canon. It had probably closed, in the form found in the Hebrew Bible, not later than the second century BCE. The threefold division of the canon, the traditional order of the books, and their standard Jewish numeration as twenty-four may well be due to Judas Maccabeus and his advisors (see 2 Macc. 2.14, and above); the slightly later numeration of the books as twenty-two, found in *Josephus, is based on the number of letters in the Hebrew alphabet, and appends Ruth to Judges and Lamentations to Jeremiah, thus reducing the number by two.

Today, the canon exists in two main forms: that found in the Hebrew Bible, followed by Jews, Protestants, and some Orthodox churches, and that found in the Septuagint, which includes the Apocrypha, followed by Roman Catholics and also some Orthodox churches. *See also* Bible.   Roger T. Beckwith

New Testament

The canon of the New Testament resulted from the interplay of various theological and historical factors. The decisive factor was the impact of the person and message of Jesus Christ, together with the Christian conviction that in him as the Lord, God had spoken his final and authoritative word in history. As the Christian movement was confronted with philosophical and religious trends current in the Mediterranean world of its time, the need for an authentic expression and preservation of the foundation of its belief became the basic motivation toward the realization of the New Testament canon. This grew more acute after the demise of the first generation of eyewitnesses. Certainly the idea of an Old Testament canon functioned as an analogy and, to a certain extent, as a stimulus in this regard. Few factors, however, expedited the growth of the idea of the canon more than the attacks from heterodox quarters, like those of Marcion, the *gnostics, and the Montanists (see below). Finally, the need for one, universally accepted holy book for the whole church also played a role.

Historical Survey. Historical processes do not lend themselves to neat chronological delineations. Nevertheless, we can roughly divide the far-reaching process through which the twenty-seven books of the New Testament were brought into a normative, carefully delineated, and ecclesiastically accepted unit, with an authority equivalent to that of the Hebrew Bible, into four periods:

The first phase (latter part of first century CE): ***Creation of various early Christian documents.*** Initially the gospel message was transmitted orally. In this period the young church was guided, in addition to the Old Testament, first by the apostolic witness, which developed into the apostolic tradition, and second by early Christian prophecy. In particular, the first of these factors was destined to play a decisive role in the eventual decisions about the extent of the New Testament canon. The authoritative writings would be those emanating from the apostles or the circle of those standing in a not too indirect relation to them. The prophetic witness is represented in the New Testament canon by the book of Revelation, although its ultimate recognition was determined by its association with John the apostle. The authors of the early Christian documents did not visualize their writings as part of a future canon. Rather they intended merely to give pastoral guidance to young churches. But as foundational documents, standing so close to the origin of Christianity, they possessed the inherent possibility of later becoming part of a normative collection.

The second phase (roughly from the close of the first century to the middle of the second): ***Growing recognition of the normative character and collection into groups of a basic number of writings.*** This period, demarcated by Clement of Rome (ca. 96 CE) on the one hand and Justin Martyr (ca. 150 CE) on the other, finds oral tradition increasingly replaced by the written *Gospels. Initially oral tradition was used alongside and even preferred to the Gospels. But as the reliability of the former declined, it was gradually replaced by the four Gospels. In 1 Clement, the Didache, Ignatius, and Papias, the "living voice" (as Papias terms it) of the oral tradition still enjoys

preference, while in Polycarp's letter to the Philippians (ca. 135 CE) the scale tips in favor of the written Gospels. In 2 Clement (ca. 140 CE) we have at least twice as many quotations from the written Gospels as from all other sources, and from the middle of the second century the written Gospels are predominant. The gnostic Gospel of Truth, for example, knows all four Gospels, while only uncertain traces of the oral tradition occur. The same holds true for Justin Martyr who makes only sporadic use of the oral tradition. Parallel to this development is the increasing use of the written Gospels for liturgical readings. Justin (*Apology* I.67.3–4) reports that the memoirs of the apostles (i.e., the Gospels) are not only read but also commented upon in public worship, which would put them on a par with the Old Testament books. The growing recognition of a substantial number of writings is also evidenced by the way references to them are made. In 2 Clement 2.4 and Barnabas 4.14 the gospel of Matthew, for instance, is referred to as on equal footing with Old Testament writings. At this stage we also find the collecting of early Christian writings around two foci, the Pauline correspondence and the Gospels. We can reasonably accept that by the middle of the second century the Pauline corpus as well as the four gospels were available in collections. All these factors serve to illustrate that they were increasingly recognized as normative ecclesiastical documents. The idea of a New Testament canon was beginning to emerge.

The third phase (ca. mid-second century to 190 CE): ***The New Testament canon becomes a reality.*** Marcion was the first person, as far as we know, who actually visualized the idea of a New Testament canon. He deliberately excluded the Old Testament from his normative collection and included only Luke and ten Pauline letters (which he purged of Jewish traits). The official church reacted by emphasizing the normative character of all four Gospels as well as all thirteen letters ascribed to Paul. Irenaeus reflects this position. In addition he probably accepted all the other New Testament books (though he does not mention all the Catholic letters) and, perhaps, also Hermas. His evaluation of 1 Clement and the Wisdom of Solomon is positive, but it is doubtful whether he regarded them as "holy scripture." It is clear, however, that by now the idea of the canon has materialized; its broad base is fixed, but uncertainty still exists over the books on its periphery.

Final stage (ca. 190–400 CE): *The closing of the canon.* It was particularly the claims to having received new revelations made by the gnostics (against whom Irenaeus already had reacted) and the Montanists, members of an apocalyptic prophetic movement, that stressed the need for a clear demarcation of the canon. Whereas the canon of Clement of Alexandria was still open, Origen and Eusebius in the Eastern church, as well as the author of the Canon of Muratori, a late second-century list, in the West, were convinced of the necessity of a clearly demarcated canon. For that reason both the former two writers, each in his own way, differentiated between three groups of writings: the generally accepted, the uncertain, and those that should be definitely excluded. In the wake of the vehement anti-Montanist reaction, many Eastern churches now began to question the position of the one prophetic-apocalyptic book in the canon, namely Revelation, a question sporadically recurring until the Middle Ages. In the West the anti-Montanist reaction took another course: in reaction against their accent on passages like Hebrews 6.4–6, the authenticity of the letter to the Hebrews became a matter of

dispute which lasted until the fourth century. Uncertainty still existed in various quarters over some of the Catholic letters and also over books like the Didache, the Shepherd of Hermas, and the Wisdom of Solomon.

In the East the uncertainty was cleared up by the thirty-ninth Paschal Letter of Athanasius, metropolitan of Alexandria, written in 367 CE, which listed all the books of the present New Testament. The writings of the apostolic fathers are excluded, but allowance is made for Hermas, the Didache, and the Wisdom of Solomon (as well as certain Old Testament *apocrypha) to be read privately. It is also noteworthy that in this letter the Greek equivalent for the verb "to canonize" (in the sense of "officially recognize as normative") is used three times of the biblical books. (Some fifteen years earlier Athanasius had used the word "canon" in a technical sense of the Bible—the first certain occurrence of this use of the word.) Although only intended for the churches under his supervision, Athanasius's influence was such that his canon was widely approved in the East, and it greatly expedited the movement toward uniformity in the whole church. In the Western church the canon of Athanasius was probably approved at the Synod of Rome in 382 CE and definitely confirmed by a papal declaration of the year 405. Under Augustine's influence the North African church followed suit at the Synods of Hippo Regius (393) and Carthage (397), and, owing to persisting uncertainties regarding Hebrews, James, and Jude, reiterated its decisions at Carthage (419). By now the New Testament canon, with its twenty-seven books, was almost universally accepted as the second part of the Christian Bible. The one exception was the Syrian National Church where the popular Diatessaron of Tatian, a second-century harmonization of the Gospels, had held sway for centuries at the cost of the four "separate gospels," and where initially strong resistance existed against some general epistles and Revelation. Here it would still take some time for the Peshitta, the official Syriac translation, to oust the Diatessaron. The small East-Syrian Nestorian church, however, persisted with a canon of twenty-two books (excluding 2 Peter, 2 and 3 John, Jude, and Revelation). The other exception was the Ethiopian church, which included Hermas, the two Clementine epistles, and the Apostolic Constitutions, and whose New Testament canon consists, up to our own day, of thirty-eight books (see Bible).

Criteria of Canonicity. In determining the content and scope of the canon various criteria were applied, e.g., that of apostolicity, the rule of faith *(regula fidei)*, and the consensus of the churches. Of these the first played the most important role. It would be a mistake, however, to deduce from this that apostolicity was, at least initially, treated as a merely formal criterion. As attested, for instance, by the Canon of Muratori, the real consideration was rather that of reliability. As primary sources the apostles and their followers were seen as the trustworthy exponents of the original revelation given in Jesus Christ. It would also be a mistake to regard the official recognition of our present twenty-seven books by the church as the act that gave them their canonical status. The decisions of the church were in reality the acknowledgement of the intrinsic authority and power of these writings.

See also Interpretation, History of, *article on* Early Christian Interpretation.
Andrie B. du Toit

CHAOS. The Hebrew word *tōhû* is generally translated in two ways. It can denote the arid wilderness, where wadis disappear, the deranged wander, and Israel was found. It can also mean the chaotic state before *creation; in this sense it can be paired with *bōhû* and by extension can mean any empty, formless reality, especially other gods or defeated nations.

These two concepts are linked in biblical tradition and in underlying mythology. Ancient Near Eastern *myths of creation frequently describe a battle between the creator, generally a storm god, and primeval forces, most frequently watery; reflexes in biblical traditions include the sea, the deep, and Leviathan, whose chaotic powers must be kept under control. Canaanite tradition in the texts from *Ugarit and elsewhere also narrates a conflict between Baal, the Canaanite storm god, and the god Mot (Death); the domain of the latter is the arid desert as well as the underworld. In biblical tradition creation can be depicted as the triumph of Yahweh over the sterile forces of drought; this is then applied to the creation of Israel and to its restoration. Thus God's defeat of the forces of chaos, both water and desert, is a necessary prelude to creation as well as an ongoing activity. (*See also* Israel, Religion of.)

The Hebrew pair *tōhû wābōhû* is also the basis of the English and French word *tohu-bohu,* meaning "chaos and confusion."
Michael D. Coogan

CHAPTER AND VERSE DIVISIONS. The complete Bible of today is ordinarily divided into chapters and verses, but such divisions were not part of the original texts. They were developed at a much later date, primarily in the interest of facilitating reference; consequently they do not always agree with the natural development of thought in the text.

Divisions in the Hebrew Text. The earliest biblical manuscripts, from Qumran, have certain divisions in the text, although they are not yet standardized and may occur at different places in copies of the same book. Eventually a system was developed (except in the Psalter) involving what are called open and closed paragraphs (*pārāšâ*, plural *pārāšiyyôt*), the purpose of which was to give assistance in understanding the flow of thought. An open (*pĕtûḥâ*) paragraph is one that begins a new line after an empty or incomplete line; a closed (*sĕtûmâ*) paragraph is separated from the preceding paragraph by a short space within the line. Later scribes ignored this distinction in the actual written format but prefixed the Hebrew letter *p* or *s* to indicate the distinction. In the Psalter the verse division depends on the parallelism (*see* Poetry, Biblical Hebrew).

Another division of the text into more lengthy sections was developed by Palestinian scholars, who provided 452 *sĕdārîm* (weekly lessons) for a three-year *lectionary cycle. In Babylonia, where the *Torah (*see* Canon, *article on* Order of Books in the Hebrew Bible) was read through each year, the division was made into fifty-four (or fifty-three) weekly lessons.

Divisions in the Greek Text. Division within books in Septuagint manuscripts was also in use at an early period. The variety in the systems used suggests that they were drawn up independently by a number of different scribes and/or editors.

In New Testament Greek manuscripts we find several different systems of division. The oldest seems to be that contained in Codex Vaticanus, in which the divisions into sections were made with reference to breaks in the sense. There are 170 in Matthew, 62 in Mark, 152 in Luke, and 80 in John.

Many manuscripts of the Gospels are provided with an ingenious system developed by Eusebius of Caesarea (ca. 260–ca. 340 CE) to aid the reader in lo-

cating parallel passages. Each gospel was divided into longer or shorter sections, depending on the relation of each section to one or more parallels in the other Gospels: 355 for Matthew, 233 for Mark, 343 for Luke, and 232 for John. Then Eusebius prepared tables, called canons. The first contains a list in which all four Gospels agree; the second, passages common to Matthew, Mark, and Luke; the third, passages in which Matthew, Luke, and John agree; the fourth, passages in which Matthew, Mark, and John agree; and so on until almost all the possible combinations were exhausted. Finally, there were references to material in each gospel alone—sixty-two in Matthew, nineteen in Mark, seventy-two in Luke, and ninety-six in John.

For the book of Acts several systems of chapter divisions are found in the manuscripts. Codex Vaticanus has two sets of chapters, one of thirty-six, the other of sixty-nine. Most of the manuscripts of the book have a system of forty chapters.

The Pauline and general letters were also divided into chapters. Codex Vaticanus has two sets of chapters—an earlier and a later. In the Pauline letters, according to the earlier division of the text, the numeration of the chapters runs continuously through the whole corpus as though the letters were regarded as constituting one book. Because of a break in the numbering between pages seventy and ninety-three of the codex, it is evident that in an ancestor of Vaticanus, the letter to the Hebrews stood between Galatians and Ephesians.

Some manuscripts of the book of Revelation are supplied with a system of divisions that was developed by Archbishop Andrew of Caesarea in Cappadocia (ca. 600), who wrote a commentary on the book that gives a "spiritual" exegesis. He divided the book into twenty-four discourses (Gk. *logoi*) and each of these into three smaller divisions, thus making seventy-two of the latter. According to Andrew's explanation, the number of the discourses corresponds to the number of elders sitting on thrones about the throne of God, and the three subdivisions symbolize the tripartite nature of the elders (body, soul, and spirit).

Development of Modern Chapter and Verse Divisions. The introduction of the present system of chapter divisions has sometimes been attributed to Cardinal Hugh of St. Cher (d. 1263) for use in his concordance to the Latin Vulgate. Before Hugh, however, the system that, with small modifications, is still in use today was introduced into the Latin Bible by a lecturer at the University of Paris, Stephen Langton, later Archbishop of Canterbury (d. 1228). Even before the invention of *printing (ca. 1456) the system began to be adopted for manuscripts of the Bible in languages other than Latin.

The chapters were at first subdivided (probably by Hugh of St. Cher) into seven portions (not paragraphs), marked in the margin by the letters *A, B, C, D, E, F,* and *G*. In the shorter Psalms, however, the division did not always extend to seven. This division (except in the Psalms) was modified by Conrad of Halberstadt (ca. 1290), who reduced the divisions of the shorter chapters from seven to four, so that the letters were always A–G or A–D. This subdivision continued long after the introduction of the present verses.

Numbered verses (for a Hebrew concordance to the *Masoretic text) were first worked out by Rabbi Isaac Nathan in about 1440. In the earlier printed Hebrew Bibles each fifth verse is marked with its Hebrew numeral. Arabic numerals were first added for the intervening verses by Joseph Athias at Amster-

dam in 1661 at the suggestion of Jan Leusden. The first portion of the Bible printed with the Masoretic verses numbered was the *Psalterium Quincuplex* of Faber Stapulensis. The *Psalterium* was beautifully printed at Paris in 1509 by Henry, father of Robert Stephanus, each verse commencing the line with a red letter and a numeral prefixed. In 1527 (or 1528) the Dominican Sanctes Paginus of Lucca published at Lyons, in quarto, his accurate translation of the Bible into Latin from the Hebrew and Greek. The verses are marked with Arabic numerals in the margin.

The current verse division in the New Testament was introduced by Robert Stephanus (Estienne), who in 1551 published at Geneva a Greek and Latin edition of the New Testament with the text of the chapters divided into separate verses. The first whole Bible divided into the present verses, and the first in which they were introduced into the *Apocrypha, was Stephanus's Latin Vulgate issued at Geneva in 1555. In the books of the Hebrew Bible Stephanus followed Paginus, but in the New Testament and in the Apocrypha he increased the number of verses. Thus, in the gospel of Matthew, Paginus has 577 verses and Stephanus 1,071; in Tobit Paginus has but 76 verses, while Stephanus has 292. According to Stephanus's son, his father made the divisions into verses *inter equitandum* on a journey from Paris to Lyons. Although some have taken this to mean "on horseback" (and have explained occasionally inappropriate verse divisions as originating when the horse bumped his pen into the wrong place!), a better interpretation is that the task was accomplished at intervals while he rested at inns along the road.

The verse divisions devised by Stephanus were widely and rapidly adopted and first appeared, for example, in English in the Geneva Bible (New Testament, 1557; Bible, 1560). Despite its utility, the system has often been criticized not only because the division sometimes occurs in the middle of a sentence, thus breaking the natural flow of thought, but also because to the reader the text appears to be a series of separate and detached statements. While it is too late to change the system to correct unfortunate verse divisions, at least the verses should never be printed each as a separate paragraph (as in most editions of the King James or Authorized Version), but the text should be continuous, in logical paragraphs, with the numerals in the margin or printed inconspicuously in the text.   *Walter F. Specht*

CHILDREN'S BIBLES. The recasting of the Bible to meet the needs of children has been a topic of increasing interest. Although children were always included within the concern of the religious communities for which the Bible served as scripture, they were understood as parts of families within which the Bible would be read and explained. In Christian circles, such an assumption lies behind the widespread production of *family Bibles and their use by parents in reading to their children. But the view of the Bible as a work to be read independently by children and the accompanying challenges for a child reading an adult book reflect a recent approach to children's Bibles. Attempts to translate the Bible in language comprehensible to children have been significant only from about 1970 on.

The education of children included a knowledge of the Bible, a goal to be carried out in the home, the church, and the school, until the nineteenth century. Since it was regularly believed that the goals of education were piety, civility, and learning, children and youth were

expected to be familiar with the Bible. The necessary knowledge of the Bible included not only its contents but also an affirmation of the *authority of scripture.

After the invention of *printing by movable type and the rise of vernacular Bibles, the widespread dissemination of Bibles was accompanied by significant study helps such as chapter summaries (Coverdale Bible, 1535) and marginal notes (Geneva Bible, 1560). A Puritan divine such as Cotton Mather (1663–1728), in his *Bonifacius: An Essay upon the Good,* proposed a number of methods intended to enable children to learn the contents of the Bible. These included Bible storytelling at the dinner table and rewards for Bible memorization—with appropriate attention to the age, interests, and abilities of particular children. The study of the Bible by children also included catechisms, psalters, and liturgies, intended to prepare them for a knowledge of the Christian faith and participation in public worship.

Among the ways used to teach children the Bible, one of the most important in England and the United States beginning in the late eighteenth century was the Sunday School in its own right and as a forerunner of the common school. Two of the popular texts used in Sunday Schools were *The Sunday School Spelling Book* (1822) and *The Union Spelling Book* (1838), both containing biblical texts and biblical diction.

In areas such as the United States where Protestants predominated through the middle of the nineteenth century, there was agreement that the reading of the Bible should be a central aspect of the public-school curriculum. The increasing religious pluralism of the United States would question this assumption and its accompanying presupposition that public reading of the Bible would be from the Authorized Version of 1611. In the United States the publication of both Roman Catholic and Jewish versions in the nineteenth century was intended, in part, to offset the exclusive use of the Authorized Version in public-school education.

By 1850 McGuffey's *Eclectic Readers* (1836) was the basic school reader in some thirty-seven states. Eighty percent of the schoolchildren of the United States used McGuffey's *Readers* for some seventy-five years. Although the majority of the material in McGuffey was non-biblical, there was still a significant degree of biblical content in the six readers.

During the nineteenth century Sunday Schools evolved a systematic approach to Bible study. The need for children's Bibles received little attention when the focus of the child's Bible study was either the memorization of Bible verses or catechetical learning that had subsumed the Bible into affirmations of the Christian faith. In the case of memorization much attention was paid to the selection of particular verses, and contextual reading of the Bible played little role. When the Bible was the primary source of moral example, this became the strongest influence in the education of children in the Sunday Schools. Initially started as interdenominational agencies, these shifted in the course of the nineteenth century to a denominational basis. Their early goals had been to improve the moral life of their students as expressed in effective citizenship. Increasingly, a knowledge of the Bible was viewed as essential for personal salvation and social stability; the Bible was a source of texts to be memorized. The texts might reflect moral themes drawn from Jesus' ministry or the lives of the ancestors and prophets. Lewis Baldwin's *The Bible Interrogatory* (1816) was one of the first attempts to system-

atize biblical study in Sunday Schools. The greatest achievement of inter-denominational Sunday Schools was the creation of the International Lesson System. A post-Civil War development, these plans stressed uniform lessons for all ages. Critics of the lesson plans noted that they ignored child psychology, and in 1894 the Lesson Committee developed a separate course for younger children.

The establishment of *Bible societies and the dissemination of Bibles, or parts of Bibles (*see* Circulation of the Bible), contributed to a consideration of the forms of Bibles for children. One result was to ensure that children have their own Bibles. This could be accomplished within the Sunday School movement by giving children Bibles as they completed one part of the Sunday School and moved to another. These presentation Bibles were usually an existing adult translation with a presentation nameplate and occasional illustrations.

Another form of children's Bible was a collection of Bible stories, selected for various emphases, and either paraphrased or completely rewritten. This has been the most popular form of children's Bible and accounts for a large part of juvenile Bibles available at any time.

A well-known example of the storybook Bible was *Child's Bible Reader* (1898), a work widely employed by three generations of Protestant Sunday School teachers in the southeastern United States. The stories in the *Reader* were attributed to the popular British writer Charlotte M. Yonge. Thousands of southern homes owned copies of this *Reader*, distributed by door-to-door salesmen of the Southwestern Company of Nashville, Tennessee. Equally popular in a later generation was Walter de la Mare's *Stories from the Bible*.

The storybook approach to children's

Bibles inevitably involves the selection of stories considered to be appealing or appropriate to children. Perennial favorites include Noah, Moses, Samson, David, Jonah, and Jesus. Common to these collections are also stories about birth and childhood, animals, and adventure stories. Such storybook Bibles generally avoid events, persons, or narratives seen as inappropriate or incomprehensible to children, such as the story of Joshua, the letters of Paul, and the book of Revelation.

The storybook Bible has encouraged the use of illustrations to complement the biblical narratives and to increase their appeal for children. Examples that have been publicly recognized for their aesthetic achievement include E. Boyd Smith's writing and illustrating of *The Story of Noah's Ark* (1905) and Dorothy Lathrop's *Animals of the Bible* (1937). (*See* Illustrated Bibles.)

The most recent development has been the production of translations specifically for children, with considerable initiative coming from the United Bible Societies. Based on the understanding of psychological, social, and intellectual development, this movement has attempted to produce readable Bibles to match the abilities and interests of various ages. In 1983 the Sweet Publishing Company issued the pioneering *International Children's Version (New Testament)* as the first translation for children. In 1986, the Worthy Publishing Company issued the *International Children's Bible, New Century Version*, noting that this was not a storybook or a paraphrased Bible but the first translation of the whole Bible prepared specifically for children. Because of its specialized vocabulary, the publishers claim that their Bible translation can be understood by children with a grade-three reading level.

Ernest S. Frerichs

CHOSEN PEOPLE. The Bible describes various individuals as "chosen" by God: Abraham, Jacob, Moses, Aaron, Saul, David, Solomon, Zerubbabel, and Jesus; Jesus, in turn, chose his disciples. These individuals are not chosen, so far as we know, for their previous virtue. All are depicted as fallible, except the shadowy Zerubbabel and the perfect Jesus. Election is usually linked with heredity; the chosen belongs to a dynasty, often as its founder. God may also choose a larger group, such as the tribe of Levi.

The most common function of this election motif is the legitimation of groups: the house of David, the Aaronic priests, the Levites, the apostles. But what does it mean to be "chosen"? There is no sign of being chosen; the election theme is primarily an assertion of God's favor.

Another body called "chosen" is Israel itself. Some consider this a later development; priestly and royal election are democratized, as all Israel becomes a "kingdom of priests" (Exod. 19.5).

The classic statement of Israel's election is Deuteronomy 7.6–9: "The Lord your God has chosen you out of all the peoples on earth to be his people, his treasured possession. It was not because you were more numerous . . . it was because the Lord loved you, and kept the oath that he swore to your ancestors." Although the verb "choose" does not appear in Deuteronomy 32.8, according to that text God gave each nation its own god (thus the Septuagint and Qumran versions), keeping Israel for himself. Ideally, this election elicits reciprocity from Israel, which in turn chooses God.

Election entails responsibility and risk as well as privilege; Deuteronomy 7.10–11 threatens punishment should Israel violate the *covenant. According to Amos 9.7–10, Israel's uniqueness lies in the fact that God will never utterly destroy it.

It is unclear when God chose Israel; one might cite the call of Abram, Jacob's vision, or the experience at Sinai. Ezekiel 20.5 dates Israel's election to God's revelation in Egypt.

Second Isaiah's concept of chosenness poses special problems. Sometimes he explicitly calls Israel "chosen," promising divine succor and numerous, pious offspring. But the prophet also describes one chosen to be a "light to the nations" (Isa. 42.1, 6; cf. 49.5–9), whose suffering atones for others' sins. Scholars debate whether this is the nation of Israel, a segment thereof, or a particular member; Christianity traditionally applies these oracles to Jesus.

While the Bible does not associate Israel's election with its intrinsic merit, later Judaism reacted to its often dire circumstances by developing a belief in the spiritual superiority of all Jews, whether by birth or by choice. Thus, the *Torah was offered to various peoples but accepted only by Israel; the eroticism of the Song of Solomon expresses God's unique love for Israel; only Israel's history is governed directly by God, other nations being subject to the laws of nature; Jewish souls derive directly from God, while the souls of gentiles are of lesser matter. Such theories, however, have never been central Jewish doctrines. The basic concept of "chosenness" has remained, as in biblical terms, that of covenant: God chose the Jews by imposing certain restrictions upon them and holding them to a higher ethical and ritual standard. Many contemporary Jewish thinkers reject even this more modest claim as irrelevant or harmful in today's pluralistic society.

The early church called its adherents "chosen," implying that they succeeded Israel as God's favored. All who embrace Jesus, Jew and gentile alike, become "chosen." Paul does not infer from the Christians' election any intrinsic greatness or virtue, and he insists that Israel retains its special status. Ironically, while many liberal Jewish thinkers disavow "chosenness," some Christian theologians today reaffirm the continuing election of the Jews.   *William H. Propp*

CHRISTIAN SCIENCE AND THE BIBLE.
Christian Science began in the United States during the latter half of the nineteenth century, appearing first as a religious teaching and later as an organized denomination. Known primarily for its practice of Christian healing, Christian Science teaches that the Bible's dominant theme is the superiority of spiritual over physical power, and that this power can be reliably—even "scientifically"—demonstrated in the lives of people today. It was founded by Mary Baker Eddy (1821–1910), a New England woman with a staunch Calvinist background and a devotion to regular study of the Bible.

Several social and personal factors help to explain the emergence of Christian Science. First, much of Eddy's early religious life was shaped by her rebellion against her Calvinist upbringing, specifically its doctrine of *predestination. Also, by midcentury, society was entering a new and scientific era, where reason, experimentation, and observable results were becoming the standard means of measuring progress and assessing truth claims. Yet for Eddy, the void left by her dissatisfaction with what she called "cruel creeds" could not be fulfilled by rational advances alone. Throughout her life she retained a characteristic Puritan piety, noted by several of her biographers, which they referred to as "a hunger and thirst for divine things."

This left her satisfied neither with the doctrinal interpretation of the Bible offered by the church nor with the more scientifically based historical-critical method of Bible analysis then gaining prominence, although she insisted that she retained whatever was valid in both. But what finally impelled her to take a radically different view of the meaning of the biblical revelation was her own suffering, including the years of near invalidism that dominated the first four decades of her life.

While she initially sought relief through almost every healing or medical system that promised comfort, including the suggestive therapeutics of the Maine mental healer Phineas Quimby, her bedrock conviction was that only the Bible offered the answer to "the great problem of being." According to her own account, she was healed of the effects of a serious accident in 1866 by reading of Jesus' healing works in the Gospels. Reflecting on her experience, she felt that she had discovered something of the underlying power, or spiritual law, that was at the very root of Christianity.

The nine years following her own healing were spent studying the Bible, writing, teaching, healing—all aimed at finding ways to articulate a metaphysics that she felt would make the Bible practical in a scientific age. Central to her view was the belief that undergirding the events of the Bible was a spiritual law, which, far from being a relic of ancient history, was dynamic and applicable in all time to bring about healing of disease and redemption from sin. She explicated her metaphysical interpretation of the Bible in her major work, *Science and Health,* first published in 1875 and eventually titled *Science and Health, with Key to the Scriptures.* She would revise and edit the book throughout the rest of her life, but it would remain the definitive statement of Christian Science.

The book became an immediate source of controversy. Critics charged

that *Science and Health,* written by a woman with no formal training, included language not found in the Bible and deviated from orthodox Christianity in its teachings. They charged Eddy with elevating her writing to the status of the Bible.

For her part, Eddy acknowledged that her book departed from certain church doctrines, but she maintained that these doctrines originated less in the Bible than in church councils, which were often guilty of "teaching as doctrines the precepts of men" (see Isa. 29.13 AV). She asserted that the way to validate an individual's understanding of God and the Bible was by examining the fruits of that understanding. Do they demonstrate a practical grasp of the power of God's word by healing and regenerating the individual? To her, this was the acid test of biblical interpretation.

In her view, from Moses' commandments to have no idols and to worship God alone, to the prophets' call for *repentance, to Christ Jesus' description of the presence of the *kingdom of God "within you," the Bible presented the *word of God, revealing the supremacy of God, Spirit, and the wholly spiritual nature of God's creation. Eddy felt that faith in this supreme and infinitely good God also implied that the very existence of *evil and *suffering, so evident in the material world, could be challenged as having no God-derived cause or legitimacy.

Eddy saw the nature of Godlike as being most perfectly manifested in the life of Christ Jesus. For her, Jesus' life was itself the unique revelation of what it means to live in authentic relation to God. She saw her own work, *Science and Health,* not as a second kind of Bible or as a replacement for it but as an offering of what she saw as the Bible's permanent and continuing meaning, making Christian discipleship a practicable possibility in the modern age. She felt that her "scientific" approach to Christianity merely made explicit what was implicit in the Bible all along, opening its message in a new and powerful way.

Today, regular study of the Bible and *Science and Health* remains central to the practice of Christian Science. Each day its adherents read a lesson made up of passages from these two books. This same lesson is read as the sermon in Sunday church services, and changes weekly.

Christian Scientists tend to reject the narrow literalism of *fundamentalism, as well as the liberal tendency to reduce biblical accounts to stories with intended morals. Instead, they assert that the Bible presents what might be called a "spiritual literal" account of the supremacy of God in human history. For example, Christian Scientists regard the *crucifixion, *resurrection, and *ascension of Christ Jesus as the central events of human history, embodying the supremacy of the law of God over all mortal existence. The first of six tenets left to the church by Eddy reads, "As adherents of Truth, we take the inspired word of the Bible as our sufficient guide to eternal Life."

Scott F. Preller

CHRISTMAS. The English word Christmas means Christ's Mass, the festival of Christ's birthday. Twenty-five December was by the fourth century CE the date of the winter solstice, celebrated in antiquity as the birthday of Mithras and of Sol Invictus. In the Julian calendar the solstice fell on 6 January, when the birthday of Osiris was celebrated at Alexandria. By about 300 CE, 6 January was the date of Epiphany in the East, a feast always closely related to Christmas. The earliest mention of 25 December for Christmas is in the Philocalian Cal-

endar of 354, part of which reflects Roman practice in 336. Celebration of Christ's birthday was not general until the fourth century; in fact, as late as the fifth century the Old Armenian Lectionary of Jerusalem still commemorated James and David on 25 December, noting "in other towns they keep the birth of Christ." When celebrated, the theme was the *Incarnation, and the scriptures were not confined to the birth or infancy narratives. To Luke 2.1–14 and Matthew 1.18–25 were added not only John 1.1–18 but also, for example, Titus 2.11–14.

The year of Christ's birth is hard to determine. The enrollment by Quirinius in that year according to Luke 2.1–5 is dated by *Josephus as equivalent to 6–7 CE (*Ant.* 18.2.26), but this enrollment was not of "all the world" (Luke 2.1), would not have taken place under Herod, during whose lifetime Quirinius was not governor of Syria, and would not have required the presence of Joseph, and still less of Mary, in Bethlehem. Although Luke 3.1–2 suggests no exact year, the passage seems to indicate between 27 and 29 CE as the times of John's baptizing and of Jesus' being about thirty years of age. Jesus' birth would then be about 4–1 BCE. The time of year is nowhere indicated. (*See also* Chronology, *article on* Early Christian Chronology.)

The place of Jesus' birth also raises problems. If we had only the gospels of Mark and John we would assume that it was Nazareth. Luke 2.1–20 tells the story of the birth in Bethlehem and Matthew 2.1 follows a similar tradition, though introducing not a birth narrative but an infancy narrative, for the account of the wise men implies that Jesus might have been as much as two years old when they arrived.

The exact place at Bethlehem is doubtful; the manger of Luke 2.7 may be rather a stall with almost no covering, or even a feeding trough in the open, the "inn" itself not being a building but a yard with partial shelter at its sides. The ox and ass of subsequent art are not in Luke's story but enter from Isaiah 1.3. Another early tradition, recorded in the second-century apocryphal Protoevangelium of James and Justin (*Trypho* 78.657), tells of a cave as the birthplace. It was apparently shown to Origen ca. 246, and by 333 Constantine had built a basilica over it, which was replaced under Justinian ca. 531. Still extant, the cave claims a stone as the manger. In early liturgies both the manger and the shepherds' fields play a part, but at the inclusive feast of the Epiphany rather than at a celebration solely of Christ's birthday.   *A. R. C. Leaney*

CHRONOLOGY. *This entry consists of two articles on dating systems used in the Bible and their correlation with modern historiography. The first article is on* Israelite Chronology *and the second,* Early Christian Chronology.

Israelite Chronology

Biblical chronology may be considered under two aspects: historical or scientific chronology, which deals with the real chronology of actual events, and theoretical or theological chronology, which considers the meanings and purposes of chronological schemes used as a literary vehicle of religious conceptions. Individual statements may often be considered from either point of view; both aspects will be taken into account here.

Dating Systems. The Hebrew Bible has no universal dating system like our BCE/CE system. There are several modes in which chronological information is given:

Simple addition from the datum point of creation: For example, Adam was 130

years old when his son Seth was born, Seth was 105 when his first son Enosh was born. By such addition, we can reckon that the *flood began in the year 1656 AM (= Anno Mundi, i.e., from creation); however, this figure is not made explicit, and readers must do their own addition. Such reckoning can produce a clear chronology, with only some uncertainties, from creation down to the start of Solomon's Temple.

Regnal years of kings, often synchronically correlated with another line of kings (e.g., years of a Judean king are stated along with years of a contemporary king of Israel). Such dates are relative, not absolute; they were doubtless adequate for people of the time, but they do not tell us the actual date unless we can bring some other source to bear.

Later books used the Seleucid era, commencing 312/311 BCE, for example, "in the one hundred thirty-seventh year of the kingdom of the Greeks" (1 Macc. 1.10); this was used long and widely in Jewish life.

Modern Jewish reckoning, by years from creation: the Jewish year 5762 is 2001–2002 CE, implying that the world was created in 3761 BCE. Although figures going back to creation were important, dates are not stated in this way in the Bible; this mode of stating dates did not come into use until long after biblical times.

Basic Data. The main body of chronological material in the Hebrew Bible falls into three great segments:

From creation to Abraham's migration from Haran into Canaan. This is easily fixed by addition of the ages of the patriarchs, mainly in the *genealogies of Genesis 5 and 11. The period is split by the central event of the flood. The figures differ in various texts, being mainly lower in the Samaritan and higher in the Septuagint (LXX); thus the flood, which is 1656 AM in the Hebrew *Masoretic text, is 1307 AM in the Samaritan and 2242 AM in the LXX. One obscurity is the "two years after the flood" of Arpachshad's birth (Gen. 11.10), which is difficult to reconcile with the dates of his father Shem.

From Abraham's migration to the start of Solomon's Temple. This segment falls into three smaller sections:

From Abraham's entry into Canaan to the entry of Jacob and his family into Egypt. This is easily calculated from the ages of the patriarchs and amounts to 215 years.

The period spent in Egypt is expressly given by Exodus 12.40 as 430 years. The Samaritan and the LXX, however, have the extra words "and in the land of Canaan" or the like; this means that the 430 years stretch back to Abraham's entry 215 years earlier, thus reducing the time in Egypt to 215 years. This reading, 430 years from Abraham to Moses, is followed by Paul. According to the Hebrew text, subject to some minor uncertainties, the *Exodus was probably in 2666 AM.

The time from the Exodus to the start of the Temple (not its completion) is clearly stated as 480 years. This comprehensive statement bridges over the times of Joshua, the Judges, Samuel, Saul, and David, for which there are many detailed chronological statements (e.g., the years of each of the Judges), but also many gaps (e.g., the dates of Joshua, Samuel, or Saul). The total of 480 bridges these uncertainties and provides a clear overarching connection between creation and Temple. The Temple building probably began in 3146 AM.

From Solomon onward we have figures for the years of each king. If we simply add up the figures for the Judean kings, from Solomon's fourth year, when the Temple construction began, to the destruction of Temple and kingdom, the figures in themselves are 430. Here, however, we can compare the figures with historical facts, and the period cannot have been more than about 372 years (Solomon's accession, 962 BCE; start of Temple, 958 BCE; destruction, 587/586 BCE). The figures amounting to 430 have been accounted for through overlaps of reigns, co-regencies, textual errors, historical mistakes, and schematic periodization. In addition, it is difficult to make the years of the Israelite kings fit exactly with those of the Judean.

After the destruction of kingdom and Temple, chronological information in the Hebrew Bible is fragmentary and sporadic. Some dates are given by the year of a Persian emperor, but the Hebrew Bible itself does not tell us how long these kings reigned or in what order they came, nor did later writers preserve an accurate memory of this. Later Jewish chronography assigned only thirty-two or fifty-two years to the entire Persian empire, which had in fact lasted over two hundred years, and similarly the number of actual Persian monarchs was unknown, hence the "four" kings of Persia. This leads to another aspect.

Dependence on Extrabiblical Information. Chronology cannot be worked out from biblical data alone; it depends on some synchronism with points established from sources other than the Bible. Traditional biblical chronology dovetailed biblical data into Greek and Roman history. Classical sources give a fairly exact dating of events back to the sixth century BCE, and this can be synchronized with the latest events recorded in Kings, thus providing an entry from extrabiblical history into biblical chronology. In modern times, knowledge of ancient Egypt and Mesopotamia, as well as *archaeological discovery, have provided a much richer network of evidence against which events reported in the Hebrew Bible can be set. Thus, an inscription of Shalmaneser III of Assyria mentions Ahab, king of Israel, in a battle (not mentioned in the Bible!) of 853 BCE, and Jehu in 841; Jehu's revolt against the dynasty of Omri is now placed in 842 BCE. This correlation of biblical data with extrabiblical information carries us back to about 1000 BCE, and without it we would not know the true duration of the kingdom. Key dates to remember are:

962 BCE	accession of Solomon
842	revolt of Jehu and crisis in royal house of both kingdoms
722	destruction of Samaria and end of kingdom of Israel
587/586	destruction of Jersualem and end of kingdom of Judah

When we go back beyond the time of David, extrabiblical information is often not sufficiently specific to provide chronological exactitude; it may suggest nothing more precise than historical circumstances or social conditions that might have fitted with an event mentioned in the Bible. Biblical dates in the earlier stages, taken alone, leave us to question whether they rest on accurate memory or on theoretical schematism. Later, in the Persian period, though the dates of kings are well known from Persian and Greek sources, the Hebrew Bible may leave it vague as to which king of a certain name was involved—for example, whether Artaxerxes I or II, an uncertainty that affects the content of Ezra and Nehemiah.

Theoretical Chronology. Taken as a whole, the chronology of the Hebrew Bible, though containing true historical data, may have been theological rather than historical in its interest, a literary or legendary device that bore a religious message. Thus, the Genesis figures are part of the genealogies, in which persons

live to ages like 930 or 969 years; this is true of Mesopotamian legend as well, in which a king in the beginnings of the world might reign for 36,000 years or more (and eight kings might last 241,000 years down to the flood), with the figures dropping rapidly after the flood. Chronology of this sort belongs to legend or myth.

Some essential dates have strikingly round figures: 215 years from Abraham to Egypt, 430 years in Egypt, 430 for the figures of the kings when added up, 40 on the march from Egypt to Canaan, 480 from the Exodus to the Temple. Are not such figures theoretical? If, as is possible, the Exodus took place in 2,666 AM, is it perhaps significant that this is almost exactly two-thirds of 4,000?

While some chronological material comes from ancient legend, there are signs that figures were being adjusted and modified at a late date, such as the variations between the Masoretic, Samaritan, and Greek texts in Genesis 5. The book of Jubilees, a rewriting of Genesis and Exodus 1–14 from the second century BCE with an intense chronological interest, measures time in "jubilees" of forty-nine years, and ends at the entry of Israel into Canaan, exactly fifty jubilees or 2,450 years from creation; like the Samaritan Pentateuch, it dates the flood to 1307 AM.

Enoch, the seventh from Adam, lived 365 years—obviously a very significant number, and markedly different from others in the same genealogy—before he was taken away by God. The book of Enoch has many contacts with jubilees, and it is concerned with the calendar and the movement of the heavenly bodies; the number of days in a year was hotly debated in this period.

Eschatological expectation forms another likely aspect; it might be thought that the world would last a total round number of years. Major events like the Flood, the Exodus, and the construction of the Temple, were linked with that coming end by significant number sequences. Such sequences might also lead not to the final end of the world but to the establishment of a basic constitution (e.g., completion of Mosaic legislation and start of tabernacle worship), or to a decisive historical stage (the entry into Canaan in Jubilees). If, as has been suggested, a figure of 4,000 was held in mind, the present biblical chronology might be predicated upon the rededication of the Temple (about 164 BCE) after its profanation by Antiochus, which would establish a connection with Daniel, as well as with the books of Enoch and Jubilees.

The antiquity of the Jewish people was an issue in Hellenistic times, when they were sometimes regarded as newcomers on the scene of world culture. Against this, *Josephus insisted on the ancient origins of the Jews; their possession of books that went back without interruption to the beginnings of the world could be a powerful argument. This may have motivated the higher figures of the chronology in the LXX.

Conclusion. Chronological interest is a very important element in the Hebrew Bible, though it is not obtrusive as in Jubilees and not all biblical sources were equally interested in it. The chronology formed an important part of the total shape of the Bible. New Testament authors were well aware of its details: Paul quoted the 430 years exactly, though he did not need the precise figure for his argument; Acts 7.4 is precise, though contrary to the natural sense of the Hebrew, in saying that Abraham migrated from Haran "after his father died" (cf. Gen. 11.26–32; 12.4). After New Testament times, biblical chronology continued as a normal and essential as-

pect of Christian culture, and was cultivated by such writers as Eusebius and Bede. Histories began with creation and continued up to what were then modern times. In the Reformation, Luther's *Supputatio annorum mundi* or chronological summary was regulative for German-speaking Protestantism. In the English-speaking world, James Ussher, Archbishop of Armagh (1581–1656), wrote his detailed chronology from creation (which he fixed in 4004 BCE) to just after the destruction of the Temple in 70 CE. In this he integrated biblical data with all known material of Greek and Roman chronology. Many English Bibles have enshrined his dates in their margins. Only in the nineteenth and twentieth centuries did biblical chronology lose its charm and come to be largely forgotten; even the more conservative and literalist reader of the Bible was no longer literal enough to take seriously the precision of biblical chronology. Now is the time for its literary and theological character to be appreciated once again.   *James Barr*

Early Christian Chronology

No special era is used by the New Testament writers. While Jewish authors were familiar with the Syrian era, which began on 1 October 312 BCE (e.g., 1 Macc. 1.20, the year 143 = 169 BCE), no references of this kind are found in the New Testament. Here, as in the works of *Josephus, dates are given simply with regard to the number of years during which a contemporary ruler had been governing when the event in question happened. Thus, John the Baptist is said to have begun preaching "in the fifteenth year of the reign of Emperor Tiberius" (Luke 3.1), which corresponds to 28 CE. Christian writers of subsequent centuries took over the Roman era in which the years were counted from the presumed foundation of Rome on 21

April 753 BCE *("ab urbe condita")*. In the sixth century CE this era was replaced by the Christian era, which is based on calculations of the Greek monk Dionysius Exiguus in Rome. Commissioned around 532 CE to coordinate the festival calendar of the church, he dated the *incarnation of Christ to 25 March of the Roman year 754, and this year became the year 1, starting from 1 January. Dionysius Exiguus made a slight error, since Matthew 2.1 dates the birth of Jesus to the days of King Herod, who died in 4 BCE.

Matthew explicitly connects the birth of Jesus with the government of King Herod, and the reference to this ruler's successor Archelaus proves that he meant Herod the Great. The years during which Herod was the king of the Jews are known from Josephus. According to his colorful reports, Herod was elected king of the Jews by the Roman senate in 40 BCE, and he died at springtime thirty-six years later, which gives us the year 4 BCE. Matthew thus reports that Jesus was born some time before the year 4 BCE. Attempts have also been made to base a more specific dating on the star discovered by the Magi, but all identifications with a comet, a constellation, or a nova seem arbitrary, so that Matthew's reference to Herod remains the only fixed datum.

Luke likewise regarded Jesus as born under Herod when he dated the birth of John the Baptist to the days of this king and indicated that Jesus was six months younger. In his infancy narrative, however, Luke connected the birth of Jesus with an enrollment for taxation ordered by Augustus and carried out under Quirinius. An enrollment arranged by Quirinius as governor of Syria is known only from 6 CE, when Judea was made the property of Augustus to be administered by a procurator in Caesarea whose task

it was to collect taxes for the emperor. This taxation of 6 CE caused a revolt in Judea, but did not involve the population of Galilee, where Joseph and Mary lived and where Herod Antipas ruled as tetrarch. Luke had probably heard of an earlier registration within the whole kingdom of Herod the Great, but was attracted by the famous taxation under Quirinius. (*See* Christmas; Tribute and Taxation, *article on* Roman Empire.)

Concerning the ministries of John the Baptist and Jesus, the only chronological information available is the above-mentioned reference to John's first preaching in 28 CE and a notice that Jesus was reproached for speaking with authority though he was not yet a senior of fifty years.

The capital punishment of the Baptist resulted from his criticism of the marriage between Herod Antipas and Herodias, whom he accused of adultery because the latter had been the wife of the former's brother. A further consequence of this marriage was that Antipas was attacked in the year 36 by the army of the Nabatean king, whose daughter the tetrarch had divorced in order to marry Herodias. John's criticism of the tetrarch cannot have been uttered many years earlier, so that his death (ibid. 116–19) will have taken place around 32 CE.

Accordingly, the death of Jesus is preferably to be dated 33 CE, and in this year the political situation favored the trial against him. Shortly before, in 31 CE, Tiberius had deposed and executed Sejanus, who had been a cruel dictator in Rome and an especially great antagonist of the Jews; subsequently and most likely in 32 the emperor had ordered his representatives in the provinces to pay attention to Jewish interests. This explains the exceptional rapport between Pilate and the Pharisees that led to the *crucifixion of Jesus.

As to a more exact dating of Jesus' last supper and his death, it has first to be observed that in Jewish tradition each day begins in the evening so that both events belonged to the same day (*see* Time, Units of). According to all four Gospels, the eucharist and the crucifixion took place just before *Passover on the so-called day of preparation (Grk. *paraskeuē*), which that year was a Friday, so that it served to prepare Passover and the Sabbath at the same time. Contrary to what is often stated, the synoptic and Johannine reports do not contradict each other in this point. In the Jewish calendar, the day of preparation for Passover, to which all four Gospels refer, had to be 14 Nisan. The beginning of this lunar month was established year by year according to the first visibility of the crescent moon in March, and though no exact timing was possible in those days, modern studies have shown that 14 Nisan fell on a Friday in two of the years in question: ca. 7 April in the year 30 and ca. 3 April in the year 33. The political factors mentioned above speak in favor of dating Jesus' last supper and crucifixion to an evening and the subsequent day around 3 April of the year 33.

The next New Testament events to be dated are the martyrdom of Stephen and the conversion of Paul, and here the circumstances justify a dating to 36 CE. In this year, troubles with the Parthians led Vitellius, the governor of Syria, to secure Jewish goodwill: he deposed Pilate in Caesarea and appointed a dynamic high priest. He allowed the latter to rule independently, and thus created a Jewish interregnum until 37 CE, when a less powerful high priest was installed and subordinated to a new imperial procurator. Since, according to Luke, the high priest who sentenced Stephen to death is not reported to have sought consent from the Roman procurator as normally

would have been required, and since he sent Paul as far as Damascus in order to arrest dissidents, he must have had unusual political authority. Thus he can be identified with the above-mentioned high priest of 36 CE, so that Stephen's martyrdom in Jerusalem and Paul's conversion at Damascus took place in that year.

Starting from the year 36, two later visits of Paul to Jerusalem can be dated with the aid of his letter to the Galatians, where he refers to a first visit "after three years" and to a second "after fourteen years" (Gal. 1.18; 2.1). As usual, the initial year is included in the numbers, so that the apostle refers to visits occurring two and thirteen years after his conversion; he thus came to Jerusalem in 38 and 49 CE. The latter date is that of the apostolic council, described from different perspectives by Luke and Paul.

Before the apostolic council, Paul had undertaken his first missionary journey under the leadership of Barnabas, and for this a suitable date is 47–48 CE. Paul's second journey can be supposed to have lasted from 50 to 54 for the following reasons: He probably came in 52 to Corinth and there met Aquila and Priscilla, who, together with other Jews, had been expelled from Rome by the emperor Claudius in 50 CE. At any rate, it was in 52 that Paul was confronted with the proconsul Gallio in Corinth, because this governor of Greece is mentioned in an inscription at Delphi as holding office during that year. The eighteen months that Paul is said to have spent in Corinth thus probably covered parts of the years 52 and 53, and so the whole second journey will have included the years 50–54.

The third journey of Paul began shortly after his second journey, or around the year 55, and it probably ended in 58 CE. During this journey the apostle spent two years in the Roman province of Asia, then a considerable time in Troas and Macedonia, and three months in Greece. The subsequent captivity in Caesarea lasted for two years, as long as Felix was procurator there, and when the new procurator Festus sent Paul to the emperor, the apostle had to spend two more years in Roman custody. Since Felix was deposed in 60 CE (when Nero had overthrown his powerful brother Pallas in Rome), Paul's captivity can be dated to parts of the years 58–60. The continuation of his trial under Festus and his journey to Rome thus probably took place in the year 60, and so the date of his custody for two years in Rome will have been 61–62.

It is also possible to give approximate dates for the death of some early Christian leaders. The apostle James was killed around 42 CE during a persecution arranged by King Agrippa I (called Herod in Acts 12.2). James, the brother of Jesus, who had presided at the apostolic council held in Jerusalem in 49 CE, was stoned in the year 62 on the initiative of the high priest. According to later sources, Peter and Paul were killed in Rome. This happened some time after the city's destruction by fire in 64 CE, which caused Nero to persecute the Christians there, probably at the beginning of the year 65.

Shortly before the Jewish war of 66–70 CE broke out, the Christians of Palestine are said to have emigrated to Transjordan. After the destruction of Jerusalem in 70 CE the separation of Judaism and Christianity became even more evident. Domitian's persecution of Christians, which took place around 94–95, is the last datable event referred to in the New Testament.

Since the New Testament books do not indicate when they were composed, their literary origin can be dated only approximately by such historical events as those mentioned above. Without this support all scholarly theories on the age of New Testament writings are speculative, and one should not accept any general tendency or common opinion as established truth.　　　　*Bo Reicke*

CHURCH. In the Greek world, the term *ekklēsia* meant a group of citizens "called out" to assemble for political purposes. In the New Testament, *ekklēsia* signifies a group of believers in Jesus who are called together, and is translated as "church." The original Greek sense survives, however, when the author of Acts describes an assembly at Ephesus in which citizens have a heated discussion about Paul and his preaching (Acts 19.32, 39, 41). The city clerk finally tells people to suspend their debate until the next regular *ekklēsia*.

In the Septuagint *ekklēsia* is used interchangeably with *synagogē* to render Hebrew terms that mean assembly. One such occurrence from Psalm 22.22 is cited by the author of Hebrews: "in the midst of the congregation *(ekklēsia)* I will praise you" (Heb. 2.12).

Paul regularly uses the term church *(ekklēsia)* in his letters to address individual communities of believers, and he uses the plural form to speak in general about groups such as "the churches of God in Christ Jesus that are in Judea" (1 Thess. 2.14) and "all the churches of the saints" (1 Cor. 14.33). Paul does not have a developed sense of the church as a universal institution but rather sees local assemblies of believers functioning independently in separate locations. In a few cases, however, especially in reference to his persecution of the church of God, Paul's use of the term seems more generalized.

The term church appears only two times in the Gospels, both in Matthew.

One occurrence refers to a local community's role in disputes between believers (Matt. 18.17), while in the other, Jesus uses the term church in a much more expansive sense. Matthew's Jesus responds to Peter's confession by saying "on this rock I will build my church" (Matt. 16.18). Whether the "rock" refers to Peter or to his confession is strongly debated, but either way, the verse conveys a sense of the church as a universal institution.

This universal sense is developed further in the deutero-Pauline letters. Ephesians and Colossians elaborate on a Pauline image by referring to the church as the body of Christ and to Christ as the head of that body. In Ephesians 5.23, Christ's headship of the church is used as justification for a husband's authority over his wife.

Ignatius of Antioch (ca. 100 CE) is the earliest known author to use the phrase "catholic church" when referring to the universality of the body of Christ (*Smyrneans,* 8). Unanimity becomes a key concept in later discussions of the church, as orthodox leaders stress catholicity in the face of challenges from various heterodox groups. Some versions of the Nicene Creed conclude with the formula "one holy catholic and apostolic church."   *Daniel N. Schowalter*

CIRCULATION OF THE BIBLE.
By the beginning of the year 2000, *translations of the entire Bible had been published in 371 languages and dialects, and portions of the Bible in 1,862 other languages and dialects. All told, these 2,233 languages account for over 80 percent of the world's population. Yet with an estimated three thousand to six thousand languages in the world, *Bible societies still face a major task in translating the scriptures.

The earliest translation of the Hebrew scriptures was into Greek (the Septuagint), made in Alexandria in the third century BCE, and it was this form that New Testament writers knew and quoted. Ensuing translations followed fairly slowly in succeeding centuries. By 600 CE, the Gospels had been translated into eight languages: Latin, Gothic, Syriac, Coptic, Armenian, Georgian, Ethiopic, and Sogdian.

When Johannes *Gutenberg invented the art of printing with movable type in about 1450, a mere thirty-three languages had any translations of the scriptures. In fact, when the Bible society movement began early in the nineteenth century, the Bible had been translated into only sixty-seven languages. Soon thereafter, however, the number skyrocketed: with the rise of the missionary movement in the nineteenth century, over four hundred languages received some part of the scriptures. By the end of the first half of the twentieth century, parts of the Bible had been published in five hundred additional languages. In many cases, the language in question had no alphabet before the Bible translator undertook to encode the language in written form.

Until relatively recently, missionaries, with the assistance of native speakers, were generally responsible for translating the Bible. Now, however, native speakers often assume primary responsibility, with missionaries sometimes serving as consultants. This has many virtues, since it is invariably easier for properly trained people to translate into their own mother tongue than into a foreign language, and the end product is likely to be more effective.

A crucial aspect of recent developments in Bible translation is the realization that cultural differences among peoples must be considered in order to assure that the text is meaningfully and

Continent or Region	Portions	Testaments	Bibles	Total
Africa	218	267	142	627
Asia.	228	212	113	553
Australasia/Pacific Islands	172	194	30	396
Europe	106	29	62	197
North & Central America/ Caribbean	41	25	7	73
South America/Mexico	135	233	16	384
Constructed Languages.	2	0	1	3
Total	902	960	371	2,233

accurately rendered. Often, a literal translation will result in wholly erroneous understanding; for instance, "the wicked will not stand in the judgment" (Ps. 1.6) was understood in one African language to mean that evil people will not be judged; and "smiting one's breast"—a sign of contrition and repentance in biblical times—was taken to mean self-congratulation. Alternately, a given language's syntax may be ill suited to convey, for example, rhetorical questions. In Hebrews 2.3, the writer is not actually looking for an escape when he asks, "How can we escape if we neglect such a great salvation?" Rather, he is declaring emphatically that there can be no escape whatsoever. In some languages and dialects, then, one must employ a negative formulation such as "There is no possible escape if we . . ."

In spite of such difficulties, the task of translators is to reproduce the message of the original text with the closest natural equivalent—an assignment that sounds simpler than it is. For instance, Amos 4.6, "I gave you cleanness of teeth in all your cities," is potentially perplexing, for it refers not to dental hygiene but to the results of a severe famine.

Over the past generation, biblical translators and revisers have often justified the preparation of several translations within a single language area, depending on the use that the rendering will serve. Basic types of translations to meet different needs are simplified translations for new readers; common language translations for evangelistic purposes; standard or traditional translations to meet the needs of traditionally oriented readers; literary-liturgical translations employing the total resources of the language and intended primarily for church use.

The following statistical summary *(see chart above)* shows the number of different languages and dialects in which publication of at least one book of the Bible (designated "portions") had been registered as of 31 December 1991.

Bruce M. Metzger

CIRCUMCISION. Circumcision is the ritualistic removal of the male's foreskin, practiced by many African, South American, and Middle Eastern peoples. Often performed at puberty, it may have originated as a rite of passage from childhood to adulthood; some biblical texts have been interpreted in this way. In Jewish tradition, following biblical commandments, males are normally circumcised at eight days of age. Proselyte males are circumcised before admission into the community.

Although some rabbis held that males who had been born Jews could maintain their status without circumcision, across the centuries others demanded excommunication for those not circumcised. According to one passage, even Moses would have died had his son not been circumcised (Exod. 4.24–26). Nevertheless, according to Joshua 5.2–9, apparently those born in the wilderness were not circumcised until they entered Canaan. Then the Lord required that they be circumcised, presumably to enable them to celebrate *Passover. Later scribes modified this tradition by improbably having them be circumcised "a second time" (Josh. 5.2).

Antiochus Epiphanes had women and their sons who had been circumcised despite his proscription killed. Some Palestinian Jews managed to have themselves uncircumcised, stood apart from the holy contract, yoked themselves to the gentiles, and sold themselves to do evil. This does not necessarily mean that they performed some sort of surgical reconstruction, for these four items are all parallel ways of making the same statement, that liberal Jews became so completely hellenized that orthodox Jews said they were no longer circumcised. This was probably insult rather than fact, just as male Jews who mingled with gentiles socially and in business were called "harlots," as if they had mingled sexually. There may, however, have been liberal Jews and Jewish Christians who stretched the remaining foreskin to make circumcision less obvious. "Circumcision" was also used metaphorically. Someone who did not accept divine teaching was said to have an uncircumcised ear, and a stubborn person had an uncircumcised heart.

Circumcision was traced back to the *covenant or contract God made with Abraham, and thus is widely practiced by Muslims as well as Jews. It was called the "sign of the covenant" (Gen. 17.11), the covenant in the flesh (Gen. 17.13), and the "covenant of circumcision" (Acts 7.8); the traditional European Jewish (i.e., Yiddish) term for circumcision, *bris,* is an alternate pronunciation of the word for "covenant" (Hebr. *bĕrît*). In earliest Christianity, there was considerable debate over the requirement of circumcision; Paul, however, held that circumcision was part of the old contract that had been superseded and was therefore no longer required, and his view ultimately became normative for Christians (*see* Law, *article on* New Testament Views). *George Wesley Buchanan*

CLEAN AND UNCLEAN. *See* Purity, Ritual.

COMPUTERS AND THE BIBLE. Just as all humanistic study of ancient texts is enhanced by the application of computing technologies, the modern study of biblical texts is increasingly being transformed by the microcomputer revolution. In particular, electronic digital media and computer programs are ideally suited to the tasks of organization, manipulation, storage, and dissemination of textual information. The democratization of "personal computer" technology enables anyone who uses a computer for writing or accounting tasks to explore scriptural texts with associated linguistic data bases and reference tools in a digital environment.

Manuscript Collation and Production of Critical Editions. Computer programs help scholars reconstruct whole "texts" from ancient manuscript fragments in the same way that programs assist archaeologists in reconstructing ceramic vessels: once the physical and textual features of manuscript fragments are described, pattern-matching programs may be used to hypothesize text reconstruction based upon groupings and physical joins. When individual texts are restored and fully encoded, programs using "genetic" knowledge may be used to suggest stemmatic (genealogical) and typological relationships, dividing texts or recensions into families. Manuscript evidence may then be manipulated programmatically to create critical editions of the text, whether on a small scale or in the production of a major edition. The advantages of creating paper critical editions from electronic data bases are great: far fewer mistakes are made in printing, and the logical and physical formats of print editions are entirely negotiable, being defined in variable sets of rules similar to electronic style sheets. (*See also* Printing and Publishing, *articles on* Production and Manufacturing; Economics.)

Data Bases for Linguistic and Literary Annotation. Biblical texts held in simple electronic format are immediately useful since they may be edited, queried, and displayed in various ways. More subtle inquiry into the text requires that words, clauses, sentences, paragraphs, pericopes—even individual characters within words—be supplied with linguistic and literary description. Computer programs have been used to "parse" texts, assigning lexical and grammatical features to words, but in general these annotations must be made manually. Morphological data bases have been created for the Hebrew Bible, New Testament, Septuagint, and related corpora. Each word might be lemmatized (given a normalized spelling and dictionary form), augmented with a morphological description and similar linguistic-literary annotations. Literary structural markers are placed within the texts, in addition

to markers used in canonical referencing schemes such as *chapters and verses. Once descriptive enhancements are made to the text, scholars may frame queries in terms of lexical, grammatical, and syntactic textual features, not merely in terms of a fixed character stream. Of course, all assignment of literary and linguistic markup is subjective, so the results of searches, however quantified, must also be qualified. In addition to the widely accessible linguistic data bases for biblical texts, rich collections of rabbinic, Greek and Latin (classical, medieval, epigraphic-ephemeral), Muslim, and Buddhist text materials are also publicly available.

Dynamic Concording. Perhaps the most popular computer applications for general users are programs that permit dynamic "concording" of texts and user-specified displays of text in *concordance formats. Whereas printed concordances are static (i.e., based upon a dictionary form or other organizing principle), a computer concordance program is dynamic. Thus, rather than scan excerpted passages containing the single word "compassion," a user specifies the search criteria, limited only by the research goals and imagination. These are some examples of searches: all sentences containing "wine" or "strong drink," as well as "joy"; all verses in the Septuagint containing more than two imperative verb forms; all conditional clauses in the book of Exodus; all interrogative sentences in the NRSV version of the book of Job. Of course, the concordance query may address only those features supported by the data base and search program.

Hypertext and Hypermedia Displays. Because the Bible has been the object of intensive textual focus for many centuries, a rich network of commentary and linguistic annotation has grown up around it. A relatively new technology for managing this network of knowledge is called "hypertext." Hypertext, and hypermedia, which includes digitized graphic images and other media formats, exploits a primary distinguishing feature of "electronic" text: nonlinearity. An electronic document may be rearranged, compressed, expanded, split into logical subdocuments, or in other ways liberated from its linear-sequential format as determined in traditional books. The concept of linking primary text with its reference works (grammar, lexicon, encyclopedia, commentary, theological wordbook) and with "parallel" texts has led to the creation of electronic books, usually scanned or keypunched, using standard reference tools. In a hypertext computer environment, each biblical verse or single word of base text is linked to portions of documents in the associated works. A hypertext application with several windows makes it possible to enjoy synchronous scrolling of several parallel texts or text versions or synchronized display of commentary text with base text. Control and navigation within such networks is not yet perfected, but hypertext technology shows great promise for individualized and interdisciplinary study of biblical texts.

Critical Study of the Bible. Most computer applications described above are general, conceptually simple, and noncontroversial. The use of quantitative and computational linguistics methodologies for the critical study of biblical texts is still immature by comparison. Within small corners of the world of biblical studies, computing techniques have been used to study such historical- and literary-critical features as textual transmission (subtle trends in spelling), authorship (unity or composite character of texts, measuring subconscious parameters of authorial style), metrical systems, translational features in ancient

versions, and syntax (word order, clause patterns). The impact on mainline biblical studies has been minimal, though not insignificant. Some of the chief obstacles to acceptance of quantitative and computational methods are the difficulty of providing formal conceptual models and text representation schemes for critical inquiry; the greater appropriateness of currently understood methods to synchronic study of texts, rather than to higher-order analytic investigation; and the preference of biblical scholars for older, proven methods of research and publishing, with concomitant slowness to embrace newer methods of working in the global electronic workspace.

Conclusion. The growing popularity of international academic networks for collaborative research, the rapidly improving software for electronic publishing, and newer conceptual models for managing multilingual text all promise a bright future for computing in biblical studies. A point of critical mass has already been reached in the popular sector among Bible enthusiasts; the equivalent threshold of scholarly involvement has nearly been crossed. As trends increase toward compact mass storage (one CD-ROM disk now contains the equivalent of 150 books) and smaller, more powerful microcomputers, the growth of humanities computing appears certain. Current reports on these developments may be found in the conference activities and publication organs of the Society of Biblical Literature's Computer Assisted Research Section and the Association Internationale Bible et Informatique, and in annual sections of the *Humanities Computing Yearbook* (Oxford).

Robin C. Cover

CONCORDANCES. The understanding of a concordance is well reflected in the title of the first concordance of the complete Bible in English, published in 1550 by John Marbeck: *A Concordance, that is to saie, a work wherein by the ordre of the letters A B C, ye maie reddly find any words conteigned in the whole Bible, so often as it is there expressed or mensioned.* A concordance lists alphabetically and in their context the words that occur in a specified writing or group of writings, with citations of where they may be found.

Concordances in general vary in what words from a corpus they include. Exhaustive concordances include every word. Some concordances exclude very frequent words, or include only words of importance for some particular purpose, or specific types of words. Thus, there can be a concordance of words that occur fewer than a hundred times, of theological terms, or of proper names.

Concordances vary in how much context they provide for each word. Works giving no context but providing citations of where the words occur have historically been called concordances, but they might more properly be called indexes.

Concordances also vary in how they list words. Graphic concordances list the form of a word as it occurs in the text. They are often satisfactory for languages that have few prefixes, like English, since most related forms of a word are listed in fairly close proximity. Lexical concordances list words by the dictionary form of the word. These are necessary for languages like Hebrew, in which the tense and person of verbs may be changed by adding prefixes.

In addition, biblical concordances vary in what books (Hebrew Bible, New Testament, Apocrypha) and what language version of the Bible (Hebrew, Greek, Latin, King James Version English, etc.) they include.

The fact that the Bible exists in many *translations has meant that users of a translation are often interested not only in a word and the contexts in which it is found, but in what word or words in the original language of the texts are being translated. A monumental work of this type is *A Concordance to the Septuagint,* begun by Edwin Hatch, completed by Henry Redpath, and published in 1897. It included several Greek versions of the Old Testament with the Hebrew words that presumably were being translated. Such a concordance is referred to as a dual language or analytical concordance.

The earliest biblical concordance known is to the Latin Bible by Antony of Padua made in the early thirteenth century. More influential, however, was the *Concordantia S. Jacobi* compiled in 1230 under the direction of Hugh of St. Cher. It was the source on which later Latin concordances were based.

The earliest Hebrew concordance was produced by Rabbi Isaac Nathan ben Kalonymos in 1448 and published in 1523. The revision by John Buxtorf in 1632 was the basis for most later Hebrew concordances.

While earlier concordances in manuscript form are mentioned, the earliest published Greek concordance of the Old Testament is *Concordantiae Graecae versionis vulgo dictae LXX interpretum* by Abraham Trommius in 1718. The first concordance of the Greek New Testament was that of Sixtus Birck (Xystus Betulejus) in 1546.

Probably the most influential and broadly published English concordance was Alexander Cruden's *A Complete Concordance to the Holy Scriptures of the Old and New Testaments* (1737).

Because of the labor and time involved and the frequency of errors, in the past it was natural that once a concordance of a text was published, later concordances of that text tended to be based on earlier concordances. This has changed radically with the introduction of the *computer and the encoding of large numbers of texts in electronic form.

The earliest computer-generated concordances were the KWIC (Key Word In Context) concordances that were generated without reference to the language of the text, except to know whether the writing goes from right to left or vice versa. The usefulness of these graphic concordances depends on the nature of the language involved.

A process called "tagging" (introducing into a text codes that give information about the individual words) has made possible the automatic production of lexical concordances. These are very similar to the KWIC concordances. In addition to information about the dictionary forms of words, tags may also include morphological and syntactic information. This creates the possibility of generating "concordances" of information other than words. One may have a concordance that arranges the nouns in the Bible together, subdividing them by how they are used in the sentence. Subjects, objects of verbs, and objects of prepositions are listed together rather than with other occurrences of the same word.

The "aligning" of texts, in which the words in two or more texts are correlated, has made possible the automatic creation of dual language or analytic concordances. By both aligning and tagging texts, a wide range of concordances can be created.

The computer has also made it practical to produce and publish concordances of other languages and groups of texts that are important to students of the Bible. Concordances exist for the *Ugaritic literature and the nonbiblical *Dead Sea Scrolls.

With tagged and/or aligned texts available in electronic form, it is possible to develop computer programs that allow the user to define the kind of concordance desired and to have the concordances generated on the spot and displayed on the screen. Today the electronic texts created by earlier scholars, rather than their concordances, are the source for new concordances.

Concordances are useful to the casual reader who wants to know where a familiar quotation is found, to the student who wants to see Paul's use of a theological term, to the preacher who is examining a biblical theme for a sermon, and to the scholar who is interested in whether the Dead Sea Scrolls use words with the same meaning that Jesus gave to them. The range of concordances is increasing at a tremendous rate, and this is likely to continue.

Richard E. Whitaker

CONVERSION. Conversion refers to two different kinds of "turning" to God: the change of allegiance from one religion (or branch of a religion) to another; and the movement from lack of faith or purely formal faith to commitment, or, with a more moral emphasis, from a life of sin to one of attempted virtue in obedience to God. In trying to understand conversion in the Bible, it is tempting to find modern individualism operating in situations where matters of group loyalty were in fact more salient. It is also easy for the modern reader to see certain biblical episodes as conversions when they are better taken as calls by God to new roles.

The complex play of these factors

may be illustrated by several examples. The stories of God's encounters with figures such as Abraham, Jacob, and Moses may, in their origins, reflect transfers of tribal allegiance to a new deity, though in their final form, they appear as calls to deeper loyalty or to a new phase in the relationship between God and his people or a particular leader. Similarly, stories such as that in Joshua 9 describe the adherence of whole groups to Israel's deity, Yahweh, inspired by what appear to us to be political and social motives. In the much later setting of the New Testament, there is evidence of people moving from other religions to Judaism, just as they moved to the Christian movement (see references to proselytes, Acts 2.10; and to gentiles on the edge of Judaism, such as Cornelius, Acts 10).

The story of Isaiah of Jerusalem is best seen as a call to a more profound allegiance to Yahweh. While it is wholly personal in its reference, it nevertheless places Isaiah in a well-authenticated tradition of holy individuals, among whom Samuel, Elijah, and Elisha are in many ways comparable earlier examples. Such figures, themselves "converted" in a charismatic act, become charismatic leaders, stirring the people, on the basis of their God-given authority, to military zeal (as in the case of Samuel or Saul), to faithfulness to Yahweh as opposed to other gods (Elijah and Elisha), or to cultic and moral purity (Isaiah, Amos, Hosea, Jeremiah). It is noteworthy that in the story of Isaiah's "conversion" a moral element is explicit as God's purity is brought home.

The so-called conversion of Paul (described in Acts 9; 22; 26; and more intimately in his own words in Gal. 1.15–16) is in many ways comparable to such prophetic calls; indeed, "call" (Grk. *kaleō*) is Paul's own most characteristic word for the summons of God both to himself and to others. It is certainly not conversion in the sense of a move from irreligion to belief, or from a life of vice to one of virtue, nor was it perceived by Paul as a move from one religion to another; there is scarcely any sign that Paul saw the new faith as other than the true Judaism, the realization of God's plan for his people. Rather, it was a call from God to serve as emissary (apostle) of Jesus Christ, whom God had sent for the purpose of drawing Jews and gentiles alike into his people.

With deep-seated origins in stories of transferred tribal allegiance and the rise of charismatic military and political leaders, there emerges in the prophetic literature—whose attitudes so deeply color the final form these stories take—a pervasive sense of God's call both to individuals and, through their activity, to his people, a call for a new loyalty to him and for a more profound moral obedience. It is evident in the preexilic prophets' summons to Israel to "turn" (see Repentance), as well as in the later optimistic promise of restoration in Second Isaiah.

This tradition of God's urgent call to turn again reaches new intensity in the ministry of Jesus. In the light of the coming *kingdom of God, Jesus summons people to unconditioned and simple allegiance to God, brushing aside competing claims such as wealth and family ties. The outcome of his summons is *salvation, seen in terms not only of the coming new age, but also of forgiveness and healing here and now. It is likely that many of the Gospel stories of healings by Jesus and other encounters with him were told and heard in terms of conversion responses to Jesus' call. It is noteworthy that precisely the same Greek words, "Your faith has saved you," are used in relation to an act of forgiveness (Luke 7.50) and an act of healing (18.42). This activity is consciously set against the prophetic background, as indeed is the language. in which the subsequent preaching of early Christian leaders is described.

Although the element of repentance and "turning" is present in much biblical material concerning people's coming to God's service, the element of "call" is more fundamental; this is clear in the portrayal of Jesus' own ministry as inaugurated by such an episode (Mark 1.9–11). Here, charisma and divine recognition are bestowed with a view to his acting as God's agent.

Adopting a perspective more keenly aware of the social realities of the world of the first century CE, we may note that in Palestine the appeal of Jesus was akin to that of a number of leaders of reform and renewal within Judaism of that period; note especially John the Baptist. In Greco-Roman society, where the Christian movement was unique among these Palestinian groups in its success in moving beyond its original setting, both the appeal and the process of "joining" were different. It is likely that a number of those attracted were people who, in one respect or another, were on the margins of society or felt themselves to be so. As Acts indicates, a number were "God-fearers," gentiles already attracted to Jewish synagogues but never able to be more than fringe members. Others may have been aliens living far from their native lands; and the power to attract women may have been linked to aspirations in earliest Christianity toward gender equality.

Such changes of religious alliance were not common in the ancient world: the open, tolerant, and undemanding nature of Greco-Roman religion made them largely incomprehensible. But there was some parallel in decisions to adhere to philosophical groups, a deci-sion that might involve a measure of commitment to a specific way of life, and in the adoption of some of the mystical paths available within the religious spectrum. In any case, the strong group identity of the Christians must have been a powerful force; and if we ask what it felt like to join the Christians in a Greek city, then the provision of a "home," centered on Christ, was a major factor, not unlike the similar provision which might be found in the synagogue or in the many guilds or clubs that abounded in city life.   *J. L. Houlden*

COVENANT. One of the fundamental theological motifs of the Hebrew and Christian scriptures. Eventually the expressions "old covenant" and "new covenant," which once referred to two eras or dispensations, came to designate the two parts of the Christian Bible, the Old Testament (Covenant) and the New.

The Hebrew term for covenant (*bĕrît*) seems to have the root meaning of "bond, fetter," indicating a binding relationship; the idea of "binding, putting together" is also suggested in the Greek term *synthēkē*. Another term used in the New Testament is *diathēkē* ("will, testament"), pointing more to the obligatory or legal aspect of a covenant. The meaning of covenant, however, is not determined primarily by etymology but by how these and related terms function in various literary contexts. In general, covenant signifies a relationship based on commitment, which includes both promises and obligations, and which has the quality of reliability and durability. The relationship is usually sealed by a rite—for example, an oath, sacred *meal, blood *sacrifice, invocation of *blessings and *curses—which makes it binding.

In the Hebrew Bible, various secular covenants are mentioned: covenants between leaders of two peoples (Abraham and Abimelech), between two heads of state (Ahab and Ben-hadad), between king and people (David and the elders of Israel), between a revolutionary priest and the army (Jehoiada), between a conquering king and a vassal (Nebuchadrezzar and a Judean prince). These treaties or pacts were usually thought to be supervised by the deity. This was the case for instance, in the covenant between Jacob and Laban, which was sealed with a sacred meal and which concluded with a prayer that God would see to it that both sides lived up to the terms of the agreement. Likewise the covenant between Jonathan and David, based on the loyalty (*ḥesed*) of friendship, was "a covenant before Yahweh" (1 Sam. 23.18).

In the ancient world, covenants or treaties often governed the relations between peoples. There were parity treaties between two equal sovereign states, and there were overlord treaties between a powerful monarch and a vassal state. Illustrative of the latter is the suzerainty treaty form of the second and first millennia, which apparently influenced Israel's Mosaic covenant theology found in the book of Deuteronomy. These treaties included such elements as a summary of the benevolent deeds of the overlord, the stipulations binding on the vassal who receives favor and protection, and the sanctions of blessings and curses in case of obedience or disobedience.

Covenant expresses a novel element of the religion of ancient Israel: the people are bound in relationship to the one God, Yahweh, who makes an exclusive ("jealous") claim upon their loyalty in worship and social life. In a larger sense, the relationship between all creatures and their creator is expressed in the universal covenant with Noah, which assures God's faithful pledge to humanity, to

nonhuman creatures, and to the earth itself. In the *Pentateuch, however, primary emphasis is given to God's covenant with the Israelite people, portrayed in the migration of Abraham and Sarah in response to the divine promise and the special relationship between God and their descendants. In the biblical narrative, the covenant with Israel's ancestors is the prelude to the crucial events of the *Exodus and the Mosaic covenant at Sinai and is supplemented by the covenant between God and the Davidic monarch, who mediates God's cosmic rule, manifest in the anointed one (the reigning ruler) and in the Temple of Zion.

The covenants between God and the people are all covenants of divine favor or *grace (Hebr. *ḥesed*). They express God's gracious commitment and faithfulness and thus establish a continuing relationship. They differ from one another theologically at the point of whether the accent falls upon God's loyalty, which endows the relationship with constancy and durability, or upon the people's response, which is subject to human weakness and sin. The Abrahamic and Davidic covenants belong to the type of the "everlasting covenant" (*běrît ʿōlām*), for they rest upon divine grace alone and are not conditioned by human behavior. On the other hand, the Mosaic covenant, set forth classically in the book of Deuteronomy, has a strong conditional note, for its endurance depends on the people's obedience to the covenant commandments.

Furthermore, all of God's covenants with Israel include divine promises, as well as human obligations, though they differ as to which is emphasized. The Abrahamic covenant is primarily a promissory covenant. In it God imposes no conditions (*circumcision is a sign, not a legal condition of the relationship) but rather gives promises: the land as an everlasting possession, numerous posterity, and a special relationship between God and the descendants of Abraham and Sarah. Similarly, the Davidic covenant, perhaps on the analogy of royal grants of the ancient Near East, does not impose legal conditions, but offers a gracious promise of an unbroken succession of kings upon the throne of David. Although unfaithful kings will be chastised if they behave badly in office, God will not abrogate the covenant promises of grace made to David (*see also* Kingship and Monarchy). The Mosaic covenant, however, like the suzerainty treaties of the ancient world, is a covenant of obligation, subject to the sanctions of blessings and curses. If the people are unfaithful and disobey the covenant stipulations, they will be punished for breaking the covenant. Carried to the extreme, this covenant could even be annulled, so that no longer would Yahweh be their God and no longer would Israel be God's people. The renewal of the covenant, in this view, would be based solely on God's forgiving grace.

The New Testament draws upon all of these covenant traditions. In some circles, however, there was a strong preference for the promissory covenants associated with Abraham and David (cf. "the covenants of promise," Eph. 2.12). Paul's interpretation of the new relationship between God and people, shown by the display of God's grace in Jesus Christ, sent him back beyond the Mosaic covenant of obligation to the Abrahamic promissory covenant. And the promissory Davidic covenant, found especially in the prophecy of the book of Isaiah, provided a theological context for the announcement that Jesus is the Messiah (Christ), the *Son of God.

See also Biblical Theology, *article on* Old Testament.   *Bernhard W. Anderson*

CREATION. The biblical accounts of the creation of the world have their background in ancient Near Eastern mythology, in which creation is often depicted as the deity's victory over the forces of *chaos, represented by threatening waters, as a result of which the god is established as a supreme king. A large number of references show that this concept was well-known in Israel also. Its immediate source was probably Canaanite mythology, and it was particularly associated with the Jerusalem Temple, where it seems likely that God's victory over primeval chaos and his royal enthronement were celebrated in a great annual festival.

Since the extended descriptions of creation in the first chapters of Genesis similarly reflect this background (*see* Myth), they are not to be viewed as providing a scientific account of the origin of the universe. They are religious statements, designed to show God's glory and greatness, the result of theological reflection by which the older mythology was radically transformed to express Israel's distinctive faith. The two accounts found together in these chapters, Genesis 1.1–2.4a and 2.4b–25, both tell of the creation of the physical world and the creation of humanity, though these were originally independent elements. The first account is generally considered to be from the hand of a sixth-century BCE priestly writer (P) who, however, depends on a much older tradition. In form it is a poem or a hymn, as the repeated refrain indicates, and its seven-day structure may be due to its having been recited during the period of the annual festival mentioned above. Although the watery chaos is still there, there is no conflict between it and God, as in ancient myth. God creates in unfettered freedom by his word or command, and creation is brought about by the separation of the elements of the universe, which produces an ordered and habitable world. Hence creation is not so much dealing with absolute beginning, creation from nothing—though this idea appears later, as in 2 Maccabees 7.28—as with the world order as perceived by human beings. An originally separate account of the creation of humankind—it does not appear as creation through the word—has been added to show human beings as the crown of creation. Humanity too is created by separation into male and female made in the image of God, a much discussed expression that probably means that God makes beings with whom he can communicate and who can respond, because, in contrast to the rest of nature, they are like him. So humanity receives the divine blessing and is given the role of God's vice-regent, in language drawn from *kingship vocabulary, to have dominion or control over the future course of the world. The final verses, which tell of God's seeing all he has made and his rest on the *Sabbath, emphasize the completeness and perfection of the created order.

The outlook of the second creation account (generally attributed to J) is essentially similar but its form is very different. It is older and it is a folktale, reflecting the concerns and interests of a peasant society, and God is described in human terms; but behind its apparent naïveté lie profound insights. It deals primarily with the creation of humanity, and the creation of the world is directed to providing a suitable agricultural environment for human beings. God molds the first man from the dust of the ground, an idea found in many other cultures; that is, he is part of the natural

order, but he is given a unique status when God breathes into him the divine breath and he becomes a living being. His naming of the animals means that he appropriates them, corresponding to the notion of dominion in Genesis 1, and the command about the trees in the garden implies responsibility toward his maker, which is part of what is meant by humanity as the image of God. No doubt the fact that woman is created secondarily from man corresponds to the position of the male in a patriarchal society. Yet even more strongly the story stresses the unity of the sexes and their mutual, complementary need. So the first creation account, with its cultic background, ends with the religious institution of the Sabbath; the second, which is directed to humankind in community, with the social institution of *marriage.

Explicit references to creation may appear to be comparatively rare in the Bible. But the creation accounts in Genesis are the starting point for the history that follows and are inseparably linked with it in the biblical narrative. The prophets and the wisdom literature also both presuppose a comprehensive world order to which they summon men and women to conform. There are, however, two particular developments in later texts to which special attention may be called.

First, the idea grows that the goal of history is to be a new creation, a return to the beginning when the creator's original intention, frustrated by human sin and rebellion, will be fulfilled. The visions of the end of time are pictured in terms of the first things. Such is a dominant theme in the later chapters of Isaiah, and it is further developed in succeeding *apocalyptic literature.

Second, in certain parts of the wisdom tradition, Wisdom comes to be represented as already existing before the creation of the world and, parallel to the divine word in Genesis 1, the means of God's creative activity. Wisdom can be strongly personified and viewed as God's personal agent in creation (Prov. 8.22–31); in Sirach 24.3 the figure of Wisdom is identified both with the word of Genesis 1 and the primary act of creation in Genesis 2.6.

It is these two developments that determine the way in which the idea of creation is transposed into a new key in the New Testament. The New Testament writers inherited the Jewish belief in the creation of the world by the one God and frequently appeal to the ordering of the world and human life that he established at the beginning. But the advent of Christ inaugurates the long awaited new creation, both of the universe and of humanity. This comes about because, on the one hand, Jesus recapitulates the former creation: he is the new Adam and the image and likeness of God. On the other hand, Christ is the agent and sustainer of all creation and is described as the word of God and the wisdom of God. But it is the figure of creative Wisdom that seems to have been most influential for the understanding of Jesus; so, like Wisdom, he is preexistent and the reflection of God's *glory. Most striking is the first chapter of John's gospel, the opening words of which echo the beginning of Genesis, with its picture of Jesus as the *Logos. This term unites the concept of the creative word of the Hebrew Bible and, from its use in Greek philosophy, the concept of Wisdom as the mediator in creation.   *J. R. Porter*

CRUCIFIXION. The act of nailing or binding a person to a cross or tree, whether for executing or for exposing the corpse. It was considered the cruelest

and most shameful method of capital punishment.

According to ancient historians such as Herodotus and Diodorus Siculus, various kinds of crucifixion (e.g., impalement) were used by the Assyrians, Scythians, Phoenicians, and Persians. The practice of crucifixion was taken over by Alexander the Great and his successors, and especially by the Romans, who reserved it for slaves in cases of robbery and rebellion. Roman citizens could be punished in this way only for the crime of high treason. In the Roman provinces crucifixion served as a means of punishing unruly people who were sentenced as "robbers." *Josephus tells of mass crucifixions in Judea under several Roman prefects, in particular Titus during the siege of Jerusalem; the same also occurred in the Jewish quarter of Alexandria, according to *Philo. Before the execution, the victim was scourged. He then had to carry the transverse beam (*patibulum*) to the place of execution, and was nailed through hands and feet to the cross, from which a wooden peg protruded to support the body; some of these literary details are confirmed by archaeological finds of the bones of crucifixion victims.

Crucifixion, though not mentioned in the list of death penalties in Jewish law, might be suggested in Deuteronomy 21.22–23, which requires that a person put to death must be hung on a tree and buried on the same day. While this is interpreted by the Mishnah as the exposure of the corpse of a man who was stoned because of blasphemy or idolatry, the order of the verbs is reversed in the Temple Scroll of Qumran: the delinquent must be hung up so that he dies, which amounts to crucifixion. The same source also specifies that it must be applied in a case of high treason, for example, if an Israelite curses his people or delivers them to a foreign nation. Although such a crime is not mentioned in the Hebrew Bible, it must be derived from the ambiguous term "God's curse" (Deut. 21.23). Delivering up or cursing Israel is also regarded as blasphemy, because the nation belongs to God.

The same interpretation of Deuteronomy 21.22–23 underlies 4QpNah, which mentions "hanging men up alive [on the tree]," presumably a reference to the atrocious deed of Alexander Janneus when he crucified eight hundred of his Pharisean enemies who, in his view, had committed high treason. Other references to crucifixion include the hanging of eighty "witches" (probably Sadducees) by Rabbi Shimon ben Shetah, the crucifixion of Rabbi Jose ben Joezer, and Matthew 23.34.

In rabbinic writings crucifixion is the death penalty for "robbers" (bandits) and for martyrs. Isaac, carrying the wood for his sacrifice, was compared to a man bearing the cross on his shoulders. Similarly, a disciple of Jesus must take up his cross and follow him.

According to Matthew 20.19 and 26.2, Jesus said that once delivered to the gentiles he would suffer crucifixion. The predictions of suffering by Jesus are not necessarily prophecies after the fact. The inscription on the cross told that Jesus was crucified as "king of the Jews" (Mark 15.26). In his trial before the high priest and before Pilate, Jesus had admitted to being the Messiah of Israel and *Son of God. The members of the Sanhedrin declared that Jesus deserved death because he had uttered blasphemy; they must have understood Deuteronomy 21.22–23 in a way similar to the Temple Scroll. A false messiah could deliver the people of Israel and the Temple to the gentiles. According to the Babylonian Talmud, Jesus was executed because he had led Israel astray, a judgment based on Deuteronomy 13.1–11.

By delivering Jesus to Pilate, the members of the Sanhedrin could expect the sentence "death by crucifixion," for the claim to be the Messiah could be understood as a rebellion against Rome. It is for this reason that Jesus was compared with the revolutionary Barabbas. After the people had asked for Barabbas, Pilate had no other choice than to crucify Jesus, who was scourged, mocked by the legionaries, and crucified together with two "robbers."

Before the crucifixion Jesus had refused wine mingled with myrrh, which was intended to ease the pain. The mockery, in which the guilt of Jesus is reiterated, may have been intended in the first place to make him understand his error and to lead him to a confession of sins. While the crucifixion was carried out by Roman soldiers, the burial in the evening of this day was done by a Jew in accordance with Deuteronomy 21.23.

Deuteronomy 21.22–23 is also related to crucifixion by Paul in Galatians 3.13. Because a person hanging on a tree is cursed by God, the cross of Jesus became a stumbling block to Jews.

See also Anti-Semitism.   *Otto Betz*

CURIOUS BIBLES.

The term "curious Bibles" is used of two types of Bibles: those that are noteworthy because of a typographical error or a peculiar translation, and those with an unusual format.

Oddities in Printing and Translation. In spite of the extreme care in proofreading Bibles, typographical errors have been found in them since the beginning of *printing history. In the 1562 folio edition of the Geneva Bible of 1560, there is an error in Matthew 5.9, which reads "Blessed are the place makers" instead of "peace makers"; hence this edition has been called the "Whig Bible." The same edition has another error in its indication of the contents of Luke 21: "Christ condemneth the poore widdowe" (for "commendeth"). Several editions of the Geneva Bible, issued by Robert Barker in London from 1608 to 1611, erroneously read "Judas" for "Jesus" at John 6.67. The first octavo edition of the King James Version (1612) reads at Psalm 119.161, "Printers have persecuted me without cause," instead of "princes."

A Bible issued in London in 1631 contains one of the most well-known typographical errors to date. This edition is known as the "Adulterous Bible" because of its omission of the word "not" in the seventh (sometimes numbered sixth) commandment, which then read, "Thou shalt commit adultery" (Exod. 20.14). For this mistake the printers, Robert Barker and associates, were fined £300 and ordered to suppress the thousand copies of the edition. Ironically, the same printers in 1641 published a Bible that omitted the word "no" in Revelation 21.1, so that it read, "And there was more sea."

John Fields of London published a Bible in 1653 that is marked by many careless errors, including the omission of "not" in 1 Corinthians 6.9, so that it reads, "Know ye not that the unrighteous shall inherit the kingdom of God?" In 1795, Thomas Bensley, also of London, issued a Bible in which Mark 7.27 read "Let the children first be killed" (instead of "filled").

The 1801 "Murderers" Bible was so named because of its use of "murderers" for "murmurers" in Jude 16. In Bibles printed in 1806, "fishers" in Ezekiel 47.10 is altered so that the text reads, "It shall come to pass that the fishes shall stand upon it." An edition of 1810 was dubbed the "Wife-Hater" Bible for its substitution of the letter *w* for *l* in Luke 14.26, so that the text reads, "If any . . . hate not . . . his own wife also."

More recent editions with noteworthy typographical errors include the first printing of volume 1 of the Old Testament published by the Episcopal Committee of the Confraternity of Christian Doctrine in 1950, in which Leviticus 11.30 includes the skunk as one of the animals that swarm upon the ground. The translation reads "skink," which is a type of lizard, but the typesetter mistakenly made an unauthorized "correction" and changed *i* to *u*. Psalm 122.6 of the 1966 *Jerusalem Bible* instructs its readers to "Pay for peace" instead of "Pray." A less obvious error in the New American Bible's first edition of 1970 omits the last verse of the letter to the Hebrews. Early printings of the 1990 New Revised Standard Version omitted the words "having ten horns and seven heads" from Revelation 13.1.

In addition to typographical errors, unusual or eccentric translations can make an edition noteworthy. Of course, many renderings are thought unusual because their use of archaic English strikes the modern reader as odd. For example, the traditional rendering "Is there no balm in Gilead?" (Jer. 8.22) appears with the word "treacle" in both the 1535 Coverdale Bible and the 1568 Bishops' Bible, and as "Is there noe rosin in Galaad?" in the 1609 Douai Bible. The use of the word "breeches" (for "aprons") in Genesis 3.7 earned the 1560 Geneva Bible and its later printings the name "Breeches Bible." (In fact, the fourteenth-century Wycliffe Bible used the same word.)

There are also twentieth-century English Bibles with eccentric renderings. In Ferrar Fenton's 1903 Bible, Acts 19.3 finds Paul and Apollos "by profession landscape painters" instead of tentmakers. In James Moffatt's revised edition of the New Testament (1935), two people sleep in "a single bed" [i.e., not a double bed] (Luke 17.34), while the first edition reads "the one bed." And, in the New English Bible (1970), Paul warns the Corinthian faithful to "have nothing to do with loose livers" (1 Cor. 5.9).

(*See also* Translations, *article on* English Language.)

Unusual Formats. There are many examples of printed Bibles in curious formats. One such grouping is hieroglyphic Bibles, which are children's picture books citing brief scripture verses, with some words of the passages represented by small pictures. The first English hieroglyphic Bible was printed before 1784, although similar volumes had already been published in Latin, German, and Dutch. A second printing, entitled *A Curious Hieroglyphic Bible*, appeared in London in 1784. Its subtitle is:

"Select Passages in the Old and New Testaments, represented with Emblematical Figures, for the Amusement of Youth: designed chiefly to familiarize tender Age, in a pleasing and diverting Manner, with early Ideas of the Holy Scriptures. To which are subjoined, a short Account of the Lives of the Evangelists, and other pieces, illustrated with Cuts."

This version of the Bible must have had popular appeal since it soon appeared in a number of editions and printings.

There exist two varieties of shorthand Bibles. The *New Testament in Shorthand*, prepared by Jeremiah Rich and issued in London in about 1665, used Rich's shorthand system throughout, except for the two dedication pages and the list of subscribers at the end. Another Bible in shorthand was published in 1904 in London by Sir Isaac Pitman and Sons Ltd., using the Pitman method.

The term "Thumb Bible" has been used to designate a synopsis, an epitome, or an abridgment of the Bible. Thumb Bibles are usually meant for children and are therefore printed in miniature volumes and decorated with pictures. The oldest recognized Thumb Bible, entitled *An Agnus Dei*, is also one of the smallest: it measures $1\frac{5}{16} \times 1\frac{1}{16}$ in (3.3 × 2.7 cm) and was issued in London in 1601. The book is made up of 128 leaves, and on each page is set about 6 lines of text, along with the running title and catch word. The text of this miniature volume, a rhymed account of Christ's life, was written by John Weever (1576–1632).

The second oldest and probably most well-known Thumb Bible is the *Verbum Sempiternum*, published in London in 1614. Presenting the Old and New Testament in versified summaries, this miniature Bible was the handiwork of John Taylor (1580–1653). *Verbum Sempiternum* was still being reprinted well into the 1800s. The first American edition (labeled "The Twelvth Edition, with Amendments") of this particular miniature Bible was published in Boston in 1786, with dimensions of $2\frac{1}{2} \times 1\frac{1}{2}$ in (5.4 × 3.8 cm). The page facing the title page reads,

"Reader, come buy this Book, for tho' it's small,
'Tis worthy the perusal of all."

Only in 1727 was the Thumb Bible published in prose. Printed in London by R. Wilkin and entitled *Biblia or a Practical Summary of ye Old & New Testaments*, this edition comprises close to three hundred pages (with sixteen engraved plates) and measures $1\frac{7}{16} \times 1\frac{5}{16}$ in (3.6 × 2.4 cm).

Longman and Co. of London seem to have originated the term "Thumb Bible," which is found on the title page of an 1849 edition. Most likely this name was borrowed from General Tom Thumb (Charles Stratton), the famous midget who visited England with P. T. Barnum in 1844. Thumb Bibles were also printed in the eighteenth and nineteenth centuries in France, Germany, Holland, and Sweden. In all, almost three hundred separate editions are known.

In 1896 the Glasgow University Press photographically reduced the complete Oxford Nonpareil Bible (Authorized Version). David Bryce and Son of Glasgow and Henry Frowde of London issued it in a printing of 25,000 copies. This version is made up of 876 pages, each of which measures 1⅝ × 1⅛ in (4.2 × 2.8 cm). In a pocket inside the front cover a magnifying glass was provided. In the same year Bryce and Frowde also published a facsimile edition of the New Testament that was even smaller, just ¾ × ⁹⁄₁₆ in (2 × 1.5 cm), and there have been many other miniature editions.

Two other curious Bibles deserve mention. The first, published in London in 1698 by Benjamin Harris, is best described by its title: *The Holy Bible in Verse, Containing the Old and New Testaments, with the Apocripha* [sic]. *For the Benefit of Weak Memories. The Whole Containing above one thousand lines, with Cuts.* In 1988, Tyndale House Publishers reprinted Kenneth Taylor's *The Living Bible, Paraphrased* (1971; *see* Paraphrases), with the books of the Bible arranged in alphabetical order, so that the volume begins with Acts of the Apostles, and ends with the book of Zephaniah.

Bruce M. Metzger

CURSE. A curse, the opposite of a *blessing, is the pronouncement of evil on someone or something. In the Hebrew Bible, nouns and verbs associated with the Hebrew roots ʾlh, ʾrr, and qll are all translated by the English word "curse." While the meanings of these three roots are related and can be interchangeable, a separate treatment of each will highlight the full range of meanings of the word "curse."

The root ʾlh occurs most frequently in legal contexts, associated with an oath and the protection of legal rights. Pronouncing a curse on a potential thief will protect property. A curse pronounced on an accused person will, if it takes effect, establish the person's guilt. Pronouncing a curse on anyone who may disobey enforces a command by persons in authority. Pronouncing a curse on anyone who may break a treaty guarantees loyalty to a treaty. It is in this last sense that curse is used in connection with Israel's *covenant with the Lord, which has similarities to a treaty. In all these senses, the curse is understood as conditional, that is, efficacious only if some legal right or agreement has been violated. Sometimes a person may be referred to as a curse, meaning that such a person is in so calamitous a situation that he or she embodies the consequence of a curse that one might wish on another.

The root ʾrr occurs most frequently in formulas that begin "Cursed be . . ." (Deut. 27.15–25; 28.16–19). In these situations, the formula is spoken by a person in authority and is directed against a subordinate. This formula functions as a way of maintaining stability within the community. Pronouncing a curse on one who has acted in ways that violate accepted social responsibility is a way of expelling that person from the community. In this sense, curse is also related to the maintenance of the covenant that the Lord made with Israel.

The root qll occurs in less technical situations; a curse can be made by private individuals against God or the king.

In the New Testament the general usage is similar. For Paul, those who adhere to the *Law are understood as being under the curse. Furthermore, it is Christ who, on the cross, became a curse in order to redeem those who live under the curse of the Law.

See also Anathema.

Edgar W. Conrad

D

DANCE AND THE BIBLE. The Bible has provided choreographers with themes and topics for their dances, and not always in a religious context: biblical characters—heroes and heroines, kings and sinners—and stories, often those with a compelling moral, provide excellent material for stage dance. They do not require copious explanatory program notes, and carry with them overtones and associations from childhood, as material learned at home or in religious education. The terse style of storytelling found in the Bible, often abounding in physical action and illuminating philosophical or moral issues, is well suited to the artistic ways and means available to the choreographer, who must deal with human movement to express aesthetic-kinetic ideas.

Salome, the daughter of Herodias who danced before Herod Antipas, is perhaps the biblical character most often encountered in the annals of choreography. She has danced onstage from medieval passion plays right to the advent of modern dance at the beginning of the twentieth century, and she has continued to dance ever since.

In 1462, René, the king of Provence, organized a choreographic religious procession called "Lou Gue" in which there was a "minuet of the Queen of Sheba," along with other biblical dances. In 1475, the Jews of the Italian town of Pesaro used the Queen of Sheba as part of

their choreographic presentation at the wedding feast of the ruler of the region.

There are only a few examples of biblical subject matter to be found in the early French court ballets of the sixteenth and seventeenth centuries. One is *Les balet* [sic] *de la Tour de Babel,* chosen perhaps because God does not appear in the story at all, and the various languages are easily represented by folk dances from diverse countries.

Audiences, as well as creators of classical ballet, regarded their art as profane, if not altogether sinful and sacrilegious, and biblical subjects are rarely found in it. The revolutionaries of modern dance —Isadora Duncan, Maud Allen, and Loie Fuller, to name a few—who brought modern dance from their native America to Europe in the first decade of the twentieth century, had no such qualms, and soon a whole flurry of Salomes occupied the dance stage.

Many other biblical figures also attracted modern choreographers. Loie Fuller used the diaphanous veils and lighting effects she invented to depict the waters in *Miriam's Dance* and *The Deluge.* Ruth St. Denis and Ted Shawn choreographed a "Salome" dance, *Jephthah's Daughter,* and their ballet *Dancer at the Court of Ahasuerus* (the story of Queen Esther) in the 1920s.

Classical ballet choreographers of the early twentieth century also turned to biblical subjects. Michel Fokine created his *Legend of Joseph* in 1914 for Diaghi-lev's Ballet Russe, and George Balanchine composed *The Prodigal Son* for the same company in 1929. Kassian Goleizovsky choreographed his innovative *Joseph the Beautiful* for the Experimental Stage of the Bolshoi Ballet in 1925. Even such philosophical writings as the book of Job served choreographers, as in Ted Shawn's *Job, a Masque for Dancing* in 1931 in the United States, and *Job* (1931) by Ninette de Valois, the founder of the British Royal Ballet.

For many leaders of American modern dance, such as Lester Horton, José Limón, and Martha Graham, the Bible was a chief source of inspiration. In particular, Graham's *Embattled Garden* and Limón's *There Is a Time* are the most perfectly wrought biblical choreographies of our time.

Not surprisingly, Israeli choreographers make frequent use of biblical themes and characters. Since the beginning of Jewish immigration to Palestine in the early part of the twentieth century, choreographers have often turned to the Bible for subjects. In the 1930s, the Russian-born ballerina Rina Nikova founded her Biblical Ballet company in Jerusalem. Several of her students were girls who had immigrated from Yemen. She soon discovered the special dance rhythms of Yemenite Jews. The teacher thus became her pupils' student, because she realized that their movement vocabulary suited the biblical stories she endeavored to depict in her works much better than did the European *danse d'école*.

Jewish-Yemenite dance traditions were also to play a decisive role in the work of the most important Israeli choreographer of her generation, Sara Levi-Tanai. She founded the Inbal Dance Theatre in 1949, and created many works based on biblical subjects, using traditional Yemenite tunes and steps to forge a personal, modern movement style that served her biblical ballets well.

The connection between ancient Yemenite artistic tradition and biblical choreography has created a commonly held fallacy, that Yemenite dance is somehow representative of dance in biblical times, of which we know little despite the many instances of dancing in the Bible. There are no less than eleven biblical Hebrew terms for dance, but hardly any further evidence that modern choreographers could use when dealing with biblical subjects.

Biblical themes also served as a source of inspiration for Israeli choreographers who since the 1940s had staged pageants, often at the very sites of the biblical events they dealt with. They combined biblical texts, music, and mass movement, in the manner and stage techniques devised by Rudolf von Laban and influenced by the "Theater of the Masses" in Soviet Russia in the 1920s and 1930s, for the kibbutzim (collective settlements). These were biblical multimedia events, staged before the term had been coined.

There is scarcely a modern choreographer of note who has not dealt with biblical materials. In recent times these include John Neumeier, Jiri Kylian, Anna Sokolow, and Laura Dean, in addition to those already mentioned. Perhaps one of the reasons modern dance artists have turned to biblical subjects is that there are so many female dramatis personae in the Bible, providing the choreographers with roles for the women in their companies.

While the Bible provides a wide cultural common denominator for all of western culture, for Israel it is in a special sense a national heritage; hence the wealth of Israeli choreographic works based on it. The Bible is indeed an excellent libretto for choreography, providing the artist with moving metaphors, in both religious and nonreligious contexts.

Giora Manor

DAY OF ATONEMENT. Known in Hebrew as *yôm (ha)kippūr(îm)*, the Day of Atonement is the most solemn festival in the Jewish religious calendar. It is celebrated on the tenth day of the seventh month, Tishri (= September/October). The name is found in Leviticus 23.27–28; 25.9 and is explained in Leviticus 16.30: "for on that day the Lord will make atonement [*yĕkappēr*] for you to purify you from all your sins." Leviticus 16 describes the elaborate rites performed by the high priest in the Temple at Jerusalem. The priest drew lots between two goats, one of which was presented as a sin offering to God, and the other dispatched to Azazel in the wilderness. It was only on this day that the high priest entered the holy of holies, the most sacred part of the *ark of the covenant was situated. He would enter bearing incense whose fragrance symbolized God's forgiveness of the sins of Israel.

In antiquity, as well as today, Yom Kippur was considered a festival of spiritual accounting. Leviticus 16.29, 31 ordains that "you shall afflict yourselves." This term was interpreted to signify a day of *fasting when all food and drink were avoided. Tradition has added to these abstentions other deprivations, such as refraining from bathing, the use of cosmetics, and sexual intercourse. The people spend the day within the synagogue reciting and chanting a specially composed liturgy, the core of which includes confessional prayers, thanksgiving hymns, and petitions to God for favor in the coming year. According to Leviticus 25.9–10, Yom Kippur was the day of the jubilee year (i.e., the fiftieth year) when slaves were freed, debts canceled, and land returned to its original owners. This aspect of the ancient festival is preserved in the modern collection of pledge contributions for the assistance of those in need.

Jewish tradition regards Yom Kippur as a day of judgment. On this day God passes judgment on the past deeds of every individual and decrees who shall live and who shall die during the ensuing year. The judgment process actually begins ten days before Yom Kippur, on the first day of Tishri, or Rosh Hashanah, the Jewish New Year, and reaches its culmination on Yom Kippur.

Even after the early Christians ceased to observe the day of fasting, some of the symbolism of Yom Kippur was retained in certain formulations. Note, for example, such New Testament expressions as "the blood of Christ" or "the *day of judgment," as well as the parallel made in Hebrews 9.1–14.

See also Feasts and Festivals.

Ben Zion Wacholder

DAY OF JUDGMENT. The "last day," the end of the present world, when God or his agent will preside over a final, universal judgment of the living and the resurrected dead. A definitive assessment of human actions will be made, and each person rewarded or punished accordingly.

Hebrew Bible. Neither the phrase "day of judgment" nor the full-blown apocalyptic *eschatology supporting it is found in the Hebrew Bible. But the cluster of ideas and images surrounding the *day of the Lord contribute significantly to its eventual development: the forensic character of "that day" when God will judge his enemies (Joel 3.2, 1, 14); its universal perspective, with judgment directed against both Israel's enemies, "the nations," and Israel herself, or at least the enemies of God in her midst (Isa. 2.6–19); and the opposing imagery of light and darkness (Amos 5.18–20), with far greater emphasis placed on the latter (Zeph. 1.14–16; the somber medieval hymn *Dies irae* draws its opening line from the Vulgate rendering of v. 15).

Early Judaism. The factors that lead eventually to the emergence of the idea of a final day of judgment in particular are as disputed as those that lead to apocalyptic eschatology in general. Some degree of foreign influence (Persian, Egyptian, and/or Hellenistic) is plausible, but difficult to prove. What is clear is that both the phrase "day of judgment" and its substance appear in a wide variety of Jewish texts of the Greco-Roman period, along with the first undisputed reference to the resurrection of the dead (*see* Afterlife and Immortality, *article on* Second Temple Judaism and Early Christianity). In Daniel, the link between resurrection and judgment is implicit. It becomes explicit in 1 Enoch, where the angel Raphael shows Enoch the places appointed for all human souls "until the day of their judgment" (22.4); this is "the great judgment" (22.5), "the great day of judgment and punishment and torment" (22.11) that will affect even the rebel angels. In these earlier strata of 1 Enoch, judgment will apparently come from God himself; in the later Similitudes, however, God's "chosen one" is repeatedly named as judge (45–55).

The apocryphal book of 2 Esdras (4 Ezra) contains the most coherent account of the day of judgment. Judgment day will be preceded by a temporary messianic kingdom, a week of "primeval silence" (7.30), and the resurrection of the dead. Only then will the Most High sit in judgment; both righteous and unrighteous deeds shall stand forth clear and unchangeable, and *paradise and *hell be disclosed. Without sun, moon,

or stars, noon or night, this "day" will in fact last "as though for a week of years" (7.43). During it, God will judge all nations, the few righteous and the many ungodly. This "day of judgment" will be definitive because it marks "the end of this age and the beginning of the immortal age to come" (7.43 *[113]*).

Other early Jewish texts that speak of a day of judgment include the Septuagint of Isaiah 34.8 (rendering the Hebrew for "day of vengeance"); Judith 16.17 (against the nations); Jubilees 5.10–14 (the great day of judgment that awaits the generation of the giants and all creation) and 22.21 (against Canaan and all his descendants); Testament of Levi 3.2–3 (the second and third heavens prepared to punish unrighteous humans and spirits at the day of judgment); and Pseudo-Philo's *Biblical Antiquities* 3.10 (following a pattern similar to that of 2 Esdras 7.30–33, 43 *[113]*).

New Testament. The New Testament references to the day of judgment are rooted in contemporary Jewish apocalyptic thought. This is evident from such texts as 2 Peter and Jude, in both of which the fate of the rebel angel Azazel is extended to his fellow rebels. In Jude 6, these angels are enchained "in deepest darkness for the judgment of the great day"; in 2 Peter 2.4, the rebels are to be kept in hellish pits "until the judgment" (expanded in 2.9 to "until the day of judgment"). And, as in 1 Enoch 22 and other texts, that same day of judgment will signal the "destruction of the godless."

In two noticeable respects, however, early Christian views of the last judgment tend to distance themselves from traditional Jewish apocalyptic. Judgment is now seen almost exclusively in individual rather than national terms, and the judge is increasingly identified as Jesus, returned to serve as God's agent (*see* Second Coming of Christ), rather than God himself. Both of these features are present in Matthew 25.31–46, where it is the *Son of man who sits on the throne of judgment, and where the nations are judged not communally but individually, based on their treatment of the needy. The second development leads also to an expansion in terminology particularly noticeable in Pauline literature. Alongside "the day" (Rom. 2.16; 1 Cor. 3.13), "that day" (2 Tim. 1.12; 4.8; cf. 4.1), and "the day of wrath" (Rom. 2.5), we find "the day of Christ" (Phil. 1.10; 2.16), "the day of Jesus Christ" (Phil. 1.6), the "day of the Lord" (1 Thess. 5.2; 2 Thess. 2.2), "the day of the Lord Jesus" (1 Cor. 5.5; 2 Cor. 1.14), and "the day of our Lord Jesus Christ" (1 Cor. 1.8). The forensic role of Jesus on the day of judgment becomes central in later Christian tradition. In the Apostles' and Nicene Creeds, Jesus "will come again (in glory) to judge the living and the dead"; and artists from Giotto and Michelangelo to William Blake have placed him at the center of their depictions of the Last Judgment.   *Paul G. Mosca*

DAY OF THE LORD. This phrase combines a strictly temporal reference to the day and a reference to the eternal (Lord). This combination, quite typical of the Bible, is an apparent contradiction that can be resolved either by giving priority to the temporal component (whether day or year)—thus imprisoning God within the slots on human calendars—or prioritizing the eternal component by thinking of this day as chosen by God to fulfill his purposes. This second option is characteristic of the Bible. The God of Israel, having created his people by sealing *covenants with them, retained authority to set a term to the period when their truancy or faithfulness would be disclosed. Typically, he would

choose a time that would surprise them, whether earlier or later than they expected. His verdicts also would be surprising, often condemnation where approval was expected, or vindication where the penitent expected punishment. The primary concern of God's spokespersons was not with the date of the accounting but with its certainty.

Often, the day of the Lord is announced as "coming." That verb denotes movement, not a movement of Israel toward a date on the calendar, but rather movement of God toward his people in order to call them to account. Where rebellion flourishes, prophets announce God's imminent coming to lay bare the secrets of hearts. Where loyalty flourishes in the midst of suffering, they provide consolation and courage by promising speedy intervention by the Most High. The approach of the day would thus be marked by both deep darkness and the shining of the dawn.

The frequent references to God's coming explain the flexibility in the use of terms. The same event could be announced as the hour, the day, the year, or the time (*see* Time, Units of). The importance of the event could be indicated by articles and adjectives: the day, that day, the great day, the last day. The fearfulness of God's judgment released an array of surreal images: lightning, thunder, earthquake, tidal waves, tumults among nations, all intended to express how terrible it is to fall into the hands of the living God. Sodom and Gomorrah become stock examples of destruction. It is impossible to organize or harmonize all pictures of God's wrath. But the expectations of doom could be reversed by surprising mercies.

In biblical as in later times, false prophets and false messiahs exploited desires to know in advance the signs of the times, but others stressed divine secrecy.

God's reckoning of time differs completely from human calculations. It was therefore wrong either to spread panic because of the day's nearness or to counsel despair because of its distance. The function of the references to the day was thus both to warn unsuspecting rebels to watch and to assure the faithful of the nearness of their salvation.

Early Christians commonly identified the biblical day of the Lord with the day of the *Son of man, when the risen Jesus would act as judge in the heavenly trial of his followers. The twelve are also pictured as sharing the throne of judgment. Some authors, however, understood the last days to have begun with the ministry of Jesus,   *Paul S. Minear*

DEAD SEA SCROLLS. Since 1947, hundreds of Hebrew and Aramaic scrolls have been discovered near the Dead Sea, at first in unorganized searches by Bedouins and later in orderly archaeological excavations. The main location where these scrolls were found is Qumran, roughly 10 mi (16 km) south of Jericho; other sites still farther to the south include Murabba'ât, Seelim, and Masada. Some of these locations are more inland, so that the term "Judean Desert Scrolls" is more appropriate than "Dead Sea Scrolls." In eleven caves at Qumran, hundreds of scrolls were discovered, some in jars and almost complete, such as the large Isaiah scroll from Cave 1, but others mere fragments, often very difficult to read. Their antiquity, disputed at first by a few scholars, is now beyond doubt, and dates between 250 BCE and 70 CE have been secured by carbon-14 tests, archaeological evidence, and paleography. The scrolls are kept in the Rockefeller and Israel Museums in Jerusalem, and only the major ones are shown to the public.

The caves in which the scrolls were found are located near the ruins of a settlement near the Dead Sea. These ruins (Khirbet Qumran) have been excavated; they consist of a walled site comprising various community buildings, such as a bakery, a potter's workshop, a dining hall, and possibly a scriptorium.

No external evidence on the settlement is available, but probably there was a close link between its buildings and the scrolls found in nearby caves. Some of the artifacts found near the scrolls are identical with artifacts found in the community buildings. Furthermore, the sectarian writings found in the caves describe the lifestyle of a community that would suit the buildings.

The identity and nature of the community of the scrolls has often been discussed by scholars, and most now agree that they are the Essenes described in ancient sources. The Essenes were an ancient Jewish sect with a status similar to that of the Samaritans, Sadducees, and early Christians, all of whom departed from mainstream Judaism, embodied in the Pharisees (*see* Judaisms of the First Century CE). While most of the Essenes lived elsewhere in Palestine, the Qumran group decided to depart physically from society when they chose to dwell in the desert of Judea. The characteristics of the Essenes (the origin of the name is unknown), described in detail by *Philo and *Josephus, agree in general with the evidence from the scrolls. These are of three types: sectarian compositions, apocryphal works, and biblical scrolls.

The sectarian compositions found in Qumran reflect a secretive community about whose life much is still unknown. The main information is found in the so-called *Manual of Discipline* (in Hebrew, "The Rule of the Community"), detailing the daily life, behavior, and hierarchy of the sect. The principal source for the history of the community is a letter supposedly written by its leader, the "Teacher of Righteousness," to the priests of Jerusalem, outlining points of difference between both groups (4QMMT). Other details can be learned from the *Damascus Covenant,* which tells about the beginning of the sect's existence, and from *pěšārîm.* The special laws of the community are outlined in the *Damascus Covenant* and in smaller legal collections. The sect's views are reflected especially in the *pěšārîm,* exegetical writings focusing on the relevance of biblical books to the sect. The *Temple Scroll,* the largest preserved scroll, rewrites the laws of the *Pentateuch in apparent agreement with some of the sect's views. The *War Scroll* depicts the future war of the "Sons of Light" (i.e., members of the sect) against the "Sons of Darkness." The sect's expectations and grievances are expressed in the *Thanksgiving Hymns.*

Among the scrolls found in Qumran and at Masada are several Hebrew and Aramaic *apocryphal and *pseudepigraphal works, previously known only in ancient translations or from medieval sources. Of these, the books of Jubilees, Enoch, Sirach, and the Testament of Levi are now known in their original Hebrew or Aramaic form.

A large group of scrolls found in Qumran and at other places in the Judean desert consists of biblical manuscripts, dating from 250 BCE until 70 CE. Similar scrolls from the beginning of the second century CE have been found in other places in the Judean Desert. These finds inaugurated a new era in the study of the text of the Hebrew Bible, previously known almost exclusively from medieval sources.

In eleven Qumran caves, roughly 190 biblical scrolls have been found, some almost complete and others very fragmentary. Different scrolls are distinguished by

their script. With the exception of Esther, all books of the Hebrew Bible are represented at Qumran, some by many scrolls (Deuteronomy, Isaiah, Psalms), others by a single copy. The great majority of the scrolls are written in the Aramaic script, while sixteen are written in the paleo-Hebrew (or Old Hebrew) script.

Most of the scrolls have the same spelling as the *Masoretic Text (MT), but a significant number are written with a previously unknown form of spelling, which frequently uses letters to indicate vowels. Some scholars argue that the scrolls displaying this special spelling were written by the Qumran scribes, for all the sectarian scrolls are written in this spelling as well. The biblical scrolls from the Dead Sea area show what the biblical text looked like in the last three centuries BCE and the first century CE.

Of similar importance are the new data about the content of the biblical scrolls, since different texts are recognizable. Some texts reflect precisely the consonantal framework of the medieval MT. Others reflect the basic framework of the MT, although their spelling is different. Still others differ in many details from the MT, while agreeing with the Septuagint or Samaritan Pentateuch. Some texts do not agree with any previously known text at all, and should be considered independent textual traditions. Thus, the textual picture presented by the Qumran scrolls represents a textual variety that was probably typical for the period.

Although most of the scrolls have been analyzed, the nature of the collection of scrolls found in the Qumran caves is still not known. While some scholars continue to refer to the contents of these caves as the "library" of the sect, others consider it a haphazard collection of works deposited there for posterity in the difficult days of the destruction of Jerusalem in 67–70 CE.

Because the nature of the collection is not known, it is also not clear how one should evaluate the fact that biblical, apocryphal, and sectarian works were found in the same caves. Probably this does not show anything about the sect's views, but some scholars believe that the sect's concept of scripture was more encompassing than the collection that eventually became the Jewish *canon.

Emanuel Tov

DEATH. The biblical concept of death is complex, like the reality it seeks to describe. Death is both natural and intrusive; it occasions no undue anxiety except in unusual circumstances such as premature departure, violence, or childless demise, and it is the greatest enemy facing humankind. In Genesis 3, death acts as punishment for primeval rebellion (*see* Fall, The). In the New Testament, one special death, that of Jesus, cancels every claim against guilty persons; hence each negative feature regarding death is balanced by its opposite. Ultimately, death is robbed of its power, and its elimination is anticipated.

Belief in the solidarity of the *family enabled ancient Israelites to accept death calmly, for in death a person simply slept with one's ancestors. Nevertheless, this sleep was subject to disturbance, prompting a cult of the dead and the effort to contact the departed. Official Yahwism condemned both, while implicitly acknowledging their efficacy. The conviction that a deed was met with an appropriate consequence gained ascendancy, particularly in prophetic and wisdom literature. This popular notion eventuated in an understanding of death as punishment, theoretically implying

that humankind could have lived forever. A *Ugaritic text, Aqhat, denies the seductive suggestion that a mortal could live forever. Such reflection about death, though rare, does occur elsewhere, especially in 2 Esdras 7 and in Paul (Rom. 5.12–21). A mythological idea of Death as combatant lies behind this development. Yahweh does battle with Mot, the Canaanite name for this foe, and subjugates the enemy. Henceforth death acts on orders from Israel's God, the ultimate source of good and evil. The result is a problem of monumental proportions, that of theodicy.

References to death in the Bible presuppose a worldview that differs from modern concepts. Life consists of well-being, and death signifies diminished life. Consequently, one must speak about degrees of death. A sick person, or a persecuted one, described the peril as death and characterized deliverance as emergence from death's grip; this convention clarifies much of the languages of the Psalms. A symbolic meaning of death thus developed. The Deuteronomist urges Israel to choose life, not death, and Ezekiel denies that God desires death for anyone. This powerful imagery for death carries over into the New Testament, where *baptism and discipleship are illuminated by speech about dying.

At first Israelites assumed that death was the end, at least of life as we know it. This somber message underlies the epic of *Gilgamesh, a story about a heroic king's efforts to obtain eternal life. Once water was spilled on the ground, none could retrieve it, to use a metaphor employed by the woman of Tekoa. Emerging individualism and harsh political realities forged a bold hope that a resurrection would take place, at least in rare instances. Greek belief in body and soul as separate entities enabled this hope to become strong conviction by Roman times (*see* Human Person).

Israel's theologians believed that God alone had authority to terminate life; those responsible for executing criminals acted in God's behalf. Suicide is rarely mentioned in the Bible, in contrast to texts from Egypt and Mesopotamia, in which suicide occurs in dire straits occasioned by shame or impending torture. In his misery Job entertains thoughts of suicide, and the author of Ecclesiastes has a fascination for death, but neither opts for early departure. Sirach recognizes that personal circumstances determine one's attitude toward death. Occasional death wishes occur—Elijah, Tobit, Jonah—and Paul confesses to having mixed feelings about death, which held many attractive features for him, in that he would then be with Christ.

*Apocalyptic thinking posits the dawn of a new age, a resurrection, and a final reckoning. The gospel of John views Jesus' presence as proof of the resurrection, and the book of Revelation proclaims the complete eradication of death, which Paul also declares. Christians therefore need not fear the isolation of death, for nothing can separate the believer from God. This attitude is not a denial of death, the plague of the human spirit, but a recognition of the sovereignty of the covenant of God despite the grim fact of death.

See also Afterlife and Immortality; Burial Customs.   *James L. Crenshaw*

DECALOGUE. *See* Ten Commandments.

DESCENT INTO HELL. The visit of a god or a hero to the underworld and the realm of death; in Christian contexts ascribed to Jesus.

Ancient Near Eastern and Greek myths know of several gods and heroes who had been in the underworld among the dead without being kept there. *Sumerian traditions include narratives of this kind about Enlil and Inanna, and in Babylonian form the motif was connected with the goddess Ishtar and the young god Tammuz. An old Egyptian text, called Amduat, depicts the sun god's journey through the underworld in a boat every night. Greek folklore cherished descent stories about heroes such as Heracles, Odysseus, Orpheus, and the daughter of Demeter called Kore or Persephone, though their visits to Hades served different purposes. Similar stories were known in the biblical world, but none of these examples are direct sources of descent motifs in the Bible.

In the Hebrew Bible, certain analogies to descent ideas appear in texts dealing with the struggle of the elect in the infernal gulfs and torrents of suffering and death. This *"de profundis"* motif is often found in the Psalms. The prophet Jonah had reason to sing a similar psalm.

In nonbiblical literature, the psalms of Qumran develop this concept of a descent into the infernal realm of suffering and death. Another form of the descent topic is found in apocalyptic teaching ascribed to Enoch. The patriarch is said to have received this message (1 Enoch 12.4–5, following the Greek text): "Enoch, you scribe of righteousness, go and tell those heavenly watchers who have left the lofty heaven [i.e., according to 1 Enoch 10.4, the fallen angels of Gen. 6.1–4, now bound in a dark prison] . . . : 'You will find neither peace nor forgiveness.'" Afterward the apocalypse describes visits of Enoch to the underworld.

In the New Testament some of the relevant biblical and nonbiblical Jewish texts were applied to Jesus. He was said to have presented himself as fulfilling the sign of Jonah. These and other reports presuppose or indicate that Jesus was in the underworld between his death and resurrection. Sometimes the descent was also described as implying a messianic activity under one of three different aspects: Hades was subdued; righteous people were delivered; Christ preached to the so-called spirits in prison and to all in the realm of death. These "spirits in prison" (1 Pet. 3.19) were meant to be understood as the fallen angels of Gen. 6.1–4, who in the Enoch tradition were treated as the initiators of paganism; the reference to Christ's going to them, therefore, was intended to strengthen the preceding exhortation to confess one's faith in front of Roman authorities.

These aspects inspired later theologians to develop doctrines of Christ's descent in corresponding ways. The affirmation "He descended into hell" first appears in the Aquileian Creed of Rufinus (ca. 400 CE); from there it gradually spread throughout the West and found a place in the Apostles' Creed.

See also Afterlife and Immortality; Hell.   *Bo Reicke*

DIVINATION. *See* Magic and Divination.

DIVORCE. In the Hebrew Bible the right of divorce is presupposed. However, like many other customs associated with family life (*see* Marriage), exactly how it was done and under what circumstances is obscure. It seems likely that Israel's practice with regard to divorce was broadly similar to that of its neighbors; certainly the laws on sexual offenses were very similar, so we can use other ancient Near Eastern laws to fill in the background to the biblical statements.

Although divorce was legitimate, it was evidently disapproved of. Genesis 2.24, the formula used at weddings ("I am [your] husband . . . forever"), and the elaborateness of the wedding ceremony itself all convey the hope that marriage would be for life. Malachi 2.16 probably reflects widespread popular antipathy to divorce. In practice divorce must have been quite rare, for it was not only socially reprehensible but expensive. If a man (normally only the husband could initiate divorce proceedings) wanted to divorce his wife for anything short of major sexual misconduct, he had to repay the dowry. This was the bride's wedding present from her father, usually larger even than the "marriage present" given by the groom's family. The dowry was given jointly to the bride and groom, but as long as the marriage remained intact, he had the use of it. However, on divorce he had to give the dowry in full to his wife and often make other large payments as well. This must have made divorce a rarity.

Laws explicitly dealing with divorce are rare. In two cases, perhaps cases in which the man has shown himself hotheaded, divorce is permanently prohibited. Some laws limit the right of a divorcée to remarry. The rules of Leviticus 18.6–18 covering the choice of marriage partners could affect divorcées as much as widow(er)s and the unmarried. But the most interesting law of all is Deuteronomy 24.1–4.

The purpose of this law is stated in v. 4, which prohibits a divorcée who has remarried from ever going back to her first husband should her second husband die or divorce her. Why this should be forbidden is obscure. Perhaps such a return would make the second marriage look like *adultery. Or perhaps because the first marriage made the couple as closely related as brother and sister (they had become one flesh), a second marriage would appear incestuous; similar principles underlie some rules in Leviticus 18.

This law also sheds light on the practice of divorce. It was initiated by the husband for whatever reasons he saw fit: "she finds no favor in his eyes" (Deut. 24.1; NRSV: "she does not please him"). "Some indecency" (NRSV: "something objectionable") is presumably something less than proven adultery, for which the death penalty was available. The husband had to give his wife a written statement of her divorce and put it in her hand. This protected her from an accusation of adultery should she later remarry, for the key phrase in a bill of divorce was "You are free to marry any man." Freedom to remarry is the essence of divorce, as opposed to separation.

By the first century CE this Deuteronomic law was the center of debate among the Pharisees. Some (the Hillelites) said it warranted divorce for any reason, for example, bad cooking. Others (the Shammaites) held that it allowed divorce only for serious sexual misconduct. According to Matthew 19 and Mark 10 Jesus was asked to comment on this controversy: "Is it lawful for a man to divorce his wife?" (Mark 10.2).

Jesus' reply dismisses the Mosaic divorce law as a concession to human sinfulness; the ideal expressed in Genesis (2.24) is that "the two shall become one flesh" and thus "what God has joined together, let no one separate" (vv. 8–9). In other words, divorce is wrong, whatever the *Law does to regulate it. According to Mark, Jesus opposed divorce more vigorously than any of the Pharisees. This is reemphasized in Mark 10.11: "Whoever divorces his wife and marries another commits adultery against

her," a revolutionary statement that puts wives on an equal basis within marriage.

Matthew's account of Jesus' teaching on divorce is geared more closely to the Jewish scene and more pointedly addresses the male chauvinism that blamed women for adultery and divorce. A man may commit adultery in the heart by looking lustfully at a woman, but by divorcing an innocent wife a man causes her to commit adultery. But Matthew also includes an exception clause that apparently modifies Jesus' total rejection of divorce in Mark: "whoever divorces his wife, except for unchastity, and marries another commits adultery" (Matt. 19.9; cf. 5.32). This has generated much discussion: what constitutes "unchastity," and does divorce after it allow one to remarry? The early church (up to 500 CE) took "unchastity" to mean serious sexual sin, typically adultery, but said that this did not allow the innocent party to remarry. Many Protestants, following Erasmus (1519), have taken "unchastity" to mean adultery, but suppose that remarriage is allowed. Many modern scholars take "unchastity" to mean marriage within the forbidden degrees of Leviticus 18, or premarital unchastity. This view sees the exception clause as specifying grounds for annulling a marriage. In this case remarriage would be allowed.

All views have their difficulties. Hardest to accept is that of Erasmus, since it makes Jesus' view little different from that of the Pharisees with whom he has just disagreed. It also fails to explain the disciples' astonishment at Jesus' harsh new teaching and the subsequent discussion of eunuchs, that is, single people who do not marry.

Paul quotes a word of Jesus opposing divorce and insisting on singleness for those who do separate. In the case of a marriage between a Christian and an unbeliever, Paul says the Christian may grant his or her partner a divorce, if the latter demands it. But he does not say that the Christian may then remarry.

Gordon J. Wenham

DREAMS. In ancient Israel, in Judaism, in the Greek world, and in the ancient Near East generally, dreams were frequently regarded as vehicles of divine *revelation, especially the dreams experienced by priests and kings. Although there is no clear example in the Hebrew Bible of this kind of revelation being sought intentionally, dreams with divine content often occurred at sanctuaries. In the book of Job, Elihu expresses the generally held view that dreams are an authentic means of divine communication. The dream was also a medium by which truth was conveyed to a prophet, though its value was thought to be inferior to revelation received from God at firsthand. According to Joel 2.28, the dreams of old men will form part of the universal and direct contact with God to be experienced in the last days.

In most cases, the content of the divine message is conveyed to the dreamer clearly and unambiguously, but in two cycles of stories—the Joseph stories and the Daniel narratives, both of which include dream phenomena reported by non-Israelites—the skills of experts or professional interpreters are required. These interpretative skills are God-given and involve an ability to construe the pattern of future events from symbolic features of the dream. In the Greek world, dreams were accorded similar respect, and subtly developed systems of interpretation were employed. Dreams and their interpretation, however, were not accepted uncritically by all. Both Jeremiah and Zechariah make scathing comments on empty or false dreamers, thus implying that the "word of the Lord" that came to a prophet in his intimate communion with God was superior to communication through dreams. A dreamer whose message encourages apostasy is, in the view of the Deuteronomic law, to be put to death. The fleeting and insubstantial character of the dream is occasionally remarked upon.

In the New Testament, interest in dreams is confined almost exclusively to Matthew's gospel, and especially its birth narratives. For Matthew, the dream is an illustration of divine intervention and guidance operating on Jesus' life from its outset; this emphasizes the distinctive Matthean theme that Jesus is God's chosen and anointed one. These dreams in Matthew 1 and 2 conform to the Greco-Roman dream pattern in which the contents of the dream usually are narrated as the dream takes place, whereas the standard pattern in the Hebrew Bible is to state a person "dreamed a dream" and then to give the contents only after the dreamer awakes. In Matthew 27.19, Pilate's wife reports to her husband the distress she suffered in a dream on account of Jesus, but the precise content of her dream is not given. In Acts, Paul receives instructions and encouragement in visions of the night, but it is not certain whether these are dreams or some other form of revelatory phenomenon.

David Hill

DRUNKENNESS. A state that is almost always viewed in a negative way. Wisdom literature associates intoxication with foolish, impractical acts, and the impropriety that emerges as a consequence is exemplified in the well-known stories of Noah and Lot. Kings are sometimes portrayed as being undone by their drunkenness, as is the case with Elah and Ben-hadad.

Drunkenness, frequently in a figurative sense, is a theme that recurs in the prophetic literature of Israel. On the one hand, the leaders of Israel (including prophets, priests, and kings) are portrayed as being drunk because their acts are viewed as irresponsible. On the other hand, those who experience the wrath of Yahweh are depicted as staggering and dazed as a drunkard. This image is applied to Israel, to the nations generally, and to specific nations such as Babylon, Nineveh, Egypt, and Moab. Those drunk with Yahweh's judgment are sometimes pictured as having drunk from the cup or bowl of his wrath and sometimes as being drunk with their own blood. Jeremiah 23.9 represents a unique image in the prophetic literature: Jeremiah likens himself, as a prophet of Yahweh overcome with the power of Yahweh's words, to a drunken man overcome with wine; note the daring application of the same image to Yahweh himself in Psalm 78.65.

In the New Testament, references to drunkenness and drunkards often occur in lists of vices, and, as in the Hebrew Bible, drunken behavior is viewed negatively. Those awaiting the *second coming of Christ should not be drunk. Paul admonishes the Corinthians not to be drunk at the *Lord's supper. In Revelation 17.2, 6, "to be drunk" is used in a figurative sense of Babylon.

See also Wine.   *Edgar W. Conrad*

E

EASTER. From Eostre, a Saxon goddess celebrated at the spring equinox. In Christianity, Easter is the annual festival commemorating the *resurrection of Christ, observed on a day related to the *Passover full moon but calculated differently in eastern and western churches.

In the Bible, the Passover (Hebr. *pesaḥ*, Grk. and late Lat. *pascha*, hence the adjective "paschal") is part of the divine order, Israel's annual commemoration of deliverance. For New Testament writers, Christ is the Christian Passover victim, and the Gospel presentation has often a Passover background; see Luke 2.41 and the synoptic passion narrative (Matt. 26.2 par.), according to which the Last Supper appears to be a Passover. In John there are three Passovers: John 2.13, which is associated with the cleansing of the Temple; John 6, where the feeding of the five thousand has paschal and eucharistic echoes (the synoptic accounts may also have a paschal origin); John 11–13; 18.28, 39; and 19.23–37, where Jesus dies on the cross, according to this Gospel's chronology, at the time when the Passover lambs were being slaughtered in preparation for the feast. Christ is thus the eternal paschal lamb (*see* Lamb of God).

Easter is therefore the Christian Passover, celebrated for some time on the night of the fourteenth of the Jewish month Nisan (Passover night), on whatever day of the week that date fell. This custom continued long in Asia Minor (as in Celtic Britain), with those maintaining it being called Quartodecimans ("fourteeners"), but in Rome Easter was observed on a Sunday from a date that is difficult to determine but earlier than 154 CE, when Polycarp of Smyrna, a Quartodeciman, on a visit discussed the different observances with Anicetus, head of the Roman church.

The transfer of Easter to the first day of the week was no doubt because Sunday had become the Christian weekly day for worship. That this was owing to the Lord's resurrection on Sunday is not provable but suggested strongly by the New Testament evidence and the absence of any convincing alternative theory. The first day of the week marks the discovery of the empty tomb, while on the same evening the meal recalls the Last Supper. See also John 20.1, 19 and 26, the last being the Sunday a week later, and Acts 20.7, which again suggests the custom of a Sunday evening Eucharist. Paul calls the Eucharist the *Lord's supper (1 Cor. 11.20); the word for "Lord's" recurs in the New Testament only in Revelation 1.10 in "the Lord's day." It was probably "the Lord's" because it was the day for the Lord's supper or Eucharist, at which the Lord had been physically present before his crucifixion, and especially on the day of his resurrection and subsequent days (to which Acts 1.4 and 10.41 probably refer), and invisibly ever since, anticipating his final coming.   *A. R. C. Leaney*

EASTERN ORTHODOXY AND THE BIBLE.
The Eastern Orthodox churches consider the Bible as the written memory of God's activity in history and of God's relationship to humankind. It does not reveal everything that God is or is not; in many respects, it is a mystery, and the main purpose it was written is so that human beings may believe and have life. There is much diversity in its accounts, style, chronologies, descriptions, poetry. But there is also unity, a centrality in its message and in its purpose. It introduces a linear approach to history and looks forward to fulfillments and the eschaton—the end of time.

As a partial memory recorded in history by human beings, the Bible cannot be understood divorced from the historical experience and the consciousness of the communities of believers, whether ancient Israel and Judaism or Christianity. It is for this reason that the Bible is considered the book of the community, depending on the community's authority and approval of its authenticity, its inspiration, and interpretation.

It was written for practical needs and under different historical circumstances. This means that the Bible is not the totality of God's word or *revelation. God's word has been revealed "in many and various ways" (Heb. 1.1), including the order and beauty of the cosmos, human conscience and natural law, the words of philosophers, poets, and prophets of many peoples, culminating in the words of the God-made-man, the incarnate *Logos of God. Thus, the *word of God can be discerned within but also outside the Bible. Natural revelation, however, is propaedeutic and preparatory to the supernatural, more direct revelation given through God's chosen prophets and finally through God's Son.

The first part of the Bible reveals that God exists, creates, and intervenes through signs and symbols, individuals, prophets and priests, kings and shepherds—in particular, through a people who serve as an example of God's providence and concern for humankind. From a Christian perspective, the Old Testament points toward a goal and a fulfillment. Its role was to prepare the way for the New Testament, which is viewed as the high point of God's revelation in Jesus Christ, who is the end of an era and the beginning of a new one.

Whether in the Old or the New Testament, divine revelation was recorded under the *inspiration of God's *Holy Spirit. But inspiration is understood in a dynamic way. The writers of the biblical books were not passive receivers of messages but energetic and conscious instruments recording the revealed message in their own styles, and through their own intellectual and linguistic presuppositions. For the Orthodox, inspiration *(theopneustia)* is an elevated state of being that makes it possible to grasp and record revelation. The Holy Spirit inspires the writers, but it is the writers who write and speak, not as mechanical, passive instruments but in full control of their senses. Thus, biblical authors may display human shortcomings, broad or limited education, and their own specific intellectual backgrounds.

For the Eastern Orthodox, then, the Bible is the inspired word of God in terms of content rather than style, grammar, history, or frame. Very few, if any, Orthodox theologians accept the word-by-word inspiration of scripture. It is for this reason that the Orthodox church has never had serious disputes concerning the application of the historical-critical method in its approach to exegesis and *hermeneutics.

The Canon and the Authority of the Bible. The Bible includes the Hebrew Palestinian canon of thirty-nine books; ten Deuterocanonicals or *Anaginoskomena* ("books that are read"; *see* Apocrypha, *article on* Jewish Apocrypha; Canon); and the New Testament of twenty-seven books.

The Greek translation of the Old Testament (Septuagint), including the Deuterocanonical books, was the Bible used by the early Christian community, and it remains the official text of the Eastern Orthodox church. The early church as a whole did not take a definite position for or against the Deuterocanonicals. Church leaders and ecclesiastical writers of both the Greek east and Latin west were not in full agreement. Some preferred the Hebrew canon, while others accepted the longer canon that included the Deuterocanonicals. The ambivalence of ecumenical and local synods (Nicea, 325 CE; Rome, 382; Laodicea, 365; Hippo, 393) was resolved by the Trullan Synod (692). It adopted deliberations of councils that had favored the shorter list, and decisions of other synods that had advocated the longer list. Ultimately, the Deuterocanonicals were adopted as inspired books, good for reading and spiritual edification and on occasions even as sources of doctrine. The most serious justification for the adoption of the Deuterocanonicals was their frequent use in the worship and life of the early church. Books such as Tobit, Judith, Wisdom of Solomon, and Sirach (or Ecclesiasticus) are frequently used in liturgical prayers and hymns.

The official text of the Old Testament used by the Eastern Orthodox churches includes the following Deuterocanonicals: 1 Esdras, Tobit, Judith, Wisdom of Solomon, Sirach, Baruch; 1–3 Maccabees; and the Letter of Jeremiah. Other Deuterocanonical texts such as Susanna, The Song of the Three Children, and Bel and the Dragon appear as parts of the book of Daniel. The canonicity of the Deuterocanonical books is still a disputed topic in Orthodox biblical theology.

The question whether or not the authority of the Bible stands above the authority of the church it serves is a serious theological issue. The prevailing opinion is that once the canon of the Bible has been established, its authority becomes absolute, but the church remains its continuous and watchful guardian. The Bible's inspiration, canonicity, and authenticity depend on the church's consent. The Bible is the book of the church. Revealed truth preexisted the written word, and the community in the sense of both the old and the new Israel (synagogue and church) preceded the writing of scripture.

The Orthodox Church continues in its teaching that revealed truth is incorporated in the apostolic tradition, in the decisions of the ecumenical councils, in the theological consensus of the church fathers, and in the sacramental life and worship of the church. The Holy Spirit that reveals the word of God cannot be confined to the pages of a book. Nevertheless, all facets of belief and life of the church have been saturated with the teachings of the scriptures. Doctrines, ethical teachings, and liturgical worship have scriptural foundations and are always in agreement with the scripture.

Ecclesial Authority and Biblical Authority. The distinction between revealed truth as written word and as tradition explains the reason why Eastern Orthodoxy emphasizes the importance of ecclesial authority. The church is the "pillar and bulwark of the truth" (1 Tim. 3.14); it proclaims and guards those divine truths, written and unwritten, scripture and tradition, which coexist in complete harmony with each other. The *ekklēsia* as a people called out by God to be God's instrument and witness existed long before the Bible's writing and codification. Whether as "the people of God" in ancient Israel or as "the new people of God" in the Christian church, it was God's people who first witnessed to God's mighty deeds in history through his prophets and finally his own Logos, who became human in order to save humanity. The Bible itself was produced within the *ekklēsia* for specific reasons and for the needs of its members. What was not incorporated in the book remained a fluid living testimony that found its way in the experience of the church as writings and commentaries of church fathers, prayers and liturgical texts, and decisions of ecumenical councils. The totality of that part of God's revelation necessary for salvation saturates the life of the church.

Notwithstanding this holistic understanding of revelation, the Bible still occupies the central position in the Orthodox church's faith and life. Doctrinal truths, ethical teachings, liturgical and prayer life all have biblical foundations. The Bible's *authority is not minimized by ecclesial authority. The church, however, remains the lawful custodian and authentic interpreter of revelation, whether it presents itself as holy scripture or sacred tradition. The indwelling Holy Spirit guides and directs the church, especially when it is assembled in a council, an ecumenical council in particular, which is the supreme authority on matters of doctrinal truth.

The Bible in the Worship of the Church and the Life of the Individual. Revelation through God's word in

prophecy, mighty deeds, and especially God's incarnate Logos, his teachings, death, and resurrection was relived by the early church assembled in worship. The human being is not only a rational animal but also a worshiping being. And worship has been of primary importance to Eastern Orthodoxy. Orthodox worship consists of the liturgy of the word and the liturgy of the mystery, the Eucharist.

The example was set by the early church. The believers devoted themselves to the teachings of the apostles, to prayers and the breaking of bread (Acts 2.42). It is not only symbolic that the book of the Gospels occupies the central place on the altar table; there is no service in the Orthodox church that does not include readings from the Psalms, prophets, and especially the Gospels and other New Testament books. Liturgical texts, hymns, and prayers are filled with biblical passages, or inspired and saturated with the spirit, images, and symbols of the Bible.

But on the same altar table we find the chalice, the tabernacle with sacred host. The liturgy of the word and the liturgy of the Eucharist are the basis of the sermons and catechetical instruction. Listening to the exposition of the written word and participating in the mystery within the community constitute the supreme religious experience for the Eastern Orthodox. The interpretation of scripture and the celebration of the Eucharist are the two principal bonds between the ancient and the ongoing life and thought of the Eastern Orthodox church.

With very few exceptions, Eastern Orthodoxy has always encouraged individual Bible reading for inspiration, edification, and the strengthening of the individual's spiritual life. "May the sun on rising find you with a Bible in your hand": these words of Evagrius Ponticus (d. 399 CE) summarize the patristic and traditional stand of Eastern Orthodoxy toward individual reading. But reading the Bible assumes a state of prayer and presupposes a sense of humility. The word of God is at once easy to understand and mysterious.

The Bible is everyone's book but not for everyone's interpretation. Subjective interpretation, which may lead to misunderstanding and extreme individualism, should be subject to the objective interpretation of the church. Subjective interpretation, usually the task of the pastor or preacher, is expected to rely on the objective exegesis of the church's theology. And there is no authentic theology outside the historic experience of the church and its teachings. It is not possible for the modern believer and the church collectively to turn their back on past centuries of accumulated wisdom and historical investigation—hence the emphasis on the value of the patristic mind and the biblical ethos of the church.   *Demetrios J. Constantelos*

EBLA. Tell Mardikh is located about 34 mi (55 km) south and slightly west of Aleppo in Syria. In antiquity it was called Ebla in cuneiform inscriptions. Naram-Sin, a conquering king of Mesopotamia in the twenty-third century BCE, records that he captured and burned Ebla.

The Italian archeologist Paolo Matthiae began work at the site in 1964 because of its size, monumental city walls, and prominent acropolis; in 1974–1975, he discovered about fifteen thousand cuneiform tablets dating from around 2300 BCE. The script is Mesopotamian cuneiform, but the language is, as a rule, Eblaite, a Semitic dialect intermediate between Babylonian and Northwest Semitic (which includes *Hebrew).

Ebla was a commercial city-state and cultural center that included a school of learned scribes who trained students in the arts and sciences not only to write the administrative records for the palace and temples but, more generally, to master and transmit a rich tradition. The brief "Age of Ebla" is contemporary with the dynasty of Sargon of Akkad (to which Naram-Sin belonged) in Mesopotamia and the Old Kingdom in Egypt (hieroglyphic names and titles of Chefren of Dynasty IV and Pepi I of Dynasty VI have been unearthed at Ebla).

From Ebla students were sent abroad to cities like Mari; and scholars, such as a mathematician from the Mesopotamian city of Kish, were also brought to Ebla. Textbooks in various subjects (including bilingual vocabularies, religion, and geography) were used at Ebla in slightly different editions than those used in Mesopotamia.

The Ebla archives have changed our concept of the background of biblical history. It used to be thought that, before the Israelites, Canaan (or Syria-Palestine) was relatively primitive, with a nomadic, or seminomadic, population. Canaan was thus regarded as a sort of cultural backwash of Mesopotamia and Egypt. Ebla shows that this was not so: the largest library that has come down to us from this period is from Ebla. The Ebla archives show that the culture of the land was urbanized; nomads did exist but were not the controlling factor.

Because the Ebla archives predate Abraham, the high level of Hebrew civilization from its outset is historically explicable: the biblical Hebrews did not go through a "primitive" period in civilization or literature. Rather, they built on the high culture that had long existed in Canaan, when Abraham migrated from Haran to the Promised Land.
          Cyrus H. Gordon

ECOLOGY. *See* Nature and Ecology.

ELECT, ELECTION. *See* Chosen People; Predestination.

ENGLISH LITERATURE. *See* Literature and the Bible, *article on* English Literature.

EPILEPSY. Epilepsy in its grand mal or major form was a well-known illness of the ancient world. Its frightening and bizarre nature seemed to defy anything other than a supernatural explanation, and it was frequently put down to the influence of evil spirits. The Greeks, however, referred to it as the "divine" or "sacred disease," considering its effects to derive from the activities of the gods; the Hippocratic school of medicine, on the other hand, considered that epilepsy was as much due to natural causes as any other illness. In view of the widespread occurrence of the disease, it is surprising that there are only two clear references to epilepsy in the Bible. There is a full account of the condition in the story of the epileptic boy (Mark 9.14–29 par.) and a passing reference at Matthew 4.24. In both cases, the disease is represented as being due to the influence of unclean spirits. Such a view mirrored contemporary thought, and in Palestinian Judaism in particular, there was a tendency to ascribe all illness to the influence of demons, although the rabbis were also aware of the familial nature of epilepsy and placed a ban on marrying a woman from an epileptic family.

The description of the epileptic boy at Mark 9, supplemented by the parallels in the other synoptic Gospels, provides such a full summary of the events of a grand mal epileptic seizure that any other diagnosis is unlikely. The account notes the immediate tonic phase of the fit with collapse and rigidity, followed by the clonic phase with its jerking convulsions, and finally a flaccid phase of deep coma before the eventual recovery of consciousness. Mark also notes the loss of weight and exhaustion characteristic of the severe form of the disease, with repeated and uncontrolled seizures. The danger to life and limb from falling into the fire or into water, which so distressed the boy's father, are well documented in such cases. In the phase of deep coma, even the most painful stimuli may elicit no response from the patient, and severe burns may result. Other injuries are not uncommon during an unrestrained fit.

Both Mark and Luke emphasize the demonic elements of the story, but Matthew plays down this interest and uses the verb *selēniazetai*, meaning "to be moonstruck" (a word occurring only here and at Matt. 4.24 in the New Testament). The verb is derived from the concept that epilepsy was under the influence of the moon, a view that persisted at least to the seventeenth century in Europe. All three versions of the story, however, preserve the tradition that Jesus ordered an unclean spirit to leave the boy in order to effect the cure.

The Markan account provides the additional information that the boy was also deaf and dumb. It is likely that this represents a conflation of two separate incidents, but if the tradition is accurate, it suggests that the boy may well have suffered from some severe congenital handicap, of which epilepsy was but one sign. Although epileptiform convulsions may sometimes be a feature of hysterical (dissociative) states, together with deafness and mutism, such a diagnosis is untenable in this case in view of the classical picture presented and the presence of the self-destructive incidents that are not found in hysterical illnesses.

The only other certain reference to epilepsy is the note at Matthew 4.24, where again the verb "to be moonstruck" is used. The text links together those who were possessed, epileptics, and those suffering from paralysis. The two latter categories should probably be construed as being descriptive of the former, so that the phrase would mean "those who were demon-possessed, such as epileptics and paralyzed persons." Although there are other references to convulsive illnesses in the synoptic Gospels, these are not presented as epilepsy and are more likely to be due to functional causes rather than organic disease.

Paul's "thorn in the flesh" (2 Cor. 12.7) has also been identified with epilepsy by some scholars. It is unlikely that this would have been idiopathic epilepsy in view of the late onset, but its clear temporal relationship to an "out of the body" experience (2 Cor. 12.2–4), possibly induced by the severe trauma of one of his many beatings or stonings, would suggest that post-traumatic epilepsy cannot be ruled out.

There is no clear evidence of epilepsy in the Hebrew Bible, although the reference to "moon stroke" in Psalm 121.6 may possibly relate to epilepsy, particularly as it is placed in parallel to "sun stroke," another serious, at times, fatal condition. It has been suggested that Saul and Ezekiel may both have suffered from epilepsy, but their abnormal behavior patterns are best explained in other ways.

See also Exorcism; Medicine; Miracles.   *J. Keir Howard*

EPISTLE. *See* Letter-writing in Antiquity.

ESCHATOLOGY. The teaching concerning last things, such as the resurrection of the dead, the Last Judgment, the end of this world, and the creation of a new one. A fully formed eschatology with all of these features emerged only late in the development of biblical traditions.

During the period of the Israelite monarchy (tenth to sixth centuries BCE), some hoped that a descendant of David would one day conquer all of Israel's enemies. They envisioned a righteous king in David's line governing a continually expanding kingdom of righteousness and peace. No Israelite king attained this messianic ideal.

The eighth-century prophet Amos predicted the fall of the northern kingdom of Israel, utilizing the image of the *day of the Lord. This had been understood as a time when God defeated Israel's enemies, but Amos transformed the motif into one of judgment against Israel itself. The Lord indeed had a day when he would defeat his enemy, but the enemy was now his own wayward people. The book of Amos ends with a promise of a new era of salvation after the time of judgment. Amos, then, is an example of prophetic eschatology; he looked for an end—not the end of the world as in later *apocalyptic literature, but the end of Israel. Beyond this end, there would be not a new world but a new period of blessing.

In 722 BCE the Assyrians crushed the northern kingdom, and in 587/586 BCE the Babylonians destroyed the southern kingdom of Judah. In the subsequent exilic period new prophetic voices arose. An anonymous prophet, known as Second Isaiah, promised a glorious return of the Jews to the land. Ezekiel also looked to a time when the Jews would return home. A supernatural river would flow from the rebuilt Temple eastward into the saline waters of the Dead Sea, making it a freshwater lake where healing trees would grow. Ezekiel foretold the transformation of ruined Judah into a new Eden and an eschatological battle in which the nations would gather against Israel and be defeated by God.

Toward the end of the sixth century, the Jews were released from captivity. But in the Israel to which they returned, conditions were far from paradisiacal. Yet they held on to the prophetic visions. During the postexilic period, the prophets Haggai and Zechariah encouraged the rebuilding of the Temple. They also stimulated messianic hope by putting their confidence in Zerubbabel, a Davidic descendant, whom they apparently expected to rule with the imminent arrival of God's kingdom. But the nations were not overthrown, the *kingdom of God did not materialize, and Zerubbabel was not crowned king. Messianic hope had to be deferred.

As time went on, some persecuted members of the Jewish community became pessimistic about an earthly kingdom of God and looked for salvation from above through direct intervention from God. This led to the development of apocalyptic eschatology, found in the Isaianic apocalypse (Isa. 24–27) and Third Isaiah (Isa. 56–66). These chapters list the following end-time events: a great cataclysm; a judgment accompanied by heavenly portents; the Lord's arrival as king on Mount Zion; an eschatological banquet; the abolition of death and sorrow; the resurrection of the dead; the destruction of Leviathan, the chaos monster; the creation of a new heaven and a new earth; a return to *paradise; and eternal punishment for God's enemies.

The prophet Joel's vision of the day of the Lord is likewise filled with destruction. The sun, moon, and stars will cease shining, and there will be a great battle involving all the nations who gather against Jerusalem, but the Lord will come down with his warriors to judge them. On the positive side, God's spirit will be given to all.

The book of Daniel was written to encourage the oppressed Jews in the second century BCE. God's kingdom would soon appear, resulting in the deliverance of the saints and the destruction of the evil kingdoms of the world. In a vision Daniel saw "one like a son of man" coming in the clouds (Dan. 7.13). Daniel speaks of an abomination that makes desolate, a time of great tribulation, a resurrection of the dead, and a Last Judgment. But once again, the kingdom of God did not arrive.

Like the prophets, apocalyptists expected an end followed by a new era of God's saving activity. But the apocalyptists saw the end as complete. The judgment would be not only on Israel but on all nations. There would be not just a restoration of Israel in the land but a resurrection from the dead and the creation of a new heaven and a new earth, not just the defeat of earthly foes but destruction of the cosmic forces of evil. Many of these elements can be found in New Testament eschatology as well.

To understand Jesus, some scholars have argued for "consistent eschatology," meaning that Jesus' eschatological teaching as presented in the Gospels refers only to what will happen at the end of the world. By contrast, "realized eschatology" holds that Jesus understood the kingdom of God to have arrived with himself. Perhaps the best viewpoint is what has been called "inaugurated eschatology." Jesus brought the dawning of the kingdom of God. Some aspects of God's reign were present in him, but other elements of the kingdom would not appear until the very end.

Jesus is described as announcing the near arrival of the kingdom of God. By casting out demons, Jesus manifested his power over Satan and showed that the kingdom had begun. Yet there would also be a future arrival of the kingdom in all its fullness. In the eschatological discourse found in Matthew 24–25 (par.; also called the synoptic apocalypse), the signs of the end are given: false prophets and false messiahs, wars, famines and earthquakes, intense persecution of Jesus' followers, apostasy, and the worldwide preaching of the gospel of the kingdom. Daniel's predictions of the abomination that makes desolate and the period of great tribulation will be fulfilled. Joel's vision of the failure of sun, moon, and stars will also come to pass. These signs will be followed by the appearance of the *Son of man in heaven (understood as Jesus himself) coming in the clouds with great power and glory accompanied by the gathering together of his chosen ones out of all the earth. According to the Gospels, Jesus' eschatological teaching also included a resurrection of the dead and a final judgment resulting in eternal life for the righteous but eternal punishment for the unrighteous.

Paul's eschatology emphasizes the resurrection. As Jesus first rose from the dead, so his followers will be raised when he comes again. As a guarantee of the coming resurrection, God has given the *Holy Spirit.

The book of Revelation is the main eschatological work of the New Testament. From Daniel it utilizes the great tribulation, the coming of the Son of man, and the resurrection and final judgment. Like Joel it contains signs of the sun, moon, and stars. Third Isaiah's influence can be seen in the new heaven and new earth. The living waters and the return to paradise with the tree of life of Ezekiel are alluded to. The eschatological battle is from the books of Ezekiel and Joel. The prophetic day of the Lord becomes "the great day of God the Almighty" (Rev. 16.14). Revelation also draws on messianic tradition, identifying Jesus as the son of David, a conquering king.

For the writers of the New Testament, Jesus' followers are situated between the inauguration of the kingdom of God and its consummation. In the meantime, they are to be busy preaching the gospel, doing good works, and purifying themselves.

See also Afterlife and Immortality; Biblical Theology; Day of Judgment; Second Coming of Christ.

William B. Nelson, Jr.

ETHICS. Biblical ethics is inalienably religious. Reflection on issues of moral conduct and character in scripture is always qualified by religious convictions and commitments. To abstract biblical ethics from its religious context is to distort it.

Biblical ethics is unyieldingly diverse. The Bible contains many books and more traditions, each addressed in a specific cultural and social context to a particular community facing concrete questions of moral conduct and character. Biblical ethics does not provide an autonomous, timeless, or coherent set of rules; it provides an account of the work, will, and way of the one God, and it evokes the creative and faithful response of those who would be God's people. The one God of scripture assures the unity of biblical ethics, but there is no simple unitive understanding even of that one God or of that one God's will. To force biblical ethics into a timeless, systematic unity is to impoverish it.

The Torah. The one God of scripture stands behind the formation and continuation of a people as liberator and ruler. The story was told in countless recitals of faith: the God of Abraham heard our groaning when we were slaves, rescued us from Egypt, and made us a people with a covenant.

The *covenant of God and the people was like an ancient suzerainty treaty, acknowledging and confirming that God will be their great king and they will be God's faithful people. Like other suzerainty treaties, the covenant begins by identifying the great king and reciting his works, continues with stipulations forbidding conflicting loyalties and assuring peace in the land, and ends with provisions for periodic renewal of the covenant and assurances of faithful *blessings upon faithful observance and *curses upon infidelity.

This story and covenant provided a framework for the gathering of stories and stipulations until the literary formation of the *Torah or *Pentateuch, the first five books of the Bible, and its acceptance as having Mosaic authority.

"Torah" is often translated "law," and much of it is legal material. Various collections can be identified (e.g., Exod. 20.22–23.19, the Book of the Covenant; Lev. 17–26, the Holiness Code; Deut. 4.44–28.68, the Deuteronomic Book of the Law) and associated with particular social contexts of Israel's history. The later collections sometimes included older material, but it is not the case that the whole Law was given once as a timeless code. Rather, the lawmakers were evidently both creative with, and faithful to, the legal traditions.

There are two forms of *law, casuistic and apodictic. The casuistic regulations are similar in form and content to other Near Eastern law codes. The apodictic prohibitions, rejecting other gods and marking out the boundaries of freedom (and so securing it), seem an innovation.

There is no simple differentiation in the Law between ceremonial and civil and moral laws. All of life is covenanted.

Ceremonially, the Torah struggles against the temptations to commit infidelity in foreign cults and nurtures a communal memory and commitment to covenant. Civilly, the Torah is fundamentally theocratic, and the theocratic conviction that the rulers are ruled too, that they are subject to law, not the final creators of it, has a democratizing effect. Morally, the Torah protects the *family and its economic participation in God's gift of the land, protects persons and property (but persons more than property), requires fairness in settling disputes and economic transactions, and provides for the care and special protection of the vulnerable, such as widows, orphans, sojourners, and the poor. This last characteristic is perhaps the most remarkable (though it is not absent from other ancient codes), but it is hardly surprising, given the story that surrounds the stipulations.

The legal materials never escape the story and its covenant, and "Torah" is, ultimately, better rendered "teachings." The narrative and covenant preserve the responsiveness of obedience to the Law; gratitude then stands behind obedience as its fundamental motive. The story, moreover, forms and informs the Law and its use. The concern about the vulnerable reflects the story of one God who heard the cries of slaves. And the stories of Moses as the champion of the oppressed were intended to shape the use of the Law by any who honored its Mosaic authority.

The narratives of the Torah, it needs finally to be said, were morally significant in their own right; artfully told, they nurtured dispositions more effectively than the stipulations themselves. The Yahwist, for example, had told the stories of the ancestors not only to trace the blessings of David's empire to God but to evoke the readiness to use the power of empire to bless the subject nations.

The Prophets. The one God who rescued and established a people visited them in the prophets. They came always with a particular word for a particular time, but the word they brought was always related to covenant. Their "Thus says the Lord" was the familiar language of diplomacy in the ancient Near East for the announcements of a messenger of a suzerain. The prophets were not social reformers, nor were they necessarily skilled in the craft and compromise of politics; they were messengers of the great king and announced his word of judgment.

The sum of that judgment was always the same: the people have forsaken the covenant. Concretely—and the message of the prophet was always concrete—some specific *idolatry or injustice was condemned as infidelity to the covenant. The infidelity of idolatry was never merely religious. The claims of Baal involved the fertility of wombs and land as well as a theory of ownership. The prophet's announcement of God's greater power freed the people to farm a land stripped of divinity but acknowledged as God's gift, and bound them to leave the edges unharvested for the poor. The infidelity of injustice was never merely moral, for faithfulness to the covenant acts justly, and the welfare of the poor and powerless is the best index of fidelity and justice. So the prophets denounced unjust rulers, greedy merchants, corrupt judges, the complacent rich, but they saved their harshest words for those who celebrated covenant in ritual and ceremony without caring about justice, without protecting the powerless, without faithfulness.

On the other side of God's judgment, the prophets saw and announced God's faithfulness to God's own good future.

God will reign and establish both peace and justice—not only in Israel but among all the nations, and not only among the nations but in nature itself. That future is not contingent on human striving, but it already affects human vision and dispositions and actions, readying the faithful even to suffer for the sake of God's cause in the world.

Wisdom Literature. The way and will of the one God can be known not only in the great events of liberation and covenant, not only in the great oracles of God's messengers, but also in the regularities of nature and experience. The moral counsel of the sage was not founded on the Torah or the covenant; reflection on moral character and conduct among the wise was grounded and tested, rather, in experience.

Careful attention to nature and experience allowed the wise to comprehend the basic principles operative in the world, the regularities to which it was both prudent and moral to conform. The one God is the creator who established and secures the order and stability of ordinary life. So the sage could give counsel about eating and drinking and sleeping and working, the way to handle money and anger, the way to relate to friends and enemies and women and kings and fools, when to speak and when to be still—in short, about everything that was a part of experience.

The ethics of wisdom literature tends to be conservative, for the experience of a community over time provides a fund of wisdom, but the immediacy of experience keeps the tradition open to challenge and revision. The ethics of wisdom tends to be prudential, but a little experience is enough to teach that the righteous may suffer and that there is no neat fit between morality and prudence (Job). The ethics of wisdom tends to delight both in the simple things of life, like the love of a man and woman (Song of Solomon), and in the quest for wisdom itself. But experience itself teaches the hard lessons that wisdom has its limit in the inscrutable and that the regularities of nature and experience cannot simply be identified with the cause of a covenanted god (Ecclesiastes).

Wisdom reflects about conduct and character quite differently than the Torah and the Prophets, but "the end of the matter," like "the beginning of knowledge" (Prov. 1.7), is a reminder of covenant: "Fear God, and keep his commandments" (Eccles. 12.13). That beginning and end keeps the wisdom literature in touch with the Torah; between that beginning and end, wisdom struggles mightily to keep Torah in touch with experience and covenant in touch with creation.

The New Testament. Jesus of Nazareth came announcing that the *kingdom of God was at hand and already making its power felt in his words and deeds. He called the people to repent, to form their conduct and character in response to the good news of that coming future.

To welcome a future where the last will be first (Mark 10.31), a future already prefigured in Jesus' humble service, is to be ready to be "servant of all" (Mark 9.35). To delight in a kingdom where the poor will be blessed is now to be carefree about riches and to give *alms. To repent before a kingdom that belongs to children, that is already prefigured in table fellowship with sinners, and that is signaled in open conversation with women, is to turn from conventional standards to bless children, welcome sinners, and treat women as equals.

Because Jesus announced and already unveiled the coming reign of God, he spoke with authority, not simply on the basis of law and tradition. And because

the coming reign of God demanded a response of the whole person and not merely external observance of the Law, his words made radical demands. So Jesus' radical demand for truthfulness replaced (and fulfilled) legal casuistry about oaths. The readiness to forgive and be reconciled set aside (and fulfilled) legal limitations on revenge. The disposition to love even enemies put aside legal debates about the meaning of "*neighbor." The ethics was based neither on the precepts of law nor the regularities of experience, nor did it discard them; law and wisdom were both qualified and fulfilled in this ethic of response to the future reign of the one God of scripture.

Jesus died on a Roman cross, but his followers proclaimed that God had raised him up in an act of power that was at once his vindication and the prelude to God's final triumph. Moral reflection in the New Testament always looks back to the vindicated Jesus and forward to God's cosmic sovereignty.

The Gospels used the traditions of Jesus' words and deeds to tell his story creatively and so to shape the conduct and character of the particular communities they addressed. Each has a distinctive emphasis. Mark represents Jesus as calling for heroic discipleship, ready to suffer and die and ready as well to live in ordinary relationships with heroic confidence in God. In Matthew, the Law holds: Jesus is presented as upholding the Law and as its best interpreter even as he demands a righteousness that "exceeds that of the scribes and Pharisees" (Matt. 5.20). Luke's emphasis falls on care for the poor, women, and sinners, as well as on the mutual respect due Jew and gentile in the community. John tells the story quite differently so that his reader might "have life" (John 20.31) and might know that this entails love for one another.

The letters of Paul make little use of the traditions of Jesus' words and deeds. Paul proclaims the gospel of the cross and *resurrection as "the power of God for salvation" (Rom. 1.16) to his churches, sometimes in the indicative mood and sometimes in the imperative. The indicative describes the power of God in the crucified and risen Christ to provide an eschatological *salvation of which Christians have the "first fruits" (Rom. 8.23) and "guarantee" (2 Cor. 5.5) in the Spirit. The imperative acknowledges that the powers of the old age still threaten Christians; so, "if we live by the Spirit, let us also be guided by the Spirit" (Gal. 5.25).

Reflection about conduct and character ought to be radically affected by God's power in the cross and resurrection. Paul provides no recipe for this new discernment, but some features are clear. Christians' self-understanding as moral agents was determined by their incorporation into Christ. Their perspective was eschatological; the Corinthian enthusiasts who claimed to be already fully in the new age were reminded of the "not yet" character of their existence, while the Colossians, tempted to submit again to angelic powers, were told that Christ was already Lord. Freedom and *love were values that provided tokens of the new age. The moral traditions of the church, the synagogue, and the Greek schools were not to be discarded, but selected, assimilated, and qualified by the gospel. Such discernment is applied to various moral issues: the relations of Jew and gentile, slave and free, male and female, rich and poor, the individual and the state. The judgments are not timeless truths in the style of either a philosopher or a code maker; they are timely applications of the gospel to specific problems in particular contexts.

The unyielding diversity of biblical ethics is only confirmed by other New Testament writings. The pastoral letters use common hellenistic moral vocabulary and urge commonplace moral judgment against the *gnostics. The letter of James is a didactic text collecting instructions into a moral miscellany. The book of Revelation provides a symbolic universe to make intelligible both the experience of injustice at the hands of the Roman emperor and the conviction that Jesus is Lord, and to make plausible both patient endurance of suffering and faithful resistance to the values of the empire.

Allen D. Verhey

EUCHARIST. *See* Lord's Supper.

EUROPEAN LITERATURE. *See* Literature and the Bible, *article on* European Literature.

EVERYDAY EXPRESSIONS FROM THE BIBLE. Over the centuries, biblical phrases and expressions have become part of the vocabulary of those for whose culture the Bible is a central text. Some idea of the Bible's influence on the English language may be gleaned from the following sample of everyday expressions, all of biblical origin, chiefly in the Authorized or King James Version (1611).

A person may be said to behave like the great I Am (Exod. 3.14), or to have "the mark of Cain" (Gen. 4:15). People are tempted to eat forbidden fruit (Gen. 2.17), desire the fleshpots of Egypt (Exod. 16.3), and give up something worth having for a mess of pottage (Gen. 25.29–34).

Yet "one does not live by bread alone" (Deut. 8.3), and finally each must go the way of all flesh (cf. Gen. 6.12; Josh. 23.14) and return to the dust (Gen. 3.19). For the moment, those who find themselves "at their wits' end" (Ps.

107.27) may still escape by the skin of their teeth (Job 19.20), but others find themselves in the position of a scapegoat (Lev. 16.8–10). Nevertheless, "a soft answer turns away wrath" (Prov. 15.1). Unfortunately, a leopard cannot change its spots (Jer. 13.23). The wicked sow the wind and reap the whirlwind (Hos. 8.7), and because they ignore the writing on the wall (Dan. 5.24), they are fated to "lick the dust" (Ps. 72.9). Inevitably "pride goeth . . . before a fall" (Prov. 16.18), and anything that hinders success is a fly in the ointment (Eccles. 10.1). The wise recall that life lasts "but threescore years and ten" (Ps. 90.10), and so they gird their loins (Job 38.3) and teach their children "the good and the right way" (1 Sam. 12.23). Such people know that "you can't take it with you" (cf. Eccles. 5.15), and that "there is nothing new under the sun" (Eccles. 1.9).

Everyday expressions from the New Testament are largely derived from the parables and other teachings of Jesus. Who has not known a good Samaritan (Luke 10.30–37), a person that will "go a second mile" (Matt. 5.41)? These individuals are "the salt of the earth" (Matt. 5.13) and often "turn the other cheek" (Matt. 5.38). Some seek the "pearl of great price" (Matt. 13.46), while others, like the Prodigal Son, waste their lives "in riotous living" (Luke 15.13). "No one can serve two masters" (Matt. 6.24). "A house divided against itself will not stand" (Mark 3.25), nor can "the blind lead the blind" (Matt. 15.14). It is useless to "cast pearls before swine" (Matt. 7.6).

In antiquity a "talent" was a unit of weight or money, but because of Jesus' parable of the talents (Matt. 25.14–30), the word has come to mean natural endowment or ability. To disregard these abilities is to hide one's light under a bushel (Matt. 5.15). Even those who have never opened a Bible recognize the *golden rule of doing to others as we would have them do to us (Matt. 7.12; Luke 6.31).

The letters of Paul are also a source of several expressions now in everyday use: "The letter kills, but the spirit gives life" (2 Cor. 3.6); "The love of money is the root of all evil" (1 Tim. 6.10); "to see through a glass darkly" (1 Cor. 13.12); "a thorn in the flesh" (2 Cor. 12.7).   *Bruce M. Metzger*

EVIL. In Israel's earliest traditions, the presence of evil in the world is taken for granted as a reality that is philosophically nonproblematic. There is no terminological distinction between moral evil and calamity, for the same Hebrew word *(ra^c or rā^{c}â)* is used for both. Evil is anything that is unpleasant, repulsive, or distorted.

Genesis 1 shows how in the beginning there already exists the darkness and the cosmic sea, pervasive symbols of evil requiring God's subjugation, and no attempt is made to explain their origin. God perceives the world as "very good" (Gen. 1.31), even though it also includes the tree of the knowledge of good and evil, along with a subtle serpent who encourages the consumption of its fruit. Although God subdues evil in the cosmos, a number of texts in the Hebrew Bible are not reluctant to identify God as the source of evil. A standard complaint when humans suffer is that God is the one who has brought the calamity on them. Since God was the undisputed master of creation, it was assumed that every occurrence was through his explicit command. It was not that God merely allowed evil to happen, for God directs evil through the mediation of supernatural beings who afflict, deceive, bring harm, and do evil in general at God's command. Both good and evil were in God's control, and he actively employed both to accomplish his ends. Although God is often depicted in conflict with evil, there is never really any doubt that God will be victorious. Philosophical dualism finds no place in biblical literature, for God has no equal, and the cosmic order that he endorses, although often in jeopardy, must inevitably be established.

There is, however, one place where evil exasperates God: the human heart, that is, a man or woman's intellectual, emotional, and spiritual center. Even here the Bible pictures God as able to manipulate humankind, but there remains a mystery that is not further explored, namely, the freedom that human beings have to direct their own hearts for good or evil.

Evil is not an intrinsic feature of the physical world, for everywhere in the Hebrew Bible creation is seen as good and submissive to the will of God. The story of Jonah is representative, for although even a prophet may stubbornly resist God, it is the fish, the winds, the plants, and the worm that dutifully cooperate. It is therefore not surprising that later *gnostic thought, which perceived the physical world as inherently evil, rejected the God of the Hebrew Bible as an evil being.

The notion that evil can characteristically be associated with a supernatural being opposed to God and God's people has roots in the Hebrew Bible but only becomes common in the New Testament. There this figure is appropriately called the "Evil One" and bears the distinctive appellatives "Adversary" (Hebr. *śāṭān*) and "Accuser" (Grk. *diabolos*). He is accompanied by a retinue of lesser supernatural creatures with a similar ethical orientation whose origins can be traced to rare references to "evil spirits," "deceiving spirits," or "evil angels" that do God's bidding.

In the New Testament, these beings are more explicitly responsible for a greater share of the evil in the world. When illness, tragedy, or calamity occurred in ancient Israel, one tended to see God at work; in the New Testament Satan and demons are generally seen as responsible. Humanity is locked in a struggle with these unseen beings who seek to crush the righteous and can manipulate human hearts. A climactic confrontation between the cosmic forces of good and evil at some time in the future will result in the eradication of all evil along with those creatures (human or otherwise) who aligned themselves with it.

Evil as a philosophical problem is never really addressed in biblical literature. Attempts in Judaism and Christianity to resolve the logical problem of the existence of evil in a world created by a compassionate, just, omnipotent, and omniscient God belong to postbiblical reflections on the text.

See also Suffering.   Samuel A. Meier

EXILE. In biblical studies, more than in the Bible itself, "the exile" looms large as a chronological hinge around 600 BCE. The decisive "preexilic" events of *covenant, *Exodus, and *kingship occupy far more space than the scanty postexilic events, but of the latter, Ezra, Haggai-Malachi, and the deuterocanonical books (see Apocrypha) are taken as the key to the final editing of the prophets and the *Pentateuch. Exile as a place was Babylonia; the earlier exile was rather an exchange of populations between the northern kingdom of Israel and subject areas of Assyria; mistrust of "the Samaritans" is justified by Jerusalemite biblical authors because of the "pagan" element thus mingled among them, and this mistrust is extended by postexilic returnees to those residents of Judah who had never gone into exile but had been ruled as a district of "Samaria."

The interchangeable Hebrew terms for exile are *gôlâ* and *gālût,* generally rendered in the Septuagint as "captivity" or "deportation." The chief deportations took place under Nebuchadrezzar in 597 BCE (2 Kings 24.14: ten thousand including all upper classes; different figures are given in Jer. 52.28–30) and in 587/ 586 (2 Kings 25.11–13: "all the rest," except the poorest). Historical details have been clarified by the Lachish ostraca and by Babylonian chronicles; also, the language of the decree of return conforms to usages attested in the Persian chancery. Dated oracles of Ezekiel fall during his life in Babylonia; he was a priest and his diction contributed to the original dating and identification of the exilic Holiness Code. Jeremiah describes the exile from within Judah (chaps. 50– 51 as Babylon's downfall and the restoration; chap. 52 a historical appendix). Isaiah 40–66 is the chief biblical portrayal of the restoration insofar as its inner unity and relation to Isaiah 1–39 can be clarified. The "law" of Ezra (7.6, 26; Neh. 8.2) was either the Priestly (P) code alone (its materials being largely early) or, more probably, its incorporation into a whole Pentateuch definitely edited toward the end of the exile. Deuteronomy also, and with it the reedited Joshua–Judges–Samuel–Kings, are varyingly related to exilic experiences; after Jerusalem and the Temple were destroyed, and David's last royal descendants executed, it could no longer be repeated that God's fidelity precluded abandoning his chosen people and land; but admission of guilt and of just punishment carried hope of restoration and a "new covenant" (Jer. 31.31).

Robert North

EXODUS, THE.

The Exodus, the escape of the Hebrews from slavery in Egypt under the leadership of Moses, is the central event of the Hebrew Bible. More space is devoted to the generation of Moses than to any other period in Israel's history, and the event itself became a model for subsequent experiences of liberation in biblical, Jewish, Christian, and Muslim traditions. The Exodus is ancient Israel's national epic, retold throughout its history, with each new narration reflecting the context in which it was rendered. The Exodus entails not only the actual events in Egypt but all those encompassed within the period from Moses to Joshua, from the actual escape from Egypt to the conquest of the land of Canaan, including the wilderness wanderings. This epic is not preserved in the *Pentateuch as such; within its boundaries the promise of land made to Abraham remains unfulfilled. But the structure of Pentateuchal narrative presumes it, and indeed the conclusion of the story is found in the book of Joshua, the beginning of the Deuteronomic history that has apparently displaced an earlier ending to Israel's original epic. The full story is also found in summary form in other passages, some of which are quite old.

Historical Context. The Bible itself is virtually devoid of concrete detail that would enable the Exodus to be dated securely. It names none of the Pharaohs with whom Joseph, the "sons of Israel," and Moses and Aaron are reported to have dealt. Egyptian records are also silent about the events described in the later chapters of the book of Genesis and the first half of the book of Exodus; they make no mention of Joseph, Moses, the Hebrews, the *plagues, or a catastrophic defeat of Pharaoh and his army. The first mention of Israel in a source other than the Bible is in an inscription written to commemorate the victory of the Egyptian Pharaoh Merneptah at the end of the thirteenth century BCE; there, Israel is associated with places in Canaan rather than in Egypt. Because of this lack of direct correlation between biblical and nonbiblical sources, scholars have to resort to indirect evidence in assigning a date to the Exodus. Two principal views have been proposed. The first associates the flight of the Hebrews with the expulsion of the Hyksos kings from Egypt at the end of the Middle Bronze Age (ca. 1550 BCE). First proposed by *Josephus (*Against Apion* 1.103), this date approximates the figure of 480 years from the Exodus to the dedication of the Temple by Solomon and, with some variations, is held by a minority of modern scholars. Biblical *chronology itself is, however, not consistent, and most scholars date the event to the mid-thirteenth century BCE, during the reign of Ramesses II, because of a convergence of probabilities, including the identification of the store cities of Pithom and Rameses with recently excavated sites in the Egyptian delta and the larger context of the history of Egypt and of the Levant.

The Narratives. The account of the Exodus in the Pentateuch is multilayered, being composed of various traditions, some very ancient, such as the "Song of the Sea" in Exodus 15, and the bulk a prose narrative combining the Pentateuchal sources J, E, and P, to be dated from the tenth to perhaps as late as the sixth century BCE. The existence of these traditions enables us to observe a virtually continuous process of revi-

sion; thus, for example, the place names vary, apparently reflecting those current when a particular tradition was set down.

Embellishment, heightening, and exaggeration can also be observed. The simplest account of the event at the Sea of Reeds is found in Exodus 14.24–25. This passage may be understood in its simplest terms as a summary of how a group of Hebrew slaves escaping on foot was pursued by Egyptian guards, who were forced to give up the chase when their chariots became mired in the swampy region east of the Nile delta. This account is ultimately transformed into a miraculous intervention of Yahweh at the sea, when through the agency of Moses he makes a path through the sea, with walls of water on both sides. Still later, in the Septuagint, the Hebrew phrase meaning "sea of reeds" is translated as "Red Sea," further enhancing the miracle. Likewise, the number of those escaping, according to Exodus 1.15 a small group whose obstetrical needs could be handled by only two midwives, becomes six hundred thousand men, as well as women and children, an impossible population of several million.

Another tendency is to mythologize. The escape of the Hebrews at the sea is recast as a historical enactment of an ancient cosmogonic *myth of a battle between the storm god and the sea, found also in biblical texts having to do with *creation (*see* Israel, Religion of). This mythology is explicitly applied to the Exodus in Psalm 114, where the adversaries of the deity are the personified Sea and Jordan River, who flee at God's approach at the head of Israel; Sea and Jordan are clearly related to Prince Sea and Judge River, the parallel titles of the adversary of the Canaanite storm god Baal in *Ugaritic mythology (note the echoes of this motif in the New Testament, in such passages as Mark 4.35–41 par.; Rev. 21.1). The adversaries of the God of Israel, however, are not cosmic but historical—the Egyptian Pharaoh and his army, and sea and river are not primeval forces but geographical realities.

The same historicizing tendency is apparent in the treatment of the *Passover, originally two separate springtime *feasts from different socioeconomic contexts now given historical etiology associated with the Exodus. The "festival of unleavened bread" was originally an agrarian pilgrimage feast in which the first spring harvest of barley was offered to a deity without being contaminated with older leaven. In the Exodus narrative, the unleavened bread is explained by the need for haste as the Hebrews left Egypt. Similarly, the slaughter of the firstborn lamb, originally an offering by pastoralists to the deity thought responsible for their flocks' increase, is linked to the protective mark of the lamb's blood on the doorposts of the Hebrews, which spared them from the last plague.

In a similar way, other laws and institutions that developed later in Israel's history were legitimated by placing their origins in the formative period of the Exodus; the formative period thus became normative. This is one way of understanding the large amount of legal and ritual material found in the books of Exodus, Leviticus, Numbers, and Deuteronomy: set in a narrative context, these laws and religious practices are thereby linked with the central event of the Exodus and with Moses, the mediator of the divinely ordained instructions.

In view of these multiple tendencies, it is impossible to determine with any certainty what may actually have occurred to Hebrews in Egypt, probably during the thirteenth century. Literary analysis of the narratives suggests that what may in fact have been several movements out of Egypt by Semitic peoples have been collapsed into one. But whatever happened, this event was also formative in the sense that ancient Israel saw its origins here. A group of runaway slaves acquired an identity that, against all odds, they have maintained even to the present. It is understandable, then, that the event would be magnified in song and story, in part to praise the God thought responsible for it. It is also understandable why the Exodus became a dominant theme of later writers, who saw in the events of their times a kind of reenactment of the original Exodus.

Allusions to the Exodus. *Hebrew Bible.* Much of biblical narrative can be seen as shaped by or alluding to the Exodus both by anticipation and in retrospect. Thus, the division of the waters and the appearance of dry land at *creation foreshadows the division of the Reed Sea; the allusion to the P account of creation in Exodus 14 is an interpretation of the Exodus itself as a new creation. Likewise, the brief story of Abram (Abraham) and Sarai (Sarah) in Egypt (Gen. 12.10–20) is a proleptic summary of the longer narrative of Israel in Egypt that will be told later in the Pentateuch: the two ancestors go down to Egypt as aliens because of a famine; subsequently, Yahweh afflicts Pharaoh and his house with great plagues so that the Egyptian ruler lets them go.

The linking of Exodus and Conquest in biblical poetry is elaborately developed in Joshua 3–4. The Deuteronomic narrative of the crossing of the Jordan River parallels that at the Reed Sea, as the conclusion to the narrative explicitly states.

Biblical literature as a whole is permeated by allusions to the Exodus. The prophet Elijah is described as returning in the darkest moment of his life to the mountain of God, called Horeb in Deuteronomic style, where the *theophany experienced by Moses is repeated, but with a difference: Yahweh is not in the wind, the earthquake, or the fire—all manifestations of his presence in Exodus —but in the "still small voice" (1 Kings 19.12). The prophet Hosea sees hope for Israel's restoration in a return to the wilderness, the scene of Israel's honeymoon with its God. Scholars have also seen echoes of the Exodus in such texts as Jonah and Psalm 23.

The most sustained set of references to the Exodus in the prophets is found in the collection of oracles attributed to Second Isaiah. Writing in the context of the Babylonian captivity in the sixth century BCE, this anonymous prophet foresaw a return of Israel to its land, describing it as a new Exodus. Yahweh, who had shown his power in the defeat of the primeval sea and at the Sea of Reeds, would act again to bring his people, in joy, through a wilderness to Zion.

Dead Sea Scrolls. The Essene community at Qumran in its sectarian writings continued the interpretive tradition of applying the experience of the Exodus to itself. These self-styled "covenanters" saw themselves as the new Israel, living in camps in the wilderness at the very edge of the Promised Land, preparing for the ultimate triumph of God after a war of forty years, reliving both Israel's original formative experience and that of the Babylonian exile, in fulfillment of the "new covenant" of Jeremiah 31.31.

New Testament. The appropriation of the Exodus as the model for prior and subsequent events in Israel's history was continued in the New Testament. The life of Jesus is frequently understood in the Gospels as a reenactment of Israel's experience. Luke 9.31 describes Jesus' passion, death, and resurrection as an

"exodus" (NRSV: "departure"), the subject of his conversation with Moses and Elijah, both associated with the original Exodus of Israel (see above). Among the *quotations from the Old Testament in the gospel of Matthew in which the evangelist explicitly describes Jesus as fulfilling, one identifies Jesus as the new Israel, come out of Egypt just as the old Israel had. There are many other allusions to events and figures of Israel's Exodus throughout Matthew's gospel. Jesus is represented as another Moses, rescued at an early age from persecutors. He gives his teaching in five major discourses like the five books of Moses (the *Torah), of which the first is a proclamation of the new law for the new Israel, the *Sermon on the Mount, just as Moses had proclaimed the original law at Mount Sinai. Like Israel in the wilderness, Jesus' followers are fed miraculously in a deserted place. The gospel of John carries this *typology further by identifying Jesus with the Passover lamb, an equation made earlier by Paul and later considerably amplified in the book of Revelation. Paul also identifies Christ with the rock from which water miraculously flowed in the wilderness.

Postbiblical traditions. It is not surprising that a similar correspondence was made between the experience of ancient Israel and the life of the Christian. *Baptism is understood as a personal exodus from slavery to sin to a new life of holiness made possible by passage through water; in the Roman liturgy the second reading of the ritual for blessing the baptismal water during the Easter vigil is Exodus 14.24–15.3. Thus, Christians, like Moses, behold the "*glory of the Lord" unveiled (2 Cor. 3.16–18). Likewise, at death, a traditional prayer asks that God save the soul of the dying person as he once saved Moses from Pharaoh. The Christian Eucharist is directly descended from the Passover service, because the Last Supper of Jesus was itself a Passover meal; the bread (often unleavened; *see* Leaven) and the wine of the Passover assume a specifically Christian symbolism, but the older Exodus themes are still present (*see* Lord's Supper).

In Islam, the *Qur³ān and subsequent traditions echo the biblical account of the Exodus in their description of the Hejira, the flight of Muhammad from Mecca to Medina.

The self-identification with the ancient community of Hebrews has continued into modern times. Various groups experiencing oppression have identified themselves with the Hebrew slaves in Egypt. Throughout the centuries of persecution and attempts at extermination, Jews have seen in the original Exodus a reason for hope: the God who had saved their ancestors would also save them. In the Diaspora, since the Roman destruction of Jerusalem in 70 CE, the longing for a return to the land of Israel has been expressed by the words "Next year in Jerusalem!" at the end of the Passover meal. Exodus symbolism was also adopted by the Zionist movement, especially in the aftermath of World War II and the *Holocaust, and continues to be used by Jews seeking to emigrate from oppressive situations.

In the ideology of the Puritans immigrating to the "New World," the Exodus also served as a model and a divine guarantee: once again a divinely chosen group had escaped from oppression across a body of water to a new Canaan, a "providence plantation"; note the many biblical place names used in New England and throughout the United States. This conviction has continued to shape the American self-image, notably in the notion of "manifest destiny": the view that the Americans of the United States are a chosen people is common-

place in American political discourse. Ironically, in the early nineteenth century, after the founding of Liberia, American blacks used the same imagery in their spirituals; the "river" to be crossed was the Atlantic Ocean, but in the opposite direction from the Pilgrims, and Africa became the goal of their journey, the "greener pastures on the other side."

Since the latter part of the twentieth century, the Exodus has been paradigmatic for liberation theology, a radical Christian movement of Latin American origin whose goals are political and social reform. Liberation theology has been criticized for its appropriation of the Exodus as sanction for views and actions espoused for other, quite legitimate, reasons. The appeal to biblical authority is highly selective and raises complicated questions: how, for example, can a God who rescues the Hebrews from Egyptian bondage be reconciled with one who immediately thereafter gives explicit commands in which the institution of slavery is not just presumed but condoned? Still, there is no denying the power of the Exodus story as a model for hope and even action to counter oppression. (*See* Politics and the Bible.)

Michael D. Coogan

EXORCISM. A belief in the existence of evil spirits or demons and their ability both to cause disease and to take possession of people has been common to most societies. Side by side with such beliefs there has usually been a recognition of the power of certain individuals to exorcise such spirits, freeing the sufferer from their malign influence. Such concepts occur in the Bible, though relatively infrequently; they are almost entirely restricted to the accounts of the ministry of Jesus in the synoptic Gospels.

There are no unequivocal examples of exorcism in the Hebrew Bible. David's use of music to calm Saul, who is described as being troubled by "an evil spirit from Yahweh" (1 Sam. 16.14–23), bears none of the characteristics of the later accounts of exorcism with their essential underlying component of a violent "casting out" of an evil spirit. Saul's behavior suggests a severe manic-depressive psychosis with marked paranoid overtones that gave rise to episodes of impulsive homicidal violence. Music could be expected to have a beneficial effect on the depression, but not on the manic paranoia.

In preexilic biblical traditions, the idea of *evil cosmic forces separate from, and against, the rule of God is not prominent. By the first century CE, however, Satan was generally viewed as ruler of the present age, having gained temporary control of the earth and holding sway over its kingdoms (a view reflected in the New Testament at Matt. 4.8–9; Luke 4.5–6; John 14.30; 2 Cor. 4.4; Eph. 6.12). This power was exercised in individual lives through demons, either in a general malevolent influence or by direct "possession." In the latter instance, the demon had to be "cast out," and thus exorcism became a dominant feature of first-century Judaism, with the professional exorcist having a recognized status. The Pharisees apparently played a significant role as adepts in exorcisms, and there is a passing reference to this at Mark 12.27. The approach was strongly magical (see Magic and Divination), using invocations and spells (foreshadowed as early as Tobit 6.17–18). In later rabbinic literature and other sources, individual demons responsible for specific illnesses are named.

Exorcism was an undisputed feature of the ministry of Jesus. The various references in the synoptic Gospels are little more than vague and generalized comments about the healing ministry of Jesus, often being simply editorial link statements in the narrative. Six specific cases of exorcism are mentioned: the Capernaum demoniac; the Gerasene demoniac; the dumb demoniac; the blind and dumb demoniac; the Syrophoenician demoniac; and the epileptic boy. The evangelists seem to have been selective in their use of the terminology of exorcism, reserving it for conditions inexplicable for them in other ways and outside the general categories of illness that Jesus healed. Although clinical details are meager, there is suggestive evidence that the synoptic exorcisms were restricted to *epilepsy and the abnormal behavior patterns that occur in hysterical (dissociative) states.

Outside the synoptic Gospels, exorcism is mentioned only in Acts: twice in general terms (5.16 and 8.7) and twice of specific incidents (16.16–18 and 19.11–19). There are no further references in the New Testament; it is noteworthy that the Jesus of the Fourth Gospel is not an exorcist, nor does he come into contact with "possessed" people. It should also be noted that in none of the discussions of spiritual gifts in the Pauline correspondence is mention made of exorcism. A general gift of healing is recognized, but there is no suggestion that this includes exorcism. The synoptic tradition is unique in suggesting that Jesus gave the twelve authority to exorcise, and this appears to have been limited to his lifetime.

Exorcism in the Bible is thus essentially a feature of the synoptic Gospels in which it is presented as an eschatological activity of Jesus, either as evidence of the arrival of God's *kingdom or in preparation for its immediate appearance. His own explanation of the phenomenon, that he cast out demons through the spirit of God, underlines this, pointing to the arrival of the promised endtime and the power of that age. Outside the synoptic tradition, the New Testament sees Satan and his unclean spirits as decisively and finally defeated in the Easter event.   *J. Keir Howard*

F

FAITH. In the Hebrew Bible, forms of the noun *ʾĕmûnâ* or the verb *ʾmn* are usually translated as "faith" or "having faith/believing." Such faith can be expressed toward God, toward a human being, or toward both: "So the people feared the Lord and believed in the Lord and in his servant Moses" (Exod. 14.31). The terms are also used to express adherence to an idea or a set of principles: "I believe in your commandments" (Ps. 119.66).

There are other ways of expressing this kind of regard for, or confidence in, someone or something. In fact, forms of the verb *bṭḥ* are much more frequent in the Hebrew Bible but are usually translated "to trust" rather than "to have faith/believe." This difference can be explained on the basis of semantic development, but there are some instances where the meanings are very close: "He [Hezekiah] trusted in the Lord, the God of Israel" (2 Kings 18.5).

One of the best-known instances of faith in the Bible concerns Abram (Abraham), who asks how God would make of him a great nation when he was old and his wife was sterile. The Lord asserts that Abraham will indeed have offspring that will be as numerous as the stars in the sky. In response to this promise and against all tangible evidence, Abram has faith in God and is considered to be a righteous person (Gen. 15.6; NJV: "he put his trust in the Lord").

Abram's willingness to trust God in this and other situations makes him a primary example of the biblical concept of faith. His willingness to believe and to obey God is the fulfillment of the *covenant that God had made with him. Throughout the Hebrew Bible, Abraham's descendants struggle with the issue of how to continue as a faithful people. The Psalms rejoice in the faithfulness of God but lament the lack of faith shown by the people. Isaiah warns the people, "If you do not stand firm in faith you shall not stand at all" (Isa. 7.8), and Habakkuk states that "the righteous live by their faith" (2.4).

The Greek translation of the Hebrew Bible, the Septuagint, usually translates the *ʾmn* family of words with a form of the Greek word *pisteuein*, "to trust" or "to believe/have faith." This same family of words is used frequently in the New Testament. The author of the letter to the Hebrews defines faith as "the assurance of things hoped for, the conviction of things not seen" (11.1) and then goes on to list the great deeds that the people of Israel had accomplished "by faith" (11.4–40).

Paul also makes use of images of faith from the Bible, especially the faith of Abraham. In the process of justifying the mission to the gentiles, Paul argues that Abraham was said to be righteous by having faith in God before he was circumcised and therefore is the father of the gentiles who believe, as well as of the Jews.

The actual content of faith—what is believed—is described in different ways in Paul's letters. In Romans, *righteousness will be credited to those who have faith in God, who raised Jesus, and to those who believe in their hearts that God raised Jesus from the dead will be saved. Elsewhere Paul refers to believing "in Christ Jesus" (Gal. 2.16), but it can be argued that this is an abbreviation for "faith in God who raised Jesus."

Several times Paul refers to faith with a grammatical construction that can be interpreted either as "faith in Christ" or "faith of Christ" (Gal. 2.16, 20; 3.22; Rom. 3.22, 26; Phil. 3.9). Scholarly debate centers on whether Jesus is referred to in the first sense as the object of faith or in the second as an example of faith. The NRSV translation includes footnotes that offer the latter reading as an alternative. It has also been suggested that Paul is being intentionally ambiguous with the construction, leaving both possibilities open. In this case it is interesting to note that later documents tend to specify "faith in Christ," eliminating the possibility for ambiguity.

In the synoptic Gospels, faith is the operative factor in many of Jesus' *miracles. Jesus is impressed by the faith of the centurion and so heals his son. Jesus marvels at the faith of those who brought the paralytic man and tells the woman with a hemorrhage that her faith has made her well. When Jesus tells the father of a demon-possessed boy that "all things are possible to the one who believes/has faith," the man responds, "I believe; help my unbelief" (Mark 9.23–24).

John's gospel emphasizes having faith (always in the verbal form) throughout, and states its purpose as leading people to believe that Jesus is the Messiah, the *Son of God.

"The faith" as a descriptive term for Christianity is found most clearly in Acts and the deutero-Pauline material.

See also Justification.

Daniel N. Schowalter

FALL, THE. The Fall refers to the disobedience and the expulsion of Adam and Eve from the garden of Eden. According to the J account of *creation (Gen. 2–3), humanity—represented by Adam and Eve—initially enjoyed a life of ease and intimacy with God, but their desire to become "like gods" (Gen 3.5) led them to disobey God's prohibition against eating from the tree of knowledge. They were punished with expulsion from *paradise and condemned to a life of *suffering that was passed on to their descendants.

The biblical myth of the Fall is similar to other legends that contrast humanity's present state of suffering with an earlier time of perfection, a lost paradise or golden age. The biblical narrative is unique, however, in implying that humanity's degradation was indirectly caused by its own free choice.

The fall of divine beings played a central role in the writings of the *gnostics (second and third centuries CE), many of whom believed that creation and even human existence were caused by a precosmic error. According to the gnostics, the physical cosmos was a concrete nightmare from which the divine sparks of humanity sought to escape.

In the New Testament, Paul explained that Adam, the man of flesh, brought sin and death to the world while Christ, the second Adam and the man of spirit, brought life. Paul's view that Adam's fall introduced sin and death led Augustine (fifth century CE) to develop the doctrine of original sin: that Adam's fall perverted all humanity and that its effects were passed by hereditary transmission from generation to generation. The belief that Adam, as a corporate personality, was responsible for the sins of humanity was never adopted by Judaism and was resisted by Christian thinkers such as Pelagius and Julian of Eclanum (fifth century CE), but Augustine's interpretation of the Fall became the accepted doctrine of Catholic Christianity. Like all myths of a lost paradise or golden age, the story of the Fall, whether of gods or humans, is an index of humanity's yearning for a better world and an attempt to account for the problems of *evil and human suffering.   *Gregory Shaw*

FAMILY. The family in ancient Israel was a fluid and open community. The most common Hebrew terms (*mišpāḥā* and *bêt*, "house") can designate the single household unit, the wider circle of consanguinity, the clan, the tribe, and the nation. This concentric usage suggests the role of the basic family in shaping the larger community. Significantly, the *Passover, Israel's foundational ritual, was essentially a family celebration.

The basis of the family is *marriage, understood as a *covenant between the husband and wife. Although some texts imply a monogamous relationship, at least in earlier periods, polygamy was an accepted practice, enlarging the scope of the family. And in a broader sense, the extended family included other relatives (grandparents, grandchildren, siblings) as well as slaves, servants, and resident foreigners.

In the extended family (the "house of the father," Hebr. *bêt ᵓāb*), the authority of the father was the strongest cohesive force. He arranged marriages for his children, generally within the clan. His patriarchal power might require drastic action against worshipers of other gods. Nevertheless, the fifth commandment demanded "honor" for mother as well as father (Exod. 20.12)—perhaps very pertinent in a family that included adult offspring—and the book of Proverbs teaches the respect due equally to each parent.

The family provided one of the most commonly used analogies for the relationship between Israel and God, as father and also as mother (*see* Metaphors).

In the New Testament, *oikia* ("house, household") is the ordinary word for family, although *patria* (from *patēr*, "father") is also used. Disobedience to parents is a sin, and caring for one's family is strongly inculcated. Yet in the teaching of Jesus, his followers must give no more than second place to even the closest family ties; the true family of Jesus are those who do his father's will.

The primary use of the word *oikia* is in reference to the *church. The solidarity of the family as the building block of the spiritual family of God is evident in "household" conversions and baptisms. Not only is the whole church the household of God, but also most early Christian congregations were family or house churches, meeting in domestic buildings and led by the householders, including women and husband-and-wife joint leaders. This helps explain the prominence given in the New Testament to appropriate relations between individuals in the family, including masters and slaves. The letters in particular are full of metaphors drawn from family life, such as childhood, adoption, sonship, and inheritance.   *David F. Wright*

FAMILY BIBLE. A product of early modern Europe still in use today, a family Bible is any edition of the Bible that includes manuscript records of genealogical and other personal information, specific to the owners of the book over several generations. It also symbolically associates the scriptures with the ideal of the Christian family, an association that began in the Reformation, was perfected by seventeenth-century English Puritans and German Pietists, and was furthered by eighteenth-century Anglo-American evangelicals.

Through the medieval period, the costly process of copying manuscripts restricted private ownership of the Bible to only the most wealthy families. Between 1450 and 1600, however, the invention of *printing and the Reformation's vernacular *translations made it possible for many families to acquire and to read the Bible. Both Protestant and Catholic reforming theologies, moreover, emphasized biblical *authority and required a greatly increased knowledge of the Bible by the laity. So the newly available vernacular Bibles soon became objects of special veneration in which facts of family history might appropriately be inscribed.

In the seventeenth and eighteenth centuries, Puritan, Pietist, and evangelical Protestants prescribed ambitious programs of doctrinal catechesis and devotional prayer for family members. The family was viewed as a spiritual commonwealth in which parents were covenantally obligated to transmit the faith to their children. Popular devotional manuals like Philip Doddridge's *On the Rise and Progress of Religion in the Soul* (1745) recommended family prayer and parental exposition of the scriptures every morning and evening. This new physical presence and spiritual authority of the scriptures in daily household rituals encouraged pious families to record the events of their lives—births, baptisms, conversions, confirmations, marriages, deaths—on the pages of their Bibles.

In the nineteenth century the enormous success of the evangelical movement, especially in Victorian Anglo-America, fashioned the Bible into a cultural icon of spiritual identity, biological continuity, and family prosperity. Since 1800 virtually every English translation of the Bible has been published in a special family edition, with commemorative pages dedicated to genealogy, marriages, births, and family history, with ornamental bindings designed for prominent display in the home. The custom of keeping a family Bible continues to be observed, especially among evangelical Protestants in the United States.

Family Bibles serve scholars as unique sources for social and religious history, but their spiritual and emotional significance was well captured by an anonymous American evangelical poet, whose popular hymn, "The Family Bible," first appeared in *The Young Christian's Companion* (1826):

How painfully pleasing the fond recollection
    Of youthful connection and innocent joy,
While blessed with parental advice and
        affection,
    Surrounded with mercy and peace from
        on high.
I still view the chairs of my father and
        mother,
    The seats of their offspring, as ranged on
        each hand,
And the richest of books, which excels
        ev'ry other,
    The family bible that stood on the stand.

                                Stephen A. Marini

FASTING. Fasting in connection with *prayer, penitence, and preparation for new ventures has been practiced from early times in many cultures and religions. The Bible recognizes it as regular in mourning for the dead, expressions of penitence, intercession, and prayer for God's aid. Fasting was undertaken for personal reasons, as a national act in the face of calamity, or as a periodic liturgical observance; normally it involved abstinence from all food to show dependence on God and submission to his will. The great national and liturgical fast was that of the *Day of Atonement, but fasting was generally recognized, especially after the *exile, as a meritorious pious practice and as a potent aid to prayer. Later, the author of Isaiah 58 claimed that if fasting was to be of value, it must be accompanied by compassion and a concern for social justice.

Jesus accepted fasting as a natural discipline, and he is described as deliberately fasting before his *temptation and the start of his ministry, similar to the action of Moses. Jesus' disciples, in contrast to the disciples of John the Baptist and those of the Pharisees, appear not to have fasted (Mark 2.18–19): they were in the presence of "the bridegroom," a parabolic reference to the Messiah, so that fasting was inappropriate. But v. 20 envisages a time of fasting "when the bridegroom is taken away from them"; this verse was probably a creation of the evangelist to justify the church's custom of fasting on Good Friday. Certainly, fasting was regularly observed in early Christianity, and Mark 9.29 (NRSV margin) shows how copyists reflected the commonly held view of the connection between fasting and prayer.

In Acts 9.9, Paul is described as fasting before his *baptism, and this became the usual practice from very early times, both for the candidates for baptism and for other members of the church. As baptism was normally celebrated at *Easter, this prebaptismal fast was probably the origin of the Lenten fast, which lasted forty days in the time of Cyril of Jerusalem (late fourth century CE), corresponding to the length of Jesus' fast at the start of his ministry.   *John N. Suggit*

FEAR. Throughout the Bible, references to fear occur in nonreligious as well as in religious contexts, with two distinct areas of meaning. The first involves emotional distress and alarm with intense concern for impending danger or evil. Thus, the Gibeonites excused themselves before Joshua saying, "We were in great fear for our lives" (Josh. 9.24). In Genesis 9.2, animals are said to be afraid of people. The signs accompanying the coming of the *Son of man are said in Luke 21.26 to cause people to faint with fear.

The other area of meaning relates to allegiance to and regard for deity. Among the many expressions in the Bible for worshiping God are some metaphors pertaining to fear. These focus on *worship as an event of profound respect with the implication of awe. In Job 15.4, Eliphaz reprimands Job saying, "But you are doing away with the fear of God." The fear of God involves worshiping the Lord with deep respect and devotion. It is a religious expression and as such implies obedience, love, and trust (*see*, for example, Deuteronomy 10.12–13). "People who feared God" became an expression for the truly religious (Mal. 3.16; Luke 18.2; Acts 10.22). Closely related is the expression "the Fear of Isaac" (Gen 31.42), an epithet for God, meaning "the one whom Isaac worships."

The phrase "fear and trembling" expresses the same two areas of meaning denoted by fear. In Psalm 55.5 and Mark 5.33, the phrase expresses great emotional distress, while in Psalm 2.11 and Philippians 2.12 the phrase signifies religious devotion.   *Johannes P. Louw*

FEASTS AND FESTIVALS. Sacred feasts and festivals punctuated the calendar of ancient Israel. New moons were a function of a lunar system in which the month functioned as the basic unit for measuring *time. The Pesaḥ festival (*Passover) in the spring, on which unleavened bread was eaten, was historical in character, a commemoration of the *Exodus from Egypt. By contrast, the spring and autumn harvest festivals were seasonal celebrations linked to the agricultural economy of ancient Israel. All three annual festivals were occasions for pilgrimage (Hebr. ḥag).

How feasts and new moons were celebrated depended in great measure on where *sacrifices could be offered. Israelites seeking to celebrate these occasions fully were required to do so at a proper cult site; in other words, to undertake a pilgrimage to an altar (bāmâ) or temple. The Bible records a protracted movement toward cult centralization and the elimination of all local and regional cult sites. The doctrine that all sacrifice should be restricted to a central temple was to have serious practical implications for the scheduling of pilgrimage festivals and all occasions when sacrifices were offered.

In 622 BCE King Josiah of Judah issued a series of edicts, recorded in 2 Kings 22–23, forbidding all sacrificial worship outside the Temple of Jerusalem. Deuteronomy 12 restricts the offering of sacrifice to a single cult place (mā-qôm) to be selected by the God of Israel. It has recently been argued that the policy of cult centralization originated in the northern Israelite kingdom of the mid- to late eighth century BCE before its fall to the Assyrians in 722 BCE. The Judean king Hezekiah had attempted to implement this policy, but since he was succeeded by Manasseh, the heterodox king who ruled throughout most of the seventh century BCE, no progress was made in eliminating the bāmôt before the

time of Josiah. A young king who had returned to the Lord sincerely, Josiah acted effectively to eliminate places of worship throughout the land.

It is logical, therefore, to conclude that most of the significant changes in the celebration of Israelite festivals went into effect only after Josiah's edicts were promulgated and that most of them were heralded in Deuteronomy. Some scholars dispute this reconstruction, however, and date the priestly codes (P), which reflect basic changes in worship, to an earlier period.

The New Moon. The new moon is sometimes referred to as "the head of the month" (Num. 28.11; etc.). By all indications, the celebration of the new moon was an important occasion in biblical times. This importance may have diminished in time, since the growing importance of the *Sabbath eventually reduced reliance on the lunar calendar, introducing the week as a unit of time.

The account in 1 Samuel 20, set in the early monarchy, suggests that the new moon was the occasion of a sacred feast (zebaḥ) celebrated by the family. Fixing the precise time of the moon's "birth" was necessary for scheduling the festivals, whose dates are formulated as numbered days of the month. According to priestly law, the new moon was to be celebrated in the public cult by a triad of sacrifices—the burnt offering, the grain offering, and the libation, preceded by the purificatory sin offering. The new moon of the seventh month, in the early autumn (Tishri), enjoyed special status because it heralded the autumn ingathering festival, the main pilgrimage festival of the year. On that new moon, the ram's horn was sounded to announce the autumn pilgrimage. In later Judaism, the new moon of the seventh month became Rosh Hashanah, the Jewish New Year.

The Festival of Unleavened Bread and the Passover. The first pilgrimage festival in the spring commemorated the Exodus from Egypt. In the Book of the Covenant, the earliest of the law codes in the Torah, this festival is called "the pilgrimage festival of unleavened bread" (ḥag hammaṣṣôt; Exod. 23.15). It is preceded on the eve of the festival by the "paschal sacrifice" ([zebaḥ] pesaḥ; Exod. 12.21–13.10).

This festival began on the new moon of the month of ripening grain ears (ʾābîb) and lasted seven days, during which only unleavened bread was to be eaten (see Leaven). The pilgrimage occurred on the seventh day. On the eve of the first day the paschal sacrifice, consisting of a lamb, was offered by the family near its home. According to Exodus 12.8–9, it was roasted whole over an open fire, a practice still followed by the Samaritans. Blood from the sacrifice was poured on the threshold and then spattered on the lintel and doorposts with a twig of hyssop. The application of the blood expressed the theme of protection. The sense of the Hebrew verb pāsaḥ, from which Pesaḥ derives, has been misunderstood to mean "skip, pass over" (whence the name "Passover"), whereas it more properly means "to straddle, stand over," hence "protect" (Isa. 31.5). The God of Israel was pictured as standing over the homes of the Israelites in Egypt to protect them from the plague of the firstborn.

Egyptian bondage was symbolized by the bitter herbs, eaten together with the unleavened bread and the paschal sacrifice. This festival is a môʿed, "appointed time," a term that indicates its observance on the same date annually, and the same is true of the other annual festivals. In Deuteronomy 16.3 a rationale is given for the unleavened bread. It symbolized affliction, and its preparation was reminiscent of the hasty departure of the fleeing Israelites. Most significant in the provisions of Deuteronomy 16.1–8 is the requirement that the paschal sacrifice be offered at the single cult place selected by God and that it be prepared in the usual manner by boiling major portions of the meat in pots, with the rest of the victim burned on the altar.

The shift of venue from the home to the central sanctuary parallels the provisions of Josiah's edict proclaiming the celebration of the paschal sacrifice in the Temple of Jerusalem, something that, we are told, had never occurred before (but see 2 Chron. 30). The paschal sacrifice now did double duty as the festival offering of the first day. This is indicated by the composite term, "the sacred feast of the pilgrimage festival of the Pesaḥ" (Exod. 34.25).

According to Deuteronomy 16, the pilgrimage began with the paschal sacrifice. Israelites would rise the next morning and return home, continuing to eat unleavened bread for the remaining six days of the festival, and observing the seventh day in their settlements as a solemn assembly, on which labor was prohibited. The result of the Deuteronomic legislation was a brief pilgrimage that allowed farmers to return home at the busiest time of the year.

The priestly prescriptions for this festival reveal even further changes in its celebration. The date is the fifteenth of the first month (Nisan), preceded by the paschal sacrifice on the fourteenth, in the late afternoon. From the formulation of these priestly laws it is clear that the paschal sacrifice, like those offered on each of the seven days, of the festival, occurred in the Temple. On both the first and the seventh days there is to be a "sacred assembly" on which labor is forbidden. Numbers 28.19–24 specifies the offerings of the public cult. The difficulty implicit in ordaining a seven-day pilgrimage to a central sanctuary would be dealt with, as we will see, by deferring the second pilgrimage. Proclaiming both the first and the seventh days as sacred assemblies satisfied the earlier pilgrimage of the Book of the Covenant as well as the Deuteronomic pilgrimage of the first night.

The Spring Harvest Festival of the First Grain Yield. In the Book of the Covenant (Exod. 23.16) this festival is named "the pilgrimage festival of reaping" *(ḥag haqqāṣîr)*, that is, of the first yield of the barley crop. No specific date is provided in Exodus, but we may assume that it would occur quite soon after the Pesaḥ, early in Iyyar.

In Deuteronomy 16.9–12 we observe the dramatic effects of the Deuteronomic requirement of celebration at a central sanctuary: the spring festival of reaping is deferred seven weeks; thus, the festival is named "the pilgrimage festival of weeks" *(ḥag šābū'ōt)*. The Israelites were to count off a period of seven weeks and then present an offering of first fruits, now consisting of wheat, not barley.

The most logical reason for the deferral was the anticipated difficulty of undertaking two extended pilgrimages to a central temple at the busiest season of the agricultural year. Priestly law, represented by Leviticus 23.9–22, retains the deferral instituted by Deuteronomy. An earlier desacralization of the new barley crop is, however, ordained for the day of the original festival of reaping, soon after the Pesaḥ festival. In Leviticus 23 the spring festival of reaping is not designated a pilgrimage at all; the first fruits were merely to be delivered to the central temple from the Israelite settlements. This celebration, on the fiftieth day of the period of counting, was rendered more elaborate by including the "sacred gifts of greeting" *(šĕlāmîm* [v. 19;

NRSV: "sacrifice of well-being"]), along with loaves made of semolina wheat. The counting of seven weeks was to commence on a Sunday and end on a Sunday, seven weeks later, so that seven actual sabbatical weeks would have passed, not merely forty-nine days. The fiftieth day is designated "a sacred assembly," on which labor is prohibited. Numbers 28.26–31 prescribes a complete regimen of sacrifices to be offered in the Temple and it curiously no longer includes the "sacred gifts of greeting."

In summary, we observe major changes in the celebration, scheduling, and essential meaning of the spring festival.

The Autumn Pilgrimage Festival of Ingathering. In the Book of the Covenant (Exod. 23.16) the autumn festival is called "the pilgrimage festival of ingathering" *(ḥag hā'āsîp)*, namely, "when you gather in your products from the field." It was to occur "at the outset of the year," more precisely, soon after the start of the two-month period of ingathering, corresponding to Tishri-Marheshvan (September–October). Psalm 81.3 indicates that this festival began on the full moon, at the middle of the month, rather than on the new moon. The pilgrimage lasted one day.

Once again, Deuteronomy (16.13–15) introduces a dramatic change. There this festival is named "the pilgrimage festival of booths" *(ḥag hassukkôt)* and is scheduled to last seven days. It was to occur somewhat later than the ingathering, at the time when the produce of the fields, vineyards, and groves was processed, in the vat and on the threshing floor.

This autumn pilgrimage was the major event of the year, bringing large numbers of Israelites to the Temple. For this reason it was an appropriate time for the dedication of Solomon's Temple.

Leviticus 23, in two successive statements, elaborates on the festival of booths, which was a particularly joyous occasion. A rationale is provided for living in booths, namely, the conditions characteristic of the wilderness experience. Greenery was utilized to symbolize the fertility of the land, and an eighth day with a solemn assembly was added. Like Leviticus, Numbers 29.12–38 specifies sacrifices for all eight days, with the first and eighth days designated as days of rest.

A more realistic approach would seem to suggest that the theme of "booths" was introduced in Deuteronomy as a consequence of the restriction of pilgrimage to one central temple, which also accounts for the extension of the festival to last longer than initially intended. Dwelling in temporary booths became necessary for the numerous pilgrims arriving in the capital from all over the land and, in later times, from the Diaspora as well.

The Day of Atonement. The first reference to the *Day of Atonement (yôm hakkippūrîm) is found in Leviticus 16, which sets forth the rites of expiation and purification to be performed by the high priest in the sanctuary. The principal function of this day was the purification of the sanctuary and priesthood, in advance of the autumn pilgrimage festival.

The rites of expiation were quite elaborate, and they included the dispatch of the scapegoat into the wilderness, bearing the sins of the people. On this day, the high priest entered the Holy of Holies to seek expiation for sins. In Zechariah 7.5 this day is referred to as "the fast-day of the seventh month," and its importance seems to have increased during the exilic and postexilic periods, in the wake of the national disaster of 587/586 BCE. The postexilic prophet

whose words are preserved in Isaiah 58 emphasizes that the God of Israel wants more than cultic purification and sets down ethical, human goals whose pursuit alone may render the atonement process acceptable to God.

Purim. The book of Esther relates the saga of deliverance that accounts for the annual Purim feast on the fourteenth day of Adar (and, in some areas, on the fifteenth day as well). Set in the reign of Ahasuerus (possibly Artaxerxes I), the Persian ruler of the fifth century BCE, the story emphasizes divine providence over Israel, in which Esther, the queen, and Mordecai, the court counselor, foil the conspiracy of Haman, the wicked enemy of the Jewish people residing in the far-flung provinces of the Achaemenid empire. Jewish custom is to read the Esther Scroll on this occasion and to exchange gifts in celebration of deliverance.

Hanukkah. There is an additional festival, unmentioned in the Hebrew Bible, which became part of later Judaism. The generic word ḥănukkâ, "dedication," occurs in such passages as Numbers 7.10–11; Psalm 30 (title); and Nehemiah 12.27; but the festival of that name is first mentioned in 1 Maccabees 4.59 in its complete form as "the Dedication of the Altar" and referred to simply as "the Dedication" in John 10.22. Hanukkah is an eight-day festival whose celebration begins on the twenty-fifth day of Chislev and which was patterned after the Tabernacles festival of the harvest season, as is indicated by statements in 2 Maccabees 1.9, 18; 2.1; 10.6–8.

Hanukkah celebrates the rededication of the Second Temple of Jerusalem in 164 BCE by the victorious Maccabees, members of the priestly Hasmoneans of Modein, after its defilement by the Seleucid ruler Antiochus IV Epiphanes, acting with the collaboration of hellenizing Jews. It is the practice to kindle lights on Hanukkah, adding one light each day throughout the eight days of the festival, and to recite psalms of praise, the Hallel.

Conclusion. After the Roman destruction of Jerusalem and of the Second Temple in 70 CE, when all sacrificial rites became inoperative, major changes in observance affect virtually all biblical feasts. Yet all biblical feasts continue to be celebrated to this day, both in Israel and wherever Jewish communities exist.

Baruch A. Levine

FEMINISM AND THE BIBLE.

History. As early as 1837, the American abolitionist lecturer Sarah Grimke suggested that biblical interpretation was deliberately biased against women in order to keep them in subjection. She urged women to become trained as scholars and to investigate the sacred text for themselves. By the end of the nineteenth century, a few women had indeed become trained as biblical scholars, but they were not generally using their expertise for the purpose of challenging scriptural arguments for traditional views of women. The foremost nineteenth-century example of such a challenge, *The Woman's Bible* (1895–1898), was largely the work of nonspecialists, twenty woman suffragists under the leadership of Elizabeth Cady Stanton. Already in this work and in the responses to it, hints of the shape of the twentieth-century discussion can be seen. Some contributors emphasized the heroic character of little-known women in the Bible. Others concentrated on historical development and change as a rationale for rejecting direct application of biblical cultural norms to their own setting. Some women biblical scholars declined to become involved in an unpopular project, while some feminists urged that the whole project was unnecessary be-

cause the Bible itself was an irrelevant relic of the past.

For about seventy years after publication of *The Woman's Bible* the question of feminist biblical interpretation received little attention. Renewed interest in women's rights in the 1960s led to renewed attention to the influence of the Bible on the status and role of women in Jewish and Christian traditions. Feminists quickly recognized the need to reassess not only the Bible but also the centuries of biblical interpretation undertaken mostly by male scholars. Published literature on the topic increased exponentially, and by the 1980s the annual output of books and articles was twentyfold the total publication list of the first half of the century.

Areas of Inquiry. Recent feminist study has contributed to biblical scholarship in at least five major areas.

1. It has emphasized more systematic historical inquiry into the status and role of women in biblical cultures. Such investigations attempt to take into account not only the paucity of biblical materials pertinent to the inquiry but also the androcentrism (whether unconscious or deliberate) of the biblical writers. They recognize that the Bible gives only occasional and indirect evidence about the everyday life of the common people, and especially about the lives of women. The inquiries make use of extrabiblical writings, while recognizing that the same limitations apply to many of these texts as well. *Archaeology and sociological studies of preindustrial societies provide additional evidence and controls for such investigations (see Social Sciences and the Bible).* The variety of lin-

guistic and other specializations required for this effort demands teamwork among scholars and the gradual building of a body of data over a period of many years.

2. A more complete and balanced picture of the actual content of the Bible has been encouraged by highlighting texts pertaining to women that were not well known even among people familiar with the Bible. Among the many examples are the inheritance and marriage of the daughters of Zelophehad (Num. 27; 36), the rape of the Levite's concubine (Judg. 19), and the frequent inclusion of women in Luke's gospel.

3. Alternative interpretations of familiar biblical texts have been introduced to show that the texts themselves do not necessarily present a negative view of women, but that biases against women have been attributed to these texts by a long succession of androcentric interpreters. Prominent examples of such studies are those arguing that male and female are created equally in the image of God and that Adam is equally responsible with his wife Eve for their disobedience in the garden, and those arguing that Paul's insistence on women's silence in church refers to a specific local problem and would not have been generalized, even by Paul, to all women in all churches.

4. A more complete and balanced picture of the God portrayed in the Bible has been encouraged by emphasizing texts in which the deity is compared to a woman (e.g., a midwife, or a woman crying out during childbirth, or one who sweeps her home to search for a lost coin). Such texts, supplemented by texts using the imagery of inanimate objects for the deity (e.g., God as rock or shield), are used to undergird and reinforce the classic teaching that God is not biologically male, but is indeed beyond male and female. The small number of texts comparing God to a woman, together with the fact that these are generally comparisons (not direct appellations), results in disagreement about the significance of these resources, particularly whether they provide a warrant for referring to the biblical deity as "mother" in contemporary theology and prayer. (*See* Metaphors.)

5. Fresh translations of all or parts of the Bible seek to reduce the amount of gender-exclusive language in the text. Some of these versions have made such changes only where scholars considered them warranted by the original Hebrew and Greek texts, while others have eliminated many more masculine references in the text. Debate about the relative merits of the two approaches focuses on the question of how an ancient text can and should be heard in a contemporary setting: should its androcentric character be left plainly visible so that it remains true to its own time and culture, or should the androcentrism be softened so that the presumed universal message can be heard more clearly?

Options in Feminist Hermeneutics. As in the time of Stanton and *The Women's Bible,* some feminists still conclude that the Bible's androcentrism is so deep-seated that the book can no longer be regarded as authoritative for their lives. These persons tend generally to break away openly from their tradition and to give attention to the Bible only as a document having a negative influence on western culture.

Many feminists, however, do continue to regard the Bible as authoritative and remain active in church or synagogue. The goal of these feminists is to describe how this biblical authority persists despite the unacceptable patriarchal context and androcentric bias they recognize in scripture. While there are many differences in detail and nuance among the approaches to the problem, these approaches may be broadly categorized into three types.

1. Close study of texts pertaining to women, with emphasis on showing that these texts do not support the patriarchal structures and assumptions of contemporary society. This approach incorporates both the highlighting of texts previously ignored and the reinterpretation of texts traditionally used to support patriarchal structures in society. The difficulties encountered in the approach are twofold. First, there is no unanimity among scholars as to the correct interpretation of many of the debated texts. Even the criteria by which correctness might be ascertained cannot be agreed upon, since some scholars would admit various interpretations that are plausible as literary readings of a text, while others would insist that the interpretation be evaluated in terms of the probable intent of the original author addressing the ancient cultural context. Second, there are some texts that present a patriarchal

view of women for which no positive reinterpretation seems possible. Thus, the question of criteria for choosing some texts as more important than others inevitably arises. Although the problem of selectivity is as old as theology based on the Bible, the difficulty of establishing criteria or the desire to avoid such selection leads some feminists to frustration with this approach.

2. Appeal to the Bible generally (not specifically to texts about women) for a critique of patriarchy. This approach is often closely associated with the concerns of liberation theology in its search to show that the Bible challenges any viewpoint or action that demeans, limits, or controls others because of their race, class, or—in this case—gender. The prophets' criticism of economic exploitation, for example, or Jesus' criticism of ethnic narrowness, is extended by analogy to authorize criticism of the oppression of women. While this approach has many adherents, others criticize what they regard as a lack of clear criteria for such extension by analogy.

3. Study of texts about women with special attention to the ways in which their patriarchal setting or androcentric worldview continues to be reflected in contemporary culture. In this approach, the texts function rather like a mirror, enabling modern readers to see their own situations more accurately by focusing on similarities between attitudes toward and treatment of women in biblical times and in the current day. Of course, it is precisely such similarity that leads some feminists to reject the Bible

as oppressive and useless as a basis for advocating change. But for those who do not reject the Bible, the mirror is expected to lead to a value judgment, the recognition that such patriarchy is wrong. The basis for this value judgment generally lies in the resources of either the first or the second approaches above.

Feminists who continue to work with the Bible as more than a historical document generally agree that the theological problem of *authority is central to their *hermeneutic task. The chief poles around which the debate is structured remain those familiar to Christian theology generally: scripture versus tradition, "canon within the canon," and letter versus spirit. A review of the areas of inquiry and hermeneutic options outlined above provides illustration of each of these themes. The scripture-versus-tradition debate, for example, takes shape in the consideration of whose interpretations of the Adam and Eve story should hold sway, whether recent feminist ones or those familiar from the New Testament and church fathers. "Canon within the canon" identifies the dilemma of those who recognize discordant perspectives on women present in scripture. The debate over Bible translation is part of the larger issue of text versus spirit. Many more illustrations could be cited. They highlight the reality that the questions posed by feminism are not peripheral, but rather are central to the understanding of the Bible by communities of faith in every generation.

Katharine Doob Sakenfeld

FESTIVALS. *See* Feasts and Festivals.

FLESH AND SPIRIT. The word "flesh" literally means soft tissue, as distinguished from skin and bones; by extension it can mean the human race and even all animal life. "Spirit" translates words that in both Hebrew and Greek mean "wind" (Gen. 8.1; cf. 1.1) or "breath" (Gen. 6.17; Ezek. 37.5), as well as vital essence. Biblical writers do not normally combine the two terms to designate the totality of human nature. The body/soul dichotomy that so fascinated Greek philosophy is not generally presupposed, even when the two terms occur in close proximity; thus, Matthew 26.41 is not a real exception to this rule. (*See* Human Person.)

In the New Testament, particularly in the letters of Paul, "flesh" and "spirit" often appear as contrasting rather than complementary terms, representing the natural and divine spheres respectively; this usage also occurs earlier. Thus, for Paul "flesh" often has a negative connotation, meaning the sphere of human rebellion against God, as contrasted with the "spirit," which is sometimes identified as the "spirit of God" (e.g., Rom. 8.9; *see* Holy Spirit).

Douglas R. A. Hare

FLOOD, THE. Today, as in the past, catastrophic floods are experienced universally, and stories are told about them. The stories share many features: land submerged, multitudes drowned, survivors in a boat. People living in basically similar ways in separate places will react similarly; hence, common features in flood stories are predictable and are not proof that all such ancient stories refer to one great flood.

On the other hand, the Babylonian and Hebrew stories share so much that a connection between them can hardly be denied. Surviving copies of the Babylonian story come from the seventeenth and seventh centuries BCE (the Epic of Atrahasis and the Epic of *Gilgamesh, respectively); the age of the account in Genesis 6–9 in its present form is debated. Both narratives have a pious hero warned by his god to build a great ship (see Ark) and to load it with his family and selected animals in order to escape the coming deluge. Once all others have perished, the ship grounds on a mountain in Armenia, a sacrifice pleases the god, and a divine oath follows never to send another flood. The later Babylonian version describes the hero releasing birds to seek vegetation, but the clay tablets on which the earlier text is recorded have been damaged where that episode might have occurred.

Both the older Babylonian account (Atrahasis) and the Hebrew account belong to larger compositions passing from the creation of human beings to later history, the flood, and its aftermath. Other Babylonian records show a wider tradition preserving names of kings from the beginning of the human race onward, interrupted by the flood. Genesis 5 and 11 present comparable lists in a comparable context. All these similarities indicate a close connection. Scholars often claim that the Hebrew flood story depends on the Babylonian, with modifications in the interest of Israel's monotheistic faith. Consideration of certain differences, however, makes it more likely that both depend upon a common original.

Whether or not such a flood occurred is impossible to prove. Archaeologists finding layers of silt in three Babylonian cities associated them with the flood, but each was confined to one place and they were not contemporary. What physical traces such a flood would leave is debatable; though Genesis may imply a global flood, it need not, for the Hebrew word translated as "earth" (6.17; etc.) also means "land, country" (e.g., 10.10), so the narrative could report a deluge limited to the writer's known world.

According to Genesis 9.8–10, God promised never again to send "a flood to destroy the earth." The *covenant with Noah sets human society on a basis of individual responsibility, and Genesis goes on to trace this concept in the special revelation that God gave to the line he chose.   *Alan Millard*

FORGIVENESS. The several Hebrew and Greek words translated "forgive" fall into two general and overlapping meanings. The first refers to financial matters and involves the annulment of the obligation to repay what is owed, as in Matthew 18.32 (see Loans and Interest). The other meaning is much more frequent and concerns the reestablishment of an interpersonal relationship that has been disrupted through some misdeed. Thus, in Genesis 50.17, Joseph is implored by his brothers to forgive the evil that they did to him.

Both meanings are applied to God's gracious pardoning of people's transgressions; note how in the two versions of the *Lord's Prayer, in Matthew's version God is asked to forgive debts, in Luke's it is sins. Various *metaphors are used to express forgiveness of sins, such as those clustered in Psalm 51: blotting out, washing, purging, hiding the face. Even more vivid language can be used, as in Micah 7.19: "he will tread our iniquities under foot . . . cast all our sins into the depths of the sea." Such expressive phrasing highlights the completeness of God's forgiveness, which is to serve as a model for human conduct.

See also Mercy of God.

Johannes P. Louw

FORNICATION. Like the Greek word *porneia* that it often translates, "fornication" means extramarital or illicit sexual intercourse; it can also mean "sexual immorality" in a broader sense.

Warnings against sexual immorality occur repeatedly in the New Testament, especially in Paul and in the book of Revelation; it was apparently an issue especially for gentile Christians.

In Matthew 5.32 and 19.9 *porneia* (NRSV: "unchastity") is a justification for *divorce, but its meaning is not clear. Is it *adultery, or some premarital conduct discovered only after *marriage? Whether committed before or after marriage, it might denote any of the offenses condemned in Leviticus 18. It is unlikely to be merely marriage within the forbidden degrees.

See also Sex.   *David F. Wright*

FREUD AND THE BIBLE. The

views of Sigmund Freud (1856–1939) on religion are well known. He proclaimed to his friend Oscar Pfister, a Lutheran pastor, that he was a "godless Jew" and that only such a one would have discovered the secrets of psychoanalysis. He prided himself on being an intrepid man of science, a conquistador of the mind, who cherished his Enlightenment attitude toward religion and clung to his avowed agnosticism until the end of his life. He admired Baruch Spinoza, the seventeenth-century thinker, who in the spirit of the philosophes proclaimed that one had to read the Bible just as critically as any other book. For all that, Freud's attitudes toward religion were not so simple—the superficial view does not take into account his own ambivalent conflicts about religion and the degree of his own obsessional superstition and even credulity. His view of the Bible reflects this ambiguity and ambivalence. We can discuss the problem in terms of Freud's early exposure to the Bible, his ambivalence toward it, his use of the Bible, and finally

the special problem of his treatment of Moses.

Early Familiarity with the Bible. Freud's frequent denials of any meaningful religious training were long accepted as authentic testimony and consistent with his staunch atheism and agnosticism. But recently material has come to light that casts this supposition in doubt, suggesting that Freud's exposure to traditional Judaism may have been more extensive than he implied. In fact, Freud's early religious formation was considerable. His parents both came from traditional Orthodox families and remained Orthodox believers, but they did not follow all the prescribed practices. According to Ernest Jones (1957), they tended to be freethinking, but only after their move from Freiberg in Moravia to Vienna did they dispense with dietary observances and rituals of their Hasidic life-style—presumably in the service of accommodation. The Seder on the eve of *Passover continued to be observed, along with Christmas and Easter.

Freud's father Jacob was a devoted student of the *Torah and was well versed in Jewish lore and tradition, and he had attained a position of considerable respect for his scholarly knowledge of scripture. His familiarity and mastery of biblical texts in the original Hebrew was exceptional. The picture of the family religious atmosphere remains unclear, with conflicting accounts from involved observers—the divergences probably relating to what phase of the family experience was being described. There seems little doubt, in the light of recent research, that little Sigmund had considerable exposure to religious practices and traditions and particularly that he was exposed to extensive and intensive study of the Bible. He was a pupil of Samuel Hammerschlag, a Hebrew scholar of moderate Reform views, and studied the Hebrew language and the Bible from age seven through thirteen. Study of Hebrew was featured in every class, and special emphasis was given to the Torah. Freud was not only Hammerschlag's prize pupil during those years, but he also enjoyed a close and affectionate relationship with his old mentor. Freud's later denials of any knowledge of Hebrew might have been due to a lapse of memory or even a retrospective distortion.

One of the prize possessions of the Freud family was the remarkable edition of the Bible by Ludwig Philippson—the biblical texts were accompanied by numerous discussions of biblical history and comparative religion. Freud would have been quite familiar with this work. He commented in his *Autobiographical Study* (1925) that he had been deeply engrossed in the Bible from as soon as he was able to read and that this experience had had a lasting effect on him.

But Freud took pains to minimize his early religious background and may thereby have promoted a shibboleth that has persisted through the subsequent years of Freud scholarship. Peter Gay, for example, in *A Godless Jew* (1987) dismisses the years of study with Hammerschlag as merely reinforcing the religious indifference of Freud's home—"Hammerschlag was far more interested in ethics than in theology, let alone the Hebrew language." This would support Freud's repeated claim that he knew no Hebrew and that his religious upbringing was negligible. He wrote in 1930, "My father spoke the sacred language as well as German or better. He let me grow up in complete ignorance of everything that concerned Judaism." It seems that this declaration cannot be taken at face value and must be reassessed in the light of new evidence to the contrary.

Attitude toward the Bible. Freud's attitude toward the Bible was mixed, reflecting his underlying ambivalence toward his father. When Freud turned thirty-five, his father sent him the family Bible with the following inscription:

My dear Son,

It was in the seventh year of your age that the spirit of God began to move you to learning. I would say that the spirit of God speaks to you: "Read in My book; there will be opened to you sources of knowledge and of the intellect." It is the Book of Books; it is the well that wise men have dug and from which lawgivers have drawn the waters of their knowledge.

You have seen in this Book the vision of the Almighty, you have heard willingly, you have done and have tried to fly high upon the wings of the Holy Spirit. Since then I have preserved the same Bible. Now, on your thirty-fifth birthday, I have brought it out from its retirement and I send it to you as a token of love from your old father.

Curiously, this inscription, so redolent with biblical allusions, was written in Hebrew. The puzzle remains why Jacob would have addressed such a poignant sentiment to his son who professed to have no knowledge of the language. Certainly one supposition is that Jacob would have known that his son could well understand his inscription. Study of Jacob's language has concluded that he was neither a devout nor nationalistic Jew, but one of the Haskalah who envisioned Judaism as the epitome of Enlightenment rationalism—a characteristic view of Freud himself. Moreover, among the books discovered in Freud's library after his death was just such a Bible in Hebrew and German, with copious marginal notes in Freud's hand. Clearly Freud was more of a student of the Bible than he admitted.

Freud could not reconcile his staunch scientific outlook with any credibility of the Bible. He wrote in a letter in 1939, "The way you are able to reconcile esteem for scientific research with belief in the reliability of the biblical report calls forth my fullest admiration. I could not manage the feat. . . . But whence do you take the right to monopolize the truth for the Bible? I suppose it simply means: I believe because I believe." Whether he was at ease with his disbelief is open to question. If he could bring no belief to the biblical texts, they continued to exercise a fascination over and attraction for him.

Use of the Bible. Freud tended to regard the Bible as a great book of the Western literary tradition, but he did not credit it with any validity or inspiration beyond that. The Bible took its place in his mind along with other great literary works of Western culture, and his use of it was much like his references to other literary sources. His knowledge of European literature in general, both ancient and modern, was extensive—he must have been a voracious reader throughout his life. But in this regard the Bible held no special place. He even quipped at one point that the writings of Karl *Marx seemed to have replaced the Bible and the Qur'ān as sources of revelation, even though they were no more free of contradictions than the sacred books.

Consequently, although scriptural references are scattered through Freud's writings, they are used in the same vein as his references to other literary sources—as allusions or images utilized to make a point, draw a comparison, or illustrate a conclusion. The references span both Testaments, suggesting that Freud had a ready familiarity with the biblical material. References to the *Pentateuch predominate, but occasional allusions to the historical books or the Psalms are also found. Use of other books of the Hebrew Bible, such as the

Song of Solomon, is incidental. The New Testament seems to have taken a back seat. The outstanding exception to this pattern is in Freud's treatment of the Moses theme.

Freud and Moses. Freud's first mention of Moses was in a letter to Carl *Jung in 1908 in which he refers to Jung as Joshua, who would lead the chosen people into the Promised Land, while Freud, like Moses, would only be able to view it from a distance. The metaphor of the Promised Land was one of Freud's favorites and was a frequent reference in his letters to Wilhelm Fliess, his longtime friend and correspondent. The meaning shifts in various contexts—at one point it is Rome, the center of Christianity; at another it becomes the meaning of dreams; and toward the end of his life it was the riddle of Moses and the birth of *monotheism.

Freud's closest engagement with the biblical texts came at the end of his life in his attempt to rewrite the Moses legend in *Moses and Monotheism* (1939). It is flawed by faulty data selection and lacks appropriate methodology and verification; its conceptual structure is built on the sand of unverifiable hypotheses. It was in fact a kind of family romance, which Freud dubbed his "historical novel." Freud had been fascinated with the figure of Moses and probably strongly identified with the great prophet who led his people into the Promised Land—a metaphor for Freud himself, who led the way into the undiscovered continent of the unconscious. In 1901, he saw Michelangelo's powerful statue of Moses and became absorbed in it; he would spend weeks studying, sketching, and analyzing the statue and finally write his essay that transformed the traditional view of Moses into Freud's own vision of restrained power—a concrete expression of Freud's own ideal of the intellectual restraint of passion. He wrote of it: "Michelangelo has placed a different Moses on the tomb of the Pope, one superior to the historical or traditional Moses. He had modified the theme of the broken tablets; he does not let Moses break them in his wrath, but makes him be influenced by the danger that they will be broken and makes him calm that wrath, or at any rate prevent it from becoming an act. In this way he has added something new and more than human to the figure of Moses; so that the giant frame with its tremendous physical power becomes only a concrete expression of the highest mental achievement that is possible in man, that of struggling successfully against an inward passion for the sake of a cause to which he has devoted himself."

Clearly, his identification with the figure of Moses was a powerful theme in Freud's thinking about himself and his religious views. The writing of *Moses and Monotheism* became a final effort to resolve his ambivalent identification with the figure of Moses and through him of his deep-seated conflict and ambivalence regarding his father. It became an act of rebellion, rising up against the religion of his father and toppling its hero. He wrote, "A hero is a man who stands up manfully against his father and in the end victoriously overcomes him." Moses was the leader of his people, the prophet who brought a new revelation and founded a new religion. The image of the prophet who was without honor in his own country, yet would finally prevail and be universally accepted, was part of Freud's vision.

Freud's writing of the Moses book reflected his deep study of the Pentateuch and the critical scholarship of his day. He was strongly influenced by the higher biblical criticism of his day—Julius Wellhausen was an important influence, along with William Robertson Smith, whom Freud quotes often. In Freud's rendering, Moses became an Egyptian and the chosen people were thus deprived of one of their great cultural heroes. Freud reviewed the story of Amenhotep IV (Akhnaton), who rebelled against the gods of his father and established the monotheistic cult of Aten. Moses would have brought the monotheistic cult with him as a new revelation to the chosen people. This rendering of the origins of monotheism has been countered by subsequent biblical research.

Moreover, following the rather flimsy thesis of Ernst Sellin, who claimed to have discovered evidence of the murder of Moses, Freud advanced the hypothesis that Moses was prevented from entering the Promised Land because the Jews had rebelled against his imposition of the worship of the Egyptian god Aten and killed the prophet. Freud's Moses does not reach the Promised Land because he was murdered by his sons—the idea recapitulates Freud's fantasy of the murder of the father of the primal horde as the origin of religion in *Totem and Taboo* (1912–1913). Only later, in the reunification at Kadesh, under the leadership of a second Moses, did they take up a new religion based on the worship of the volcano god Yahweh. The result was the preservation of elements of Egyptian monotheism in the worship of Yahweh, including the practice of *circumcision.

Psychoanalysts have speculated that, in addition to his identification with Moses, this argument reflects Freud's underlying guilt for his own hostile wishes against his father. Freud would have been struggling to overcome his guilt and ambivalence by his wish to become another messiah, another Moses, who would lead his people out of psychological bondage by the new revelation of psychoanalysis. But this required the destruction of the religion of the fathers. He wrote, "There was no place in the framework of the religion of Moses for a direct expression of the murderous hatred of the father. All that could come to light was a mighty reaction against it—a sense of guilt on account of that hostility, a bad conscience for having sinned against God and for not ceasing to sin. This sense of guilt . . . had yet another superficial motivation, which nearly disguised its true origin. Things were going badly for the people; the hopes resting on the favour of God failed in fulfillment; it was not easy to maintain an illusion . . . of being God's Chosen People. If they wished to avoid renouncing the happiness, a sense of guilt on account of their own sinfulness offered a welcome means of exculpating God: . . . they deserved no better than to be punished by him since they had not obeyed his commandments."

Acceptance of Sellin's fabricated account suggests a strong need to believe on Freud's part, deriving from his identification of Moses with his father and his own unconscious hostility. The murder of Moses thus expresses a fitting punishment for Freud's own parricidal wishes. The identification with the slain Moses-father would have been intensified by Freud's advanced age and the progressive deterioration caused by his painful cancer.

Conclusion. Freud could never resolve his ambivalence toward things religious; his attitudes toward the Bible bear eloquent testimony to this conflict. He refused to acknowledge holy writ as bearing any significance beyond its status as an ancient and traditional literary masterpiece. Yet despite his skeptical and agnostic stance, he could not leave the Bible alone. He returned at the end of his life to immerse himself in the figure of

Moses and the mystery of the religion he brought to God's chosen people. He created a psychoanalytic myth of the origins of monotheistic belief in the primal murder of the father in the person of Moses. If this imaginative fiction cannot bear the weight of critical appraisal as a contribution to biblical studies, the question still remains whether Freud was touching on something more profound and meaningful about the human religious condition. Certainly, the Freudian encounter with scripture carries its own lesson—that the reading and interpretation of the biblical texts may not be divorced from the motives, sometimes hidden, of the reader.　　　*William W. Meissner, S.J.*

FUNDAMENTALISM. A theological movement among conservative Protestants, largely in North America. Despite its broad, amorphous, and decentralized character, fundamentalism has the following features:

1. A strong emphasis on the *inspiration and *authority of the Bible, which is to be understood "literally" and which is held to be "inerrant"—totally free from any error whatsoever, whether historical, theological, or scientific. It is not surprising that fundamentalists strongly repudiate the conclusions of modern biblical criticism, seeing them as implicitly, if not explicitly, undermining the beliefs of traditional Christianity (*see* Interpretation, History of, *article on* Modern Biblical Criticism).

2. A marked, at times militant, impulse toward separatism from the other branches of Christianity. Inasmuch as the large mainline Protestant denominations were perceived in the early twentieth century to be drifting toward

"modernism" or "liberalism," fundamentalists often withdrew fellowship from them, eventually creating rival Bible colleges, seminaries, publishing houses, and even entire denominations. In 1941, for example, they founded the American Council of Christian Churches, explicitly separate from its mainline counterpart, the Federal (later National) Council of Churches of Christ.

3. With a few exceptions, mostly among some Calvinist churches, fundamentalists tend to embrace the dispensationalist school of biblical interpretation, especially as popularized by the *Scofield Reference Bible. Again understanding the Bible "literally," particularly the many prophecies concerning the land of Israel as yet seemingly unfulfilled, fundamentalists tend to be premillennialists, looking forward to a literal thousand-year future reign of the Messiah (the *second coming of Christ) over a restored Jewish nation. Thus, a strong emphasis on future fulfillment of biblical prophecy usually characterizes fundamentalists. A perhaps inevitable corollary to this type of premillennialism is a strong sense of pessimism concerning contemporary human history, which is expected only to degenerate further and further until Christ's return.

4. In accord with this last point, fundamentalists tend to emphasize personal piety and holiness over the social concerns of the mainline churches. Typically, fundamentalists promote evangelistic revivals and missionary activity, both foreign and domestic, while they heavily inveigh against smoking, drinking (see Wine), the theater, card playing, and the like. Somewhat paradoxical, however, is their strong sense of patriotism, often identifying American values and traditions closely with Christianity. Ever since the 1960s, for example, fundamentalists have bitterly denounced the United States Supreme Court ban on prayer in the public schools as "un-American" as well as "anti-Christian."

The term "fundamentalist" first appeared in the early 1920s to describe those who subscribed to the "fundamentals" of Christian faith, especially the tenets promulgated in a twelve-volume work, entitled *The Fundamentals,* which had been printed and mailed to thousands of ministers and laypersons during the years 1910–1915 by two California oil millionaires, Lyman and Milton Stewart. These booklets took issue with a wide list of enemies of Christianity—Romanism, socialism, atheism, Mormonism, and most of all naturalism, which was held to be the basis of contemporary theological liberalism. The volumes also reaffirmed what were deemed to be "fundamental" truths of traditional Christianity, especially the inspiration and authority of scripture. Historians of fundamentalism commonly link the publishing of these volumes to the "five fundamentals" that had been previously adopted by the General Assembly of the (northern) Presbyterian Church in the U.S.A. in 1910 (later reaffirmed in 1916 and 1923), namely, the inerrancy of scripture, the deity of Jesus Christ and his *virgin birth, Christ's substitutionary atonement, his physical (bodily) *resurrection, and the historicity of his *miracles. But, as Ernest R. Sandeen has pointed out, any such listing of the "five points" of fundamentalism, and still less the twelve volumes of *The Fundamentals,* never typified the leadership of this era. Nonetheless, by the early 1920s, various lists of "the fundamentals" had indeed been drawn up, and they were meant to represent the essential, and hence nonnegotiable, doctrines of Christianity.

Throughout the 1920s, fundamentalists exerted a surprisingly powerful force on American religion and politics, especially in several of the larger Protestant denominations such as the northern Presbyterians and northern Baptists. As Sandeen notes, the origins of fundamentalism were largely to be found in the northeastern region of North America in metropolitan areas, not, as commonly argued, in agrarian or southern locales. Nonetheless, the real strength of fundamentalistic religion eventually did manifest itself among the Southern Baptists and the countless independent Bible churches that began to spring up throughout North America during this time, especially in the southern and midwestern regions of the United States. Politically, the fundamentalists flexed their muscles as well, strongly opposing, for example, the teaching in public schools of Darwinian evolution (*see* Science and the Bible). This opposition led eventually to the notorious "Scopes Monkey Trial" of 1925, in which William Jennings Bryan, a Presbyterian layperson and three-time Democratic party presidential candidate, argued unsuccessfully against the teaching of evolution in the public schools of Tennessee. Other famous fundamentalists of the era included the colorful and popular evangelist Billy Sunday and Princeton seminary professor John Gresham Machen, who personally resisted being called a fundamentalist, saying that it sounded like a new religion.

By the 1940s, less militant fundamentalists were also chafing under the term, regarding it as connoting anti-intellectualism, combativeness, extremism, and paranoia. Calling themselves "evangelicals," they banded together in 1942 to found the National Association of Evangelicals as a more moderate counterpart to the fundamentalist American Council of Christian Churches founded the previous year. Evangelicals still reckoned themselves as the heirs of true, historic Christianity, but they were more willing to work within and among the mainline denominations. The well-known contemporary evangelist Billy Graham, a moderate fundamentalist, has been repeatedly and bitterly denounced by his more conservative counterparts for such compromise.

Fundamentalism is still a force within modern North American Protestant Christianity. In 1976, Jimmy Carter, a self-styled "born again" evangelical Christian, was elected president of the United States, and both of Ronald Reagan's subsequent presidential victories were due in part to the votes of evangelicals and fundamentalists. In 2000, the very narrow victory of George W. Bush, who made his evangelical Protestant faith no secret throughout his campaign, would fall into this category as well. The beginning of the twenty-first century finds evangelical churches and organizations continuing to grow and thrive, and Billy Graham, now semiretired, is regularly singled out as one of the most respected figures in American life.

William H. Barnes

G

GENEALOGIES. *This entry consists of two articles, the first on genealogies in the Hebrew Bible, especially in the book of Genesis, and the second on genealogies in the New Testament.*

Hebrew Bible

A genealogy is a catalogue of the most important information about the successive members of a family's lineage, including their birth, marriage, offspring, age achieved, and death (with many variations). This listing of biographical facts serves to preserve the continuity of a family in its progression through time. Genesis 11.10–11 (P) is an example of a simple genealogy: "These are the descendants of Shem. When Shem was one hundred years old, he became the father of Arpachshad two years after the flood; and Shem lived after the birth of Arpachshad five hundred years, and had other sons and daughters." Originally, genealogies simply preserved a family's generational succession; later they also came to express kinship and social, political, and religious relationships, as well as connections within larger communities.

Genealogies are an independent genre whose origins go back to nomadic tribes; evidence is found mainly among Arab nomads and African tribes, in some cases to this day. They represent the history of a "prehistoric" period and lose their function after the creation of a state, to be replaced by historical facts.

There are two main types of genealogy. In the linear form, family heads are given in a straight progression from the founder of the clan down to the last or currently living representative; this serves simply to establish the lineage of the latest descendant. The other form follows the diverging branches of a family and exhibits the divisions among the communities descended from the sons of a single ancestor (e.g., Noah in Gen. 10). Genealogies, which were transmitted orally, are intrinsically mutable; changes in the relationships of groups within a larger community are expressed as changes in their genealogies. This capacity for change explains the contradictions between some genealogies: they reflect actual developments in the history of such groups.

Genealogies are an important component of the Bible and of Genesis in particular, establishing the continuity of events through the succession of generations. The original locus of genealogy is the history of the ancestors in Genesis 12–50, where generational succession provides the framework for the narrative; subsequently, genealogies were used in accounts of primeval history as well. In religious-historical terms, this corresponds to the depiction of cosmogony as theogony; in some religions, as in those of Egypt and Mesopotamia, the origin of the world and its elements is attributed to a succession of divine births. An echo of this can still be found in the Hebrew designation of creation as *tôlēdôt* ("generations" in the literal sense) of heaven and earth. Genealogies, however, occur in the Bible only after the creation of humankind; primeval events have been shifted from divine to human history. The genealogies in Genesis depict all of humanity as the effect of the creator's blessing, from Adam to Noah (chap. 5: linear genealogy) and then branching out from Noah's sons to cover the entire known world (chap. 10: branching genealogy). These genealogies knit the individual accounts of primeval events in Genesis 1–11 into a coherent narrative.

Genealogies enclose the history of the ancestors as a whole, as well as framing each of the smaller sections; they thus serve as formal elements in the composition of narrative units. Narratives sometimes begin and/or end with genealogies. Genealogical information delineates the lives of Abraham and his sons. A genealogy marks the transition from primeval times to the history of the ancestors (Shem to Terah in Gen. 11.10–26 and Terah's sons in 11.27–32). Difficulties concerning the genealogies within the ancestral history arise primarily because they reflect two stages: first, the development of a small kinship group (as in Gen. 25.19–20), and second, the formation of the tribes (e.g., the twelve sons of Jacob as the fathers of the later twelve tribes of Israel).

In earlier stages of the development of the genre, genealogy and narrative are more tightly integrated. Genealogical information anchors the narrative in a continuous temporal progression. One can merge into the other; a narrative frequently grows out of an item in a ge-

nealogy. The proximity of genealogy to narrative is demonstrated in the short elaborations within genealogies, including references to an occupation, as in Genesis 4.2 and 10.9; mention of a contemporaneous event, as in 10.25; or a remark concerning childlessness, as in 11.30. Thus, in the early stages, genealogies contained quite a few narrative elements. In subsequent traditions (P in particular), they follow a fixed format of identical or near-identical sentences, as in Genesis 5.6–8: "When Seth had lived one hundred five years, he became the father of Enoch. Seth lived after the birth of Enoch eight hundred seven years, and had other sons and daughters. Thus all the days of Seth were nine hundred twelve years; and he died." Although limited to a few facts, this form still preserves the life histories of those making up the chain of generations. In a final, later stage, all that remains is a list of names—no longer genealogy in the true sense of the word. A variant development is illustrated by the story of Joseph, in which genealogy has so completely merged with the narrative as to lose its independent existence.

The developmental phases of the genre of genealogy can be observed in the line of Esau's descendants, where a kinship phase (his sons) is followed by one of tribes (the chiefs) and then by one of kings; the format changes accordingly.

After the formation of a state, genealogies, having been reduced to mere lists, tend to lose their importance. In a monarchy, they serve a political function in securing the succession to the throne; for a priesthood they have religious significance in securing succession to sacred office. In these contexts, genealogies still play a role in the life of the community; the lists of names in 1 Chronicles 1–9, however, are a purely literary device.

See also Chronology, *article on* Israelite Chronology.   *Claus Westermann*

New Testament

The New Testament contains two genealogies of Jesus: one in Matthew 1.1–16, which traces his descent from Abraham, and one in Luke 3.23–38, which reverses the order. While Matthew's genealogy is limited to the Abrahamic line, Luke's goes back to Adam. Perhaps as a mnemonic device, Matthew or his source divided the generations from Abraham to Jesus into three groups of fourteen: fourteen generations from Abraham to David, fourteen from David to the Babylonian *exile, and fourteen from the Babylonian exile to Jesus. In order to maintain the symmetry, the names of the kings Ahaziah, Joash, and Amaziah were dropped from the second list of fourteen between Joram (Jehoram) and Uzziah. Other omissions may have occurred in Matthew's third list of fourteen, because Luke, who presents a different lineage between Zerubbabel and Joseph, records nineteen names for the same period.

Matthew's genealogy seems to be intentionally formed around a predetermined number. Most likely he meant to show that Jesus is a royal descendant of Abraham and David, in fact a new David: the sum of the numerical value of the Hebrew consonants in the name "David" ($d + w + d = 4 + 6 + 4$) is fourteen, and Jesus is frequently called "son of David" throughout the gospel of Matthew.

Four women appear in Matthew's list, though they are not found in Luke's. This is notable because in biblical times lineage was traced through males. Even more surprising is that three of these women were non-Israelites: Rahab the Canaanite, Ruth the Moabite, and (presumably) Bathsheba, the wife of Uriah the Hittite. Their mention anticipates the inclusion of gentiles among Jesus' disciples.

The genealogy in Luke 3.23–38 has variations in different textual traditions. According to most Greek manuscripts (followed by the United Bible Societies' *Greek New Testament*), there are 11×7 generations from Adam to Jesus (that is, from Adam to Abraham, 3×7 generations; from Isaac to David, 2×7 generations; from Nathan to Salathiel (preexilic), 3×7 generations; from Zerubbabel (postexilic) to Jesus, 3×7 generations). Other Greek manuscripts, the Latin Vulgate, and the Syriac Peshitta record 76 generations, and some Latin manuscripts list 72 generations. Most likely Luke traces Jesus' genealogy back through Abraham to Adam to show that Jesus is not only the fulfillment of the history of Israel, but also that he is the savior of the world.

Many attempts have been made to reconcile the two genealogies, which after David agree in only two names (Shealtiel [Salathiel] and Zerubbabel). Because none of these attempts have been generally accepted, it is likely that these inconsistent genealogies serve separate literary functions and are not to be interpreted like modern registers of pedigree. Matthew's genealogy is meant to show Jesus' Davidic, royal descent, and Luke's to underscore the universal role of Jesus as *Son of God.

The word genealogy occurs twice in a disparaging sense: in 1 Timothy 1.4 ("endless genealogies that promote speculations"), and in Titus 3.9 ("avoid . . . genealogies . . . for they are unprofitable"). Because the larger contexts refer to *myths, the allusions may be to the various emanations ("aeons") between

God and humankind in *gnostic belief. Or, since Titus 1.14 relates to Jewish myths and 1 Timothy 1.7 calls into question the claims of those who desire to be teachers of the *Law, the genealogies referred to may be based on biblical sources but elaborated in the same way as the Book of Jubilees and more generally *aggadah.* Bruce M. Metzger

GIDEONS, THE. The Gideons are an organization of laypeople dedicated to Christian evangelism through the distribution of scripture. They got their start through a chance encounter between two traveling salesmen at the Central Hotel in Boscobel, Wisconsin, in 1898. John H. Nicholson and Samuel Hill, who had stumbled into a raucous convention of lumberjacks, discovered that they shared a common love of the scriptures. The next year, along with W. J. Knights, they founded the Christian Commercial Travelers Association of America. Later the organization was named after Gideon who (according to Judg. 7) led Israel, armed only with torches and pitchers, to victory over the Midianites. The Gideons began distributing Bibles in 1908, with their first order for twenty-five copies assigned to the Superior Hotel in Iron Mountain, Montana. Since then, they have put the Bible into hotels and motels in more than 150 countries. They have also distributed millions of New Testaments to schoolchildren and to men and women entering the military. Their Bibles have gone to prisons, inner-city rescue missions, hospitals (in large print), and airplanes, ships, and trains. The ubiquitous presence of the Gideon Bible in hotel rooms has been the occasion of much humor, some of it risqué, but also of reassurance to countless travelers. The organization is active in 175 countries, and distributes more than 56 million copies of the scriptures annually.

Mark A. Noll

GILGAMESH EPIC. The Gilgamesh Epic is the greatest masterpiece of literature prior to the Bible and Homer. Episodes of Gilgamesh such as the *flood (from which Genesis 6–8 is in part derived) have survived in older *Sumerian tablets, but the epic as a whole was the later creation of the Semitic Babylonians and Assyrians. It circulated widely in the ancient Near East, and was translated into other languages, including Hittite and Hurrian. As the foremost classic of Mesopotamian civilization, it penetrated Palestine prior to the Israelite conquest, and Anatolia, where it was available to the Ionian Greeks of Asia Minor.

The twelve tablets of the Gilgamesh Epic form a unified composition dealing with the serious problems of life and death as experienced by the hero Gilgamesh. The milieu of the epic is urban: Gilgamesh is the king of Uruk (biblical Erech), described as a well-planned, walled city of superb construction.

The Gilgamesh Epic deals with heroic values. Gilgamesh gives up selfish tyranny for the noble but dangerous aim of eliminating evil from the face of the earth. Because he needs a friend to help him in this awesome mission, a worthy companion, named Enkidu, is created for him out of clay. Together they triumph over the forces of evil in the forms of monsters and dragons.

For offending the goddess Ishtar, Enkidu dies, which reminds Gilgamesh that he too is mortal and will someday perish. For, like Adam, Gilgamesh has gained knowledge but not immortality. Frightened by the prospect of death, Gilgamesh undertakes a perilous journey to the hero Utnapishtim, who survived the flood and had immortality conferred on him by the assembled gods. On the way, Gilgamesh stops at the tavern run by the goddess Siduri, who tells him to make the most of life: to eat, drink, be merry; to wed and sire children whose little hands he could hold. Such are the joys within the grasp of mortals; but the gods had reserved immortality for themselves. Nevertheless, Gilgamesh persists in traversing land and sea until he finds old Utnapishtim, who explains that the gods had made him immortal because of a unique event, the flood, which would never be repeated. The gods could not be reconvened merely to immortalize Gilgamesh. So Gilgamesh returns to Uruk, whose magnificence he admires. If we mortals cannot have heaven, we can at least enjoy the comforts of our native city.

The final tablet tells how Gilgamesh interviews the dead Enkidu and learns that the underworld is dreary at best, but utterly wretched for those who die without progeny to offer them food and drink. One's state there is alleviated by leaving children on earth—and the more, the better.

The message is clear: Make the most of the life that is given to us. Ecclesiastes makes the same point.

Cyrus H. Gordon

GLORY OF GOD. While *holiness expresses God's transcendence, his glory concerns rather his immanence to the world. One text can be seen to combine both concepts: "Holy, holy, holy is the Lord of hosts; the whole earth is full of his glory" (Isa. 6.3). God is invisible, but his glory (Hebr. *kābôd*) manifests itself in *theophanies, usually associated with storms, fire, and earthquake. Such resplendent events both reveal God's presence and reflect his transcendence, concealing him as it were. In the Yahwist (J)

tradition, God shows himself present in a pillar of cloud or of fire, while for the Priestly (P) tradition "the glory of the Lord" settled on Mount Sinai and appeared to the Israelites below "like a devouring fire" (Exod. 24.17). Also according to this tradition, the radiant glory of the Lord so transfigured Moses' face that he had to wear a veil to conceal it. It was this same manifestation of the divine presence that filled the Temple when it was dedicated; Ezekiel described it as leaving the Temple, going into *exile with Israel, an exile from which it would return.

Although the universal character of the divine glory is often referred to, in later biblical traditions this universality is particularly stressed. When Paul speaks of "an eternal weight of glory" (2 Cor. 4.17), he is recalling the etymology of the Hebrew word (which is derived from the root *kbd*, whose primary meaning is "to be heavy"). For Paul, the "glory of Christ" (2 Cor. 4.4), particularly the risen Christ, is a manifestation of the glory of the Father. In the gospel of John, on the other hand, the glory of God, possessed by Christ in his preexistence, now dwells in him on earth. The prologue to this Gospel continues the statement that the "Word became flesh and pitched his tent among us" with another regarding seeing the glory of the Son (1.14), and the rest of the Gospel describes particular manifestations of that glory. Similarly, for the author of the letter to the Hebrews, the Son "is the reflection of God's glory and the exact imprint of God's very being" (1.3), somewhat like personified Wisdom, "a pure emanation of the glory of the Almighty" (Wisd. of Sol. 7.25).

Leopold Sabourin, S.J.

GLOSSOLALIA. Glossolalia (from Grk. *glōssai*, "tongues, languages," and *lalein,* "to speak") is a phenomenon of intense religious experience expressing itself in ecstatic speech. It is found in several religions, and in Christianity is understood to be a manifestation of the *Holy Spirit.

Explicit New Testament references to speaking in tongues are confined to 1 Corinthians 12–14 and three passages in Acts (2.1–13; 10.46; 19.6). While Paul and the author of Acts both affirm that tongues are a gift of the Spirit, their portrayals of the experience are very different. Paul, who himself had shared the experience, describes speaking in tongues as unintelligible to others unless a further gift of interpretation enables it to be more than private devotion, and he contrasts tongues and prophecy. Luke's description of *Pentecost understands these "other tongues" (Acts 2.4) as intelligible proclamation, and he links tongues and prophecy.

Paul replies to questions and assertions put to him by the Corinthian church. As with other matters in Corinth, Paul is disturbed by the self-centeredness of those who prize and parade their piety while neglecting the love that builds up the community. Accordingly, his chapter on *love as the more excellent way is at the heart of his discussion, and in the list of gifts of the Spirit he places tongues and the interpretation of tongues last. He suggests that undue preoccupation with tongues represents immaturity rather than maturity, and he limits the use of tongues in the church's assembly.

Luke's account of Pentecost may include residual traces of the unintelligible speech that Paul describes, for he reports that some had charged those who had received the Spirit with drunkenness. But Luke interprets the tongues as known languages, and Pentecost as the reversal of Babel, where a confusion of languages had divided the human community. Each of the three passages of Acts in which explicit mention is made of tongues represents a breakthrough in the church's mission. At Pentecost, the first three thousand were baptized. The second mention represents the beginning of the gentile mission. The third occurs when the Christian mission is clearly differentiated from that of the followers of John the Baptist.   *John Frederick Jansen*

GNOSTICISM. A modern designation for a religious movement of the early centuries CE, though only some of the groups involved actually called themselves "gnostics" (from Greek *gnōsis,* "knowledge"). Initially it was regarded as a heresy within early Christianity, opposed by Irenaeus, Hippolytus, and others, the "falsely called knowledge" of 1 Timothy 6.20. A false knowledge, however, implies the existence of a true knowledge, and Clement of Alexandria in fact uses the term "gnostic" for a Christian who has penetrated more deeply than the ordinary believer into the knowledge of the truth (*Stromata* 7.1–2). Further complications have arisen with increasing knowledge of the religious life of the ancient world, comparative study of ancient religions, and the attempt to account for the origins of gnosticism. One common error of method has been to identify terms or concepts as "gnostic" because of their appearance in developed gnostic systems, and then to trace them back through Greek philosophy or the religions of Egypt, Persia, or Babylonia. This is to ignore the fact that the gnostics adapted and transformed motifs that they borrowed; some such terms and concepts are "gnostic" only in a gnostic context. More recently, increased attention has been paid to possible Jewish origins; but while there is no doubt of the importance of the Jewish contribution, for example in gnostic use and reinterpretation of the Hebrew Bible, it is by no means certain that the movement originated within Judaism or was initiated by Jews. The Septuagint was the Bible also of early gentile Christians.

What is now clear is that the movement did not suddenly emerge in the second century CE, when it was opposed by early church fathers. There are affinities in the writings of *Philo of Alexandria, and there is evidence that there was a good deal of "gnosticizing" thought, even in the first century CE. A question still in debate is the extent of "gnostic" influence on the New Testament, since the evidence has to be found in the New Testament itself, and there is always a danger of interpreting it in light of later systems, which may be to impose on it the ideas of a later period. There is still no gnostic document that in its present form can be dated prior to the New Testament.

The chief characteristics common to all the developed systems are (1) a radical cosmic dualism that rejects this world and all that belongs to it: the body is a prison from which the soul longs to escape; (2) a distinction between the unknown transcendent true God and the creator or Demiurge, commonly identified with the God of the Hebrew Bible; (3) the belief that the human race is essentially akin to the divine, being a spark of heavenly light imprisoned in a material body; (4) a myth, often narrating a premundane *fall, to account for the present human predicament; and (5) the saving knowledge by which deliverance is effected and the gnostic awakened to recognition of his or her true nature and heavenly origin. At one time it was thought, as the church fathers sometimes allege, that the gnostic was "saved by nature," and that morality was

therefore of no importance; indeed, since ethics is largely a matter of obedience to the law of the creator, who seeks to hold the human race in slavery, it could be seen as a positive duty for the gnostic to disobey all such commands. The evidence of the *Nag Hammadi documents, however, suggests that while some gnostics may have shown libertine tendencies, the main direction of the movement was toward asceticism. Some of the characteristics listed can be identified in other systems of thought, but that does not make these gnostic; it is the combination of those ideas into a new synthesis that is gnosticism.

The classic period of gnosticism is the second century CE, with such figures as Basilides and Valentinus, and the latter's disciples Ptolemy and Heracleon, but this was the culmination of a long development. The later books of the New Testament (e.g., the Pastorals, Jude, 1 John) show signs of resistance to an incipient gnosticism, but it is a mistake to think of clear distinctions between orthodoxy and heresy at such an early stage; differing points of view may well coexist for a period, interacting with one another, before it finally becomes clear that they are incompatible. The gospel of John makes frequent use of the verb "to know," but never employs the noun *gnōsis*, which may perhaps be significant; Paul uses the noun quite often, but we need to ask whether he is speaking of a specifically gnostic knowledge. Most religions do profess to convey some kind of knowledge! While there may be doubts about gnostic influence in the New Testament, there can be no question of the significance of New Testament influence on gnosticism; this is shown by numerous allusions and direct quotations in the sources, to which the Nag Hammadi library has added greatly.

Gnosticism has often been regarded as bizarre and outlandish, and certainly it is not easily understood until it is examined in its contemporary setting. It was, however, no mere playing with words and ideas, but a serious attempt to resolve real problems: the nature and destiny of the human race, the problem of *evil, the human predicament. To a gnostic it brought a release and joy and hope, as if awakening from a nightmare. One later offshoot, Manicheism, became for a time a world religion, reaching as far as China, and there are at least elements of gnosticism in such medieval movements as those of the Bogomiles and the Cathari. Gnostic influence has been seen in various works of modern literature, such as those of William Blake and W. B. Yeats, and is also to be found in the Theosophy of Madame Blavatsky and the Anthroposophy of Rudolph Steiner. Gnosticism was of lifelong interest to the psychologist C. G. *Jung, and one of the Nag Hammadi codices (the Jung Codex) was for a time in the Jung Institute in Zurich.

Robert McL. Wilson

GOLDEN CALF. Three "golden calves" appear in the Bible. The first is fashioned by Aaron at Sinai to replace Moses and Yahweh, and the second and third are a pair commissioned by Jeroboam, leader of the northern secession, to replace the *ark; they were worshiped respectively at Dan and Bethel.

Hebrew ‛ēgel is generally rendered "calf," but a more mature beast may be intended. On the one hand, an ‛ēgel can be a prancing, untrained one year old. On the other hand, the feminine ‛eglâ can denote a three-year-old heifer, trained for plowing or threshing. Hosea 10.5 calls Jeroboam's images "heifers," although the reading is uncertain; elsewhere, Hosea describes the animals as male. Most likely, the golden "calves"

are young bulls, as the Septuagint renders in 1 Kings 12.

It is uncertain from 1 Kings 12.28 whether Jeroboam's images are solid gold or gold-plated wood; 2 Kings 17.16 calls them "molten." Aaron's image is "molten," yet it is destroyed by grinding and burning, as if partly wooden. Hosea 13.2 refers to molten image(s), idols, and calves (it is unclear whether these are the same), and speaks of silver, not gold, while Hosea 8.4 mentions both silver and gold, probably the constituents of the calf in 8.5. Judges 17–18 describes a molten silver image worshiped in Dan, conceivably a forerunner of Jeroboam's calf. In 1990 a silver-coated molten bronze bull 4 in (10 cm) high dated to ca. 1550 BCE was discovered at Ashkelon.

Aaron's and Jeroboam's calves are symbols of Yahweh; Aaron declares a "festival to Yahweh" (Exod. 32.5) and, throughout its history, the northern kingdom of Israel worshiped Yahweh, even while venerating the calves. But it is unclear whether the calves represent Yahweh himself or a supernatural bovine on which he stands; Jeroboam's calves may even constitute the armrests of God's throne. All three interpretations have parallels in ancient Near Eastern art and literature, and perhaps more than one was current in Israel. The nonbiblical name ‛Egel-yo appears in the Samaria ostraca (eighth century BCE) and could mean either "calf of Yahweh" or "Yahweh is a calf."

The calf stories in Exodus 32 and 1 Kings 12 are closely related. Both extol "your gods, O Israel, who brought you up out of the land of Egypt," and both culminate in priestly ordination. The simplest explanation is that Exodus 32 is a polemic against Jeroboam's movement; this would explain the plural "your gods" in Exodus 32.4 (contrast the singular in Neh. 9.18). Alternatively, Exodus 32 might be a polemic against an older cult revived by Jeroboam—conceivably that of Judges 17–18.

See also Graven Image; Idols, Idolatry.
William H. Propp

GOLDEN RULE. Since the eighteenth century CE the familiar saying "Do unto others as you would have them do unto you" has been known as the "Golden Rule." Often cited as the sum of Jesus' ethics, the saying also occurs in ancient Greek, Roman, and Jewish writings. For example, Rabbi Hillel (first century BCE) answered a question about the Law's central teaching with the statement: "What is hateful to you, do not do to your fellow creature. That is the whole Law; the rest is commentary" (*b. Sabb.* 31a).

Some seek to distinguish between the more common negative form just cited and the positive form found in Jesus' teaching by attributing the former to common sense based on self-interest and the latter to Jesus' higher ethical concerns. This distinction, however, fails to hold because the positive form also occurs in extrabiblical writings (*Letter of Aristeas* 207; *T. Naph.* 1; and 2 Enoch 61.1), and the negative form appears in Christian literature, such as a variant reading in Acts 15.20, 29; and *Didache* 1.1.

By itself, the rule could indeed reflect a commonsense principle of conduct based on self-interest rather than conduct based on concern for others. But a closer look at New Testament usage reveals that the Golden Rule occurs in contexts calling for *love for others. Matthew and Luke have the saying as part of Jesus' teaching in the *Sermon on the Mount. In Luke 6.31 it is integral to Jesus' teaching about love for one's enemies. In Matthew 7.12 it comes at the conclusion of a series of demands pertaining to one's relation with others and with God.

Probably, therefore, Matthew took the saying from its traditional context of love for one's enemies and used it as a summary of the preceding list of Jesus' demands. By adding the phrase, "for this is the law and the prophets," Matthew places the rule in the broader context of the Sermon on the Mount as well as of his entire gospel. In 5.17 he introduces the series of Jesus' demands by noting that Jesus had come to "fulfill the law and the prophets"; a "greater righteousness" (5.20) is now demanded in one's relationship with others (5.21–48) and with God (6.1–7.11). In 22.40 Matthew directly relates the rule to the love commandment by having Jesus declare that the "law and the prophets" depend on the love commandment.

In the context of Jesus' teaching, therefore, the Golden Rule, rather than being merely a commonsense, ethical rule of thumb, is a practical expression of the love commandment growing out of love for God and one's neighbor. The same connection between the Golden Rule and the love commandment is found in *Didache* 1.2, as well as in the variant reading in Acts 15.20, 29.
Robert A. Guelich

GOSPEL, GENRE OF. The term "gospel" (Grk. *euaggelion*) is used in Christian tradition to designate the canonical Gospels, Matthew, Mark, Luke, and John, presumably written between 65 and 100 CE. Some source-critical theories suggest the existence of a precanonical gospel, that is, a hypothetical primitive gospel or protogospel underlying one or more of the four canonical Gospels. Other gospels were produced in the second century (and perhaps the first), but they are not recognized as canonical. (*See also* Apocrypha, *article on* Christian Apocrypha; Canon, *article on* New Testament.)

The four Gospels are grouped together in the New Testament canon, apart from the letters and Revelation and also distinct from the other narrative book, Acts of Apostles. The Gospels include stories about Jesus, sayings of Jesus, and a passion narrative; they describe the career of Jesus in a connected narrative from the preaching of John the Baptist to Jesus' death and *resurrection. This is commonly accepted as the characteristic gospel form. Justin Martyr, about 150 CE, refers to the "gospels" (the first attestation of the term in the plural) as "the memoirs of the apostles," and this historical or biographical definition remained popular through the centuries: the gospel is the story of Jesus, the account of the life and teaching of Jesus Christ.

According to the modern critical consensus, the Gospels constitute their own literary genre: they are sui generis, sharing a distinctive form and content. Three factors seem to have been of influence. First, the study of the literary relationship among the synoptic Gospels has led to the widely accepted view that both Matthew and Luke depend on Mark, and thus the problem of the gospel genre has become, to a large extent, a problem of the origin of Mark. Second, form critics emphasize, on the one hand, the role of the kerygma (preaching) in the early church, and on the other, the oral origin and the unliterary character of the pre-Markan gospel material (short anecdotes, small units, and probably a primitive passion narrative). The author of Mark, by combining this traditional material into a framework, created the gospel genre. Third, the Christian gospel form is apparently not influenced by the genres of the Hellenistic literature. The kerygmatic hypothesis has taken two opposing forms. The majority opinion ascribes the gospel framework to Markan

redaction. For C. H. Dodd, on the other hand, Mark serves as a commentary on the kerygma. The basic outline of the gospel corresponds to the historical section in the traditional kerygmatic scheme of the sermons in Acts. The story of the passion is prefaced in Mark 1–8, as it is in Acts 10, by an account of the ministry of Jesus in Galilee. The debate is not closed, but Lucan redaction in Acts 10.36–43 can hardly be denied.

There is, however, a growing dissatisfaction with this form-critical approach. The definition of the gospel of Mark as a passion narrative with an extended introduction is no longer acceptable. There is a renewed interest in the search for parallels to Mark's genre, especially for possible associations with Hellenistic biographical literature, in its variegated forms, including the popular biography; a biography subtype written to dispel a false image of the teacher and to provide a true model to follow; an encomium biography; and the epideictic type of biography. For other scholars, connections with Hellenistic biography remain unproved. Yet it can be recognized that the Gospels are biographical in a broader sense. Some analogies can be found in the biblical tradition: the life of Moses, or the biography of the suffering righteous one. Biography in its various types, however, is only one of the models suggested for the gospel. The *apocalyptic genre, the *Passover haggadah, the calendrical cycles, and, in Greco-Roman literature, the Socratic dialogues, the Greek tragedy, the tragicomedy, and rhetorical conventions are other suggestions. The aretalogy deserves special consideration. Mark and John are supposed to have corrected the divineman christology of their sources, the pre-Markan collection of miracles and the pre-Johannine signs-source. The gospel thus becomes an antiaretalogy, an adaptation of the existing aretalogical genre. On the other hand, however, the source-critical and other presuppositions of these Markan and Johannine trajectories are far from certain. John's dependence on the Synoptics, at least with regard to the gospel form, is a more likely hypothesis.

The gospel of Mark is used in Matthew and Luke in combination with a second source, the hypothetical Q document. The narrative framework, typical of the gospel form, is lacking in this sayings collection, and designations such as "wisdom gospel" or "aphoristic gospel" are inappropriate. The Q material is blocked together with special material in three interpolations in Luke and mainly in five (or six) discourses in Matthew. The Markan gospel's general outline is preserved in both, with an expansion of the biographical element in the birth stories and the genealogies at the beginning and the appearances of the risen Lord at the end. Luke and Acts explicitly form a two-volume work by one author, and some influence of the literary conventions of Greek historiography is undeniable.

Each of the four Gospels has its own individuality. Redaction criticism and narrative analysis uncover differences of language, style, and composition; differing theological concepts; and differing authorial intentions. Their anonymity is a common characteristic. The present superscriptions (Gospel according to Matthew, etc.) were affixed at an early stage of the tradition, probably under the influence of Mark 1.1, extending the use of the term gospel proclamation to the literary form of the gospel book.

The gospel genre implies a similarity of form and content. For some of the so-called noncanonical gospels—namely for those that embody stories without kerygmatic outlook or those that present sayings and dialogues without a narrative—the term gospel is used improperly.

Frans Neirynck

GRACE. In the Bible, the term grace combines ideas in tension that point to profound mystery. Grace names the undeserved gift that creates relationships and the sustaining, responding, forbearing attitude-plus-action that nurtures relationships. Grace concerns the interaction between gracious person and graced recipient, involving the wills of both. The motives of the grace giver; the acceptance, rejection, or forgetfulness of the recipient; the forbearance of the giver; the entire dynamic of forgiveness; the life-renewing impact of the gift—all these are at issue. All pertain whether the gracious one is divine or human. English translations interchange "grace," "favor," "mercy," "compassion," "kindness," and "love" in probing the theme.

There is a slight distinction among the Hebrew and Greek words translated "grace, graciousness, show grace," but more significant is the large degree of overlap in meaning. The Hebrew roots *ḥnn* ("favor, grace"), *ḥsd* ("loyalty, steadfast love"), *rḥm* ("compassion, mercy"), *rṣh* ("pleasure in, favor toward"), and *ʾhb* ("love") point to the grace theme, as do Greek *charis* ("grace"), *eleos* ("mercy"), *oiktirmos* ("pity, mercy"), and *eudokia* ("pleasure in"). Close in meaning are Hebrew *ʾmn* ("steadiness, trustworthiness"), and *ḥml* and *ḥus* ("to pity, to spare").

Much of the Bible portrays grace rather than naming it. In Hosea 11.1–9, the metaphor of parenting dominates, involving compassion and anger, disappointment and chagrin, intervention and forbearance. In Matthew and Mark, Jesus' *parables and person display grace; *charis* is not used, and *eleos* appears very rarely. The prophets seldom use grace vocabulary, wrestling instead in beautiful word pictures with the past, present, and future tension between divine wrath and divine yearning love, as well as with the tension in human relationships between care and violation of neighbors. When they do employ grace vocabulary, they sometimes, as Hosea does with *ḥesed*, select a word for special probing of graced relationships.

It is often said that the *ḥnn* group pertains to the gifted initiation of relationship, while the maintenance of relationship is named by *ḥesed*. Note the Septuagint translations: *charis* for *ḥen*, *eleos* for *ḥesed*. In lament and thanksgiving psalms, however, frequently the poet implores divine grace/mercy with an imperative of *ḥnn* paralleling other imperatives, showing that God's gracing sustains and refurbishes the existing relationship. God is asked to turn back to the one who has lost favor; to hear/answer appeals based on prior experience of God's favor; to heal, redeem, blot out transgressions in the one graced. Whether the worshiper is contrite about transgression or bewildered by the undeserved absence of God, continuance of a prior relationship is sought.

In virtually all instances, one who does/gives/shows grace has a superior capacity to act, while the one imploring is in need. Hence the frequent idiom of a needy one "finding favor/grace in the eyes of" someone. A gracious one reaches out to the poor, the needy, the oppressed, the forsaken—a movement intrinsic to God and to righteous humans.

To understand grace best, one can begin with human or divine instances. Proverbs 22.9 and 19.7 display human action: a gracing (NRSV: "generous") person is blessed for sharing bread with the poor; a person gracious (NRSV: "kind") to the poor lends to the Lord and will be appropriately recompensed.

But grace does not act to deserve reward; grace is intrinsic to the righteous. One senses God's graciousness by observing the best of human action, but divine and human paradigms of grace inform one another: human grace imitates and depicts God's grace; God's grace calls forth human imitation.

Yet there are heightened dimensions to God's grace. One indication is the intensity of appeal to God's grace and favor in psalms and liturgical compositions. Another is the number of proper names compounded of grace vocabulary and a divine name, such as Hananiah (Ananias), Hananel and Hanniel, and the short forms Hanan, Hanun, Hanani, and Hannah; a dozen names contain the element *rḥm*, "compassion."

Three liturgical passages are especially expressive. Exodus 33.19, "I will be gracious to whom I will be gracious, will show mercy on whom I will show mercy," combines affirmation of God's freedom with the promise that grace and *mercy are intrinsic to God. Exodus 34.6–7, using a rich range of grace language in a divine self-affirmation, is recalled in Psalms 86.15; 103.8; 111.4; 145.8; Nehemiah 9.17; Joel 2.13; Jonah 4.2; the affirmation is echoed in part in several other passages and questioned in Psalm 77.7–9. Numbers 6.24–26, the Aaronic blessing, emphasizes the continuance of God's grace and the expected consequence: *šālôm* (NRSV: "peace").

Grace and mercy in the New Testament, as well as the combination "grace and truth" in the prologue to John (1.14–17), are deeply influenced by Hebrew usage. The noun *charis* in Luke 1.30; 2.40; 2.52; and 4.22, together with verb forms in 7.21, 42, and many Lucan uses of the term in Acts, reflect the semantic range of the Hebrew Bible. A special emphasis appears in Paul's and Peter's speeches in Acts 13.43 and 15.11

and in nearby narratives about the apostles. Here grace as emanating from God, with a commending and sanctifying impact on those who have received it, accords with Paul's use of *charis* in Romans (fourteen times), 1 and 2 Corinthians, Galatians, and Philippians, developed in Deutero-Pauline Ephesians and Colossians. Paul's polemical emphasis is on the free gift of God's grace, a means of salvation that ought not be resisted, which impels its recipient to new, spontaneous righteousness. Thus grace is both the gift of Jesus Christ and the gift(s) of consequent righteous living in vocation. Paul's aim is to recapture the primacy of God's yearning search for humankind and the bestowal of power to become disciples. Grace, *charis*, bestows gifts, *charismata*. Paul has moved God's initiative of relationship to such prominence that "seeking God's favor" or "imploring God's mercy" fades. But Paul will go on wrestling with human response, the use made of God's gift, and the expectation of consequential, thankful living.

The tensions in the dynamic of grace characterize much of the theological wrestling of synagogue and church across the centuries. Grace can be deemed all-sufficient ("grace alone"), but repentance, merit, and reward play their part in its dynamic. Grace can seem to be irresistible in its attractiveness and yet be resisted mightily. Humans who accept God's grace can do dastardly things in God's name. God can be perceived to have run out of favor and patience, and yet new mercy appears. The freedom of God and the perplexity of human behavior have meant that both biblical authors and theologians fail, finally, to penetrate the depth of mystery in grace.

Edward F. Campbell

GRAVEN IMAGE. Hebrew *pesel* is variously translated as "graven image," "idol," or "statue." Three-dimensional

sacred images of metal, stone, wood, or clay were ubiquitously venerated in antiquity.

The Bible misrepresents *idolatry by ascribing to worshipers the naive belief that the image is the deity. Egyptians, Canaanites, and Mesopotamians believed a god's spirit inhabited a statue after consecration, causing it to move, speak, or sweat. While the statue was the god in many respects, the god was not limited to its image. The idol's purpose was to allow the mortal a vision of the divine and to help god and worshiper focus their attention on each other. A few idols had moving parts—such as a movable jaw or dribbling breast—enabling priests to generate "miraculous" divine responses.

Since almost all ancient gods, including Yahweh, resembled humans, most idols were anthropomorphic. Some, however, portrayed animals, and Egyptian divine images often combined human and animal aspects. While humanoid idols depicted the god him- or herself, the wholly or partly animal representations metaphorically expressed aspects of its nature: a lion for ferocity, a frog for fecundity, a ram for virility, a hawk for mobility, and so forth.

The Bible forbids idolatry to Israelites. In Roman times, this proscription prevented compliance with the state cult of worshiping the emperor's statue. Although archaeologists have uncovered virtually no representations of male gods from Israelite times, female figurines, probably representing goddesses, are common. Some equate these statuettes with biblical Asherah or teraphim.

Prayers might be spoken before the idol or food set before it, later to be removed for consumption by priests and/or worshipers. Among Jews and Christians of the Roman period, such food was strictly forbidden.

The avoidance of divine images is

called aniconism. While there is no inevitable link between *monotheism and aniconism, it cannot be coincidence that the first monotheist, Pharaoh Akhnaton (1363–1347 BCE), abolished idolatry. Apparently both he and the biblical authors believed figurative representations limited the divine to a particular conception and place or encouraged identification of the one true God with other nonexistent deities. But while Akhnaton's god, the sun, was visible to all in the sky, Yahweh was hidden in his fiery cloud.

Although there were few if any images of Yahweh, Israelite shrines featured statues, carvings, and embroidery depicting celestial beasts associated with Yahweh: cherubim (winged sphinxes), bull calves (see Golden Calf), and perhaps seraphim (winged snakes). The Bible preserves vestiges of a debate over their significance: Are the cherubim God's throne or canopy? Are the calves pedestals or depictions of God? Is Nehushtan a seraph sheltering Yahweh or a venomous serpent?

Jewish ritual *art, like Muslim art, has generally avoided human images, but the third-century CE synagogue of Dura Europos features realistic illustrations of Bible scenes. Periodically, Christians have banned holy statues and pictures (iconoclasm), but they are still venerated in Roman Catholicism and Eastern Orthodoxy.   *William H. Propp*

GREEK. This language belongs to the western branch of the Indo-European language group, along with the Germanic, Italic, and Celtic families. It evolved into a relatively distinct and unified language ca. 2000 BCE, when Indo-European speakers mixed with earlier inhabitants in the Aegean area, especially on the Greek mainland. Extensive contact with Minoan culture ca. 1650–1450 BCE led to the development of the Mycenaean dialect recorded in the pre-alphabetic Linear B syllabary. With the collapse of Mycenaean civilization ca. 1250–1200 BCE, the Mycenaean dialect was largely replaced by Doric dialects, except in the interior mountainous region of the Peloponnese and in Cyprus, to which it spread. From the Doric dialects gradually developed Northwest Greek, comprising the dialects of Phocian, Locrian, and Elean, and the West Greek dialects, or Doric proper, including Laconian, Heraclean, Argolic, Corinthian, Megarian, Rhodian, Coan, Theran, Cretan, and other lesser dialects of the west, such as Syracusan and Corcyran. In the east, a dialect akin to Mycenaean, which had already reflected innovations characteristic of the east Greek dialects of classical times, evolved in the Cycladic area into historical Ionic, from which Attic later developed; and in Thessaly another dialect, which was the origin of Aeolic, spread by migrations to Boeotia and Lesbos, where it underwent further modifications through convergence with Ionic.

Only a few dialects were used in literature, and then generally in a somewhat artificial form not corresponding exactly to the spoken language. Further, these literary dialects were associated with certain classes of literature and were so used, regardless of the author's native dialect.

First and foremost among these was the Homeric dialect (well developed before 700 BCE), an amalgam of Ionic and Aeolic, a development of centuries of epic and bardic tradition based on a substratum of Mycenaean. The language of Hesiod (seventh century BCE) is substantially that of Homeric epic but with some Aeolic forms and peculiarities found in Doric and Boeotian. The epic dialect is also used, with some modifications, by elegiac and iambic poets, and to some extent it influenced all of Greek poetry.

The melic poets Alcaeus and Sappho wrote in the Lesbian dialect, with some traces of epic forms. Their language too was imitated by later writers, including Theocritus.

The language of the choral lyric is an artificial composite of Doric characteristics with the elimination of local features and some admixture of Lesbian and epic forms. It was used by the Boeotian Pindar and the Ionians Simonides and Bacchylides, as well. The first prose writers were the Ionic philosophers of the sixth century BCE, and in the fifth century the historian Herodotus and Hippocrates of Cos, a Dorian, wrote in Ionic. With the political hegemony and intellectual supremacy of Athens, the Attic dialect became the language of drama, and by the end of the fifth century it was also used in prose, but earlier prose writers such as the historian Thucydides, the tragedians Aeschylus, Sophocles, and Euripides, and the comedian Aristophanes avoided Attic peculiarities. Among the other great Attic prose writers were the orators Lysias, Isocrates, Aeschines, and Demosthenes, the philosopher Plato, and the historian Xenophon.

Some few other dialects were cultivated in local literature, but the majority of dialects are known only from inscriptions and play no role in literature.

From the welter of classical dialects emerged the Koine. Also called Hellenistic Greek, koinē, "the common (dialect)," designates the prevalent form of the Greek language from the time of Alexander the Great (late fourth century BCE) to the Byzantine period (sixth-seventh century CE). The Koine emerged largely through a process of leveling and assimilation. Based primarily upon the Attic dialect, the Koine also incorporated elements from other dialects, including Ionic, Doric, and Boeotian. Features peculiar to a single dialect tended to be lost in the formation of a universal Greek vernacular, while those shared by several important dialects left their mark on it. It was spread by the Macedonian conquests over a vast area and became the vehicle of communication for diplomacy and commerce. With the adoption of Hellenic culture it became established in the leading centers of Greek civilization. Its widespread use, especially by nonnative Greek speakers, led to extensive modifications in the living language, which is best preserved in more than fifty thousand papyri, ostraca, and inscriptions from the fourth century BCE to the eighth century CE.

This largely homogenous dialect continued to develop as a living language, but a literary form of the Koine was created in imitation of classical Attic idiom. Among the leading Koine authors using this elevated language were the historians Polybius, Diodorus Siculus, *Josephus, and Arrian; the biographer Plutarch; the rhetorician Dionysus of Halicarnassus; the geographer Strabo; the philosophers Philodemus, *Philo, and Epictetus; and the Sophists Lucian, Philostratus, and Philostratus the Younger. The Atticistic movement, an artificial revival of the classical language, flourished especially in the second century CE as a reaction to the natural developments and innovations of the spoken language that impinged increasingly upon even the literary form of the Koine.

Much more akin to the living Koine is biblical Greek. Hardly a unity in itself, the language of the various Greek translations of the Hebrew scriptures, the writings of the New Testament, the Jewish and Christian *apocrypha and *pseudepigrapha does not constitute a special Jewish dialect of the Koine, much less a language outside the mainstream of the development of Greek. But like the papyri, ostraca, and inscriptions from Egypt subject to extensive bilingual interference from Egyptian (Coptic), biblical Greek in varying degrees preserves a Semitic tone and flavor, adopts Semitic modes of speech, and reflects Semitic interference in grammar. It diverges from the rest of the Koine most noticeably in vocabulary, as it coins new words to express specifically biblical concepts or uses older terms with new Jewish or Christian meanings.

The Koine is the direct ancestor of medieval and Modern Greek, except for the Tsaconian dialect descended from classical Laconian. Although the Modern Greek vernacular language (*dimotiki*) contains very many Latin and especially Turkish loanwords and is itself split into numerous dialects, it represents the latest phase in the development of the Greek language over an unbroken period of some four thousand years. Alongside the Modern Greek vernacular, there is an archaizing form of the language called the *katharevousa*, which long served as the standard learned and literary language but no longer enjoys its former official status.   *Francis T. Gignac*

GUTENBERG, JOHANNES GENSFLEISCH ZUM. (ca. 1396–

ca. 1468). German printer and inventor of movable type. Gutenberg was born in Mainz and trained as a goldsmith. Around 1430, he moved to Strassburg, where, along with three others, he began to experiment with printing. By the time he returned to Mainz in about 1449, he apparently had movable metal type formed in separate letters, and had invented a typecasting machine along with an oil-based ink printer. In Mainz he became partners with Johannes Fust, a banker, so that he could have funding for a large Latin Bible in two-column format, with each page containing forty-two lines. The types he prepared comprised not only the 24 capital and 24 lowercase letters of the Latin alphabet, but 290 different characters (47 capitals and 243 lowercase letters). Gutenberg cast such a great number of types because he wanted to reproduce as accurately as possible the detail of letters in sumptuous medieval manuscripts—and, if he could, to surpass their beauty through his new art. According to most critics, Gutenberg's Bible is better-proportioned and harmonized than any of the manuscripts, including those transcribed with the greatest care. Because he printed with an exceptional deep black ink, the Bibles retain their fresh luster to this day. After first trying to print the headings and initial letters of chapters in red, he hired artisans to illuminate these unadorned spaces in red and blue by hand.

Generally bound in two massive folio volumes, the Gutenberg Bible comprises 1,282 double-columned pages. The pages measure 15½ × 11⅛ in (39.4 × 28.3 cm). It is believed that approximately 150 copies were printed on paper and about 35 on parchment (vellum). To print each copy, 340 sheets of four pages each were required. Since one calfskin provided only two good sheets of this size, almost 6,000 calves were needed to supply enough vellum for the 35 parchment copies of this Bible. Printing of the Bible began in approximately 1452, but financing problems, as well as the use of Gutenberg's six presses for the production of school grammars, calendars, letters of indulgence, and other small print jobs, postponed the completion of the printing of the Bible until late 1455 or early 1456. Only twelve parchment and thirty-six paper copies of the original Gutenberg Bible are known to exist worldwide; four of the parchment copies are complete, as are seventeen of the paper copies.

See Printing and Publishing, *article on* The Printed Bible.   *Bruce M. Metzger*

H

HADES. *See* Hell.

HANDS, LAYING ON OF. *See* Laying on of Hands.

HARDENING OF HEART. Hebrew expresses moral and intellectual obtuseness by calling the heart "hard" (or "strong," "firm," "fat," or "bold"). "Hardness of heart" primarily connotes inflexibility of purpose or perception, often but not necessarily leading to *sin. There is no nuance of cruelty, however, as might be inferred from English "hardhearted." Such obtuseness hinders, for example, Jesus' disciples from understanding his *miracles. The rejection of the Christian movement by Jews and gentiles is also blamed upon their "hardness" and "stubbornness," as is subsequent dissension within the church.

A heart can be made hard by God or by sinners themselves. In general, the Bible attributes misconduct both to human initiative and to divine intervention. Psalm 81.12 describes God abandoning the sinful to their stubbornness. Thus, sometimes the Pharaoh of the *Exodus hardens his own heart, sometimes it is hardened for him by Yahweh, and sometimes it simply "becomes hard." God's intervention and Pharaoh's native stubbornness together lead the king to his doom.

In Isaiah 6.9–10, Isaiah is told that the purpose of his prophecy is to make the Israelites obtuse, lest they evade their deserved punishment. Jesus cites this verse as the reason he speaks not clearly but only in *parables. In other words, God has decided that some will be impervious to his message and fated for perdition.

This may seem unfair, and the book of Jonah in fact dramatizes the converse theory: while the prophet would deny sinners the opportunity to repent, God insists that they be given a chance. Similarly, Ezekiel maintains that Yahweh desires each sinner's *repentance; to bring this about is the prophet's job. This more benevolent picture of God contributed in the Persian period and later to the evolution of the image of Satan, who largely relieved Yahweh of his role of tempter. But the notion of the divine origin of human sin and obtuseness survives in the New Testament. Paul addresses the question of fairness in Romans 9 but reaches no clear conclusion, merely affirming God's absolute power and inscrutable justice: "Who indeed are you, a human being to argue with God?" (Rom. 9.20); compare the divine response to Job from the whirlwind (Job 38–41): "Where were you when I laid the foundations of the earth?" (38.4).   *William H. Propp*

HEAVEN. It is important to note that in the Hebrew Bible the word (*šāmayim*) is plural; English translations sometimes use "heaven," sometimes "the heavens."

In Genesis 1.6–8, the creation of the firmament (NRSV: "dome") is described, "and God called the firmament Heaven [NRSV: Sky]." This was regarded as an overarching vault resting on pillars at the ends of the earth. Above it was the celestial ocean, and above this the dwelling of God. In the firmament were openings or "windows" through which the upper waters came down in the form of rain. At times, the term "the heavens" refers to the expanse in which the birds fly, at times to the starry heavens, and at other times still to the highest heaven above the firmament. The context decides which meaning is appropriate.

The starry heavens are regarded as a witness to God's being and creative power; continually they "are telling the glory of God" (Ps. 19.1). These heavens remind humans of their littleness and the wonder of God's concern for them. Humans' ignorance of "the ordinances of the heavens" (Job 38.33) helps to fill them with awe.

In the course of the biblical period, more transcendent ideas of God developed, and Jeremiah declares, "Do not I fill heaven and earth? says the Lord" (23.24). But even when the concept of God's omnipresence was expressed, other expressions were retained. According to 1 Kings 8.27, Solomon recognizes that heaven and the highest heaven cannot contain God; but later in the same prayer he repeatedly asks, "Hear in heaven your dwelling place" (8.30, etc.). Isaiah 65.17 speaks of "new heavens and a new earth"; this hope for a new, or renewed, *creation had important developments in later *apocalyptic literature.

With respect to heaven as the final abode of God's people, this is hardly to be found in the Hebrew Bible, where for the most part, the fate of everyone, good or bad, was the shadowy realm of Sheol

(see Hell). After the *exile, however, Persian and Greek ideas stimulated Jewish thinking in new directions, and this is seen in some of the apocalypses of the period. Bitter persecution also produced the conviction that God would not leave without some vindication of those who had died for their faith. The doctrine of resurrection was at first associated with the hope of life on a renewed earth (see Afterlife and Immortality).

By the Roman period, a blessed future holds a sure place in Jewish thinking, particularly among the Pharisees; the Sadducees retained the conception of a universal Sheol. In the New Testament, generally, the servants of God are encouraged to look forward to a blissful eternity with God, but the word "heaven" is used sparingly in this connection, other terms such as "eternal life," "glory," "my Father's house," being preferred. Hebrews 11.16 speaks of those who "desire a better country, that is, a heavenly one." Paul is more concerned with the company than the place and speaks of the future life as being "with Christ" (Phil. 1.23) and as seeing "face to face" (1 Cor. 13.12).

The term "heaven" still occurs in the New Testament in the sense of "sky" (e.g., Mark 13.25; Luke 13.19 [NRSV: "air"]). In the letter to the Hebrews, mention is made of the heavens of the present creation that are destined to perish, the heavens through which Jesus passed, and the realm beyond, where he sits on the right hand of God "in heaven." The last of these resembles in some ways the Platonic heaven of ultimate realities, of which earthly things are copies.

The word "heaven" does not necessarily refer to a literal place, for already the Christian sits with Christ in the heavenly places. Jesus, who has "all authority in heaven and on earth" (Matt.

28.18), shares the omnipresence of the Father; he "ascended far above all the heavens, so that he might fill all things" (Eph. 4.10).

There is more about heaven in the book of Revelation than in any other book of the Bible, and vivid pictures are given of the throne of God and the *Lamb, with living creatures and elders, angelic hosts and multitudes of the redeemed, drawn from every nation, bringing homage and praise. Popular conceptions of heaven have been derived largely from the imagery of this book.

Two other matters need mention. Some of the noncanonical writings give detailed descriptions of multiple heavens, up to seven or more. But Paul was not necessarily thinking of these when he wrote of his mystical transport into the third heaven (2 Cor. 12.2); an alternate explanation is that the expression indicates a high degree of spiritual exaltation. Second, Jewish tradition came to have such reverence for the name of God that "heaven" and other substitutes were used; thus, for example, the prodigal son says, "I have sinned against heaven and before you" (Luke 15.18, 21); and Matthew generally uses "kingdom of heaven" and only four times "*kingdom of God."

See also Paradise.

Thomas Francis Glasson

HEBREW. The Hebrew language is written from right to left in an alphabet of twenty-two letters. They all originally denoted only consonants, but *w*, *y*, and *h* have also been used to represent certain long vowels at the end of words (*w* = "u"; *y* = "i"; *h* = "a," "o," and "e"; *w* and *y* were later used for "o" and "e," respectively) since at least the tenth century BCE and *w* and *y* within words since the ninth. In texts from Qumran and in

later writings, letters are used more extensively to represent vowels. The full system of representing vowels by adding points to the consonants developed much later, between the fifth and tenth centuries CE. The present system of vocalization thus reproduces the pronunciation current about a thousand years after the end of the biblical period, though it is doubtless based on earlier traditions of reading the Bible.

Among the differences between Hebrew (along with other Semitic languages) and English are the presence in the former of the guttural consonants *ᶜayin* and *ḥēt* (the latter is like "ch" in Scottish "loch"); the emphatic consonants *ṭēt*, *ṣādeh*, and *qōp* (kinds of "t" and "s" that do not occur in English, and a kind of "k" that is not distinguished in English from any other kind of "k"); the sibilant *śĩn* (probably the same as a consonant in Modern South Arabian dialects) alongside *sāmek* (s) and *šĩn* (š); the presence of two grammatical genders, masculine and feminine; the use of the dual form for certain nouns that go in pairs (e.g., eyes, ears, and feet); the fact that many words are derived from roots of three consonants; and a verbal system in which the use of certain vowels and consonants denotes differences in meaning (e.g., *kātab*, "he wrote"; *niktab*, "it was written"; *hiktîb*, "he caused to write"), and in which there are two forms, the so-called perfect and imperfect, which were used in later times to denote the past and the future, but were employed in earlier times in ways that are still debated.

Within the Northwest Semitic group of languages, Hebrew belongs to the Canaanite family, which includes Phoenician, Moabite, and Ammonite (some would add *Ugaritic). The other major Northwest Semitic language family is *Aramaic. The word "Hebrew" (*ᶜibrît*) is not used of the language until the Hellenistic period, but we read of "the language of Canaan" in Isaiah 19.18; and in 2 Kings 18.26, 28 (= Isa. 36.11, 13; 2 Chron. 32.18) and Nehemiah 13.24 Jerusalemites speak *yĕhûdît*, that is, "Judean" (later "Jewish"). Certainly, the similarity between Biblical Hebrew and Phoenician and some Canaanite words that appear in the *Amarna letters from the fourteenth century BCE shows that the Israelites' language did not differ much, if at all, from that of the Canaanites. Some have inferred from the common characteristics of Hebrew and Canaanite, and from the words "A wandering Aramean was my father" (Deut. 26.5) that the ancestors of the Israelites spoke Aramaic and that they adopted from the Canaanites the language later known as Hebrew. It is doubtful, however, whether Deuteronomy 26.5 is intended to convey information about linguistic history, and the affinities of Hebrew with what was spoken by the Canaanites may be explained on the hypothesis that the Israelites and their ancestors already spoke a language closely related to that of the Canaanites.

While the Bible is the principal source for Classical Hebrew, the same language is used in inscriptions. Among the best known are the Gezer Calendar (tenth century BCE), a list of months defined by the characteristic agricultural work performed in them—this text may not have been written by an Israelite; the Kuntillet ᶜAjrud and Khirbet el-Qom inscriptions (late ninth or early eighth century BCE), which mention Yahweh and his Asherah; the Samaria ostraca (eighth century BCE) recording payments of wine, oil, and so on; the Siloam Tunnel inscription (late eighth century BCE), found in the tunnel built by Hezekiah under the city of David to bring water from the spring of Gihon to the Pool of Siloam; the Lachish ostraca (early sixth century BCE) with military messages before the Babylonian invasion; and the Arad ostraca (same period) recording the provisions supplied to soldiers. The Moabite Stone (ca. 830 BCE), in which King Mesha of Moab boasts of his victories over the Israelites, is in a language almost identical with Biblical Hebrew.

There were differences of dialect among the Israelites. Judges 11.5–6 reports that the Ephraimite fugitives were unable to say "*shibboleth" but said "sibboleth" and so betrayed their origin to their Gileadite enemies. The Hebrew Bible was transmitted by people in Judah, but traces of another—presumably northern—dialect have been preserved in the Bible. The Song of Deborah (Judg. 5), which appears to be of northern origin, uses the masculine plural ending *-în* in v. 10, and the relative particle *šă-* in v. 7, where the dialect of Judah would have used *-îm* and *ᵓăšer*, respectively. There were other differences between southern and northern Hebrew, as in the second-person feminine singular pronoun and pronominal suffix. A northern story such as 2 Kings 4 (in which the northern prophet Elisha appears) has thus retained something of its northern dialect. Further, northern inscriptions show dialectal differences. For example, the Biblical Hebrew word for house is *bayit*, but northern inscriptions have *bt*, which probably reflects a pronunciation *bēt*, and "year" is *št* in contrast to the southern *šnh*. The book of Hosea contains many linguistic and textual difficulties, and some of them can probably be explained as resulting from the prophet's northern dialect.

Hebrew changed with the passing of time. The language of the books of Chronicles, for example, is different from that of Kings. Aramaic became the dominant language in the Syro-

Palestinian region and it influenced Hebrew and eventually displaced it in some areas. Nehemiah 13.24 complains that some children of mixed marriages could no longer speak the language of Judah but spoke "the language of Ashdod." It is possible that this refers not to a survival of the Philistine language (though that cannot be excluded) but to Aramaic. The language of Ecclesiastes differs markedly from that of preexilic texts, and the linguistic peculiarities of the Song of Solomon are often attributed to a late date. Some people, however, could still write in the earlier style, as may be seen in the book of Sirach, written around 180 BCE, and in the sectarian writings from Qumran. Yet such essays in composition in Classical Hebrew were attempts at archaizing. The prologue to the Greek translation of Sirach also contains the earliest use of the term Hebrew for the language of ancient Israel.

Rabbinical writings of the first few centuries CE use a form of Hebrew that is usually known as Mishnaic Hebrew (from the collection of legal tractates known as the Mishnah, of ca. 200 CE). It was once widely believed that this language was never used by the common people but was a scholarly language created under the influence of Aramaic. Now it is generally recognized that the rabbis did not concoct a scholarly language but used a form of Hebrew that developed in the last few centuries BCE. This conclusion arises from a study of the nature of the language and from references in rabbinic texts to its use by ordinary people, and this vernacular use doubtless lies behind its presence in the Copper Scroll from Qumran and in some letters from the Second Jewish Revolt (132–135 CE). Although Hebrew was used in Judah in the first century CE as a vernacular, Aramaic and *Greek were also spoken, and there is evidence

that Aramaic was dominant in Galilee in the north. Jesus came from Galilee, and normally he probably spoke Aramaic. Indeed, some of his words quoted in the Gospels are Aramaic, though some (such as "*abba" and "ephphatha") can be explained as either Hebrew or Aramaic. It is not unlikely that he also spoke Hebrew, especially when visiting Judea.

Several verses in the New Testament appear at first sight to refer to the Hebrew language, and the Greek word translated as "Hebrew" (hebraisti) does indeed refer to that language in Revelation 9.11; 10.16. But it is also used of the Aramaic words Gabbatha and Golgotha in John 19.13, 17, and it probably denotes a Semitic (as distinct from Greek) language spoken by Jews, including both Hebrew and Aramaic, rather than referring to Hebrew in distinction from Aramaic. Similarly, the Aramaic expression Akeldema is said in Acts 1.19 to be "in their language," that is, the language of the people of Jerusalem.

Some time after the Second Jewish Revolt, Hebrew died out as a vernacular in Palestine, probably in the late second or the third century CE. It continued, however, to be used by Jews as a religious, scholarly, and literary language, and was also spoken in certain circumstances. It was revived as a vernacular only in the later nineteenth century, and it is now the living language of the state of Israel.   J. A. Emerton

HEBREW BIBLE. See Bible; Canon.

HELL. Hell (from a Germanic root meaning "to cover") is the traditional English translation of the Hebrew word Sheol, found sixty-five times in the Hebrew Bible, and of the Greek word Hades, used twenty-six times in the *Apocrypha and ten times in the New Testament. In the NRSV these words are simply transliterated into English, and the translation "hell" is reserved for Gehenna.

Both Sheol and Hades refer to a general dwelling place of souls after *death. Since this sphere was mainly supposed to be found in the underworld, it was also called "the pit" (Isa. 38.18), "the bottomless place" (Luke 8.31; Rom. 10.7; see Abyss), or "the lower parts" (of the world; Ps. 63.10; Eph 4.9 [Latin *inferiores partes,* cf. "inferno"]).

Postexilic Judaism reserved a particular section of hell for the punishment of sinners. In the New Testament, the synoptic Gospels and James in twelve cases name this place of pain Gehenna. Among the New Testament examples of Hades, there are three in which punishment is the point, so that Hades corresponds to Gehenna. In the other passages where Hades occurs, however, it is used in the neutral sense of a space where all the dead are kept.

Concerning the location of hell, the biblical references are colored by the usual cosmology of antiquity, which divided the universe into *heaven, earth, and underworld. The concept of hell, however, did not depend on cosmology, but rather on concern for the destiny of the dead. There was a general conviction that existence continued in some way after its separation from earthly life, an event that implied separation from God, the source of all life. The connection of God with heaven and the *burial of the dead in the ground gave reason generally to localize the realm of death in the underworld, and eventually to let the souls of the wicked dwell in a deeper section than those of the righteous. Such spatial aspects of hell were meant to give the distance of the deceased from God or their nearness to God concrete expression.

In the course of time, several different perspectives on hell emerge in the Bible. From a neutral viewpoint, Sheol was regarded in Israel as the dwelling place of all the dead, independent of their character. Jacob is reported to have said when he believed his son Joseph dead: "I shall go down to Sheol to my son, mourning" (Gen. 37.35). A similar pessimism is found in various types of literature. The probable etymology of the word (from the verb *šāʾal,* "to ask") reflects this universalism: the underworld is never sated, but keeps asking for more. Postexilic Judaism and the New Testament also presupposed this general place of the dead, but made it provisional because of the belief in a coming resurrection.

When ethical viewpoints are involved, however, Sheol is said to be a place of punishment. Korah and his companions were swallowed up by "the earth" (a term that can also mean "the underworld"), while their supporters were burned in fire. Psalmists and prophets threatened the godless with destruction in hell, and wisdom teachers warned the youth to avoid hell; originally, this probably meant that untimely death was the deserved fate of the wicked, but many of these texts could also be interpreted to mean punishment after death. As indicated above, Judaism also developed the idea of different sections for righteous and sinful people in hell, and especially ascribed the punishment of blasphemers to a cursed and flaming gorge, later called Gehenna. In the New Testament, the story of Lazarus illustrates the different places reserved for the righteous and sinners in the realm of death. Parenetic concerns of Jesus and his followers dominate other passages in which hell (called Hades, the abyss, Gehenna, and, in 2 Peter, also *tartaros*) is represented as an instrument of divine punishment. Matthew was especially concerned with this negative aspect of hell, but neither John in his Gospel nor Paul in his letters developed it.

Hell was even seen as a power that endeavors to attack life on earth. This found expression in psalms dealing with *salvation from mortal danger; for example: "The cords of Sheol entangled me" (2 Sam. 22.6 = Ps. 18.5), or "The pangs of Sheol laid hold on me" (Ps. 116.3). In postexilic Judaism, the topic was further developed by the community of Qumran, which also let the "gates" of hell represent the aggressiveness of the underworld. According to Matthew 16.18, these gates of hell will not be able to subdue the church. It is Gehenna that inspires false teachers and inflames evil tongues, and powers of destruction ascend from hell to rage on earth.

Ultimately, however, God is the one who controls hell. His own fire is able to destroy it, and hell is never hidden from his eyes. The almighty God of Israel is often praised for his ability to rescue a pious soul from death and hell.

Gradually, the conviction of God's omnipotence led to a belief in the resurrection of the dead. These expectations were prepared for by prophetic sayings like the following: God "will swallow up death" (Isa. 25.7; cf. 1 Cor. 15.54); "Your dead will live, their corpses shall rise" (Isa. 26.19); "He [the Servant] shall prolong his days" (Isa. 53.10); "I will open your graves" (Ezek. 37.12). Influenced to some extent by Persian religion, Judaism then developed various doctrines of a resurrection and judgment, implying that hell will deliver the righteous and rearrest the sinful, for example: "Many . . . shall awake, some to everlasting life, and some to shame and everlasting contempt" (Dan. 12.2); "the king of the universe will raise us up . . . because we have died for his laws"

(2 Macc. 7.9); the souls will be kept in hell "until the great judgment" (1 Enoch 22.4).

In the New Testament, a new perspective is opened by the witness of the apostles that God had raised his Christ from death, confirmed by the information that some women had found the tomb empty and that several disciples had "seen" the risen Lord. These experiences were understood to indicate that hell and death had already been defeated by the Lord of life, as Peter was reported to have proclaimed at *Pentecost. Some of the righteous were also reported to have risen together with him. The provisional and the definitive victory of Christ over death and related powers was a central point for Paul, and he exclaimed with great joy: "O death, where is your victory?" (1 Cor. 15.55 [see Hos. 13.14]). Although he avoided expressions for hell, Paul certainly reserved some place for the dead until their resurrection, describing this as a peaceful sleep or a punishment in fire. Christ's final victory over hell is described in more detail in the book of Revelation. Although the destructive powers of hell increase their attacks on humankind before the approaching end, the final conflict will lead to the complete disappearance of death and hell.

See also Afterlife and Immortality; Day of Judgment; Descent into Hell; Resurrection of Christ.   Bo Reicke

HERMENEUTICS.

Hermeneutics may be defined as the theory of interpretation. More precisely, biblical hermeneutics inquires into the conditions under which the interpretation of biblical texts may be judged possible, faithful, accurate, responsible, or productive in relation to some specified goal. Whereas exegesis involves the actual process of interpretation, biblical hermeneutics moves beyond interpretation. It entails a study of method, inviting reflection on the nature, methods, and goals of biblical interpretation. It also draws on general hermeneutic theory, that is, on traditions of scholarship—within philosophy, the social sciences, theories of literature, and semiotics—that shed light on questions about meaning and understanding. The subject embodies a proper concern to understand the biblical writings not only as particular historical documents of the past but also as texts that address the present with a living and transforming voice. This has often been described as the task of "application," though some prefer to speak of "recontextualization." Finally, theological questions about the status and nature of the Bible also shape hermeneutics. Whether or in what sense the Bible is seen as the authoritative word of God shapes the ways in which issues are explored. (*See* Authority of the Bible.)

Up to the end of the eighteenth century, three sets of issues assumed particular importance in the history of biblical hermeneutics. First, the Hebrew Bible could be seen either as part of the Christian scriptures or as Jewish scripture only. For Jesus and the earliest Christian communities, the Hebrew Bible was their only scripture, providing among other things the frame of reference within which the gospel was to be understood. These Christians saw it as applying to their situation and interpreted it in the light of the ministry of Jesus Christ. In the second century CE, Marcion challenged the status of the Old Testament as part of Christian scripture. But Irenaeus and other church fathers reaffirmed the unity of the two testaments as the message of the one God, who had revealed himself preeminently in Christ (*see* Interpretation, History of, *article on* Early Christian Interpretation).

The second issue concerns allegorical interpretation. Allegory presents a meaning other (Grk. *allos*) than that which might be immediately apparent in the text. For example, John Bunyan's *The Pilgrim's Progress*, which portrays a spiritual journey through language, at first sight seems to describe physical travel from place to place. In such cases, allegorical interpretation constitutes the appropriate hermeneutic method. But this method was also used extensively in the ancient and medieval world as a device with which to seek out other meanings from biblical and classical texts. It was used in classical Greece to draw "higher" meanings from Homer's narratives about petty squabbles among the Greek deities. The Alexandrian church fathers, especially Clement and Origen, were among those who inherited and used this interpretative device. Clement of Rome allegorized the scarlet thread in Rahab's window into a symbol of the blood of Christ. More subtly, many narrative *parables were interpreted as if they had been spoken as allegories in which each element of narrative description carried some independent or self-contained spiritual meaning. The Antiochene fathers, and subsequently also Luther, used the method, though more cautiously. Calvin dismissed the approach on the ground that it allows the interpreter to shape scripture in accordance with human judgments. In this respect allegory is less constrained than *typology: whereas allegory rests on parallels between ideas, typology depends on correspondences or parallels between events.

A third persistent issue in hermeneutics concerns the role of interpretative tradition. Does the way in which the Bible is read and understood depend decisively on the tradition of expectations and assumptions in which the interpreter stands? On one side, the church fathers insisted, against the *gnostics, that the Bible can be understood rightly only when it is seen as the scriptures of the catholic or universal church. On the other side, the reformers, while respecting early tradition, insisted that the Bible could stand on its own feet (*see* Interpretation, History of, *article on* Christian Interpretation from the Middle Ages to the Reformation). Its message was not to be equated with how it might already be understood within some given ecclesiastical tradition. In the modern era, it is widely recognized that interpreters must take seriously both the right of the text to speak from within its own historical particularity and the role of traditions in shaping the horizons of interpreters and their questions.

In the modern era, several movements have profoundly influenced biblical hermeneutics. Following the rise of Romanticism in the eighteenth century, Friedrich Schleiermacher and Wilhelm Dilthey argued that to understand a text we must seek out the circumstances or creative vision that caused the author to produce it. This involves sympathetic imagination, or the capacity to place oneself in the author's shoes. The Romantic theorists rightly saw that in the process of interpretation there is a progressive interaction between understanding elements of a written text and provisionally grasping the sense of the whole. In biblical study, this means interaction between an analytical study of words or phrases and an attempt to grasp the message of a book or an author as a whole.

In the mid-twentieth century, a number of writers explored existentialist models of hermeneutics. Most notably, Rudolf Bultmann insisted that a narrative or descriptive mode of writing in the Bible can mislead us into failing to notice where such material serves primarily not to describe but to evoke some practical response from the reader. Thus "myth" (a descriptive or narrative mode) needs to be "demythologized," in other words, interpreted as preaching or *kerygma*. The strength of this approach is that it takes seriously the practical function of the Bible for its writers and earliest audiences. Its weaknesses are that it makes claims about the definition and use of "myth" that are open to question, and that it underplays the importance of historical report and factual truth claims in the New Testament.

Bultmann's pupil, Ernst Fuchs, together with Gerhard Ebeling, pioneered a movement that came to be known in the 1960s as the "new hermeneutic." It had close affinities with the philosophical hermeneutics of the later Martin Heidegger and Hans-Georg Gadamer. They argued that language does not merely communicate ideas; it creates a "world." Biblical language draws the interpreter into a world within which a new reality comes to life. This creative experience is described as a "language-event."

From the late 1960s to the late 1980s, various other hermeneutic models were explored. Liberation theology has taken up the sociocritical models of the social sciences by raising questions about the use of texts for the social control of communities. Paul Ricoeur and others have seen the earliest origins of a "hermeneutic of suspicion" in Marx, Nietzsche, and Freud. On the other hand, Ricoeur and, from a different angle, liberation theologians also seek to bring the situation of the present to bear on the text in order to produce positive meaning. Thus, feminist hermeneutics expresses suspicion of masculine interest and have attempted to derive feminist significance from new readings (*see* Feminism and the Bible). One critical question for such movements is whether the desire for change represents any less an "interest" than does desire to perpetuate the status quo.

Reader-response criticism in literary studies represents another model in process of exploration. The capacity of biblical texts to shape, revise, or confirm readers' expectations is seen as one further aspect of hermeneutic inquiry. Each of the models explored in the modern era underlines, in different ways, the many levels at which understanding, transformation, and action may take place in the encounter between the reader and the text.

See also Interpretation, History of, *article on* Modern Biblical Criticism.

Anthony C. Thiselton

HOLINESS. When the seraphim before God's throne cry "Holy, holy, holy" (Isa. 6.3; cf. Rev. 4.8), they are engaging in an ascriptive tautology. God is holy and by that fact defines holiness. "Hallowed be thy name" is a prayer that the intrinsic holiness of God be established and recognized within creation, that is, that God's kingdom come and God's will be done (Matt. 6.9–10 par.; *see* Lord's Prayer).

In *The Idea of the Holy,* Rudolph Otto argues that the experience of the holy is irreducible to other categories. What he calls "the numinous" is a *mysterium tremendum et fascinans,* an awe-inspiring phenomenon that both repels and attracts. The voice from the burning bush tells Moses to take off his shoes, for he is standing on holy ground, and Moses hides his face. In the Bible, the elementary religious experience takes on a personal and ethical tone. The "wholly other," the incomparable "Holy One" (Isa. 40.25), is also the transcendent creator. God's holy name is vindicated by his acts in history. If God inspires fear, it is on account of his power and *purity; if God attracts, it is by his creating love

and redeeming *grace. More precisely, God's power shows itself as love for the creature; God's purity shows itself as grace to transform the sinner. In his vision of "the King," Isaiah finds his lips touched with a burning coal and his guilt is taken away (Isa. 6.5–7). The prophet is then set in God's service.

God's active claim upon a creature consecrates it. That is preeminently true of God's elect people. Yahweh is, especially in the book of Isaiah, "the Holy One of Israel." He is "God and no mortal, the Holy One in [their] midst" (Hos. 11.9). Out of love, he has chosen this people for his own. Belonging to the God who dwells among them, they are a holy nation. The divine gift brings an obligation: "You shall be holy for I am holy" (Lev. 11.44; 19.2; 20.7, 26).

According to the New Testament, Jesus is "the Holy One of God" (John 6.69; cf. Mark 1.24 par.; Luke 1.35; Acts 3.14), and through him God's favor has been extended to believing gentiles. The church's vocation is to holiness. This again entails a way of life that distinguishes its members from the world.

The way of holiness follows God by imitation and even participation. Believers are "called [to be] saints" (Rom. 1.7; 1 Cor. 1.2; Col. 3.12). Having been sanctified in *baptism, Christians are to yield themselves to the righteousness of God for their sanctification to continue. Their sanctification is the work within them of the Holy Spirit who has been given to them. The promise is that of being made "partakers of the divine nature" (2 Pet. 1.3–11).

From the Exodus on, the *ark of the covenant was a sign—and a dangerous one—of Yahweh's presence with Israel. In the Jerusalem Temple, it belonged in the "holy of holies" (1 Kings 8.6). Divinely significant objects, places, times, and people were "holy," and the adjective became practically formulaic in the priestly documents of the postexilic period: God's holy house or Temple stood on God's holy mountain; it was served by a holy priesthood, and the feasts were holy days. A matching ethic was a prophetic concern. In the New Testament, cultic terminology is turned toward conduct: "Present your bodies as a living sacrifice, holy and acceptable to God" (Rom. 12.1; cf. 1 Cor. 6.19–20; Eph. 2.21–22).   *Geoffrey Wainwright*

HOLOCAUST. The English word *holocaust* is derived from Latin *holocaustum* and Greek *holocaustos / holokautos* (*holos,* "whole," and *kaustos / kautos,* "burnt"). Forms of the latter appear more than two hundred times in the Septuagint, generally to translate Hebrew *ʿōlâ* (literally, that which goes up), the burnt offering, one of the most common, multipurpose, and ancient forms of Israelite *sacrifice. The slaughtered sacrificial *animals, birds, or unblemished male quadrupeds such as sheep, goats, or cattle were wholly burned on the altar, with the exception of the skin, which was given to the priest who performed the ritual. The holocaust offering is mentioned three times in the New Testament. Although the sacrificial system ceased with the destruction of the Temple in 70 CE, rabbinic literature includes traditions about and discussions of the burnt offering, the earliest of which is in the Mishnah, especially tractates Zebaḥim and Tamid.

The meaning of "holocaust" has evolved from complete burnt consumption in sacrifice to include complete or massive destruction, especially of people. It was used in this context in the aftermaths of World War I and II. Since the 1950s, "The Holocaust" has come to refer to the Nazi murder of European Jewry (1941–1945). By extension, "ho-

locaust" is sometimes used to designate massive atrocities against or destruction of large numbers of people. The biblical religious-sacrificial origins and connotations of the term are troubling to some who prefer the word used most often in modern Hebrew to refer to the Nazi murder of European Jewry, *Shoʾah,* whose biblical meanings include devastation, desolation, and ruin.

Barbara Geller Nathanson

HOLY SPIRIT. There is no distinct term for spirit in the languages of the Bible; the concept was expressed by a metaphorical use of words that mean, literally, wind and breath (Hebr. *rûaḥ*; Grk. *pneuma*); the English word "spirit" is simply an Anglicized form of the Latin word for breath *(spiritus).* Wind is an invisible, unpredictable, uncontrollable force, which bears down on everything in its path; and people found early that they are exposed to influences that affect them like the wind. Breath is a miniature wind, and from this the metaphorical use of the term acquired a more precise and positive direction, for breath is essential to life.

The Spirit of God in the Hebrew Bible. The action of the spirit is seen in a broad range of experiences, some of which seem less than "spiritual" as we now understand the word. Thus the source of (physical) strength that enabled Samson to kill a lion is ascribed to the spirit of God. And there are several places where it is not clear whether *rûaḥ* bears the literal sense of wind or the metaphorical sense of spirit. The action of spirit is more often seen in inner experiences, but some of these too are ambiguous (e.g., the evil spirit from the Lord that seized Saul, 1 Sam. 16.14; the lying spirit that the Lord put in the mouth of certain prophets, 1 Kings 22.22). Among the most distinctive experiences ascribed to the action of the spirit are the raptures that drove people to ecstatic speech and behavior (e.g., Saul after his anointing, 1 Sam. 10.6–11; the seventy elders, Num. 11.25); this was the original meaning of "prophecy."

None of the prophets of Israel before the exile ascribe their vocation to the action of the spirit or, indeed, have much to say about the spirit at all. Some references of a critical or ironical nature seem to indicate that these prophets wished to dissociate their prophetic calling from the ecstatic raptures that earlier went under the name. It is only in the later prophets that the spirit comes into prominence, notably in Ezekiel. Ezekiel mostly used the term *rûaḥ* without the qualification "of God," and in many cases the literal and metaphorical senses of the term are hard to disentangle. A high point in the prophecy of Ezekiel is his vision of the valley of dry bones, over which he was commanded to invoke the life-giving breath, or wind, or spirit of God (Ezek. 37.1–14; the three words all render *rûaḥ*). The hope so dramatically envisaged here becomes a major theme in the latest phase of biblical prophecy. Recognizing that the renewal of God's people could come only from God, the prophets came to look for a general outpouring of his spirit. In no case is the fulfillment of this hope ascribed to the mediation of an expected messianic king; but in the portrayal of this figure in the prophecy of Isaiah, he is to be the permanent bearer of the spirit—perhaps in contrast to the charismatic leaders of Israel, such as Saul, from whom the spirit departed. The distinctive mark of the messianic era will be the bestowal of God's spirit on all, high and low, old and young, male and female.

The designation "holy spirit" occurs only in Psalm 51.11 and Isaiah 63.10–11.

The Holy Spirit in the New Testament. The New Testament announces the fulfillment of the eschatological hope of the spirit proclaimed by the prophets. Two elements are emphasized: the coming of the one who is the permanent bearer of the spirit and the outpouring of the spirit on "all flesh"; and both are linked.

Jesus is identified as the promised one on whom the Spirit will remain. This identification took place at his *baptism by the visible descent of the Holy Spirit on him in the form of a dove. The story need not imply that the association of the Spirit with Jesus began at his baptism and that he was at that moment adopted as *Son of God; John especially saw in the baptism of Jesus the epiphany of the preexisting Son, the one in whom the prophetic hope was fulfilled. According to Luke, Jesus explicitly claimed this identity in his sermon at Nazareth; and it is indicated in the nativity stories, where the emphasis is on the conception by the Holy Spirit rather than on the virginity of Mary (*see* Virgin Birth of Christ). Further references to the Holy Spirit are not frequent in the Gospels, but they occur at significant points, especially in Luke. It is preeminently in the presence and operation of the Holy Spirit in him that Jesus is authenticated; and thus to refuse the testimony of the Spirit is a sin that is infinitely graver than the sin of refusing the testimony of Jesus to himself. The life of Jesus is presented as wholly directed by the Holy Spirit, and this note recurs in the apostolic preaching in Acts.

Jesus is not only the permanent bearer of the Holy Spirit; he is also the one who will dispense the gift of the Holy Spirit to others. But this action of Jesus (which is expressed in the future tense in the first three Gospels) does not coincide with his manifestation as the bearer of the Spirit; it is projected into a future beyond the earthly mission of Jesus. There is a stated interval between the epiphany of Jesus and the general distribution of the Holy Spirit. Luke concludes his account of the ministry of Jesus with his command to the disciples to wait for the promise of the Father, and in the sequel he measures the period of waiting as fifty days after Easter. John expressed the same point in a different way, even though he records the promise made at the baptism of Jesus in the present tense, and he disagrees with the Lucan chronology in placing the gift of the Spirit to the disciples on the evening of Easter; early in his gospel John states that the gift of the Spirit could not be bestowed before Jesus was "glorified," that is, before he had completed his mission (John 7.39), and later, in one of the Paraclete sayings (see below), he stressed that the departure of Jesus must take place first, no matter how that grieves the disciples.

The five sayings about the Paraclete, perhaps a separate collection before their inclusion in the gospel according to John, contain the only formal teaching about the Holy Spirit in the New Testament. The term "Paraclete" (NRSV: "Advocate") belongs to the language of the law courts, and means a defending counsel, or attorney, as opposed to the accuser, who is called *diabolos* ("devil," Rev. 12.10). Paraclete is applied directly to Jesus himself in 1 John 2.1, and, indirectly, in John 14.16, where the word "another" implies a similarity between the Paraclete and Jesus himself; the Paraclete will be to the disciples what Jesus himself has been, and the coming of the Paraclete will be equivalent to a coming of Jesus himself (John 14.18, unless this is an allusion to the return of Jesus to the disciples after the Resurrection). But there are important differences, in addition to the sequential relation. The similarities and the differences may be listed summarily: the teaching of the Paraclete will be centered on Jesus and his teaching; the Paraclete will extend the range of Jesus' teaching to the world; the Paraclete will advance the disciples' understanding of "the truth," which is identical with Jesus; the presence of the Paraclete with the disciples will be permanent, in contrast to that of Jesus, which had to be withdrawn; the presence of the Paraclete will be invisible and inward.

The relation between Christ and the Holy Spirit is also close in Paul. The mission of Christ and the mission of the Holy Spirit are virtually indistinguishable; the presence of the Holy Spirit is equivalent to the presence of Christ. The Christ who is designated Son of God in power according to the Holy Spirit is no longer to be known according to the flesh.

The distinction between Christ and the Holy Spirit, where it appears in Paul, is nowhere expressed in terms of a sequence but rather as one between two sides or aspects of the same act of God; the mission of Christ presents its objective, or exterior, aspect, the mission of the Spirit its subjective, or interior, aspect. Paul's main concern is with the reality of Christ for faith; for the reality of Christ is accessible only to faith, and it is made accessible through the Holy Spirit. Thus to be "in Christ" (Rom. 8.1) is the same as to be "in the Spirit" (Rom. 8.9).

The notion of the "seven gifts" of the Holy Spirit, which was developed in Christian liturgical tradition, is based on Isaiah 11.2 (where the Septuagint and the Vulgate add "piety" after "knowledge"), but this number does not cover the endowments granted to different members of the church for the good of the whole; lists of these gifts, called "charismata," are found at various places in the New Testament.

George S. Hendry

HOLY WAR. *See* War.

HOMOSEXUALITY. Leviticus 20.13 prohibits sexual relations between men, defines them as an "abomination," and places them under the death penalty (see also Lev. 18.22). Ethical considerations such as consent, coercion, or the power imbalance inherent in adult-child relations are not legally relevant in these passages (nor in the surrounding levitical laws on adultery, incest, and bestiality). Thus, regardless of the sexual relationship of the participants (a man and his consenting male partner, an adult male whom he had raped, or a child victim), all are equally culpable, since all are equally defiled (see Philo, *De spec. leg.* 3.7.37–42).

Like Leviticus, Paul does not employ the ethical categories of consent or age for distinguishing between sanctioned and condemned sexual relations. His letters contain linguistic and conceptual parallels to the levitical laws about same-sex sexual relations. Thus, 1 Corinthians 6.9–10 states that "the ones who lie with men" (NRSV: "sodomites"; cf. Lev. 20.13) will not "inherit the kingdom of God." Paul describes male-male sexual relations as "impurity" and asserts that such men "deserve to die" (Rom. 1.24–32). Paul extends the prohibition to include sexual relations between women as do other postbiblical Jewish writings. Like other writers in the Roman world such as *Philo, Ptolemy, and Martial, Paul sees same-sex sexual relations as transgressions of hierarchical gender boundaries. For example, "unnatural" (Rom. 1.26) most likely refers to the women's attempt to transcend the passive, subordinate role accorded to them by nature. Similarly, the men have relinquished the superordinate, active role and have descended to the level of women.

Some postbiblical Jewish and early Christian writers specifically define the sin of Sodom and Gomorrah as same-sex relations rather than as rape or inhospitality; see, for example, Jude 7 and Philo, *De Abrahamo* 26.134–36 (cf. 2 Pet. 2.6; *Testament of Naphtali* 3.4–5; 4.1).

Biblical prohibitions of same-sex love directly influenced later Roman law and, indeed, Western legal statutes until the present (e.g., sodomy statutes in U.S. criminal law).

See also Sex.   *Bernadette J. Brooten*

HOPE. An attitude toward the future, an assurance that God's promises will be kept, a confidence that what is bad will pass and that what is good will be preserved. Hope is a theme in many places in the Bible, even when specific words for hope are not used.

In the Hebrew Bible, a number of words are translated into English as hope. As in English, hope can be a verb or a noun—the act of hoping, the thing hoped for, or the person or thing in whom one hopes. There is no single root word that carries the major responsibility for conveying this concept. Each word provides a slightly different nuance to the process of hoping, though we may not be able to identify each subtle distinction. The related words *qāwâ* (verb) and *tiqwâ* (noun) may be connected with meanings like "twist," "cord," or "rope," possibly referring to the tension of a time of hoping or the rope to which one clings when in need of hope. The root of the words *yāḥal* (verb) and *tôḥelet* (noun) may mean simply "to wait," being neutral about what will happen at the end of the waiting. Similarly, the verb *šābar* means "to watch," "wait," "expect"; it becomes hope when one waits with a positive expectation about what will come.

Two words sometimes translated as hope show the relational quality of hope. The verb *ḥāsâ* can mean "to flee for protection," "to take refuge," "to put trust." The word *bāṭaḥ* is usually translated as "trust," but it can be understood as "hope," as the Septuagint often does. In the New Testament, the noun *elpis* and the verb *elpizein* are virtually the only words translated as hope. They are used widely in the epistles, rarely in the Gospels, and not at all in the book of Revelation. This shows clearly that hope may be expressed by a text (such as in the words of Jesus or in Revelation) even when the specific word for hope is not present.

Hope has both an objective and subjective aspect. There are promises from God to which one clings as one faces the unknown and often forbidding future. But as suggested by a word like *bāṭaḥ*, hope is also an inner sense of confidence in God, a serenity despite terrible present circumstances. Whatever strengthens *faith will also increase hope. Experiences that bring on a crisis of faith, like the *exile or persecution of the early Christians, will also make hope more difficult.

God's promises form the basis for the content of biblical hope. From the objective side, hope is dependent on the confidence that God will provide: (1) The necessities of life—food, *water, land. Without food and water, there is no hope even for life. Land plays an important part in biblical hope—it is promised, given, removed, and promised again. (2) Protection from danger—both as a community called by God and as individuals. God sends leaders—judges, kings—to protect the nation. When the nation falls, God promises a new and better king from the line of David, one who will outdo his illustrious ancestor (messianic promises in Isaiah, Jeremiah, Micah, and elsewhere). God will also protect individuals from all that can hurt them. (3) Justice—the good will be rewarded and the wicked will be restrained and punished. (4) Community—the assurance that God will never abandon the people he has chosen, and that they will live in peace and love with other human beings.

Generally speaking, there is in the Bible a growing pessimism that God's promises will be kept within historical time; this is most clearly seen in *apocalyptic writings. Confidence in God remains and hope as relationship survives, but language that had been used to articulate hope for this world is now projected into a world beyond human experience: the land becomes a heavenly home, food and water become heavenly food and the water of life; the Messiah becomes a divine being; heaven and *hell are the final solution to the problem of justice; communities broken by death and tragedy and sin can be restored in heaven. In spite of the failures and disillusionments of this life, however, there is still hope. God will win the heavenly battle. There will be a resurrection, life after death, and a new age where God reigns.

See also Afterlife and Immortality.

Daniel J. Simundson

HUMAN PERSON. The idea of the human person, so important in modern times thanks especially to the study of psychology, was not a focus of ancient Israelite thought. Because of the corporate identity of the people of Israel, the individual person did not receive much attention in the literature of Israel. However, as Israel moved into a later period, and particularly after its encounter with Hellenism, the nature of the individual and his or her fate became much more prominent both in Second Temple Judaism and early Christianity.

The Hebrew word for the human being is *nepeš*, which among its wide range of meanings connotes both flesh and soul as inseparable components of a person. A *nepeš*, or person, is first of all a living being, animated by breath. The life of a person is seen as residing in the *blood as well as in the breath; therefore, it is unlawful to shed or to eat blood. Thus, an essential component of the person is the flesh (Hebr. *bāśār*), which is separate from God and carries a connotation of weakness. All animals are composed of flesh, and the human animal is no different in this regard.

However, a person is also composed of "soul," so that less concrete attributes also belong to the person. Appetites such as hunger and thirst; emotions like desire, loathing, sorrow, joy, and love; and thought or mental activity all belong to the *nepeš*. This is how the human differs from animals, who are only flesh; the human, who has been animated by the breath of God, shares in the attributes of God.

At death, the person's flesh dies, and the soul dwells in Sheol, a shadowy place for the dead (*see* Afterlife and Immortality; Hell). There is no notion in what may be called orthodox Israelite religion of a separate existence for the soul after death. Death is accepted as a natural part of the life cycle, but it is not welcomed, for the person who dies loses his or her being. In a prayer of thanksgiving, the psalmist says to the Lord, "What profit is there in my death, if I go down to the Pit? Will the dust praise you? Will it tell of your faithfulness?" (Ps. 30.9). Death is thus perceived to be the end of all sentient life. In later times, a doctrine of the resurrection of the dead developed, so that the best hope of the person after death lay in resurrection, when the soul and body would be reunited and live again.

With the introduction of Hellenism into the ancient Near East, Israelite thought began to espouse the notion of a separation of soul and body. In Greek thought, body (*sōma*) is separate from soul (*psychē*), and the soul contains the true essence of a person. At death, the soul flees the prison of the body to seek a higher life, so that death is truly the liberation of the soul. As Jewish thought began to be influenced by Greek, these concepts emerge in its literature. *Philo, an Alexandrian Jewish philosopher of the first century CE, assumes throughout his works a complete separation of soul and body, with flesh the chief cause of ignorance and soul the vehicle for a higher life. *Josephus, the first-century CE Jewish historian, states that the Pharisees believe that souls have the power to survive death (*Ant.* 18.1.14), and that the Essenes believe that the soul is immortal (*Ant.* 18.1.18). It is probable, however, that the immortality both of these groups anticipate includes a bodily resurrection.

In the New Testament, the still prominent idea of bodily resurrection (*see* especially the resurrection narratives in the Gospels and also 1 Cor. 15) implies that the soul and body are inseparable, but the notion of a human being composed of a separate soul and body slowly gains ascendancy. There are several Greek words used to explain different aspects of the human person. The Greek word *sarx*, the equivalent of Hebrew *bāśār*, denotes the flesh of both animals and humans. It often appears with the word "blood," as in "flesh and blood," to signify the physical being of the human (as opposed to a supernatural being such as an angel, which is not composed of flesh and blood). As early as Paul, the word "flesh" begins to receive negative connotations, as the vehicle for *sin in the human being.

The body is the physical being of the person animated by the soul. As such, it is both physical and spiritual, and sometimes is used as the equivalent of *nepeš*. Paul uses the term *sōma* in his metaphor of the church as the body of Christ, animated by Christ's spirit.

The word *psychē,* or soul, occurs over a hundred times in the New Testament, illustrating its importance in early Christian thought. The soul is the seat and center of the inner life of the human, and the location of the feelings and emotions, especially love. The soul is that part of the human person that survives after the death of the body, and receives the rewards and punishments of the afterlife. Thus the soul is the vehicle of *salvation. It cannot be injured by human instrumentality, but God can hand it over for destruction. Therefore the soul is the most important possession a person has. Thus the New Testament has moved beyond the Hebrew Bible concept of an inseparable *nepeš,* to the idea of a separate soul and body. The soul survives after death, but may be reunited with the body in a physical resurrection.

The last word associated with the makeup of the human being in the New Testament is *pneuma,* or spirit. The spirit is the breath, that which gives life to the body; in fact, it is often used with "flesh" or "body" to denote the whole person (1 Cor. 5.3–5). The spirit is the seat of insight, often giving persons glimpses of things not visible to the naked eye. The spirit is also the location of feeling (particularly of love and grief) and will, so that at times the spirit and the flesh are in conflict: "the spirit indeed is willing, but the flesh is weak" (Matt. 26.41). The usage of the word "spirit" often overlaps with that of "soul," and the two together divide the inner life between them. The use of the term "spirit" in connection with Jesus, however, emphasizes the most important aspect of "spirit": it is the divine attribute of the human being. God, who is spiritual, breathed his own spirit into the human at creation, and now the human spirit and the divine spirit are related. Often, it is the spirit of God that animates the life of the Christian, as at *Pentecost. And it is the *Holy Spirit which calls to the human spirit: "it is that very Spirit bearing witness with our spirit that we are children of God" (Rom. 8.16). Thus, early Christian writers pictured the human person as composed of flesh, soul, and spirit, with the flesh, as the vehicle of sin, as something to be tamed, and the soul and spirit, as the vehicles for salvation and participation in the divine, as those parts of the human to be emphasized and nurtured.

Sidnie Ann White

I

IDOLS, IDOLATRY. An idol is a figure or image worshiped as the representation of a deity. Idols normally take the form of figures in the round or in relief. Strictly prohibited in the Bible, idolatry was widely practiced in the religions of the ancient Near East. Because of their popular appeal, idols became the frequent object of attack in biblical literature.

More than ten different Hebrew words in the Bible designate various types of idols. Some are distinguished according to the method of their construction: "carved image" of stone, clay, wood, or metal; "cast idol" of metal; "pillar," usually an unhewn stone set erect. Other terms have a more general meaning of "shape, form," and thus "representation." The few with a distinctly pejorative sense are not technical names but terms conveying contempt for idolatry: "abominations," "dung-pellets," or "worthless things."

In the religions of ancient Israel's neighbors, idolatry constituted a primary component of public and private piety, and archaeological excavations throughout the region have recovered examples from earliest times onward. These range from crude to elaborate artistic productions of figures in human or animal form, or a mixture of both. Unworked pieces, such as a meteorite rock or a simple wood pillar, could also serve as idols. Egyptian idols, normally kept in temples,

were cultically awakened at daybreak, nourished through sacrifices, dressed and adorned with jewels, and carried about on festive occasions. In Babylonia, idols could also serve as oracles and were placed at the entrances of homes to guard against witches and evil spirits. The Canaanites, as did others, formed some of their idols with explicit sexual features, consistent with their fertility cult's concern to ensure the fruitfulness of the land and the womb.

It is not always easy to determine how idols were interpreted in the various religions. In an Egyptian text known as "The Theology of Memphis," the high god Ptah is said to have created not only all other gods but also the idols in which they were to live. This notion—that the idols are not themselves the gods but rather represent them or house them—was probably present in many religions, though such a distinction may not have been made by all believers, as the various cultic practices of caring for the idols seem to suggest. Several later Greek and Roman thinkers wrote polemically to the effect that weak and ignorant people need idols to help them imagine their gods, maintain faith in them, and have the magical means for securing blessing and avoiding disaster.

Strict prohibition of idolatry is one of the most distinctive features of Israelite religion: Yahweh, the God of Israel, could not be represented in physical form and would not tolerate the idols of any other gods. This aniconic principle is articulated in the *Ten Commandments: "You shall not make for yourself an idol, or any likeness of anything . . . ; you shall not bow down to them or serve them" (Exod. 20.4–5 [RSV]). Historically, it is uncertain when and why this prohibition first arose. Probably it is early and is directly connected to the demand for exclusive worship of Yahweh alone. Monolatry, while implicitly recognizing the existence of other gods, did not allow for worshiping them, and this perhaps led to banning idolatry altogether in the official cult of Israel.

Nonetheless, there are records of the presence of idols throughout Israel's history. Rachel's cunning theft of her father's household gods is perhaps less an instance of idolatry than of the usurping of the father's traditional cultic and legal powers in the family. The *golden calves erected first by Aaron in the wilderness and later by Jeroboam I at Dan and Bethel were, on the other hand, regarded as flagrant violations, at least in some Judean circles. Idolatry occurred also in later periods of the monarchy and became the object of reforms by King Hezekiah and King Josiah. With the impending fall of Jerusalem, Ezekiel reported that the people again reverted to idols in hope of escaping destruction. In biting sarcasm, both Jeremiah and Second Isaiah exposed the futility of worshiping the products of human hands.

The line between idol representations and permissible cultic objects may at points seem unclear; the *ark, with its gold cherubim, was not considered an idol but a manifestation of God's presence; similarly ambiguous were the teraphim, the ephod, the Nehushtan or bronze serpent, and the oxen supporting the molten sea in Solomon's Temple.

The criterion for illicit use of such cultic objects apparently lay in whether they were worshiped directly as manipulable substitutes for Yahweh. Theologically, aniconism became a means for insisting that Yahweh cannot—by virtue of the chasm between creator and creation—be rendered adequately in any physical form. The nature of Israel's God must be reflected not in an image but in all aspects of the people's socioeconomic, political, legal, and domestic life. The prohibition of idolatry was thus coupled with commands for alternate types of religious and moral behavior.

The New Testament polemic against idolatry was primarily related to the opposition to Greco-Roman gods. The "desolating sacrilege" in Mark 13.14 may be an allusion to the Roman emperor cult. Paul discussed at some length the problem of whether Christians should eat meat sacrificed to idols, and he concluded that, while such food was untainted because the idols represented nonexistent gods, Christians should be cautious not to let this practice undermine weaker believers. Figuratively, idolatry designated a shifting of reverence to worldly things, including covetousness and gluttony.

The prohibition against representation of divine or human beings has been observed in synagogue ornamentation in most periods, and is strictly complied with in Islamic religious architecture as well. In Christianity, strict observance of the prohibition has surfaced in such movements as iconoclasm and Puritanism, and there are significant differences in practice between Roman Catholic and Orthodox churches, on the one hand, and some Protestant churches, on the other.

See also Graven Image; Monotheism.
    Douglas A. Knight

ILLUSTRATED BIBLES. The subject of illustrations to the Bible includes not only two-dimensional designs, such as paintings, drawings, engravings, photographs, stained-glass windows, and mosaics, but three-dimensional works as well, such as statues and bas-reliefs. Raphael's madonnas, Michelangelo's Moses, the windows of Chartres Cathedral, the ceiling mosaics of the Santa Sophia in Istanbul, and Ghiberti's great doors to the Baptistry in Florence are all, in a sense, Bible illustrations. Annotations to the Bible are also illustrations of it, and originally this was perhaps the primary meaning of "Bible illustrations." In at least one of these senses, there have been "illustrations" of the Bible since it was written and canonized. Not only were there biblical commentaries from the earliest times, but the interpretation of the commandment against *graven images as a total prohibition of visual representation of sacred (or perhaps any other) scenes was not uniform even in Jewish tradition—note, for example, the cycle of paintings of scenes from the Hebrew Bible on the walls of the Dura-Europos synagogue, destroyed by the Persians in 256 CE.

The earliest Christian visual representations of the Bible were apparently emblematic, with Jesus depicted as "the fish" (the Greek word for fish, *ichthus,* was understood as an acronym for "Jesus Christ, God's Son, savior"), and up to the fifth century the *crucifixion was always shown symbolically rather than literally. The first narrative cycle of biblical illustrations is the mosaics in Santa Maria Maggiore in Rome, 432–440 CE, and narrative art is much more common in the West than in the eastern churches. Often postbiblical traditions are also represented; for example, Job is depicted as a bishop and as the patron saint of music.

We are concerned in this article with illustrations *in* Bibles, largely a Christian phenomenon. The earliest such illustrations now known, from about 400 CE, are for separate sections of the Bible, particularly the *Pentateuch, the Gospels, and the book of Revelation. Complete illustrated Bibles first appear in the Carolingian period in the eighth century.

The visual matter in such illuminated manuscript Bibles generally consists of three kinds of work: illuminated initial letters, particularly the first word of a book, often merely formal but sometimes representing more or less relevant scenes, such as Paul preaching; decorated borders, with flowers or scrolls or beasts, usually not closely related to their texts; and miniature pictures representing a scene in the text. The illuminated Romanesque Bibles were often very fine, but in them the illustrations were generally less important than the decorations. The illuminated initials in Bibles of the seventh and eighth centuries indicate the dominance of the text over the designs. Among the best-known early illustrated Bibles are the seventh-century Lindisfarne Gospels in the British Museum and the eighth-century Book of Kells in Trinity College, Dublin.

In some cases, the illustrations were not only derived from the text but were more extensive and perhaps even more important than it. The *Bible Moralisée,* made for Louis IX about 1240, had some five thousand illustrations, now scattered among the Bodleian Library, the British Museum, and the Bibliothèque Nationale. Indeed, the *Biblia pauperum,* the Bible for the illiterate poor, consisted chiefly of illustrations. The *Biblia pauperum* was a textbook of Christian *typology, often showing two Old Testament exempla or types (such as Moses in the wilderness) flanking their New Testament echo or antitype (such as Christ in the wilderness), accompanied by appropriate quotations and an explanatory verse in Latin. These were particularly popular in Germany in the thirteenth century. Later, books printed from engraved blocks of wood (not from movable type) with biblical illustrations were also popular in Germany, though they. are comparatively rare in Italy and Spain. These block books were enormously influential in the fifteenth and sixteenth centuries; their images were copied in sculpture (e.g., misericords), tapestry, stained glass, and paintings. They became the visual lingua franca of the medieval church.

The first printed Bible, that by Johannes *Gutenberg in the mid-fifteenth century, had no printed illustrations, but in some copies, manuscript borders and initials were added to make the work as beautiful as the manuscript Bibles that it was imitating. There were woodcuts in a German Bible of 1478–1479, and later illustrators included Hans Holbein in a Bible of 1522–1523 and Hans Burgkmair in a Bible of 1523. Since then, many great artists have made at least some biblical illustrations; among the best known are those by Raphael and Gustave Doré, and, in the modern period, Georges Rouault and Marc Chagall.

In England, Winchester was the most important center for early book illustration and its artisans produced innovative and very fine work, particularly about 1000, remarkable especially for depictions of the *Ascension and the creator. The Bible itself was central for Protestant reformers, and Luther's translation of the Bible was one of the most popular books ever published. Further, Luther actively encouraged illustration of the Bible, so long as the text was followed meticu-

lously. But biblical illustration was slow to develop in England, partly because the country was aesthetically backward and partly because the English Puritans were strongly iconoclastic, deploring all visual representations of holy subjects. It was not until the Restoration of Charles II in 1660 that significant illustrated Bibles were printed in England.

The first great illustrated Bible of the Restoration is the two-volume folio of *The Holy Bible* printed at Cambridge by John Field with a hundred marvelous double-page plates by Jan Visscher; a splendid copy bound in 1673 in velvet with watered silk endpapers is in the Norwich Cathedral Library. As in most fine book illustration in England before 1750, the artists and even the engravers were from the Continent, chiefly from Holland and France. An equally ambitious folio edition of *The Holy Bible* was published at Oxford by John Baskett in 1716–1717 with sixty-seven plates mostly designed by Louis Cheron and engraved by Michael Van der Gucht and Claude Du Bosc, as well as engraved initial letters. This was issued on two sizes of page and with two suites of designs, and the magnificent copy in the Bodleian is printed on vellum, lined in red throughout, and bound in velvet with the arms of the university in silver plaques on the covers.

Before 1750, however, the illustrations in most English Bibles came from separately published suites of designs engraved by John Sturt (1716) and James Cole (1724) and added to plain texts of the Bible by the bookseller or the purchaser. One reason for this may have been that copyright of the King James translation of the Bible belonged to the crown and was assigned only to the university presses at Oxford and Cambridge and to the royal printer in London. As John Reeves, "One of the Patentees" (*see* Printing and Publishing, *article on* Royal Printer's Patent), explained in his great, nonillustrated *Holy Bible* of 1802, "These privileged persons have confined themselves to reprinting the bare text, in which they have an exclusive right; forbearing to publish it with notes, which, it is deemed, may be done by any of the King's subjects as well as themselves." Toward the middle of the eighteenth century, enterprising publishers began publishing the King James translation with notes and with illustrations, and, to distinguish their productions from those protected by the crown's perpetual copyright, called them *The Family Bible* or even *The Royal Universal Family Bible* (1780–1782). Other ways of evading the copyright were to publish a *History of the Holy Bible,* or a paraphrase, or an abridgment. Frequently, perhaps normally, these works were published in inexpensive parts, often sixpence each, in folio, with extensive illustrations, sometimes a hundred and more engravings. There were scores of these bulky publications during the eighteenth century; among the most impressive editions were those printed in Birmingham by John Baskerville (1769–1772), with engravings by James Fittler (London, 1795), and with plates after Richard Corbould and Charles R. Ryley (London, 1795). But the most ambitious illustrated Bible ever published in Britain was that undertaken by Thomas Macklin and published in parts from 1791 to 1800 with seventy huge and splendid plates designed by the greatest English artists, such as Benjamin West and Sir Joshua Reynolds, and engraved by the best of the English engravers. Macklin's influence on English artists and publishers was great. For instance, in the first twenty-one years of Royal Academy exhibitions (1769–1789), there had been an average of six or seven biblical illustrations per year,

but in the eleven years from Macklin's announcement of his great undertaking in 1789 until its completion in 1800, seventeen biblical subjects were exhibited per year. In addition Macklin held his own exhibition of the biblical pictures he had commissioned. There were later popular Bible illustrators in England, most notably perhaps John Martin, but no illustrated edition of the Bible in England has surpassed that of Thomas Macklin.

See also Art and the Bible; Children's Bibles.   *G. E. Bentley, Jr.*

IMAGE. *See* Graven Image.

IMMORTALITY. *See* Afterlife and Immortality.

INCARNATION. Literally meaning "enfleshment," incarnation is the entry of divinity into human form and life. In some religions this is thought of as something that happens repeatedly, but in the New Testament, incarnation is a once-and-for-all occurrence in Jesus Christ.

The earliest Christian terms for interpreting Jesus had been drawn from the eschatological hope for a future transformation of existence. In the gospel of John this hope became secondary, and incarnation—the bringing together of the human and divine in a specific person, Jesus—became the central way of interpreting the divine presence in him.

The effort to express the full presence of God in Jesus led to the conclusion that this specific mode of presence had existed with God prior to the life of Jesus; this preexistent figure had been God's agent in creating the world. The existence of Christ before the creation is already present in Paul's writings as they are commonly interpreted and in the non-Pauline Hebrews 1.1–3. Some question the presence of a clear belief in the preexistence of Christ before the relatively late gospel of John. According to this view, the belief developed gradually among Christians from Jewish wisdom theology, which was first applied to the full preexistence of Christ in John. But wisdom and word (*see* Logos) were spoken of in Jewish and early Christian circles as personified entities, and most scholars hold that this imagery had already provided a way of thinking about a preexistent Christ.

Incarnation is meaningful when the distance between the divine and the human is strongly held. This dualism of *flesh and spirit and its overcoming in the incarnation opened the way for the development of later incarnational theology, which held that the goal of the incarnation was the transformation of the human into a nature compatible with the divine.

The Johannine theology of incarnation served as a focal point in the thought of the early church. It became a unifying center for the development of the doctrine of the full divinity and full humanity of Christ and the doctrine of the *Trinity.

The theology of incarnation has been actively debated in modern times. Some regard incarnation as an ancient mythological form of thought; others see in the incarnation a clue to the universal entering of God into human life; still others see the particularity of the incarnation in Jesus Christ as the distinctive core of Christianity.   *William A. Beardslee*

INCENSE. Incense is formed from the resin and gums of certain trees that, when burned, give off a fragrant odor. Incense was widely used in the ancient Near East both domestically, as a perfume, and in religious rites, as a *sacrifice or as a means of driving away demons.

The use of incense in Israelite worship parallels its widespread use in Canaanite ritual. The prophets' denunciation of it relates to their denunciation of sacrifices offered by unethical persons, or because incense was being burned before *idols. The reference in Ezekiel 16.18 to "my [i.e., God's] incense" shows that the offering, which should have been made to God, was being blasphemously misused.

In the Hebrew Bible, we find three main uses of incense. First, it supplemented the grain offering, for which pure frankincense was prescribed. Doubtless, some form of incense was used with animal sacrifices to counteract the stench of burning flesh. Second, its use in censers was part of Egyptian ritual, and was included in Israelite worship, probably from an early period. Finally, as part of the sacrificial system, incense was burned on the golden altar within the sanctuary; it was burned regularly twice a day. This offering was restricted to the priests who officiated according to a roster. On the *Day of Atonement, the high priest entered the holy of holies with a censer to cover the mercy seat with a cloud of smoke, lest he be exposed to the presence of God and die.

In the New Testament there are few references to the use of incense. Most concern Israelite practices, though Revelation 5.8 and 8.3–4, describing the worship of heaven, may reflect early Christian ritual. After the destruction of the Temple and the cessation of the sacrificial system, however, incense is unlikely to have been used by Jews or Christians; its use in other religions, and especially in the imperial cult, would have made it suspect. There are no references to Christian use of incense in the first four centuries CE.

Its use in worship from the fifth century onward probably derived from its ordinary use to show respect for eminent persons, who were sometimes preceded by servants with censers. It is therefore significant that it has been used especially in the Eucharist to cense the ministers, the people, the gospel book, the altar, and the eucharistic elements, all of which are regarded as representations of Christ himself to whom honor is due. This conception was perhaps helped by the understanding of incense as symbolizing the prayers of God's people.

John N. Suggit

INERRANCY. *See* Inspiration and Inerrancy.

INHERITANCE. In its secular sense, inheritance is the transmission of property on the owner's death to those entitled to receive it. In Israel this was the right of those related by blood, generally the sons, among whom the firstborn received a double portion. The Hebrew word for inheritance, *naḥălâ*, can also mean possession or portion. There are, however, few legal provisions concerning inheritance in the Hebrew Bible, and its meaning there is primarily theological.

Thus, the land of Canaan is frequently mentioned as the territory that God gives to Israel. God had promised it to the ancestors, first to Abra(ha)m, then to each succeeding patriarch and to Moses. It was divided up among the tribes, so that each received its own inheritance. The nation, too, is often described as the Lord's inheritance and therefore holy. Only if the people maintain their *holiness by keeping God's commandments can they keep possession of the land. Thus, the inheritance of the land is a sign of God's faithfulness in fulfilling his promises and a reminder of Israel's duties toward him as the true owner of the land.

After the *exile, various developments occur in the concept of inheritance. With the dispersion of many of the nation from the land of Israel, possession of the Promised Land increasingly becomes a future hope. With the full development of *monotheism, the inheritance that God gives to Israel includes all peoples and countries. He is the portion of the individual believer as representative of the righteous *remnant that can trust only in God. In the book of Wisdom and other writings, the inheritance of the righteous is eternal life.

Various aspects of these ideas are resumed in the New Testament. The promise of inheritance to Abraham is fulfilled in Christ, so that he is the promised inheritance. Similarly, in the parable of the evil tenants, Christ is the son to whom inheritance rightly belongs, and after his death it passes to his followers.

For Paul, Christians are the real descendants of Abraham, because they share in the inheritance with Christ, to whom the promise to Abraham properly refers. This means that the inheritance now belongs not just to Abraham's physical descendants but also to faithful non-Israelites, the gentiles.

Finally, the concept of inheritance is eschatological. Although a present reality, it is more commonly viewed as something Christians will receive only in the heavenly realm beyond this world. Thus, it is defined as "eternal life" or "the kingdom," which are to be possessed when the *Son of man returns at the end of time (Matt. 19.29; 25.34). Similarly, the letter to the Hebrews reinterprets the promise to Abraham to refer not to Canaan but to the heavenly city (Heb. 11.8–10). *Hope is the link between present and future, as is the sealing by the Holy Spirit that guarantees to Christians their promised inheritance until they can finally possess it.

J. R. Porter

INSPIRATION AND INER-RANCY. With regard to the Bible, inspiration denotes the doctrine that the human authors and editors of canonical scripture were led or influenced by the Deity, with the result that their writings may be designated in some sense the *word of God. The theological corollary of inspiration, inerrancy, indicates that these writings have been thereby supernaturally protected from error, thus implying that scripture is entirely trustworthy and uniquely authoritative for a given community of faith. The categories of inspiration and inerrancy derive from traditional Christian theology, although analogous conclusions concerning their scriptures would be held by most Orthodox and Conservative Jews.

By far, the most comprehensive of the two terms is inspiration, which is derived from a Latin word meaning "to breathe into or upon." More focused than general usage, in which a literary or artistic work, or the like, is said to be inspired if it is intellectually, emotionally, or volitionally moving, the theological term designates what for the community of faith would have been an objective reality: the sacred scriptures are nothing less than authentic communication from the Deity, or, as the First Vatican Council (1868–1870) simply expressed it, "they have God as their author." In Christian theology, with its traditional trinitarian understanding of the one God as three persons (Father, Son, and Holy Spirit), it is usually the third person of the *Trinity who is specified as having inspired the scriptures.

The theological category of inerrancy is of less venerable vintage; the term does not appear either in Latin or in English before the nineteenth century, and modern Protestant fundamentalists often employ it in a separative and polemical way. Inerrancy denotes the quality of er-

rorlessness (hence, truthfulness) in all the scripture affirms. Related theological concepts such as *authority and infallibility also seek to define the utter dependability of the Bible as uniquely the word of God. Many contemporary theologians avoid the term inerrancy on the grounds that, on the one hand, too much is claimed by it (a focus on the total exclusion of mistakes rather than on the complete absence of deception, as the early church fathers emphasized), and, on the other hand, too little (typically, only the now nonexistent autographs, or original manuscripts, are deemed inerrant; all admit that the later copies contain errors).

Nonetheless, even if the term inerrant itself is of recent and controversial pedigree, the underlying concept of the complete truthfulness and dependability of all that scripture affirms has long been a part of both Jewish and Christian tradition. (Traditional Muslims would enthusiastically categorize the *Qurʾān with the same terms.) Those books that the rabbis categorized as "defiling the hands," and hence sacred scripture, were highly revered by the late first century CE, as *Josephus indicates: "We have given practical proof of our reverence for our own scriptures. For, although such long ages have now passed, no one has ventured either to add, or to remove, or to alter a syllable; and it is an instinct with every Jew, from the day of his birth, to regard them as the decrees of God, to abide by them, and, if need be, cheerfully to die for them" (*Ag. Ap.* 1.42).

The Jewish scriptures were of course sacred for Jesus and his followers, and gospel traditions present him as regarding them as humanly inalterable and inviolate. For Jesus and the New Testament writers, the sacred books were "the scriptures" par excellence, and in the words of these scriptures the Holy Spirit of God spoke through human agency. Typically, words from the mouth of Yahweh found in the Hebrew Bible are labeled "scripture" in the New Testament, and even quotations not originally from the mouth of God are sometimes designated as such. Indeed, the Hebrew Bible as a whole is twice designated the "oracles of God" (Rom. 3.2; Heb 5.12), and in the classic New Testament text concerning God's inspiration of the Hebrew scriptures, 2 Timothy 3.14–17, Paul is pictured exhorting Timothy, his Jewish convert, to remember the "sacred writings" he has known since childhood, for "all scripture" (evidently a reference to all, or nearly all, of the books now included in the Hebrew *canon) is "inspired by God" (Grk. *theopneustos,* probably meaning "breathed out by God") and therefore "useful for both doctrinal instruction and ethical guidance." Similarly, the divine origin of the scripture is clearly emphasized in 2 Peter 1.21.

To be sure, the human origins of the scriptures were not altogether ignored. The personalities of the prophets Jeremiah and Ezekiel vividly shine through much of the literature attributed to them, and few readers of any age would confuse the writings of one with those of the other, even though they were contemporaries and often spoke about the same topics. The same could be said for the eighth-century BCE Judahite prophets Micah and Isaiah. Considerably later, probably in the early first century BCE, the writer of 2 Maccabees provided a memorable description of the human cost of authorship (2.24–32), including "sweat and loss of sleep," and he concluded his book as follows: "If it is well told and to the point, that is what I myself desired; if it is poorly done and mediocre, that was the best I could do. For just as it is harmful to drink wine alone, or, again, to drink water alone, while

wine mixed with water is sweet and delicious and enhances one's enjoyment, so also the style of the story delights the ears of those who read the work" (15.38–39). As for the New Testament, a roundabout and not altogether complimentary attestation of the scriptural status of Paul's letters may be found in 2 Peter 3.15–16. Likewise Luke's own efforts at research are recalled in his preface to his gospel. Indeed, apostolic authorship, whether actual or pseudonymous, of the New Testament writings served as a major criterion for later acceptance into the canon. Nevertheless, the relationship between the divine and human "authors" of scripture has never been easily delineated.

The subordination of the human author to the divine is clearly assumed in the New Testament. Not surprisingly, later Christian theological speculation attempted to refine the nature of this subordination, and the early church fathers utilized images for the human author such as the mouth, finger, lyre, minister, or deacon of God. Rabbinic Judaism also recognized the heavenly origin of scripture, especially the *Torah. In a discussion of interpretations of the harsh denunciation of the "high-handed" sinner of Numbers 15.30–31, the Babylonian Talmud observes, "This refers to him who maintains that the Torah is not from Heaven. And even if he asserts that the whole Torah is from Heaven, excepting a particular verse, which [he maintains] was not uttered by God but by Moses himself, he is included in 'because he has despised the word of the Lord'" (*b. Sanh.* 99a).

Already in the first century CE, the Hellenistic Jewish philosopher *Philo of Alexandria proposed what may be termed the "mantic theory" of the inspiration of the scriptures, in which the human author becomes possessed by

God and loses consciousness of self, surrendering to the divine spirit and its communicatory powers. The second-century Christian apologist Athenagoras also subscribed to such a theory, as did the Montanists, most notably Tertullian (d. ca. 225). But this was a minority position, with both Hippolytus (ca. 170–236) and Origen (ca. 185–254) denying that the biblical writers lost their free will under the force of divine pressure. In the Middle Ages emphasis was usually given only to the divine origin of the Bible, with little interest given to its human writers, although Henry of Ghent (d. 1293) did assert that the human authors were true, if secondary, authors of the books of scripture, not merely organs or channels for the divine message.

But it was not until the Renaissance and Reformation that serious speculation as to the nature of biblical inspiration took place. One of the principal theories popular then was what may be termed the dictation theory, in which God communicated to the human writer the very words of scripture, the human contribution merely being the exact and conscious reception of the divine message. Other views included that of Sixtus of Siena (1520–1569) that hypothetically a book of scripture could have been composed by purely human means, with the later approval of the church attesting to its inspiration; and Jacques Bonfrère (1573–1642), who suggested that some parts of the Bible were written only under the negative assistance of the Holy Spirit, which kept the writers from error but otherwise exerted no influence on them. The christological emphasis of Martin Luther (1483–1546) should probably be mentioned at this point; he adopted what may be termed an incarnational view of biblical inspiration, with the divinity and power of God embedded in scripture in the same way as it

was in Christ's body. Luther's scorn for the letter of James, which in his opinion did not preach Christ sufficiently, is well known: he termed it a "right strawy epistle." John Calvin (1509–1564) returned to an emphasis on the divine origin of scripture, but he also stressed the concept of accommodation, God adapting the divine message to human capacity through words that accommodated their limited understanding. Post-Reformation Protestant theologians, however, tended to return to the scholasticism of the Middle Ages, describing the inspiration of the Bible as "verbal" (the very words are those chosen by God) and "plenary" (every word, even every letter of scripture is inspired). This view is akin to that of contemporary Protestant fundamentalists.

As a result of the Enlightenment, theologians have focused on issues of biblical authority; for example, whether the Bible, the product of ancient cultures, has any claim on modern humanity. Supernatural revelation was often denied in whole or in part, with such views gaining further support from the rise of modern biblical criticism in the nineteenth century (*see* Interpretation, History of, *article on* Modern Biblical Criticism). To be sure, there were exceptions such as millenarians and pietists, but for most the overarching question became and still remains whether and to what degree the Bible is inspired by God, not by what manner such inspiration took place. Today all but the most extreme Jewish and Christian fundamentalists recognize the complicated and heterogeneous origins of the Bible and that it contains statements that in any other literary work would be considered erroneous. Modern biblical criticism has immeasurably enriched our understanding of biblical backgrounds, customs, and mores, but it has inevitably raised other issues. Most modern believers acknowledge that in the end the issue of biblical inspiration is ultimately a mystery—truly a matter of faith.   *William H. Barnes*

INTEREST, LOANS AND. *See* Loans and Interest.

INTERPRETATION, HISTORY OF. *This entry consists of four articles that survey the history of the interpretation of the Bible:*

> Jewish Interpretation
> Early Christian Interpretation
> Christian Interpretation from the
>   Middle Ages to the Reformation
> Modern Biblical Criticism

For further treatment of the general topic, see Hermeneutics, and for discussion of particulars, see Anti-Semitism; Feminism and the Bible; Fundamentalism.

Jewish Interpretation

The Earliest Commentaries. Although the process of interpretation may be traced within scripture itself (in the reinterpretation of earlier laws and oracles, and in the reuse of earlier narratives), for practical purposes the earliest phase of commentary on the Hebrew Bible extended from ca. 250 BCE to ca. 500 CE. Commentary was the primary medium of Jewish religious discourse in this period, and ideas, both new and old, were presented in the form of comments on the Bible. The commentaries were of several types.

The "rewritten Bible" texts. Into this category fall works such as Jubilees (see below), the *Liber antiquitatum biblicarum*, the Genesis Apocryphon, and the biblical sections of *Josephus's Antiquities of the Jews.* These offer an interpretative retelling of the Bible in the interpreter's own words, and they mirror the basic form of the original. The paradigm of

this type of commentary is already found within scripture, notably in the books of Chronicles, which rework the history of the books of Samuel and Kings. Certain sections of the *apocalyptic writings should also, perhaps, be included here, as well as the Temple Scroll from Qumran, which codifies Temple law.

The Qumran pesharim. These are in true commentary form, in that they quote the original in full and attach to it comments introduced by such formulae as "the interpretation of the matter is" (Hebr. *pēšer haddābār*). The interpretation is mantological: interpreters see in the text of scripture cryptic allusions to events in their own time, and they decode it in the way they would decode a dream. The interpretation itself is presented in oracular style.

The commentaries of Philo. The commentaries on the Pentateuch by the Alexandrian Jewish scholar *Philo (ca. 15 BCE–50 CE) are, like the pesharim, in true commentary form, and consist of biblical lemma plus comment. They are philosophical in content and attempt, by extensive use of allegory, to read middle Platonism into the Bible. Unlike the rewritten Bible texts or the pesharim, Philonic commentary is argumentative (i.e., it presents its exegetical reasoning, not just its conclusions), and it offers multiple interpretations of the same verse.

The Targums. These Bible translations (which are sometimes very paraphrastic) were used to render the Hebrew lections simultaneously into *Aramaic in the synagogue. Like the rewritten Bible texts, they mirror the form of the original, but in terms of content they are close to the midrashim (see below), and clearly emanate from a rabbinic milieu. (*See* Translations, *article on* Targums.)

The midrashim. These works, products of the rabbinic schools of Palestine in the Tannaitic (ca. 70–200 CE) and Amoraic (ca. 200–500 CE) periods, constitute by far the largest corpus of early Jewish biblical commentary. In form they are true commentaries, proceeding by way of lemma plus comment. They are intensely argumentative, at pains to make clear their exegetical reasoning, and quote divergent, and often contradictory, opinions of various scholars. They contain both ʾaggādâ (narrative/homiletic material) and hālākâ (legal material). Important texts belonging to this category are the Mekhilta of Rabbi Ishmael (on Exodus), Sifra (on Leviticus), Sifre (on Numbers and Deuteronomy), Genesis Rabba, and Pesiqta de Rab Kahana (on the readings for the festivals and special Sabbaths).

Classical Hermeneutics. Care must be taken in analyzing the hermeneutics of such a complex phenomenon as early Jewish biblical interpretation. Much of the theory, and indeed the practice, is not explicit, and this opens the door to guesswork and subjectivity. It is also important to distinguish between descriptions of the phenomenon from outside and from inside the tradition, since descriptions stemming from these two standpoints will not always coincide. In external description, one need not accept at face value any explicit hermeneutic statements the commentators happen to make, for what they say they are doing and what they actually do are not necessarily the same. In many cases it is clear, from an external standpoint, that the commentators are reading ideas into scripture: they are engaged in eisegesis rather than exegesis. The Jewish tradition of Bible interpretation oscillates between two contrary tendencies—one centrifugal, the other centripetal. In the centrifugal tendency, the tradition moves further and further from the text of scripture, and its links with scripture become increasingly tenuous. In the centripetal tendency, the centrifugal forces are checked and an attempt is made to reintegrate the tradition with scripture. The book of Jubilees is an early example of a centripetal text: it attempts to fuse with the biblical narrative extrabiblical traditions (e.g., legends about Noah) that had grown up in the preceding one hundred or more years, and so to halt the fragmentation of the tradition. In a similar manner, the rabbinic midrashim of the third century CE and later attempt to reintegrate Mishnah with scripture (note especially Sifra). So, too, in the Middle Ages the Zohar checked the centrifugal movement of qabbalistic literature by reading qabbalistic ideas into scripture. From an external standpoint, eisegesis is a central feature of the tradition. From within the tradition, however, eisegesis is always presented as exegesis: in order to validate the tradition it is necessary to create the illusion that the tradition is already present in scripture, and has been discovered there through meditation.

A fruitful way to analyze early Jewish biblical hermeneutics is to use rabbinic midrash as a yardstick. Rabbinic midrash serves this purpose well because it is massively documented, its underlying worldview is accessible through the living tradition of the synagogue, and, of all the traditions, it is the most explicit as to its hermeneutical theory and practice.

Midrash can be seen as a game like chess, played to strict but complex rules: it has a field of play (the chessboard); aims and objectives (checkmating the king); forces to be deployed and strategies followed to achieve the aims and objectives (the chess pieces, their moves and set patterns of play).

Two axioms define the midrashic field of play. The first is that midrash is an activity performed on the Bible, which is regarded as a fixed, canonical text. For the rabbis, prophecy has ceased and the *canon of scripture is closed. God no longer speaks directly to humankind; his will can be discovered only through the interpretation of scripture. The scribe replaces the prophet as the central authority in Judaism. This is the simple, traditional view of the matter. In reality, however, the situation is rather more complicated. To solve the problem of authority and to preempt readings of scripture with which they could not agree, the rabbis were forced to elevate their interpretations to the same status as scripture itself: their interpretations became Oral Torah, and were traced back in principle to Moses. In effect, the scholar, too, was inspired, though care was taken to distinguish his inspiration from that of the prophet. (See, however, *b. B. Bat.* 12a: "Since the destruction of the Temple, prophecy has been taken from the prophets and given to the sages"!) Moreover, in actual fact the rabbis did not confine midrash to scripture. There is an element in midrashic practice that simply represents the standard hermeneutics of the Greco-Roman world, and parallels to it can easily be found in Alexandrian Greek scholarship. To a certain extent, the rabbis would have interpreted any text in the way they interpret scripture. In fact, in the Gemara they apply midrashic methods to the exegesis of the Mishnah.

The second axiom is that scripture is divine speech: it has its origin in the mind of God. The human element in scripture is minimal. The prophet was invaded by a divine power—the "holy spirit" or "spirit of prophecy"—that neutralized human imperfections. "Moses fulfilled the function of a scribe receiving dictation, and he wrote the whole Torah, its histories, its narratives, and its commandments, and that is why he is called a 'copyist' [Deut. 33.21]" (Maimonides, *Commentary on Mishnah Sanhedrin, Ḥeleq*).

From this axiom a number of inferences were deemed to flow:

1. Scripture is inerrant: it can contain no errors of fact. Errors can be only apparent, not real.
2. Scripture is coherent: each part agrees with all the other parts. Scripture forms a harmonious, interlocking text. Contradictions can be only apparent, not real.
3. Scripture is unalterable. At one level, this means that it is inviolable: it forms a closed text, which should not be changed or rewritten in any way. Interpretation must be clearly distinguished from the actual text of scripture, not integrated with it. Elaborate techniques, culminating in the full-blown Masorah of the early Middle Ages, were devised to ensure the exact transmission of the received text of the *Torah. At another level, the unalterability of scripture means that it remains eternally relevant: since it originated in the mind of God it can never become obsolescent or be superseded. The rabbis did not admit a doctrine of abrogation. The contrast with Islam is instructive. Abrogation in Islam originally referred to the abrogation of both Judaism and Christianity by the superior revelation brought by Muhammad, the "seal" of the prophets. But it was also used by Islamic lawyers as a way of reconciling conflicts within the *Qurʾān and *hadith*: early laws are sometimes said to have been abrogated by laws promulgated later by the prophet. The rabbis could

have used such a strategy to resolve the contradictions within scripture, but they never did. Perhaps they shied away from implying that God contradicted himself.

4. Scripture is "all music and no noise." Every minute detail is significant—even whether a word is spelled fully or defectively. Mountains of religious law can be deduced even from the "crowns" added to the letters as decorative embellishment. The language of scripture does not contain any redundancy. Repetitions are regularly nuanced to give a slightly different sense.

5. Scripture is polyvalent: it does not have one, fixed, original meaning but, rather, can mean many things at once. Even when two contradictory conclusions are drawn from it, both can be seen as "words of the living God." Although interpreters have great freedom before the text, they are not totally free: they cannot simply deduce what they like from scripture. There is a tendency to stress the primacy of the literal meaning: "no verse can ever lose its plain sense (*pĕšaṭ*)" (b. *Šabb.* 63a; *Sanh.* 34a). With few exceptions, the cantillation and vocalization of the biblical text reflect *pĕšaṭ*. Latent meanings must be congruent with the *pĕšaṭ*. The influential dictum that "Torah speaks according to human language" (b. *Ber.* 31b) implies that Torah communicates like ordinary speech, and should be interpreted like ordinary speech. Halaka (religious law) also exercised a restraining hand on midrash: it was forbidden to disclose aspects of Torah that did not accord with

halaka. But the ultimate restraint was the power of tradition. Correct interpretation could be given only by the rabbis—by scholars who had studied in the right schools, and who were recipients of a tradition going back through the ages to Moses himself.

The aims of the "game" of midrash can, from an internal standpoint, be defined as drawing out the meaning of scripture and applying it to the heart and life of the Jew. This involves resolving the obscurities and contradictions of scripture, displaying its coherence, and bringing it to bear on everyday life. From an external standpoint, the aims can be seen largely in terms of validating tradition from scripture, of finding ways of attaching contemporary custom and belief to the sacred text.

The moves in the "game" of midrash are in part laid down in "rulebooks." From an early date, the rabbis drew up lists of hermeneutical norms (*middôt*) by which the Torah is to be interpreted. Three of these lists were particularly influential—the Seven Middot of Hillel, the Thirteen Middot of Rabbi Ishmael, and the Thirty-Two Middot of Rabbi Eliezer ben Yose ha-Gelili. The introduction to Eliezer's list categorically states that its norms are to be employed in the exegesis of aggada (i.e., nonlegal texts in the Torah). The lists in Hillel and Ishmael, by contrast, have always been regarded as applying to the exegesis of halaka (i.e., legal texts), though not exclusively. This distinction should not be pressed too far, for some of Eliezer's norms are employed in the interpretation of halaka. There is, however, a discernible reluctance to use some of the more fanciful aggadic techniques, such as *gĕmaṭriâ* (computation of the numerical values of words or phrases) and *nôṭārîqôn* (treating biblical words as acronyms) in legal argument. Wherever possible the simple sense *(pěšaṭ)* of a law prevailed.

The dates of these lists are very uncertain, for their attributions cannot be taken at face value. The Seven Middot of Hillel—almost certainly the earliest of the three lists—illustrates the nature of the rabbinic exegetical norms:

1. *Qāl wāḥōmer,* inference from a less important case *(qal)* to a more important one *(ḥōmer):* For example, if the perpetual offering, neglect of which is not punished by cutting off, overrides the *Sabbath, then the *Passover offering, neglect of which is punished by cutting off, will also override the Sabbath.

2. *Gězērâ šāwâ,* inference based on the presence in two different laws of a common term: For example, the expression "in its appointed time" is used in connection with both the Passover (Num. 9.2) and the perpetual offering (Num. 28.2). Since the expression "in its appointed time" used of the perpetual offering involves overriding the Sabbath, so the same term when used of Passover must equally involve overriding the Sabbath.

3. *Binyan ʾāb mikkātûb ʾeḥād ûbinyan ʾāb miššěnê kětûbîm,* construction of a category (literally, a "father") on the basis of one text, and construction of a category on the basis of two texts: For example, if a master intentionally knocks out a slave's tooth or blinds him in one eye, the slave goes free in compensation. "Tooth" and "eye" are cited by scripture merely as examples. Their common features

are that they are chief organs, they are visible, and loss of them would constitute a permanent defect. Therefore, if a master injures the slave in any of his principal organs, which are visible and loss of which would cause a permanent defect, the slave is entitled to go free.

4. *Kělāl ûpěrāṭ,* when a general term *(kělāl)* is followed by a specific term *(pěrāṭ),* the general includes only what is contained in the specific: For example, in Leviticus 1.2, "When any of you bring an offering of beasts to the Lord, even of the herd and of the flock . . . ," "beasts" (the *kělāl*) on its own could include "wild beasts," but the addition of "herd" and "flock" (the *pěrāṭ*) limits sacrifice to domestic animals.

5. *Pěrāṭ ûkělāl,* when a specific term is followed by a general term, the general adds to the specific, and everything contained in the general term is included: For example, Exodus 22.10 (Hebr. 22.9), "If a man deliver to his neighbor an ass, or an ox, or a sheep [the *pěrāṭ*], or any beast [the *kělāl*] . . ." The bailee is liable for any animal falling within the general category of "beast," not just for the specific animals mentioned.

6. *Kayôsēʾ bô běmāqôm ʾaḥēr,* the same interpretation applies in another place: For example, consecration of the firstborn to God does not make them God's, since they already belong to him. Rather, this act was instituted so that one can receive a reward for obeying a divine commandment. The same interpretation applies to kindling the fire on the altar. This act cannot do anything for God, since

"Lebanon would not provide fuel enough, nor are its animals enough for a burnt offering" to God (Isa. 40.16). Rather, it gives a person the opportunity to receive a reward for fulfilling a commandment.

7. *Dābār hallāmēd mēⁱinyānô*, the meaning of a statement may be determined from its context: For example, "You shall not steal" in Exodus 20.15 must denote a capital offense, since the two preceding offenses in the same verse (murder and adultery) are capital offenses. It denotes, therefore, theft of persons (kidnapping). In Leviticus 19.11, however, "You shall not steal" must refer to theft of property, since the context there is concerned with property.

As a description of the exegetical techniques employed in midrash, these lists of *middôt* have drawbacks: they are by no means exhaustive, and they do not include norms such as *heqqēš* (analogy) and *sĕmûkîm* (inference based on juxtaposition of verses). Sherira Gaon (tenth-eleventh centuries CE), in his famous *Epistle*, gives a list of exegetical norms (designated *ⁱiqqārîn* rather than *middôt*), many of which are not found in any of our three lists. Even if all the norms articulated in rabbinic literature were gathered together, they would not necessarily give a total account of the methods of the *daršānîm*. The rabbinic norms are prescriptive as well as descriptive: they are as much concerned with what should happen in midrash as with what actually does happen. Some of them are largely academic, since examples in actual midrashic texts can be found only with difficulty. Modern analysis has detected ex-

egetical processes at work in midrash that are nowhere formally acknowledged in rabbinic hermeneutical theory. The lists of norms are useful, but they should be supplemented by direct analysis of the midrashic texts themselves. Studying the rulebooks is no substitute for watching the game actually played.

Broadly speaking, rabbinic hermeneutics appear to hold good for the early nonrabbinic Bible commentaries as well. Many of the exegetical techniques of midrash certainly seem to apply. These are so numerous and so varied that it would be surprising if the methods of the nonrabbinic exegetes could not be paralleled from somewhere in rabbinic midrash. At two points, however, differences of emphasis may be detected. The polyvalent character of scripture is stressed less in the nonrabbinic texts: they tend to offer a unitary reading of scripture. Philo comes closest to the rabbinic position by giving a variety of interpretations of a single verse. Second, in some cases the nonrabbinic commentaries appear less committed than the rabbis to the principle of the unalterability of scripture. The way in which Jubilees and the Temple Scroll rewrite the Bible in classical Hebrew would probably have been frowned upon by the rabbis. This practice raises the suspicion that a new Torah, designed to supersede the old, is being promulgated. In general, however, the aim appears not to have been to supersede the canonical text, but rather to add to it. Jubilees claims to be of divine origin—a second Torah that supplements the first. The book known as 2 Esdras also implies that it is a secret book of Moses, worthy of canonical status. These assertions differ perhaps in degree, but hardly in kind, from the rabbis' claim that their traditions are oral Torah, or from Pesher Habakkuk's and Philo's statements that their comments on scripture are inspired.

Medieval Developments. The aims and basic methods of rabbinic biblical interpretation as defined in the Talmudic period persisted in Judaism down to modern times. The continuity of the tradition is seen in Rashi (1045–1105), the most influential of all the medieval Jewish commentators. Living in a rather hostile Christian environment in northern France at the time of the First Crusade, Rashi had little incentive to innovate. Although he has his own approach that tends to stress the plain sense (*pĕšaṭ*) of scripture, and to introduce only "sober" *dĕraš*, the general intention of his work is to digest and conserve the tradition. The first really radical break with tradition comes with Baruch Spinoza (1632–1677), who, notably in his *Tractatus Theologico-Politicus*, adumbrates a critical, historical approach to the Bible.

Despite the broad continuity down to the time of Spinoza, significant developments occurred in a number of areas.

Philology. Karaism, founded at Baghdad ca. 765 by Anan ben David, who rejected rabbinic tradition and turned back afresh to scripture, stimulated an interest among Rabbanite scholars in philology. Especially in Spain, Jewish philologians, such as Jonah ibn Janāḥ (first half of eleventh century), began to clarify the grammar of classical Hebrew by using contemporary Arabic linguistic theory; for example, they established once and for all the triliteral nature of the Hebrew verb. The new philology was championed by the Spanish scholar Abraham ibn Ezra (1089–1164). In the Introduction to his Commentary on the Pentateuch, he outlines five ways to approach the Bible—the Geonic, the Karaite, the Christian, the midrashic, and the philological—and makes clear his preference for the philological: "The fifth way is the one upon which I will base my commentary. Before God, whom alone I fear, it is in my view the right way. I will defer to no one when it comes to interpreting the Torah, but, to my utmost ability, will seek out the grammar of every word and then do my best to explain it." However, the most influential of the grammatical commentators was the French scholar David Kimḥi (ca. 1160–1235). His lucid grammatical analyses, much consulted by Christian scholars at the time of the Renaissance and Reformation, have sometimes a curiously modern ring; note, for example, his comments at Genesis 10.9 on the use of the word "God" to express the superlative in classical Hebrew.

Philosophy. Philosophical interpretation of scripture, which had remained largely dormant in mainstream Judaism since Philo, reemerged powerfully in the Middle Ages. Here, too, Karaism provided the initial stimulus. Through the influence of Saadiah Gaon (882–942), the great opponent of Karaism, the leading ideas of Arabic scholastic theology (Qalām) were made acceptable to rabbinic thought. Philosophical interpretation involved reading the Bible allegorically from a certain philosophical standpoint; thus, Maimonides interprets Ezekiel's vision of the chariot as an allegorical account of his own Neoplatonic form of Aristotelianism. The pre-existing philosophical system, whatever it was, functioned as a hermeneutic key to unlock scripture.

Mysticism. The rise of the mystical system of qabbalistic literature also powerfully affected biblical interpretation. The Zohar, the most influential mystical commentary, was compiled by Moses de Leon in Spain at the end of the thirteenth century. In formal terms, mystical commentary is similar to philosophical commentary: a preexistent system of ideas is used as a hermeneutic key to determine the sense of scripture, and elements of that system (e.g., the qabbalistic doctrine of the Sefirot: see Zohar 2. 42b–43a) are read into scripture using allegorical methods.

Hermeneutic theory in the Middle Ages was much concerned with identifying the various types of approach to scripture. The most famous classification, known by the mnemonic "PaRDeS," probably goes back to Moses de Leon: Pěšaṭ = literal interpretation; Remez = allegorical interpretation; Děraš = homiletic interpretation; Sôd = mystical interpretation. The Spanish scholar Bahya ben Asher (late thirteenth century) produced a slightly different fourfold classification: literal interpretation (pěšaṭ); homiletic (midrāš); rational, i.e., philosophical (sekel); and mystical (called "the way of the Lord" = Qabbalah).

In general, the various approaches to scripture were seen not as exclusive or contradictory but as complementary; the polyvalency of scripture continued to be stressed. There was a tendency, however, to rank them in hierarchical order, depending on the interpreter's standpoint. Even Maimonides, who cautioned against trying to separate the "kernel" from the "husk" in scripture, acknowledged that there was an "apparent" and a "latent" sense in scripture. The Zohar uses the analogy of the human body to illustrate the relationship between the various levels of meaning in scripture. Foolish people look only at the tales of the Torah, which are its outer garments; those who are wiser look at the commandments, which are the body of the Torah. But the true sages look only at the inner mystical sense of the Torah, the soul of the Torah. And lest it should be

supposed that the meaning of divine speech could ever be exhausted, the Zohar concludes, "and in the world to come they [the mystics] are destined to look at the soul of the soul of the Torah."
                                    Philip S. Alexander

Early Christian Interpretation

The Bible of the earliest Christians was identical with the Hebrew scriptures of the Jewish communities. When Jesus and the writers of the apostolic period speak of "scripture(s)," they mean the *canon of Torah, Prophets, and Writings that Jews regarded as divinely inspired, that is, written under the immediate dictate or influence of God. *Inspiration was also claimed for the Greek translation of the "Seventy" (Septuagint [LXX]), which was endorsed by Alexandrian Jewish authorities. In Christian eyes, the legend of the Septuagint's miraculous origin, first told in the Letter of Aristeas (late second century BCE), then elaborated by *Philo, and further embellished by Christian authors such as Justin Martyr, Irenaeus of Lyons, Tertullian, and Augustine, even rendered the Septuagint superior to the Hebrew original.

Jewish interpretation of the Hellenistic and Roman periods took three forms. Midrashic exegesis as practiced by the rabbis searched the holy text for clues to authoritative rules for living (hālākâ) or to a broadly edifying meaning in the present (ʿaggādâ), guided by tradition. The hermeneutical center was *Torah, the Law of God. Second, Jewish scholars in the Greek-speaking diaspora, exemplified by Philo, tried to harmonize the texts with the truths of Platonic or Stoic natural philosophy and ethics. Finally, the Essene sectarians at Qumran, relying on the authority of their "Teacher of Righteousness," read the biblical texts as divine oracles predicting their own end-time existence in the post-Maccabean period; here, the hermeneutical center was moving away from Torah to the prophetic literature. *(See also article on Jewish Interpretation above.)*

Traces of all three forms can be found in the earliest Christian literature. The synoptic Gospels portray Jesus as a rabbinical teacher who routinely answered questions about the *Law. Paul used both halakic and aggadic modes in interpreting biblical texts, even the seven rules attributed to Rabbi Hillel. The letter to the Hebrews, in its vision of the Temple cult as a shadow of the heavenly reality, seems to fuse the eschatology of an earlier generation with a Platonic worldview akin to Philo. Most important, the central Christian affirmation of Jesus of Nazareth as being the promised Messiah and the hermeneutics of promise and fulfillment share the tendency to shift the hermeneutical center from the Law to the Prophets. The prophets, including Moses, David, and other prophetic voices in the scriptures, predicted what was to happen "in these last days" (Heb. 1.2) and thus opened up the *apocalyptic meaning of the present in the context of the overarching plan of God; for example, "Today this scripture has been fulfilled in your hearing" (Luke 4.21; cf. Isa. 61.1). The proof from prophecy very quickly became a major tool of Christian missionaries. It appealed to Jewish hearers loyal to their divine scriptures as well as to non-Jews impressed by the antiquity of such writings. Although Christians might have discarded the Jewish scriptures and started with the experience of new revelation in the person of Jesus, they retained them as a valuable tool for Christian apologetics, which, understood as divine oracles, not only appealed to potential converts but also gave Christians themselves the interpretive categories for understanding the life,

death, and resurrection of Jesus the Christ *(see* Quotations of the Jewish Scriptures in the New Testament).

It was Paul who spelled out most powerfully the theological basis of this unified vision of God's purpose in history and the meaning of Christian practices such as *baptism and the common *meal. The old *covenant of the Law had been crowned by the revelation of the new covenant predicted by the prophets. But this fulfillment for Paul was not only linked to the story of Jesus and the Christian present; it also included the *second coming. Beyond a limited store of messianic passages that had governed the formation of the earliest Christian traditions about Jesus, Paul identified further predictions and anticipations of the new era in the scriptures. He also suggested the procedures for their apocalyptic interpretation through which later generations would continue to understand biblical passages as applicable to their own situation.

Typology. Explaining the experience of Israel as a warning to Christians of his own generation, Paul used the language of "type" or "typical" (1 Cor. 10.6, 11 [NRSV: "example"]), equating it with the "spiritual" understanding of those who have the Holy Spirit (Rom. 8.9, 23; 1 Cor. 2.13–15; 7.40). This kind of *typology, which was not without Jewish antecedents, gained an immense popularity in second-century Christian interpretation. The Greek term "antitype" for Christian baptism as the counterpart of Noah's rescue already appears in 1 Peter 3.21 (NRSV: "prefigured"). The apostolic fathers, especially the letter of Barnabas, show the rapid development of the concept. 1 Clement 25 even calls on an image of classical mythology, the phoenix, as a type of Christ's *resurrection. In the middle of the second century CE, the writings of Justin Martyr reveal the wide scope of possible types: Justin not only defended the traditional Christian use of messianic passages such as Genesis 49.10–12; Isaiah 7.14; 9.6; 11.1–3; 53; Psalms 2.7; 110.4; he also found "types," for example, of the cross, in almost every piece of wood mentioned in the Jewish scriptures. The Easter Homily by Melito of Sardis (late second century CE) demonstrates the same wealth of imagination when the author reads the *Exodus traditions as types of Christ's death and resurrection. It is likely that second-century Christians had *testimonia*, collections that grouped together for convenience messianic predictions or other texts yielding "types." Cyprian's treatise *Ad Quirinum* provides an example; its second part contains a list of "stone" testimonies from the Jewish scriptures that are interpreted as types of Christ, as well as a collection of passages that mention mountain, *lamb, or bridegroom. Typological traditions also inform the earliest representations of Christian *art, especially the funerary paintings and monuments of the catacombs. The pictures frequently can be interpreted as types of salvation using biblical figures such as Noah in the ark, Daniel between the lions, Susanna rescued from the elders, Jonah saved from the fish, or New Testament stories such as the raising of Lazarus and healing *miracles as pointers to the Christian hope beyond the grave.

Allegory. Paul also introduced the term "allegory" into the vocabulary of Christian exegesis. Galatians 4.21–26 refers to the story of Sarah and Hagar with the claim that it has to be understood "allegorically" as speaking of two covenants. The interpretation of an authoritative text as having a deeper meaning *(hyponoia)* than what its words seem to suggest was an old practice among Greeks in the appropriation of Homer

and the early poets. The *Homeric Allegories* of Pseudo-Heraclitus were probably written by a contemporary of Paul. Allegory as a writer's device, an "extended metaphor" in Quintilian's definition (*Instit. Rhetor.* 9.2.46), appeared with such stories as "Heracles at the crossroads" by Prodikos the Sophist (fourth century BCE). The allegorical interpretation of Homer was the hallmark of Stoic scholarship and later dominated Jewish and Christian interpretation at Alexandria. Philo's main interpretation of the Torah was entitled "Allegories of the Law"; like other allegorizers, Philo found the key to deeper meanings in etymological phenomena, numbers, and unusual terms.

Paul's use of the technical term *allēgoroumena* in Galatians 4.24 does not clearly distinguish allegory from typology. Sarah and Hagar function here as types in the same way as the wilderness generation in 1 Corinthians 10. Hellenistic allegorization, however, was deliberately employed by other Christian writers. The author of Hebrews interprets the key texts about the role of the high priest as speaking of Jesus Christ. The letter of Barnabas declares the entire cultic law of Judaism superseded and moralizes all its precepts. It seems that *gnostic teachers developed the apologetic potential of allegory to the fullest extent. Christian gnosis such as that represented by Clement of Alexandria in the early third century freely used the term *allēgoria* for exegetical endeavors that included extensive reinterpretation of biblical texts as teaching general and timeless truths.

Origen of Alexandria (ca. 185–254), the most prolific exegete of the early church, gave Christian allegory its theoretical foundation. In Book 4 of his treatise *On First Principles,* he claimed total inspiration by divine providence not only for the canonical scriptures themselves but even for their textual transmission with all its variants and scribal errors. Passages that present "stumbling blocks" in content and wording alert the reader that a spiritual, not a literal meaning must be sought in the holy texts. An "inspired" text requires "spiritual" interpretation that leads the soul upward (Grk. *anagōgē*) from the realm of the flesh to that of the Spirit. Origen assumed that much of the biblical revelation concerned the fate of souls, their fallen condition, and their redemption. Thus, in his commentaries on the Jewish scriptures, he allegorized the story of Israel as speaking of the journey of the soul, which, leaving the sensual world of "Egypt," seeks the Promised Land of blessedness. The teachings of Jesus and the apostles had the same goal: they pointed, directly or allegorically, to the *hope by which Christians live.

Authority and Canon. The wide use of allegory among gnostics, however, raised early doubts about the procedure. Marcion of Pontus, who founded a successful counterchurch in the middle of the second century CE, rejected the Jewish scriptures as the revelation of an "alien" God and based his thought on a revised Paul and a purged gospel of Luke. Such interpretation by textual revision was not uncommon; Tatian the Syrian applied it in his *Diatessaron*, an attempt to merge the four separate gospel accounts into one. To curb gnostic "misuses" of the Bible, church writers appealed to three authorities for its proper understanding: an approved canon of the "Old" Testament together with a "New" that assembled writings believed to be of apostolic origin; the "Rule of Faith," a creedal summary of accepted teachings; and the episcopal office, which was expected to decide among competing claims to authoritative exegesis. "Apostolicity" was invoked by Irenaeus and Tertullian as a central criterion against Marcion's reduced canon, a docetic Christology, or gnostic cosmological speculations. Both accused their opponents of arbitrary interpretation and displayed their strong disapproval of unchecked gnostic allegory.

They also shared a concern to apply the apostolic norm to the expansion of the Christian canon through apocrypha. Such writings were not only part of the growing gnostic literature but were also produced and read by catholic Christians. Apocryphal gospels filled in the blanks about Jesus' family and childhood, the forty days after his resurrection, and his journey into hell and heaven (*see* Descent into Hell). Apocryphal acts interpreted the witness of the apostles as supporting ascetic ideals, especially virginity; in this way they perpetuated the strong accent on moral exhortation that was at the heart of the biblical interpretation of the apostolic fathers (1 and 2 Clement; Didache; Ignatius; Barnabas; Shepherd of Hermas). The earliest canon list of New Testament books, the Canon Muratori (ca. 200 CE), already rejects a large number of apocrypha, but despite constant attempts at curbing the genre, apocryphal books such as the Protevangelium of James, the Acts of Pilate, the Gospel of Bartholomew, and the Apocalypses of Peter and Paul influenced biblical interpretation for centuries to come. (*See also* Apocrypha, *article on* Christian Apocrypha.)

The School of Alexandria. During the first two centuries, Christian biblical interpretation was guided by practical concerns: the needs of missionary preaching, the instruction of new converts, apologetics directed at non-Christians, and polemics against "heretical" teachings. In the third and fourth centuries it came to be dominated by a conflict of "schools" analogous to the rivalry of philosophical schools in the Hellenistic world. The conflict clarified some basic options in expounding canonical scriptures in a Christian framework. An ancient but unreliable tradition claimed that Alexandria had a Christian catechetical school with a succession of famous teachers, beginning with Pantaenus in the late second century, Clement of Alexandria, and Origen. Reports by Gregory the Wonderworker, Pamphilus of Caesarea, and Eusebius suggest that Origen taught a curriculum of higher Christian studies that included classical disciplines such as grammar, Greek literature, and philosophy as a basis and the study of biblical texts as the crown. *Textual criticism was as much part of this endeavor as literary analysis and spiritual interpretation. Through Jewish converts, Origen was also aware of the exegetical traditions of rabbinic Judaism and was able to draw on them.

The Alexandrian school of the fourth century carried on the interpretive methods of Origen, including the use of allegory. Major theologians, such as Athanasius, Eusebius, Apollinaris, the Cappadocian fathers, and Cyril of Alexandria, wrote interpretations of biblical books for a broad educated public in the spirit of Origen's anagogical dynamics: scripture instructs the spiritual quest of the soul for an ascent to God who, through Christ the eternal *Logos, has revealed this "way" in the holy writings. Gregory of Nyssa's *Life of Moses* presents a reading of the Exodus story in two parts, first recounting the details in their historical sequence and then opening up their spiritual meaning as a description of the soul's journey to God in its various stages. Didymus the Blind (d. 398 CE) expounded numerous books of the Bible in a similar way. Alexandrian hermeneutics shows a keen interest in philological detail. The precise wording of a biblical passage as well as its stylistic peculiarities was of utmost importance because the inspired words themselves contained the key to their divinely intended meaning. For these scholars, allegorization was a science, not an arbitrary flight of fancy.

The School of Antioch. This understanding of Christian allegory became the polemical target of Alexandria's rival, the school of Antioch, in the fourth century. Antioch, important for earliest Christian history, could boast of a long tradition of Hellenistic scholarship. The emphasis seems to have been on the rhetorical arts; Aristotelian and Jewish influences were important. We hear of Christian teachers in Antioch from the late third century onward: Malchion; Lucian, whose recension of the Greek Bible acquired something of a normative status; Dorotheus; Eustathius; and especially Diodore of Tarsus (d. ca. 390 CE), whose ascetic community became the seedbed of the distinctive Antiochian tradition of biblical exegesis. Diodore taught a generation of great scholars, among them Theodore of Mopsuestia, John Chrysostom, and Theodoret of Cyrrhus.

Through the association of Antiochian teachers with the names of heretics such as Arius and Nestorius, many of the works of the school have perished. From the remnants we can infer a sober appreciation of the Bible as a valuable historical document in addition to its spiritual meaning. The Antiochian exegetes took note of the times and circumstances of a particular biblical book. Diodore, for example, tried to rearrange the biblical Psalms according to their true historical sequence, which he gleaned from internal and external clues, especially the titles. Theodore considered only four Psalms as messianic and understood the Song of Solomon as a love poem composed by Solomon for the Queen of Sheba. This did not exclude a divinely intended accommodation of the texts to later times or the need to search for a spiritual sense, which the Antiochians called theōria. But their respect for the historical setting nourished a deep-seated distrust of Alexandrian allegorism. Diodore wrote a (lost) treatise "On the Difference Between Theōria and Allēgoria," and Theodore deplored the dissolution of historical reality at the hand of Alexandrian exegetes, especially in the Genesis account of *creation and *fall, on which he thought the entire Christian message of sin, salvation, and human responsibility depended.

While suspicion of Antiochian theologians remained high during the christological struggles of the fifth and sixth centuries, their moral and ascetic fervor continued to be influential, thanks to the universal reception of the work of John Chrysostom. Chrysostom's sermons on biblical books were avidly copied and were known in the West through Latin translations, the earliest of which probably go back to his lifetime. The school itself found refuge first at Ephraem's school in Edessa, where it was represented by Syrian teachers such as Ibas and Narsai the Great, and later even farther East at Nisibis between the Euphrates and Tigris, where eminent scholars such as Babi the Great and Ishoᶜdad of Merv upheld the great tradition through the end of the patristic period.

The Latin Church. The Western church did not participate directly in the war of the schools. Some of its great theologians, such as Ambrose of Milan, Hilary of Poitiers, and Jerome, studied under, or drew on, scholars of both traditions for their moral and spiritual interpretations but did not take sides: Greek learning in any form was still greatly admired. Cassiodorus's list of hermeneutical textbooks for the use of students in the early sixth century includes "Alexandrian" works such as Hilary's Treatise of Mysteries and Eucherius of Lyon's Varieties of Spiritual Understanding, as well as "Antiochian" handbooks such as those of Hadrian and Junilius Africanus. There can be no question, however, that the influence of Origen and his program of spiritual exegesis was central in giving direction to Western biblical interpretation. Translations by Jerome's erstwhile friend Rufinus toned down offensive features of Origen's On First Principles and several of his commentaries, and the contacts with Alexandrian exegetes were never interrupted.

The indigenous Latin tradition, especially in North Africa, reflected an emphasis on catechetical instruction and apologetics, as the writings of Tertullian demonstrate. A rich store of typological exegesis, inherited from the church of the second century, seems to have served these interests; Cyprian's biblicism drew its substance from it. Western exegesis also remained more traditional in its apocalyptic tendencies. While the expectation of an imminent end met with heavy criticism in the East after the Montanist crisis of the late second century, and the book of Revelation was still of doubtful canonicity to Eusebius at the beginning of the fourth century because of its chiliasm, apocalyptic expectations and millennial themes remained popular in the West. At the time when Greek was still the language of the Christian community in Rome, Hippolytus (early third century) wrote on the prophet Daniel and on the Antichrist against an upsurge of apocalyptic fervor in response to the persecutions. The first Latin exegesis of the book of Revelation was written in the early fourth century by Victorinus of Pettau in Dalmatia; it is known to us through Jerome's revision, stripped of its pronounced chiliasm.

The late fourth century saw the emergence of an independent mind among Latin exegetes in Tyconius the Donatist. His *Book of Rules* did not follow Origen's allegorical principles but gathered clues from a rational analysis of biblical language to separate fulfilled messianic prophecies from the divinely intended message of the texts for the church of his day. Tyconius was guided by a vision of history that included the beginnings, the story of Israel, Christ, and the church in one great redemptive movement, understood in terms of the final victory of good over evil. The fragments of his commentary on the book of Revelation show that, while he interpreted its apocalyptic prophecy as applicable to any age, he retained a sophisticated imminent expectation of the eschatological exodus of the true church (the Donatist) from the false.

Another feature of the Western development was a rise of interest in the Pauline letters at a time when such interest was relatively low in the East. We know of five major efforts between 365 and 410 in the West at interpreting the letter to the Romans: those of Marius Victorinus, the so-called Ambrosiaster, the Budapest Anonymous, Pelagius, and Augustine, who wrote only two fragments on Romans, but the importance of Paul for the formation of his mature theology is amply documented. By his own admission, Augustine was indebted to Tyconius in formulating his exegetical principles. He also shared the Alexandrian emphasis on the spiritual sense, even though he tended to replace the terminology of allegorization with that of "figuration." According to Augustine, scripture speaks not only of promise and fulfillment in the person of Jesus but contains literally or figuratively the an-

swer to all basic questions of humanity. In God's providence, it is given as a means to incite believers to the double love of God and neighbor, which is the goal of the soul's journey. Its human language with all its ambiguities requires careful work by the interpreter. Augustine's plea for competence in biblical languages and the liberal arts, especially rhetoric and logic, became the charter of early medieval monastic education in the West. His exegetical writings, circulating in numerous manuscripts, constituted one of the main patristic authorities for exegetes down to the Reformation. They stressed the priority of the spiritual goal of reading scripture without discouraging the investigation of the plain sense of its words. The medieval theory of a fourfold sense—literal, allegorical, tropological (moral), and anagogical— did not originate with Augustine, however. The first writer to mention it was John Cassian in the fifth century (*Conferences* 14.8), who used the four biblical meanings of Jerusalem as an illustration: the actual city, the church, the human soul, and the heavenly city, our final home.

Interpretive Genres. The literary forms of biblical interpretation during the early centuries show a bewildering variety. At first, biblical interpretation was a function of the missionary proclamation by apostles and evangelists, the instruction of converts by teachers and elders, and the itinerant ministry of prophets. The expansion of Christianity beyond its original Jewish context brought with it the need for apologetics and polemics and moved scriptural interpretation quite naturally into the writing of the more literate members of the church, who could serve as advocates and apologists for the movement. The basic task of interpreting scripture within the Christian congregations, however, was not so much a matter of a developing Christian literature but of the living voice of bishop, elder, and teacher. The exegetical writings of Hippolytus consist of homiletical reflections on biblical texts, often fragmentary and incomplete, as they would relate to the life of his church members. They were not biblical commentaries. On the contrary, the bishop denounced the genre of "commentary" as an invention of the pagan schools and a heretical practice.

Literary attempts at a coherent interpretation of entire canonical books in a Christian vein were first made by Christian gnostics who took the case for their esoteric theological systems to a literate non-Christian audience through detailed analysis of authoritative texts, among which the Bible held a special place. Even the gnostic interpretation of the Fourth Gospel by the Valentinian Heracleon (end of second century), the first such piece of which we have textual evidence, was, however, far more an apologetic treatise than an exegetical commentary. Commentaries in the strict sense were the product of the Hellenistic school tradition, as Hippolytus suggested. Christian biblical commentaries were the fruit of such traditions on Christian soil, as in Alexandria and Antioch. It seems that Origen created the genre, following classical precedent and employing the three standard forms of scholia, homilies, and *tomoi*, that is, philological explanations of an entire biblical book at a time. Wherever some form of Christian education took shape in Christian "schools," monastic communities, at the residence of bishops, or in learned circles of ascetic women, biblical interpretation as a scholarly enterprise was a highly valued activity.

The fourth and fifth centuries became the golden age of commentary writing. Jerome deliberately conveyed

the impression that even earlier Christians had already produced a respectable body of "commentaries" on the scriptures. Ostensibly building on this treasure, but especially on Origen and the admired exegetes of the Eastern schools, he nourished the dream of creating a Latin Christian literature equal to that of the Romans, based on the Bible and its eternal truths but matching Virgil, Cicero, and Horace in style and form. He gave this endeavor a solid foundation by providing a new Latin translation of major parts of the Bible in his Vulgate and adapted the forms of classical textual scholarship in his own exegetical work, drawing up tools for the study of biblical chronology, prosopography, geography, and languages, as well as commentaries, in which he made use of his vast learning.

As Jerome himself had feared, his ambitious project fell victim to the new pluralism of a barbarian age that superseded the cultural unity of the crumbling Empire. In Christianity, the syntheses of the following centuries tended to look to the past for their canons of biblical exegesis before they encouraged new attempts at taking up the task. In the East, compilations of the exegetical heritage began to appear in the sixth century with Procopius of Gaza. To this literature of "chains" *(catenae)*, the gathering of patristic interpretations by biblical book and chapter, we owe the preservation of precious fragments of lost commentaries. Even the outstanding theological writers of the Byzantine age rarely wrote fresh commentaries themselves. Similarly, the West experienced a decline in commentary writing after Jerome. The shining exceptions were Cassiodorus and Pope Gregory I in the sixth century. It was the educational zeal of the great monasteries in the British Isles and of the Carolingian rulers on the Continent in the eighth and ninth centuries that created the conditions for a new flowering of serious exegetical work.   *Karlfried Froehlich*

Christian Interpretation from the Middle Ages to the Reformation

During the period from 600 to 1600 CE, the interpretation of the Bible reflected the broader institutional developments and intellectual concerns of western Christianity. During the earliest part of that period, students of the scriptures relied almost exclusively on the guidance of patristic authority. As a distinctive medieval civilization developed, commentators found positions in schools and universities, where they geared their work to the educational and theological needs of their world. Toward the end of the period, biblical interpretation reflected the fresh influences of critical reason and the spiritual demands that emerged during the epoch of the Protestant and Catholic Reformations. Throughout the whole period, the scriptures helped to shape western culture in all its dimensions. Little wonder, then, that commentators continuously sought to adjust their understanding of the Bible and to expound it in the light of the most advanced information available to them.

Patristic Influence. The most advanced information available during the early Middle Ages came from the church fathers. Only rarely did Christian commentators of the late first millennium CE understand more than a smattering of Greek or Hebrew, and even less frequently did they possess the intellectual self-confidence to develop fresh interpretations. The Venerable Bede (672–735) knew some Greek, which he employed in his exposition of Acts, and Remigius of Auxerre (d. 908) seems to have compared the Latin Psalter with the Hebrew text. John Scotus Erigena (d. 877)

stood alone, however, as a commentator possessing both language skills and a powerful critical faculty. He consulted the writings of the Greek fathers and based his own commentary of John's gospel on the Greek text; furthermore, he displayed a willingness to correct Latin exegesis on the basis of Greek sources. Most other early medieval commentators, however, worked in an extremely conservative vein. Even the best known of them—Alcuin (d. 804), Claude of Turin (d. 827), and Rabanus Maurus (d. 856)—did little more than reproduce the views of the Latin fathers, particularly those of Jerome and Augustine. Most commentators of the period recognized the literal sense as the foundation of scriptural exegesis, but all of them considered a literal exposition fully compatible with one or more modes of moral, allegorical, or mystical interpretation. Indeed, given the general absence of linguistic skills and philological concern, expositors had little alternative but to develop the various spiritual senses of scripture, which they did with considerable zeal.

Scholasticism. The establishment of monastic and cathedral schools encouraged several new developments in biblical interpretation. In the first place, they created a demand for textbooks. Masters in the schools recognized the need for standardized interpretations that could serve as a common foundation for all students. The result was the compilation of the *Glossa ordinaria,* which presented a brief exposition of the entire Bible. The chief figure in the preparation of this work was Anselm of Laon (d. 1117), master in the cathedral school at Laon, though several other twelfth-century theologians and commentators also contributed to the effort. The *Glossa* drew extracts from patristic and early medieval expositions, so that it possessed no claim to originality. It exercised an enormous influence, however, since it served for half a millennium as the basic text for students embarked on their introduction to the Bible.

More important, the medieval schools fostered an intellectual and theological creativity that deeply influenced biblical interpretation. Expertise in grammar, logic, and dialectic imparted to the masters a new self-confidence in their intellectual abilities, and equipped them with the tools to fashion a new kind of exegesis. Twelfth-century commentators progressively abandoned the patristic style of running exposition in favor of explanations that concentrated on well-defined theological issues. Exegetes such as Gilbert de la Porrée (d. 1154) and Robert of Melun (d. 1167) organized their commentaries around *quaestiones*—doctrinal issues requiring explanation on the basis of reason and grounded in some source of authority—so that exposition served the interests of theological accuracy. The culmination of this practice came in the *Sentences* of Peter Lombard (d. 1160), who organized biblical and patristic doctrine into a veritable compendium of Christian theology.

The most impressive school of interpreters of this sort was that centered in the Abbey of St. Victor in Paris. Hugh of St. Victor (d. 1141), founder of the school, called for systematic, scholarly study of the scriptures. He placed equal weight on literal and spiritual exposition: the exegete must carefully employ all the relevant arts and sciences in establishing the literal sense of the text; whenever appropriate, however, its moral or theological significance should also be developed. Hugh's successors did not take so balanced an approach as their master:

Richard of St. Victor (d. 1173) devoted himself to allegorical and mystical exegesis, while Andrew of St. Victor (d. 1175) insisted on a scientifically accurate exposition of the literal and historical sense of the scriptures. In preparing himself for his work, Andrew consulted Jewish scholars and steeped himself in Hebrew, thus setting an example followed by numerous Christian exegetes through the following two centuries.

Whatever their attitude toward spiritual exegesis, expositors in the schools generally geared their work toward theological and doctrinal issues. As a result, biblical interpretation became an increasingly specialized activity. Expositors developed impressive skills in language and reasoning, which they then applied in scriptural analysis. In doing so, they emphasized the significance of the scriptures for the correct understanding of Christian doctrine—rather than seeking, for example, to develop materials for homiletic or teaching purposes—so that exegesis increasingly assumed the status of a subdiscipline of theology.

The establishment of universities in the thirteenth century strongly encouraged the further development of a professional, scientific variety of biblical interpretation. Some commentators, such as Stephen Langton (1155–1228) and Hugh of St. Cher (1200–1263), continued to expound allegorical and spiritual senses of scripture. Generally speaking, however, the universities' heavy emphasis on theology encouraged interpreters to concentrate on the literal sense and to focus their commentaries on important doctrinal issues. The introduction of Aristotelian thought and subsequent development of scholastic theology worked toward the same end. Thus, Albertus Magnus (1193–1280) and Thomas Aquinas (1225–1274) brought Aristotelian science and analysis to bear on the scriptures; both produced literal expositions that plumbed the scriptures in search of support for scholastic explanations of Christian doctrine and mysteries.

The culmination of this variety of exegesis came in the work of Nicholas of Lyra (1270–1349), best known for his monumental *Postilla litteralis,* which provided an exhaustive literal exposition of the entire Bible. Lyra by no means abandoned spiritual exposition: he set great store by accurate exegesis of the spiritual senses of scripture, and as a supplement to his *Postilla litteralis* he even prepared a work that briefly outlined the moral and allegorical significance of the entire Bible. Like Albertus and Aquinas, however, Lyra concentrated on literal exposition, and he took pains whenever possible to show that the scriptures supported the scholastic understanding of theology. Yet Lyra also considerably advanced comprehension of the Hebrew Bible in particular because of his solid command of Hebrew. Lyra also closely studied rabbinic commentaries, particularly those of Rashi (1030–1105), one of the greatest of the medieval Jewish exegetes *(see article on* Jewish Interpretation, *above).* His language skills enabled him to provide both proper translations and accurate explanations of numerous biblical passages. Similar clarification of the New Testament did not become available until the fifteenth and sixteenth centuries, when Renaissance humanists brought their newly acquired knowledge of Greek to bear on the Christian scriptures.

Renaissance and Reformation. During the later Middle Ages, theologians such as Roger Bacon (1220–1292) and Pierre d'Ailly (1350–1421) called for increased emphasis on Hebrew and Greek as a propaedeutic for biblical interpretation. Regular instruction in biblical languages did not, however, become widely available until the sixteenth century, and by then new cultural forces ensured that scholastic theology would no longer dominate exegesis. Pico della Mirandola (1463–1494) and Johann Reuchlin (1455–1522) became enchanted not only with Hebrew, but also with qabbalistic ideas, which they sought to introduce into Christian exegesis. Meanwhile, expertise in Greek enabled the Renaissance humanists to make important contributions to the understanding of the New Testament. Lorenzo Valla (1407–1457) and especially Erasmus of Rotterdam (1466–1536) inaugurated the modern tradition of New Testament interpretation: they rejected the guidance of scholastic theology, studied the Greek text of the New Testament, and offered expositions that depended on a combination of linguistic, philological, and historical considerations. Both placed high value on the derivation of moral and theological doctrine from the scriptures. Like most of their humanist colleagues, though, they also denied the usefulness of elaborate allegorical or spiritual exegesis, insisting instead on the primacy of literal and historical expositions. Their work made possible a vastly improved understanding of the New Testament. On the basis of their knowledge of Greek and their well-developed critical faculties, they corrected the texts of the Greek and Latin New Testament, offered new Latin translations superior to those of the Vulgate, and clarified numerous points of history and doctrine in their exegesis of the New Testament.

The Reformation movements of the sixteenth century had deep implications for biblical interpretation, as theologians of all persuasions sought scriptural support for their religious views. To some extent, both Protestant and Catholic reformers continued to work in the tradition of Erasmus and other Renaissance scholars who had brought linguistic skills and philological analysis to bear on the scriptures. Both John Calvin (1509–1564) and Cardinal Cajetan (1468–1534), for example, produced extensive commentaries based on the study of scriptural texts in their original languages and informed by all the advances the humanists had registered in the explanation of the Bible.

Inevitably, however, sixteenth-century commentaries generally betrayed the theological, controversial, or confessional intentions of their authors. Rebels against the authority of the Roman Catholic church, including John Wycliffe (1330–1384) and John Hus (1370–1415) among many others, had traditionally appealed to scripture in justifying their defiance of the pope and the institutional church. Martin Luther (1483–1546) recognized the Bible as the ultimate authority in matters of Christian doctrine, and his expositions—especially of the Psalms and Pauline letters—helped him to develop his understanding of *faith and *grace. All the major Protestant theologians—Ulrich Zwingli (1484–1531), Martin Bucer (1491–1551), Philip Melanchthon (1497–1560), Heinrich Bullinger (1503–1575), and especially John Calvin—followed Luther's example. Protestants generally rejected the practice of developing elaborate allegorical explanations of the scriptures, but they eagerly scrutinized both the Hebrew Bible and the New Testament in search of authoritative support for Protestant doctrine. Their lectures, sermons, and commentaries on the Bible helped all the founders of Protestant Christianity to develop and solidify their theological views.

Roman Catholic theologians, of course, did not view scriptural authority as a substitute for papal primacy, but during the sixteenth century they too turned their attention to the Bible with special urgency. Jacques Lefèvre d'Étaples (1455–1536), Gasparo Contarini (1483–1542), and Juan de Valdés (1500–1541) all produced commentaries or exegetical works of a highly spiritual character. All three responded especially warmly to the Pauline letters and sought to encourage spiritual reform within the Roman church, while incidentally rendering the scriptures an instrument of Catholic as well as Protestant controversial literature. Cardinals Reginald Pole (1500–1558) and Girolamo Seripando (1492–1563) strongly encouraged delegates at the Council of Trent (1545–1564) to reform the education of clergy: a curriculum based on humanist study of the Bible rather than scholastic theology, they argued, would lead to general reform and eventually to the religious reunion of Christianity. Meanwhile, Cardinal Cajetan undertook a more direct challenge to Protestant Christianity. In long commentaries on the Gospels and Pauline letters, Cajetan depended upon the methods of humanist scholarship to argue that the New Testament proved the truth of Roman Catholic doctrine and confuted the Protestant alternative.

By the late sixteenth century, then, biblical exegesis clearly reflected the theological division of western Christianity. Although it certainly became the focal point of unpleasant disputes, the Bible also retained its status as the prime source of Christian doctrine and moral teaching. Indeed, the disputes themselves testify to the point that, just as throughout the previous thousand years, the Bible still stood at the center of Christian culture.

Jerry H. Bentley

Modern Biblical Criticism

Biblical criticism is a very general term, and not easy to define; it covers a wide range of scholarly activities. Its ultimate basis lies in the linguistic and literary character of the Bible. Scripture, though understood to be the word of God, is in human language (*Hebrew, *Aramaic, and *Greek) and in the literary, rhetorical, and poetic patterns of human expression, which can and must be interpreted by human understanding. God speaks through scripture, but its meanings function within the structures of ordinary human language. Criticism depends on a grasp of style, of the relation of part to whole, of expression to genre; it takes the biblical diction very seriously and moves from the detail of language to the larger overarching themes. Approached in this way, the Bible is sometimes found to have meanings other than those that traditional or superficial interpretations have suggested. Criticism is thus "critical," not in the sense that it "criticizes" the Bible (it often reveres it as the basic and holy text), but in the sense that it assumes freedom to derive from the Bible, seen in itself, meanings other than those that traditional religion has seen in it. Biblical criticism thus uncovers new questions about the Bible, even as it offers fresh answers in place of old solutions.

Criticism and Conflict. Biblical criticism need not conflict with long-accepted understandings, but it may do so. This will mean that some traditional interpretations have been ill-grounded in scripture and that some new interpretation should be suggested if justice is to be done to the facts of scripture. Criticism has thus often disturbed existing religion; yet it is also intrinsic to the religious belief in biblical *authority. Far from being a nontheological activity, it is essential to proper theological evaluation. We momentarily suspend the existing theological conviction to see whether it stands the test of questioning against the biblical material itself.

Not surprisingly, therefore, religious conflict has been a great stimulus to critical questioning. Two groups share the same scripture but have widely differing religious convictions. Each may then appeal to the scripture and argue that it cannot mean what others have taken it to mean. According to Matthew 23.23, Jesus himself says that the "weightier matters of the law" are neglected if one concentrates on the implementation of details—an appeal to the general tenor of the text against its detailed literality. As against the Christian understanding of Isaiah 7.14 as a prediction of Christ's *virgin birth, the Jew Trypho (second century CE) insisted that the Hebrew word means simply "young woman," that no virgin birth is involved, and that the reference is to the natural birth of Hezekiah.

The religious conflicts that most stimulated the rise of biblical criticism were, however, the Catholic-Protestant conflict within Christianity and, later, the disputes among the many different directions within Protestantism, for these particularly emphasized the unique role of scripture and the implications of reading it for and from itself.

Obstacles to Criticism. The main factors with which criticism has had to contend have included the following:

General ideas or principles concerning the Bible, such as the conviction that, being the word of God, it must necessarily be perfect and thus inerrant in all its parts (*see* Inspiration and Inerrancy). As against these theoretical convictions, criticism works with the factual realities of the Bible.

Harmonizations that universalize ideas and meanings throughout the Bible, obscuring differences between one part and another. Criticism notices these differences, such as that between documents affirming a virgin birth (Matthew, less clearly Luke) and others that appear not to do so (Mark, Paul, John).

Midrash and allegorical interpretations that decontextualize the words of scripture, ascribing to them senses that may be found elsewhere but do not fit this context. Criticism takes the actual context to be decisive.

Failure to perceive the literary form of the texts, and, in particular, failure to give weight to the silences of scripture, the absences of elements that are commonly read in; for example, the absence from the Hebrew Bible of Adam's disobedience as an explanation for *evil, the absence of any birth narrative in Mark, the absence from other Gospels of the clause "except for unchastity" (Matt. 19.9; cf. 5.32; *see* Divorce).

Anachronistic reading into the text of meanings, ideas, and situations of a later age; for example, to understand bishop in the New Testament as if this were identical with medieval episcopacy, or "scripture" in 2 Timothy 3.16 as if it meant exactly the same set of books that are canonical in modern Protestantism (*see* Canon). Criticism insists on starting with the words in the meanings that they had in biblical times.

Rationalistic apologetic arguments supposed to overcome discrepancies; for example, the idea that, since the ejection of merchants from the temple by Jesus is placed early in the ministry by John, late by the other Gospels, the event happened several times. Criticism, on the other hand, suggests that the differential placing of the story was for reasons of theological meaning within the narrative.

Authorship. Classical biblical criticism has been much interested in matters

of authorship. The *Pentateuch was not written by Moses himself; the book of Isaiah contains materials from a time long after that prophet lived; the Gospels were not necessarily written by the disciples whose names they bear. This realization at once changes our picture of the sort of book the Bible is: it is not a once-and-for-all, divinely dictated report but a product of tradition developed over some time within communities of faith. Relations between documents like the synoptic Gospels are literary relations, involving revision, change of emphasis, selection, and theological difference. The feature of pseudepigraphy must be recognized as a fact: that is, that books may be written in the name of, and attributed to, some great person of the past who presides over that genre. Thus, almost all Israelite *law, of whatever time, was attached to the name of Moses, as were wisdom writings to that of Solomon; some letters written in the name of Paul or Peter may have been written by followers, perhaps using some material from the apostle himself, rather than by him directly.

Style has been an important criterion from the beginning. Already in the ancient church it was obvious that 2 Peter was not in a style that Peter used, that the letter to the Hebrews differed in style from Paul, and that the book of Revelation differed vastly in style from the gospel and letters of John; and this observation was already used in early arguments about the canonicity of such books. These ancient observations formed a basis for similar discussions later, especially in Renaissance and Reformation (*see article on* Christian Interpretation from the Middle Ages to the Reformation, *above*), when the appreciation of ancient styles had been greatly quickened.

Sources. That books had been formed by the combination of earlier sources was an obvious corollary of these ideas. Chronicles used Samuel-Kings, revising sometimes slightly, sometimes drastically, and adding material of its own. Mark is most commonly believed to have been used and rewritten by Matthew and Luke. And the sources used could be works that had long disappeared. The books of Kings mention other historical sources known to them. Material common to Matthew and Luke, but absent from Mark, could go back to a source now lost. Within the Pentateuch the different strata, marked by very different language, style, and ideas, could be explained if different sources from different times had been gradually combined. The detection of different sources within a book may thus explain discrepancies and divergent theological viewpoints. Source criticism of this kind is a highly characteristic form of classical biblical criticism. It, along with questions of authorship and date, is sometimes called "higher criticism," in contrast to "lower criticism," the study of text and textual variations (*see* Textual Criticism), but these terms are now old-fashioned. Indeed, from about the 1930s on, source criticism itself became somewhat old-fashioned and less work was done on it; uncertainties in its conclusions were noted, and rivals to the widely accepted views came to be more commonly supported. Nevertheless, source-critical results continue to be used as a normal framework of discussion by the great majority of scholars, and the broad outlines of source identification in the key areas—the Pentateuch, Isaiah, and the synoptic Gospels—are very generally accepted; such alternatives as there are equally critical, but in a different way.

Cosmology and Miracle. The rise of biblical criticism ran parallel with

changing ideas about the world we live in. New scientific knowledge made it seem impossible that the world could have originated as recently as the date (5000–3600 BCE) implied by the Bible's own *chronology, and the vast majority accepted this: the world was not exactly as Genesis had made it seem (*see* Science and the Bible). Similarly, it was debated just how exactly factual biblical depictions of miraculous events were. Critics noted the literary aspect: scripture is quite uneven in the degree to which it brings in miracle stories, and it may describe the same event in ways that are more sheerly miraculous or less so. This suggests that the element of miracle is again in part a matter of style. Biblical criticism is not in principle skeptical about *miracles, but it takes it as clear that not all miracle stories are to be taken literally just because they are in the Bible. On the whole, critical scholarship leaves the question aside; for, in its developed form, it concentrates mainly on the meaning or function that the miracle story had within the work of the writer. For this purpose, it finds it unnecessary either to defend or to deny the reality of miracles; the exegetical process works in the same way in either case.

History has often been looked on as the essential component in biblical criticism, though we have maintained that its foundations rest more in language and in literary form. The literary perceptions thus stimulated often could not produce solutions without a historical account of what had taken place. Thus, in the method of Julius Wellhausen (1844–1918), Pentateuchal sources identified through linguistic and literary criteria were matched with the evidence of different stages in the development of religious institutions in Israel, producing a likely sequence and dating. Dating sources and setting them within the framework of known world history thus provides a strong frame of reference for biblical study and a way in which evidence can be marshaled and ordered for discussion and theological evaluation. In particular, the knowledge, even if only approximate, of what lay before and after makes it possible to understand the presuppositions of biblical writers and the situation for which they wrote.

The centrality of this frame, and the importance of the perspective it afforded, has often caused the entire operation of biblical criticism to be understood as "historical criticism." But this exaggerates the degree to which the ideals of historical research dominate biblical study. Historical investigation is only one aspect of traditional criticism. Much critical work is basically the exegesis of biblical books; for this, complete historical precision is often impossible, and in any case is not attained, often hardly attempted. More important is a rough and general historical location; the gross distortion of total anachronism is to be avoided. Words must be understood to mean what they meant in the language of the texts, and that means in the time of the texts; texts should be seen against the situation in life for which they were written. In fact, biblical scholars, even when they insist on a historical approach, are often not very historical; they tend to let theological predilection overcome historical realism, and their motivation is commonly the religious scholar's devotion to texts rather than pure historical rigor. It was from traditional theology that there came the emphasis on what had "really happened" in biblical times, on the persons of authority who were behind the writings, on history as the milieu of God's activity. Conversely, the historical perspective on the Bible that biblical criticism has brought about is important primarily as a major fact

within theology itself, rather than as a purely historical achievement.

The Canon. One important historical aspect is the perception of the canon of scripture: the canon came about historically and can be understood historically. The pioneering studies of Johann S. Semler (1725–1791) in this area were a vital step in the development of modern biblical studies. The boundaries of scripture are not something eternally and unchangeably established by God; what scripture included at one time and place was not entirely identical with what it included at another; the study of scripture and the study of church history are not separable. That the origins of the canon can be investigated as a human undertaking is correlative with a similar study of the books themselves. The canon can still be understood as God-given, just as the contents of scripture are God-given, but not purely and supernaturally so—rather, only indirectly and through the mediation of human intentions and meanings. Biblical critics have not rejected the canon; on the whole they have continued to uphold it, maintaining that the religious content of the Bible (i.e., the canonical books) is, broadly speaking, vastly superior in quality to that of any other set of written texts.

Theological Differentiation. Central to biblical criticism, and even more important than its historical orientation, is its use of the perception that theological views and emphases differ between one part of scripture and another. The Bible is not a monochrome and unvarying photograph of the being and will of God; it is more like a choir, each member of which has a different part to sing. Thus, in spite of much common subject matter, the P stratum of the Pentateuch has a theology quite different from that of Deuteronomy, and Matthew presents quite a different picture of Jesus from that of Luke. This in itself is no novel or revolutionary insight; but, rather than being content merely to admire the complementary character of the theologies of the books, biblical criticism uses it as a valuable index for the identification of strata and their relative dating, situations, and problems. Equally, it strives to perceive, understand, and evaluate these different theologies as crucial stages in the understanding of scripture as a whole, seen in a dimension of depth.

Theological Roots of Biblical Criticism. Although biblical criticism may appear as something new, in fact it has deep theological roots. The interest in personal authorship went back to early times and was part of the argument over canonicity. Style was also known as a criterion from early times; later, on the basis of style, John Calvin doubted that Peter had written 2 Peter, just as, on grounds of content, he thought that Psalms 74 and 79 came from the Maccabean period (a view later regarded as drastically critical). The emphasis on history and actual events was also part of general Christian tradition: Christianity, people thought, was a peculiarly historical religion, and the importance of the actual words and deeds of Jesus was overwhelmingly accepted and stressed. If biblical criticism noticed and used the theological differences within the Bible, this was an extension from the practice of all theologies; for all, even when accepting the total canon of scripture, had picked out portions as more essential and dominant, while treating others as derivative or of secondary importance. As for the canon, the first obvious fact was that theological tradition had not agreed about it; there had been variations in canons throughout the early centuries, and again as between Roman Catholic and Orthodox on one side, and Protestant on the other.

This fact was accentuated when Martin Luther, impressed by theological differentiation, effectively demoted from the New Testament canon James, Hebrews (not by Paul), and Revelation on the ground of their inadequate understanding of the essential principle of *justification. Difference in emphasis between Old Testament and New Testament was also traditional and universal in Christianity.

The impetus toward biblical criticism given by the Reformation was substantial. Stressing scripture alone—as against mediation through church tradition—meant that everything seemed to depend on scripture. The grammar and wording of the original was reemphasized and a learned ministry capable of handling these words was demanded. The Reformation rejected allegorical methods that had covered over cracks in the surface of scripture, and in the Hebrew Bible it mediated influences from medieval Jewish exegesis (seen, e.g., in the KJV), which in this respect also favored literal understanding *(see article in this entry on Jewish Interpretation, above)*. It asserted the freedom of the interpreter to take a stand on the biblical words as against traditional and authoritative interpretations. But, despite the reformers' insistence on biblical authority, they failed to produce doctrinal agreement; on the contrary, they created a wide variety of conflicting doctrinal positions, all claiming a basis in infallible scripture. The wide variation of ideas and hypotheses within later biblical criticism is a reflection of the same situation.

Rise and Reception of Criticism. The ancient and early modern anticipations of critical views are not in themselves very important. It could be obvious enough that the statement that "at that time the Canaanites were in the land" (Gen. 12.6) was not written by

Moses but was a later note; so argued Abraham ibn Ezra (1089–1164), an opinion on which Baruch Spinoza (1632–1677) later built much more. Such observations were often only minor annotations and do not amount to a critical vision of any scale. More important was the growth of the general atmosphere of thought in which it seemed permissible and even normal to argue on the basis of the language and literary form of scripture, with freedom to offer the interpretations that emerged from them. This tradition may go back to Erasmus (1466–1536), and is well represented by Hugo Grotius (1583–1645), who belonged to the Arminian current in the Dutch church. In France, Richard Simon (1638–1712) argued that uncertainties about scripture undermined the Protestant reliance upon it, while freedom in biblical study produced no clash with Catholic dogma; alongside this, his argument against Moses' authorship of the entire Pentateuch is a minor point. Jean Astruc (1684–1766) pioneered the systematic source analysis of the Pentateuch, the different documents being isolated but understood to have been combined by Moses himself.

An especially active locus of new ideas about scripture was England in the seventeenth and eighteenth centuries. In conflicts over church polity, civil government, and religious freedom there were manifold viewpoints, all of which sought legitimation from scripture, and the ensuing controversies evoked an efflorescence of new ideas and arguments. Thomas Hobbes (1588–1679) is a distinguished representative. For him there is no doubting the authority of the Bible as the law of God; but equally, in the matter of authorship and date, it is simply obvious that the only light we have must come from the books themselves, and from this it is manifest that the books

of Moses were written after his time, and similarly with other books. Other important exegetical ideas come from John Locke (1632–1704), who noted, among other things, how Jesus kept secret his messianic status until late in his career (*see* Messianic Secret); Sir Isaac Newton (1642–1727), who worked on biblical chronology and also thought that the idea of the *Trinity could be disproved from the New Testament; and many others.

In Germany, these ideas were followed up in the later eighteenth century by university professors, who applied them in a much more systematic way. A typical genre was the "introduction," which would cover in turn each book of Old Testament or New Testament and discuss methodically all matters of authorship, source analysis, and dates on the basis of language and content; a pioneer of such work was by Johann Gottfried Eichhorn (published 1780–1783). Central names in Old Testament scholarship are Wilhelm Martin Leberecht de Wette (1780–1849), noted for his work on the key book of Deuteronomy, and Julius Wellhausen, whose solution (the "P" document is the latest of the Pentateuchal sources) remains the point of reference for all discussion of the subject. In New Testament studies, a central figure was Ferdinand Christian Baur (1792–1860), who saw a conflict between Pauline and Petrine traditions as decisive for early Christianity. Of the "quest for the historical Jesus," it is hard to know whether it counts as biblical criticism or as speculative theology; the claim of Johannes Weiss (1863–1914) that Jesus' mission was dominated by eschatological expectation is a more clearly critical standpoint.

The return of this developed biblical criticism to the English-speaking world was not without conflict. W. Robertson

Smith was removed from his professorship in Scotland in 1881, and Charles A. Briggs from his clerical functions in the United States in 1893. But soon after these events, critical approaches had clearly won the day in these same churches. In Oxford, from 1883, the cautious and erudite scholarship of Samuel Rolles Driver commended the critical reading of the Old Testament, and *Lux mundi* (1889) aligned the Catholic tradition of Anglicanism with the same. By the early twentieth century, critical perspectives, though not always easily accepted, were overwhelmingly dominant in academic study and serious publishing throughout the western non-Roman Catholic world.

Although biblical criticism made a deep difference to the handling of the Bible, this did not have the feared serious effects on doctrine. This was partly because many traditional doctrines were not nearly as solely dependent on the Bible as had been supposed. Shifts in the mode of understanding the Bible left it possible for these same doctrines to still be maintained. Indeed, biblical criticism fitted in well with certain important doctrinal emphases: in Lutheranism with justification by faith, in Anglicanism with the centrality of *incarnation, in Calvinism with the appreciation of Israel and the Old Testament. Moreover, though much biblical criticism grew up in association with latitudinarian views, with deism, and later with liberal theology, the achievements of criticism showed themselves to be separable from these origins and to be fully maintainable by those who repudiated them. Thus "dialectical" or "neo-orthodox" theology, bitterly hostile to "liberal" theology, accepted the legitimacy of critical procedures and, though itself often cool toward biblical scholarship, on the whole

created an atmosphere in which it could flourish very freely.

In the Roman Catholic world, Richard Simon's argument that critical freedom favored the Catholic position was little accepted by his superiors, and critical work was muted until the rise of Catholic modernism, especially in France in the late nineteenth century with Alfred F. Loisy (1857–1940). The modernist movement was formally condemned by Pius X in 1907, and the dogmatic necessity of traditional authorships and dates was reasserted. But since the encyclical *Divino afflante spiritu* (1943) and especially since the Second Vatican Council, the critical freedom of the Catholic exegete has been acknowledged, and today Catholic and Protestant biblical scholarship form one total constituency (*see also* Pontifical Biblical Commission).

Jewish academic scholarship has often differed from the solutions favored in Christian work; examples include opposition to Pentateuchal source criticism from Moses Hirsch Segal (1876–1968) and Umberto Cassuto (1883–1951), and different reconstruction of Israelite religious history from Yehezkel Kaufmann (1889–1963). Non-Jewish scholarship was often felt to be too much influenced by Christian theological traditions. But the alternative positions advanced by Jewish scholars are in their own way just as critical, and offer no support to a consistent anticritical mode of study.

Biblical Theology. Biblical criticism has often been understood primarily as an analytical discipline, but equally it is linked with the discipline of *biblical theology, which is the synthetic side of the same movement. Biblical theology seeks to see the common elements that run through the texts, whether through a historical or developmental scheme or through the perception of an inner structure. No serious biblical theology has arisen except in conjunction with the critical approach. Biblical theology, like criticism, is an exploratory approach; the true inner theology of the Bible is not already known, but must be discovered. For opponents of critical study, the theology of scripture is already known, fixed in older creeds and traditions. Although twentieth-century biblical theology felt itself to be in contrast with biblical criticism, they are in fact two sides of the same coin.

Religious Environment. All the above may count as a depiction of "classical" biblical criticism; there remain some more recent developments to be mentioned. The older critics worked largely from the Bible itself; later, increasing knowledge from Mesopotamia and Syria, from Hellenistic *mystery religions, and from *gnosticism was added. Clearly, there is some overlap in religious ideas and institutions, in legends, myths, and poetic forms. The "history of religions" school explored this area; a central name is that of Hermann Gunkel (1862–1932).

Form Criticism, influential from the 1920s on, is interested in the smaller literary units that have a function in their "situation in life," through which one penetrates to the underlying purpose. Thus, a gospel story might be of a form fitted for controversy with Jews, a psalm might be of a form belonging to an enthronement ceremony. Important form critics are Gunkel for the Hebrew Bible, and Rudolf Bultmann (1884–1976) for the New Testament. For the New Testament, form criticism often seemed to be skeptical in character, suggesting that stories were generated for these purposes rather than actually spoken by Jesus; in the Hebrew Bible its effects were more

conservative, suggesting ways in which poems might have functioned in ancient cult and liturgy.

Tradition Criticism concentrates on the way in which traditions have altered and grown, the places to which they are attached, and the social and cultic relations within which they have been meaningful. It is less interested in documentary hypotheses, more in oral stages of tradition, and it illuminates the deep underlying forces that have molded the Bible into its present form. It has been particularly exemplified in Scandinavian scholarship.

Redaction Criticism is interested in the work of the final editors, who molded the earlier sources into the text that we now have. The method depends on some view of the sources used by the redactor, but the interest falls less on these sources in themselves and more on the way in which they have been adapted into the final text. The object is therefore the shape and structure of the book as we now have it; yet the perception of this depends on a perspective in time, going back to an earlier stage or earlier revisional activity.

Modern Literary Readings. Although the literary character of biblical criticism has been emphasized here, from about 1960 on it has been increasingly felt that it is out of step with modern trends in the appreciation of literature. Literary critics from outside the technical biblical sphere—for example, Frank Kermode, Robert Alter, and Northrop Frye—have made powerful contributions and some biblical scholars are following similar lines. Most of this literary movement is interested in the final, the present, stage of the text, not in historical reconstruction; nor does it share the theological interests characteristic of most biblical criticism. The stress is on the styles, the patterns, the narrative techniques. The text, some think, does not "refer" to anything external to itself, but operates within "the world of the text" (*see also* Literature, The Bible as). Some of this overlaps with ideas coming from *structuralism, a movement centered in France. Structuralism is interested in the code, the set of structures, that are used in all social and literary complexes, as they are in language itself. It stresses the synchronic, the structures visible within one text at one time, rather than its development over a span of time, though it can also be extended to deal with historical change. These types of reading, in general, differ widely from traditional biblical criticism and especially from its historical interests; on the other hand, their reluctance to say anything informative about the world "outside the text" leaves it doubtful how they can fit with the older theological needs served by biblical criticism.

Canonical Criticism. This approach, advocated principally by Brevard S. Childs, insists on the canon of scripture as the essential key to interpretation. Canonicity is interested in the final text, not in earlier stages that have led up to it. The canon of books, which brings them all together as holy scripture of the community, means that taken together they provide a "construal" of all their contents. Traditional biblical criticism is legitimate, providing, as it does, the starting points from which Childs reasons toward the canonical sense; but its perspective and direction are basically erroneous. Common areas with redaction criticism and with modern literary readings and structuralism seem obvious; but Childs is anxious to disclaim support from these quarters, for canonical criticism is not at all literary in character, and its validation comes entirely from the theological status of scripture. Although

it appears to seek a connection with much earlier exegesis, canonical criticism is a clearly modern phenomenon, working entirely from the tradition of biblical criticism even when it seeks to depart from it.

Conclusion. Biblical criticism has proved to be a dynamic field of study. New approaches and perspectives continue to appear. Areas undergoing fresh examination include the nature of Hebrew poetic form (stimulated by our knowledge of *Ugaritic poetry; *see also* Poetry, Biblical Hebrew); the character of Judaism at the time when Christianity originated; the character of scripture as story rather than as history. Results believed to have been established will be reconsidered. Yet some of the main positions achieved have remained as essential reference points for the discussion, and no alternatives have been proposed that have gained anything like the same degree of assent. Still more important, the general intellectual atmosphere of criticism, with its base in language and literary form, its reference grid in history, and its lifeblood in freedom to follow what the text actually says, has established itself as without serious challenge. Serious work on scripture can be done only in continuity with the tradition of biblical criticism.

See also Social Sciences and the Bible.

James Barr

ISRAEL, RELIGION OF.

Ancient Israel and Its Ancient Near Eastern Setting. Scholarship on ancient Israelite religion seems to swing back and forth, as if attached to a great pendulum, between those who advocate the uniqueness of the biblical revelation (the "biblical theology" approach) and those who assert that ancient Israelite religion is cut from the same cloth as other ancient Near Eastern religions (the "history of religions" approach). Much of the swing toward the latter was occasioned by archaeological discoveries that correlate the Bible and its ancient Near Eastern setting.

Most scholars of ancient Israelite religion argue that we should no longer refer to the Bible *and* the ancient Near East, as if the former were not a part of the latter. By affirming Israel's cultural and material solidarity with its neighbors, scholars have underscored that the study of ancient Israelite religion must be anchored in its historical ancient Near Eastern moorings. This need not prevent us from affirming that ancient Israel developed uniquely; by definition, all societies form cultural configurations that are distinct. The belief system that emerged from ancient Israel, especially in its conception of the divine, was indeed radical in its context.

The Formative Period. Scholars have been able to document the Canaanite heritage of ancient Israelite religion. Ancestral religion, for example, with its worship of El (as exemplified by titles found in Genesis such as El Shadday, El Elyon, El Bethel, and El, the God of Israel), is directly related to the Canaanite deity El described in the *Ugaritic texts.

Yet scholars have found it more difficult to describe the underlying reasons that led Israel to come up with a configuration of beliefs, such as *monotheism and the absence of divine sex and death, that was radical in its West Semitic Canaanite context. A closely related debate is the date assigned to the formative period for these beliefs. Scholars such as Julius Wellhausen reconstructed an evolutionary process whereby a gradual progression from polytheism and then henotheism eventually led to the "ethical monotheism" of the prophets of the eighth century BCE and later. Others,

such as W. F. Albright and Yehezkel Kaufmann, argued for an early crystallization of revolutionary beliefs such as monotheism during the time of Moses. Such debates have continued and always involve various theories on the settlement of Palestine and the archaeological evidence for the transition from the Late Bronze to the Iron Age.

Nature and Scope. Past treatments of ancient Israelite religion were excessively narrow, treating only the "orthodox" religion described by the majority of biblical texts. While the biblical Yahwism that eventually emerged as normative takes center stage for most people, today emphasis is also placed on religious conceptions that were very much a part of ancient Israelite society yet were eventually seen as nonnormative (e.g., Asherah, cults of the dead; see below). In other words, scholars now argue that Israelite religion must be studied from its earliest times to its latest. One should not opt for late Israelite religion (e.g., Deuteronomic or prophetic) while ignoring early forms, even if it seems that the religion of the early period cannot be easily divorced from Canaanite religion.

Sources. The Hebrew Bible is the most important document for studying ancient Israelite religion, yet it has its limitations. It must be understood as collections selected and edited according to certain criteria (e.g., Judean ideology, Deuteronomic theology). Yet this is hardly different from most other ancient Near Eastern texts or even modern literature in which writers selectively edit their material.

Current scholarship runs the full spectrum from pessimism to optimism about our ability to uncover early Israelite religion. Some scholars emphasize that the majority of texts stem from later times and are more or less useless for reconstructing the earlier stages. Others, such as Albright, Frank Moore Cross, David Noel Freedman, and Johannes C. de Moor, argue that some texts, primarily poetic ones, do contain material from the earliest periods of ancient Israel's existence. All scholars face an array of questions when working with material that has an overlay of late editing. To what degree can we unearth the earlier stages of the religion? Can we uncover nonorthodox viewpoints? Does later editing, even later reworking of material, obscure every trace of early beliefs or practices that might have been more at home in the family worship than in the cult which became normative?

*Archaeology provides windows into the diversity of ancient Israelite religion. It uncovers physical remains of temples and various cult paraphernalia regardless of whether such sanctuaries and cultic objects were considered legitimate or apostate. Household shrines, foundations deposits, funeral offerings, and *burials provide new dates on which to reconstruct practices characteristic of family worship and thus outside the scope of most biblical writers. Inscriptional evidence gives us empirical data (such as theophoric elements in personal names) free from the heavy editing of most literary works. But archaeology also has its limitations, such as a simple lack of evidence. At times the extant material remains can be just as restrictive as the biblical texts. The interpretation of the evidence is also subjective and sometimes even dogmatic. But archaeology's biggest shortcoming for reconstructing religion is that it is hard-pressed to comment on underlying causes and ideologies such as monotheism.

It has been widely assumed that a great deal can be learned about a religion by looking at theophoric elements (divine names or titles) in personal names,

for the ancients often gave their children names reflecting the deity or deities whom they worshiped. Yet because of social convention, personal names do not necessarily provide full and accurate evidence of explicit religious devotion. Even polytheists such as Ahab, Jezebel, and Athaliah could give their children Yahwistic names. One should ask to what degree this might have been a widespread practice among polytheists, who for some reason (e.g., political motivation, fear of repression) adopted the name of the national deity, yet in practice worshiped other deities. The absence of naming after goddesses, especially that of Asherah, has been considered significant. Yet at ancient Ugarit there was a vibrant cult dedicated to Asherah but only one attestation of her name as the theophoric element in a personal name.

Key Concepts. *Monotheism.* The Israelite deity goes by the names of El/Elohim (a common Semitic noun for "god") and Yahweh. There is universal agreement that Yahweh is derived from the verb "to be," but scholars differ over whether the verb underlying the name is noncausative or causative, "the one who causes to come into being," that is, a reference to the deity's role as creator; the latter seems preferable. Scholars emphasizing the Canaanite heritage also draw parallels between Israelite El/Elohim and Yahweh and the Amorite/Canaanite deities El and Baal. A correlative issue is the relation of the names Elohim and Yahweh and their connection to the "god of the fathers" of Israelite ancestral tradition. Some, such as Cross, see in Yahweh an original epithet of the ancestral deity El ("El, who causes the heavenly hosts to come into being"). Others, such as de Moor, have argued for Yahweh-El as a south Canaanite form of the gods of the fathers.

Tracing the development of monotheism in ancient Israel is a complex endeavor with little consensus among scholars. One can easily find an advocate for placing the origin of monotheism in every age from the ancestral down to the exilic. Often, one's views of monotheism are tied to equally difficult issues, such as the historicity of the ancestors, the person of Moses, the makeup of the tribal league, kinship relations, the settlement of the land of Israel, and the social function of the prophets.

In the early period, there are clear indications of henotheism or monolatry, the worship of a single deity though recognizing the existence of others. Ancestral religion with its focus on the worship of El seems to point to a monolatrous El cult. Other texts emphasize the presence of other deities. In Psalm 29 we read of the beckoning of the gods to praise Yahweh, and Psalm 82 represents Yahweh judging the gods (see Son of God).

Recently scholars have emphasized the role of the monarchy in the development of nationalistic exclusivity and corresponding monolatrous tendencies. Baruch Halpern sees in Josiah's reform a "self-conscious monotheism" (see Kingship and Monarchy). Further examples of explicit monotheism can be found in relatively late texts. Thus, Jeremiah no longer describes other deities as options but rather as "cracked cisterns that can hold no water" (Jer. 2.13). Explicit monotheism finds its most articulate voice in Second Isaiah: "I am Yahweh, and there is no other; besides me there is no god" (Isa. 45.5).

The goddess Asherah. The goddess Asherah has always been known in the Bible through curious references to some type of cult object usually translated as "asherah pole." Some scholars see hints of her in Genesis 49.25 and Amos 8.14, but these verses are textually very difficult. The absence of any destruction of

the prophets of Asherah in the Elijah narrative is intriguing. Similarly, Jehu destroys the Baal from Israel, yet no mention is made of Asherah.

Recently, the goddess and her possible roles have been studied intensively, owing to the discovery of enigmatic inscriptions referring to "Yahweh and his/ its(?) Asherah/asherah" at Kuntillet Ajrud and Khirbet el-Qom. As a result some scholars have concluded that Asherah was worshiped in ancient Israel as the consort of Yahweh. But others have argued for an understanding of the word "asherah" as a symbol within the cult of Yahweh rather than a reference to the goddess herself.

Asherah/asherah was certainly present in monarchic Israel. But ancient Israelite society was more pluralistic than we usually assume. There were probably numerous differing viewpoints, many at odds with each other, and they most likely differed from city to city. The asherah symbol in its origin is not easily divorced from the goddess Asherah. Different groups may have had differing degrees of toleration when someone mentioned "Yahweh and his asherah." Some may have believed Yahweh to be the national deity, yet had no problem in worshiping local Asherah deities, especially in cults dealing with fertility and agriculture. Other circles freely appropriated mythic imagery apart from mythic content, and thus for them the symbol was a legitimate part of Yahwistic religion. For yet others, such as certain prophetic groups and the Deuteronomist, who argued for exclusive worship of Yahweh, any hint of the goddess deserved condemnation.

The break with ancient Near Eastern myth. Some scholars of Israelite religion, such as Yehezkel Kaufmann and Michael Fishbane, have been struck by the Bible's break with ancient Near Eastern mythical consciousness. This new paradigm was characterized by a "creator-creature distinction" in which an autonomous God is portrayed as distinct from the created world. In addition, sex and death are conspicuously absent when the biblical god is depicted, in contrast to the prevalence of these motifs in other ancient Near Eastern literatures. Admitting henotheism in the early period, one must still recognize that the deity of the Hebrew Bible is not part of a pantheon and is not described as having any sexual relations with any consort, nor does he impregnate animals as does Baal in one of the Ugaritic texts. He is not a "dying and rising god" like Canaanite Baal or Egyptian Osiris. The biblical deity does not imbibe, unlike Canaanite El, described in another text as a pathetic drunkard. In short, the divine is portrayed more transcendently; God is not dependent on any outside power. (*See also* Myth.)

The development of this new paradigm was part of a process whereby Israelite religion emerged from its Canaanite context and changed from polytheism to monolatry and eventually to monotheism. From all indications this differentiation appeared quite early, although this is not to say that mythic imagery, especially with regard to fertility and *death, does not permeate the Bible, as Marvin Pope showed.

The aniconic tradition. The novelty of the absence of divine iconography in Israelite religion was not lost even on the ancients. The Roman historian Tacitus thought it bizarre that the Jews would prohibit portrayal of the divine. Modern scholars have a better footing to debate the question thanks to archaeological evidence. In addition to the biblical description of Yahweh invisibly enthroned on the cherubim, scholars have also looked to data such as an incense stand

from Taanach as a depiction of an unseen deity. The most relevant archaeological material is the plethora of bronze and terra cotta figurines depicting Canaanite deities. In light of these, it is remarkable how few material remains exist that document the physical portrayal of Yahweh.

The scholarly debate over the origin of the aniconic tradition goes hand in hand with the debate over the origin of monotheism. Tryvge N. D. Mettinger has noted that the theology associated with the *ark of the covenant was centered on an aniconic deity. Yet he argues that the polemic against images did not reach its full force until the prophet Hosea. Ronald S. Hendel has underscored the role of divine iconography in legitimating royalty throughout the ancient Near East, and thus he traces the origin of the aniconic tradition in Israel back to the bias against kingship.

God versus the dragon and the sea. Some of the clearest examples of mythic imagery in the Bible are the descriptions of God battling a personified sea as well as a dragonlike creature called Leviathan and Rahab. Cross has stressed that God's battle with Leviathan, Sea, and Death are alloforms of one basic cosmogonic myth in which the Divine Warrior is victorious over the forces of *chaos, found for example in Mesopotamia (Marduk vs. Tiamat) and Canaanite (Baal and Anat vs. Sea, Lotan, and Mot) mythologies. In Psalm 74.13–14 God crushes the heads of Leviathan, a close parallel to the seven-headed dragon creature of the same name known from Ugaritic. Chaos imagery is applied to historical forces (often Egypt), which Yahweh defeats in like manner, and is often projected into future eschatological battles. Isaiah 27.1 describes such a battle in which Yahweh will destroy the twisting serpent Leviathan with his mighty sword. The longevity of the theme can be seen in the account in Revelation 12–13 of the defeat of the seven-headed dragon and the seven-headed beast.

The cult and abode of the dead. The biblical idioms for death, "being gathered to one's kin" and "sleeping with one's fathers," underscore the clan solidarity within ancient Israel. Nevertheless, the Yahwism that emerged as normative condemned the worship of the deceased and any form of necromancy. On the other hand, the Hebrew Bible also gives witness to the practice of certain death rituals. Note especially 1 Samuel 28, where Saul has a necromancer conjure the dead Samuel from the grave; the Deuteronomic historian used this well-known tale to underscore the demise of Saul, yet he left the efficacy of the practice intact.

Various Hebrew terms are used, often in parallelism, to describe the abode of the dead, including Sheol, Death, and two words meaning "the Pit." Both Sheol and Death are also used for the personified chthonic power behind death (cf. the Ugaritic god Mot, whose name means "Death"). As a location, Sheol is described as the lowest place imaginable, often in contrast with the highest heavens. Sheol is frequently associated with water images, often echoing the stories of divine combat. The gates of the underworld frequently mentioned in Egyptian and Mesopotamian accounts are also found in the Bible. Thus Sheol is a place of imprisonment from which one cannot escape. The personification of Sheol and Death can be seen in descriptions of their insatiable appetites, remarkably reminiscent of the Canaanite deity Mot's voracious appetite. (*See also* Afterlife and Immortality; Hell.)

Conclusion. Many scholars have looked to the premonarchic league period to find the origins of ancient Israel's unique configuration, and have produced an array of hypotheses dependent on their views of the conquest/settlement of ancient Israel. Recently archaeologists have re-emphasized the indigenous nature of early Israel, yet outside influences certainly played a substantial role. Thus, many look for the key to unlock Israel's radical configuration in the early league (Cross), Mosaic (Freedman), or even pre-Mosaic (de Moor) periods. It will remain difficult, however, to illuminate the social and political background of this period given the paucity of textual and material evidence and the fact that the texts we do have may not constitute plausible historical witnesses.

Ancient Israelite religion encompasses the full spectrum of religious belief and practice, and in addition to the cross-references given above, the reader should look to specialized entries such as the following for a more complete picture: Apocalyptic Literature; Circumcision; Covenant; Creation; Dreams; Eschatology; Feasts and Festivals; Graven Image; Heaven; Idols, Idolatry; Magic and Divination; Passover; Prayer(s); Righteousness; Sabbath; Sacrifice; Sin; Theophany.   *Theodore J. Lewis*

J

JOSEPHUS, FLAVIUS. Our knowledge of the life of Josephus stems directly from his own writings, four of which have survived. These works form the most important sources of contemporary information about Jewish religious life, history, and culture during the last two pre-Christian and first post-Christian centuries.

The life of Josephus (37–ca. 100 CE) divides itself into two parts: his dramatic and controversial years in Judea and his residence in Rome as a client of the Flavian emperors. He was born in Jerusalem as Yosef ben Mattityahu. While still a teenager he spent some time in the wilderness as a member of the Essenes, whose austere life and devotion to scripture Josephus found romantic. Later he classified himself as a member of the Pharisees. When the great revolt against Rome began in 66 CE, Josephus was appointed as general to take charge of the defense of Galilee in the northern part of the country. His preparations, however, were nullified when Vespasian overran the Jewish forces. This rout resulted, according to Josephus, from the martial superiority of the Roman army and the tactical skill of their commander. On the other hand, the detractors of Josephus asserted that the Roman victory derived from treachery by Josephus himself, and this suspicion of Josephus's patriotism would haunt him the remainder of his public life. Josephus and some of his companions escaped the besieged town of Jotapata and formed a suicide pact in order to escape capture by the Romans. Somehow Josephus managed to become the sole survivor of this scheme and then promptly surrendered himself to the Romans. He managed to win the attention of Vespasian by forecasting that the Roman commander would become emperor, and when this prediction proved true, Josephus became a permanent fixture in the entourage first of Vespasian and then of Titus. He played a prominent role in the eventual subjugation of Judea.

Josephus spent the remainder of his life residing in Rome as a pensioner of the imperial family. He devoted himself to writing, producing his works under the name of Flavius Josephus. His first surviving work is *The Jewish War,* a seven-book account of the great rebellion in which he played so prominent a part. Josephus exhibits his skill as a historian by beginning his account two-and-a-half centuries before the actual revolt in order to portray the historical background of the unrest in Judea. His account of the war itself veers in two directions: he manages to defend and magnify the deeds of the Roman generals while simultaneously depicting the courage and heroism of the Jewish defenders of Jerusalem.

Josephus found in Roman society a considerable interest in Jewish history and in Judaism, and to satisfy this curiosity he wrote *The Jewish Antiquities.* This work lacks the skillful writing and dramatic excitement of the *War* but makes up for this lack in sheer comprehensiveness. The first ten of its twenty books are an expanded and embellished paraphrase of the historical writings of the Hebrew Bible. Josephus supplements the biblical narrative with Jewish lore known as *haggadah* as well as with selections from Greek and other sources relevant to the biblical story. In the second half of the *Antiquities* Josephus devotes a great deal of space to the rise and reign of Herod the Great. This section is largely dependent on the histories of Nicolaus of Damascus, a secretary to Herod.

The most charming work of Josephus is a two-book tractate in which he defends the Jewish people and religion against their ancient detractors. Something akin to *anti-Semitism had reared its head in antiquity, and Josephus records some of these ancient slanders in this work, entitled *Against Apion.* Apion was a popular publicist whose writings featured a number of these calumnies, and the essay of Josephus was intended to be a reply.

Finally, Josephus composed an autobiography originally appended to the *Antiquities,* which now circulates independently under the title of *Life.* Much of what is contained in the *Life* was previously reported in the *War.* Yet there is some additional material here as well, such as Josephus's version of his dispute with Justus of Tiberias, a rival historian.

The writings of Josephus played an important role in the culture of the Radical Reformation. If Puritan arrivals to New England possessed a book in addition to their Bibles, it was usually Josephus.

See also Judaisms of the First Century CE.

Ben Zion Wacholder

JUDAISMS OF THE FIRST CENTURY CE.

The title of this article indicates a change in an earlier scholarly consensus. Why Judaisms and not Judaism? It has become clear that in the first century CE Judaism was not monolithic but highly variegated throughout the Greco-Roman world, and diverse and complex even within the borders of Roman Palestine. No longer valid is George Foot Moore's characterization of "normative Judaism," by which he meant that Pharisaic-Rabbinic Judaism was the dominant and legitimate expression, against which all other Judaisms were judged to be aberrations or variants. Instead, the picture that has emerged is of multiple Judaisms, distinct Jewish religious systems, yet with connecting threads, indicators that they share a common legacy. Another characterization to be rejected is "late Judaism." This early twentieth-century terminology was used to brand Judaism in the Greco-Roman period as a legalistic degeneration of earlier prophetic religion, moving toward the end of Judaism with its lack of acceptance of Jesus as the Messiah. Scholars today recognize that the Judaisms of the first century are early and not late, that they are much more at the beginning than at the end. Yet another contrast that has been laid aside is that of Palestinian versus Hellenistic Judaism; this is an artificial opposition which reduces an enormously complex picture into a simplistic one. Hellenization and its attendant issues were not confined to the Diaspora. Still, while the overlap between the Judaisms inside and outside of Palestine is significant, one should not deny the distinctive features of Diaspora Judaism, many of which were an outgrowth of two issues: the great distance between the Jerusalem Temple and most Diaspora Jews, and the fact that Diaspora Judaism was a minority religion in a heavily hellenized and polytheistic setting. In short, it is difficult to compose a coherent picture of the Judaisms of this time because of the very diversity, complexity, and dynamic character that lead us to speak of Judaisms rather than Judaism, and also because of the nature of the sources.

Sources. The primary literary sources for the Judaisms of the first century provide only a limited picture. Those preserved are those which were important to the victors of history. From the Jewish perspective this is rabbinic literature (which dates from the third century CE on, though it may preserve earlier traditions), the foundational literature of what is known as Orthodox Judaism. It gradually came to regard itself as the heir to Pharisaic Judaism, and therefore either ignored or was hostile to other varieties of Judaism in the first century. From a Christian perspective, there is mid-first to second century evidence in the New Testament and other early Christian writings. These view first-century Judaisms through the lenses of various Christian communities struggling to establish identities independent of the Judaism out of which they are emerging or with which they are competing, often polemically. Additional sources include two first-century Jewish figures, the historian Flavius *Josephus and the philosopher *Philo of Alexandria, the *Dead Sea Scrolls, the Jewish literature written between the Bible and the Mishnah and preserved in the *apocrypha and in the *pseudepigrapha, and archeological and inscriptional evidence. Each source has its own problems of interpretation, and there are major gaps, such as data concerning women. Nevertheless, there is a wealth and variety of sources for the Judaisms of the first century that reflect diverse socioeconomic perspectives. Ironically, it is the very diversity of these perspectives which often limits historical reconstructions, because of their disagreements with one another and the gaping holes that they leave in their wake.

Pharisees. Of the named Judaisms of the first century, the best known are the Pharisees, attested in Josephus, the New Testament, and rabbinic literature. The evidence reveals nothing of the internal organization of this group—their criteria for membership, leadership structure, or educational system. Only two known individuals claim that they were themselves Pharisees: Josephus and Paul. There are reasons to question Josephus's claim that at the age of nineteen he became a Pharisee, and certainly many of his writings do not seem to be those of a Pharisee or someone who is more than neutral toward the Pharisees. Still, his later writings show a change of attitude and could support a later Pharisaic affiliation. Paul wrote from the perspective of one who had left Pharisaic Judaism. Josephus's and Paul's claims to be Pharisees open up the possibility that Pharisaic Judaism was found not only in Roman Palestine but in the Diaspora, possibly as a way of responding to the wider world of Greco-Roman culture with a consciously Jewish way of life.

Josephus mentions the Pharisees fewer than twenty times, and the portrait that emerges is of a relatively small group (six thousand at the time of Herod the Great) that for most of the first century played a minor role in Jewish society. They are portrayed as one of three philosophical schools of thought, alongside the Sadducees and Essenes, but seem to have been primarily a political interest group. Lacking their own political power, the Pharisees sought influence with the ruling class to achieve their goals for Jewish society, especially during the latter part of Hasmonean rule, and at various other times up through the beginning of the revolt against Rome in 66 CE. Josephus's selective description of Pharisaic beliefs—they believe in fate, free will, and God; that the soul is imperishable; and that the souls of the wicked will be punished—reflects the interests of his Greco-Roman audience. A hint of the Pharisees' overall goals is that they had a reputation for interpreting traditional laws not recorded in the books of Moses; unfortunately Josephus does not elaborate.

Other clues concerning the Pharisees' goals for a renewed Judaism and their own internal rules come from the Gospels and rabbinic Judaism. The depiction of the Pharisees in the Gospels as the opponents of Jesus focuses the contention between Jesus and the Pharisees around issues of *fasting and *tithing, *purity, and *Sabbath observance, issues that overlap with the agenda of early rabbinic law. Further, the early rabbinic evidence for the Pharisees presents them as applying their own tradition of priestly piety to everyday life and business. According to Anthony Saldarini, "the Pharisees drew on an old tradition of using priestly laws concerning purity, food, and marriage in order to separate, protect, and identify Judaism" ("Pharisees," *Anchor Bible Dictionary*). Without denying that the rabbis are the ideological descendants of the Pharisees, the precise relationship between the Pharisees and the early rabbis who came after them is problematic, and there are considerable differences between the rabbis and the Pharisees. Apparently Pharisaic Judaism's rise to prominence is gradual, beginning after the war with Rome.

Sadducees. Evidence for the Sadducees is more meager and much more difficult to interpret than that for the Pharisees. None of the sources (Josephus, the New Testament, rabbinic literature) were written from a Sadducean point of view; the Sadducees rarely appear alone in them; and they are generally hostile in their treatment of the Sadducees. The sources agree, however, that the Sadducees were a recognized and well-established group of first-century Jews. Josephus further notes that while they had limited influence, they were respected within Jewish society. Their origins and history are obscure, though we hear of them as a political party during the Hasmonean rule of John Hyrcanus (134–104 BCE) and continue to hear of them throughout the first century CE until sometime after the war with Rome. Josephus portrays the Sadducees as drawn from the ruling class and therefore not popular with the masses. Several sources suggest some sort of connection between the Sadducees and the priestly establishment, and Acts 5 associates them with the high priest and makes them the dominant group on the Sanhedrin (though Acts 23 envisions the Sanhedrin as more evenly divided). Caution is needed here: the Sadducees cannot be equated with the priesthood and the ruling class. Not all Sadducees were priests and at best only a very small number of the ruling class were Sadducees. In rabbinic literature the Sadducees are identified with the even less well known Boethusians. It is unclear whether these were two distinct groups or whether the rabbis have conflated two sets of opponents. The little we can glean of Sadducean beliefs comports well with the conservative nature of a group drawn from the ruling class and with some connection to the priesthood: they rejected resurrection, the *afterlife, and judgment—a position connecting them with older Israelite religion and pitting them against newer beliefs. Josephus portrays them as denying fate and the traditions of the Pharisees and accepting no observance "apart from the laws." This hardly makes them scriptural literalists, and most likely they had their own traditions of interpretation opposed to those of the Pharisees. Certainly early rabbinic sources claim that the Sadducees differ from the Pharisees concerning ritual purity and Sabbath observance. Other beliefs concerning rituals such as those related to the Temple and the Sadducean/Boethusian method of reckoning Pentecost coincide with priestly practices.

Essenes. Largely due to the discovery of the Dead Sea Scrolls at Qumran, the best-known group from ancient sources is the Essenes. The identification of the Qumran community with Essenes is not found in the Scrolls; rather, the impressive agreement of the evidence in the scrolls with that of the other key sources for Essenes (the Roman geographer Pliny the Elder, Philo, and Josephus) makes highly probable the identification of the Qumran community as Essenes. Still, discrepancies remain and the portrait that emerges is far from complete. Both Philo and Josephus number the Essenes at more than four thousand and say that the Essene communities were found throughout Palestine. Pliny locates a major settlement of the Essenes on the northwest corner of the Dead Sea, between Jericho and Engedi, which all but names the site at Qumran. That site could accommodate about two hundred members at any one time; the majority of Essenes must have lived elsewhere. Both the Scrolls and Josephus seem to provide for two orders of Essenes: celibate men and those who married and had families. It is presumed that Qumran was a celibate community of Essenes and may have served as a center for Essenes from other locations—

though the evidence does not rule out other interpretations. The history of the group is only imprecisely known. The Essenes may have originated in the early second century BCE. Even though the Qumran site was destroyed in the war against Rome, because the majority of Essenes lived at other settlements it is not impossible that the group persisted after 70 CE, though evidence to support their survival is hard to find.

Both the Qumran community and the other Essene groups were tightly organized. Those living outside of Qumran offered hospitality to other members, and in general the Essenes studiously avoided contact with outsiders. The penalties were severe for those who violated the rules and purity regulations of the community and for those who denigrated the community in any way. The Essenes were hierarchically organized according to seniority, standing within the community, and "perfection of spirit," with priests at the top. Admission to the group entailed a graduated process over two to three years, which was carefully regulated; there was also provision for expulsion. Full membership involved some form of communal property (even though there appears to have been some private ownership allowed), as well as communal meals and communal funds. The Essenes rigorously kept the Sabbath. The evidence concerning the attitude of the Essenes toward animal *sacrifice and Temple worship is confusing. Possible interpretations include: there were times in the history of the group when they sent offerings to the Temple and times when they did not; or, the Qumran community dissented from the official Temple ritual, whereas the other Essene communities did not. Among their beliefs were theological determinism, present participation in "eternal life" as well as one which extended beyond the grave, and the notion of a final and universal conflagration.

Other Groups. Philo mentions the Therapeutae, a celibate community of men and women living outside of Alexandria. Their piety and communal practices resemble those of celibate Essenes, with whom there may be some connection. The evidence for scribes in the first century CE is at best sparse and confusing, and the portrait that emerges from the various sources is incoherent. Despite the presentation of the scribes in the New Testament, scribes do not seem to have formed an organization with its own membership. Rather, scribalism was a profession and a class of literate individuals who functioned as personal secretaries and public officials at all levels of Jewish society. Scribes who worked with the ruling class would most likely have been learned in all aspects of Judaism.

There are also first-century Jewish groups whose activity seems to have been primarily political during the time leading up to and throughout the First Jewish Revolt. Josephus wrote of the Zealots mainly as a group in Jerusalem from 68–70 CE, who spent most of their energy struggling with other Jewish revolutionary groups until Jerusalem was surrounded, when they united against the Romans and mostly died fighting. Josephus also mentions the Fourth Philosophy, a group similar to the Pharisees except for their belief that only God should be acknowledged as king and ruler. The Fourth Philosophy spawned the Sicarii, who specialized in assassinating Jews who collaborated with the Romans. They may have been motivated in part by eschatological and messianic expectations.

Just as there was no "normative Judaism" in the first century CE, so too the borders of first-century Judaism were not impermeable. Several groups attest to the porous nature of first-century Jewish identity. Most clearly on the "outside" from all but their own perspective are the Samaritans, yet there are many reasons to view them as among the Judaisms of the age. The Samaritans believed themselves to be the authentic representatives of Mosaic religion. They are characterized by the building of their temple on Mount Gerizim and worship there rather than in Jerusalem, and by limiting themselves to their own version of the Pentateuch, which emphasizes the divine sanctity of Gerizim as the center for Israel's cultic life. Ranging from "inside" to "just outside" from a first-century perspective, and yet clearly on the outside from modern Jewish and Christian perspectives are Jewish Christians, a label that encompasses a complex situation and a great variety. Examples include a number of named Jewish Christian groups mentioned in early patristic sources who share their adherence to Jewish beliefs and practices alongside their messianic understanding of Jesus and often a virulent anti-Pauline strain; the community underlying the gospel of Matthew, who seem to have understood themselves as recently and bitterly separated from the local synagogue because of their messianic beliefs, despite the fact that they were better at practicing their Judaism; the gospel of John may be appealing to Jews who have a secret and incipient belief in Jesus (represented by Nicodemus, the parents of the man born blind, and Joseph of Arimathea), urging them to grow in their understanding and not to be afraid of expulsion from the synagogue or of leaving their Jewish roots behind.

The above Judaisms present only a partial picture of the diversity of the first century. Josephus and Philo are examples of individuals who do not give us a clear sense of what, if any, Jewish group they might represent (despite Josephus's claim to have been a Pharisee from the age of nineteen). Most of the first-century Jewish writings preserved in the apocrypha and pseudepigrapha are not linked to the above-named groups, yet they add significantly to the diversity and complexity of the picture. The several apocalypses and the apocalyptic features of other writings add another substantial dimension. There seem to have been a number of small groups that placed an emphasis on *baptism, whether for ritual purification, initiation, or both. We have only glimpses of other features of the Judaisms of the first century: possible Jewish-*Gnostic tendencies, peasant social banditry groups, popular messianic movements, prophetic movements, and groups that formed around a wide range of charismatic leaders.

Common Elements. What do these diverse groups share? In part it is what Lester Grabbe has termed "personal Jewish identity": belief in one God; the concept of being part of the chosen people—Israel; the rejection of images in worship; the centrality of *Torah; and the practice of *circumcision. But even these characteristics are complex. Torah is a good example. The third part of Jewish *canon (the Writings) was not yet closed; in general, different Jews had different ideas about what to include, which text or translation to read, which parts of the Torah, Prophets, and Writings were more authoritative, and how they should be interpreted. Also connecting the various first-century Judaisms was the Jerusalem Temple. The Temple was central both within Roman Palestine and in the Diaspora, despite the obvious problem of distance. In Jewish writings the Temple varies from concrete reality to metaphor to idealization. Long after its destruction, the Mishnah discusses the Temple as if it were still stand-

ing. Even those who were critical of current Temple practices, such as the Qumran community, did not contemplate permanently abandoning it. There are exceptions, like the Samaritans, who rejected the Jerusalem Temple, or the community of Leontopolis in Egypt, who built another. Yet even for such dissidents, temple cult in some form was central.

See also Anti-Semitism.

Sarah J. Tanzer

JUDGMENT. *See* Day of Judgment.

JUNG AND THE BIBLE. There would be little challenge to the proposition that Carl Jung (1875–1961) paid more attention to the Bible than any other psychoanalytic thinker or that his views of the Bible provoked more commentary from his followers and other religious scholars than those of any comparable figure. All of Jung's discussions of biblical texts bear the unique mark of his psychological views and his theories of symbolic meaning. As is so often the case, Jung's immersion in the Bible reflects aspects of his personality and life experience.

Early Development. Jung's familiarity with the Bible came at an early age. He was born in Keswill on Lake Constance in Switzerland in 1875. His father was a minister and pastor of the Lutheran church there, but within six months moved to Laufen, where Jung spent his early years. Of this early experience, Jung wrote, "In my mother's family there were six parsons, and on my father's side not only was my father a parson but two of my uncles also. Thus I heard many religious conversations, theological discussions, and sermons."

Jung's relationship with his pastor father was not the happiest. The pastor was a pious and conservative man of

God, but for all his religiosity he was unable to help his son with the childhood terrors and emotional turmoil, the severe nightmares and choking fits, that made life in the parsonage all but unbearable. Theological issues became a sticking point between them. Jung's curiosity and inquisitive mind led him to question his father's traditional beliefs, to which the older Jung would reply that one should not bother about thinking in religious matters, but should devote oneself to believing. Jung's early religious doubts seem to have centered around his conflicts toward his father and his deep-seated ambivalence, both toward his father and his father's religious views. For the son the religion of the father was a doctrine about God and had little to do with the living experience of God. In Jung's view, his father "had taken the Bible's commandments as his guide; he believed in God as the Bible prescribed and as his forefathers had taught him" but without any sense of "the immediate living God who stands, omnipotent and free above His Bible and His Church, who calls upon man to partake of His freedom." Much of Jung's later writing about religion reflects his underlying ambivalence toward his father and his constant effort to contest approaches to religion and the Bible that resulted in no more than stale doctrines and scientific facts and did not foster the life of the spirit and the enrichment of psychic life to which Jung devoted his life.

If Jung's religiously conservative father became the object of Jung's ambivalent conflicts, his mother played an important if opposite role. Her religious views were less rigid and little concerned with conventional piety. She introduced her son to works from other religious traditions and gave him a copy of Goethe's *Faust* when he was a university student. She also seems to have encouraged Jung's interest in spiritualism and parapsychological phenomena.

Jung's Approach. One cannot help but be impressed by the extent to which Jung was steeped in biblical lore. In none of his writings is he ever very far from the discussion of biblical themes or from the use of scriptural references to make his point. In the preface of *Answer to Job*, he stated, "I do not write as a biblical scholar (which I am not), but as a layman and physician who has been privileged to see deeply into the psychic life of many people." He was not interested in the usual questions of biblical research—the meaning, origins, cultural background, and history behind biblical texts. He sought to find that meaning of the texts that would speak to modern men and women in their present historical and cultural experience. He was less concerned with the origins of the texts than with their effects on the lives of contemporary readers.

His familiarity with the Bible is impressive. References can be found from all but thirteen of the sixty-six books in the Hebrew Bible and New Testament. The gospel of John was his favorite—he cited it more than 120 times. He was well acquainted with the *Apocrypha and *Pseudepigrapha, quoting from the books of Enoch, 2 Esdras, Tobit, and the Wisdom of Solomon. He also made references to the New Testament apocryphal writings, quoting from the Gospel of the Egyptians, the book of the Apostle Bartholomew, the Gospel of Peter, the Acts of Peter, the Acts of John, the Gospel of Philip, and the Acts of Thomas. References to biblical figures and biblical phrases flowed easily from his pen. Further testimony to the significance of holy writ in Jung's life are the inscriptions on the family tomb in Küsnacht. The first reads *Vocatus atque non vocatus Deus aderit* ("Summoned or not, God will be here")—the same words were inscribed on Jung's bookplate and over the entrance to his home. The second is *Primus homo terrenus de terra; secundus homo coelestis de coelo* ("The first man was earthly, from the earth; the second man was heavenly, from heaven"; 1 Cor. 15.47). In explaining the first inscription over his doorway, he said, "I have put the inscription there to remind my patients and myself: *timor dei initium sapientiae* ['The fear of God is the beginning of wisdom']. Here another not less important road begins, not the approach to Christianity, but to God himself and this seems to be the ultimate question."

Certainly Jung's use of the Bible was idiosyncratic. For him it was a primary source of material that could be translated into terms of his psychological system—with particular emphasis on the symbolic dimension of scriptural references and events that he was able to connect with aspects of his own views about the role of myths and symbols in human psychic functioning and their connection with the collective unconscious and archetypal symbols. Myths were not mere words or stories but living truths and psychic realities that exercise their power on the human soul by their use of symbolic language. Symbols thus served as the vehicles of psychic transformation that extended beyond the communication of meaning to the level of psychic integration and spiritual revitalization.

His effort was consistently directed to viewing scripture in such a way as to make it relevant to psychic concerns. He argued that the religious propositions in the Bible had their origin in the human psyche and that their meaning was in some sense determined by psychic roots, whether conscious or unconscious. They are in effect psychic facts and relevant to psychic truths that are concerned with the illumination of the soul. Their aim

and purpose is not to provide information but to bring about psychic change. Jung endorsed the view that "all scripture is inspired by God and useful for teaching, for reproof, for correction, and for training in righteousness, so that everyone who belongs to God may be proficient, equipped for every good work" (2 Tim. 3.16). Insofar as religious statements are "psychic confessions" deriving from the unconscious, they are like dreams that enter consciousness to inspire new insight and illumination. Thus, the prophets spoke of being seized by the *word or spirit of God. The psyche becomes the place where the divine and human interact—transcendence is replaced by immanence. The scripture becomes the vehicle and means of God's presence and action in the soul. Behind and in the words there is the Word.

Christ as Archetype of the Self. A good example of this usage is Jung's development of Christ as the symbol for the integrated self. The Self in Jung's psychology represents the unity and wholeness of the personality, embracing all psychic phenomena. It stands for the goal of integration of the total personality and individuality. This archetypal image is expressed in mandalas and in the heroes of myth and legend but above all in the image of Christ who "exemplifies the archetype of the Self." As Jung comments in *Answer to Job*, "Christ would never have made the impression he did on his followers if he had not expressed something that was alive and at work in their unconscious. Christianity itself would never have spread through the pagan world with such astonishing rapidity had its ideas not found an analogous psychic readiness to receive them."

He makes use of the Johannine theme of Christ as the way, the truth, and the light. Christ thus comes to symbolize the way of love, service, the life of the Spirit, salvation, and reconciliation. Christ thus becomes the archetype of the Self—the Christ-event not only speaks to the soul but acts within it to awaken, revive, cleanse, and save. In psychological terms, the Christ-event means that to become true Selves we must acquire a broader consciousness that connects the sense of identity and wholeness with love of the neighbor. Love is the mark of the Christian. Jung observes, "The men of that age were ripe for identification with the word made flesh, for the founding of a community united by an idea, in the name of which they could love one another and call each other brothers. The old idea of . . . a mediator in whose name new ways of love would be opened, became a fact, and with that human society took an immense stride forward."

In this fashion Jung strove to bring the scripture closer to vital interests and make it a force for psychic enrichment and integration—far different from his father's stale reverence for the words of scripture rather than the relation of the Bible to real life and the God of life. As he put it, "The Bible is not the words of God, but the Word of God." As the archetype of the Self, Christ becomes a real event in the life of the soul. Christ acts in the soul to draw out real effects and changes. The Christ symbol brings with it a power through *grace to become what one could not become on one's own.

Answer to Job. Despite his frequent allusions to scripture, the *Answer*, written in 1952, was his only work based exclusively on a scriptural text. It was meant to be his interpretation of the Old Testament God-image of Judaism and its transformation into the Christian God. His portrayal of God in this work was controversial and provocative, challenging the traditional Christian view of God

by its theory of the "dark side" of God. Jung's God, from one perspective, is like a reflection of *gnostic dualism, ruling the world by the forces of good, embodied in the figure of Christ, and evil, embodied in the figure of Satan. The dualism of good and evil is integrated in the unified image of God.

From another point of view, he saw God and the *Trinity in terms of a symbolic dynamic pertaining to the individual soul and the whole of Judeo-Christian culture. In the first stage God is Yahweh of the Old Testament; in the second stage the image of the Son and behind him the loving Father dominates the New Testament and its historical developments; and finally, with the doctrine of the Holy Spirit we enter the post–New Testament era of Christian history and development. We can hear the echoes of Joachim di Fiore and his preaching of the final and consummate age of the Holy Spirit that stirred millennial visions in the twelfth century. In Jung's eyes the trinitarian doctrine was rooted in archetypal symbols that characterize the collective unconscious of humanity. Despite his disclaimer that he was only addressing the image of God as a psychological construct and not as a reality outside the mind, Jung's treatment of the subject often seems to forget or ignore his own qualifications.

To recapitulate the story of *Answer to Job:* the adversary of God, Satan, casts doubt on the faithfulness of God's mortal servant Job. Jung puzzles as to why Yahweh accepts the testimony of the father of lies and seems not to know Job's true character. Why should God believe Satan rather than his own omniscience? In any event, God turns Job over to the torments of the devil in order to win the wager with Satan. All Job's possessions and even his children are destroyed before his face, yet he still cries out in his grief, "The Lord gave and the Lord has taken away; blessed be the name of the Lord" (Job 1.21). Satan ups the ante, and Job is subjected to further torments and afflictions. In his misery Job turns to his friends for solace, but they are helpless to explain his poor fortune, appealing to conventional wisdom which proves inadequate.

Yahweh answers Job's appeals for mercy not by rejecting the deceptions of Satan but by majestic declarations of his omnipotence. But, asks Jung, what of the missing omniscience? The compensatory outpouring of rich gifts, the thousands of head of cattle, camels, oxen, and so on, even the blessings of new sons and daughters, hardly measure up to the loss of the others whom Job had loved and cherished. This God, says Jung, has no feeling, so lost in his own omnipotence is he.

The drama progresses as the figure of Sophia, a feminine figure representing Wisdom as found in the wisdom literature, enters. If Yahweh had consulted her rather than Satan, he would have known Job's faithfulness. Her task is to help undo the damage caused by God's omnipotence. Under her influence, Yahweh wishes to become human in order to make recompense for the torments he inflicted on Job, to restore the moral balance, and particularly to avoid the consequence of becoming a discredited and disregarded god. Most of all, he wishes to save himself from his own terrible and heartless indifference to human fate and sufferings. He can become human only through the help of Sophia, the prototype of Mary. Sophia helps him see that his first creation went awry because of the devices of Satan in the guise of the serpent. To avoid the taint of Satan's influence, God would have to be born of a *virgin by an immaculate conception.

Answer to Job was essentially Jung's culminating effort to join his conflictual struggle with God and at another remove his father. His view of God was transmuted into a cultural crisis of modernity. He commented, "Later generations could afford to ignore the dark side of the Apocalypse, because the specifically Christian achievement was something that was not to be frivolously endangered. But for modern man the case is quite otherwise. We have experienced things so unheard of and so staggering that the question of whether such things are in any way reconcilable with the idea of a good God has become burningly topical."

Thus, Jung argues, the insistence on the concept of God as all good has lost its meaning for contemporary men and women and has led to the abandonment of God. The result is a mechanistic view of the universe, a decline of spiritual values, and a sense of the meaninglessness of human existence. The presence of *evil in the world creates a crisis for Christian consciousness: If God is omnipotent and all good, why does evil exist? Jung's answer is that God is not all good, but that he encompasses both good and evil. We can see the reflection of Jung's father's face in the face of the God he portrays in the *Answer.* It is a face compounded of good and evil that presents itself as a mystery and an enigma, just as his own father's difficult character had been for Jung as a child.

Conclusion. The Bible was for Jung not just another book to be read critically and skeptically, as *Freud might have done. It was a book of faith, of hope, of inspiration, in which Jung found the words and images that carried him along his fevered search for meaning, psychological truth, and wholeness in his own and in his contemporaries' psychic lives. His concerns were far removed from the more scientific objectives of biblical *hermeneutics and exegesis. He sought what was for him a psychological cause, a lifelong crusade, to translate the God of his father into a living God of Jung's own making. The success of his effort and the validity of his accomplishment remain enigmatic.

William W. Meissner, S.J.

JUSTICE. See Righteousness.

JUSTIFICATION. The concept of justification is based on that of *righteousness; in fact, both can translate the same Greek word *(dikaiosunē)*. As applied to human beings, this connotes the status of being in the right when tested or judged by God. That condition lies at the heart of the covenantal relationship between Yahweh and his people, Israel. For the maintenance of *covenant relations, righteousness on Israel's part is also required, with the prospect of attaining approval from God both in this life and, in later literature, at the final judgment.

Paul opposed this construction for two reasons. The claim that those who keep God's law will be set right with God and given approved status before God is considered by Paul to be a vain hope, inasmuch as this class of "righteous" persons has no qualified member, for "all have sinned and fall short of the glory of God" (Rom. 3.23). There is no prospect of being set right with God as long as a person stays with nomistic religion. Instead, the outlook on such a basis is one of universal condemnation for both Jews and gentiles, since all have become sinners. All stand under divine judgment, and must remain so unless God takes action on their behalf.

The second reason why Paul opposed nomistic religion is that he believed a new era had dawned with the coming of the Messiah. What Judaism anticipated as God's gracious intervention at the end-time, Paul now declares as a present reality for all who are of faith, in the sure confidence that at the future tribunal the past verdict of acceptance and amnesty will be confirmed. In this way the tension of the Christian life ("already justified . . . not yet finally 'saved' ") is maintained as a part of Paul's proclamation.

Justification has been defined as "the gracious action of God accepting persons as righteous in consequence of faith resting upon His redemptive activity in Christ" (Vincent Taylor). This definition needs strengthening by a recognition that Paul constantly lays a basis for what he believed about God's "redemptive activity" in Christ's obedience or righteousness. Consequently, more should be said in any summary statement about Paul's insistence on "imputation" as providing a rationale for the divine enterprise in canceling human guilt and providing acceptance in his holy presence. Romans 3.21–26 and 2 Corinthians 5.18–21 stand out as central to Paul's teaching. Also, Paul's thought is as much conditioned by promises of rectification of personal relationships as by assurances of forensic acquittal. Indeed, the term acquittal is best avoided if it conjures up the notion of treating sinners as though they were not sinners. Plainly, in Paul's theology there is no room for such exonerating considerations. "Amnesty," therefore, is a term preferred by some scholars, and it recalls that justification is above all a royal act by which pardon is freely bestowed on the undeserving. God's royal rule is displayed in releasing offenders from guilt out of respect for his Son, who stands as their sponsor. Jesus Christ by his undertaking arranges a new network of divine-human relations—the element of novelty is seen by Paul's statement that God's righteousness (i.e., his saving power) is shown "apart from law" (Rom. 3.21)—and the whole enterprise springs from his free favor, his "grace" (Rom. 3.24; 11.6). The fresh start made by Christ's action ushers in a new order that consists of a whole series of events involving both forensic and dynamic acts on the part of God. The refusal to delimit justification to the initial act of acquittal and remission of guilt, thought of in exclusively legal terms and played out in a courtroom drama, paves the way for a much richer understanding of the term. It certainly will include a forensic release from sin's penalty, but will also entail the entire process of the rectification of the human relationship to God, who dynamically releases a power to set this relationship in a new orbit. For Paul, the new sphere of living is one of sonship within a family context and no longer that of slavery under the taskmaster's stern eye.

Two consequences flow from these considerations, as Ernst Käsemann has observed. First, God's righteousness is a gift that has the character of power. In fact, the actual term is associated with other words, such as "love," "peace," and "wrath," that are used in personified form and often connote divine power. That is to say, what God does in rectifying sinners is characteristically a regal fiat, announcing a new day when past failures are put away, debts and liabilities canceled, and guilt removed from those who otherwise must pay the price. According to Romans 1.17 and 3.21, a new order has come into existence, one that sets human relationships on a different footing from that of strict justice and merit. The divine power now released and known in human experience is what the Pauline gospel is all about.

Second, God's righteousness is characterized by universality. Paul stands directly in the tradition of the exilic prophet known as Second Isaiah, for whom divine ṣĕdāqâ (righteousness) spills over into Yahweh's saving activity put forth on Israel's behalf and issuing in the promise of a new world. The apocalyptic dimension of Paul's thought is clear in his celebration of God's power in reaching out to capture the entire world for the sovereignty of God. What seems a limited teaching in the Jewish Christian fragment of Romans 3.24–25 is taken over editorially by Paul and enlarged to cover God's faithfulness not only to the covenant people of Israel but also to the whole creation. And that statement of a new creation brought into existence at God's command will play a significant part in Paul's developed teaching on reconciliation as Paul elaborates the cosmic scope of Christ's salvific work.

In summary, justification by faith is a relational term. Talk of forensic acquittal, often suggesting a sterile setting free from immediate punishment, is misplaced and merits the criticism brought by some that Paul's teaching is little short of a legal fiction. But such criticism is deflected once we recall how this terminology is basically couched in the framework of interpersonal relationships, and carries for Paul a dynamic nuance of a new attitude of God to human beings, as of humans to God, which in both instances leads to a chain of events. God, for his part, takes steps to carry through the enterprise of human recovery and renewal, while on the human side the initial act of "rightwising"—to use an old English term—begins a process of moral transformation associated with union with Christ that will ultimately reach its goal in the final homecoming of the people of God at the last day.

Paul's teaching was so finely balanced that it was capable of being distorted and misrepresented. The evidence for this comes in Romans 3.8; 6.1–15; Galatians 5.13, where his stress on the sufficiency of God's justifying grace was understood by some as an invitation to moral laxity. Pauline extremists are evidently the subject of James's debate on faith and works. The need to have justification by faith set in the context of the call to a new life of obedience and the fruit of holy living (already anticipated in Gal. 5.6) led to the teachings of the Pauline school of the Pastoral letters and possibly accounts for the stress on good works in 1 Peter and Matthew.   *Ralph P. Martin*

K

KINGDOM OF GOD. There is clear agreement among the synoptic Gospels that the kingdom of God was the principal theme within Jesus' message, although each attests to this fact distinctively. In aggregate, they present some fifty sayings and *parables of Jesus concerning the kingdom. In the gospel of John Jesus refers only once to the kingdom expressly, though the saying is repeated (3.3, 5). In that instance, however, the kingdom is presented as something that even the Pharisee Nicodemus is assumed to understand; the point at issue is not the nature of the kingdom but how it might be entered. It is, then, a matter of consensus within the canon that the kingdom constituted a primary focus of Jesus' theology.

The notion that God is king and as such rules, or wishes to rule, his people is evident in the scriptures of Israel. In the books of Judges and Samuel, the Lord's kingship is even held to exclude human monarchy as the appropriate government of the covenantal people. It requires a distinctive fiat, by prophetic anointing, to establish Davidic *kingship as the seal of the divine *covenant. In no sense, then, does the Davidic royal house supplant God's ultimate rule. God could still be conceived of as reigning over all things, and as about to reign on behalf of Israel. In both Hebrew and Aramaic the verb "reigns" or "rules" is cognate with the nouns "king" and "kingdom"

(all from the root *mlk*); furthermore, the noun "kingdom" refers more to the fact or force of rule than to the territory governed. The phrasing of the New Testament, although distinctive, is conceptually rooted in the Hebrew Bible.

The future orientation found in Isaiah 52.7 may be perplexing. Alongside the conviction of God's continuing, royal care, there was also the hope that God would finally—and unambiguously—be disclosed as king. Just that hope, in an ultimate and irrefutable exertion of the divine reign, is characteristic of early *eschatology. Within that perspective, the end of time is not dreaded but is rather the object of longing. The dissolution of the present age is a frightening prospect only for those who enjoy the rewards of this world; for Israel, the chosen people who had been denied the fruits of divine promise as a result of their sin and foreign domination, the end of this age—and the beginning of another—increasingly became an urgent hope. Only then, it was believed, would the promised peace of God reign supreme. Their hope seemed only to increase the more critical became the absence of a Davidic king, the presence of the Romans, and confusing controversies concerning the efficacy of worship in the Temple. Eschatological urgency was a function of two collateral axioms within the faith of Israel: that God was just and that Israel is the elect people of God. Within their own understanding, the people of Israel could not agree that contemporary circumstances were consistent with either axiom. God, they felt, must be about to act in vindication of both his people and his own integrity.

"The kingdom of God" (or "the kingdom of the Lord") is precisely the phrase used in certain documents of early Judaism in order to express hope in God's ultimate disclosure as king. The Targums use the phrase chiefly to convey that eschatological hope. The early (perhaps first-century CE) prayer known as the Kaddish also refers to the kingdom in that sense: "May He make his kingdom reign in your lifetime!" Later rabbinic texts conventionally use the phrase "kingdom of the heavens," as in Matthew. No difference in meaning is implied by replacing the word "God" or "Lord"; "heavens" appears to be a reverential periphrasis. In most rabbinic texts, however, the kingdom appears less as an eschatological than as a moral concept; the language refers to accepting God as one's king (by reciting the *Shema) rather than to readying oneself for his rule.

The preaching of Jesus is far closer to eschatological expectation than to the moral emphasis of later rabbis. Although, in Jesus' thinking, the kingdom "has come near" (Mark 1.15), or has made itself available, it was part of his programmatic prayer that the kingdom's coming should be sought. Care must be taken, however, to do justice to Jesus' distinctiveness as a rabbi or teacher as well as to his context within Judaism. By speaking of the kingdom, Jesus adopted the language of scripture (as used in synagogues) and of prayer and made that language his own. The kingdom in his preaching was not merely promised but announced as a divine activity that demanded repentance and that could be entered into by participating in its divine force. That stance is represented not only by the programmatic descriptions of his teaching but also by the parables. Those that involve images of growth or process particularly insist that the kingdom must not be limited to any single temporality, be it present or future. Such limitation would betray the dynamic unfolding such parables are designed to convey. For that reason, to describe the kingdom in Jesus' expectation as apocalyptic, in the sense of an anticipated calendar of divine unveilings in which God's rule can be dated, is misleading. The dearth of references to the kingdom in *apocalyptic literature undermines that position, and much of the teaching attributed to Jesus militates against it.

A last element of Jesus' theology of the kingdom must be mentioned, which also tells against an apocalyptic construal of his message. Jesus' teaching was not simply futuristic in its eschatological orientation; he was also known as an ethical teacher. Many of his parables show how, within his vision of a single kingdom, Jesus could be both expectant of the future and demanding in the present. Parables of growth or process involve expectant readiness as the appropriate attitude toward the climax; a king or lord who invites people to a banquet expects those invited to be prepared; even absent rulers anticipate their subjects' willing obedience during their absence. The ethical themes implicit in such parables make sense once one appreciates that Jesus conveys by them a self-disclosing kingdom whose focus is irreducibly future and whose implications are pressingly present. Just as his claim to speak on behalf of that kingdom is perhaps the most obvious root of Christology, so his message gave to the movement that succeeded him a characteristic attitude of expectancy in respect of the future and, consequently, of responsibility within the present.   *Bruce D. Chilton*

KINGDOM OF HEAVEN. *See* Kingdom of God.

KINGSHIP AND MONARCHY.

Ancient Near Eastern Background. Ancient Near Eastern texts almost unanimously presuppose the institution of kingship as a social organizing principle. Kingship in Mesopotamia is "lowered from heaven" or is coeval with *creation. The Assyrian King List, for example, can hypothesize a time when kings "lived in tents," but not a time before kingship. The image of the "first man" as the "image of God" and as lord over creation (Gen. 1.26–28) is not unrelated: YHWH is often portrayed in Israelite literature and iconography in solar terms; just as the sun, the "major" astral body, "rules" over the sky (Gen. 1.16–18), just as YHWH rules over creation, so the relationship between humanity and the world is modeled as one of royal domination from the very outset.

Near Eastern myths, too, principally portray the order of divine organization as monarchic. Egyptian, Greek, Hittite, *Ugaritic, and Mesopotamian myths all recount tales of martial conflict whereby one of the gods emerges as their king. In most instances, the monarchic order is portrayed as an innovation, replacing an earlier paternal domination of children. Interestingly, in the cases of Mesopotamian and Greek myth, the new kingship is functionally elective: the pantheon appoint a king-elect from among their number, to lead them into battle; the appointee wins the battle; and, as a result, the appointee wins confirmation on the throne. The royal ideal is thus one of elective autocracy. In Babylonian myth, the winning of the throne is also the starting point for the creation of the cosmos, which is the foundation for the heavenly structure that serves as the high god's palace, the counterpart of his earthly temple.

Kings and other administrators in the ancient Near East regularly portray themselves, like the state gods, as champions of the weak and the oppressed. The king was the upholder of the social order—much like the divine king who resisted the threats and encroachments of *chaos. But fixing the social order, to judge from Mesopotamian law codes, involved attempting to fix prices and attempting to ensure the inviolability of property. It also involved occasional amnesties, and general release from debt. Ultimately, the king presented himself as the personification and defender of what was just, the supreme judicial authority.

Near Eastern kingship was overwhelmingly an urban phenomenon. Cities lent themselves to monarchic organization precisely because of the complexity of administration involved. Kings took responsibility for, and pride in, the fortification of towns: the *Gilgamesh Epic ends with a return to the subject of the mighty walls of Uruk, which were the hero's immortality. Kings thus enjoyed the right not to tax, but to direct corvée and conscription for the public good—for defense, conquest, and the construction of irrigation and navigation systems.

Claiming the right to govern by divine election, kings also relate their temple-building activities. The completion of a temple is modeled by them as a mundane repetition of the heavenly creation myth. The building of a temple also is taken as a sign of the gods' imprimatur on the builder's royal dynasty. Likewise, the New Year ritual in Babylon, and, later, in Assyria, combines a rehearsal of the creation myth with a renewal of the high god's temple: the king leads the high god in procession to reoccupy the temple, and at the same time renews his own kingship, after a ritual battle against chaos. The king consistently presents himself as warrior, builder, creator, favorite, even adoptee of the gods.

Biblical Traditions. Israelite conceptions of kingship reflect both continuity with, and departure from, earlier traditions. For one thing, earliest Israel was decidedly nonurban, consisting of small agricultural settlements principally in the central hill country, Transjordan, and the upper Galilee. It is impossible to identify any major urban center as Israelite before David's conquest of Jerusalem. Israelite monarchy, therefore, originated as a national monarchy, not as a city-state kingship. Correspondingly, Israel is the only ancient Near Eastern culture to have preserved written memories of a time before the evolution of kingship or to have constructed any account of a transition from what later tradition would construe as a theocracy to monarchic organization. (There were, however, periods when Assyrian kings presented themselves as stewards of the gods, rather than as kings, and early *Sumerian kings adopted the same recourse.)

In this connection, a number of Israelite texts express reservations about the institution of kingship—a sentiment elsewhere unparalleled. Offered a dynasty, for example, the premonarchic warrior Gideon makes the paradigmatic reply, "I will not rule over you, and my son will not rule over you; YHWH will rule over you" (Judg. 8.24). Although the text proceeds to condemn Gideon for appropriating priestly status and constructing an ephod, similar sentiments recur in an account of the transition to monarchy: the urge to enthrone a human king conflicts on this theory with the ideal of YHWH's kingship over Israel.

Scholars for the most part find two sources underlying the account of the origins of Israelite kingship in 1 Samuel 8–12, but differ about their precise delineation. Nevertheless, both sources seem to replicate the pattern for divine kingship: in one, Saul is elected king with YHWH's approval, defeats Ammon, and is confirmed as king; in the other, Saul is anointed king-designate, defeats the Philistines, and is said to have "captured the kingship" (1 Sam. 14.47). There is a homology with YHWH's kingship over Israel, said to have originated in his election in order to bring Israel out of Egypt and into Canaan, and confirmed at the completion of the *Exodus; the same pattern already occurs in the Song of the Sea (Exod. 15; twelfth-eleventh century BCE), where YHWH's perpetual kingship and acquisition of a shrine is predicated on his defeat of Egypt and the establishment of Israel in Canaan.

Numerous psalms follow the same pattern, praising YHWH as the creator or as the victor in some cosmic or mundane martial conflict, in the context of the celebration of his kingship. Likewise, the book of Judges describes the pattern of mundane leadership in terms of a leader's election by YHWH, defeat of a threat or oppressor, and assumption of administrative power. And the books of Samuel-Kings let the same myth inform their historiography: kings whose succession is irregular win battles or overcome obstacles and threats, before their accession formulary (that is, their historiographic confirmation on the throne) appears. The "myth of the Divine Warrior" regularly informs Israelite views of mundane, as well as divine, leadership.

Kings and Temples. Other Near Eastern conceptions of kingship are equally pervasive among the Israelites. The first Israelite kings eschewed temple-building, no doubt out of deference to their constituents' distributed and varied cultic traditions. David did bring a central icon, the *ark, to his capital. But Solomon was the first to build a temple, and in the capital, which articulated claims of an eternal Davidic dynasty—as well as claims that Solomon, and the later Davidides, are sons of YHWH, entrants into the court of the divine king (see Son of God). Notably, the Israelite kingdom established by Jeroboam by secession from the kingship of Solomon's successor prescinded from establishing its cultic centers in the political capital. Yet the leader of the secession, Jeroboam, was moved to erect cultic establishments at Bethel and Dan to establish himself, too, as a temple builder (see Golden Calf). His actions implied independence from Judah yet disavowed any unchangeable divine election of his dynasty. When Omri's son, Ahab, later erected a temple in Samaria, his capital, the same dynamic was in effect. The revolutionary, Jehu, destroyed the temple in the capital, ensuring a separation of capital and temple in the northern kingdom for the rest of its duration.

Limits on Royal Power. In the Israelite ideal, the king is one nominated (or anointed) by YHWH, by prophetic means, and adopted by the people—YHWH proposes and the people dispose. But the opportunity exists, in the aftermath of divine designation, for popular elements responsible for confirming the king to impose conditions on the king's sovereignty. The operation of this principle is evident in 1 Kings 12, where the Israelites propose to elect Rehoboam as their king, on the condition that he lower taxes. Rehoboam refuses; the people therefore reject him as king, and elect Jeroboam. Similarly, both David and Absalom campaign for election; David actually campaigns for reelection after Absalom's revolt. Although elements of the royal establishment laid claim to a perpetual divine dynastic grant, even the laws of Deuteronomy 17.14–20 acknowledge that kingship, given divine nomination of the candidate, was elective. In practice, this often meant that the king was made by army democracy—as in the cases of Solomon, Baasha, Omri, Jehu, Uzziah, and others.

The laws of Deuteronomy 17–18 also attempt to limit the king's latitude in forming policy. They limit priesthood to "Levites," install Levitic priests as the supreme judiciary, and protect the institution of prophecy. They further attempt to restrict the king's ability to accumulate wealth. Scholars concur that the Deuteronomic law code is late in origin. Still, the attempt to limit the ability to tax, the urge to restrict the king's right to disenfranchise priesthoods, the urge to protect prophets—all reflect traditional ideals and rural views of central governmental authority.

Royal Prerogatives. Notwithstanding popular resistance to royal encroachments on the economy in particular, Israelite kings enjoyed the power both to tax and to conscript for warfare and for public works. Moreover, archaeological remains at important towns, such as Megiddo and Hazor, indicate that the kings projected their power into the countryside in the form of massive fortifications and impressive public buildings. To date, this phenomenon is less well represented in the Israelite heartland, the hill country. Starting in the tenth century BCE, however, and accelerating in the eighth century, public buildings are constructed in proximity to the gate complexes of some urban centers, such as Tell Beit Mirsim, Lachish, and Tell el-Far‘ah (biblical Tirzah).

In the same period, increasing royal intervention in local economies is documented by the standardization of weights, and probably, by indications of incipient industrialization, as at the site of Horvat Rosh Zayit, inland from Akko. And, at the end of the eighth century, Hezekiah of Judah was able to concentrate the rural population of his kingdom in a set of fortresses.

There had always been some tension between the royal establishment and the kinship structures—the rural lineages—which were the seat of succession and conflict resolution before the monarchy and continued to function as such after the introduction of kingship. Early on, the state acknowledged an interest in restricting the feud, one of the nonstate forms of conflict resolution in the society. But as the revolt of Absalom ended with the complete triumph of the professional royal army over the irregulars of the countryside, central control could be asserted over not only the succession but other aspects of statecraft as well. As early as the time of Solomon, a system of royal administrators was set in place for the purpose of extracting taxation and corvée, bypassing traditional tribal forms of organization. It is likely that Jeroboam and the later kings of the northern kingdom undid this innovation; the Samaria ostraca furnish evidence of at least dabblings in a system of such administrators only in the eighth century (one group of ostraca reflects administration through the lineages at that time). However, even the lineage heads through whom some kings administered taxation would have been royal appointees in some sense, and certainly familiars of the establishment.

It was only in the seventh century, after Hezekiah's emergency urbanization, that the monarchy achieved complete domination over the lineages. The urban geography of that era in Judah (Israel having been deported) reflects the resettlement of Judah, after its depopulation by Assyria in 701 BCE, by state orchestration. Gone are the extended-family compounds that characterize Israelite settlements until the late eighth century. Gone are the large, rambling settlements of that earlier era. Instead, the state, and the kingship, were able to stamp the ideals of the royal cult, the Jerusalem Temple, onto the country as a whole, resulting in a policy, under Josiah, of centralization of worship and of power. This development, and the disappearance of the monarchy in the restoration community (538 BCE), paved the way for the detachment of the monarchic ideology from its origins in relations with the agrarian hinterlands of the capital. In the Second Temple period, the idea of YHWH's anointed—the messiah, notionally a son of YHWH—was transferred from the human king whose election was a matter of negotiation and limitation, to a future king, not wholly human, whose reign would usher in a regime of justice, of the defense of the oppressed, and of requital of the guilty. In the myth of a kingless postexilic Judah, the old, high ideals of Near Eastern kingship took renewed hold, without the brake of political realities to restrain the ambitions or the imaginings of their adherents.

Baruch Halpern

KNOW. The biblical Hebrew verb most commonly translated "to know" is *yāda͑*. Besides the neutral or secular sense of being aware of or acquainted with, the verb and its derivatives have a complex range of meanings.

Knowledge becomes a biblical topic as early as Genesis 2.9 with the tree of the knowledge of good and evil. The tree's name is probably a merismus, a literary device to describe the totality of something by naming the first and the last in its semantic spectrum (here, the full range of knowledge).

In Genesis 4.1, sexual knowledge comes from Adam and Eve's experience of the greatest possible intimacy, namely *sexual intercourse. The verb in this sense may have either a man or a woman as its subject, includes homosexual intercourse, and can occasionally signify rape (of women and men).

The organ of knowledge is the heart, which suggests that knowledge is experiential and not merely speculative. One knows war or God's displeasure by experiencing it. Yahweh's special relationship with Moses is described as knowing Moses face to face. While Samuel certainly knows who Yahweh is, he does not know God until he experiences a *theophany.

Yahweh wants to be known, reaching out to Israel by revelatory acts, most importantly delivering Israel from Egyptian slavery and by joining with Israel in the theophanic *covenant ceremony at Sinai. In biblical terminology, the response to *revelation is knowledge; knowledge is akin to what elsewhere might be called *faith.

Beginning in the book of Exodus, the motif of knowing Yahweh becomes a dominant biblical theme, recurring especially in Deuteronomy, Hosea (who deliberately blurs the sexual and religious meanings of knowing to illustrate God's closeness to Israel), Isaiah, Jeremiah, and Ezekiel. Knowledge and knowing in this case have a technical connection to the language of covenant-making. Hosea 4.1–6 equates knowledge with keeping the covenant laws, the *Ten Commandments: Yahweh will reject those who reject knowledge. Isaiah 5.12–13 warns that *exile, a covenant curse, is the consequence of lack of knowledge. In Jeremiah's famous "new covenant" oracle, Yahweh declares that the law will be written on all hearts and "all shall know me" (Jer. 31.31–34).

In the New Testament, the revealed Christ becomes the source of the knowledge of God, a theme developed most notably in the gospel of John and in Paul's letters.

See also Gnosticism.

Mary Joan Winn Leith

KORAN. See Qurān and Bible, The.

L

LAMB OF GOD. Being common in the Near East, lambs were one of the most usual sacrificial animals in ancient Israel. Twice a day a lamb was slaughtered in the Temple; a lamb could be offered as a sin offering; each family annually slaughtered a paschal lamb for *Passover. Thus, the lamb is often a biblical symbol of meekness, obedience, and the need for protection. But in *apocalyptic language and probably as an expression of the final victory promised by God to the elect in spite of their weakness, the lamb is occasionally a conquering figure that is to overcome all the evil beasts that symbolize sin and revolt against God. Some scholars think that, as an apocalyptic preacher, John the Baptist, who announced the one who was mightier than he, may have applied the title "the Lamb of God" to this mysterious person in that sense, whatever nuances later Christian interpretations may have added. The apocalyptic writer of the book of Revelation used the Greek word *arnion*, meaning lamb, to describe the risen Christ as ruler of the world (twenty-eight occurrences); although in the saying of John the Baptist another term (*amnos*) is used, the idea is the same. But the lamb of Revelation is also a slain lamb, whose death has redeeming power.

The Fourth Evangelist, who adapted to his own purposes a number of traditions concerning John the Baptist, added an extensive commentary to his first mention of the phrase "the lamb of God" (John 1.29–34). In his view, the final words of v. 29, "who takes away the sin of the world," refer to the redemption brought about by Jesus' death; but they might originally have been part of the Baptist's saying, referring to the victory over evil by the apocalyptic "lamb of God." Vv. 30–31 have an apologetic flavor: they try to account for the failure of the Baptist to identify Jesus as the apocalyptic lamb and suggest that he did so after the baptism of Jesus. The designation of Jesus as lamb of God at the beginning of his ministry is balanced by the allusion to the Passover lamb at his death (John 19.33–37).

See also Sacrifice.   *Etienne Trocmé*

LAST SUPPER. *See* Lord's Supper.

LATIN. The language of imperial Rome and ancestor of the Romance languages. Because of its use by the Roman army and civil administration, Latin had some currency in the eastern Mediterranean in the first century CE, in such provinces as Syria and Judea. Latin inscriptions marked mileposts on roadways, and warned gentiles against entry into the Temple courts in Jerusalem. Other inscriptions survive from military camps and buildings dedicated by Roman officials, such as the aqueduct and the temple for emperor worship at Caesarea Maritima. The charge for which Jesus was condemned was written on a plaque above his cross in Latin, *Greek, and *Hebrew (*Aramaic), according to John 19.20.

Several words of Latin origin are found in the Greek New Testament. Some had become familiar through the spread of Roman influence in the East, including words like *denarius,* found in Jesus' parables and in his dispute over paying taxes to Caesar. Despite the presence and influence of Roman institutions, some terms of Latin origin, such as *praetorium* in Philippians 1.13, or *census, centurion, legion,* and *speculator* in the gospel of Mark, are thought by some scholars to prove that those works were written in Rome.

Most Christians of the Mediterranean basin were Greek speakers at the start (Paul wrote to the Christians of Rome in Greek). Western Christians began to write in Latin only in the third century CE.   *Philip Sellew*

LAW. *This entry consists of two articles, the first on* Israelite Law *in its ancient Near Eastern context, and the second on* New Testament Views *of what came to be known as "the Law." For discussion of the influence of the Bible on later legal systems, see* Law and the Bible.

Israelite Law

Although laws and the concept of law played an overwhelmingly important role in the Hebrew Bible and in the life of ancient Israel, the Hebrew Bible has no term exactly equivalent to the English word "law." The Hebrew word most often translated as "law," *tôrâ* (*Torah), actually means teaching or instruction. As such it expresses the morally and socially didactic nature of God's demands on the Israelite people. The misleading translation of *tôrâ* as law entered Western

thought through the Greek translation (Septuagint) of the term as *nomos,* as in the name of the book of Deuteronomy ("the second law"). That the word *tôrâ* is a loose concept is indicated by its use for the first five books of the Hebrew scriptures, which contain the bulk of ancient Israel's purely legal material, as well as for the Hebrew Bible as a whole. The vibrant nature of the legal tradition is indicated by the later Jewish distinction between the written Torah, namely the Hebrew Bible, and the oral Torah, the legal and religious traditions which were eventually codified in the Mishnah (ca. 200 CE) and developed in the Gemara (ca. 500 CE; together they form the Talmud) and later commentaries. The human intermediary between the people and their God in both cases is viewed as Moses, through the revelation at Sinai and later in a valedictory address in Transjordan before his death (Deuteronomy).

Among other terms employed in the Hebrew Bible that belong to the legal sphere and refer to specific practices and enactments are *ḥoq* "statute," *mišpāṭ* "ordinance," *miṣwâ* "commandment," and *dābār* "word."

Law in the Ancient Near East. Although it was once felt that biblical Israel's legal and moral traditions were unique in the ancient world, archaeological activity over the course of the last century has brought to light a large number of texts, mainly written in cuneiform script on clay tablets, which help to place biblical law in its ancient Near Eastern context. These include texts that have erroneously been termed "law codes," in addition to international treaties, royal edicts, and documents from the daily legal sphere.

The Babylonian Laws of Hammurapi (eighteenth century BCE, copies of which have been found dating up to a millennium later) remain the most famous and comprehensive of the ancient legal collections, and include close to three hundred laws, in addition to a lengthy prologue and epilogue in which the divine mission of providing laws for the land is given to Hammurapi. Other important "codes" include the Laws of Urnammu, a *Sumerian collection dating to ca. 2100 BCE; the Laws of Lipit-Ishtar, also in Sumerian, ca. 1900 BCE; the Laws of the city of Eshnunna, written in Akkadian and to be dated in the nineteenth century; the Hittite Laws, which date in their original form to ca. 1600 BCE; and the Middle Assyrian Laws from the reign of Tiglath-pileser I, ca. 1200 BCE.

These so-called law codes are not comprehensive codices in the Roman sense. They are rather miscellaneous collections of laws, compiled in order to enhance the stature of the ruler as the originator of order in his land. Although they preserve important evidence of individual stipulations and of the legal structure of a given society, these legal compilations are best viewed as literary texts. In spite of the ancient fame of a text such as the Babylonian Laws of Hammurapi, it is significant that among the thousands of legal documents known from ancient Mesopotamia not one refers to that collection for a precedent, nor to any other.

Ancient Near Eastern treaties, while important as historical, political, and legal sources, have also played a role in understanding the nature of Israel's *covenant with God as one of vassal with suzerain. Elements in treaties that have been found in the Hebrew Bible include the identification of the parties to the treaty, a historical prologue in which God's actions on behalf of Israel are listed, the treaty stipulations (i.e., the laws), and the *blessings and *curses to be expected as a consequence of obedience or of noncompliance to the terms of the covenant. Among the most important treaties are those of the Hittite empire of the second millennium BCE, to which many scholars look for the origin of the genre as a whole, and the Neo-Assyrian vassal treaties, especially those of Esarhaddon (early seventh century BCE).

By far the largest number of ancient documents come from the daily practice of law. Tens of thousands of documents have been found recording economic and social transactions of all kinds, many of which can be compared to biblical practices. The closest biblical parallel to the actual practice of documenting transactions may be found in the account of Jeremiah's purchase of a plot of land in his home town of Anathoth, a transaction recorded in duplicate as were countless cuneiform documents. Although most of the documents found were written on cuneiform tablets in Mesopotamia, documents written on papyrus and other perishable materials have been found in Egypt, for example at the site of the Jewish military colony at Elephantine, and in caves in the Judean desert, near the Dead Sea (see Writing in Antiquity).

Israel's Laws in Modern Research. In addition to the comparative study of Israel's legal traditions, which seeks to shed light upon Israel's laws in their ancient context through a comparison of similarities and differences with nonbiblical legal materials, two major trends can be identified in modern research on ancient Israel's legal traditions. The first is form-critical and concerns itself with the classification of Israel's laws according to form and syntax. The second attempts to identify the basic principles of Israel's legal tradition that set it apart from its surrounding cultures.

Basic for the study of the forms of Israelite law is the work of Albrecht Alt.

In his essay on "The Origins of Israelite Law" (1934), Alt identified two basic patterns of legal formulations in the Bible. The first he termed "casuistic" law, since it arose from the sphere of case law. These are the laws formulated in the "if . . . then . . ." pattern. Alt sought the origin of these laws in Canaanite and general ancient Near Eastern traditions, which the Israelites took over after their "conquest" of the land. The second he termed "apodictic" law. These are laws formulated as absolute pronouncements, such as the *Ten Commandments. They are mostly formed in the imperative: "You shall (not) . . ." Alt sought the origin of these formulations in Israel's ancient Yahwistic law, originating in Israel's preconquest traditions. While Alt's analysis of the origins of these two types of law has not withstood the test of time, since both casuistic and apodictic laws are to be found in most ancient Semitic legal collections in varying relative percentages, his basic form-critical distinction continues to serve as the starting point of contemporary discussion.

Once it could be shown that ancient Israel belonged to the cultural milieu of the world in which it lived, the question arose whether there was any aspect of Israelite law which could be identified as distinguishing it from its neighbors. Two considerations are basic to the discussion.

First is the issue of authority. Although in ancient Mesopotamia the king was guided by divine will in the establishment of (secular) justice, the source of law was the king himself. In the Bible, on the other hand, the source of law was conceived of as God. In distinction to other ancient Near Eastern practice, in Israel the king was not conceived of as the promulgator of law. Moses and others were simply intermediaries who transmitted God's rules to the people. Thus both secular and religious law were

given divine origin. Obeying laws was hence both a legal and a religious requirement. Breaking a law was not simply a secular delict, but an infraction of the will of God, hence a sin. (*See* Kingship and Monarchy.)

The second is the valuation of human life, for which the case of the goring ox (Exod. 21.28–32) may serve as example. The case of an ox that injured or killed a human being appears in a number of ancient legal collections. There are differences between the various laws regarding the liability of the owner of the goring ox according to its prior behavior and to the status of the person gored. However, only in the biblical law, upon which similar medieval European legislation was based, is the ox itself subject to the death penalty for killing a human being, its flesh not to be eaten. Since the ox murdered a human being, it became taboo and hence not fit for human consumption, in spite of the fact that that inflicted a great financial loss on its owner. To give another example, in the code of Hammurapi the death penalty is adduced for theft. The killing of another human being did not necessarily warrant such severe punishment (depending on the relative societal status of the individuals involved). In the Bible, capital punishment is reserved for cultic offenses, which included *murder. Theft of property, as long it was not cultic or under the ban (see the story of Achan in Josh. 7), was not punishable by death. Theft of another human being, however, was. Thus it is postulated by Moshe Greenberg that, whereas the protection of property belonging to the upper echelons of society was of paramount concern in Babylonian law, in Israelite law the sanctity of the individual formed in the image of God was primary.

Major Collections of Biblical Laws. Among the many legal passages in the Bible are a number that have been identified as independent units by modern scholars. These include the Ten Commandments, the Book of the Covenant, the Holiness Code, and the Deuteronomic laws. The Ten Commandments can be understood as the heart of Israel's covenantal relationship with God, since they include an identification of the suzerain, God's acts on behalf of Israel, and Israel's obligations to God formulated in apodictic style. Most of the obligations incumbent upon Israel in the Decalogue deal not with cultic issues, but with the relations between people in an orderly society. The Book of the Covenant (Exod. 20.22–23.19), containing casuistic laws with many parallels in other ancient Near Eastern traditions, is assumed by many to be the oldest collection of laws in the Bible. The Holiness Code (Lev. 17–26) forms the oldest core of Priestly (P) legislation and is so named on account of its concern with Israelite ritual *purity and *holiness. The Deuteronomic laws (Deut. 12–26), although presented as a speech delivered by Moses in Transjordan before his death, are associated in modern scholarship with the cultic reforms of King Josiah of Judah (640–609 BCE). The major concern of this corpus of religious legislation is with the centralization and purification of the cult and its sacrificial system in the Temple in Jerusalem.

Carl S. Ehrlich

New Testament Views

The modern New Testament is a fourth-century anthology of mid- to late first-century documents, composed in Greek and reflecting the social and religious stresses of a new religious movement seeking to define and eventually to distinguish itself from Greek-speaking synagogue communities. In such a charged and changing context, "the Law" (Grk.

nomos) received widely divergent treatments, although its definition remains constant: the Law is God's revelation through Moses to Israel.

Paul. The earliest and most problematic source is Paul. Written to predominantly gentile communities, his letters often address questions of *ethics and authority. On these occasions, Paul's statements concerning the Law can only be seen as unself-consciously positive. The Law is the key to decent community life and the standard for group behavior. Gentiles "in Christ" should strive to fulfill it and keep its commandments. One can—and Paul did—obtain *righteousness under the Law. *Faith in Christ, Paul says, upholds the Law. In the largest sense, the redemption in Christ comes to gentiles in order to confirm God's promises to Israel's ancestors as preserved in Genesis, the first of the five books of *Torah.

Yet elsewhere Paul virtually equates the Law with sin, death, and the flesh—the worst aspects of the "old aeon" that, through Christ's death, *resurrection, and imminent *parousia, is about to be overcome. God gave the Law on account of transgression and in order to condemn: it is the "old dispensation," inglorious and incomplete, compared to the gospel of Christ. How then can this same author possibly maintain that "the Law is holy, and the commandment is holy and just and good" (Rom. 7.12)?

Scholars have attempted to resolve this tension. Some, at one extreme, take Paul's negative statements as definitive of his (hence, the) gospel and his positive statements as the measure of an unthought-out sentimental attachment to his community of origin. Some at the other end maintain that Paul preached a two-covenant theology: Torah for Jews, Christ for gentiles. On this view, his only objection to the Law would be if Christian gentiles chose it, that is, opted as Christians for conversion to Judaism. But Paul's own statements—forceful, passionate, at times intemperate—defy a consistent interpretation. He himself seems aware of the tensions in his position. As Paul saw it, however, history would soon relieve him of the necessity to make sense of God's plan in electing Israel, giving the Torah, and then sending Christ. For Christ, Paul urged, was about to return, end history, and bring all under the dominion of God. This conviction, and not his statements on the Law, is the one consistent theme in all of Paul's letters, from first to last. It spared him having to work out a "theology" of the Law.

The Gospels. The evangelists, writing some forty to seventy years after Jesus' death, turned a negative attitude toward the Law (or the Jewish understanding of it) into the touchstone of Christian identity. This tendency makes for considerable confusion when one tries to reconstruct the views of the historical Jesus. Jesus of Nazareth, living and working in a predominantly Jewish environment, very likely had his own views on the correct interpretation of Torah, and these views may well have differed from those of his contemporaries. Argument about the Law between Jews was and is a timeless Jewish occupation: controversy implies inclusion. Transposed to a gentile context, however, argument can seem like repudiation.

Thus Mark's Jesus turns an unexceptional observation (people are morally defiled by what they do or say, not by what they eat, 7.15–23) into a repudiation of the Law regarding kosher food ("Thus he declared all foods clean"; v. 19). John's Jesus condemns his Jewish audience as sons of the lower cosmos and children of the devil: the Law, charac-terized throughout as that "of Moses" is, implicitly, not "of God," from whom comes grace, peace, and the Son (1.16; 7.19–24). In his *Sermon on the Mount, Matthew's Jesus presents his intensification of Torah ethics as if in contradistinction to Torah and Jewish tradition ("You have heard it said . . . but I say"; chap. 5). Luke, although retaining the theme of Jewish guilt for the death of Jesus both in his Gospel and in Acts, nonetheless wishes to present the new movement as continuous with a Jewish view of biblical revelation. Consequently he edits out or softens many of Mark's anti-Law statements. And all the Gospels, no matter how strong their individual polemic against Jews and Judaism (see Anti-Semitism), and hence the Law, still present a Jesus who worships at synagogue on the *Sabbath, observes Temple sacrifice, pilgrimage holidays, and *Passover rituals, and whose followers, honoring the Sabbath, come to his tomb only on the Sunday after his death.

Later Traditions. Both within the New Testament and without, later traditions are similarly ambivalent. Negative statements tend to occur in those passages where these new communities seek to establish their identity vis-à-vis Jews and Judaism; positive statements emerge where Christians wish to distance themselves from their Greco-Roman environment. Christian ethics are in the latter case a judaizing of gentile populations according to the principles of Torah: shunning *idols, sorcery, astrology, hetero- and homosexual *fornication; keeping litigation within the community; supporting the poor, especially widows; and so on—all themes found especially in Paul's Corinthian correspondence.

In the early decades of the second century, Christian dualists such as Marcion and Valentinus took the position that the God of the Jews, the God of the Law, was a second, lower, cosmic deity; God the father of Jesus, they held, thus had nothing directly to do with material creation and, thus, with the events and legislation given in scripture. Other Christians, committed to the unity of *creation and redemption, argued that the Law was of divine origin: only their particular group, however, knew how to interpret it correctly (that is, for the most part, allegorically: see esp. Justin Martyr, *Dialogue with Trypho*, and *see* Interpretation, History of, *article on* Early Christian Interpretation). The church's ambivalence toward the Law eventually determined the structure of the Christian *canon itself. Retaining the Septuagint even as it repudiated Judaism, the church incorporated the Law into its "Old" Testament, while maintaining that it was superseded or perfected by the "New."

Paula Fredriksen

LAW AND THE BIBLE. Municipal or national law is the set of rules that, within a state, orders its affairs and those of persons under its jurisdiction, and that, when necessary, is enforced by special organs of the state. There may be more than one municipal law in a state, as in the United Kingdom, which contains the Scottish, English, and Northern Irish legal systems, or in the United States, where each state has its own legal system in addition to the federal system. Other states, such as India, have special rules for special communities (e.g., for Christians). International law is the law between states and between states and other international entities.

Municipal law can be divided into the law that regulates the affairs of the state itself and that which deals with the rights and duties, privileges, and immunities of persons within it. This division is often described as one between public

and private law, though these categories overlap.

The Bible has influenced all those systems of law that can be traced, sometimes tortuously, to western European sources. By and large, the legal systems of other societies have been less subject to its influence, though sometimes that influence was historically present, as with the Russian system, in which a traditional Christianity molded society in former centuries and is still to be discerned in such rules as those regarding contract.

There are two main groups within the broad European legal tradition. Civilian legal systems form one group. These owe much to the legacy of Roman Civil Law, particularly as that Law was rediscovered and developed by scholars from the twelfth to the sixteenth century. The Civil Law lays emphasis on rationality and principle, and for that reason the civilian tradition has been adopted by many states that have consciously chosen their law. The other group, roughly encompassing the Anglo-American tradition, stems in large part from the English Common Law, and like it has tended to concentrate more on remedies. This group has spread more by conquest and imposition than by conscious adoption. There is also a third group, that of the "mixed" legal systems, which draws from both main traditions. Scots Law and that of Louisiana are examples of these.

The remote history of any legal system is obscure, for much of our understanding of particular influences at specific times is conditional upon the accidental survival of documentation, and deductions therefrom. It is, however, undeniable that the influence of the Bible on the legal systems that trace themselves to a western European root is extensive, though nowadays often diffuse. Biblical principles form a part of the foundations, which, like all good foundations, are well buried. Indeed, many in the twentieth century would deny biblical influence on many legal principles, which in former years were held to be sufficiently justified by the Bible. Much depends upon a willingness to accept parallels as indicative of influence and not a simple coincidence of result. Jews or Christians interpret the evidence differently from those who proceed from rationalist, agnostic, or atheist presuppositions.

When the modern legal systems of the European family were being formed, three main bodies of law influenced their development, namely the indigenous law of the community, Roman law, and canon law. The Bible's influence was mediated through each of these.

Indigenous Law. Indigenous law was that obtaining within a community, refined in accordance with the expectation of the community as to what was right in a given situation. Naturally, such expectations had much to do with religious belief and presuppositions. In each legal system, therefore, there came to be a body of "common law" manifested and developed through the decisions of judges and the reasoning that supported those decisions. Since the early judges in most countries were in holy orders (though they were not usually canonists), the opportunity for biblical influence was great. Specific recourse to the Bible as authority was unusual, but the principles it contained exercised their influence. Within the English tradition, the common law came to be highly significant, and it is only in comparatively recent times that the legislature has come to be considered of greater authority than the common law in the sense that what Parliament legislates takes precedence over the common law. By contrast, in the American tradition, the

Constitution operates as the brake upon the lawmaking power of the Congress or of state legislatures.

Roman Law. Throughout Europe, indigenous law was directly influenced by Roman law, particularly as enunciated in the *Corpus Iuris Civilis* (529–545 CE), the product of scholars working under instructions from the Emperor Justinian. Naturally, the empire having become Christian, there was a desire on the part of these scholars to make the civil law congruent with church teachings. Biblical influences therefore were strong. From the twelfth century onward, scholars (known collectively as the Glossators) worked on the *Corpus*, expanding its precepts through commentary, with considerable effect on their contemporary municipal law.

Canon Law. The indigenous law was also influenced to a greater or lesser degree by the canon law, a major contribution of the church to civilization. The Roman Catholic church had extended its authority even as the Roman empire waned and disintegrated, and it was considered by many to be the only body that could continue a tradition of universal law. The sources of church law, however, were many and various, and it was only as the church organized itself on a monarchic principle under the papacy that the need for systematization was dealt with. The eleventh-century rediscovery of Roman Law in the form of the Justinianic legislation, and notably the *Digest* of 533 CE, provided a model that eventually resulted in the *Corpus Iuris Canonici*, though that was constantly augmented by interpretation and further legislation. Much of the canon law had to do with church organization, but large portions affected the daily life of the laity and influenced the development of national laws in various areas. The aim of the canonists was to make their system of law correspond as closely as possible to right Christian conduct, and to minimize the separation of law and morals. The Bible influenced their deliberations, though its principles were often mediated through the teachings of the Roman Catholic church.

One area of law affected by the canonists was the law of *marriage, an area important in every society and subject to church procedures. Another was the law of wills, where the church rules were much simpler than those of the civil law. Naturally the canonists, keen to keep law and morals together, were concerned with matters of intention and good and bad faith. In contracts, therefore, good faith was made a major requirement, and bargains were enforced through the church courts without the insistence upon the formalities for their constitution that had grown up previously. (It has to be said, however, that this development took greater hold in the civilian tradition than in the Anglo-American, which has retained certain elements of formal requirements such as the notion of "consideration," and which does not recognize a unilateral contract unless entered into under appropriate ceremonial.) Again, the canonists' stress on responsibility for the consequences of one's actions helped root the concepts of tort.

In the area of crime, intention also came to be insisted upon as a prerequisite for criminality of conduct, thereby bringing crime into closer association with notions of *sin and allowing actions to be differently weighed in any consideration of "blame," and therefore also of punishment. (A modern extrapolation from such concepts is the Scottish defense to a criminal charge of "diminished responsibility," which stems from that root, and was only lately taken over into English law.) The emphasis on sin also produced a change in attitude to punishment. In more and more instances, prison as a place of *repentance was accorded a higher priority than vengeance exacted through physical unpleasantness. In criminal procedure, the notion of God as judge, weighing the evidence, came to be accepted as a model, and human judges were given a greater freedom in their conduct of trials than former formalities permitted.

Finally, like the theologians and philosophers, the canonists gave consideration to such social questions as the doctrine of the "just price" and the "just wage." Price fluctuations in response to market forces alone were considered contrary to notions of intrinsic value. Such matters and their attempted solutions are, of course, still with us, and still echo.

The Reformation. The Reformation produced an interest in principles taken directly from the Bible in contrast to those mediated through church tradition and canon law. In some instances, this interest produced formal legislation. To take examples from one "reformed" jurisdiction, in 1567 in the Scots law the "degrees of relationship" within which marriage could lawfully be contracted were set out in terms of Leviticus 20 and "the Law of God," and the "prohibited degrees of relationship" for the purpose of defining incest were set out specifically in terms of Leviticus 18—though inaccurately, since the Geneva version (1560) of the Bible was the source used. Again, marriage between divorced persons and their paramours was made unlawful, though this was soon administratively avoided, and *adultery was made a crime. *Divorce on the grounds of adultery or desertion was introduced. In 1563, witchcraft was made a capital crime in terms of Exodus 22.18, and various Sunday observance statutes were passed. In 1649, 1661, and 1695 *blasphemy was made a capital offence, though the full penalty was exacted only once.

The other major element that the Reformation took from the Bible was the concept of the priesthood of all believers, which eventually filters down to the modern institutions of democratic government.

The law books of the sixteenth to eighteenth centuries, in which the roots of much modern law are laid, contain a considerable mixture of sources for the principles that they assert. The Bible is often quoted, as is the Roman law. However, appeal is also frequently made to a "natural law," containing principles that are treated as axiomatic. At first, such "law" was said by writers to be given by God, but in 1625, in the *Prolegomena* to his *De Iure belli ac pacis* ("The Law of War and Peace"), Hugo Grotius pointed out that the legal principles so identified would have a degree of validity even if there were no God. Reason would deduce such principles from a consideration of the nature of human beings and from their needs in society. Others acted on that observation, and drove a wedge between "natural law" and any religious source. This was not, however, a sudden or complete change of emphasis. Blackstone's *Commentaries on the Laws of England* (1765), for example, discusses law as stemming from God (Intro. s.2), but makes little appeal to biblical texts. Stair's *Institutions of the Law of Scotland* (2d ed., 1693), written from a Presbyterian background, also links law to God, making a number of biblical citations in so doing (e.g., Book I, tit. 1, 2–9), but again the bulk of the work treats such matters as a base to be acknowledged and not as an active source of law. In that train, Puritanism influenced English and American law in the seventeenth and eighteenth centuries, but since then the deduction of legal principle from biblical or theological sources has been largely abandoned by lawyers. The principles remain, but their source is usually not acknowledged or is otherwise explained on bases of social, economic, or political necessity. In Europe, anticlericalism gave that trend further impetus.

Modern Issues. In the twentieth century, major advances in securing biblical principles were made in international law, particularly through the United Nations' Universal Declaration of Human Rights, and other international Human Rights Covenants and Conventions following in its wake. In some measure, these have provided a statement of fundamental principles for human conduct that draw on biblical ideas among their unacknowledged sources. They provide a base from which municipal law can be criticized, and even, under certain human rights treaties, a remedy and change can be obtained.

Within the municipal law of most states of the European tradition, the law generally now proceeds upon unexamined assumptions. The biblical roots acknowledged in the early texts are taken for granted, and go unmentioned in modern discussions of matters such as tort, contract, marriage, divorce, wills, and the like, where the canonists did their job well in former centuries. In some areas, however, there has been a revival of appeal to biblical notions, often with explicit citation of biblical texts. Thus medical ethics, euthanasia, *abortion, and surrogacy are controverted legal matters. Curiously, it is in the United States, where the Constitution requires a separation of church and state, that most modern legislation and court action has had a clear biblical base. The debate on such matters as school prayer, abortion, and the teaching of science in schools (creationism verses evolution; *see* Science and the Bible) has had a considerable emphasis on biblical precept. In other states, the influence of the Bible and of Christianity is left as something inarticulate but nonetheless real. The principles are there, but only those who are willing to do so acknowledge their source. Legislators and judges act on them, but without reference to their origin. As noted, effective foundations are well buried. *Francis Lyall*

LAYING ON OF HANDS. The laying on of hands was a ceremonial act that conferred a special favor or function on the person for whom it was performed.

In the Hebrew Bible the ceremony often conveyed a personal blessing or function. Israel (Jacob), with his hands crossed on their heads, blessed Ephraim and Manasseh. Several ideas are related to this. Aaron's outstretched hands conveyed a blessing on the people, and the psalmist was enraptured after he felt God's hand laid on him.

Sometimes the ceremony conveyed the transfer of authority from one person to another. Witnesses laid their hands on criminals to testify against them before judgment for crime.

In sacrificial worship either officials in the Temple or the sacrificers themselves laid their hands on the animals before they were slaughtered. The basic idea was that of dedicating the victim to God to obtain the forgiveness of sins. With the scapegoat, the ceremony signified the transfer of sins from the sacrificers to the victims.

In the New Testament the laying on of hands served some of the same functions. Laying his hands on them, Jesus blessed the children, and while lifting up his hands he blessed the disciples.

The ceremony occurs most fre-quently in stories of healing, both by Jesus and his followers, reflecting the belief that through the ritual act of a person with divine favor healing power passes to a sick person. (*See also* Medicine.)

According to Acts 8.14–19; 19.6, the ceremony was understood as supplementing *baptism by the giving of the Holy Spirit. The act also conveyed authority to persons who already had the Holy Spirit: the seven and Barnabas and Saul (Paul).

The ceremony became more formal, and officials used it to impart spiritual gifts, or, perhaps, as a reconciliation of sinners who no longer were in the church but who wanted to return. It is still used in ecclesiastical ceremonies such as ordination and the sacrament of confirmation. *Edwin D. Freed*

LEAVEN. The translation of two Hebrew terms used in reference to the fermenting of bread dough. One word (*śĕʾōr*) designates the leavening agent, a piece of old dough set aside to ferment. This produces sourdough, which itself is inedible. The other, more frequently used word (*ḥāmēṣ*), designates the mixture of flour and water to which a piece of the old or fermented dough is added to facilitate rising.

Leaven in the Bible is most prominent in texts dealing with the annual springtime *Passover (*pesaḥ*) celebration, which incorporated an ancient and originally separate agricultural festival, the Feast of Unleavened Bread. During this seven-day feast, a flat unleavened bread called *maṣṣâ* was to be eaten instead of leavened bread. The Pentateuchal texts historicize this practice by relating it to the *Exodus event, when the haste of the Israelites' departure precluded sufficient time for bread dough to rise.

The Passover ban on leaven can be understood in relation to other biblical rituals forbidding the use of leaven. As a rule, *sacrifices containing leaven were never to be offered. The only exceptions were offerings meant for the offerer and priest, hence they were not offered to God. The ban on leaven in sacrifices in general and on *maṣṣâ* in particular is probably related to the association of leavening with decomposition and putrefaction. Sourdough is clearly unsavory, despite its useful role in bread preparation. Leaven may thus have come to symbolize corruption, and thus an element to be consciously omitted from a feast involving spiritual rejuvenation and also from sacrifices involving communion with God. The Hebrew Bible does not make such a notion explicit, but early Jewish sources and the New Testament assume that leaven represents *evil.

See also Feasts and Festivals.

Carol L. Meyers

LECTIONARIES. *This entry consists of two articles on readings from the Bible in liturgical contexts, the first in* Jewish Tradition, *and the second in* Christian Tradition.

Jewish Tradition

Although it has no lectionary in the formal sense, Jewish liturgy draws extensively on the Hebrew Bible with readings, direct quotations, and textual references to explain the significance of portions of the service.

One of the oldest uses of the biblical text within the liturgy is Deuteronomy 6.4–9, the *Shema. These verses express the essential Jewish belief in a single God and provide a course of action for demonstrating this belief. This paragraph is followed in the traditional prayer service (omitted in Reform Judaism) by two other biblical passages, Deuteronomy 11.13–21 and Numbers 15.37–41, that state the consequences both of following

God and of disobeying Him. The Shema is the focus of the first part of the service.

Similar to the Christian lectionary is the annual Jewish cycle of *Torah readings. The Torah is a handwritten scroll containing the *Pentateuch. The fifty-four pentateuchal readings progress weekly, with successive portions of the Pentateuch, some weeks having double readings. Special Sabbaths and holy days have their own Torah readings, conveying the meaning of the holy day and replacing the weekly reading. For example, the reading for the holiday of Shavuᶜot (*Pentecost) is Exodus 19–20, which includes the *Ten Commandments. This reading emphasizes the meaning of Shavuᶜot as celebrating the acceptance of the Torah by the people of Israel. The Torah is traditionally read on Monday, Thursday, and Ṣabbath mornings. On Sabbath afternoon, the reading for the following week is begun.

On the Sabbath and holy days there is an additional reading from the Prophets called the Haftarah. Each Torah reading has a designated Haftarah that is meant to parallel and illuminate the message of the Torah reading. Thus, the Torah portion mentioning the building of the *tabernacle in the wilderness is accompanied by a Haftarah about the building of the Temple in Jerusalem. Holy days have special Haftarah readings.

The Torah reading, central to the Jewish service, is accompanied by Devar Torah ("word of Torah"), a sermon drawing upon the weekly portion in order to teach a lesson for daily life. The portion is also used as a focus for study during the week.

Five other biblical books, collectively known as *megillot ("scrolls") are read in full during the year. The scroll of Esther is read on the festival of Purim, commemorating the salvation of Persian

Jewry. Song of Songs is read on *Passover. In ancient Israel, Passover took place at the early spring harvest, alluded to in Song of Songs. This book is understood as an allegory of God's relationship with the Jewish people, a relationship that began with the *Exodus celebrated on Passover. The book of Ruth is read on Shavuʿot (Pentecost), a holiday that celebrated the late spring harvest, mentioned in Ruth. In addition, it is the holiday of accepting the Torah, and Ruth in Jewish tradition is an exemplary model of a convert who accepts God's teachings. The book of Lamentations is read on Tishʿah BeʾAv (the ninth of Ab), the day commemorating the destruction of the First and Second Temples in Jerusalem. Ecclesiastes is read on the holiday of Sukkot (Booths), because the holiday takes place in the fall and Ecclesiastes is written in the autumn of the preacher's life.

The service surrounding the actual reading from the Torah draws on numerous biblical verses. The introductory part of the service on Sabbath and holidays strings together verses thematically emphasizing God's eternal rule and his relationship with the people of Israel. This is followed by a series of verses tied to the idea of bringing out God's teaching. Numbers 10.35 is chanted in imitation of Moses' action when the *ark traveled. Then Isaiah 2.3 is chanted, describing the Torah as being the word of God emanating from Zion. This is followed by the Shema, emphasizing God's unity; Psalm 34.4 (3), a call to exalt God's name; and Psalm 99.5, 9, in response to the call. After the Torah reading, Deuteronomy 4.44 and Numbers 9.23 are sung in confirmation that the Torah was given to the people of Israel by God through Moses. As the scroll is returned to its ark, the liturgy mirrors the beginning of the service with a call

to exalt God's name followed by a song of exaltation. When the scroll is placed back in the ark, there is another selection of verses strung together thematically referring to the ark being brought to rest. This selection emphasizes the centrality of the Torah to the relation between God and Israel, reaffirming the Torah as the "tree of life."

Within the central part of the service called the Amidah (standing prayer), Isaiah 6.3, Ezekiel 3.12, and Psalms 146.10 are the focal point in the Kedushah ("sanctification"). The priestly blessing (Num. 6.24–26) appears on special occasions. Numerous other verses are interpolated into the prayers as well.

Psalms are also widely used in Jewish liturgy. There is a psalm for each day of the week, a psalm for the Sabbath day, a series of psalms recited Friday evening to represent the weekdays, psalms recited in the introductory service on the Sabbath morning. There is also a special addition to the service on holy days called the Hallel ("praise"), consisting of Psalms 113–118. While all the psalms give word to the individual's desire to praise God, those appearing in the introductory portions of the service help prepare the individual spiritually for the service.

Often the influence of the Bible on liturgy is interpretive. The public reading of the Torah is said to be based on Exodus 24.3 and Deuteronomy 5.1 and 31.11–12, all examples of Moses reciting commandments or laws to the people of Israel. The action and wording of the call to prayer at the beginning of the service is based on Nehemiah 9.5. The essential portion of the prayer service is recited standing, attributed to Phinehas's action in Psalm 106.30, the interpretation being that the act of standing will be counted in one's favor. The prayers of supplication in the daily service are based on Daniel 9.3–19; Ezra 9.6–15; and Nehemiah 1.4–11. The inclusion of a prayer for the welfare of the government in the Sabbath service is derived from Jeremiah 29.7, where the exiles are told to seek the welfare of the country in which they reside. Even relatively late additions to the prayer book use biblical verses as their foundation. *Michal Shekel*

Christian Tradition

A lectionary is a set selection of passages from the Bible to be read aloud in public worship over a fixed period of time. The designation may refer to a book in which is actually printed each assigned reading or simply to a list of chapters and verses that are then read from a Bible. Sometimes the specific pericopes (selected passages) for the lay reader, deacon/priest, and cantor are printed in separate books (the Lectionary, the Book of Gospels, and the Gradual, respectively). A community may employ multiple lectionaries, with different sets of readings for Sunday, for weekdays, for celebrations of the Eucharist, and for Services of the Word. Not all Christian communities follow a formal lectionary.

The practice of reading scripture when Christians gather for worship can be traced back very early, and is related to some extent to the Jewish practice of continuous Torah reading in the synagogue (*see previous article in this entry on* Jewish Tradition). Already in the second century CE, Justin Martyr described how "the memoirs of the apostles and the writings of the prophets are read for as long as possible" (*Apol.* 67). The pilgrim Egeria, in recounting her visit to Jerusalem in the fourth century, noted that in the church there the biblical readings were chosen so as to be appropriate for the feast or the place. Various early tables of readings are attested from both the Eastern and Western churches and exhibit great diversity in both the number

and selection of readings according to language, region, and liturgical rite. In Augustine's church of the fifth century, for instance, the bishop exercised some freedom of choice, but the readings for the major feasts were basically already fixed. More complete lists have survived from the eighth century, most notably the Comes of Wurzburg, the *Liber Commicus* of Spain, and the *Lectionary of Luxeuil* from Gaul.

After the Reformation, distinctive lectionary traditions developed in the Lutheran and Anglican communities, while most of the "Free Churches" abandoned the imposition of a lectionary. The Greek churches have largely maintained the Byzantine lectionary of the eighth century. The Roman church of the West retained the Missal of Pope Paul V from 1570, with a one-year cycle of New Testament readings.

In subsequent centuries relatively little attention was paid to the lectionary until the Second Vatican Council of the Roman Catholic church called for a major reform of the entire lectionary, with the intent that "the treasures of the Bible are to be opened up more lavishly" (*Constitution on the Sacred Liturgy* 51). A complete revision for Sundays, weekdays, feasts, sacraments, and other rites was completed in 1969 and prepared for worldwide use in 1971; some slight revisions and a more extensive introduction were published in 1981. Various Protestant churches, particularly in North America, quickly adopted this lectionary, usually with minor changes (especially in the structure of the liturgical year and substitutions for the apocryphal/deuterocanonical books). The most important of these adaptations of the Roman lectionary is the *Common Lectionary* of 1983 and the *Revised Common Lectionary* of 1992, prepared by the Consultation on Common Texts, an ecumenical forum of Christian churches in North America. In addition, numerous other lectionaries, independent of the Roman lectionary, have been developed in the last decades, often on a regional or denominational basis; one of the most widely used is the two-year thematic-type lectionary proposed by the Joint Working Group in Britain in 1967, revised to a four-year cycle in 1990.

Certain fundamental principles guide modern lectionary planning and revision: a desire to read extensively and widely from the Bible in public worship; assignment of the more important biblical passages to Sundays and solemnities; maintenance of certain pericopes that historically have been long associated with major feasts; and a doxological, Christocentric orientation that reflects the doxological nature of liturgy rather than an academic or didactic orientation. In the Roman lectionary and its adaptations, these principles find expression in the Sunday lectionary in the development of a three-year cycle, with one gospel read in a semicontinuous fashion over each year and the gospel of John used to supplement Mark and for much of the Lenten and Easter season. A second New Testament reading from the Epistles is also semicontinuous. The Roman lectionary has a first reading, chosen from the Old Testament (except during the Easter season when it is from Acts) on the basis of a thematic connection with the Gospel; the *Revised Common Lectionary* now offers an alternative system of semicontinuous reading of Old Testament narratives for the Sundays after *Pentecost. In addition, a psalm is provided for each Sunday as a congregational response between the first and second reading. The weekday lectionary is based on a two-year cycle of two semicontinuous pericopes, except for the Advent-Christmas and Lent-Easter cycle, where the readings fit the liturgical season.

Ongoing discussion and critique have focused on the fundamental nature of a lectionary as such and on the specific choices of a certain lectionary. A lectionary implies an inherent element of selectivity; it always excludes as well as includes, and to that extent it establishes its own canon of texts that form the basis for popular knowledge, preaching, and even catechetical instruction. The most problematic issues raised about specific lectionaries are questions concerning the presence or absence of biblical passages about women; the use or nonuse of passages that speak negatively about the Jews (*see* Anti-Semitism); problems in the typological use of the Old Testament; and the difficulty of preaching on the basis of two or three virtually independent readings. Yet for many Christians the revised Roman lectionary is recognized as one of the major achievements of the Second Vatican Council. Its adoption and adaptation by many Protestant churches, even those churches that traditionally had not used a lectionary, has brought an unforeseen degree of ecumenical convergence in the scriptures that are read each Sunday throughout a large portion of the Christian church.

Eileen Schuller

LETTER-WRITING IN ANTIQUITY.
Letter-writing arose in antiquity to serve official purposes. There were three broad types of official correspondence: royal or diplomatic letters, military orders and reports, and administrative correspondence used in managing internal affairs. Most letters embedded in the Hebrew Bible, along with several other nonbiblical Israelite and Jewish letters, are official in nature. Solomon's correspondence with King Hiram of Tyre, for example, is diplomatic. The Lachish

letters, written when Judah was under siege by Babylonia, are military communiqués. We may add to these the letter from the Jewish military settlement in Egypt at Elephantine, which was sent to the Persian governor of Judah, requesting his intervention against attacks on a Jewish temple.

Originally, messages were oral, carried by trusted couriers. With the passage of time, the principal message of the letter was delivered in written form, but the letter's sender continued to be identified orally by the messenger with the phrase, "Thus says . . ." A written message provided confirmation of the letter's authenticity, especially when signed with the sender's seal. The written message carried by Uriah from King David to the military commander Joab was clearly closed, because it commanded Uriah's own death.

Although professional couriers were used by ancient states from the beginning of recorded history, the first organized postal system was not established until the sixth century BCE, when the Persian king Cyrus set up a network of highways and relay stations. This postal system served as a model for Alexander the Great and his successors, as well as for the Roman empire.

Even when the entirety of the letter was written, the messenger often continued to play a supplemental role. This was certainly the case with Paul, who usually employed trusted coworkers as couriers and who expected messengers to represent him to his correspondents.

Various materials were used for written messages. Correspondence in Mesopotamia was written on clay tablets in cuneiform script by means of a reed with a wedge-shaped tip. It was common in a number of places to write with a brush or reed pen on potsherds (ostraca). Parchment and vellum (skins) were used for more important correspondence. Papyrus was the most widely used material during the Persian and Greco-Roman periods. When Hellenistic rulers proclaimed benefactions and edicts worthy of permanent record, they were inscribed on stone after delivery. (*See* Books and Bookmaking in Antiquity; Writing in Antiquity.)

Gradually, the letter was adapted to serve personal and nonofficial purposes. We know from archaeological discoveries that, at least in Greco-Roman Egypt, all levels of society sent letters. Although many were written by scribes, literacy was not as rare as was formerly believed. Nonetheless, ancient postal systems existed to serve only state business, not private correspondence. Whereas wealthy families and business firms could use employees or servants to carry their mail, ordinary people depended on those traveling on business (e.g., by ship or caravan) or on friends and passing strangers.

Greek and Roman rhetoricians regarded the cultivated letter of friendship as the most authentic form of correspondence. The letter was conceived as a substitute for the sender's actual presence. Since the recipient, however, could not ask for immediate clarification on epistolary subjects, it was recognized that the letter had to be more articulate than face-to-face talk. Despite the more studied style of letter-writing relative to conversation, theorists warned that the discussion of technical subjects was not appropriate in a letter. Nonetheless, the democratization of knowledge in late antiquity, along with the dialogic character of popular philosophy at the time, made it almost inevitable that much philosophical and religious instruction would be communicated in epistolary form.

While none of the books of the Hebrew Bible takes the form of a letter, twenty-one of the twenty-seven New Testament books are letters (also known as "epistles"). This difference stems in part from the fact that New Testament letters were written by Greek-speaking Jewish Christians who were influenced by the Hellenistic practice of writing instruction in the form of letters. Moreover, letters were often used by Christian leaders, such as Paul, to maintain contact with widely separated congregations. Some of the letters are known as "catholic" or "general" (Grk. *katholikos*) epistles, because they were written to early Christianity at large, rather than to specific congregations (like the letters of Paul and Rev. 2–3). The New Testament contains seven catholic letters: James, traditionally ascribed to "the brother of Jesus"; 1 and 2 Peter, ascribed to Jesus' disciple; 1, 2, and 3 John, which are related to the gospel of John; and Jude, ascribed to the brother of James.

The New Testament letters and patristic letters of the first three centuries CE are much longer than most pieces of ancient Greek correspondence. This length corresponds directly to their purpose as letters of instruction. In this respect, Christian letters are more like philosophical letters of instruction than ordinary letters. On the other hand, the hortatory rhetoric used in Christian letters differs significantly from that in literary letters. For example, the emphasis on the whole community's spiritual maturation brought about by Christ's return, rather than on building one's individual character, shows that Christian letters were written by a specific religious subgroup with an *apocalyptic Jewish coloring. Their special character is evident in the way traditional Jewish materials are cited within the letter (doxologies, benedictions, hymns), as well as in the tone of familiarity and equality that frequently described Christian recipients and their senders as family members. Later, in the fourth and fifth centuries CE, letters from Christian leaders conformed much more to Greek literary models of letters. *John L. White*

LITERACY IN ANCIENT ISRAEL.

The invention of the alphabet in the Levant in the second millennium BCE and its subsequent adoption as the preferred *writing system in various regions by the beginning of the first millennium led to significant changes in education and literature. The use of a limited acrophonic system of graphemic representation led to relatively widespread literacy in ancient Israel, and everywhere where the originally Canaanite alphabet, spread by the Phoenicians, was adopted. Nevertheless, the boundary between oral and literate cultures is not sharp, and there is no doubt that orality continued to be important even after literacy became widespread; in *Hebrew as in other languages the verb meaning "to read" *(qārāʾ)* literally means "to say aloud."

The evidence for writing in ancient Israel is fragmentary, largely because of the use of perishable writing materials. Papyrus, leather, and occasionally wood and plaster were the surfaces most frequently used, but these materials were usually destroyed in conflagrations or by natural decomposition over the centuries. Dramatic evidence for this is found in a number of seal impressions from archaeological strata in Jerusalem dated to the time of the Babylonian destruction of the city in 587/586 BCE. The small globs of clay with their seal impressions have survived, aided by the fire that hardened them, but the documents to which they were attached were burnt; these bullae sometimes still have the impression of the strings used to tie the papyrus and occasionally impressions of the papyrus itself. Only in relatively isolated and dry locales do leather and papyrus documents like the *Dead Sea Scrolls survive. Most of the inscriptions that have been uncovered, therefore, are on stone or pottery, and they represent only a small proportion of written materials produced at any given time.

On the basis of the surviving epigraphic evidence the democratization of literacy can be dated to about the eighth century BCE. Rapid changes in the forms of letters and a statistically significant increase in the number of extant inscriptions suggest frequent and diffuse use of the alphabet beginning in this period. Certainly by the sixth century literacy is so much a reality that, for example, a soldier can boast in a letter to his superior that he has never needed a scribe to read for him (Lachish Letter 3). Datable references to reading and writing in the Bible also become more frequent in this period.

These developments had profound effects on the formation, transmission, and reception of biblical traditions. From the mid-eighth century BCE onward, there are more and more frequent references to reading and writing in both biblical and epigraphic sources; these provide further evidence of the spread of literacy beyond a scribal and socioeconomic elite. In earlier traditions, for example, God is the writer of his commandments, or Moses is his scribe. But by the time of the composition of the book of Deuteronomy, the *tôrâ* ("teaching," or "law"; *see* Torah), while read aloud in the universal ancient mode, was accessible in written form to the larger population. They are prohibited from adding to or removing any of its stipulations and are thus themselves capable of writing. Noteworthy in this connection is the command in Deuteronomy 6.9 (*see* Shema): "You [pl.] shall write them on the doorposts of your house and on your gates" (cf. 11.19–20).

It is in addition more than coincidental that the rise of "classical" prophecy in the mid-eighth century BCE is simultaneous with the spread of writing; in other words, the rise of new forms of, literally, literature is due to the availability of writing in the process of composition. The spread of literacy may also mean that the written traditions of which the Bible preserves a sample may have been accessible not only to elite scribal and priestly groups but more and more to ordinary citizens as well; as an example there is the seventh-century letter from Yavneh Yam in which a field hand shows familiarity with the legal traditions found in Exodus 22:26, Deuteronomy 24:12–13, and Amos 2:8.

Scribal schools continued to function and to flourish, especially in the palace and Temple, but individuals also employed scribes, the most famous of whom is Baruch. It is presumably to such professional writers that we should attribute the acrostic poems in the Bible. But the teaching and learning of reading and writing would have taken place in domestic and village contexts as well. It is significant that one word meaning both "to learn" and in the causal form "to teach" is derived from the name of the first letter of the alphabet (*ʾālep*); it is attested from the eighth century BCE onward in both *Aramaic and Hebrew.

See also Books and Bookmaking in Antiquity.   *Michael D. Coogan*

LITERATURE AND THE BIBLE.
This entry consists of four articles that survey, by geographical region, the uses of the Bible in and its influences on literature:

English Literature
British Commonwealth Literature

European Literature
North American Literature

For discussion of the literary interpretation of the Bible, see Literature, The Bible as *and* Interpretation, History of, *article on* Modern Biblical Criticism.

English Literature

From the swift Christianization of Britain in the seventh century CE, at the beginning of which native writing of texts had not yet begun, down to the present "post-Christian" era in which textuality is almost exclusively the preserve of literary traditions, the Bible has been by far the most important of foundational texts for English literature. In the earliest days of written English, it may be said that the Bible effectively established the literary canon; and until the time of the Enlightenment, it largely continued to shape its outer contours. In the modern period, though this definitive influence has declined dramatically, we may still say that the Bible remains the most widely alluded to of all texts in works by English-speaking authors.

Anglo-Saxon Period. This vast influence is attributable in part to the formative role "free translation" of the Bible had in the development of self-conscious English narrative style. Bede (673–735), in his *Ecclesiastical History of the English People,* offers as paradigm the case of Caedmon, an unlettered cowherd who was miraculously transformed overnight into an accomplished poet: Caedmon's first composition was a hymn drawing on Genesis in praise of *creation, and his name was subsequently attached to the relatively large body of Anglo-Saxon hexameral poetry that reflected patristic commentaries on Genesis (especially the *Hexameron* of Basil). The chief literary themes of this tradition—the six days of creation, the revolt and fall of the angels, and the temptation and *fall of Adam and Eve—are felt in the Caedmonian versification of *Genesis* (A and B), or paraphrase-abridgement of *Exodus, Daniel* (1–5), and dramatic *Christ and Satan,* with its three-part relation of the revolt and fall of the angels, Christ's *temptation, and the harrowing of *hell. Later Christian poems associated with the author Cynewulf (ninth and tenth century) tend to concern saints' lives, miracles, and lyrical parables, with the notable exception of the three-part poem, *Christ.* The third section of this poem is a powerful treatment of the contest between Christ and Satan, culminating in the Last Judgment. The Exeter *Harrowing of Hell* draws heavily on the apocalyptic gospel of Nicodemus, while another tenth-century poem, *Solomon and Satan,* applies the prevalent theme of holy war between Christ and his adversary in a debate between Christian and non-Christian wisdom. As a type of Christ, Solomon interprets biblical narratives (e.g., the tower of Babel) as well as wisdom literature in such a way as to confound his opponent's resistance to the gospel. All these works, as much as the sermons of Wulfstan and Aelfric, the beautiful *Advent Lyrics* or more literal translations of the Psalter and Gospels, reflect a desire to transmit biblical knowledge. The authors of Anglo-Saxon literature were for the most part missionaries, monks, or lay brothers trained in monasteries, and much of their work can be seen as an outgrowth of the evangelization of Britain. Even in the great non-Christian epic *Beowulf* (which occurs in the same manuscript as a retelling of the apocryphal narrative, *Judith*), biblical allusion is a significant feature.

Later Middle Ages. After 1066, with the massive cultural and linguistic upheaval occasioned by the Norman invasion, there followed a quiet period for English literature. (The great *Jeu d'Adam*, perhaps the first biblical play in the vernacular to be written in England, was written in Anglo-Norman French.) Yet in the twelfth century, revival of interest in late Roman Christian learning (especially the works of Augustine and Gregory the Great) provided an opportunity for substantial progress in the development of Christian literary theory. Initially, this was applied to reading the Bible itself. But the Augustinian notion that classical literature ought to be appropriated to Christian use, "baptized" by subordination to biblical and catechetical rewriting, had also been defended in his *On Christian Doctrine* by analogy with the divine command to the Jews exiting from Egypt to take with them vessels of Egyptian gold and silver, later to put them to ordinary uses. Under the continued tutelage of Hugh of St. Victor in France and, in England, John of Salisbury (d. 1180), "Egyptian gold" became a major emphasis in late-medieval Christian ideas about literature and shaped the interaction of scripture and vernacular writing in England until well into the Renaissance. The principle of discrimination in all reading, non-Christian as well as Christian, was held to be the Augustinian test of *love. Richard de Bury (1287–1345) reflects these ideas in his treatise on the love of books *(Philobiblion)* in which "the fables of the poets" are integrated with a canon of humane learning whose basis is scriptural and patristic. Ovid, for example, is subjected to biblical allegory, both in vernacular *(Ovide moralisé)* and Latin versions (Petrus Berchorius). Within the context provided by these developments, as well as by the striking growth of commentary on the Bible itself reflected in central textbooks such as Peter Lombard's *Sentences on the Gospels* (1150), the

Ordinary Gloss, and Nicholas Lyra's extensive commentaries on scripture (early fourteenth century), the influence of the Bible on vernacular English literature that began to flourish again in the fourteenth century split into two main lines of development.

As in the Anglo-Saxon period, there was still a strong tradition of narrative works that may be described as biblical paraphrase and abridgement. This includes works of biblical extrapolation and sacred tradition: *Cursor mundi,* the *South English Legendary,* the 10,840-line *Stanzaic Life of Christ,* and also the famous biblical cycle plays of York, Chester, Wakefield, Lincoln, and Coventry. Multiday pageants covering the biblical history of salvation from creation to the Last Judgment, these plays represent the most extensive adaptation of the Bible to vernacular literary use in the history of English letters. While the Bible provides the principal content, the treatment is free, with more or less skillful interpolation or narrative and dramatic expansion effecting the historiographical or homiletic purpose of the authors. (By 1350, few priests and almost no female religious had sufficient Latin to read the Vulgate even if available; for many, such vernacular works were accordingly a principal source of their biblical knowledge.) Other writers, sometimes with much greater skill and sophistication, might take individual Bible stories and craft them into romance narratives. Two such poems are by the anonymous "Pearl-poet," probably a north-country priest: *Patience,* a retelling of the story of Jonah, and *Cleanness,* a fierce denunciation of sin which employs biblical narratives (Sodom and Gomorrah; the fall of Babylon; the parable of the wedding feast; Nebuchadnezzar and Belshazzar) to underscore the perils of profanation. *Pearl,* in the same verse form and by the same author, is an exquisite Gothic exposition of the parables of the pearl of great price and the penny-hire, blended with material from the book of Revelation to address the relationship between present life and future hope, time, and eternity.

The second stream of biblical influence, flowing from the revival of Christian literary theory in the twelfth to the fourteenth centuries, is illustrated well in a fourth poem by the Pearl-poet, *Sir Gawain and the Green Knight*. In it Celtic myth and the conventions of ancestral romance narrative are blended with New Testament themes. Although neither biblical narrative nor extended biblical allegory is present, biblical interpretation in the Augustinian tradition heavily flavors the treatment of non-Christian narrative.

The preeminent poet of the fourteenth century, Geoffrey Chaucer (1340–1400), reveals a rich appreciation of biblical literature, yet his poetry involves rather a "baptism" of worldly tales by Christian thought and purpose than simple allegory or biblical paraphrase. In his *Canterbury Tales,* various pilgrim narrators use biblical idiom and figure in such a way as to characterize their attitudes toward justice, mercy, love, and forgiveness. The humor and the "moralite" of the Miller's use of Noah's *Flood and the Song of Solomon, like the outrageous and funny misreadings of the gospel of Matthew and the church fathers by the Wife of Bath, equally with the Parson's sober sermon on repentance (from Jeremiah 6), toward which the collection moves, depend both upon a veridical reading of the biblical text and also upon the more elaborate hermeneutic encoding that is the product of later biblical scholarship and commentary. That how one reads the Bible can be a subject for lively cognizance and considerably so-

phisticated humor in English court circles is a striking measure of biblical literacy in the fourteenth century. Further, in the deliberate superimposing of biblical text over familiar classical myth, as in Chaucer's *Maunciples's Tale* or in the anonymous Christian reversal of the Orpheus and Eurydice legend, *Sir Orfeo*, we see a dependence upon Augustinian notions of how the Bible might be expected to transform non-Christian story.

For less cultured readers, the same techniques could be adapted to biblically directed social criticism. In Langland's apocalyptic *Piers Plowman* (1369; 1378; 1386), simple moral and political allegories are projected from the Gospels and Pauline epistles onto contemporary crises in church and state. Here the reader is invited to refer both text and events of contemporary life to the Bible for understanding; Langland not only assumes biblical knowledge but, much like Richard Rolle (d. 1349) and Walter Hilton (d. 1396) among spiritual writers and John Wycliffe among Oxford academics, urges his readers toward direct, personal reading of the scriptures. The Wycliffite Bible translation (1384; 1396) by Nicholas Hereford, John Purvey, and others not only contributed to but depended upon widespread interest in the Bible among nonclerical readers.

The fifteenth century is almost as unremarkable for English literature as were the years immediately following 1066. With the stiff suppression of Lollardry and condemnation of the Wycliffite Bible, it became unfashionable to exhibit biblical influence with the freedom known in the fourteenth century; one could be arrested on suspicion of heresy even for owning a copy of *The Canterbury Tales*. With the exception of continuation, for a time, of the cycle plays and allegorical morality plays, the most notable examples of biblical influence may be two surviving saints' plays, *The Conversion of St. Paul* and *The Play of Mary Magdalene*. Although true saints' plays in form, they are from the very end of the period and probably owe their preservation in Protestant times to the fact that the principals were biblical figures; the St. Paul play is particularly careful to hew close to the account in Acts and at pains to advertise this in its preface. Some of the religious poetry of the Scots poets, such as William Dunbar, and that of English writer John Skelton show indebtedness to biblical story, and among the first printed English works of William Caxton is included an apocryphal narrative on the *Infancy of Jesus* and another translation from Latin, *The Mirror of the Blessed Life of Jesus Christ*. But central, vital influence of the Bible upon the main fabric of English literature degenerated almost entirely until after the stormiest years of the Reformation.

Reformation and Renaissance. In the sixteenth century, with the translations of Tyndale (1525–1530), Coverdale (1535), Rogers and Taverner, the "Great Bible" (1539), the Geneva Bible (1560), and finally the Bishop's Bible (1568) (*see* Translations, *article on* English Language), the combination of controversial interest and accessibility assured a fresh infusion of literary interest. While Cranmer's *Book of Common Prayer* (1564) aided in the increase of biblical knowledge among ordinary persons, its largely liturgical organization of biblical story no longer governed patterns of influence as had its Latin predecessors. The accessible English Bible now invited reading through, like other books, and the success of the King James Version (1611), rightly regarded as the high-water mark of English literary prose, merely confirmed this new type of literary enjoyment of the Bible. Thus, though there are still examples of poet-translators of

scripture, such as Sir Philip Sidney and the Countess of Pembroke in their rendition of the Psalms (1586; 1589), and Joshua Sylvester's translation (1605) of the Frenchman Du Bartas' *Divine Weeks and Works* (a highly successful Protestantized version of medieval hexameral literature), the true influence of the Bible is in this period internalized, revealing itself not merely in the emergence of previously neglected themes and narratives (such as the stories of Jephthah, Samson, Ruth, Deborah, and the theme of the covenant) but in the actual force of idiom, phrase, and cadence of the Coverdale, Geneva, and finally King James Versions working their way into English poetic diction. Spenser's sonnets (66; 68; 70) and *Epithalamion* (1595) offer exquisite examples, as do, somewhat later, many poems of George Herbert in *The Temple* (1633); biblical idiom shapes also the prose of Hooker's *Laws of Ecclesiastical Polity* (1593; 1597), Decker's *The Seven Deadly Sins of London* (1606), the *Devotions* of John Donne (1624), and, more extravagantly, Jeremy Taylor's *Holy Living and Holy Dying* (1650; 1651), to cite but a few luminous examples. It can truly be said of the seventeenth century in England that nowhere else has the effect of the Bible on literary language been so all-pervasive. Both writers and readers savor the flavor of "biblical" English; even playwrights are able to depend on an intimate familiarity with the Bible on the part of popular audiences. As Christopher Marlowe in the opening speeches of *Dr. Faustus* (1604) can characterize his proud and self-damning protagonist by his misquotation of key biblical texts, so also William Shakespeare is able, in *Measure for Measure,* to critique the theology of the Puritans by setting his text from Matthew 7 in a rich context of quotations from Paul's letter to the Romans, such as were frequently featured in the Puritans' own sermons. Throughout his work, Shakespeare draws heavily on the Geneva Bible to encode and enrich his work, whether in romances like *The Winter's Tale* or history plays like *Henry IV* (Parts 1 and 2).

Biblical allusion in post-Reformation England, at least until the time of Milton and Bunyan, is ubiquitous, and it salts every kind of learned discourse. Poetry in the service of biblical interpretation or theological controversy, though more easily delineated as an expression of the influence of the Bible on the growth of humane letters, is almost as impossible to summarize; it must be kept in mind that between 1480 and 1660 more than half of all books printed in England were devoted to theological or ethical subjects, and typically copiously indebted to biblical "evidences" and discourse. Many of these works were dedicated to lay readership, and a large portion elected one or another genre of poetry as a medium. The younger Giles Fletcher's long serial poem, *Christ's Victorie and Triumph in Heaven and Earth* (1618) and, to a lesser extent, his brother Phineas's *The Locusts of Apollyonists* (1627) exemplify Protestant allegorical treatments of major biblical themes.

Such adaptations of the *agon* motif familiar from earlier English portrayals of the cosmic battle between Christ and Satan may have helped redirect the classically trained John Milton (1608–1674) in his desire to write a great English epic. Milton goes beyond Spenser, not only rejecting a plot from Greek or Roman literature but choosing the biblical story of fall and redemption over the national Arthurian myth. *Paradise Lost* (1667) and *Paradise Regained* (1671) represent a high point, then, of biblical influence on English literature, perhaps the greatest exemplar of a national culture that by this point had come to see the Bible as chief

amongst its foundational texts. From the "war in heaven" to the "last battle," major epic themes from the Bible were adorned with Latinate diction and humane learning of such a high order as to reinforce the centrality of biblical influence through subsequent, much less religious periods in English letters. In his short drama *Samson Agonistes* and lesser poems as well, Milton offers a shaping of biblical influence so distinctive that many subsequent authors have effectively read their Bible in Milton's "version"—which is also to say, of course, that the Bible became strongly identified in the minds of some with Milton's brand of Protestant theology.

The once-vigorous tradition of biblical drama did not entirely die out with the Reformation but was substantially adapted to serve the emphases of Protestant interpretations of the Bible. Thus, while the saints' plays probably dominated religious drama in the fifteenth century, they now gave way entirely, to be replaced by plays about heroic figures from the Hebrew Bible; individual Tudor plays, many now lost, were dedicated to the stories of Ruth, Esther, Darius, Hezekiah, Jephthah, Joshua, Samson, Absalom, and Susanna, as well as the more familiar Abraham and Lot, Jacob and Esau, and a variety of plays about Joseph and his brothers. Common to these plays, as to those with New Testament subjects (such as *John the Baptist, Pontius Pilate,* and *The Prodigal Son*), is a movement away from salvation history to a focus on individual spiritual struggle of heroic proportions, ending either in repentance, conversion, and triumph or in hardening of the heart and tragedy. Almost the sole Tudor survival of the classical saints' play is the mediocre *Life and Repentance of Mary Magdalene* (1566) by Lewis Wager. John Bale, protégé of Thomas Cromwell, employed his Antichrist play, *King Johan,* as anti-Catholic polemic. His *God's Promises* (1577), an interesting reworking of the earlier prophet plays, concerns itself with promises to the individual believer rather than the fulfillment of salvation history in Christ. Among a smaller number of surviving Elizabethan plays on biblical subjects are *Susanna* (1578) by Thomas Carter, *Absalon* by Thomas Watson, *David and Bathsabe* (1594) by George Peele, and *Herod and Antipater* (1622) by Markham and Sampson. After this period, until Milton, biblical influence tends to be less direct yet, as J. H. Sims (*Dramatic Uses of Biblical Allusions in Marlowe and Shakespeare* [1966]) shows, entirely pervasive.

In the late sixteenth and seventeenth centuries, the English sermon was a high art form, and some of the finest examples of biblically influenced prose from this period come from the pens of Lancelot Andrewes, Richard Baxter, Isaac Barrow, the authorized homilists of the Church of England, and from poet-preachers such as John Donne (1572–1631) and George Herbert (1593–1633). The lyric poetry of the latter is replete with biblical imagery and subject, as is Henry Vaughan's postconversion *Silex Scintillans* (1655). Also, the characteristically apologetic use of the Bible in this period led to its use in political writings too numerous to contemplate here, including those of major figures such as Parker, Baxter, and Harrington. Even Hobbes's *Leviathan* (1651) is rich in biblical quotation and allusion. In no period of English literary history is literary language in every subject and genre so thoroughly indebted to the Bible; from autobiographies like the magnificent *Religio Medici* (1642) of Thomas Browne to praises of science and progress like Abraham Cowley's poem *To the Royal Society* (1677), or Francis Bacon's essay *New At-*

lantis (1627), to Isaac Walton's biography of John Donne, the images, words, and accents of the English Bible echo on nearly every page of English literature.

Enlightenment. After the dismal failure of the Puritan Commonwealth under Oliver Cromwell and the Restoration under Charles II (1660) of Anglican church-state government, there was a marked turning away from anything that resembled piety in public life and the arts. Accordingly, biblical influence upon an increasingly secular literature suffered a sharp demise; while still felt at the level of language and allusion, biblical subject matter and titles almost entirely disappear, or else, in a case like Dryden's satiric political allegory, *Absalom and Achitophel* (1681), the reference of the allegory is curiously reversed: biblical story becomes a diaphanous screen for contemporary political miscreance. The notable counterpoint in this period is John Bunyan (1628–1688), whose prison writings were directed not to fashionable taste but to persons as humble as their author, whose literacy lay almost exclusively in knowledge of the Bible. Here again the device was allegory but, after *Grace Abounding to the Chief of Sinners* (1666), characterized by moral psychomachia rooted in a pattern of familiar biblical *typology. The Pilgrim's Progress* (1678; 1684), *The Life and Death of Mr. Badman* (1680), and *The Holy War* (1682), though enduring classics, stand apart from rather than represent the pattern of biblical influence on English literature going into the eighteenth century, in that they are undisguisedly a species of evangelical tract. An allied literary form favored by the Puritans, spiritual autobiography, was to receive its best-known popular adaptation in Daniel Defoe's *Robinson Crusoe* (1719), a progenitor of the modern novel, in which the protagonist's experience is a progress from original sin and alienation through exile, wandering, and providential intervention to a discovery and reading of the Bible, which then interprets life retrospectively, bringing about repentance, conversion, and rescue.

Further erosion of biblical influence on the mainstream of English literature was occasioned not only by increasing political isolation of the Puritans, with whom it had now become so closely associated, but by the rise of religious skepticism and critical attack on the scientific reliability of the biblical texts themselves. Thus, the skeptical modernism that began as a trickle in works such as Lord Herbert of Cherbury's protodeist *De Veritate* (1623), when coupled with biblical criticism such as Richard Simon's *Critical History of the Old Testament* (translated in 1682) and the philosophical writings of John Locke, was to grow into a flood of challenges to the authority and relevance of the Bible in writers of major influence, such as Shaftesbury, Bolingbroke, and, later, David Hume and Edward Gibbon. Gibbon's *Decline and Fall of the Roman Empire* (1776–1788) celebrates the reinstitution of Roman as opposed to biblical models and values, and English evolution in literature from an era dominated by Christian and biblical influences to one in which they become marginal, from the Puritan to the "Augustan" age. Oliver Goldsmith, who coined the latter term in one of his essays (1759), reflects nostalgically on the fading of core biblical values from contemporary social and literary life in his *Vicar of Wakefield* (1764); his own oratorio on the *Exodus narrative was not published in his lifetime. As in Jonathan Swift's *Tale of a Tub* (1704) and *Argument against Abolishing Christianity* (1711) or the urbane criticism of Alexander Pope's quasi-deistic *Essay on Man* (1731–1735), the residual influence is institutional Chris-

tianity rather than biblical narrative or language. Throughout the period a scattering of poems inspired by progress in science employ biblical paraphrases, often in an attempt to show the correspondence of Newton and scripture, and William Broome's *A Paraphrase of Parts of Job* (ca. 1720) makes the author of Job, in turn, sound like a lecturer to the Royal Society.

Within the Established Church there was a continuing tradition of biblical verse both narrative and lyric, and though much less distinguished than their predecessors, poet-priests like the nonjuror Bishop Thomas Ken (1637–1711), John Norris (1657–1711), and, at a lesser rank, Samuel Wesley the elder, wrote moral, biblically inspired verse. Among influential poets in the biblical tradition, however, Isaac Watts, scion of the dissenting tradition, and Charles Wesley, whose work is a fusion of Puritan and Catholic sensibility, must be counted as of a higher rank. Watts, a favorite of Samuel Johnson, wrote on biblical themes in his *Horae lyricae* (1706), and is remembered for his imitation of the Psalms (1719) as well as numerous celebrated hymns. Charles Wesley, cofounder of Methodism and Watts's only peer as a writer of hymns in this period, also wrote a distinguished biblical poem, *Wrestling Jacob* (1742). In eighteenth-century poetry, however, biblical influence was often accompanied by melancholic self-absorption, as in Edward Young's *Night Thoughts* (1742–1745), Robert Blair's *The Grave* (1743), James Hervey's *Meditations and Contemplations* (1747), Christopher Smart's *Jubilate Agno* and *Song to David* (1763), and, preeminent in this vein, William Cowper's *Task* (1785) and *Olney Hymns* (1779), coauthored with the Reverend John Newton. In none of this later poetry is there much of the formative power of the biblical texts so familiar to the seventeenth century and, like the biblical fictions and poems of Elizabeth Rowe (1737) or even the later ones of the considerably more crisp Hannah More (1745–1833), it pales in comparison with Milton or Herbert. As with Johnson's use of biblical allusion to fortify temperate rationalism in *Rasselas* (1759) or James Thomson's in *Aeolus' Harp* (1748) to universalize sentiment, not only the focus but also the expectation of readers' familiarity with the Bible has significantly faded. Only rarely in the eighteenth century, and that most memorably in the novel, with Henry Fielding's *Joseph Andrews* (1742) and *Tom Jones* (1749), does biblical influence extend to narrative structure, governing paradigms, themes, and substance of the discourse. When this happens, as in the adaptation in *Joseph Andrews* of the Joseph story from Genesis applied with the aid of New Testament pericopes like the parable of the Good Samaritan, the effect is to create a text with two or more levels, in which the livelier intertextual relationships seem not merely to encode a moral but ally the novel with an earlier tradition of biblically underwritten narrative.

Romanticism and the Modern Era. With William Blake (1757–1827), English literature enters an entirely new phase of relationship with the Bible. Blake, in *Songs of Experience* (1794) as well as his *Book of Thel* (1789), *Marriage of Heaven and Hell* (1793), and the revisionist *Milton* (1808), *Jerusalem* (1820), and *The Everlasting Gospel* (1818), created his "own myth," as he put it, to avoid being "enslaved by that of another man." In Blake's reading, authority is transferred from foundational text to the poet of genius, who creates his own "reading," obliterating traditional understanding: the Bible is "rewritten" to suit his myth. (*See also* Art and the Bible.) As Northrop Frye (*The Great Code* [1982]) and others have indicated, Blake becomes in this way a harbinger not only of modernist approaches to the Bible in literature, but also of postmodernism in both literature and criticism. In his reading of Milton's *Paradise Lost,* Satan becomes the real hero. Subsequent romantic poets, such as Byron in *Manfred* (1816) and *Cain* (1821), and Shelley in *Prometheus Unbound* (1820), follow suit. Coleridge, in his "Satanic Hero," reflects on certain consequences.

Within a more conservative biblical tradition was James Hogg, the Scottish shepherd whose *Pilgrims of the Sun* (1815) and *Private Memoirs and Confessions of a Justified Sinner* (1824) afford a glimpse of prevalent tensions between a biblical view of the human condition and the intensely personalistic romantic quest for identity. Walter Scott's novel *Old Mortality* (1816) studies, in language rich with the Scottish covenanters' fluent biblicism, social strife attendant upon strict literal application of the "Calvinist" Bible to politics.

Coleridge was a theologically sophisticated reader of the Bible, as chapter 13 of his *Biographia litteraria* suggests; Wordsworth, as may be seen in "Intimations Ode" and "Westminster Bridge" (1807), comparatively naive. With the second wave of Wesleyan revival in the first part of the nineteenth century, however, and the consolidation of religious values in curriculum and canon in the early years of Queen Victoria's reign, the Bible became both more widely acceptable in literary theme or motif, and much more visible in literary language. Yet R. W. Buchanan's "Ballad of Judas Iscariot" (1863) and Thomas Beddoe's "Old Adam the Crow" (1828), like Browning's *Saul* (1847) or "Death in the Desert," put the Bible to characteristically broad-church purposes. Tennyson's "Rizpah" prefers the Bible to Calvinist interpretations of it, though Tennyson's characteristic reading of the Bible is governed, in fact, by what he called "Higher Pantheism" and other presuppositions similar to Browning's. Browning's analysis of biblical notions of worship in "Epilogue of Dramatis Personae" reveals his interest in German biblical criticism as much as "Abt Volger" does his fascination with Feuerbachian eschatology. In the 1860s a poet like Charles Tennyson might be, as Hoxie Fairchild puts it (in his six-volume *Religious Trends in English Poetry: 1700–1965*), "much less troubled by Darwinism than by the extension of scientific method to biblical criticism and the comparative study of religion."

Some of the more peculiar adaptations of the Bible as literary influence in this period are to be found in the work of minor poets such as the spiritualist F. W. H. Myers's "St. Paul" or the medieval romanticist R. W. Dixon's *Christ's Company* (1861) with its angular and psychological poems on Mary Magdalene, John, and the *Stabat mater* theme. An early harbinger of liberation theology is Arthur O'Shaughnessy, especially in "Christ Will Return" from his *Songs of a Worker* (1881). The evangelical poets of earlier in the period, whose best effort is probably Elizabeth Barrett's tedious *The Seraphim* (1838) and pseudo-Miltonic *A Drama of Exile* (1844), are the only ones to contribute work of substantially biblical theme and subject. Robert Pollok's *The Course of Time* (1827), Robert Montgomery's *Satan* (1830) and *Messiah* (1832), and John Heraud's *Descent into Hell* (1830) and *The Judgement of the Flood* (1834) illustrate a continuing appetite for Miltonic adaptations of the Bible, but also, as does C. J. Wells's *Joseph and His Brethren* (1824), an exhaustion of that taste and talent.

The vital continuance of biblical influence upon English literature at the close of the century is in some ways shown less vividly in the popularity of evidently Christian works such as Francis Thompson's "Hound of Heaven" (1893) or the poems of John Cardinal Newman, Arthur Hugh Clough, and the Rossettis than in the rich mastery of biblical idiom, motif, and allusion by writers notably antagonistic to orthodox religion. Partly this owes to a substantial attempt by Matthew Arnold in his *Literature and Dogma* (1873), *St. Paul and Protestantism* (1890), and *God and the Bible* (1899) to separate the Bible from its association with Puritan or Calvinistic religion and grant it supremely literary value in an English canon. Partly it owes to the training in these orthodox traditions, and their subsequent partial or complete rejection by numerous major authors: George Eliot's *Silas Marner* (1861) and Thomas Hardy's *Jude the Obscure* (1895), like Swinburne's "Hymn to Proserpine," are rich in biblical influence despite explicit aversion to biblical religion, and George MacDonald in *Lilith* (1895) treats Jewish *apocrypha in a New Testament context in such a way as to challenge his Calvinist colleagues with a hypothesis of universal salvation.

A measure of the literary power of the "English" Bible in overcoming religious considerations is the complete dominance of the King James Version from its first publication until well into the twentieth century; even James Joyce, who makes copious use of the Bible, prefers the cadences of this English translation to facilitate his inversions. This remains the pattern through W. B. Yeats ("Adam's Curse," "The Second Coming") and the fiction of D. H. Lawrence; it is visible in Robert Graves's *King Jesus* as well as in works such as Edwin Muir's *One Foot in Eden* (1956) or, more recently, Ted Hughes's *Crow* (1970). Blakean rewriting of biblical narrative had become by World War I perhaps the significant tradition in modern English literature. The type of fiction represented by George A. Moore's *The Brook Kerith* (1916), which interweaves the lives of a Christ who survives the cross with those of Paul and Joseph of Arimathea, has grown abundantly in the twentieth century; examples are too numerous to list and most lack significant literary merit. Differing literary responses to the Bible have made their mark, however, including the poems of Gerard Manley Hopkins and perhaps most notably T. S. Eliot's "Ash Wednesday" (1930), "Journey of the Magi" (1927), and the magisterial *Four Quartets* (1935–1942). The *Anathemata* (1952) of David Jones and R. S. Thomas's *Stones of the Field* (1946), *Pieta* (1966), and *Laboratories of the Spirit* (1975) exemplify a revival of biblical voice in modern British poetry, and may come to be seen as part of a neo-Christian revival of biblical influence. To some extent, the novels of Joyce Carey, notably his second trilogy, *Prisoner of Grace* (1952), *Except the Lord* (1953), and *Not Honour More* (1955), reflect a dissenting tradition, while the fiction of C. S. Lewis, exemplified in his Miltonic retelling of the Eden story, *Perelandra, or Voyage to Venus* (1940), and the plays of Dorothy Sayers, including *The Man Born to Be King* (1943) and *The Zeal of Thy House* (1948), offer explicit representations of biblical narrative. A resonant incorporation of biblical theme, motif, and language is provided by J. R. R. Tolkien's evocation of Nordic saga, *The Lord of the Rings* (1954–1955). Discernably then, the shaping of biblical influence by Miltonic Puritanism, Anglo-Saxon monasticism, Anglican historicism, and Anglo-Catholic sacramentalism, all find continued expression in contemporary literature. Since World War II, however, the influence of the Bible on English literature has been markedly reduced in comparison with its influence on literature being written in America and the Commonwealth (*see the corresponding articles in this entry*). For a detailed tracing of the development of biblical allusion, narrative, and typology from Anglo-Saxon to contemporary English and American literature, as well as extensive annotated bibliography of critical studies on the use of the Bible by English authors, see D. L. Jeffrey, *A Dictionary of Biblical Tradition in English Literature* (1992).   *David Lyle Jeffrey*

British Commonwealth Literature

The influence of the Bible on British Commonwealth literature is complicated by the relatively late development of the British empire. The rise of British control of Australia and New Zealand, India, and substantial parts of Africa, accomplished chiefly in the nineteenth century, coincided with the decline of biblical authority in the West, especially among the educated classes responsible for the production of written literature. Thus, one might expect that Commonwealth literature would owe very little to the Bible; this expectation is often, but not always, fulfilled.

In Australia, for instance, literature is dominated, well into the twentieth century, by the overriding themes of that culture's history: the experiences of the convicts who first colonized Australia and of the bushrangers who soon populated the outback. Many writers understood the Bible to have little relevance to their circumstances—but not all: A. D. Hope (b. 1907), though not a believer, often makes vivid use of biblical themes and imagery (see, for instance, his "Imperial Adam"); James McAuley (1917–1976), an adult convert to Catholicism, attempts to reconstitute in modern terms, though in traditional forms, the devotional verse of Donne and Herbert:

> Since all our keys are lost or broken,
> Shall it be thought absurd
> If for an art of words I turn
> Discreetly to the Word?
> ["An Art of Poetry," II. 1–4]

And the continent's most prominent novelist, Patrick White (b. 1912), is noted for his use of biblical symbolism, for instance in his novel *Voss* (1957), whose title character is gradually revealed as a Christ-figure of significant dimensions.

In Anglophone Indian literature the situation is much more complex, for three dominant reasons. First is cultural independence: the rise of this literature was simultaneous with a powerful renewal of pride among Indian (especially Hindu) intellectuals in their traditional culture, a renewal strongly encouraged by visitors from the West, especially members of the Theosophical movement. Thus, the typical Anglo-Indian novel—for example, by R. K. Narayan (b. 1907)—will use European forms to express traditionally Indian ideas and ideals. Second is familial resemblance. Some Indian literature, such as the poetry of Rabindranath Tagore (1861–1941), may closely resemble certain kinds of biblical literature, especially the poetry exemplified by the Song of Solomon; but direct influence is a less likely explanation for this phenomenon than a shared use of sexual and natural imagery. Last is Hindu syncretism; again Tagore will provide an example. His philosophical-poetic meditations on the one God often sound like a variety of Jewish or Christian mysticism, but monotheism has always been one of Hinduism's many facets. It has never

been consistently emphasized throughout India, but neither has any other facet of Hinduism. That religion's syncretic ability to absorb multifarious influences makes biblical influences upon it extremely difficult to trace or fix.

In African literature, however, the influence of the Bible has been nothing less than enormous. The oral tradition in Africa is exceptionally powerful, and written literature appeared only after the coming of the Europeans. Since those Europeans, especially the British, favored literacy in the natives chiefly for religious purposes—reading the Bible and the prayer book—it should not be surprising that the earliest written literature in Africa served evangelical aims. This age of didactic literature eventually passed, replaced by novels, plays, and poems that stand at the forefront of post–World War II literature; but the influence of the Bible has remained strong in the countries once or still associated with the British Commonwealth. Nigeria's two best-known writers, the novelist Chinua Achebe (b. 1930) and the Nobel Prize–winning playwright Wole Soyinka (b. 1934), are of different tribes, but both were raised as Christians; biblical themes and language echo throughout their work. For instance, Achebe's second novel *No Longer at Ease* presents its protagonist Obi Oknokwo in terms of the prodigal son and of the Magi returning to their kingdoms (as described in T. S. Eliot's poem "Journey of the Magi"); further, it skillfully presents the competing languages of the traditional Ibo proverb-oriented culture and the Christian culture of biblical quotation, sometimes seeing the two in direct conflict but often as witness to the Ibos' ability to synthesize the two. Soyinka repeatedly uses biblical archetypes; he too presents the theme of the prodigal (and the larger biblical theme of two brothers in conflict) in *The Swamp Dwellers,* and writes a profound variation on the Christ-theme of sacrificial, redemptive death in one of his finest plays, *The Strong Breed.*

Likewise, in South Africa we see writers, such as the novelist and autobiographer Peter Abrahams, who claim to have learned their prose style and, what is more important, a vocabulary of justice and injustice, power, and oppression, from the King James Bible; and we also see the prodigal once again, this time fused with elements of the David-Absalom story, in Alan Paton's forthrightly Christian plea for compassion in his land, *Cry, the Beloved Country.* Paton is white, Abrahams what the South African regime called "coloured"; it would appear that for South Africans of whatever color, the Bible provided a complex literary vocabulary with which to confront a harsh and difficult society.

Alan Jacobs

European Literature

The influence of the Bible on continental European literature has been so pervasive as to be almost incalculable. Both as a collection of sacred texts and as the source of the various creeds, codes, and cults of Judaism and Christianity, the Bible is the most essential document in the Western world. To begin with, the spread of Christianity generated a gigantic (and still growing) corpus of liturgies, sermons, pamphlets, prayer books, practical guides, and every conceivable form of theology, which, supplementing and accompanying the Bible, have served as the foundation for Western Christian culture. The bulk of this corpus, as enshrined, for example, in the 383 volumes of Jacques-Paul Migne's (1800–1875) monumental *Patrologiae Cursus Completus,* which collects the writings of the church fathers from the apostolic era to

the early thirteenth century, may be a dead letter except for historians and students of religion, but significant portions have survived and remain noteworthy.

The *Missale Romanum,* for instance, which was organized and edited by the Council of Trent (1545–1563), contains —apart from many biblical texts arranged to fit the cycle of the liturgical year—some memorable poetry (e.g., the powerful symbols and ceremonies of the Easter Vigil, the "sequences," etc.) and many prayers marked by a distinctive spare eloquence. Missals, breviaries, and books of hours have made the Bible (particularly the Gospels and the Psalms) an integral part of the consciousness of both clergy and pious lay people for centuries. The liturgy, like the cathedrals (each a *Biblia pauperum*) that were its supreme setting, and the church *music (from before Palestrina to after Fauré) that expressed it, mediated the Bible to the world at large.

Church Fathers. The Bible obviously played a key role in the work of early Christian authors. In the pre-Nicene period (i.e., up to 325 CE) perhaps only Tertullian (ca. 160–225), moralist, apologist, and fierce controversialist, has retained an important place in the Western literary canon. He is remembered for, among other things, the notorious paradox, "Certum est quia impossibile," and for asking the pregnant question, "Quid ergo Athenis et Ierosolymis?"

Jerome (ca. 342–420) not only produced the first great translation of the Bible, the Vulgate, but some of the most brilliantly rhetorical letters in any language. He is generally considered the supreme stylist of Christian Latinity. In a famous nightmare (Letter XXII) Jerome saw himself being dragged before the judgment seat and asked about his condition. Claiming to be a Christian, he was abruptly contradicted, "You lie. You are a Ciceronian. 'Where your treasure is, there will your heart be also' [Matt. 6.21]." The scene aptly conveys Jerome's ambivalence and guilt (and that of countless Christian intellectuals like him) about his love of classical literature—which persisted, despite this warning from on high.

Although, like Tertullian, he was born in North Africa, Augustine (354–430) spent his crucial formative years (384–390) in Italy; and, like Tertullian's, his works became European classics. He is naturally best remembered for his *Confessions* and for his great rambling encyclopedic philosophy of history, *The City of God*. Augustine is the direct progenitor of countless spiritual autobiographies, from Teresa of Avila's *Libro de su vida* (1587) to Leo Tolstoy's *A Confession* (completed in 1882) and, through Jean-Jacques Rousseau (1712–1778), of modern autobiography. Beyond this, the teachings in Augustine's huge oeuvre of ninety-three works reverberated long and fatefully in Western intellectual history—to choose but one example, in the seventeenth-century Jansenist controversy, which in turn spawned such diverse masterpieces as Pascal's *Provincial Letters* (1656 and after) and Sainte-Beuve's magisterial history of *Port-Royal* (1840–1859).

Marian Literature. One of the most remarkable offshoots of the New Testament was the cult of Mary. After modest beginnings in early Christianity it made enormous advances once Mary was defined by the Council of Ephesus (431) as "God-bearer" (Grk. *theotokos*). By the twelfth century Bernard of Clairvaux (1090–1153) could exclaim, "De Maria numquam satis," and medieval Christian writers seem to have taken this maxim to heart. There is an enormous and varied body of Marian literature, with fa-

mous tributes from writers from all over the Christian world, from Aimar, bishop of Le Puy (ca. 1087), author of the great hymn "Salve, regina," to Dante (d. 1321), who has Bernard address Mary as, "Vergine madre, figlia di tuo figlio," in the final canto of the *Paradiso*. And the tradition was continued by many later writers, in works as diverse as Cardinal Duperron's (1556–1618) "Cantique de la Vierge Marie," Anatole France's (1884–1924) *Le Jongleur de Notre-Dame,* and Rainer Maria Rilke's (1875–1926) *Das Marien-Leben.*

Hymnic Poetry. On a much smaller scale than the patristic writings there is a venerable tradition of hymnology and religious poetry in Latin, from Ambrose's (339–397) "Aeterne rerum conditor" to Thomas Aquinas's (1225–1274) "Lauda Sion" and "Pange, lingua, gloriosi." Other names worth recalling here include Caelius Sedulius (fl. ca. 450), Columba (521–597), Venantius Fortunatus (ca. 530–610), Peter Damian (1007–1072), Bernard of Cluny (fl. 1140), Adam of St. Victor (fl. 1140), Peter Abelard (1079–1142), Philip the Chancellor (d. 1236), and Thomas of Celano (ca. 1190–1260), author of the immortal "Dies irae," which borrows from Matthew 25:31–46 and other New Testament texts to create a haunting vision of the *day of judgment. There were also many fine anonymous poets, authors of such familiar pieces as "Ave maris stella," "Veni creator spiritus," "Alma redemptoris mater," "Stabat mater," and "Dulcis Iesu memoria." This poetry is simple, direct, and unassuming. Consider the Easter sequence by Wipo (d. ca. 1050), who was chaplain to two Holy Roman Emperors: "Victimae paschali laudes / immolent Christiani. / Agnus redemit oves: / Christus innocens Patri / reconciliavit peccatores. / Mors et vita duello / conflixere mirando: / dux vitae mortuus / regnat vivus," etc. While not true folk art, many of these hymns, heard continually in church services and learned by heart, became an integral part of popular European culture. Some, notably the "Dies irae," which was integrated into the Mass for the Dead, were set to music by composers such as Mozart and Verdi; the Gregorian chant "Dies irae" resounds menacingly in Berlioz's *Symphonie Fantastique.* These Latin hymns also introduced the use of rhyme, which was then adopted by writers of vernacular verse.

Religious Orders. Another vital element of European literature (in the broad sense) inspired by the Bible was the unique genre of the "rule" for monastic or religious orders, such as Benedict of Nursia's (d. ca. 543) *Regula Monachorum,* and its many successors, including the rules of the Franciscans, Dominicans, and Jesuits, along with Ignatius Loyola's (1491–1556) extremely influential *Spiritual Exercises,* with its numerous echoes in later literature, such as James Joyce's *Portrait of the Artist as a Young Man* (1914–1915). This sort of Christian "torah"—with its distinctly utopian cast—was not merely, or even primarily, reading material, though many generations of religious read them over and over again, down through the centuries. They were the constitutions and codes of communities that attempted, despite repeated and inevitable failures (as lampooned, e.g., in Robert Browning's hilarious "Soliloquy of the Spanish Cloister"), to rebuild Jerusalem in the various "green and pleasant lands" of Europe.

Among the founders of religious orders Francis of Assisi (1181–1226) holds a unique literary position. The author of various important works, he is best known for the "Canticle of the Sun" (a sublime variation on Ps. 148 and similar texts), which Ernest Hatch Wilkins called "the first noble composition in an Italian dialect." Francis's idiosyncratic, stunningly literal attempt to live the "evangelical counsels" made him a dubious administrator, but his poetic celebration of "Lady Poverty" (combining the *Sermon on the Mount with courtly love) and his notion of friars as God's minstrels have fired the imagination of countless writers and readers. The *Fioretti,* an anonymous fourteenth-century collection of Franciscan legends (e.g., how Francis tamed the man-eating wolf of Gubbio), is perhaps the most colorful and charming volume of Western hagiography.

Medieval Literature. With the rise of the vernacular languages the influence of the Bible was extended through the medieval mystery (or miracle) plays, which began as severely restrained liturgical dramas on the life of Christ and the Virgin Mary, written by clerics and performed in the churches in Latin. They later moved outdoors, shedding both their Latin and their restraint. In the twelfth century, to cite just one example, the *Jeu d'Adam* dramatized the *Fall, Cain's fratricide, and the supposed biblical prophecies about Jesus. In the later morality plays (fifteenth century), allegorical figures representing Virtue and Vice struggled for the human soul, sometimes accompanied by crowd-pleasing horseplay. While this primitive theater is little read today (continental literature has nothing to rival the delightful Wakefield *Second Shepherds' Play,* ca. 1400–1450), it served as a bridge to the splendid flowering of drama in the Renaissance.

Religion of a crude chauvinistic sort played a major role in the *chansons de geste,* with their bellicose bishops and cast-iron conviction, as in *The Song of Roland* (early twelfth century), that

"Paiien ont tort et chrestiens ont dreit." In *The Poem of the Cid* (ca. 1140), the Cid addresses his Castilian vassals: "I pray to God, to our spiritual Father / That you who for my sake have left your homes and lands / May, before I die, get some good of me / That you may regain double what you have lost." On the enemy side, "The King of Morocco is distressed at my Cid Don Rodrigo: / 'He has violated my territories / And gives thanks to no one, except Jesus Christ.'"

In the immense corpus of medieval chivalric literature, religion—that is, mystical Christianity—played a large role, especially in the Arthurian cycle. The quest for the Holy Grail (the cup in which Joseph of Arimathea supposedly received the blood from Christ's side), which was told in the legend of Parsifal both by Chrétien de Troyes (latter half of twelfth century) and Wolfram von Eschenbach (d. ca. 1220), is one of the most famous chivalric tales. For many years Wagner's *Parsifal* (1882) was regularly performed on Good Friday. But the heart of chivalry was full of war, lust, and self-aggrandizement—Tristan and Iseult's irreproachable piety is helpless to check their adulterous desire—and hence alien to Christian ideals. This point was irrefutably made by no less a critic than Sancho Panza, who told Don Quixote (Part II, Chap. viii): "And so, my lord, it's better to be a humble little friar, of any order whatever, than a valiant and wandering knight; God gives more credit for two dozen blows with a lash than for two thousand thrusts with a lance—be they at giants, monsters, or dragons." Don Quixote feebly responds that there are many paths to heavenly glory, but Sancho has dogma on his side.

Mystical Writings. Much more directly inspired by the Bible was the richly varied medieval mystical tradition. Some of its crucial figures include Bernard of Clairvaux, Francis of Assisi, Bonaventure (ca. 1217–1274), and the Germans Hildegard of Bingen (1098–1179), Meister Eckhart (ca. 1260–1327), and Nicholas of Cusa (1401–1464). Germany undoubtedly had the most highly developed schools of mysticism, but the later Spanish Carmelites Teresa of Avila (1515–1582) and John of the Cross (1542–1591) reached a wider audience and have a more distinguished place in the literary canon. Teresa's mystical writings include *The Path of Perfection* and *The Interior Castle*. John is best known today for three of his poems, "Dark Night of the Soul," a phrase now naturalized in English; "The Spiritual Canticle," based on the Song of Solomon; and "Flame of Living Love," which, like the previous two, borrows the vocabulary of sexual passion to describe the soul's encounter with God. An Augustinian contemporary of John, Luis de León (1527–1591), was perhaps an even greater poet, and like him found particular inspiration in the Song of Solomon. For translating that book from the Hebrew (and his "judaizing" tendencies) he was imprisoned for almost five years, during which time he wrote a prose masterpiece, *Los Nombres de Cristo*, a Platonic dialogue on the meaning of such titles ascribed to Christ as "Prince of Peace" and "Son of God." Fray Luis also wrote a powerful *Exposition on the Book of Job*. Mystical literature is vast and of considerable importance in the later development of individualism, religious and otherwise. But most of it belongs more properly in the realm of theology or, in some cases, philosophy.

Dante. The supreme literary work of the late Middle Ages–early Renaissance is Dante's *Divine Comedy* (finished some time before 1321), which is literally in a class by itself. Dante's poem draws upon science, philosophy, and history, as well as theology, but it is supremely indebted to the Bible. Dante works leading figures from the Bible into his vast tapestry. For example, he shows us Judas locked in the jaws of Satan at the frozen bottom of *hell; in the *Purgatorio* he evokes the scene of Michal scorning David's dance before the *ark; and he populates his *Paradiso* with all sorts of biblical figures, from Adam and Eve to Rachel, Rebekah, and Rahab. But the work as a whole is dogged by the devil's disconcerting way of having all the good tunes: just as Satan is, despite everything, the most interesting and eloquent character in *Paradise Lost*, so Dante's *Inferno* is superior to the other two *cantiche* in dramatic power. And Dante's grandest moments come when he has the damned (e.g., Francesca da Rimini, Farinata, Ulysses, and Ugolino) tell their tragic stories—with a greatness of soul not lessened by the fact that they stand under God's eternal condemnation.

Thomas à Kempis. The late Middle Ages also witnessed the appearance of what has been perhaps the most popular of all books inspired by the Bible, the *Imitation of Christ*, written in Latin and commonly attributed to Thomas Hammerken (ca. 1380–1471), a German Augustinian monk known to history as Thomas à Kempis. Kempis was profoundly influenced by the years (1392–1397) he spent with the Brothers of the Common Life, a community of pious laymen in Deventer, near Utrecht. In a simple, pellucid style, interwoven with quotations from the New Testament, the *Imitation* champions an intensely personal love of Jesus (culminating in a quasi-erotic mystical union) that focuses on the Eucharist. The book urges its readers to seek imitation in literal adhesion to the Gospels, particularly stressing humility, self-denial, rejection of the "world," and constant prayer. Kempis's highly individ-

ualistic version of Christianity, which no doubt reflects his own retiring nature (see his famous dictum, "Cella continuata dulcescit"), seems to be oblivious of social justice and the outside world in general; and this has contributed to its current status as an unread, or seldom read, classic. Devotional literature since Kempis has been a fantastically prolific but mostly undistinguished genre. One exception to this rule is the *Introduction to the Devout Life* by Francis de Sales (1567–1622), an agreeably written and more accommodating handbook of Christian piety for the layperson.

Reformation Literature. During the Middle Ages direct access to the Bible was limited to those who knew Latin. With the coming of the Reformation and the discovery of the *printing press, this would change forever. The act of reading one's own copy of the Bible and shaping one's own interpretation of it would eventually become a kind of sacramental symbol of intellectual freedom. In Germany Martin Luther's (1483–1546) *translation of the Bible, drawing on the chancery style of Saxony, which laid the groundwork for modern High German, was of unparalleled importance. It is partly thanks to Luther that Germany has been and still is the most biblically literate country in the world. His vigorous, earthy, impetuous prose style, in his pamphlets and controversial works, along with his fine hymns ("Ein' feste Burg," "Vom Himmel hoch," etc.) earned him a large niche in German cultural history. At the same time, the power of his pen gave broad currency to his vitriolic *anti-Semitism (as in his pamphlet *On the Jews and Their Lies*).

The more irenic Desiderius Erasmus (ca. 1469–1536), a peripatetic Dutch Augustinian, published a Greek New Testament with a Latin translation that, while beneath modern standards, helped to focus scholarly attention on the original. His wonderful *Praise of Folly* (1516) is a satirical hodgepodge, ultimately inspired by 1 Corinthians 1.18–25. And John Calvin's (1509–1564) *Institutes of the Christian Religion* (1536, first written in Latin) is a radical Protestant reading of the Bible, an assault on Catholicism, and a powerful piece of French prose. Partly as the result of Calvin's influence, French Protestant writers, even such a black sheep as André Gide (1869–1951), have been better versed in the Bible than their Catholic or unbelieving counterparts. And the Calvinistic practice of relentless, lonely self-scrutiny bore autobiographical and biographical fruit in later centuries. It is no accident that both Jean-Jacques Rousseau and James Boswell (1740–1795) were raised in the Calvinist fortresses of Geneva and Edinburgh.

The Seventeenth Century. The seventeenth century saw the last great age of biblically based religious literature. The tradition of religious theater survived in the seventeenth century in Spain, with Calderón (1600–1681) and his *autos sacramentales*, and France, with such masterpieces as Corneille's (1606–1684) *Polyeucte* (1641), and Racine's (1639–1699) *Esther* (1689) and *Athalie* (1691). The latter, with its exquisite formal artifice and courtly grandeur ("O divine, ô charmante loi! / O justice! ô bonté suprême! / Que de raisons, quelle douceur extrême / D'engager à ce Dieu son amour et sa foi!"), seems far removed from the Bible; but Racine handles his sources in 2 Kings and 2 Chronicles with intelligence and discretion. In the seventeenth and eighteenth centuries the Jesuits wrote and staged learned, edifying Latin plays on biblical themes all over Europe. Perhaps the last surviving specimens of popular Christian drama are the Passion Play of Oberammergau (which

is based in part on a sixteenth-century model and has now been sanitized of its worst anti-Semitic features) and Hugo von Hofmannsthal's *Jedermann* (1911), an effective reworking of the great fifteenth-century Dutch morality play of the same name *(Elckerlijk)*.

The seventeenth century was also a great age of pulpit oratory. Jacques Bénigne Bossuet (1627–1704) is still remembered for his solemn sermons delivered at the funerals of the aristocracy, full of resonant maxims on the passing of worldly glory ("Tout ce qui se mesure finit, et tout ce qui est né pour finir n'est pas tout à fait sorti du néant, où il est sitôt replongé"). Bossuet retired just about the time that the Jesuit preacher Louis Bourdaloue (1632–1704) was coming into vogue. Bourdaloue may have been the better reasoner and rhetorician, but posterity (although not Voltaire) gave the palm to Bossuet. In Portugal (and later in Brazil and Rome) a still more gifted Jesuit, António Vieira (1608–1697) wrote clear, vivid, sharply reasoned sermons that rank with the finest specimens of Portuguese prose.

The age also saw at least two great, if uneven, Protestant poets. Andreas Gryphius (1616–1664) lamented the horrors of the Thirty Years War and gave moving expression to his stalwart, deeply humanistic Lutheran piety. In *Les Tragiques*, a bitterly satirical epic, Agrippa d'Aubigné (1551–1630) anticipated the Last Judgment, as he championed the long-suffering Huguenots and chastised evil Catholic rulers, especially Catherine de Médicis, who launched the St. Bartholomew's Day massacre in 1572.

Pascal's *Pensées*, one of the most brilliant instances of the French talent for treating serious philosophical questions on a level accessible to the layperson, are an undeniable masterpiece, even though its proof-text treatment of scripture is its least impressive part. Pascal argued that without the apparently irrational Pauline doctrine of original sin there is no way to understand the mysteries of human nature. Pascal's most memorable device is his dramatized figure of the *libertin*— a seventeenth-century descendant of the ungodly gentiles savaged by Paul in Romans 1:18–32—desperately fleeing thoughts of death in "diversion" and terrified by "the eternal silence of those infinite spaces." Pascal is still read enthusiastically by believers and unbelievers alike, but the fact that the fideistic and pessimistic *Pensées* were a rear-guard action against an increasingly triumphant secularism did not bode well for the philosophical future of Christianity.

The Enlightenment. After more than a century of exhausting religious wars, the Enlightenment brought the first large-scale rejection of the Bible and biblical religion, along with numerous apologetic counterattacks. This had the inevitable if paradoxical effect that the *philosophes* spent a great deal of time discussing Holy Writ. Voltaire (1694–1778), a rebellious product of the Jesuit Collège Louis le Grand, devoted much of his prodigious energy to mocking "l'infâme" (well defined by George Saintsbury as "privileged and persecuting orthodoxy") and everything connected with it. *Candide* (1759) pronounces all biblical theodicy bankrupt. In one of his gentler pieces, *Ingenuous* (1767), he taunts contemporary Christians for their deviations from apostolic practice. More benign critics such as Rousseau, in his "Profession of Faith of a Savoyard Vicar" in *Émile* (1762), tried to rationalize and demythologize the God of the Bible.

In one of the greatest Enlightenment texts, *Foundations of the Metaphysics of Morals,* Immanuel Kant (1724–1804) claimed to reject all external moral authority (such as churches and scriptures)

in favor of a "categorical imperative" that supposedly applied to all rational beings on earth (or anywhere else), but this "universal" ethics had deep and obvious roots in the German Pietism Kant knew from his youth and in the age-old Christian tradition of self-denial.

Even as Kant was condemning all fixed theological statements as "heteronomous," his almost exact contemporary, Friedrich Gottlieb Klopstock (1724–1803) was attempting, in a grandly anachronistic (twenty cantos in hexameter) orthodox epic, *Der Messias,* to do for Germany what Milton had done for England. Drawing mainly from the New Testament, *Paradise Lost,* and the topoi of classical and Renaissance epics, the poem recounts the passion, death, resurrection, and enthronement of Jesus at the right hand of the Father. But traditional epic and biblical narrative (as Erich Auerbach showed in *Mimesis*) are scarcely compatible, and in any case Klopstock was essentially a lyricist; and so *Der Messias,* except for the first three cantos, is generally acknowledged to be a well-intentioned failure.

Jewish Writers. The eighteenth century witnessed the Haskalah, the Jewish Enlightenment, which eventually brought millions of European Jews into the mainstream of European culture. It also led to a painful state of deracination that can be observed in two of the greatest modern Jewish writers, Heinrich Heine (1797–1856) and Franz Kafka (1883–1924). Heine cynically accepted baptism, but never found a satisfactory home in Judaism, Christianity, or unbelief. His scintillating, relentlessly ironic prose records the contradiction of his love for the gods of Greece and his sometimes begrudging attachment to his Jewish roots. In his *Confessions* (1854) he explains, "In my earlier days I hadn't felt any special love for Moses, possibly because I was under the sway of the Hellenic spirit, and I couldn't forgive the Lawgiver of the Jews his hatred for image-making and the plastic arts. I failed to see that . . . he himself was nevertheless a great artist, with the true artistic spirit. Only he, like his Egyptian compatriots, turned his artistic genius exclusively toward the realm of the colossal and the indestructible." Self-exiled in Paris for a quarter-century, Heine summed up his impossible position in his oft-quoted deathbed words, "Dieu me pardonnera: c'est son métier."

Kafka, who has been hailed by some critics as the twentieth-century novelist par excellence, had a love-hate relation with Judaism characteristic of his assimilated contemporaries in Austro-Hungary. Although his work seems to be marked by a blank, uncanny lack of any frame of reference, some pieces, such as his fragment "Before the Law" (later integrated into *The Trial*) evoke explicitly, as his other stories and novels do implicitly, a haunted, absurd, Job-like demand for justice. Elsewhere in *The Trial*, Joseph K., searching for the "law books" studied by his mysterious accusers (and later executioners) can find only clumsy pornography. To the extent that Kafka's dark parables refer to the Bible ("In the Penal Colony" speaks of the old and new "Commandant," sacred but unintelligible "scripts," an impossible commandment to "BE JUST!" etc.), the tone is consistently hostile. But while he was free to carp and complain—in eerily reasonable prose—about the failure of his world to resemble the Bible's, this "religious humorist," as Thomas Mann called him, was never free to leave the subject alone.

For Marcel Proust (1871–1922), whose mother was Jewish and who strongly identified with her, religion was only a source of aesthetic sensations—and guilt. Still, *Remembrance of Things Past* (1913–1928) has many biblical echoes, most obviously and painfully in its longest single section, *Sodome et Gomorrhe,* where Proust projects his own horror of "inversion" onto the doomed inhabitants of *The Cities of the Plain* (as the original three volumes are called in the Montcrieff translation; see Gen. 19.29). The famous scene of the madeleine cookie and the lime tea in *Swann's Way* is a nostalgic transformation of both the *Passover seder and the Eucharist: an attempt to redeem lost time (and create "sacred history," in the absence of God and revelation) through art.

For Isaac Bashevis Singer (1904–1991), the son of a Polish rabbi, biblical faith, as preserved and embodied in the *shtetl,* is unspeakably precious (especially in the horrific light of the *Holocaust), but salvation is, at best, a leap in the dark. Singer's Gimpel the fool is a model absurdist, believing for belief's sake. One of Singer's many devout atheists, Rabbi Nechemia in "Something Is There," inevitably quotes Ecclesiastes 3:19 to himself, "For the fate of the sons of men and the fate of beasts is the same; as one dies, so dies the other"—before its terrible truth breaks his heart.

Romanticism. The Romantic movement, with its validation of the primitive, the irrational, and the noumenal, often took a positive view of biblical religion. In Italy *Saul* (very freely adapted from 1 Samuel) by Vittorio Alfieri (1749–1803) may well be the finest modern poetic treatment of any biblical figure. Alfieri's pure, severe style proved a splendid match for his subject. Alessandro Manzoni's *I promessi sposi* (1825–1826) deserves mention because, although perhaps marginally "biblical" (it recounts the successful struggle of a pious Catholic couple in early seventeenth-century Lombardy to get married despite the formidable obstacles placed in their way by a villainous aristocrat and a spineless parish priest), the grandness of its conception and the richness of its execution have led to its being ranked as the greatest Italian novel.

In the early Romantic period Germany had two outstanding poets who grappled with the conflict between the Bible and secular culture (in various guises). Friedrich Hölderlin (1770–1843) is remembered for his impassioned evocation of the gods of Greece. But in his last creative years (he went incurably insane in 1806) Hölderlin wrote enigmatic hymns to an agonizing Christ ("For suffering colors the purity of this man who is as pure as a sword"), the last of the gods, joining them in a hopeful, heretical synthesis against a cruel God the Father.

In *Christendom or Europe,* Novalis (Friedrich von Hardenberg, 1772–1801) conjured up a "new golden age with dark infinite eyes, a prophetic, wonder-working and wound-healing comforting time that sparks eternal life—a great time of reconciliation." This was not meant to be a reactionary restoration of medieval Catholicism, but a kind of sacred dream come true. Novalis also had a vision of the individual as the locus of literally divine possibilities. "The history of each person," he wrote, "should be a Bible—aims to be a Bible."

In his *Essay on Criticism* (1711) Alexander Pope mocked people who "to church repair, / Not for the doctrine, but the music there." This stricture would apply to the many Romantics who loved the Bible primarily for its symbols. A crucial instance of this is Goethe's (1749–1832) *Faust* (1808, 1832). The "Prologue in Heaven," which frames the entire narrative, is freely adapted from the book of Job. But "der Herr" is less the Lord than the embodiment of cosmic optimism and paternal benevolence, and Mephistopheles

is emphatically not the New Testament Satan. He represents instead a destructive, cynical antihumanism. Similarly, Goethe borrows from both the Virgin Mary and Mary Magdalene to create Gretchen. The "Eternal Feminine" that draws Faust upward is a universal Madonna. T. S. Eliot claimed that bad poets borrow but good poets steal; and Goethe shows no compunction about ransacking the Bible for whatever he needed. In any case, nineteenth-century literature is full of Madonna-substitutes, like Solveig in Ibsen's *Peer Gynt* (1867), and Magdalene figures, such as Sonya in Dostoyevsky's *Crime and Punishment* (1866).

Similarly, other Romantic writers could be classified as in one sense or other "religious"; but upon closer inspection the role of the Bible in their work often proves to be secondary. François René de Chateaubriand (1768–1848) was a Romantic apologist for Christianity, who celebrated its aesthetic appeal in an erstwhile classic, *The Genius of Christianity, or The Poetic and Moral Beauties of the Christian Religion* (1802). In this fervent miscellany Chateaubriand extols the Bible for its "sublimity," but his two most famous works that originally formed part of the book, *Atala* and *René,* show him on more congenial ground, describing the sexual torment, guilt, and despair, in awesomely beautiful natural settings, of young Catholic characters who are projections of himself.

Kierkegaard. One of the greatest nineteenth-century religious writers is Søren Kierkegaard (1813–1855), whose work is without parallel. Although essentially a philosopher-theologian, Kierkegaard's style—passionate, prodigiously energetic, dramatic, and often ironic—qualifies him as a literary figure. A sort of Danish Don Quixote, Kierkegaard's reading of the Bible "turned his head" (cf. his famous "teleological suspension of the ethical" interpretation of the binding of Isaac in Gen. 22; *see also* Aqedah), and impelled him to spend his short life campaigning against the deformation of Christianity into Christendom, and proclaiming the "contemporaneousness" of the Gospels. But as with Pascal before him and Dostoyevsky after, the secular reader may wonder why Kierkegaard's eloquence is so often fired by anxiety and doubt.

Flaubert. In an entirely different sense Gustave Flaubert (1821–1880) found frequent inspiration in the Bible. Religion for Flaubert may be an exploded illusion, but its vivid mythology is immeasurably superior to the desiccation and meanness of contemporary life. *Madame Bovary* (1857), who has been bitterly disillusioned by her banal, soulless lovers, gives the most passionate kiss of her life to the crucifix proffered to her as she dies. In Flaubert's final masterpiece, *Three Tales* (1877), the failure of biblical religion is still an open wound. The ironically named Félicité in "A Simple Heart" is a self-immolating (and totally ignorant) believer. Enslaved by her employer, mistreated or abandoned by almost everyone in a nominally Christian society, she dies during a senile fantasy of her stuffed pet parrot as the Holy Ghost. "The Legend of St. Julian the Hospitaller" retells the mysterious, harrowing life of a sort of Christian Oedipus, but the concluding lines dismiss the story as a stained-glass fairy tale. Worst of all, in "Herodias," a skillful fictionalization of the beheading of John the Baptist, Flaubert curses all parties—Jews, Romans, Pharisees, Sadducees, Essenes, and proto-Christians—as bigoted, brutal, and deluded.

Russian Writers. Nineteenth-century Russia produced two great instances of literature shaped by the Bible: the work of the tortured believer Fyodor Dostoyevsky (1821–1881) and of the aristocratic convert to evangelical simplicity, Leo Tolstoy (1828–1910). Orthodox critics have praised Dostoyevsky's "Christ-figures," such as Prince Leo Myshkin from *The Idiot* (1868–1869) and the former monk Alyosha Karamazov (1880), but the voice of his naysayers, such as the Underground Man (1864) or the antitheist Ivan Karamazov strikes most readers as far more compelling. Ivan, to be sure, is as God-haunted as any Dostoyevskyan character, and in his prose poem, "The Grand Inquisitor," he imagines Jesus returning to sixteenth-century Spain. Yet though he kisses the Grand Inquisitor (who wants to protect his infantilized, anesthetized, but beloved flock from the dangers of Christian freedom), Dostoyevsky's Christ has literally nothing to say.

Tolstoy's peculiar brand of deism, discarding most of Christian dogma but borrowing freely from the New Testament, preaching nonresistance to evil and exalting Christ-like self-donation to others, won followers around the world, but he suffers from the archetypal liberal Christian problem of deriving the inspiration and motivating energy of his work from a source in which he himself no longer believes. In two of his best stories, "The Death of Ivan Ilych" (1886) and "Master and Man" (1895), Tolstoy creates blindly materialistic protagonists who transcend their bourgeois egoism on the point of death by imitating their altruistic servants. Tolstoy's acid depiction of the lives of Ivan Ilych Golovin and Vasili Andreevich Brekhunov has an angry prophetic power, but the vague redemption they achieve (in lieu of death Ivan Ilych finds a mysterious "light," and an unnamed "Someone" comes to visit Brekhunov) seems like a biblical deus ex machina.

Doubters and Atheists. Then there is the unique and paradoxical case of the "antitheists," the greatest of whom is

Friedrich Nietzsche (1844–1900). Like Kierkegaard, Nietzsche has secured a place in the literary canon thanks to his unique brand of philosophizing—"with a hammer," as he put it. While grimly declaring that "God is dead," and brutally insisting that the slave morality of Jews and Christians has to give way to the master morality of "the blond beast," Nietzsche, who was the son of a Lutheran pastor, produced an epochal body of work that weirdly mirrors the Bible. His aphorisms have the alternately angry, exultant, or scornful ring of the prophets. His superman is a secular messiah. His doctrine of eternal recurrence is a fantastic substitute for an eternal afterlife. And Nietzsche's life had both the suicidal courage of the Christian martyr as well as the fierce self-denial and misogynistic celibacy of a Christian hermit.

Miguel de Unamuno (1864–1936) is a paradoxical heir of Pascal, Kierkegaard, and Nietzsche, who turns doubt into a category of religious experience, an ex-believer who cannot stop wrestling with the Bible. Early on in *The Agony of Christianity* (1924) he writes, "Agony, then, is struggle. And Christ came to bring us agony, struggle, and not peace. He told us as much. 'Do not think that I have come to bring peace on earth' [Matt. 10.34]." And he concludes, "Christ, our Christ! Why hast thou forsaken us?" In *Saint Manuel the Good* (1931) Unamuno describes an utterly devoted but unbelieving priest whose honesty forces him to keep silent as his congregation recites the Creed but who is (almost) buoyed up and borne ahead by the wave of their faith.

A number of other twentieth-century atheistic writers, such as Jean-Paul Sartre (1905–1980), Albert Camus (1913–1960), and the practitioners of the "Theatre of the Absurd" (e.g., Luigi Pirandello, Eugène Ionesco, Samuel Beckett),

can be seen as conducting a lifelong argument with the biblical version of the world, shaking their fists at an empty heaven. The "nausea" experienced by Sartre's autobiographical hero, Antoine Roquentin (1938), is a kind of metaphysical malaise caused by the fact that "every thing in existence is born without reason, prolongs itself out of weakness, and dies by accident." Although Roquentin, like Proust, decides to seek relief from a godless universe in art, he nevertheless defines himself by what he rejects: the idea of *creation.

Beckett's play *Waiting for Godot* (1952) is full of futile nostalgia for the world of the Bible. Vladimir wonders why only one of the evangelists tells the story of the good thief, and he can't remember a verse from Proverbs: "Hope deferred maketh the something sick." Although Beckett himself defined Godot as whatever one hopes for, he is clearly a tragicomically incompetent/nonexistent biblical God with an unreliable and very nervous young boy as his angel. Like Kafka, Beckett plays endless variations on the theme of being condemned to hope. But while for Kafka hope is a sort of cruel and crazy mitzvah, for Beckett it is an incurable tic douleureux from which all humans suffer.

Nikos Kazantzakis (1885–1957) is a different and unusual case. At times resembling an incoherent Unamuno, Kazantzakis was a nihilist whose obsession with Christianity knew no bounds (see *The Greek Passion, The Last Temptation of Christ,* and *Report to Greco*), but with the passage of time his work strikes many readers as embarrassingly full of sound and fury.

Conclusion: The Bible and Modern Literature. The most significant influence of the Bible on modern literature (roughly from the late eighteenth century to the present) may well be the persistence of Jewish and Christian symbols and allusions—as in Ibsen's *Brand* (1866), the story of a noble, but self-destructive zealot, or in the title *The Road to Damascus* (1898–1904) by August Strindberg, who had nothing in common with Paul except a hair-trigger emotional sensitivity.

All in all, this biblical influence is so varied and complex that it is hard to assess. The texts, as we have already seen, run a staggeringly broad gamut, from *Nathan der Weise* by Gotthold Ephraim Lessing (1729–1781), a Christian who idealized his friend, the great *maskil* and "Jewish Socrates," Moses Mendelssohn (1729–1786), to the philo-Christian "Nazarene" novels of the Yiddish writer Sholem Asch (1880–1957). Biblical themes appear in myriad guises. Ernest Renan (1823–1892) had an immense, scandalous success with his *Vie de Jésus* (1863) and its vision of Jesus as the "divine charmer" and Jewish Orpheus (cf. the rapturous Hellenism of Renan's "Prayer on the Acropolis" in his *Souvenirs d'Enfance et de Jeunesse* [1883]) but, although dated, it remains the most widely read popular-scholarly life of Christ. Thomas Mann (1875–1955) created an extraordinarily ambitious, sympathetic, and thoughtful, if not always aesthetically compelling, picture of the world of the ancestors of Israel in his immense novel *Joseph and his Brothers* (1934–1942). When all is said and done, no one can predict what forms the influence of the Bible on future writers may take, but it may be safe to predict that such influence will be both continuous and attenuated. *Peter D. Heinegg*

North American Literature

American literature, in its use of the Bible, is not notably characterized by medieval or Miltonic retellings of scriptural narratives. Drawing epic and dramatic material rather from frontier life, New World authors often chose to invest immediate and local experience with eternal significance by encoding it with biblical *typology. It is this typological biblicizing of national life, and the theological worldview that such a biblical typology implies, that facilitates the connection of important individual texts to the development of a larger public "myth" in the United States. In Canada, by contrast, where the wilderness seemed more resistant to subjugation, and survival rather than triumph the visible goal, the use of the Bible by literary authors does not follow from a typological worldview; hence it is more tentative, less schematic, and, where involved with questions of identity, more concerned to relate personal rather than public experience to the transvaluation afforded by biblical references.

The United States. American literature branched off from English literature just at that point in the seventeenth century when the influence of the Bible upon secular texts was at its zenith in Britain. The Puritans who settled in New England and dominated its literary culture for several generations, were, moreover, of English speakers among the most biblically literate. Extensive mastery of the entire biblical corpus in the King James (Authorized) Version was common among ordinary people in the colonies, and individuals who had memorized entire books, or, as in the case of John Cotton, large portions of both Testaments, were far from rare.

The writing of the Puritans themselves was confined largely to diaries, chronicles, and well-wrought sermons, but a few, such as Anne Bradstreet, with her sense of struggle between "The Flesh and the Spirit" (1678), and Edward Taylor, so heavily influenced (like his English metaphysical counterparts) by the

Song of Solomon, wrote reflective and devotional poetry rich in biblical theme and idiom. Almost any kind of American text in this period, from chronicle to court judgment, might not only quote the Bible extensively but be characterized throughout by biblical diction.

Biblical typology, as Sacvan Bercovitch (*Biblical Typology in Early American Literature* [1972]) and others have shown, provided a means whereby life in the colonies became literal realization of scriptural metaphor: *Fall, *exile, *Exodus, pilgrim history, Promised Land, and even millennial kingdom are worked almost seamlessly into the narratives of William Bradford, John Winthrop, Roger Williams, Michael Wigglesworth (*The Day of Doom* [1662]), Cotton Mather, Samuel Sewall, and Jonathan Edwards. In Wigglesworth, whose text was buttressed throughout by marginal references to precise biblical texts, or later, in Edwards's dramatic "Sinners in the Hands of an Angry God" (1741), one sees the incipient apocalypticism as well as a hellfire and brimstone call to repentance that the Puritan style of Calvinism was to bequeath to American literary consciousness. In Bradford, Winthrop, and Taylor, one observes paradoxically that America was also seen as a recovered Eden, a new Canaan, or Promised Land in the here and now. In this early period, it is clearly typology and allusion to the Hebrew Bible that predominates: even a poem such as Edward Taylor's *Christographia* (ca. 1690), a fourteen-sermon "portrait" of Christ, each sermon preceded by a poetic meditation, tends to be structured according to types, promises, and prophecies of the Hebrew scriptures.

Bercovitch has shown that developmental typology in Puritan literature relates figures from the Hebrew Bible not only to the *incarnation but, in a form of *sensus plenior,* to the *second coming of Christ. Thus, typical narratives, such as those of the Babylonian captivity and Promised Land, come to prefigure end-time events as well as aspects of the story of Christ. America is Eden "in the last days." This historiographic view is complemented by "the static biographical parallelism offered by correlative typology, in which the focus is not primarily upon Christ but upon certain Old Testament heroes . . . as they become, *through* Christ, 'redivivus' in contemporary heroes." This second typology, visible in actual names as well as the names of literary characters, relies as much as the first on *covenant theology. Typology thus becomes a link between the concept of "a recurrent national covenant and the concept of an unchanging covenant of grace manifest in succeeding stages of the history of redemption" (Bercovitch, p. 25). Thomas Shepard's *The Covenant of Grace* (1651) reads current frontier events as if they were superimposed upon the lineated covenant history of the Bible; Cotton Mather's *Magnalia Christi Americana* (1702) looks back already to the golden age of Puritanism as a lost Eden or New Canaan, as from a pilgrim prospect from which the intervention of providence must be sought to ensure against the temptation to return—even at Harvard College—to the luxurious entrapments of Egypt. For America to realize its destiny as the land of promise, the conversion of American experience into a text about God's unfolding plan of redemption, emergent in Edward Johnson's *Wonder-Working Providence of Sion's Savior* (1654), was coupled with a tendency to read the text of the Bible itself as though it were chiefly about Americans, or, as Giles Gunn puts it in *The Bible and American Arts and Letters* (1983), as if "the Bible was proleptically American."

The American jeremiad, a political sermon that joins social criticism to spiritual renewal (as well as public dream to private identity), has come to be recognized as a foundational mythopoeic American literary genre. From the frontier outpost sermons of Peter Bulkeley in the mid-seventeenth century to the television evangelists of the late twentieth century it has tended to read contemporary events as though they were written down in an unfolding text to which the Bible is the master code and ultimate governing form. Characterized not only by biblical rhetoric and diction but also formed upon biblical narrative and dependent for its wide appeal on extensive popular knowledge of the Bible, the jeremiad has in turn had a powerful influence upon other literary genres throughout the history of American letters.

This was less apparent in the second half of the eighteenth century, however, than later. The dominant American writings in this period of consolidation continued to be political, but of a decidedly Enlightenment stripe. Allusions to the Bible occur only rarely in the works of Franklin and Jefferson; classical literature, as in England, usurped the fashion. Even in poetry, dominated by the "Yale poets" (Trumbull, Dwight, Barlow, Humphreys, and Hopkins), despite their uniformly Calvinist upbringing, literary use of the Bible is as marginal as it is in the poetry of Philip Freneau who, in the spirit of his time, eulogized "On the Religion of Nature." Timothy Dwight's Miltonic allegorical epic, *The Conquest of Canaan* (ca. 1775), populated with eighteenth-century Americans with Hebrew names and perhaps the most self-consciously biblical poem of the period, was unsuccessfully archaic, a relic of his grandfather Jonathan Edwards's day, displaced in popularity by Dwight's own rather conventional pastoral verse. Only the black slave poet Phillis Wheatley ("Thoughts on the Works of Providence" [1770]) wrote popular verse that adhered to the Puritan vision and its biblical themes and language, and it too looked backward, as in her most famous poem, "On the Death of the Rev. Mr. George Whitefield, 1770."

The nineteenth century brought a notable revival in biblical allusion in the works of writers of diverse religious persuasions; easily recognizable from the Calvinist William Cullen Bryant to the Quaker John Greenleaf Whittier, it is richly present in the most popular poet of the nineteenth century, Henry Wadsworth Longfellow. Each of these poets wrote verse heavily marked by biblical idiom and diction, if not always devoted to a biblical theme; Whittier, however, in his concern with *slavery, readily invoked the captivity, Exodus, and wilderness themes in poems such as "Song of Slaves in the Desert" (1847), "Ichabod" (1850), and "First Day Thoughts" (1852), while Longfellow, author of *The Divine Tragedy* (1871), a Passion drama, related *Pentecost and the atonement in his verse-sermon, "The Children of the Lord's Supper." In James Russell Lowell's then famous Harvard "Oration Ode" (1810), the old Puritan vision of America as "the Promised Land / That flows with Freedom's honey and milk" buttresses both the rhetoric and Lowell's moral: " 'Tis not the grapes of Canaan that repay, / But the high faith that failed not by the way."

Side by side with these sentiments, the growth of romantic naturalism and transcendentalism expressed in Henry David Thoreau and Ralph Waldo Emerson respectively is supported by a subtle recasting of selected biblical verities. Thoreau, in the prophetic sense of mission, evidenced particularly in *Walden*

(1854) and *Civil Disobedience* (1849), shows familiarity with Genesis, Ecclesiastes, and the gospel of Matthew, though he characteristically edits according to his strong dislike of any emphasis on *repentance. Emerson, son of a Unitarian minister and descended from Puritans, began his career as a Unitarian preacher but, in a crisis of vocation, shortly resigned to pursue an interest in Montaigne and certain writers of the English Romantic movement. As a colloquial philosopher in an era when the popular lecture was displacing the sermon in literary importance, he perceived where his future lay: "I believe that wherever we go, whatever we do, self is the sole subject we study and learn . . . but as self means Devil, so it means God." In his pursuit of the "God within," and despite his railing at "sulphurous Calvinism," he found, in his poem "The Problem" (1839), that "Out from the heart of nature rolled / the burdens of the Bible old." Although his antinomian redefinition of those burdens, most memorably expressed in his famous essay "On Self-Reliance" (1841), is what he has most contributed to the "biblical tradition" in American literature, Emerson could on occasion quickly revert to Puritan humility before an omnipotent God, as in "Grace" (1842).

In prose fiction, the novels of James Fenimore Cooper make extended use of biblical analogy for frontier experience. In a recrudescence of the Puritan pattern, Amer of *The Oak Openings* (1848) thinks the Bible addresses itself particularly to him, directing that he should lead the Indians, descendants of the lost tribes of Israel, back to Palestine. In *The Last of the Mohicans* (1826) Gamut is a singer of psalms who idolizes King David. Yet Cooper is critical of the Puritan instinct for typological autobiography in *The Deerslayer* (1841), where he rejects the

appropriation to the self of divine authority on the basis of forced biblical analogy. Despite their anti-Christian stance, Nathaniel Hawthorne's novels and short stories are rich in biblical allusions, though often as parody: in "Roger Malvin's Burial," the character Reuben is not only a superficial parallel to his biblical namesake, but a type of Israel seeking redemption from "Cyrus." In Herman Melville's epic-novel *Moby-Dick* (1851), notwithstanding a fierce resistance to Calvinistic religion, a rich synthesis of biblical narrative and typology reveals a knowledge of the Bible that might almost have done credit to a Puritan divine; Melville's text opens with the evocative words, "Call me Ishmael." In *Pierre* (1852), he explores the theme of failed "imitation of Christ," to which he returns in the posthumously published *Billy Budd* (1924); in *The Confidence Man* (1857) he has the prototypical beguiler, Satan himself, come on board the American ship of faith, *Fidele,* and, by arguing that there are no trustworthy texts (in that the Bible itself is a devilish beguiler), demonstrate that there are in fact no real Christians aboard. The writings of Edgar Allan Poe, who refers to the Qurʾān more approvingly than the Bible, are surprisingly rich in biblicisms, and one story, "The Cask of Amontillado" (1846), has been read as a demonic parody of the Passion.

The work of these major fiction writers illustrates that if resistance to the formidable biblical inclusiveness of Puritan views of history and writing had been largely passive in the years from the mid-eighteenth century through the first quarter of the nineteenth century, it began to take on a more strident antinomian flavor during the period known as the American Literary Renaissance. This is particularly evident in the poets, of whom (beside Poe) Walt Whitman and

Emily Dickinson suffice as illustration. The debt of Whitman's prosody, rhythm, and diction to the language of the King James Bible, along with his special interest in Judaism, does not hinder his Emersonian vindication of "the plain old Adam, the simple genuine self against the whole world." In "A Backward Glance O'er Traveled Roads," he tells us that in preparation for *Leaves of Grass* (1855) he grounded himself in both testaments, and the influence is clear enough at the level of structure. His tendency to see himself as a Christ or prophet, as in the climactic thirty-third section of *Song of Myself*, "I am the man, I suffered, I was there," is reinforced by his appreciation of the role of biblical prophets as visionary denouncers of social privilege and cultural hypocrisy.

Dickinson, as Herbert Schneidau has observed, presents an extreme case of the familiar paradox so apparent in Melville: "the more antinomian the American poet, the more he or she falls back upon the traditional guidebook." Her poetry requires extensive verbal familiarity with the Bible if its full import as a rejection of conformity with received traditions is to be fully understood. Following her years at Mount Holyoke Female Seminary, she sees the Bible as "an antique volume / Written by faded men / At the suggestion of Holy Spectres," rejecting with bitter ironies the orthodox and Calvinistic appropriation of the Bible in which she had been educated.

The presence of the Bible in nineteenth-century literature is largely a function of educational formation; still living off the spiritual and literary capital of the Puritan era, and possessed thereby of a biblical literacy paralleled today only in certain parts of the English-speaking third world, American writers almost unavoidably wrote in biblical language, whatever their subject. Yet "the one serious Christian novel of the age," and most seriously biblical, was Harriet Beecher Stowe's *Uncle Tom's Cabin* (1851–1852). Its actual plot turns upon a biblical treatment of the problem of evil, specifically recollected in a crisis reading of Psalm 73, and the hero Tom is made to be the paragon of the imitation of Christ in his nonviolent resistance to persecution and oppression. Yet this enormously popular work—as to a lesser extent the work of George Washington Cable and Joseph Holy Ingraham's epistolary, sensationalist and trivializing life of Christ, *The Prince of the House of David* (1855)—is, despite its success in the marketplace, an exception that merely defines the literary mainstream of the later nineteenth century, as represented by the realists Mark Twain, W. D. Howells, and Henry James. Twain (Samuel Clemens), especially in *Innocents Abroad* (1869), *Adventures of Huckleberry Finn* (1883), and *A Connecticut Yankee in King Arthur's Court* (1889), offers narrators who seem to know much about the Bible, yet for strategic purposes deploy it incorrectly. Twain's notorious antireligiosity grows steadily less covert and less comic (but note *Eve's Diary* [1906]) toward the end of his life, obliterating even this use of the Bible in the despairing cynicism of *A Mysterious Stranger* (1916). W. D. Howells, raised a Swedenborgian and matured as an agnostic, is said to have known much of the Bible by heart, and his *Rise of Silas Lapham* (1885) loosely rewords the story of Jacob and Esau. Henry James, whose "A Passionate Pilgrim" (1871) is heading back to the European "Egypt," makes almost no significant use of the Bible, except perhaps in the title only of *The Golden Bowl* (1904), which may be an enigmatic residue of Ecclesiastes 12.6. The Bible is largely displaced in the novels of the 1890s—in Hamlin Garland, Kate Chopin, Frank Norris, Jack London; even in the work of Stephen Crane, son of a Methodist minister, there are few traceable echoes. Exceptions to this generalization in "serious" literature were historical novels based upon biblical times, of which General Lew Wallace's *Ben-Hur* (1880) was the most successful, followed by Henry K. Sienkiewicz's *Quo Vadis?* (1896), based upon the apostolic labors of Peter. Even Henry Adams attempted a religious-historical novel, though his *Esther* (1884) was not popular.

Among the American poets writing between the two world wars, Robert Frost reflects an ambivalent attitude toward the Bible as a source, choosing the painful paradoxes of Job as the material for his most overtly biblical poem, *A Masque of Reason* (1945). On the one hand, popular taste was being formed by the popular religious novels of Lloyd C. Douglas, notably *The Robe* (1942) and *The Fisherman* (1949), the first of which was made into a movie, and more thoughtfully in the novels of Sholem Asch, including *The Nazarene* (1939), *The Apostle* (1943), *Mary* (1949), and *Moses* (1951). On the other, the poetry and celebrated conversion of T. S. Eliot was prompting the renewal of intellectual interest in the Bible among poets and dramatists in some ways unprecedented since the Puritans. Marianne Moore was by 1920 the "poet's poet" in America. Her poetry, fluent in biblical story and idiom, reached the height of its achievement toward the end of World War II, and is exemplified in poems rich in allusion to Jonah ("Sojourn in a Whale") and Job ("In Distrust of Merits"). Biblical allusions nonetheless waned in the poetry of Vachel Lindsay, after *General William Booth Enters into Heaven* (1913), and is of small consequence in the work of e. e. cummings, Edna St. Vincent Millay, and Hart Crane—even John Crowe Ransome and Allen Tate—though biblical phrasing flavors the work of William Carlos Williams. In quite different accents it persists in some of the writers of the Harlem Renaissance, such as Langston Hughes and Countee Cullen.

In the drama, meanwhile, as in the popular novel, there had merged a tradition of modern retelling of biblical stories: George Cabot Lodge's *Cain* (1904), F. E. Pierce's *The World That God Destroyed* (1911), William Ford Manley's *The Mess of Pottage* (1928), Richard Burton's *Rahab* (1906), Sholem Asch's *Jephthah's Daughter* (1915), and R. G. Moulton's *The Book of Job* (1918). Marc Connelly's famous *Green Pastures* (1929), Eugene O'Neill's *Belshazzar* (1915), and Archibald MacLeish's acclaimed *J.B.*, a modernization of the Job story (1958), along with his earlier *Nobodaddy* (1926), a verse play using Adam, Eve, Cain, and Abel (cf. his volume *Songs for Eve* [1954]), illustrate something of the diversity of dramatizations of subjects from the Hebrew Bible. Plays on New Testament subjects, though less numerous, were more influential: O'Neill's *Lazarus Laughed* (1925), Thornton Wilder's *Now the Servant's Name Was Malchus* (1928) and *Hast Thou Considered My Servant Job?* (a play about Christ, Satan, and Judas), Robinson Jeffers's dramatic poem *Dear Judas* (1929), along with Marie Doran's *Quo Vadis?* (1928), a dramatic adaptation of the novel of Sienkiewicz, highlight a flurry of activity in the 1920s. These plays, with their tendency to recharacterize New Testament narratives, are a sharp contrast to the still traditional biblical drama of the prewar period, well represented in Charles Kennedy's *The Terrible Meek* (1912), and anticipate successful cinematic and musical adaptations of the Christ-Judas-Peter narrative in the 1960s and 1970s.

Biblical motif more than biblical language or narrative plot marks a residual influence of the Bible on American fiction of the modern period, often hearkening back to the old Puritan typology and theology of a "God-blessed America." In Walker Percy's *Love in the Ruins* (1971), a biblically encoded national mythology is called up nostalgically in a time when it seems actually to have lost much of its cultural and religious power. In titles that are evocative rather than indicative, biblical allusion is often used as if to borrow a mythological authority for writing unsure of how to proceed without a shareable literary foundation: F. Scott Fitzgerald's *This Side of Paradise* (1920) and *The Beautiful and the Damned* (1922), John Steinbeck's *East of Eden* (1952) and *Grapes of Wrath* (1939), Katherine Anne Porter's *Pale Horse, Pale Rider* (1939), James Baldwin's *The Fire Next Time* (1963), William Faulkner's *Go Down, Moses* (1942), Saul Bellow's *The Victim* (1947), and Walker Percy's *The Second Coming* (1980), all indicate a tendency to call upon biblical points of reference—and a specific mode—to express *apocalyptic apprehension. Elsewhere the biblical titles call up a mood of lamentation in Faulkner's *Absalom, Absalom!* (1936) or, as in Ernest Hemingway's use of Ecclesiastes, an experience of undermined foundations and lost identities, in *The Sun Also Rises* (1926). James Agee's *Let Us Now Praise Famous Men* (1941), in a related vein, makes use of Sirach 44 to create a jeremiad on a lost sense of national covenant history.

The *parable has become another discernible mode in modern American fiction, with Hemingway's *The Old Man and the Sea* (1952) as perhaps the most eminent modern example. Biblical titles continue to appear, as in Wright Morris's "The Ram in the Thicket" (1951), with

only a loosely allusive function; even in writers with notably religious concerns, such as Percy or Flannery O'Connor ("The Lame Shall Enter First"; *The Violent Bear It Away* [1960]), substantive use of biblical material is rare.

What Ursula Brumm describes as "the figure of Christ in American literature" (*Partisan Review* 24 [1957]), notably in Hemingway, Faulkner, and Ralph Ellison's *Invisible Man* (1952), is in effect an attempt to give transcendent meaning to the chaotic complexity of ordinary life in which the innocent are made to suffer. Theodore Ziolkowski had identified Gore Vidal's *Messiah* (1954) and John Barth's *Giles Goat Boy* (1966) as "demonic parodies of the life of Christ," works in which "all questions of meaning aside, the events as set down immutably in the Gospels prefigure the action of the plot" (*Fictional Transfigurations of Jesus* [1972], p. 26). Such works, however much narrative analogues to the Bible, are in effect "anti-Gospels"—diametrically opposite to the imitation of Christ such as is represented in American fiction by Charles M. Sheldon's "Bible Belt" classic *In His Steps* (1896). By the second half of the twentieth century, the "Christ-figure" has often become "Antichrist."

The Bible continues, nonetheless, to shape and texture American fiction in more traditional fashion. John Updike, in novels whose protagonists bear the consistent character of the fallen Adam—*Rabbit, Run* (1960), *Rabbit Redux* (1971), *Rabbit Is Rich* (1981), and *Rabbit at Rest* (1990)—as well as *The Centaur* (1963) and *Roger's Version* (1987), uses biblical allusion and elements of ancestral saga in the shaping of narrative; in his *Couples* (1968) the hero is identified with Lot living in the cities of the plain (the coast near Boston), fleeing Sodom with his two daughters, and leaving behind his wife turned to salt. Another writer who demands considerable biblical literacy from his readers and whose use of the Bible extends from title to precept and narrative elements as well as significant allusion, is Chaim Potok, notably in his novels of Jewish life in New York, *The Chosen* (1967) and *The Promise* (1969). American Jewish fiction born of more recent immigrant experience readily employs biblical analogue for covenant saga, jeremiad, even apocalyptic (Saul Bellows's *Mr. Sammler's Planet* [1969]), and, in the stories of Isaac Bashevis Singer, parable. The reemergence of these biblically informed genres lends an appearance of continuity with forms of literary imagination familiar in American literature from its seventeenth-century Puritan beginnings.

Canada. Canadian literature grew up slowly at the end of the eighteenth century and the beginning of the nineteenth; thus, heavily influenced by enlightenment taste and romantic self-consciousness, it did not turn readily to the Bible as a foundational literature. The dramatic poem *Jephthah's Daughter* (1865), published by Charles Heavysege shortly after his arrival in Canada, is perhaps the only significant example of biblical influence before the twentieth century. Without any equivalent to the Puritan legacy of American writers, English Canadian authors begin to take a significant interest in the Bible only after its "rediscovery," following the influence of Matthew Arnold in Britain, as a "secular" literature, and, subsequently, the success of Jewish writers in Canada following World War II. French Canadian authors have made even less use of scriptural sources, even by way of allusion, although Yves Theriault, in *Aaron* (1954), a novel about an orthodox Jew who loses his son to gentiles, is a notable

parallel to contemporary developments in English Canadian fiction.

While Morley Callaghan incorporated religious ideas and even doctrines into some of his many novels, his conspicuous use of biblical allusion is peripheral: in *Such Is My Beloved* (1934), for example, the priest-protagonist concludes his frustrated idealism in a mental hospital working on a commentary on the Song of Solomon; other of Callaghan's suggestively biblical titles fit their plots still more loosely, as is the case in *They Shall Inherit the Earth* (1935) and *More Joy in Heaven* (1937). Howard O'Hagan's *Tay John* (1939) draws on Native American mythology as well as biblical sources in a story of suffering and self-generated attempts at atonement that contrasts sharply with E. J. Pratt's use of similar sources in his poem *Brebeuf and His Brethren* (1940). Other more or less gratuitously allusive titles include Sinclair Ross's *As for Me and My House* (1941), W. O. Mitchell's *Who Has Seen the Wind* (1947), and, with varying degrees of apropos, Hugh MacLennan's *The Watch That Ends the Night* (1959) and Marian Engel's *The Glassy Sea* (1978).

Beyond the echoing allusions of writers such as Archibald Lampman, E. J. Pratt, P. K. Page, and James Reaney, Canadian poetry and drama have produced few examples of formative biblical influence. Among these may be counted Jay Macpherson's *The Boatman* (1957) and Margaret Avison's *Sunblue* (1980), in the latter of which the poet still gladly countenances "The Bible to Be Believed." Renewal of Canadian literary interest in the Arnoldian tradition, evidenced in Northrop Frye's discussion of the Bible as foundational literature in *The Great Code* (1982) and *Words with Power* (1990), is necessarily oblique to the generative power of the Bible for those writing out of an immediate experience of it as textual authority, such as Avison, Rudy Wiebe, or, most centrally, A. M. Klein. Klein's "Five Characters" is a penetrating analysis of the book of Esther, and his "Koheleth" is a reading back of the dark sayings of Ecclesiastes into the mind behind the utterances. He writes in imitation of the Psalms in *The Psalter of Avram Haketani* (1948; a volume that has in turn influenced the prose psalms of Jubilee repentance of Leonard Cohen, *A Book of Mercy* [1984]), in whimsical parody of "Jonah," and in moving evocation of Hebrew apocalyptic in *A Voice Was Heard in Ramah* (1948).

A revival of more substantial engagement of the Bible in Canadian fiction may be traced to A. M. Klein's novel of Jewish covenant history, *The Second Scroll* (1951), a "double tale" composed of five books named for those of the *Torah and five "glosses." While Ernest Buckler's *The Mountain and the Valley* (1952), with its artist protagonist David Canaan, is recognizably influenced by New England writers, it is an exception proving the rule that Puritan covenant theology has had little impact on Canadian literary consciousness. *The Second Scroll* was followed by another novel of diaspora Jewish life, Adele Wiseman's *The Sacrifice* (1956), in which Abraham and Sarah flee pogroms in the Ukraine during which their sons Jacob and Moses are murdered at Easter (Passover) by Christians only to have their son of later years, Isaac, die while saving a copy of the Torah from the flames. Rudy Wiebe's *Peace Shall Destroy Many* (1962) and subsequent *The Blue Mountains of China* (1970), with its own epic recounting of family/covenant history of the Mennonite diaspora, follow Klein and Wiseman in the way in which contemporary life is grafted directly onto biblical narrative, or made to seem an outgrowth of it. Margaret Laurence's *The Stone Angel* (1964), whose heroine Hagar is a rebel not only against her husband Bram but against God and the world, is a tale from without, a novel molded by the protagonist's sense of covenantal exclusion. It is not, however, like Timothy Findley's grisly and angry redrafting of the story of Noah, *Not Wanted on the Voyage* (1984), a demonic parody of the Bible, or like Wiebe's *My Lovely Enemy* (1983), a desacralization and inversion of biblical salvation history.

Resistance to the influence of the Bible, especially as represented by the American Puritan legacy in political life, reaches its zenith in Margaret Atwood's *The Handmaid's Tale* (1985), a dystopia in which American fundamentalists have erected a society based on a rigid implementation of biblical law and social custom. Atwood's apocalyptic tale is an antijeremiad, expressing Canadian fears of a biblicist America declaring itself the only "chosen," and serves to indicate much of the basis for the strikingly divergent uses of biblical tradition in Canadian and American literature.

David Lyle Jeffrey

LITERATURE, THE BIBLE AS.

An appreciation for the literary artistry of the Bible began early in the history of interpretation. It reached a high water mark during the era of the Renaissance and Protestant Reformation, when poets and storytellers viewed the Bible as a literary model to be emulated, and when interpreters of the Bible were sensitive to its literary style and genres.

The idea of the Bible as literature received sporadic attention throughout the twentieth century, but its most notable revival began in the late 1960s, when high school and college courses in the literature of the Bible became popular.

By the 1980s, the literary approach had attracted the allegiance of biblical scholars, whose traditional methods became strongly influenced by, and often replaced by, tools of analysis long practiced by literary critics in the humanities.

How Literary Is the Bible? Acceptance of a literary approach to the Bible has always been rendered difficult (and sometimes suspect) because of the mixed nature of biblical writing. Three impulses and three corresponding types of material exist side by side in the Bible: the didactic or theological impulse to teach religious truth, the historical impulse to record and interpret historical events, and the literary/aesthetic impulse to recreate experiences and be artistically beautiful. This combination of religious, documentary, and literary interests in the Bible has made the literary study of the Bible different from the study of other literature. Literary critics of the Bible find themselves sharing the same book with scholars who approach it with very different methods.

Despite this complexity, the literary approach to the Bible can be defined with precision. It is rooted in an awareness that literature is itself a genre with identifying traits. These include the impulse to image reality and human experience instead of conveying abstract information, the presence of literary genres, reliance on figurative language and rhetorical devices, an interest in artistry as something intrinsically valuable (with special emphasis on unity), and stylistic excellence. A literary approach to the Bible begins with these features as its agenda of concerns and proceeds to apply familiar tools of literary analysis to the parts of the Bible that are most thoroughly literary in nature.

An Imaginative Book. To say that the Bible is an imaginative book is to call attention to the most important differentia of literature—its impulse to image reality. Whereas expository or informational writing tends toward abstraction and proposition, the aim of literature is to recreate an experience as concretely as possible. Literature takes human experience rather than abstract thought as its subject, and it puts a reader through an experience instead of appealing primarily to a grasp of ideas. The truth that literature portrays is primarily truthfulness to human experience in the world.

Biblical writing as a whole exists on a continuum between the poles of the expository and the literary, or between propositions and images (including characters and events), but the literary impulse to incarnate meaning—to image experience—probably dominates. Wherever we turn in the Bible, we find appeals to our image-making and image-perceiving capacity. The Bible is consistently rooted in the concrete realities of human life in this world, and a literary approach is sensitive to this experiential dimension.

It is a truism that whereas history tells us what happened, literature tells us what happens. Literature portrays universal human experience and as a result does not go out of date. A literary approach to the Bible is therefore interested in the universal, always-recognizable human experiences that are portrayed. In the Bible, we see ourselves, not only characters and events from the past. Adam and Jacob, David and Ruth are paradigms of the human condition as well as figures in historical narrative.

Because biblical literature embodies its meanings in characters, events, and images, it communicates by indirectness. It gives example rather than precept. The result is that literature puts a greater burden of interpretation on a reader than straightforward expository prose does. Even such a simple literary form as *metaphor ("God is light") requires a reader to interpret how one thing is like another. Here, too, the Bible shows itself to be a work of imagination. Again and again we find that biblical writers entrust their utterance to a literary medium in order to achieve the memorability, affective power, and truthfulness to lived experience that are characteristic of literature.

Literary Genres in the Bible. The commonest way to define literature is by its genres or literary types. Through the centuries, people have agreed that certain genres (such as story, poetry, and drama) are literary in nature. Other types, such as historical chronicles, theological essays, and genealogies, are expository (informational). Still others can fall into either category. Letters, sermons, and orations, for example, can move in the direction of literature by virtue of experiential concreteness, figurative language, and artistic style.

The Bible is a mixture of genres, some of them literary in nature. The major literary genres in the Bible are narrative or story, *poetry (especially lyric poetry), proverb, and visionary writing (including prophecy and *apocalypse). The New Testament *letters frequently become literary because of their occasional nature, figurative language, and rhetorical or artistic patterning. Other literary genres of note in the Bible include epic, tragedy, *gospel, *parable, satire, pastoral, oratory, encomium, epithalamion (wedding poem), elegy (funeral poem), and a host of subtypes of lyric poetry (such as nature poem, psalm of praise, lament, love poem, psalm of worship, hymn).

Genre study is central to any literary approach to the Bible because every genre has its own conventions, expectations, and corresponding rules of interpretation. A biblical story, for example, is a sequence of events, not a series of ideas. It is structured around a plot conflict, not a logical argument. It communicates by means of setting, character, and event, not propositions. In short, the literary genres of the Bible require us to approach them in terms of the conventions and procedures that they possess.

Literary Language and Rhetoric. Literature uses distinctive resources of language. This is most evident in poetry. Poets, for example, think in images and figures of speech: God is a shepherd, people are sheep, the tongue is a fire. It is noteworthy how much of the Bible is poetic in form, including books in which it dominates: Job, Psalms, Proverbs, Ecclesiastes, Song of Solomon, and most of the prophets.

The whole realm of figurative language looms large in any consideration of the Bible as literature. Figurative language in the Bible includes metaphor, simile, symbol, hyperbole, apostrophe (address to someone or something absent as though they or it were present), personification, paradox, pun, irony, and wordplay. These resources of language are not limited to poetry but pervade the entire Bible, including parts of it that would not be considered primarily literary. Everywhere we turn in the Bible—in narrative, in the prophets, in the Gospels, in the New Testament epistles, in apocalypse—we find figurative language. In fact, it is hard to find a page of the Bible that does not contain figurative language.

The literary use of language also includes rhetorical devices, or language arranged by stylized patterns. Examples include parallel sentences or clauses (the standard verse form in biblical poetry), any highly patterned arrangement of clauses or words or phrases, rhetorical questions, question and answer constructions, imaginary dialogues, and the aphoristic conciseness of a proverb. These rhetorical forms pervade the Bible, lending a literary quality to the Bible as a whole, giving it qualities of conscious artistry and heightening the audience's attention.

Artistry in the Bible. Literature is an art form, and one of the criteria by which we classify something as literary is the presence of beauty, form, craft, and technique. The elements of artistic form include pattern or design, unity, theme and variation, balance, contrast, symmetry, repetition or recurrence, coherence, and unified progression. The artistic spirit regards these as having inherent value.

When judged by these criteria of aesthetic form or beauty, the Bible contains artistic and literary masterpieces. The stories of the Bible are models of concise shapeliness, with every detail contributing to the total effect. Biblical poetry, as well as some of its prose (notably the discourses of Jesus), is composed with conscious artistry in the form known as parallelism, in which two or more lines use different words to express the same idea in similar grammatical form. Whole books of the Bible show similar evidence of artistic patterning, with the gospel according to Matthew, for example, alternating between sections of narrative and sections of discourse.

The most basic of all artistic principles is unity, and one of the things that has set off the literary approach to the Bible from other approaches is a preoccupation with unifying patterns and literary wholes. Literary unity consists of various things: the structure of a work or passage, a dominant theme, an image pattern, or progressive development of a motif. Whatever form it takes, unity is evidence of an artistic urge for order, shapeliness, and wholeness of effect.

Several functions are served by the artistry that we find in the Bible. Artistry intensifies the impact of what is said, but it also serves the purposes of pleasure, delight, and enjoyment. These purposes are abundantly satisfied when we read the Bible, as has been repeatedly shown by literary critics, who assume and find conscious artistry and design there.

The Literary Unity of the Bible. The central protagonist in the overall story of the Bible is God. The characterization of God is the central literary concern of the Bible, and it is pursued from beginning to end. Hardly anything is viewed apart from its relation to the deity.

The Bible is also unified by its religious orientation. It is pervaded by a consciousness of the presence of God. Human experience is constantly viewed in a religious and moral light. One result is that the literature of the Bible invests human experience with a sense of ultimacy. A vivid consciousness of values pervades biblical literature.

Literary archetypes also unify the Bible. Archetypes are master images that recur throughout the Bible and throughout literature. They are either images (light, water, hill), character types (hero, villain, king), or plot motifs (journey, rescue, temptation). The Bible is filled with such archetypes or master images, which lend an elemental quality to the Bible and make its world strongly unified in a reader's imagination.

The Necessity of a Literary Approach. The foregoing discussion suggests why a literary approach to the Bible is necessary. The Bible is, in significant ways, a work of literature. It will yield its meanings fully only if explored in terms of its kinds of writing. Understanding it depends partly on the reader's ability to be receptive to concrete pictures of human experience, to know what to expect from various literary genres, to interpret figurative language and recognize rhetorical patterns. Finally, a literary approach can also enhance the enjoyment of the Bible.   *Leland Ryken*

LOANS AND INTEREST. Indebtedness arose variously, but in loans the lender had discretion whether to show "grace and favor" when approached with a request. Terms would naturally tend to depend on one's relationship with the borrower. Because of the Israelites' acceptance of God's plan for their welfare and their remembrance of him, they must be generous in lending, in taking and keeping any pledge, and in the use of landed security.

There are three main classes of loan: for use, as distinct from hire; for consumption; and for business. The Bible does not deal with the third. The others demanded attention, for the parties were seldom on equal terms. The sabbatical year was intended to cancel all loans; but so benevolent a provision impaired borrowers' credit until Hillel invented a form of agreement to protect it. Biblical traditions extol the granting of loans, praising all who are ready to lend even though the "wicked" may not repay or restore a loaned object. The parties' interests tended to be opposed; a loan could sour relationships. Accordingly, "righteous" lenders must not profit from their neighbors by charging interest (KJV "usury"), enriching themselves from others' calamities. Usurers did charge interest, although a Jewish court would reject a usurious transaction between Jews. But since the lender had the upper hand and since "righteousness" was reputable, society favored interest-free loans. God had promised that, if his people obeyed him, they would always lend to foreigners, who would defer to them.

The *Torah allowed lending at interest to non-Jews. It certainly protected indigent Jews from exploitation; but all loans, including commercial loans, fell under regulation by Pharisees. To evade this, capital was sometimes invested with entrepreneurs on the basis that the parties became partners and that the party with capital hired the other as an employee. The return on such capital was not, technically, "usury."

Another scheme obliged debtors who owed rent or advances of cash to acknowledge a duty to supply commodities, the value of which incorporated, in effect, capital and interest—a device found in Egyptian papyri. It would be righteous to scale such debts down, for concealed usury violated the spirit of the Torah.

The New Testament urges the ready granting of loans without speculating whether the borrower will ever reciprocate. The Hebrew Bible distinguishes gifts and loans, but even a loan can be a good deed. He who shows kindness to the poor lends to the Lord. Such is the religious dimension of a legal transaction, that even a thoughtful cancellation of an insolvent's debts can prove the creditor's mindfulness of God.

J. Duncan M. Derrett

LOGOS. Grk. "word." In the prologue of the gospel according to John, the *logos* is the divine word, a self-communicating divine presence that existed with God and was uniquely manifested in Jesus Christ. The Johannine *logos* is strongly parallel to the concept of wisdom in Hellenistic Jewish thought, where already wisdom and word were associated. Wisdom or Word was God's creative presence through which the world came into being. John's gospel affirms that this same divine presence was fully and (in contrast to the usual thinking about wisdom) uniquely present in Jesus Christ. It was a redemptive presence that was necessary because the world had rejected the original creative presence. The word was not in Jesus simply as verbal communication, but entered fully into human life. The *incarnation of the word brought life to human beings, to whom it was otherwise unavailable.

The Johannine prologue is the only fully explicit statement of the theme of incarnation in the New Testament, though the rest of the gospel of John shows in narrative form what the coming of the *logos* meant. The prologue of the gospel is echoed in 1 John 1.1 ("the word of life") and in the imagery of Revelation 19.13, where Christ, "the Word of God," appears as a warrior.

In the Hebrew Bible, the *word of God is both creative and commanding. This background contributed to the general usage of the term *logos* in the New Testament, where the "word" often signifies the Christian message. This field of meaning was drawn into the interpretation of the *logos* of John's prologue, but was only indirectly in its background.

In Greek, *logos* meant both spoken word and pervading principle. Stoic philosophy, using the latter meaning, saw the *logos* as the ordering principle of the universe; the wise person aims to live in harmony with it. This meaning, though not a direct background for John's *logos*, was quickly drawn into the interpretation of John as "*logos* theology" developed in the second century CE. This was a principal means of making Christian thought intelligible to its environment; but this later *logos* theology was more rationalistic than was the gospel of John.

Christ as the *logos* was an important avenue of development of the doctrine of the *Trinity, but *logos* was eventually largely replaced by other terms ("hypostasis," "person,") because *logos* appeared to make of Christ a second God.

See also Creation; Philo.
                    William A. Beardslee

LORD'S PRAYER. Also known as the "Our Father" (Latin *Pater noster*) from its first words, the Lord's Prayer occurs in the New Testament in two slightly different forms. The longer form is included in Matthew's account of Jesus' *Sermon on the Mount (6.9–13) and reads (in the NRSV):

> Our Father in heaven,
>   hallowed be your name.
>   Your kingdom come.
>   Your will be done,
>   on earth as it is in heaven.
>   Give us this day our daily bread.
>   And forgive us our debts,
>   as we also have forgiven our debtors.
>   And do not bring us to the time of trial,
>   but rescue us from the evil one.

The doxology at the close ("For the kingdom and the power and the glory are yours forever. Amen") is absent in ancient and important Greek manuscripts, and is not mentioned in early commentaries on the Lord's Prayer by Tertullian, Cyprian, and Origen. It occurs in twofold form ("power and glory") in the Didache (8.2). In liturgical use, some kind of doxology (perhaps composed on the model of 1 Chron. 29.11–13) could have concluded such a prayer as this.

The shorter form of the Lord's Prayer is given in Luke 11.2–4, where Jesus responds to a disciple's request, "Lord, teach us to pray," with the following:

> Father, hallowed be your name.
>   Your kingdom come.
>   Give us each day our daily bread.
>   And forgive us our sins,
>   for we ourselves forgive everyone
>   indebted to us.
>   And do not bring us to the time of trial.

Later manuscripts, on which the King James Version depends, include additions that assimilate the Lucan form of the Prayer to that in Matthew. Furthermore, two Greek manuscripts of the Gospels replace the petition "Your kingdom come" with "Your holy Spirit come upon us and cleanse us." This adaptation may have been used when celebrating the rite of *baptism or the *laying on of hands.

It is likely that Luke's shorter version is closer to the original and that Matthew's is an elaboration. But, of course, Jesus may well have given the prayer in different forms on different occasions.

It would seem that the mode of address that Jesus habitually used in prayer to God was "*Abba, dear Father" (the only exception is Mark 15.34, itself a quotation from Ps. 22.1). It seems that nowhere in the literature of the *prayers of ancient Judaism does the invocation of God as "Abba" occur. Perhaps there is an intimacy of relationship implied here that others had hesitated to use. However, in teaching his followers to address God in this way, Jesus lets them share in his own communion with God. That they rejoiced to do so is apparent in the letters of Paul. Ancient Christian liturgies reflect something of the sense of privilege in using this approach when they preface the Lord's Prayer with the words "We are bold to say 'Our Father.'"

But if the address "Our Father" suggests intimacy, not to say familiarity, the next words, "in heaven," speak of the "otherness," the holiness, the awesomeness of God. It is when these two aspects of approach to God are held together in creative tension that real prayer can be engaged in. Further, the plural "our" should be noted—not, at least in this instance, "my." This is the prayer that Jesus' followers as members of one family are bidden to say together; the Father presides over the family unit.

Following the invocation in the Matthean form of the prayer, the petitions fall into two parts: three "you" petitions are followed by "we" petitions. The former focus on God and his purposes in the world; the latter pertain to our provision, pardon, and protection. In other words, before any thought is given to human need ("our daily bread") or even to divine forgiveness of sins or to the problem of temptation, God's name, God's kingdom, God's will must first engage our attention. This is the order of precedence when human beings engage in communication with the God who is at once immanent and transcendent.

"Your will be done" is not a prayer of resignation, but one for the full accomplishment of the divine purpose. The words "on earth as it is in heaven" may be taken with all three preceding petitions.

The Greek adjective (epiousios), usually translated "daily," is extremely rare; it may mean "[the bread we need] for tomorrow." In either case, the sense is that we are to pray for one day's rations, perhaps with the implied suggestion that asking for more would be to engage in needless concern for the future.

The petition for God's forgiveness is closely linked with our forgiveness of one another (the difference in tenses between the Matthean and Lucan versions should be noted); Matthew elaborates the teaching in the following verses. The *Aramaic word for "debt" is used in rabbinic writings to mean "sin," and would be so understood by Jesus' hearers.

The petition often translated "lead us not into temptation" is best understood as a prayer to be kept in the hour of severe trial; it is an acknowledgment of spiritual frailty in the face of the evil one (or evil, for the Greek can mean either; see Temptation). *Donald Coggan*

LORD'S SUPPER.

Paul. In 1 Corinthians 11.20 Paul refers to a gathering of church members at Corinth to eat "the Lord's supper," complaining that the way in which they did so was not consistent with the true character of the *meal. What was meant to be a proclamation of the Lord's death was being celebrated as an occasion for gluttony and even *drunkenness. This is the only passage in the New Testament where the meal is described by this name. In what is no doubt a reference to the same meal, Paul states (1 Cor. 10.16) that the Christians came together to "break bread"; hence, we can assume that "the breaking of bread" (Acts 2.46) was another name for the same occasion. The same verse, with its reference to sharing (Grk. *koinōnia*) in the body and blood of Christ, is the source of the name "(Holy) Communion" for the meal, and the association with thanksgiving (Grk. *eucharistoun*) in 1 Corinthians 11.24 is the rationale for calling it the Eucharist.

The only full discussion of this meal in the New Testament is in 1 Corinthians 11.17–34, where Paul deals with irregularities that had arisen in the congregation at Corinth. They met, doubtless in the home of one of their members, to have a communal meal, and it is likely that the practice of meeting weekly on the first day of the week was developing. It was a full meal, but apparently each person brought his or her own food. Since the church consisted of richer and poorer members, differences in the amount and quality of the food and drink existed, so that the social differences in the church were emphasized rather than diminished by this communal occasion. At some point in the meal there was a more formal sharing in a loaf of bread and a cup of wine, which became the focus of significant symbolism.

Already in 1 Corinthians 10.16–17, Paul commented that those who shared in the loaf and the cup, for which thanks had been given to God, were participating in the body and blood of Christ. The reference must be to experiencing the benefits resulting from the death of Jesus, in which he gave himself and shed his *blood for the sake of others. At the same time Paul emphasized that those who took part in this way constituted one body; their common participation in the gift of salvation, as symbolized by the one loaf, meant that they belonged together in a way that should overcome the social and other differences that had arisen in the church. Thus, the meal was a powerful sign of unity within the local congregation.

Synoptic Gospels. The tradition that Paul had passed on to the church at the time of his visit there is found here in its oldest written form. We also have it in slightly divergent forms in the three synoptic Gospels (Matt. 26.26–29; Mark 14.22–25; Luke 22.15–20, reversing the order of wine and bread). In all of these cases, we have a tradition of what Jesus said and did at his Last Supper with his twelve disciples shortly before his death. Analysis of the differences between the accounts shows that we have two basic forms of the tradition, one given by Mark (who is substantially followed by Matthew), and the other found in 1 Corinthians and Luke (though Luke has also been influenced by Mark). The major difference between the two traditions lies in the two sayings of Jesus:

MARK	I CORINTHIANS
This is my body.	This is my body that is for you. Do this in remembrance of me.
This is my blood of the covenant	This cup is the new covenant in my blood

which is poured
out for many.

(Luke: + which is
poured out for you.)
Do this, as often as you
drink it, in remem-
brance of me.

There is no agreement among scholars as to which is the older form of the
tradition, but the differences are not too
significant.

What we have here, then, is an account of the essential elements in the
Last Supper that formed the pattern for
the church's meal. It has been argued
that the story in the Gospels is not so
much a part of the story of Jesus as a
liturgical text that was preserved on its
own and then inserted into the gospel
narrative. Some scholars would go further and claim that the story is based on
early Christian liturgies rather than on
history, the accounts of what the church
did having been read back into the lifetime of Jesus. Still others claim that the
uncertainty in the tradition of Jesus' sayings and how they express early Christian theology suggest that they are the
creation of the early church (or at least
that the original form has been heavily
modified in transmission), with the result
that we can no longer be sure what Jesus
said. For example, the presence of the
command to "do this" in remembrance
of Jesus, which is lacking from Mark's
account, given once in Luke and twice
in 1 Corinthians, could be due to the
early church putting into words what it
took to be the intention of Jesus. Even
if this is the case, we would still be left
with a tradition of Jesus' sharing a loaf
and a cup with his disciples, and these
actions would invite interpretation. In
other words, to account for the origin of
the church meal and the early Christians'
appeal to Jesus we must surely postulate
the historicity of some kind of meal he
held.

Theological Themes. The Gospels
all suggest that the Last Supper of Jesus
was associated in some way with the
Jewish *Passover, though the Synoptics
and John disagree on the date of that festival. Like other Jewish formal meals, it
began with the breaking and distribution
of bread to the accompaniment of a
prayer of thanksgiving, and it included
the drinking of *wine. If it was a Passover meal, the main items of food would
have been treated as symbols whose significance needed to be explained. There
would then be a precedent for Jesus' explaining the significance of the loaf and
the cup. Whether or not a Passover lamb
was served (as Luke 22.15 and the story
of the preparations for the meal clearly
imply), no record has survived of any interpretation of it. Instead, Jesus made
three main comments. First, he spoke of
this meal as the last that he would eat
with his disciples until he ate with them
in the *kingdom of God. This may suggest his imminent death. Second, he
made the loaf a symbol of his body, and
his distribution of the broken pieces suggests his giving of himself for others.
Third, he made the cup a symbol of his
blood. Blood, however, signifies death.
Jesus associated it with a new *covenant,
and the echoes of Exodus 24.8 suggest a
sacrificial death inaugurating a new covenant. The words "for many" are an allusion to the self-giving of the Servant
of the Lord "for many" in Isaiah 53.11–
12. And the way in which Jesus performed this act before his death implies
that he was giving his disciples a way of
remembering him and enjoying some
kind of association with him after his
death and during the period before they
would share together in the kingdom of
God. Hence, the meal that his disciples were to celebrate could be regarded as in some sense an anticipation
of the meal that the Messiah would celebrate with his disciples in the new age.
Such a meal would not be merely a sym-

bol or picture of the future meal but would be a real anticipation of it. This is clear from the language of 1 Corinthians 10.16. Here the believers who receive the loaf and the cup participate in the body and blood of Jesus. The language must not be pressed literally, since the body in fact includes the blood; rather, Paul is saying in two ways that believers have a share in Jesus who died for them. This interpretation is confirmed by his point that it is inconsistent for believers to take part also in meals at which food sacrificed to *idols was consumed: such a meal was a means of being "partners with demons" (1 Cor. 10.20), that is, having some kind of spiritual relationship to them. It is also confirmed by Luke's implication that the "breaking of bread" in Acts is a continuation of the meals described in the appearances of Jesus after the *resurrection.

We can now see how Paul meant the meal to be celebrated at Corinth. It certainly was an occasion for joyful celebration rather than a funeral meal, but some of the Corinthian Christians carried this element to excess. But it was supremely a way of proclaiming the death of Jesus as a sacrifice on their behalf and the inauguration of the new covenant. It was an occasion for bringing believers together in unity rather than in disharmony. It was a meal for the temporary period before the Lord would return in triumph, and during that period it was one of the ways in which the union between the Lord and his people was expressed.

Other Traditions. In Acts we have further evidence that the believers met regularly to break bread. Since there is no reference in Acts to the cup or to any relevant sayings of Jesus, it is sometimes argued that here we have evidence of a somewhat different meal from the Pauline Lord's Supper, a joyful celebration

of fellowship with the risen Lord rather than a memorial of his death. There is, however, nothing incompatible between the two types of account, and the combination of solemn remembrance of the Lord's death and joyful communion with him is entirely appropriate.

John's account of the Last Supper lacks the eucharistic elements found in the other Gospels, because for John it was not a Passover meal; John recorded elsewhere teaching ascribed to Jesus about eating his flesh and drinking his blood.

There are other allusions to the Lord's Supper in the New Testament. For example, the way in which the stories of Jesus feeding the multitudes are told suggests that the evangelists saw a parallel between Jesus' feeding the people with bread and his spiritual nourishment of the church. And the development of the understanding of the death of Jesus that we find in the New Testament most probably had its roots in the words of institution where the basic concepts of sacrifice and covenant are to be found.

See also Love-feast; Sacrament.

I. Howard Marshall

LOVE (Hebr. *'āhābâ; ḥesed*). Human loves in all their rich variety fill the passages of biblical narrative: love at first sight (Gen. 29.18–20: Jacob and Rachel); sexual obsession (2 Sam. 13: Amnon and Tamar); family affection across generations (Gen. 22.2; 37.3; Ruth 4.15: between mother and daughter-in-law); long marital intimacy (1 Sam. 1: Elkanah and Hannah); servile devotion (Exod. 21.5); intense same-sex friendship (1 Sam. 18.1, 3; 20.17: David and Jonathan); enthusiastic loyalty toward a leader (1 Sam. 18.16, 28: Israel and Judah's love of David). But the religious significance of the Bible's view of love lies preeminently with its ways of speaking about

God and most particularly about God's relationship with Israel. Israel's election, their redemption from Egypt (and, eventually, Babylon), the giving of the *Torah, the promise of the land—all are ascribed in biblical narrative and later rabbinic commentary to the fundamental and mysterious fact of God's love for Israel and the people's reciprocal love of God.

Human love serves as the readiest analogy when speaking of this relationship. God loves Israel as a husband loves his wife, a father his firstborn son, a mother the child of her womb. God manifests his love in and through his saving acts, most especially in his bringing Israel up from Egypt. Narratively and theologically, this liberation culminates in the Sinai *covenant, when God gives Israel his *tôrâ* (literally, "teaching"), instructing Israel on their social and religious obligations in light of their election. Chosen by God's love, Israel is to respond in kind: loving the God who redeemed them and revealed his will to them, teaching his ways to all future generations.

The covenant binding God and Israel likewise binds together society. The individual is charged to "love your neighbor as yourself," kindred and foreigner both (Lev. 19.18, 34). The Bible specifies the concrete actions through which this love is to be expressed: support for the poor; honesty in measurements and in social interactions; prompt payment to laborers; just law courts, favoring neither rich nor poor; respect for the elderly. A system of tithes underlay the welfare both of the poor, the fatherless, and the widowed, and of priests and Levites who, unendowed with land, are "the Lord's portion" (Num. 18.20; Deut. 18.1–2). Right behavior, group affection, and communal social responsibility are thus the concrete measure of Israel's

commitment to the covenant. And God, in turn, "keeps" or "guards" his steadfast love for Israel. Ultimately, Israel's confidence in redemption rests in her conviction that God's love is unwavering, his covenant eternal, his promises sure.

Much of this tradition, both social and theological, comes into the earliest strata of New Testament writings. Paul urges his gentiles in Galatia to be "servants of one another through love [Grk. *agapē*], for the whole law is fulfilled in one word, 'You shall love your neighbor as yourself'" (Gal. 5.13–14, quoting Lev. 19.18). In powerfully poetic language, he exhorts the Corinthians to be knit together as a community through love. Mark's Jesus sums up the Torah with the first line of the *Shema (love of God) and Leviticus 19.18 (love of neighbor; Mark 12.28–31). The Q material of the later synoptic Gospels extends this last: followers of Jesus are to love not just their *neighbor but also and even their enemies. Perhaps, by the criterion of multiple attestation, this ethic of passive—indeed, even active—nonresistance may go back to the historical Jesus himself. Paul teaches similarly: persecutors should be blessed; vengeance eschewed; injustice tolerated (so too other first-century Jewish texts).

Love became the theological lodestone of nascent Christianity. Christ's sacrifice on the cross was understood as the ultimate sign of God's love for humanity. The eucharist (a community meal celebrating this sacrifice) was referred to as the *agapē*, or "*love-feast." Christians exhorted themselves to love one another, calling each other brothers and sisters. Such designations and community enthusiasms, misheard at a hostile distance, fueled dislike of the new groups, who were often accused of expressing love carnally at their convocations. Yet in their care for both their own poor and the poor of the late Roman city, Christians, like their Jewish contemporaries, distinguished themselves by acts of public philanthropy—a fact noted with some irritation by the non-Christian emperor Julian (the Apostate, ca. 360). This philanthropy was the social expression of the scriptural injunction to love the neighbor.

The Christian concept of love, in both its social and its theological applications, underwent elaborate and idiosyncratic development in the work of Augustine. In the unprecedented ecclesiastical situation after Constantine (d. 337), with the church increasingly merging with late Roman imperial culture, Augustine argued that the state coercion of heretics (by which he meant most especially his schismatic rivals, the Donatists) at the behest of the church is an act of Christian love, since it is done for their ultimate spiritual welfare. Theologically, he explored the concept of the *Trinity as a dynamic of divine (and, ultimately, of human) loves: the Trinity should be understood on the analogy of the relations between and process of human self-knowledge and self-love. Finally, and most influentially, Augustine came to analyze all humanity (and thus, given his theological anthropocentrism, all reality) according to loves: those enabled by God's love to love God belong to the "heavenly city"; those whom God leaves to their own fallen state love carnal things and thus belong to the "earthly city."

The City of God, Augustine's great masterwork, may thus be seen as a lengthy survey of the history of love, from angels through pagan culture to Israel and finally to the ultimate revelation of God's love through Christ. Fifteen centuries of Western religious thinkers, such as Bernard, Francis, Dante, and Simone Weil, attest to the power of this essentially Augustinian notion of *caritas* and *amor Dei* as the Christian virtues par excellence.   *Paula Fredriksen*

LOVE-FEAST. The love-feast (Grk. *agapē*, which also means "love") is the common *meal with which Christians first followed Christ's command at the Last Supper to "do this in remembrance of me" (e.g., Luke 22.19, 1 Cor. 11.24), and later to "feed my sheep" (e.g., John 21.17). According to Paul, Christians repeat the "*Lord's supper" to "proclaim the Lord's death until he comes" (1 Cor. 11.20, 26). In Acts (2.43–47; 20.7), "breaking bread . . . with glad and generous hearts" is associated with distributing goods "to all, as any had need"; only Jude 12 uses *agapē* to refer to the meal. Most scholars agree that Paul is ironic in advising the "hungry," wealthy Corinthians to "eat at home" (1 Cor. 11.34): he sees the loving inseparably from the eating. Eating in *agapē* (1 Cor. 13), Christians will "discern" Christ's presence in themselves and others together (1 Cor. 11.29, 31), just as the elders of Israel finally "saw God, and ate and drank" in making the first *covenant (Luke 24.30–31, 35–36; John 21.12; see Exod. 24:11).

The love-feasts of early Christians draw on metaphors in Israelite scripture and sectarian practice linking food and law, commensalism, and covenanted communities, with concerns about how to see "face to face" the ineffable, imageless presence of God in daily life. The New Testament writers' visions of epiphany in loving-eating are inseparable from their sectarian assumptions about incarnation and universalism. Love-feasts were intended less to mark boundaries than to cross them by fostering "loving" relations among infinitely disparate people, Abraham's descendants in the "many nations" (Rom. 4.17; Gen. 17.5).

Paul shows how Corinthians, untutored in midrashic debates about the bodiliness of fleshly spirits whom God may feed or consume in a moment, and committed to their own views of commensalism and community, could be blindly indiscriminate eaters of Jewish-Christian feasts. Reports of Jesus as "a glutton and a drunkard, a friend of tax collectors and sinners" (Matt. 11:19 par.), like Peter's vision, show how Jewish-Christian feasts could be blatantly indiscriminate to fellow Jews who shared their view of the body as a temple but not their abrogation of all the laws epitomized in the dietary rules, except "the law of love" and its new creation.

Underlying the conflicts that New Testament writers attributed to differences among and between Jews and gentiles are deeper visions of the complexities of humans and their unions seen in the presence of Judas and Peter at Christ's table, a juxtaposition that suggests the kinds of conflicts that led to the historical separation of the "loving" meal *(agapē)* from the blessing and distribution of the bread and wine, or "thanksgiving" *(eucharistia)*, as Ignatius (ca. 115 CE) called it. With the incorporation of the church into the Roman empire during the fourth century CE., those well fed enough to abstain from millennial dreams of banquets gradually replaced the feast encompassed in the bread and wine with a preparatory fast.

Gillian Feeley-Harnik

M

MAGIC AND DIVINATION.
Magic is based on the assumption that
one can achieve desired results through
the recitation of proper formulas or by
the performance of certain prescribed
actions. In most cases, the effect sought
is something that will either harm others
(especially an enemy or one who is a potential threat) or ward off harm that an
opponent may be plotting. The essential
feature for success is to repeat the formulaic words or actions exactly. Magic
is evident in many cultures, ancient and
modern, and was especially prevalent in
the second century CE and subsequent
centuries, as the abundance of Greek
magical papyri attest.

In the Hebrew Bible, magic can be
associated with disbelief in the power
and purpose of Yahweh. Thus, in Genesis 41 the power and wisdom of the
God of Joseph are contrasted sharply
with the inability of Pharaoh's wise men
and magicians to understand his dream.
The God who is in control of the world
and of history discloses through Joseph
what his intention is, thereby thoroughly
discrediting the Egyptian magicians and
diviners. A similar contest takes place in
Exodus 7, where the diviners and magicians gathered by Pharaoh are able to
change rods into snakes, as Aaron did,
but Aaron's rod-become-snake swallows
all the others. The clear implication is
that God's power and purpose are
stronger than the powers of the Egyptian
magicians. Magical practices are prohibited in the Law of Moses. The contrast
between Yahweh's power and the claims
of the magicians is set out in Balaam's
song (Num. 23.23), where after recounting God's acts in delivering his people
from Egypt, he declares, "Surely there is
no enchantment against Jacob, no divination against Israel; now it shall be said
of Jacob and Israel, 'See what God has
done!'"

The historical and prophetic books
contain occasional denunciations of
those who practice magic. King Manasseh of Judah practiced soothsaying and
augury, burned his son as an offering,
and consulted mediums and wizards. An
important dimension of this kind of occult practice, as we can infer from the
prophets, was divination. This was a
means of direct determination of the divine will, usually by the interpretation of
some object (perceived as a sign) such as
a marked stone or the entrails of a sacrificial animal. Jeremiah groups together
false prophets, soothsayers, diviners, and
sorcerers as those to whom Judah must
not turn for counsel in the face of exile
and deportation. Similar warnings are
given in Ezekiel 13 and Malachi 3.5.
The frequency of references to this practice attests to the continuing appeal that
magic and divination held for leaders and
populace, and points up the sharp difference that the legal and prophetic
traditions of Israel saw between these oc-

cult practices and Yahweh's determination of his will for his people.

In the New Testament, the prophecies, visions, and *miracles of Jesus are set within the framework of the present evidence of God's rule, rather than as performances of magic, as has sometimes been asserted. The gospel narratives are characterized by a virtual absence of the formulas and techniques of magic (with the description of the healings by Jesus in the gospel of Mark being a partial exception). Encounters with magic and magicians are explicitly mentioned only in Acts, where their work is denounced and the perpetrator is struck blind.

In the *Law of Moses there were prescribed certain means by which the divine will could be communicated. These include the Urim and Thummim, the ephod and the teraphim. The inability of scholars to agree on the translation of these terms is an indication of uncertainty as to how these items were used and understood. The Urim and Thummim were probably a set of dice or flat stones that were marked in such a way as to indicate "yes" or "no" when thrown down by the priest in order to ascertain God's will in a specific case. The ephod (a sacred garment, perhaps with some special adornment or attachment) and the teraphim (portable representations of deities) were also consulted by priests and others in order to discover the divine plan at a crucial juncture in personal or national history. The Israelites' persistence in consulting diviners and sorcerers is given as one of the chief reasons for their being carried off to Babylon. Yet Ezra 2.63 (= Neh. 7.65) seems to indicate that the use of Urim and Thummim to learn God's will was to be resumed after the return of Israel from the *exile.

The attitude toward diviners in the New Testament is unambiguous: their capacity to discern is the result of their being possessed by evil spirits, as Paul's *exorcism of the soothsaying spirit that possessed the young slave woman in Acts 16 shows. The subsequent miracle of deliverance, whereby Paul and Silas are released from prison by divine intervention in the form of an earthquake and a loosening of their bonds, demonstrates for the author of Acts that God is the protector of his own.

See also Sortes Biblicae.

Howard Clark Kee

MANNA. Of uncertain origin, in Exodus 16.15 the word "manna" is given a popular etymology by Israelites who asked, when they saw it, "What is it?" (Hebr. *mān hûʾ*). This was the miraculous food supplied by the Lord to the Israelites during the forty years of their wandering in the wilderness from Egypt to Canaan. Manna is also called, poetically, "bread of the mighty ones [NRSV: angels]" (Ps. 78.25) and "food of angels" (Wisd. of Sol. 16.20).

Early in their *Exodus from Egypt, the Israelites came to the wilderness of Sin. There the whole congregation accused Moses and Aaron of bringing them into the wilderness to kill them with hunger. In response the Lord promised to rain down bread for them from heaven. Manna came six days a week. Only one day's portion was to be gathered except on the sixth day; a double portion gathered that day permitted Israel to keep the *Sabbath rest. Each morning when the dew had vanished, "there on the surface of the wilderness was a fine flaky substance, as fine as frost on the ground" (Exod. 16.14). It was "like coriander seed, white, and the taste of it was like wafers made with honey" (Exod. 16.31). Its appearance was like "gum resin" (Num. 11.7). The people "ground it in mills or beat it in mortars, then boiled it in pots and made cakes of it; and the taste of it was like the taste of cakes baked with oil" (Num. 11.8). An urn containing a quantity of manna was kept in or in front of the *ark of the covenant as a reminder of this divine provision.

From ancient to modern times, manna has been linked with natural phenomena in the Sinai region. The traditional identification has been with a granular type of sweet substance thought to be secreted in early summer by the tamarisk bush. More recent investigations suggest that this "manna" is produced by the excretion of two kinds of scale insects that feed on the sap of the tamarisk. Because the sap is poor in nitrogen, the insects must ingest large amounts of carbohydrate-rich sap in order to consume enough nitrogen. The excess carbohydrate is then excreted as honeydew rich in three basic sugars and pectin. The amount of the substance thus produced would, of course, fall far short of Israel's need for bread; in any case, to give a natural explanation for what the Bible describes as miraculous is perhaps to miss the point.

According to the gospel of John, when Jesus was challenged to validate his ministry with a sign comparable to that of manna, he identified himself as the "true bread from heaven," come down to give life to the world (John 6.32–35).

James I. Cook

MAPS OF THE BIBLICAL WORLD.

Maps in the conventional sense of scale drawings based on accurate ground measurements did not exist before the modern era. There were, however, written maps that served, like drawn maps, as abstract representations of space.

The Hebrew Bible contains three kinds of written maps: administrative maps, campaign itineraries, and historical or ethnographic geographies. These distinctions are based on inferences about their differing origins and functions. The first two concern real places and are approximately contemporary with the landscape they describe; the last are retrospective or anachronizing descriptions of places and peoples either real or imagined.

Administrative maps were either boundary maps defining territorial limits or lists of towns and/or tribes within specific districts. Boundary maps usually follow the formula "from point A to point B, then to point C," and so on, returning ultimately to point A. The simplest biblical boundary map, the familiar description of Canaan "from Dan to Beer-sheba" (2 Sam. 24.2), has only two elements. The most complex, a detailed delineation of Canaan's boundaries in Numbers 34.1–12, enumerates multiple consecutive points. Town lists were not sequences of connected points but inclusive catalogues probably compiled by a central authority for purposes of calculating revenue or population size in a given district. These probably originated in the royal administration begun by David (e.g., the Levitical cities in Josh. 21; 1 Chron. 6) and continued by Solomon (1 Kings 4.7–19; e.g., the Galilean and Transjordanian tribes and northern Benjamin in Josh. 13; 18; 19) and later kings (e.g., the districts of Judah in Josh. 15.20–62; the towns of Simeon and Dan in Josh. 19; 1 Chron. 4).

Itineraries of military expeditions, based probably on contemporary sources, include the campaign of Benhadad of Aram-Damascus into northern Israel, the invasion of Israel by Tiglathpileser III of Assyria, Uzziah's conquests in Philistia, and the Philistine retaliation against Judah in the reign of Ahaz. Abraham's legendary war with the kings of the east contains topographic information about the southern Dead Sea region, although the historicity and geographical details of this account are disputed.

Finally, there are historical and ethnographic geographies that depict, accurately or imperfectly, real places and peoples or portray cosmic realms outside human experience. The former include the "Table of Nations" tracing Noah's descendants after the *Flood, Israelite wanderings after their *Exodus from Egypt, the roster of Canaanite kings opposing the Israelite invaders, tribal allotments awarded after the conquest of Canaan, and the land that remained unconquered. Ezekiel's oracle against Tyre describes not only the city but also its far-flung trading connections. Cosmic geographies include descriptions of the rivers of the garden of Eden and Ezekiel's vision of the new Jerusalem coupled with the idealized boundaries of the land of Israel. Revelation 21 is a New Testament version of Ezekiel's visionary map of the heavenly Jerusalem. Biblical word maps of real or imagined space were perhaps accompanied originally by drawings, but none of these have survived.

Drawn maps from ancient Mesopotamia do however exist. These were inscribed on clay, like most other Mesopotamian written documents. The oldest (late third millennium BCE), excavated at Nuzi in northeastern Iraq, depicts an agricultural estate east of Nuzi belonging to "Arzala." Two additional maps, both dated to the mid-second millennium BCE, are from Nippur in southern Iraq. One shows the city itself and its adjacent canals; another locates twelve agricultural plots in the vicinity and names their owners. These maps represent cadastral (land measurement) maps, identifying plots to record ownership and perhaps

for purposes of taxation, like modern land deeds. In ancient Syria-Palestine such cadastral maps may also have existed. They were probably drawn on perishable parchment or papyrus and thus have not survived.

The existence of maps, whether written or drawn, implies an underlying notion of spatial orientation. In the biblical world that orientation was eastward, not northward as with modern maps. Others directions were related to this primary one. Since east was "front" (Gen. 2.8), west was "behind" (Job 18.20), north was "on the left hand" (Gen. 14.15), and south "on the right hand" (1 Sam. 23.24). The etymologies of the biblical words frequently used to express cardinal directions conform to this orientation. An alternate orientation, toward the rising of the sun, also existed. East was the direction of the sun's rising, and west, of its setting. The two orientations, one solar and one based on an observer's position, may be connected through the sacral significance, common throughout the ancient Near East, of facing the sunrise.

The best-known extant map of the biblical world is the sixth-century CE mosaic map discovered in Madaba (Medeba), Jordan. Even in its present fragmentary state, the Madaba map is a recognizable although schematic representation of Palestine on both sides of the Dead Sea. Byzantine Jerusalem, labeled "the holy city," is the focal point of the map. Not coincidentally, place names written on it are intended to be read as the viewer looks east, facing the mosaic.

Medieval maps of Palestine, both Jewish and Christian, were, like the Madaba map, created after the region's religious significance had been established. Such maps were concerned primarily with locations mentioned in biblical narrative and not with precise mapping of the landscape.

Modern mapping of the biblical world began in the eighteenth century CE as biblical geographers attempted to relate word maps to contemporary locations in Palestine and neighboring lands. The first accurate topographic maps of Palestine, based on field surveys conducted by C. R. Conder and H. H. Kitchener in 1872–1877, were published by the Palestine Exploration Fund in 1880. After World War I, Britain and France established topographic surveys in Palestine and Syria, respectively, which produced maps of the region that are, with improvements, still the basis for archaeological exploration in the region. (See further R. North, *A History of Biblical Map Making,* Wiesbaden, 1979.)

Joseph A. Greene

MARI TABLETS. The magnificent palace of Mari with its royal archives of cuneiform tablets is the most significant archaeological find from French excavations at Tell Hariri, which is situated about a mile west of the Middle Euphrates in Syria. Most of these tablets, numbering in the tens of thousands, are royal correspondence dealing with domestic and international matters and economic, administrative, and juridical records of the palace. These texts have supplied important historical, chronological, geographic, ethnolinguistic, and cultural data concerning northern Mesopotamia and Syria-Palestine from the mid-nineteenth to the mid-eighteenth century BCE, a period just before the rise of Hammurapi of Babylon and culminating in the formation of his Old Babylonian Empire.

Part of the significance of the Mari tablets for the interpretation of the Bible stems from the information that they provide about the West Semitic Amur-

rites, who began a massive infiltration into Mesopotamia at the beginning of the second millennium BCE. The Mari archives document a wide spectrum of Amurrites. They depict confederacies of seminomadic West Semitic tribes such as the Yaminites, who were untouched by Mesopotamian civilization and remained hostile to the central authorities. At the other extreme, they record the rule of thoroughly Mesopotamianized West Semitic kings, such as Shamasi-addu of Assyria, Zimri-lim of Mari, and Hammurapi of Babylon, who remained Amurrite only in name. They also describe the West Semitic Haneans in the process of sedentarization, who accepted the authority of the Mesopotamian kings but retained many of the ways of the Amurrites. In recording the activities of all these Amurrites, the Mari archives provide rich documentation of West Semitic personal names, vocabulary, tribal structure and organization, and institutions and practices, such as *covenant making and census taking. In the cultic sphere, there is a small but significant group of prophecy texts, which attest to the existence of intuitive divination by "ecstatics" and "answerers" at Mari, who inform the king of the deity's message.

Some scholars have sought to place the events described in Genesis 12–50 within the West Semitic context of Mari, thus dating the ancestors of Israel to the early second millennium. While one must acknowledge the invaluable contributions of the Mari tablets in illuminating the ancient West Semitic background of biblical traditions, parallels alone cannot establish contemporaneity. Until the distinguishing particularities of Amurrite and Aramean cultures can be clarified by new discoveries, we must be content to utilize the Mari data for the insights and perspectives they provide without drawing chronological conclusions that cannot be proved.

Barry L. Eichler

MARRIAGE.

Ancient Israel. The institution of marriage is intimately related to kinship in the Hebrew Bible. There are indications that marriage was thought of as an extension of kinship through an informal or written covenant or agreement. Language that is used in connection with the *covenant, such as "love" and "hate" (for the latter, see Deut. 24.3 [NRSV "dislike"]; Judg. 15.2 [NRSV "reject"]), is also used of the marriage relationship and its dissolution. From at least the eighth century BCE onward, the covenantal relationship between Yahweh and Israel is likened to a covenanted marriage; this analogous usage begins in Hosea 1–3 and continues in later materials. By analyzing the analogy we can deduce some of the ideals concerning marriage in ancient Israel, at least for those who produced the texts. Two characteristics may be noted. First, the relationship was monogamous. Israel had only one God, and God had chosen Israel over all other peoples. Second, mutual fidelity was expected. *Adultery was accepted as grounds for dissolving the relationship (*see* Divorce). Hosea implies that the relationship should be one of mutual love, respect, and fidelity, and that the wife would call her husband "my man" and not "my master" (Hebr. *ba*ᶜ*al*) (2.16).

The status of women in ancient Israel is an important factor in understanding the institution of marriage. A woman seems always to have been under the authority and protection of her nearest male kin; for the wife, this was the husband. Some texts may imply that the status of women changed for the better over time.

Although monogamy may have been the ideal, polygamy was accepted and practiced throughout Israel's history, although to what extent we cannot be sure, since the sources for the most part are derived from and describe the elite ruling and upper classes. The patriarchs took more than one wife, and the kings of Israel and Judah maintained harems, of which Solomon's was the most notorious. By the Roman period, monogamy seems to have been the common practice.

Endogamy and exogamy. Endogamy is marriage within one's group, however that may be defined, and exogamy is marriage outside it; both are attested in the Bible. In the ancestral narratives, endogamy was apparently the dominant practice; for example, in Genesis 24 Abraham sends his servant back to Mesopotamia to find a wife for his son Isaac from among his own kin. Yet exogamy is also reported, as by Esau and Joseph. Exogamy was practiced by the kings of Israel and Judah, such as David, few of whose marriages were endogamous (beginning with Michal, Saul's daughter), Solomon, and Ahab.

The Deuteronomic view of exogamy was hostile, expressly because of a fear of apostasy, a view also found in postexilic literature. The book of Ruth, on the other hand, has been interpreted as espousing a position in which exogamy is acceptable.

New Testament. No detailed teaching concerning marriage is found in the Gospels; we may infer from discussions concerning divorce and other passages that Jesus viewed it positively, with monogamy as the ideal. Paul's views are more developed, and more controversial. The most detailed discussion is in 1 Corinthians 7, where Paul argues that marriage is an antidote to sexual immorality, but that celibacy is preferable. As v. 26 makes clear, in part this view was due to

Paul's belief in an imminent *second coming of Christ, but other factors no doubt were also at work, including Paul's own unmarried state. The "household codes" of the post-Pauline letters exhibit a conventional view of marriage, and the subordinate position of women within it.

As in the Hebrew Bible, the marriage relationship is used in the New Testament to describe the bond between the community and God, in this case expressed as the church and Christ.

See also Sex.   *Russell Fuller*

MARX AND THE BIBLE.

What did Karl Marx (1818–1883) make of the Bible? Was it a book that he knew and used? Did the Bible have any influence on him, a person who became estranged from all religion, especially from Judaism and Christianity? These two religious traditions were part of his heritage, and there is evidence that Marx knew the Bible and used it in various ways for his own purposes. But, of course, a knowledge of the Bible implies neither a regard for its teaching nor a recognition of its authority. No one who was capable of writing, as Marx did in 1844, that "the criticism of religion ends with the precept that the supreme being for man is man" is likely to have had much sympathy for a collection of writings that expresses a distinctly different point of view. He believed that human beings must unite in a revolutionary struggle to free themselves from exploitation, from belief in God, and from the illusory comforts of religion.

Marx's Jewish and Christian Background. Born in Trier on 5 May 1818, Marx was the son of a Jewish lawyer, Heinrich (Heschel) Marx, who converted to Lutheranism in 1817. The law did not permit Jews to work as civil servants or as lawyers, and those who did not convert to Christianity were obliged to accept subordinate positions in society. Conversion was not easy for either of Marx's parents, several of whose forebears in Germany and Holland had served their communities as rabbis. It was not until August 1824 that the children, including Karl, were baptized. Out of respect for her parents, Marx's mother postponed her own baptism for another fifteen months. Marx's early upbringing thus provided him with opportunities to observe both Jewish and Christian traditions.

Like Friedrich Engels, as a young man Marx was by no means hostile to Christianity. In a youthful piece, *The Union of Believers with Christ* (1835), he speaks of how Christians are able to turn to their fellow believers because they share with them an inner bond, through the sacrificial love of Christ. Union with Christ can bring "inner elevation, comfort in sorrow, calm trust, and a heart susceptible to human love, to everything noble and great, not for the sake of ambition and glory, but only for the sake of Christ." Was this an expression of genuine Christian conviction? Or was it an early example of his ability to parody the devotional language of Christian contemporaries? If it is parody, it helps to account for the apparent shift in Marx from belief to unbelief, from Christian commitment to militant atheism. The change in Marx's beliefs came when his Promethean instincts surfaced. In his doctoral dissertation at Jena (1841) he uses the words of Aeschylus's Prometheus, "In one word—I hate all the gods." Above all, he hated the God of the Bible: the creator God, who created humans in his own image, was, in Marx's analysis, the enemy of humanity, a human projection that served only to delay progress toward final liberation.

Approaches to Alienation. Marx's concept of *Entfremdung* (alienation) is not unknown in the Bible, although there it finds a very different focus in the estrangement of human beings from their creator. The prophets inveighed against all forms of idolatry in which human beings rendered to lifeless images the worship due alone to the living God. These *idols were the work of human hands. For Marx, God was an idol, worshiped by its creator; it distracted men and women from the realization of their own potential. Marx insisted that the alienation experienced by human beings was alienation, not from God, but from themselves. Like the biblical writers, Marx's themes were those of deliverance, liberation, justice, and equality, but his conclusions were different from theirs because he held that we live in a universe without God.

The eschatological aspects of his prophetic vision of the classless society are thus very different from those in the Bible. His was a belief in a secular eschatology, a belief that in the future the difference between human essence and human existence would be eliminated. The theology of the *incarnation would be turned on its head in the deification of the human. Marx believed that salvation lies within history, not beyond it. Insofar as he used biblical concepts, and employed stylistic devices reminiscent of the prophets, Marx was at pains to correct, if not expressly, what the Bible had to say to those looking for justice and liberation from oppression. What is missing in Marx is the biblical recognition of the individual's value in eternity as well as in time. The New Testament's emphasis on the redeeming activity of Jesus, on the full life to be enjoyed by the believer, and on the reconciling work of God in Christ, found neither echo nor acknowledgment in Marx. In place of this he repudiated biblical teaching by means of quotation out of context, carefully selected allusions, a tendentious use of theological interpretation, and outright parody.

All of this served Marx's purpose by diminishing the value of the Bible as a credible historical record of the events it contains or as a repository of wisdom. In this he gained support from an unexpected source. While he did not acknowledge any indebtedness to the criticism of the New Testament that came into prominence in the middle of the nineteenth century in Germany (see. Interpretation, History of, article on Modern Biblical Criticism), there is, nonetheless, in the subsequent attention that he gave to theologians like David F. Strauss (1808–1874) and Bruno Bauer (1809–1882), a recognition of the implications of their criticism. The spirit of this criticism was congenial to Marx because it served the interests of his attack on religion.

Marx's Use of the Bible. Several of Marx's works are replete with biblical quotations and allusions. In using them, Marx attempted to expose the naïveté of any lingering religious sentiments in other writers and political activists, employing an idiom with which he presumed them to be familiar, yet in a way that destroyed the original emphasis. To this end he alluded to biblical subjects and themes such as justice, equality, and deliverance, and echoed familiar phrases from the scriptures, well-known hymns, and the language of Christian piety.

The language of the *Sermon on the Mount and of the beatitudes features in his criticism of the attitudes of the poor, who delude themselves with promises of a heavenly inheritance. Texts such as Colossians 1.26 were given an interpretation more in line with his own concept of reality for a new generation of "saints." Similarly, "the time is fulfilled" (Mark 1.15) is interpreted in terms very different from those of the realized eschatology of the gospel. The emphasis on faith rather than works in Romans 3.28 is identified as a weakness typical of those who continue to accept false views of human existence. The struggles for human liberation, and the creation of a new order foreseen in Revelation 21.1, are accommodated to Marx's own vision of the future.

Despite Marx's atheism and his despisal of all religions—Judaism and Christianity especially—because they had become instruments of oppression in the struggle between workers and capitalists, there is little doubt that from time to time biblical memories came back to his consciousness. Later, his daughter Eleanor Marx-Aveling recalled how her father dealt with her "religious qualms" after she had been to a Roman Catholic church "to hear the beautiful music," when she was about six years old. Marx "quietly made everything clear and straight, so that from that hour to this no doubt could ever cross my mind again." But she adds the following note that sheds a different light on Marx's residual memory of a religious revelation that he despised.

And how I remember his telling the story— I do not think it could ever have been so told before or since—of the carpenter whom rich men killed, and many and many a time saying, "After all we can forgive Christianity much, because it taught us the worship of the child." And Marx could himself have said, "Suffer little children to come unto me," for wherever he went, there children somehow would turn up also.

To the themes of justice, equality, and the value of labor Marx brought his own perceptions. These are also biblical themes, but when Paul, for instance, addressed himself to those in the Christian community who were content to enjoy the fruits of the labors of others, he spoke in response to a different vision. Marx insisted that if anyone would not work, he should not eat, but this was a note of warning, sounded from the logic of his own dualistic anthropology. Marx held that human was set against human, as enemy against enemy, as worker against capitalist.

For the Bible's essential message Marx had only derision. Yet he was obliged to admit that the transformation of the world would require more than reliance on the processes of historical materialism. Above all, it would require a new kind of human creature with the capacity, as well as the desire, to build a society in which swords are beaten into plowshares.   *Edward Hulmes*

MASORETIC TEXT. The Masoretic Text (MT) refers to the textual product elaborated by schools of scholars (Masoretes) who in the early Middle Ages integrated vowel signs, accent markings, and marginal notes (the Masorah) into the received consonantal text of the Hebrew Bible. It is the text both of rabbinic Bibles and of modern scholarship.

There are thirty-one extant Masoretic manuscripts of the Hebrew Bible, complete or fragmentary, dating from the late ninth century to 1100 CE, and some three thousand thereafter. In the sixteenth century, Eliahu ha-Levi noted that there were thousands of Masoretes over a long period of time, neither the beginning nor the end of which is known; their work began toward the end of the Talmudic period (ca. 600 CE) and found its crown in the work of the ben Asher family at the beginning of the tenth century.

The complete MT is included in a manuscript discovered in a synagogue in Cairo during the nineteenth century and now housed in the public library in St. Petersburg (formerly Leningrad, hence called Leningradensis [L]). It dates to 1009 CE and derives from the work of Aaron ben Asher. It is the text of the third Kittel-Kahle edition of *Biblia Hebraica* (1937) and of *Biblia Hebraica Stuttgartensia* (1976), its successor. Two facsimile editions have been published. The printed edition of the Second Rabbinic Bible of Jacob ben Hayyim ben Adoniyahu (Venice, 1524–1525), which was based in large part on the ben Asher tradition, had been the text of the first two editions of the Kittel Bible.

Older than L by about three-quarters of a century is the partially preserved Aleppensis (A), which was brought in 1948 to Jerusalem from Aleppo. It is believed that this represents the text of which Maimonides (twelfth century) approved; it is the text of the *Hebrew University Bible* (1975–).

The oldest manuscripts of the Hebrew Bible, from the *Dead Sea Scrolls, date from the third century BCE to the beginning of the second century CE, and have only consonants; most are pre-Masoretic. Those from other caves in the same area, dating to a period after 70 CE, are proto-Masoretic and reflect the stabilization of the consonantal text taking place at the time. It was this stabilized and exceptionally well-preserved consonantal text to which the Masorah was later added.   *James A. Sanders*

MEALS. Meals—from the apple in Eden to Ezekiel's scroll, from the *Passover to Jesus' Last Supper to the messianic wedding banquet—are still among the Bible's most powerful images, despite centuries of radical change. Indeed, as most explicitly stated in the Lord's command to the Israelites to tell their children about the Passover sacrifice and in

Jesus' command "Do this in remembrance of me" (Luke 22.19), these meals embody, translate, and reinterpret scripture. They speak to an ongoing process of turning water into *wine, drawing the living *Torah from daily life, but also, in the New Testament, turning the blood and wine of the *crucifixion back into the milk and water of plain speech. Biblical meals express an intensely dialogic and historical view of religious understanding, in which human responses approach the divine status of the original revelations.

Nineteenth-century evolutionists explained the prominence of food imagery in the Bible by arguing that the ancient Israelites represented earlier stages of the development from concrete to abstract forms of reasoning; taboos on meat were alleged to be the remnants of animal worship antedating *monotheism. Subsequent research has shown that symbolic or metaphorical reasoning is basic to human cognition, and food imagery is central to most known religions. Commensalism is synonymous with community; but particular cultural evaluations of who should eat what with whom, when, where, and why take many different forms, often subject to close scrutiny and debate precisely because of their critical social role.

Most scholarship on biblical meals has focused on the dietary rules concerning "clean" and "unclean" *animals, probably because of their salience in debates over the *Law that lead to the eventual differentiation of Judaism and Christianity. The most fruitful scholarship follows Leviticus 11.44 and Deuteronomy 14.2, 21, and some early rabbis, in seeing the rules as expressing and achieving *holiness by mandating the consumption of animals that are "clean" because they conform wholly to the cosmic order of the *creation and prohibiting the "unclean" anomalies (see, e.g., Mary Douglas, *Purity and Danger,* 1966; R. Bulmer in *Man* 24 [1989]: 302–20; *see also* Purity, Ritual).

Other scholars have emphasized the need for open-ended approaches, taking into account the diversity of Israelites, the paradoxical complexity of their Law, and the ways in which the Law has been continuously reinterpreted over time. For Robert Alter (*Commentary* 68/2 [1979]: 46–52) the holiness achieved by observing the dietary rules includes "vitalism," imitation of God's life-giving powers, expressed in prohibiting *blood and creatures found dead, and restricting, but not completely forbidding, the consumption of animals, especially carnivores. Samuel Cooper (in Harvey E. Goldberg, ed., *Judaism Viewed from Within and from Without,* 1987) sees the "laws of mixture" on the separation of meat and milk, linen and wool, and grain and grape as mediating similar contradictions in life giving and taking. Howard Eilberg-Schwartz (*The Savage in Judaism,* 1990) is still more comprehensive, seeing Israelite animal and plant classifications as root metaphors about a people brought into being by a God with no body.

Gillian Feeley-Harnik (*The Lord's Table,* 1981) emphasizes the need to look beyond the dietary rules at the broader significance of biblical meals in the light of participants' views of their moral dilemmas—notably, "Who is the true Israelite?" and "Who is my neighbor?"—and in terms of their own modes of analysis—notably *midrash*—in changing social and historical circumstances. Food, articulated in meals, was the embodiment of God's word, divine Wisdom, for people who would have no *graven images. The food that God provided was the foundation of the *covenant rela-

tionship in scripture and in sectarianism; the food God prohibited was *idolatry. During and after the Babylonian *exile (sixth century BCE), as God's word became increasingly identified with the Law, food law came to represent the whole Law. Sectarianism was expressed above all through differing interpretations of the dietary rules. Christians of the first century CE, as observant Jews, used the language of meals to establish both the legitimacy of Jesus and the novelty of his interpretation of the Law, which required different kinds of relations among human beings and God from those advocated by other sectarians.

Biblical meals are part of a larger semantic field, thought-action as a landscape, laid out in Genesis 1–2. The creation embodies not only vital categories but also vital creative, transformative processes that endow specific foods with particular social values, conveyed in meals. God, as the preeminent gardener, works to produce vital, edible wisdom-food, engendering and sustaining humans who should respond to God and each other in kind. Biblical meals express bodily processes of understanding and communicating that accompany and may even transcend words in the fullest "face-to-face" encounters. Peter's vision of the sheet filled with clean and unclean animals (Acts 10.9–11.18) is one striking example of how early Jewish-Christians used biblical meals to communicate their "face-to-face" understanding of the Law across the babel of tongues and stomachs that characterize humankind.

See also Lord's Supper.

Gillian Feeley-Harnik

MEDICINE. Although the existence of survivable surgical procedures on the skull (trephination) is attested from the Neolithic through the Arab periods, it is particularly difficult to identify and evaluate the therapeutic value of most specific treatments mentioned in the Bible. Such healing practices include the use of "balsam" from Gilead (Jer. 46.11), "mandrakes" for infertility (Gen. 30.14), and "bandages" (Ezek. 30.21).

Archaeoparasitologists have recently established the probable existence of certain intestinal diseases (e.g., tapeworm [taenia] and whipworm [trichuris trichiura] infections) in ancient Israel, but the precise identification of most diseases in the Bible has been notoriously difficult, especially in cases of epidemics. The condition usually translated as "leprosy" (Hebr. ṣāraʿat) receives the most attention in the Bible, but it does not have a simple modern equivalent because it probably encompassed a large variety of diseases, especially those manifesting chronic discoloration of the skin. Infertility was viewed as an illness that diminished the social status of the afflicted woman.

The Hebrew Bible has at least two principal explanations for illness. One, represented by Deuteronomy 28, affirms that health (Hebr. šālôm) encompasses a physical state associated with the fulfillment of *covenant stipulations that are fully disclosed to the members of the society, and illness stems from the violation of those stipulations. Therapy includes reviewing one's actions in light of the covenant. The book of Job offers a contrasting yet complementary view, which argues that illness may be rooted in divine plans that may not be disclosed to the patient at all and not in the transgression of published rules. The patient must trust that God's undisclosed reasons are just.

Perhaps the most distinctive feature of the Israelite health-care system depicted in the canonical texts is the division into legitimate and illegitimate consultative options for the patient. This dichotomy is partly related to monolatry, insofar as illness and healing rest ultimately on Yahweh's control and insofar as non-Yahwistic options are prohibited. Since it was accessible and inexpensive, *prayer to Yahweh was probably the most common legitimate option for a patient. Petitions and thanksgiving prayers uttered from the viewpoint of the patient are attested in the Bible.

Illegitimate options included consultants designated as "healers" (2 Chron. 16.12: Hebr. rōpĕʾîm, NRSV: "physicians"), non-Yahwistic temples (2 Kings 1.2–4), and probably a large variety of "sorcerers" (Deut. 18.10–12). Warnings in the canonical texts, along with archaeological evidence for fertility cults, indicate that such "illegitimate" options were used widely in ancient Israel.

The foremost legitimate consultants in the canonical texts are commonly designated as prophets, and they were often in fierce competition with "illegitimate" consultants. Stories of healing *miracles may reflect an effort to promote prophets as the legitimate consultants. Their function was to provide prognoses and intercede on behalf of the patient. Unlike some of the principal healing consultants in other Near Eastern societies, the efficacy of the Israelite prophets resided more in their relationship with God than in technical expertise. The demise of the prophetic office early in the Second Temple period probably led to the wide legitimation of the rōpĕʾîm.

Another accepted option for some illnesses, particularly in the preexilic period, was the temple. In 1 Samuel 1, Hannah visited the temple at Shiloh to help reverse her infertility. 2 Kings 18.4 indicates that, prior to Hezekiah, the bronze serpent made by Moses as a therapeutic device was involved in acceptable therapeutic rituals in the Temple of Jerusalem. Bronze serpents have been found in temples known to have been used for therapy during the first millennium BCE (e.g., the Asclepieion at Pergamon).

By the postexilic period the Priestly code (P) severely restricted access to the Temple for the chronically ill (e.g., "lepers" in Lev. 13–14; cf. 2 Sam. 5.7 on the blind and the lame) because of fear of "impurity." "Leprosy" alone probably encompassed a wide variety of patients. The theology of impurity, as a system of social boundaries, could serve to remove socioeconomically burdensome populations from society, the chronically ill perhaps being the most prominent. In effect, the Priestly code minimizes state responsibility for the chronically ill, leaving the eradication of illness for the future. (*See* Purity, Ritual.)

Thanksgiving or "well-being" offerings (Lev. 7.11–36) after an illness were probably always acceptable and economically advantageous for the Temple. Offerings after an illness also may have served as public notice of the readmission of previously ostracized patients to society.

The community responsible for the *Dead Sea Scrolls added to the priestly list of illnesses that excluded from the normal community and expanded the restrictions for "leprosy," the blind, and the lame. Socioeconomic reasons, as well as the fear of magical contamination, may be responsible for such increased restrictions.

Perhaps the most far-reaching consequence of the Priestly code was the growth of chronically ill populations with little access to the Temple. Since Jesus and his disciples appear to target these populations, early Christianity may be seen, in part, as a critique of the priestly health-care system. In early Christianity illness may be caused by numerous demonic entities who are not always acting at Yahweh's command (*see* Exorcism) and not necessarily by the violation of covenant stipulations. Emphasizing that the cure for illness may be found in this world, early Christianity preserved many older Jewish traditions regarding miraculous healings and collective health, although the influence of Hellenistic healing cults (e.g., the Asclepius cult) also may be seen.

Hector Ignacio Avalos

MEDICINE AND THE BIBLE. It is generally agreed that modern Western medicine takes its origin from two main sources, the Greek ideals enshrined in the Hippocratic tradition, to which was added the influence of the biblical teaching of love of one's *neighbor. Thus, although Western medicine owes much to its classical heritage, especially as this has been reinterpreted since the Renaissance, it was the added dimension of a biblically based ethic that gave it a distinctive approach, centered in a profound respect for the person.

The pragmatism of Greek ideals is reflected in writings dealing with the exposure of unwanted or weak infants and with solutions to the problems of the chronically ill. The latter, being useless to themselves and to the state, should be allowed to die without medical attention. Biblical religion, on the other hand, had the frame of reference of a transcendent God to whom humankind was ultimately answerable; this gives rise to a profound respect for the dignity and innate value of the individual, seen as created in the image of God. The responsibilities of biblical faith, whether Jewish or Christian, in the relations of people with one another are summed up in texts like "you shall love your neighbor as yourself" (Lev. 19.18) and "Do to others as you would have them do to you" (Matt. 7.12; *see* Golden Rule). From the standpoint of medicine, this was admirably summed up in the prayer of the great Jewish physician Maimonides (1135–1204 CE): "May I never see in my patient anything else than a fellow creature in pain."

The influence of such biblical precepts introduces an element of moral obligation into medical ethics as it developed in parallel with the rising influence of Christianity in the later Roman empire and throughout the medieval period in Europe. It also provided the spur to the church to establish hospitals that provided care for the sick; refuges that gave shelter to the blind, sufferers from leprosy, the mentally ill, and others outcast from society; and dispensaries for the poor. This same obligation, at a much later stage, led to the development of medical missionary work in conjunction with, yet distinct from, the growth of evangelistic concern that took place in the nineteenth century.

In providing a moral base for such developments, the Bible has given to modern medicine a great deal more than it might now care to acknowledge. Nevertheless, the centrality of respect for the person that originates in the Bible has now become enshrined in modern medical codes, such as the Geneva Convention Code of Ethics (1949) and the Helsinki Convention (1964) of the World Medical Association.

On the other hand, as a result of the ways in which the Bible has been interpreted and applied, there have been times when its influence on medicine has been negative. Until there was any proper understanding of the causative factors in disease and the actual disease processes themselves, there was a tendency to see sickness as the result of divine visitations and punishment for wrongdoing. The Bible itself knows little of physicians as such (*see* Medicine), and

in the faith of Israel it was God alone who was the healer and giver of life. Most references to physicians are uncomplimentary (as in Mark 5.25–26, more temperately put in Luke 8.43) or at best neutral. Other than the reference to Luke "the beloved physician" (Col. 4.14), the only positive remarks about medical practitioners occur in Sirach 38.1–15, where the reader is exhorted to "honor physicians for their services." Even in this passage, however, the emphasis is on the need for confession of sin before any true healing could take place and the role of God as healer. (Note the much later dictum of Ambroise Paré [1510–1590]: "I treated the patient, but God healed him.")

In the Bible itself, it is the religious component that dominates in a situation where religion and medicine are inextricably bound together. This is seen particularly in Israel's legal codes, which did not separate physical disease from ritual *purity. Thus, while the sanitary code of the *Torah contains regulations that were of major importance in the promotion of health and the prevention of epidemic diseases in the community, they are set within a religious framework. Ultimately, it was God alone who sent disease and disaster as a punishment for wrongdoing or, alternatively, rewarded the good with health and well-being.

The establishment of such a causal relationship between disease and a failure to meet religious and moral obligations was, in some sense, an attempt to answer the unanswerable question, "Why me?" It was seen especially with regard to contagious and disfiguring diseases, of which the best example is the disease complex unfortunately called leprosy in most English translations. Various ritual prescriptions were applied to such diseases in order to avoid the contamination of the community, which was seen as more important than the healing of the sick person. Similar ritual restrictions were also imposed in relation to normal physiological functions. Thus, consulting a physician for help could be construed as denial of the primary role of God and evidence of lack of faith in him, as well as lack of willingness to acknowledge personal sin.

Many of these concepts were perpetuated in Christianity, even though such a simplistic viewpoint was challenged in the Bible. The early church, however, undoubtedly interpreted such views too literally, and medical treatment was displaced by an emphasis on prayer and fasting in order to chasten the individual. From the Renaissance onward, however, medicine and theology became increasingly divorced from one another, allowing the development of medicine along the now-familiar lines of scientific principles from the sixteenth or seventeenth centuries onward. Nonetheless, there has always been in Christianity a healing ministry that has been seen as biblically based. In general, this has not been considered as in competition with orthodox medicine but rather as complementary to it. Some more recent developments in healing ministries derived from biblical literalism, however, seem to be an attempt to return to a prescientific worldview, and will inevitably be in conflict with modern medical practice.
J. Keir Howard

MEEK. The English word "meek" is now largely archaic, and recent translations of the Bible use it far less frequently than earlier versions. Its connotations of gentleness and humility are not entirely accurate representations of the word it generally translates in the Hebrew Bible, where ᶜānāw and its cognates refer primarily to socioeconomic and political deprivation; the ᶜānāwîm are the poor,

the oppressed, whose special protector is God. They are both individuals within the community and Israel as a totality as well: their persecutors will be defeated and they will inherit the land. Earlier suggestions that they were an identifiable political group are now generally rejected.

On occasion the Hebrew words in question seem to refer to an inner attitude of humility as well; the "meek" are somehow closer to God. This spiritual connotation is dominant in the word used to translate ᶜānāw in the Septuagint. The word *praos* and its cognates are widely used in Greek literature to describe an admirable moral quality of gentle and genial composure, and this is its dominant sense in the New Testament, where it is used of both Jesus and his followers.

The beatitude in Matthew 5.5 that describes the meek inheriting the earth is clearly derived from Psalm 37.11, and Jesus probably intended its original, concrete sense, but in view of Matthew's spiritualization of other beatitudes with parallels in Luke 6.20–23, the meek seem for Matthew at least to be those who are not only socioeconomically deprived but patiently accepting of their status as well. (*See* Sermon on the Mount.)   *Michael D. Coogan*

MEGILLOT. The name, meaning "scrolls," given to the collection of the five shortest books of the Writings, the third section of the Hebrew Bible. The Megillot are Song of Solomon, Ruth, Lamentations, Ecclesiastes, and Esther. Although the current order of the books in printed Bibles follows their order in the annual Jewish liturgical cycle, in some older traditions they were arranged according to traditional chronology: Ruth, Song of Solomon, Ecclesiastes, Lamentations, Esther. The Song of Solomon is read on the feast of *Passover, as well as preceding the service welcoming the *Sabbath on Friday evenings; the love poetry of the Song is thought to represent in the former case the marriage of God and Israel and in the latter the marriage of Israel and Queen Sabbath. Ruth is read at *Pentecost (Shavuᶜot); among the reasons given are the setting of Ruth at the time of the barley harvest, the tradition that King David, one of Ruth's descendants, was born and died at this time, and the relationship between Israel's assumption of the *Torah at Mount Sinai seven weeks after the *Exodus and Ruth's acceptance of Judaism. Lamentations, a series of dirges commemorating the destruction of Jerusalem and the Temple, is read on the ninth of the month of Ab, a fast day on which these events, and the destruction of the Second Temple as well, are said to have taken place. The somber mood of Ecclesiastes, read in the fall on the Feast of Booths (Sukkot), is thought to be a reflection of the season. Esther is read on Purim, the joyous holiday celebrating the salvation of the Jews as related in the book.

See also Canon, article on Order of Books in the Hebrew Bible; Lectionaries, article on Jewish Tradition.

Carl S. Ehrlich

MENE, MENE, TEKEL, AND PARSIN. The banquet of King Belshazzar, described in Daniel 5, was disrupted by a divine apparition; a hand etching the words "Mene Mene Teqel Upharsin" (u being a form of the common Semitic conjunction meaning "and") on the plaster of a wall.

Ancient evidence suggests that the repetition of "mene" in v. 25 may be scribal error (see v. 26). Others interpret the first "mene" as a verbal form meaning "he has weighed."

The inability of the various diviners to elicit sense from the inscription was most likely rooted in their failure to understand the meaning behind the words rather than to read the words themselves. In 1886, Charles Clermont-Ganneau suggested that the terms reflect ancient weights or measures: mina, shekel, and half-shekel; this view is now widely held. The meaning of the inscription as interpreted by Daniel, however, lies not in these nouns but in the verbal notions behind them: Belshazzar's kingdom was numbered (mnh): he was weighed (tql); his kingdom was divided (prs) between the Medes and the Persians.

James H. Platt

MENORAH. The seven-branched candelabrum of the wilderness *tabernacle and Jerusalem Temples, it was typical of Iron Age elevated metal structures combining the functions of lampstand and lamp. The tabernacle menorah, anachronistically described in the postexilic Priestly code (P), was said to have been hammered, together with all of its lamps and utensils, from one whole talent (ca. 96 lb [44 kg]) of pure gold by the craftsman Bezalel. Based on a tripod, three branches curved from both sides of a vertical shaft; these, with the central stem, were decorated with cups carved in the shape of open almond blossoms, the uppermost holding the lamps. These botanical motifs may reflect tree of life symbolism, common in the ancient Near East.

According to 1 Kings 7.39 (and 2 Chron. 4.7), ten pure gold lampstands, which are not described in detail, together with gold accoutrements, adorned Solomon's Temple, five on the south side of the main hall, and five on the north. The Second Temple, following the priestly directions for the wilderness tabernacle, had one golden menorah. According to Josephus, three of its lamps burned all day; the rest were lit in the evening. The Talmud relates that the westernmost lamp, closest to the Holy of Holies, was never extinguished. The menorah was removed in 169 BCE by Antiochus Epiphanes IV during his desecration of the Temple. Judas Maccabee supplied a new menorah, together with other vessels, during the Temple's cleansing. Josephus recounts that when Herod's Temple was destroyed in 70 CE, the menorah was carried by the Romans in Titus's triumphal march. The Temple menorah seems to be depicted on the Arch of Titus in Rome, although there is some controversy over this rendition's accuracy, particularly regarding the double octagonal pedestal, since according to all Jewish sources and considerable archeological evidence, the menorah stood on three legs. After 70 CE, the menorah became an enduring Jewish religious and national symbol, frequently appearing in synagogue, domestic, and funerary art; it appears today on the emblem of the State of Israel.   *Judith R. Baskin*

MERCY OF GOD. The concept of a loving and merciful god is ancient, found in hymns to Egyptian, *Sumerian, and Babylonian deities. In the *Ugaritic texts, the high god El is formulaically described as merciful and compassionate, with a cognate of the same word used two millennia later in Muslim characterization of God. Several Hebrew words have traditionally been translated by the English word "mercy," including *ḥānan, ḥesed,* and especially *rāḥamîm.* The last is derived from the word for uterus *(reḥem),* and is remarkable both for its maternal nuance and for its persistence in biblical and nonbiblical descriptions of male deities. The nuance is made explicit in Isa-

iah 49.14–15, a rare instance of maternal *metaphor to describe the God of Israel.

One of the oldest characterizations of Yahweh is found in Exodus 34.6–7, quoted or alluded to frequently. This ancient liturgical fragment describes Yahweh as "merciful *(raḥûm)* and gracious *(ḥannûn),* slow to anger, and abounding in steadfast love . . . forgiving iniquity and transgression and sin . . . yet by no means clearing the guilty, but visiting the iniquity of the parents upon the children and the children's children," and thus raises one of the most profound dilemmas of monotheism, the tension between divine mercy and justice. Biblical tradition itself offers a partial corrective to the theory of inherited, and thus implicitly collective, guilt, notably in Ezekiel 18. But the more profound paradox of a God believed to be merciful and forgiving on the one hand and ultimately just on the other remains unresolved. The Bible is of course not an abstract theological treatise, and so it is not surprising that there is no detailed exposition of the problem. But it is one to which biblical writers frequently return, in narratives, dialogue, and especially in *prayers, where the hope of the worshiper is that God's mercy will prevail over his justice. This hope is based on the realization of the essential unworthiness of those chosen by God; the election of Israel, and the *salvation of the Christian, were motivated by gratuitous divine love.

God's mercy is also a model for human conduct. "Those who fear the Lord" are characterized as "gracious *(ḥannûn),* merciful *(raḥûm),* and righteous" in Psalm 112.4, phrasing that echoes the immediately preceding description of Yahweh in the similarly acrostic Psalm 111.4. Resuming this theme, Jesus commands his followers to imitate divine mercy according to Luke 6.36.

See also Covenant; Evil; Grace; Suffering.   *Michael D. Coogan*

MESSIANIC SECRET. The use of the term "messianic secret" arose at the beginning of the twentieth century with the publication of Wilhelm Wrede's *Das Messiasgeheimnis in den Evangelien* (1901), translated into English under the title *The Messianic Secret* (Cambridge, 1971). Wrede started from an assumption that was widely held in critical biblical studies, namely, that the historical Jesus was not conscious of being more than a Jewish prophet, and that his claims were in no way messianic. After his *crucifixion, however, his disciples were convinced that he had risen from the dead and therefore must have been the Messiah who was foretold in scripture.

When looking back, Christians of the first generation were, according to Wrede, puzzled by the lack of consistency between the picture of Jesus of Nazareth that was presented by the traditions of his earthly life and their own belief in a risen Lord. Therefore Mark, the author of the oldest written gospel, removed the offense by introducing into his narrative sayings in which Jesus told his followers and people he dealt with not to disclose his true nature. The injunctions to silence in different sayings are therefore not historical reminiscences but an editorial device created by the evangelist. This means that Wrede's thesis is one of the earliest attempts to elucidate the process of redaction in the formation of the Gospels. Matthew and Luke have retained, though not consistently, the core of Mark's redactional scheme.

According to Wrede, the texts that have been arranged with the intention to portray Jesus as attempting to conceal his messiahship include the following: *exorcisms where Jesus silences the confessions pronounced by demons, miraculous healings, intentional retirement, a command to keep silent addressed to a disciple, private teaching given to the disciples, and the saying about parabolic teaching. All these passages are interpreted in light of Mark 9.9: "He ordered them to tell no one about what they had seen, until the Son of Man had risen from the dead. So they kept the matter to themselves."

Since Wrede published his book it has become evident that the presentation of Jesus in the synoptic Gospels is more complicated and cannot be explained by assuming a simple redactional pattern. In only one narrative, Peter's confession, does the injunction to silence refer explicitly to messiahship. On the other hand, there are numerous instances where the "messianic character" of a saying or an action is by no means being concealed: the feeding of the five thousand, the triumphal entry into Jerusalem, and, not least, the trial and condemnation of Jesus, when he was found guilty of claiming to be the king of the Jews. It can be said that in the public ministry of Jesus there is constant paradox of secrecy and revelation, of concealment and proclamation. Mark reports exorcisms where no command to keep silent is given.

The same paradox can be observed in narratives where miraculous healings are reported. In these cases the injunctions to silence, when given, have obviously nothing to do with a messianic secret. Not one of the healing *miracles performed publicly gives the impression that Jesus was the Messiah. When the blind Bartimaeus twice hails him as Son of David, it is not Jesus who silences him

(Mark 10.47–49). When Jesus cured sick people, the injunction to secrecy was primarily a matter of privacy. The raising of Jairus's daughter shows the paradox inherent in one single narrative (5.35–43).

Teaching in *parables is another context where the motif of secrecy is apparent, yet in another modulation and without reference to messiahship. As used in Mark 4.1–13, the quotation from Isaiah 6.9 does not simply imply that Jesus' parables were intended to conceal a mystery. What is meant is that parables were a way by which to test the serious intention of the listeners: "To those who have, more will be given; and from those who have not, even what they have will be taken away" (Mark 4.25; cf. 4.33–34). It is a question of response, which is essentially different from concealment as a literary device. The paradox of secrecy and publicity appears also in Jesus' sayings about the *Son of man, as they are presented by Mark. The reference to Daniel 7 is clear, and in that text a heavenly figure corresponds to the suffering saints. In the sayings that were publicly pronounced, the enigmatic symbol of the Son of man stands for authority. In the instruction given privately to the disciples, the Son of man and his followers are to face trials, suffering, and death on their way to the final kingdom.

In the final analysis, the paradox of secrecy and publicity is inherent in different layers of reminiscences from the earthly life of Jesus, layers that precede the christological interpretation worked out by the early church. Jesus stands out as possessing more than human authority. His words and his actions are charged with a transcendent rather than a messianic significance. This is intimated in his private teaching, but he did not want it to be proclaimed. When unclean spirits and demons recognized him as more than human, they were silenced and defeated. The motif of secrecy can thus be discerned in the synoptic Gospels in different variations, apparently more original in Mark, sublimated by continuing christological reflection in Matthew and Luke. The underlying prerequisite is the essential choice by those confronted with Jesus, between belief and unbelief.

Harald Riesenfeld

METAPHORS. The principal subject of the Bible is God in his relation to his world, his people, and humanity. But the God of the Bible is holy, transcendent, other, unlike anything in all creation. It follows, then, that language about God must be figurative, because it attempts to describe in terms of this world one who is totally different from this world.

We can speak about God and our relation to him, however, because he has revealed himself through his own words and deeds in the history recorded in the scriptures. All metaphoric language about God must be consonant with that self-revelation in order to be true.

God is known in the biblical account only in relationship. The five most frequent metaphors of his relationship with his people are king/subject, judge/litigant, husband/wife, father/child, and lord or master/servant. All are commissive metaphors, implying an obligation in the relationship described.

Yet every metaphoric term for God breaks its limits and transforms the way in which it is ordinarily understood. For example, when God is described as father, the term is filled with the meaning given it by God's self-revelation, and human fathers then become responsible for growing up into the measure of God's compassionate and loving fatherhood. In short, metaphors for God come to define the goal of human life, which is to conform to the image of God.

None of the metaphors for God are intended to be taken literally in their human sense, a fact sometimes overlooked. For example, God as father or husband is never literally male, nor does he exercise sexual functions. Similarly, the use of metaphoric language for God says nothing about the historicity of his deeds and words.

Many terms for God participate in metaphoric systems and undergo rich development in the scriptures. God as father is source of life, names, care, love, discipline, family unity, and an example to children; he feeds, clothes, and gives *inheritance, legal rights, property, home, and a sense of belonging. Because such a metaphoric system is involved, God is never called mother in the Bible, though he exercises mother-like love and care for his children. Female terms for God are used in the Bible only in similes, pointing to one activity (see Feminism and the Bible). If they are interpreted as metaphors, the deity is then connected with the images of birth and suckling, and they erroneously result in the view of a goddess giving birth to all things and persons, who then participate in the divine being. The distinction that the Bible insists on between creator and creature is then lost.

Figures for God can have a high or low degree of correspondence with their referents. When God is described as like a bear, lion, leopard, moth, withering wind, devouring fire, eagle, or even dry rot, the correspondence is low, and such images are used for their shock or surprise value. More appropriate are the descriptions of God as rock, sun, living water, fortress, refuge; similarly, the descriptions of his actions in terms of those of a healer, potter, vintner, builder, farmer, tailor, shepherd, or warrior yield vivid pictures. Indeed, God is most often portrayed in anthropomorphic terms; this prevents his identification with some diffuse soul of nature, and it expresses the fact that he meets us person to person and demands from us the full depth of our personal devotion and love.

Some metaphors for God have lost their meaning because they have lost their context, such as the metaphor "*redeemer," which originally referred to a relative who bought back a family member from *slavery. The metaphor is recovered when the original context is recalled. Similarly, some figures become objectionable to some groups, for example, those of God as mighty warrior or as judge or, for feminists, as father or lord. But such metaphors are indispensable to the canonical witness to God and should be recovered by an explication of their full biblical content.

Human beings' relation to God is also described metaphorically because it deals with that which is evident only to the eyes of the faithful and must describe the unknown in terms of the known. Thus, God's faithful people are called in the Bible his adopted sons or children, his bride, kingdom of priests, holy nation, peculiar treasure, servants, jewels, witnesses, noble vine, pleasant planting, fruitful trees, and so on.

The church, in the New Testament, is called the new Jerusalem, the bride of Christ, the true *circumcision, the Israel of God, the body of Christ, God's temple, building, field, his covenant people, new creation, or colony of heaven. Church members are pilgrims, aliens, exiles, strangers on the earth, slaves of righteousness or of Christ, heirs, fools for Christ, citizens of heaven, or ministers of reconciliation. Christ himself is their righteousness, sanctification, redemption, first fruits, covenant, temple, high priest, sacrifice, word, or wisdom and power of God. He is called priest after the order of Melchizedek, man of heaven, *Son of God, servant, last Adam, *Son of man, Messiah, and Lord.

The life of faith is described in an almost limitless stock of pictures. It is soaring or being set in a broad place or on the heights. It is enjoying freedom, light, order, joy, life. It is being granted never-failing water and food, knowing shade and rest. It is experiencing the gift of a new heart and spirit.

On the other hand, the life of faithlessness is described as slavery to sin and death, and sinners are compared to rebels, disobedient sons, adulterous wives, whores, worms, backsliders, dead bones, waterless clouds, fruitless trees, wild waves, wandering stars, restless young camels, plunging horses, wild asses, rudderless ships, stubborn heifers, dogs, wilting grass, and choking tares. They are the old Adam, those of the flesh, cursed by God, and slaves to the principalities and powers of this present evil darkness.

Some metaphor systems permeate the Bible from beginning to end, for example, those connected with the *Exodus, or with the Temple and sacrificial system, or the *law court. Other metaphors, such as those of light and darkness, are given expression by many different words (cf. morning star, dayspring on high), while others draw on the perennial relationships and rounds of family life, as well as birth and death.

Metaphors may change their meaning from one context to another. Thus, the wilderness can be an expression of danger and judgment or of love and care; a yoke can be a figure of sin or of faithfulness. Meanings can be determined only by the context and by the intention of the author.

Other metaphorical forms, such as those of synecdoche, eponymy, metonomy, *parable, and allegory are frequent in the scriptures. The Bible is rich in fig-urative terms, of which we use only a very small portion.

See also Literature, The Bible as.

Elizabeth Achtemeier

MIRACLES. A miracle is an extraordinary event, perceived to be the result of the direct, purposeful action of a god or the agent of a god. Miracles are a common feature of literature and religious tradition in every culture, from the simplest to the most sophisticated societies, and from earliest historical times to the present. The questions raised by the occurrence of an event that is understood to be a miracle are not only "What happened?" but also "What does it mean?" or more specifically, "What is the divine message imparted through this event?"

It is inappropriate to describe a miracle as a violation of natural law, since most societies, including those represented in the Bible, believed in the direct action of God (or gods) in history. What happens in the world and in human experience is seen as the outworking of the divine will rather than an immutable law running its course. Even when among the Stoics there arose the idea of natural law as a fixed, basic process by which the universe operated, allowance was still made for the direct action of the gods. Thus, for example, in the circumstances surrounding the accession to power of Julius Caesar or in the birth and attainment of the imperial authority by Augustus, contemporary accounts by Roman historians describe the miracles that accompanied these historical developments as an indication of the active interest of the gods in human affairs.

In the Hebrew Bible, several types of miracle are reported. Among these are confirmatory miracles, through which God shows his choice and support of certain individuals or groups. Examples are the direct visions of God that are granted to Abraham, Jacob, and especially Moses. Thus, Abraham is given assurance by the appearance of the smoking fire pot and flaming torch that the *covenant with Yahweh will be fulfilled. Sarah's giving birth to Isaac after years of infertility is a confirming sign that the covenant will be established. Similarly, the burning bush confirms Moses' call by God to lead his people out of slavery in Egypt. The confirmation of God's promise to the covenant people is given in their safe passage through the sea and in the provision of *manna and *water for them in the Sinai desert. Or again, the power of the God whom Elijah serves is confirmed by the fire from Yahweh that consumes the altar and the offering upon it.

A second type of miracle is judgmental, as in the *plagues that befall the Egyptians until the release of the Israelites or the fall of the walls of Jericho when its inhabitants resist Israel's entry into the Promised Land. Another type is the act of mercy, through which some basic human need is met, as in the healings performed by Elisha.

Yet another type of miracle is the divine act of deliverance of individuals, as when Daniel and his friends are preserved from the fiery furnace, from starvation, and from the lion's den. Of a different sort are the miracles of divine vision, in which God and his purposes for his people are disclosed to certain persons, such as Isaiah, Ezekiel, and Daniel. In each case, the miracle is described as taking place in order to reveal God's purpose for his people, or to achieve some form of deliverance or punishment in behalf of individuals, of the Israelite nation, of her enemies, or of the minority who remain faithful to God.

In the New Testament, miracle is central to the earliest understanding of who Jesus is and his role in the inauguration of God's rule in the world. In the Q source, for example, when Jesus is asked by the followers of John the Baptist to explain who he is, he replies by pointing to his miracles of healing as evidences of the fulfillment of the prophetic promises of benefits to the needy and the outcasts. He also points to his *exorcisms as the major sign of the beginning of the defeat of the evil powers and the establishment of the *kingdom of God. Indeed, he refers to his own power to heal and to expel demons by the same phrase, "the finger of God," used of God's action in delivering Israel from Egypt (Exod. 8.19). There are miracle stories in the New Testament that directly parallel those in the Hebrew Bible. For example, the feeding of the five thousand shares details and overall aim with God's miraculous feeding of Israel in the desert. In both cases, a covenant people about to be reconstituted are taken out into a barren territory, where God meets their needs and where they are joined in covenant as his special people; this connection is made explicit in John's version of the story. The covenantal significance is underscored by the use within the feeding story of what become technical terms at the Last Supper: he took, he blessed, he broke, he gave. In the gospel of John, the emphasis of the miracle stories falls on their symbolic significance, as in the story of the healing of the man born blind, who symbolizes the blindness of traditional Jewish piety as to who Jesus is, and the light of understanding that faith brings. And the raising of Lazarus from the dead is, of course, the symbol of the triumph over death accomplished through Jesus. The symbolic significance of Jesus' miracles for John is made explicit in John 20.30–31, where the writer tells us that he has chosen to report these particular signs in order that readers might see Jesus as the anointed one (Messiah) of God, through whom new life is given.

In Paul's letters, his encounter with the risen Lord and his being taken up into the presence of God resemble the miracles of revelation and confirmation in the Hebrew Bible. The ability to heal, to perform miracles, and to prophesy is seen by Paul as the gift that God grants through the Spirit. Paul's apostolic office is confirmed through "signs and wonders and mighty works" (2 Cor. 12.12). It is surprising, therefore, that Paul makes no reference to the miracles performed by Jesus, though the miracle of his *resurrection by God is central to Paul's gospel.

Miracles of various kinds abound in Acts. Foremost are the confirmatory type, as when the miraculous hearing of those speaking in tongues at the outpouring of the Spirit enables people from many lands to understand in spite of linguistic differences (*see* Glossolalia). The healing of the man at the Temple gate by Peter and John is interpreted by their followers as God's attestation of the gospel. Similarly, Philip's evangelization of the Samaritans is confirmed through the many healings that accompany his preaching there. And the gentile mission as a whole is acknowledged by the Jerusalem leaders to be of God, by virtue of the signs and wonders that accompanied the work of Paul and his associates. At the same time, judgmental miracles are also depicted, as in the death of Ananias and Sapphira for their duplicity and failure to meet their obligations to the community. The deliverance of Paul and his associates from the shipwreck and the viper shows God's care and concern for those doing his work, since by thus preserving Paul, he is enabled to reach with the gospel the center of the world, Rome itself.

Throughout the Bible, therefore, miracles are presented as a means by which God discloses and fulfills his purpose in the world, especially in behalf of his people and for the redemption of those who respond in faith to his activity in their behalf.   *Howard Clark Kee*

MONARCHY. *See* Kingship and Monarchy.

MONOTHEISM. Discussion of monotheism in the ancient world sometimes blurs the distinction between theology and religion. In non-Western settings, religion is a complex of behaviors that mark a culture. Theology, however, involves cohesive ideological speculation to justify behaviors. A single religion can have many competing or complementary theologies.

Scholars have traditionally taken a theological and prescriptive approach to the issue of Israelite monotheism: monotheism is the conviction that only one god exists, and no others. This conviction is, however, difficult to document.

Ancient Near Eastern Background. Egyptian, Mesopotamian, Hittite, Greek, and early Canaanite myths all present developed pantheons. These texts relate how one generation of gods succeeds the next just as humans succeed one another; this succession entails war among the gods. In Mesopotamia, the creation of the universe results from this conflict. Mesopotamian, Hittite, and Canaanite myths relate how the storm god defeats the sea god (in Egypt, the battle is essentially between the Nile and the desert): a god responsible for life-giving *water wins control of the cosmos. The focus in all of these myths is the succession of a patriarchal high god's royal son.

These pantheons all have a high god, under whose direction other gods—of the sun, of pestilence, and so forth—act, often independently. The high god is usually the state god. In some cases, the subordinate gods in the state pantheon represent local high gods, of areas in an empire. Thus different states may share essentially identical pantheons but identify different high gods: in Mesopotamia, the Babylonian high god was Marduk; the Assyrian high god was Ashur. Sennacherib had the Babylonian creation epic rewritten to award Marduk's role in it to Ashur.

Yet state myths did not reflect the subjective experience of a worshiper in a god's cult. Mesopotamian literature is filled with pleas to gods and goddesses, such as Ishtar of Arbela, Ishtar of Nineveh, Shamash (the sun god), and Addu (biblical Hadad). In prayer, the god being addressed is the sole object of devotion.

Scholars refer to this phenomenon as effective henotheism, devotion to one god conceding the potency of others. This principle was elevated to state policy in Egypt under Akhnaton (ca. 1350 BCE), the pharaoh who channeled resources into the cult of the solar disk at a cost to competing cults. A similar attempt to impose a god atop a state pantheon, under the sixth-century BCE Babylonian king Nabonidus, exhibits the same characteristics, with statues of all the other gods being brought to Babylon, possibly for the New Year. Nabonidus's attempt, like Akhnaton's, proved abortive.

These failures, however, show that the line between monotheism and polytheism should not be too precisely drawn. Akhnaton and Nabonidus, the two great religious reformers of Near Eastern antiquity, focused the cult on their respective gods. Not dissimilar are the monotheistic traditions of Judaism, Christianity, and Islam: all admit the existence of subordinate divinities—saints, angels, demons, and, in Christianity and Islam, Satan, the eternal antagonist of the high god. But if these traditions are not monotheistic, no religion (as opposed to theology) is. The term monotheism loses its meaning.

Monotheism, Yehezkel Kaufmann observed, postulates multiple deities, subordinated to the one; it tolerates myths of primordial struggle for cosmic supremacy. Two elements distinguish it from polytheism: a conviction that the one controls the pantheon, and the idea of false gods.

Ancient Israel and Its Immediate Neighbors. From the outset, Israelites identified themselves as "the people of YHWH" (Judg. 5.13). The expression implies a societal commitment to a single, national god. Israelite personal names offer confirmation: these include either the name of a god or a divine epithet. Almost uniformly, the god in Israelite personal names is YHWH or an epithet of YHWH, such as "god" (ʾēl), "lord" (baʿal), or "(divine) kinsman" (ʿamm).

This practice resembles that of the Transjordanian nations of Ammon, Moab, and Edom, Israel's nearest neighbors and, in the folklore of Genesis 12–25, closest relations. Conversely, in Canaanite and Phoenician city-states, personal names include the names and epithets of a variety of gods and goddesses. The ethnic nations that emerged in Canaan in the thirteenth-twelfth centuries BCE, unlike the states of Syria and Mesopotamia, are early tied to national gods.

None of these cultures, however, denied the existence of divinities other than the high god. The ninth-century Moabite Stone, though treating the national god, Chemosh, as Israel treated YHWH, nevertheless mentions sacrifice to a subordinate of his. An eighth-century inscription from Deir ᶜAllā, in the Israelite-Ammonite border area, mentions a pantheon, or group of gods, called Shaddayin. Similarly, many biblical texts, from the twelfth century down to the Babylonian *exile, describe the divine court over which YHWH presides as the council of the gods: these report to and suggest strategy to YHWH, praise YHWH, and are assessed by YHWH. In monarchic theologies, the subordinate gods administered other nations for YHWH. But they also received Israelite homage—the sun, moon, and host of heaven, the stars who fought as YHWH's army against Canaan: the host was YHWH's astral army, and YHWH was regularly represented through solar imagery.

The astral gods—the host of heaven—figure prominently in early sources. The meaning of YHWH's name has long been in dispute. However, the name associated with the *ark of the covenant, and prevalent throughout the era of the monarchy, is YHWH Sebaᵓot ("Lord of Hosts"). On the most common interpretation of the name YHWH, this means, "He [who] summons the hosts [of heaven] into being." If so, the full name of Israel's god in the Pentateuch's Yahwistic source (J), YHWH Elohim, means, "He [who] summons the gods into being." And before the revelation of the name YHWH to Moses, the Priestly (P) source calls the high god El Shadday: originally, this, too, associated YHWH with sky gods, Shaddayin, known from the Deir ᶜAllā inscription.

The Israelite cult also embraced the ancestors. Israelites invoked the ancestors for aid in matters familial, agricultural, and political. The ancestral spirits could intervene with YHWH, to the benefit of the family, the landholding corporation that inherited its resources from the fathers. (*See* Israel, Religion of.)

The Emergence of Monotheism. Starting apparently in the ninth century BCE, Israelites began to distinguish YHWH starkly from other gods. It is unknown whether the distinction originated from the opposition between YHWH and foreign high gods or between YHWH and local ancestral gods. Still, the alienation of the local gods from YHWH ensued, as subordinate gods were identified as foreign.

Our first indications of the cleavage come from a ninth-century nativist revolution against the house of Omri, the ruling dynasty of the northern kingdom of Israel. Solomon had earlier constructed a Temple in Jerusalem. This Temple incorporated representations of cherubim and, judging from later developments, probably of YHWH's asherah, or consort, Ashtoret (Astarte). Opposite the Temple, Solomon also consecrated shrines to YHWH's subordinates—Ashtoret, Milkom, and Chemosh. After seceding from Jerusalem under Jeroboam I, the kingdom of Israel had maintained a more conservative separation of state shrines from the capital. Ahab, however, installed a new temple in Samaria; in the Near East, a temple in the capital signified a divine grant of dynasty. Jehu's revolt, however, destroyed the temple and reaffirmed Jeroboam's cultic policy. (*See* Kingship and Monarchy.)

The earliest biblical writer to contrast YHWH with his subordinate deities is Hosea. This eighth-century prophet rejects calling YHWH Israel's "baal" (lord) and claims that attention to the "baals" (YHWH's subordinate gods) deflects attention from the deity responsible for their ministrations. The alienation of the subordinates (who in the traditional theology administer other nations for YHWH) from YHWH, who administers Israel, permits Hosea to identify pursuit of the "baals" with foreign political alliances. Intellectually, the same alienation was part of a critique of traditional culture leveled by the "classical," that is, the literary, prophets.

In the eighth century, Israel enjoyed a trading network embracing the Assyrian empire in western Asia and Phoenician trade outposts around the Mediterranean. As a bridge on the spice trade route to the south, and as a producer of cash crops such as olives and grapes, Israel underwent incipient industrialization, developing capital reserves. Foreign goods, texts, and practices became increasingly familiar to a growing middle class. In reaction, the elite was impelled to define distinctively Israelite values and culture. Groping for its identity, the elite discovered the gap between the elite theology, in which YHWH was completely sovereign, and popular practice, with its devotions to subordinate deities and ancestors; between theology, in which repentance was increasingly individuated, and ritual repentance, a matter of behavior, not attitude; between theology, in which one worshiped an unseen god, and a cult employing icons. The critique by the literary prophets thus predicated that the symbol or manifestation—the icon, the ritual, the subordinate god—was alien from, and not to be mistaken for, the Reality—the high god, or one's own inner essence. (*See* Graven Image.)

Ahaz of Judah first implemented this critique, removing plastic imagery from the Temple nave. In preparation for the Assyrian invasion of 701, his successor Hezekiah concentrated the Judahite population in fortified towns; his ideologians articulated attacks on the high places, the centers of traditional rural worship, and on the ancestral cult, linked to the agricultural areas he planned to abandon to the aggressor. Assyria then deported most of the population outside of Jerusalem; Hezekiah's spokesmen took this as YHWH's judgment on the rural cult, which they interpreted to be identical with the cult of the northern kingdom—Samaria had fallen prey to total deportation in 720. Jerusalem's survival, by contrast, represented YHWH's imprimatur on the state cult.

Some scholars hypothesize that Israelite monotheism was husbanded by a small, "Yahweh-alone" party until the time of Hezekiah or even Josiah. No text indicates such a doctrine before Josiah's reign, however, and the chief indices suggest its gradual development rather than some perpetual keeping of a flame. Solomon's high places, for example, survived Hezekiah's reform, although the "Mosaic" snake-icon, Nehushtan, did not. Child sacrifice continued in the Jerusalem Topheth—an activity directed toward the host of heaven. Personal seals continued to include astronomical imagery, though this was increasingly astral rather than solar as earlier.

In the seventh century, however, Josiah destroyed Solomon's shrines to gods now identified as foreign and dismantled state shrines in the countryside. Josiah's campaign against the ancestral cult included tomb desecration and the exposure of bones for the first time in Israelite history. A term previously reserved for the ancestors, Rephaim, was now applied to the Canaanite aborigines allegedly proscribed by YHWH. Deuteronomy, the legal program of Josiah's court or of a later extension of it, enjoined the worship of YHWH alone. Deuteronomy, Jeremiah, and Zephaniah explicitly identified the host of heaven as foreign, as objects of apostasy. The Priestly source of the Pentateuch rewrote the traditional ancestral lore, suppressing all references to superhuman agencies other than YHWH; it forbids any imagery in the cult—correspondingly, seals are increasingly aniconic.

Sennacherib's deportations and the processes of industrialization and cash cropping had destroyed the effectiveness of the old kinship groups among whom the traditional religion, with its multiple divinities, was rooted. The imposition of state dogma of exclusive loyalty to the state god reflects the state's ambition to deal directly with the individual, bypassing the centers of resistance, the lineages. Thus, Deuteronomy 13.6–11 instructs the Israelite to inform on brothers, children, or wives who worship other gods, such as the host of heaven.

In this period, not in the exile as earlier scholars claimed, the notion of reliance on a single god took root. That idea survived, as a doctrine distinguishing Israel from other, polytheistic nations, through the exile and over the course of the restoration. Some of the elite, such as Second Isaiah, accepted the implications of philosophical monotheism, identifying YHWH as the source of evil as well as good. Yet even in sources that accept the activity of subordinate deities, such as Job 1–2, the concept of exclusive loyalty to the state god had taken hold. Affirmation of the cult of the one god— the ultimate cause of events—could persist despite the assumption that other divinities existed, too. The doctrine of a *Trinity, or of angels in heaven, or of a devil, coexisted happily with the idea in Judaism, Christianity, and Islam of an enlightened community distinguished from others by its monotheism.

Baruch Halpern

MORMONISM AND THE BIBLE.

Objecting to views of the *Torah as a closed world, Martin Buber wrote, "To you God is One who created once and not again; but to us God is he who 'renews the work of creation every day.' To you God is One who revealed Himself once and no more; but to us He speaks out of the burning thornbush of the present." Buber's passion parallels a quintessential dimension of Mormon thought: a deep respect for biblical *revelation supporting an even-higher regard for ongoing revelation.

Mormonism came into being through a man (Joseph Smith, 1805–1844) and a culture (antebellum upstate New York) that shared a profound reverence for the Bible. This reverence was thus genetically part of the movement and has not greatly dissipated in the rapidly expanding tradition even at present. Among other things, this means that Mormons have fundamental allegiances in common with many other Christians and also with Jews. Mormons tend to take what they interpret as the Bible's essential truths for granted. They are enjoined to study the testaments regularly and, excepting errors of transmission and translation, consider them to be inspired, in some sense "the word of God." Their interpretation of the Bible informs their worship, their personal and social ethics, their polity, their theology, and their overall self-consciousness.

It was in fact Joseph Smith's attachment to the Bible that led him to seek God directly during the religious confusion of his youth. This search resulted, Mormons believe, in a vision of God and Jesus (1820) and the organization of a new (or a "restored") religious tradition: The Church of Jesus Christ of Latter-day Saints (1830). This church and its belief system would be incomprehensible without its biblically inspired basis.

Despite this enduring biblical foundation, Mormon attitudes are distinct from those of other biblically based faiths. Most centrally, Mormonism rejects the notion of a closed *canon. With what he described as divine guidance, Joseph Smith translated and published (1830) the abridged records of ancient Israelites who had escaped the Babylonian captivity by traveling to the Americas around 600 BCE, spawning a civilization that flourished until about 400 CE. This record, known as the Book of Mormon (after its ancient prophet-editor), was itself scripture and was inextricably entwined with the traditional Bible: at once challenging the Bible's uniqueness and yet witnessing to the Bible's authority, echoing its themes, interpreting its passages, sharing its content, correcting its errors, filling its gaps, adopting its language, and restoring its methods, namely, the prophetic process itself.

Many of Smith's later revelations—saturated with biblical themes, phrases, and figures—were also subsequently canonized (*The Doctrine and Covenants; The Pearl of Great Price*). This precedent of expanding the canon quickly broadened to belief in an open-ended canon. One basic Mormon tenet is that divine-human contact is an ongoing process not subject to closure at an arbitrary point by any human council: "We believe all that God has revealed, all that he does now reveal, and we believe that He will yet reveal many great and important things."

It is, however, not simply an open canon that distinguishes Mormon biblical usage. Joseph Smith's understanding of the very nature of scripture was expansive. For instance, Smith did not believe that "scripture," despite its etymology, need necessarily be written to be true and authoritative. Thus, said one of his revelations, "Whatsoever [those who hold the priesthood] shall speak when moved upon by the Holy Ghost shall be scripture, shall be the will of the Lord, shall be the mind of the Lord, shall be the word of the Lord, shall be the voice of the Lord, and the power of God

unto salvation." The idea of oral scripture contrasts with contemporary Christian practice but bears historical comparison with the treatment of sacred materials in other world religions.

Moreover, scripture for Smith was not the static, final, untouchable word of God that it was for many believers of his time. The Mormon prophet considered scripture to be sacred yet provisional, subject to refinement and addition, as both the evolving texts of his own revelations and the progressive stages of his inspired revision of the Bible (never published in his lifetime) demonstrate. For Mormons, the record of God's actions with humankind is to be highly prized, but this record is necessarily subordinate to direct experience with God—the lifespring of such records—and therefore subject to expansion, clarification, and correction. Mormon leaders further observe that not all of holy writ applies beyond the local and temporal context for which it was formulated.

Since Mormonism is not fond of creeds, Mormon perceptions of scripture are not monolithic. Many Latter-day Saints, for example, assume complete theological harmony within the Bible and between the Bible and other Mormon scriptures. Others champion the priority of modern revelation when apparent conflicts surface or attribute discrepancies to corruptions in the received biblical text. Still others give broad leeway to the human element in both ancient and contemporary revelation. Brigham Young (1801–1877) dismissed parts of the Bible as "baby stories" while remaining loyal to the biblical tradition in general. Joseph Smith, emboldened by his prophetic consciousness, solved various contradictions within the Bible and between his revelations and the biblical text by rewriting portions of the Bible. In the modern context, historical-critical studies of scripture have inspired a predominantly cool, antagonistic, or even oblivious reaction in Mormonism as a whole, particularly where those studies are controlled by naturalistic assumptions. Yet the attitudes of influential leaders and lay members toward serious biblical scholarship have been as divergent as those of any denomination, ranging from enthusiastic to scandalized.

Since the time of Joseph Smith, the Mormon use of scripture has combined a traditional faith in the Bible with more "conservative" elements (like an extra dose of literalism), some liberal components (such as Joseph Smith's insistence, anticipating the thought of Horace Bushnell, on the radical limits of human language), and some radical ingredients (an open canon, an oral scripture, the subjugation of biblical assertions to experiential truth or the pronouncements of living authorities). All of this links the Saints with other religious traditions yet separates them too. Mormons in the modern world remain Bible-believing Christians but with a difference.

Philip L. Barlow

MURDER. The biblical concept of the image of God lay at the heart of abhorrence to the taking of a human life. However the idea of a divine image was understood—physical likeness, self-transcendence, capacity to communicate, authoritative rule—it implied that one dare not destroy another person who bore God's image. The story of the first murder, Cain's slaying of his brother Abel, insists that spilt *blood cries out to the creator, who acts to ensure vindication but not at the expense of compassion. This tension between revenge and mercy produced responses to murder that lack consistency precisely because they take mitigating circumstances into consideration.

The *Ten Commandments prohibit murder categorically and without exception. Nevertheless, in Israel's day-to-day existence distinctions were made, and killing was held to be justified in at least two situations, warfare and execution for capital offenses. The first of these was fortified by the conviction that Israelites engaged in holy wars, with Yahweh as their commander-in-chief. In these circumstances compassion had no place, particularly when the enemy was placed under ḥērem (the ban). Saul's sparing of the Amalekite king Agag, whatever its motive, was deemed an act of disobedience, and the prophet Samuel carried out Yahweh's execution of Agag. Israel's recorders of sacred history did not balk at depicting Yahweh as sanctioning, even ordering, such action. Elijah's slaughter of competing prophets raised no objections that were rooted in the Ten Commandments. The same leniency occurs with respect to cases of capital punishment. In fact, the blessing of Noah actually contains a stipulation that murderers are to be executed.

The practical implementing of this sentence resulted in elaborate rituals and numerous distinctions. Premeditated violence differed from an act in the heat of anger or from accidental injury. From early times an institution, the avenger of blood (gōʾēl), assured vindication within each family. The next of kin assumed responsibility for avenging a death, and society sanctioned this means of obtaining revenge for grievous wrong. In time, ransom of the guilty person's life introduced the principle of monetary compensation for the loss.

In cases of accidental homicide, provision was made for the establishment of cities of refuge, thus enabling society to combine revenge and mercy. Persons who accidentally caused a death or who killed another person in a fit of anger could flee to a city of refuge and, after satisfactorily convincing officials that asylum was appropriate, entered the city and remained there until the high priest's death; thereafter the individual could return home without harm. Of course, these institutions of a redeemer and of cities of refuge sometimes failed, for not everyone respected the laws governing both.

In cases in which a murder occurred but the murderer was not known, the nearest town had a special ritual by which the people were exonerated of collective guilt. The problem of adjudicating responsibility for murder was no simple matter. If an owner of a dangerous ox had been warned because of its habitual goring but failed to keep the ox under control so that it killed someone, the owner was held responsible for the death. Similarly, if two persons fought and one was injured but was later able to get up and walk around, the offender could go free even though death occurred a short time later. Owners of slaves were not culpable if they beat them to death, provided that a day or so lapsed between beating and death. Moreover, a person who killed a thief in the night was not held responsible for the action.

The older institution of blood revenge gradually disappeared. By Ezra's time officials of the state handled such matters. The Romans seem to have restricted Jewish authority in cases of capital punishment, and by insisting that the murderer had to be warned immediately before the crime, the rabbis made it virtually impossible to take human life. Jesus broadened the prohibition of murder to include anger.   *James L. Crenshaw*

MUSIC AND MUSICAL INSTRUMENTS. The most significant survival of the music of biblical times is its lyrical material. The Bible gives no indication of the actual melodies used in ancient times by singers for the rendition of the lyrical and only random reference to the range and character of music, musical instruments, and musical patterns. In the Hebrew Bible, however, there are a variety of musical expressions during the monarchic period and a treasure house of hymns after the *exile, and the New Testament contains several examples of hymns as well.

Premonarchic Period. The musical tradition of Israel began in the premonarchic period. Israel's ancestors are depicted as seminomads, traveling long distances within their territorial boundaries in search of grazing land and watering places for their herds of sheep and goats. The Song of the Well (Num. 21.17–18), for example, reveals their constant search for water, and disputes over territory are reflected in their war songs, ranging from shouts associated with the banner and with the *ark to the skillfully composed Song of Deborah (Judg. 5); note also the reference to the lost "Book of Wars of the Lord" mentioned in Numbers 21.14–15, where a few lines are quoted. The purpose of the brief war shouts was to enable members of a tribe to identify themselves with their own group, and that of the Song of Lamech to incite them to execute the law of blood vengeance. In the case of Miriam's brief song of triumph, the biblical author reports that women in her entourage danced and beat their tambourines. This suggests a sharp, strident, staccato rendering of brief war refrains. In the case of longer war odes it seems likely that they had a more elaborate instrumental setting, and, as Genesis 4.21 suggests, such instruments as harps and pipes were used from an early time. In fact the reference in Genesis 4.21 to Jubal as the "father of all who play" these instruments is particularly important for its implication of organized guilds of professional musicians in the premonarchic period.

Monarchic Period. The centralization of the monarchy brought about changes in Israel's social, economic, and cultural life. Court musicians were remembered for their participation in such functions as coronations, weddings, funerals, and banquets; note, for example, 2 Samuel 19.35. The coronation of a king was a joyous occasion: a trumpet's blast gave the signal for the crowd's acclamation, and the noise of pipes and trumpets was so great that "the earth quaked" (1 Kings 1.40). For celebrations of his enthronement, musicians sang odes of praise for his just rule and victory over the nation's enemies. They also sang laments for slain warriors. Court musicians performed at royal weddings. The summoning of David to the court to calm Saul's violent temper by playing the lyre was an exceptional command performance. By the time of Hezekiah's reign, court singers and instrumentalists had been so widely acclaimed that they had the unfortunate honor of being included among the royal treasures taken from the palace of Jerusalem by Sennacherib to his capital at Nineveh (701 BCE).

During the monarchic period the second important center for the development of Hebrew music was the Temple at Jerusalem. Familiar in this connection are the stories of how David brought the ark to Jerusalem in a religious procession with dancing, shouts of joy, and the sound of the ram's horn, and how Solomon dedicated the sanctuary in which it was housed. Although the music of the Temple was undoubtedly not as elaborate in Solomonic times as the later, postexilic Chronicler imagined, it is likely that the king had a major role in organizing the musical elements of the service. The blowing of the silver trumpets both summoned the congregation to the Temple and indicated the times for the offering of *sacrifice. To the accompaniment of stringed instruments the priestly choir sang hymns, which were probably the familiar ones of praise, petition, and thanksgiving.

Hymns were composed according to the metrical scheme of traditional Hebrew *poetry: that is, in couplets of two lines having an accentual rhythm of three or four beats to each line and exhibiting a "parallelism of members," whether synonymous, antithetical, or progressive (step-parallelism). A much-used variation of this metrical scheme is the extension of the three-beat line by two beats, which gives the structural unit a limping or elegiac character. The 3:3 accentual pattern of a single structural unit whose lines express an idea in synonymous parallelism may be illustrated by the passage:

The heavens are telling the glory of God,
    and the firmament proclaims his handiwork.
                                    [Ps. 19.1]

In Psalm 150 the lyricist lists many, but not all, instruments used by musicians: among the strings, the lyre *(kinnôr)* and the harp with ten strings *(nēbel);* among the wind instruments, the ram's horn *(šōpār)* and the flute *(ʿûgāb),* but not the metal trumpet *(ḥāṣōṣĕrâ)* and the double oboe *(ḥālîl);* and among the percussion instruments, the tambourine *(tōp)* and cymbals *(ṣelṣĕlîm),* but not the sistrum *(mĕnaʿanʿîm).*

The Prophets. Prophecy and the prophetic movement give us two interesting sidelights on the development of music that occurred apart from the king's patronage: first, on the association of religion and music, and second, on the use of secular music. In the early years of the monarchy, guilds of prophets found that the playing of such instruments as harps, lyres, tambourines, and flutes induced a trancelike state during which individuals were seized by God's spirit and prophesied ecstatically; in the later period none of the prophets whose oracles are recorded is known to have used music for this purpose. This did not deter them from using effectively metrical forms of lyrics for their pronouncements. Amos, for example, used the *qînâ* meter of professional musicians for his lament over the imminent destruction of Israel:

> Fállen no móre to ríse
> is maíden Ísrael;
> fórsaken ón her lánd
> with nóne to upraíse her.
> [Amos 5.2]

These later prophets also allude to secular music of urban and rural communities: songs associated with agricultural life, wedding songs, and songs for feasts that were accompanied by such instruments as harps, lyres, tambourines, and flutes. An example of a harvest song is Isaiah's famous Song of the Vineyard (Isa. 5.1–4).

Exilic and Postexilic Periods. We hear next of the development of music two centuries after the destruction of the Temple, the fall of the monarchy, and the taking captive of its leaders to Babylon. In the Persian period, exiles returning to Jerusalem were given permission to rebuild the Temple and organize their corporate life under the leadership of the high priest. It is natural, therefore, that the Temple and the Law became the two foci of Jewish existence. For the development of music during this period the two outstanding sources are the books of Chronicles and Psalms, the latter sometimes called the "hymn book of the Second Temple."

According to these two sources it seems that from the fourth century BCE on music became an even more important feature of worship at the Temple than in the earlier period. Vocal and instrumental music was performed by guilds of professional musicians who associated themselves by descent with Heman, Asaph, and Jeduthun (and Korah), and thus ultimately with Levi, and claimed that they had been commissioned by David himself. They apparently collected psalms (e.g., Pss. 73–82, attributed to Asaph) and added musical and liturgical notations, some of which are obscure, like, for example, the term selah, which probably indicates a pause in the singing of a psalm for a brief instrumental interlude. Titles to the psalms were also added to indicate how the lyrics were to be performed and used. Some psalms were to be sung with the accompaniment of stringed instruments or flutes; others sung to known tunes (e.g., "The Deer of the Dawn," Ps. 22); and still others for religious occasions (for pilgrimages, Pss. 120–134; for the dedication of the Temple, Ps. 30; for the *Sabbath, Ps. 92). So well established is the relation of Temple worship and music that the psalmists associated the act of coming to the place of God's presence with that of making "a joyful noise to him with songs of praise" (Ps. 95.2) and of "making melody to him with tambourine and lyre" (Ps. 149.3).

Earliest Christianity. The development of music and its use in early Christianity can be reconstructed only tentatively from materials in the New Testament, which, in comparison with those of the Hebrew Bible, cover a very short span of time and are so closely associated with the purposes of Christian missionary activity that they contain little information about the subject. In general, it seems that the music of early Christians, like that of the synagogue, was entirely vocal and consisted of psalms (cf. the frequent quotations from the Psalter in the New Testament) and of their own lyrics, especially those to be used for baptismal and eucharistic rites.

Examples of Christian lyrics appear to represent three types of hymnody that originated in the churches of Palestine or of the Greek world beyond Palestinian borders. For the first, we have five hymnic passages that probably came from the Jewish Christian churches, having been translated into *Greek from *Aramaic and exhibiting the characteristics of biblical psalmody. Two are preserved in the infancy narrative of Luke (1.46–55; 2.29–32; cf. 1.68–79, probably sung at one time by disciples of John the Baptist). Three in the book of Revelation are a song of thanksgiving (Rev. 5.3–4), a song in praise of the slain *Lamb (Rev. 5.9–10), and hymnic material in Revelation 19.1–7, which used responses of "Hallelujah" and "*Amen" and is about the marriage of the Lamb. The last two were probably used during the eucharistic rite.

From the churches of the Greek world there are no examples in New Testament literature of a hymn using the quantitative metric form of the Greeks, but there is hymnic material that seems to reflect mixed forms developed from the fusion of biblical and Hellenistic elements. An example that may have been translated from Aramaic but departs slightly from Jewish tradition is the fragment of a confessional hymn preserved in 1 Timothy 3.16. Here the structure is still biblical, as probably was the music, but the parallelism is that of Hellenistic rhetorical construction.

The third type of hymn is found in lyrics in praise of Christ as Lord (Phil. 2.6–11), as the image of God (Col. 1.15–20), and as the eternal *Logos (John 1.1–18). These hymns seem to be even more remote from Jewish psalmody, for they are characterized by the absence of parallelism, the brevity and equality of the lines, and the stanza-form. These hymns come from the Christian community in its formative years.

See also Music and the Bible.

Lucetta Mowry

MUSIC AND THE BIBLE. This entry focuses on the use of the Bible in sacred and secular Western music. For music in biblical times, see Music and Musical Instruments.

The Bible has been used in Western music for several purposes: (1) At worship Christians and Jews frequently sing biblical passages in psalms or hymns. (2) Biblical material in liturgy is also accompanied and, in effect, interpreted by music. (3) The Bible is present in music intended not for worship but for the opera house or concert hall.

Liturgy. Both Judaism and Christianity have used biblical texts for liturgical purposes. The Psalms were composed for ritual singing, as some of the superscriptions show: "To the Choirmaster" (NRSV: "To the leader"; Pss. 18–22; etc.) probably designates a collection of songs and also suggests organized liturgical music. Exodus 15.1–18 is a psalm concluding the narrative of the *Passover celebration. Early Christians sang "psalms and hymns and spiritual songs" (Eph. 5.19), doubtless psalms in translation and Christian hymnody, such as the Magnificat and Benedictus (Luke 1.46–55, 68–79) or musical outbursts like Revelation 11.17–18; 19.1–2, 5, 6–8.

Although Judaism and Christianity generated other texts for liturgical singing, biblical language had great importance. Not all of the canon of the Mass is derived from the Bible (e.g., Kyrie eleison and Credo), but the opening lines of the Gloria are from Luke 2.14, and the Agnus Dei augments John the Baptist's remark in John 1.29.

We know very little about the music

of late antiquity. Ambrose (Bishop of Milan, 374–397 CE) introduced antiphonal singing of psalms and hymns, and the Ambrosian liturgy strongly influenced liturgical practice in France and Spain. The great figure of medieval liturgical music was Pope Gregory I (590–604 CE), who had chants collected and assigned to liturgical occasions, bringing liturgical music into a systematic whole (hence "Gregorian" chant). Music was understood as the servant of faith; it was not intended to interpret the text. Thus, melismatic embellishments on certain syllables in the chant, far from calling attention to important religious concepts in the text, fell mostly on unstressed syllables. Music, expected to dispose the mind to truth and open the heart to pious feelings, was subordinate to words. Thus, though the psalms refer to instruments, and secular music freely used them, Christian liturgy was purely vocal until the thirteenth-century revival of the organ to accompany singing. The organ, known from Hellenistic times, had been used earlier for ecclesiastical processions, and organs were known in some European churches well before the thirteenth century.

When polyphony (Greek, "many voices") replaced the older monophony ("single voice") with more complex musical textures, around 1000 CE, greater freedom to interpret the text words became possible. Sounding several musical lines simultaneously, polyphony enlarged the expressive potential of the music and became the distinctive mark of European music. It was performed in monasteries, where the monks were trained to sing, or by choirs in churches. Congregations were not expected to sing polyphony, and its introduction made the congregation in most cases the silent partner in worship.

Early polyphony consisted of one to three voices weaving faster-moving melodic lines above a slower voice holding (Lat. *tenere*, hence "tenor") a Gregorian chant melody. In the thirteenth-century polyphony of the Notre Dame school, the quick rhythms of upper voices above the long notes of the chant produce emotional depth in the psalm text. The effect is not interpretation of the words but a more emotional aspect to the experience. Polyphonic music became even less accessible to ordinary people, and the Reformation aimed to revive congregational hymn-singing. Lutheran chorales and Reformed hymns and psalms continued to be polyphonic, in that voices sang different notes at the same time, but the melody was sung by one voice (originally the tenor), with other voices in chordal accompaniment. Interpretive scope was limited.

Since the Reformation, the liturgical settings of biblical words have been mainly hymns and anthems, the former sung by congregations, the latter by choirs. Hymn melodies are conventionally sung by the soprano, not the tenor, with the other voices accompanying in chords. Many hymns have been metrical paraphrases of psalms (some Protestant, especially Calvinist, groups would sing nothing but psalms). Metrical psalms were often stilted in wording, with the meter taking precedence over clarity of sense. They usually used standardized metrical patterns in order to fit more than one tune. Some perennially favorite hymns are psalm paraphrases. For example, "Our God, our help in ages past" derives from Psalm 90, and "A mighty fortress is our God," for which Martin Luther wrote both words and melody, is a paraphrase of Psalm 46. Tunes might be written for the words, but frequently secular melodies were employed. When a melody has become traditionally associated with certain words, the melody itself is enough to recall the words to those trained in the tradition. The hymn tune "St. Anne" brings immediately to Protestant minds "Our God, our help in ages past," and the association arouses emotional resonance in the hearers.

Since the eighteenth century, congregational singing has usually been accompanied by organs, sometimes by other instruments, though a few sects refuse instruments altogether. Pianos may appear in less formal settings. Since the latter twentieth century, many churches have introduced even into major liturgical occasions unison hymns accompanied by a guitar instead of an organ. Increasingly, such hymns are contemporary religious verse and not paraphrases of the Bible.

Musical Interpretation. With polyphony came more complex interpretation in the musical settings of the Bible. Voices accompanying the chant melody (*cantus firmus*, "fixed song") of the polyphonic motet might sing different, even secular, words. In a thirteenth-century motet on *Haec dies quam fecit Dominus* ("This is the day that the Lord has made," Ps. 118.24), from a gradual for Easter Sunday, the middle voice sings of the Virgin Mary as bringer of grace, the upper one a plaintive love song about "fair Marion." Easter suggested Christ's grace mediated by the Virgin, and springtime justified a declaration of love for "fair Marion," whose name echoes Mary. Simultaneous different texts might seem confused cacophony, but they lent a symbolic and interpretive depth to the "day that the Lord has made."

Understanding such a work depended on conventional frames of reference. Those who knew the Easter reference of *Haec dies* would grasp the other symbolism. Music refined its conventions of reference, making interpretive

gestures familiar to congregations. Every system of musical style has such conventions. In European-derived music of the last several centuries, a reed instrument playing slowly in a ⅝, ⅜, or ¹²⁄₈ rhythm conveys the pastoral, a shepherd's song or a meadow scene. Music featuring horns and drums in a heavily accented duple meter is recognized as a march, and so on. The music by itself cannot show whether the shepherd be Greek, Palestinian, or Scandinavian, or whether the marchers are Egyptian soldiers, English constables, or an American marching band.

Complex polyphony has been sung by choirs, which can be trained to sing expressively interpretive music, rather than by congregations. In addition to "anthems" (a word corrupted from the medieval and Renaissance "antiphon") set to biblical words—some of which are no harder than hymns, though others are extremely difficult (e.g., Charles Ives's *Psalm 90* [1923])—Christian churches developed more elaborate musical forms to present biblical texts. The term "motet" came to refer to almost any liturgical choral composition, and especially in the eighteenth and nineteenth centuries, to an unaccompanied choral work on a biblical text. Johann Sebastian Bach's *"Jesu, meine Freude"* (1723?) has no biblical text, but Johannes Brahms wrote beautiful motets (e.g., *Psalm 51* [1860]). In the late Renaissance, *cantata* meant merely something "sung" (Ital. *cantare*), whereas in northern Europe, the term came to mean a multimovement religious choral work, accompanied by organ or orchestra, often with solos. In J. S. Bach's busy hands (he wrote hundreds), the cantatas meditated musically on a theme in the lectionary reading for a given Sunday, or focused on an apt chorale (e.g., Cantata no. 140, *"Wachet auf"* [1731], alluding to Isa. 40.9). The text often refers to the prescribed biblical reading, and the recitatives and arias expand upon its religious meaning to the pious soul. This kind of cantata, especially characteristic of pietistic Lutheranism, was extended in the *Passions* by Lutheran composers. Bach probably wrote five Passion settings, though only those on *St. Matthew* (1727) and *St. John* (1724) are complete, one on *St. Mark* is reconstructed, and two are lost. They intersperse narration with chorales (possibly sung by congregation and choir), interpretive recitatives, arias, and duets set to devotional words. Solo voices sing words of the characters in recitative, and words of Jesus are always accompanied by the special timbre of the orchestral strings. The chorus sings the words of groups—disciples, priests, or the crowd—to orchestral accompaniment.

A more dramatic form, often with biblical contents, was the oratorio. Originally a musical morality play performed in an oratory, a room devoted to prayer to a saint, the form developed in the seventeenth century into something like a sacred opera. Giacomo Carissimi's *Jephtha* (1650), based on Judges 11, has recitatives, arias, duets, choruses, and a narrator. Whether oratorios were staged remains uncertain. From the seventeenth century to the present many have been biblical stories or extended comment on biblical themes. The text of George F. Handel's *Messiah* (1742), the most familiar of the latter kind, is a catena of biblical verses, and the music combines vast choruses, arias, duets, and orchestral pieces. His *Saul* (1739) and *Judas Maccabaeus* (1747) dramatically interpret the biblical stories. Hundreds if not thousands of oratorios have biblical content. Franz Joseph Haydn's *The Creation* (1798), Felix Mendelssohn's *Elijah* (1846), Hector Berlioz's *L'Enfance du Christ* (1854), César Franck's *Béatitudes*

(1869–1879), John Knowles Paine's *St. Peter* (1873), and Charles Gounod's *Redemption* (1882) are examples from a list that could be extended for pages. Brahms's *A German Requiem* (1868) is an oratorio like the *Messiah*, that is, an interpretation of biblical texts about death. Many oratorios, including Handel's, were written for performance not in church but in music halls or concert rooms.

In the nineteenth century, it was sometimes argued that religious music ought to be stylistically distinct from secular music. Some composers were criticized for liturgical works indistinguishable from their operas. Gioacchino Rossini's *Stabat mater* (second version, 1841) and Giuseppe Verdi's *Requiem* (1874) are perhaps the textbook examples. The argument rested both on liturgical conservatism perceptible in a Christianity that felt beleaguered by secularity's growing self-confidence and on the theological principle, always present in Christianity, that the life of faith is distinct from the life of the world.

Secular Biblical Music. Early sacred cantatas were like small operas, and oratorios like larger ones. Opera was originally drama continuously accompanied by music, the work of Florentines around 1600 intending to revive Greek drama. As the form moved beyond Florence, we find opera on religious subjects in Rome as early as Stefano Landi's *Sant'Alessio* (1632). We might have expected North German Protestants to pioneer biblical operas, but there were only sporadic compositions. Hamburg saw such works as Johann Theile's *Der erschaffene, gefallene, und wieder aufgerichtete Mensch* ("Created, Fallen, and Restored Humanity," 1678). Paris had Marc-Antoine Charpentier's *David et Jonathan* (1688). Energy that might have gone into biblical opera in the eighteenth century was apparently put mostly into the oratorio (*Jephté* by Michel Montéclair [1732] is a rare operatic exception). Perhaps the line between "sacred" and "secular" handling of biblical matters was becoming fainter.

Biblical operas proliferated in the nineteenth century, and a long list might begin with Etienne Méhul's *Joseph* (1807) and continue through such works as Rossini's *Moses in Egypt* (1818), Verdi's *Nabucco* (Nebuchadnezzar, 1842), Gounod's *The Queen of Sheba* (1861), Camille Saint-Saëns's *Samson and Delilah* (1877), Jules Massenet's *Hérodiade* (1881), Richard Strauss's *Salome* (1905, based on Oscar Wilde's one-act play on the New Testament story), Artur Honegger's *King David* (1921), to Arnold Schoenberg's incomplete masterpiece, *Moses und Aron* (1931–1932). Carlisle Floyd's Tennessee-mountain setting of the story of Susanna and the elders in *Susannah* (1955) is perhaps the most successful American biblical opera.

"Secular" biblical music includes such orchestral works as Ralph Vaughan Williams's *Job, A Mask for Dancing* (1931), Ernest Bloch's *Schelomo* (Solomon) for cello and orchestra (1916), and Leonard Bernstein's *Jeremiah Symphony* (1942), in which a mezzo-soprano sings part of Lamentations in Hebrew. Some vocal works intended for the concert hall are Zoltán Kodály's *Psalmus hungaricus* (Ps. 55, an old Hungarian translation [1923]); Igor Stravinsky's *Symphony of Psalms* (1930, rev. 1948), using Vulgate texts; Aaron Copland's "In the Beginning" (1947, Gen. 1.1–2.7); Luigi Dallapiccola's remarkable *Job* (1950); and Mario Davidovsky's *Scenes from Shir Hashirim* (1975–1976, Song of Solomon). Dvořák's *Biblical Songs* (1894) and Brahms's *Four Serious Songs* (1896), for voice and piano, set biblical passages in a style not different from their other songs.

Johann Kuhnau wrote six sonatas for harpsichord (1700), dramatically narrating biblical episodes: "Saul's Madness Cured by Music," "David and Goliath," and others. Instrumental music conveying biblical atmospheres must use referential conventions or composers' programmatic titles. There are few such works. Jaromír Weinberger published *Bible Poems* (1939) for organ, and the Black American composer R. Nathaniel Dett wrote *Eight Bible Vignettes* (1941–1943) for solo piano, an attractive set in a Late Romantic style.

Such a survey can only drop a few names and make a few generalities. Western music has used the Bible mostly to enrich the liturgies of Christianity and Judaism. In the past century or two, the Bible has provided composers more comfortably than before with material for music other than "religious." Modern music shows the Bible's secure place as an artifact of the culture rather than as the exclusive possession of religious associations.   *Edwin M. Good*

MYSTERY. In the *Aramaic section of Daniel, the Aramaic word *rāz*, translated in the Septuagint by the *Greek word *mystērion*, "mystery," has a specialized meaning, denoting primarily that what God has decreed shall take place in the future, that is, the eschatological secret to be made known. This use in Daniel of "mystery" with the correlative "solution" or "interpretation" is paralleled at Qumran. Whereas in ordinary discourse "mystery" generally means a secret for which no answer can be found, this is not its sense in Greek, in which the term "mysteries" denotes the sacred rites or teachings of the *mystery religions in which only the initiated shared.

In the New Testament, therefore, *mystērion* signifies a divine secret that is being (or has been) revealed in God's good time, an open secret in some sense. The word thus paradoxically comes close to the word for revelation, *apokalypsis,* and can almost be equivalent to the Christian gospel. The only occurrence of the word in the Gospels is Mark 4.11 (= Matt. 13.11; Luke 8.10; plural in both of the latter). It refers to the *kingdom of God, the knowledge of which is reserved for those to whom it is given; at least the Markan usage appears to mean that the secret revealed is that in some sense Jesus himself in his ministry should be identified with the kingdom of God (*see* Messianic Secret).

If "mystery" is read (instead of "testimony") in 1 Corinthians 2.1, it must mean the gospel, the subject of Paul's proclamation. In Romans 11.25, the "mystery" is a special aspect of the divine plan, namely, the partial eclipse of Israel until the gentiles are won; in Ephesians the mystery is, in particular, that aspect of God's plan which consists of the unification of the universe, including Jews and gentiles. Romans 16.25–26 is a clear example of the meaning of "mystery" as the divine plan in the process of being divulged; and in Colossians 1.26–27 and 2.2, this seems to be daringly identified with Christ himself. Perhaps 2 Thessalonians 2.7 should be included here, if by "the mystery of lawlessness" is meant a satanic parody of God's mystery, a sort of demonic gospel to be destroyed by Jesus at his coming.

Elsewhere the word can mean a more private, exclusive, and less generally divulged religious secret. According to 1 Corinthians 14.2, a person who utters unintelligible sounds is speaking "mysteries in the Spirit" (cf. 1 Cor. 13.2; *see* Glossolalia). In Ephesians 5.32, "mystery" appears to apply to the exegesis of Genesis 2.24, quoted in the preceding verse, thus denoting the inner meaning of a passage whose more obvious sense is something other; there is an analogous sense in Revelation 1.20; 17.5, 13.

The use of the word "mystery" with reference to the *sacraments (the Vulgate sometimes translates *mystērion* by *sacramentum*) is postbiblical, but an understandable development from the abovementioned usage of the word to denote the inner meaning of a phrase or symbol.
David Hill

MYSTERY RELIGIONS. Mystery religions, practiced throughout the Mediterranean from the seventh century BCE to the fifth century CE, were secret and voluntary rites of initiation entered by those seeking an intensified form of worship in addition to their inherited traditions dedicated to deities of family, community, and place.

The term "mystery" derives from the Greek *mystēria,* which described the oldest initiation rites at Eleusis. The Eleusinian and Dionysian mysteries were Greek, while those of Isis, Mithras, Kybele, and Attis came from the East. Common to each of the mysteries was the prohibition against revealing its secrets to noninitiates. They were literally unspeakable because it was not knowledge but an experience that was transmitted through specific ritual acts, with each cult offering a different experience through the performance of an initiatory rite.

The participant in the mysteries ritually reenacted the drama and suffering of the deity honored in the rites, which ensured a connection with the deity and a significant change of status for the initiate. The Eleusinian mysteries promised blessedness and a guarantee of immortality, while the mysteries of Isis promised rebirth and freedom from fate.

The influence of the mysteries can be seen in both Judaism and Christianity. Jewish scriptures of the Hellenistic era employed the terminology of the mysteries to portray the wisdom of God that remains hidden from the ungodly (Wisd. of Sol. 2.22; 6.22). The influence in this case is terminological, as also in Daniel 2.27–30, 47.

Far more problematic is the question of how far the Greco-Roman mysteries influenced the early Christian community not only in terminology but also in the rites that secured salvation with Christ. Paul's explanation that *baptism united the initiate with the death and *resurrection of Christ (Rom. 6.3–5) has elicited heated debate from scholars who have asserted or denied Paul's dependence on the mysteries. The terminological influence of the mystery cults on early Christianity is not disputed, but the degree to which they influenced the content of Christian baptism and celebration of the Eucharist has still not been resolved.

Like their modern counterparts, early apologists sought to distinguish the Christian rites of initiation from those celebrated by others. Justin Martyr (ca. 150 CE), for example, claimed that the pagan mysteries were demonic counterfeits of the true mysteries of Christ. Yet by the fourth century, as the church adapted to Hellenistic culture, the *mystēria* of Christ reflected both the terminology and the structure of the ancient mystery cults.

See also Mystery.   *Gregory Shaw*

MYTH. A story, usually originally transmitted orally, that has as its main actors superhuman beings and that is typically set in otherworldly time and space.

Historians of religion, while often differing on how to interpret any specific myth, tend to agree that all myths, through the use of symbolic language, communicate transcendent meaning within a culture, revealing its cosmic dimensions. In the New Testament, however, Greek *mythos* (Engl. "myth") is used negatively to mean an invented story, a rumor, or a fable.

Hebrew Bible. At first glance, there seems very little narrative in the Hebrew Bible that can, on the basis of the definition above, be classified as myth. Only Genesis 1.1–2.4a, the story of *creation, is set in cosmic time and space and features a superhuman being, God, as its main actor. Elsewhere biblical narratives ostensibly focus on human actors living on earth during historical time. Still, it can be argued that Genesis 2.4b–11.9, including the stories of the garden of Eden, Noah, and the tower of Babel, is myth. Humanity's first home in Eden and the plain of Shinar, where the tower of Babel is built, cannot really be understood as this-worldly locations; the date of the expulsion from *paradise and the year of the *Flood are not points that can be fixed on a historical time line. Moreover, while Adam, Eve, Noah, and the people of Babel are not gods, their existence is surely not limited by the kinds of constraints that define normal human experience: they have extraordinarily long life spans, and God makes clothes for Adam and Eve and speaks directly to Noah.

This conclusion concerning the mythic nature of Genesis 1–11 is enhanced by looking at the mythologies of Israel's ancient Near Eastern neighbors: Egypt, Canaan, and, in particular, Mesopotamia. The story of creation in Genesis 1.1–2.4a, which begins with the wind of God hovering over a watery *chaos (Hebr. *tĕhôm*), finds parallels in the Babylonian creation myth, *Enuma elish,* which describes a primordial battle between a goddess of watery chaos, Tiamat (etymologically related to Hebr. *tĕhôm*), and Marduk, a god of wind and storm. The story of Noah should be compared to a fragmentary third-millennium flood myth from *Sumer, the myth of Ziusudra, and to two later Akkadian versions of the same myth found in the epics of Atrahasis and *Gilgamesh. Both the Atrahasis and Gilgamesh epics also contain parallels to the story of Eden: in Atrahasis, as in Genesis 2.7, humans are molded from the clay of the earth (this tradition can also be found in Egyptian myths about the potter god of creation, Khnum); in the Gilgamesh epic, as in Genesis 3.22, there is a magical plant that, once eaten, yields a god-like state of immortality. The story of the tower of Babel similarly finds its roots in Mesopotamian sources, as the very name Babel, the Hebrew equivalent of Babylon, suggests.

While it is difficult, beyond Genesis 1–11, to speak of myth as such in Hebrew Bible narrative, scholars have identified ways in which the language and patterns of myths from the ancient Near East are present even in seemingly historical accounts. Most significant is the common Semitic myth of a fight between a storm deity and a sea deity, the Babylonian exemplar of which, *Enuma elish,* is described above. The same basic plot is known from second-millennium BCE Canaan, in *Ugaritic texts depicting a battle between a god of the waters of chaos, called both Yamm, "Sea," and Nahar, "River," and Baal, the god of the storm. In the Hebrew Bible, while the overt polytheism of these Mesopotamian and Canaanite prototypes is rejected, scholars have argued that the ancient mythic conception of storm versus sea stands behind Exodus 15.1–18, an account of the Israelite *Exodus from Egypt that culminates with God routing the Egyptians by sending a storm to drown them in the Reed Sea.

This same notion of a battle between Yahweh, the god of Israel, and some sort of watery enemy is also alluded to frequently in poetic passages, particularly in prophetic texts, in certain psalms, and in Job. In these texts the foe is most often described as a primordial water monster. Again, the myths of Israel's neighbors provide crucial comparative data: the biblical sea monster is at points called *yam,* "sea," and *nāhār,* "river," the same names given to Baal's watery foe at Ugarit; also in Ugaritic myth Yamm/Nahar is called Lotan, cognate to Hebrew Leviathan, and Tannin, cognate to Hebrew *tannîn,* "serpent," both terms used in biblical poetry of the primordial monster. And, as in Psalm 74.13, both Ugaritic Yamm/Nahar and Tiamat, the watery enemy of *Enuma elish,* are depicted as multiheaded dragons.

Among poetic texts the theme of Yahweh's battle with the dragon often occurs in *apocalyptic literature, both poetry and prose, in which mythological language and imagery are common. For example, the collection of apocalypses found in Daniel 7–12 is full of mythological allusions: Daniel 7.9–10, 13–14 reflects, it has been argued, myths concerning a younger god who assumes power from an older deity; also mythological is the notion that the divine patrons of the nations fight in the heavens while their earthly counterparts battle below. Mythic motifs manifest themselves similarly even in protoapocalyptic texts from the exilic and postexilic periods. One notable example comes from Isaiah 25.7, which describes how Yahweh, at the eschatological banquet at the end of time, will swallow up death forever; this is an allusion to a passage found in the Baal myth from Ugarit, in which it is said that the god of death, Mot, will swallow up Baal into the underworld. Yet simultaneous with allusion, there is reversal, for in the Canaanite myth, the god of storm and fertility, Baal, is rendered a prisoner through the power of death; in Israel, however, Yahweh, who shares with Baal attributes of fertility and storm god, vanquishes death through swallowing rather than being swallowed up.

The observation concerning attributes Yahweh shares with Baal suggests one final way in which older mythic traditions are reflected in biblical literature: the characteristics of ancient Near Eastern gods, in particular the gods of Canaan, are used in Israel to describe the character of Yahweh. Thus, like Baal, Yahweh is said to ride in a chariot of clouds, to speak with a voice of thunder, and to appear in a *theophany of storm. Yahweh is also depicted as creator and a granter of children, as lawgiver, as judge among the divine council of the gods (see Son of God), and as a deity of graciousness and compassion, language reminiscent of El, the high god of the Canaanite pantheon.

New Testament. While, as noted above, the term "myth" is used in New Testament literature with negative connotations, much in the New Testament is in fact mythic in character. The New Testament, for example, inherits from the Hebrew Bible a mythological conception of the universe as having three tiers: heaven, earth, and underworld. Each of these three regions, according to

New Testament thought, has its proper denizens (God and the angels, humanity, and Satan and the demons, respectively), and this notion of divine and demonic forces also has its antecedents in mythological patternings found in the Hebrew Bible, especially in apocalyptic literature. Apocalyptic also infuses New Testament thought with a mythological view of time, in particular with a belief that time has reached its fullness and the eschaton is imminent.

Moreover, the fundamental narrative that inspires the New Testament, the story of Jesus, could be understood as mythic in character. Thus various New Testament writers, although they differ in details, depict a Jesus who is superhuman in nature, the product of a miraculous birth, able to effect healings and *exorcisms, and, most important, a being resurrected on the third day after his death (see Resurrection of Christ). Moreover, according especially to Paul and to the author of the gospel of John, there is found in Jesus even before he is born a cosmic dimension that transcends this worldly space and time (see Logos). Thus the Jesus of Paul and John is described as one who was preexistent, present in the heavens with God from the beginning of time. Paul, along with the author of the book of Revelation and others, adds an eschatological, even apocalyptic component to this cosmic description of Jesus by arguing for the return of Jesus as heavenly judge at the end of creation.

See also Israel, Religion of.

                                    Susan Ackerman

N

NAG HAMMADI LIBRARY. Before the publication of the Berlin Codex 8502, resources for the study of *gnosticism were almost entirely limited to the refutations of the early church fathers, with such extracts and quotations as they chose to include. The only original gnostic material in Coptic—the Pistis Sophia in the Askew Codex, the two Books of Jeu, and an anonymous treatise in the Bruce Codex—was late and from a time when the movement had long since faltered. The patristic refutations were inevitably open to suspicion as the propaganda of the winning side, while the Coptic material left the impression that the whole movement was both tedious and bizarre. The Berlin Codex, known as far back as 1896 but published only in 1955, yielded three new documents: a fragmentary gospel of Mary, the Apocryphon of John, and the Sophia Jesu Christi. In contrast, the Nag Hammadi library, discovered in 1945 and gradually made available between 1956 and 1977, contains some forty previously unknown documents together with copies of several texts already known. Fragments used to stiffen the binding of some of the codices suggest a date of about the middle of the fourth century CE, but the Greek originals from which these Coptic texts were translated probably go back in some cases to the second century CE. Thus, the library's significance for the study of some aspects of early Christianity is comparable to that of the *Dead Sea Scrolls for the Judaism of an earlier period. The library derives its name from the modern Egyptian town of Nag Hammadi on the Nile north of Luxor, which was the nearest town to the place of the discovery.

The collection consists of twelve codices in their original bindings, plus eight leaves of a thirteenth (Codex XIII), which were apparently found inside the cover of Codex VI. The total amounts to over one thousand pages, in varying states of preservation: some are almost complete, while others are more or less fragmentary. Most of one codex (Codex I = the Jung Codex) was smuggled out of Egypt, but has now been returned for preservation with the others in the Coptic Museum in Cairo. A complete facsimile edition has been published, and translations have been made into various modern languages.

Not all the documents in the library are strictly gnostic. One (Codex VI,5) is a rather poor translation of a short section of Plato's *Republic;* another (VI,8) is part of the Hermetic tractate Asclepius, previously known from a Latin version. The Teachings of Silvanus (VII,4) is an early Christian wisdom text, while XII,1 is part of the Sentences of Sextus, already known in the original Greek and in versions in other ancient languages. The strongly ascetic tone of the latter work, with the similar ascetic emphasis in other documents, indicates that the collection belonged to a group that stressed asceticism, in contrast to the accusations of libertinism often made against the gnostics in patristic sources. Of the strictly gnostic documents, some are clearly Valentinian in character, such as the gospel of Philip (II,3), the Tripartite Tractate (I,5), and the Valentinian Exposition (XI,2), though there are often variations on the Valentinian system described by Irenaeus. It has been suggested that some texts, such as the Gospel of Truth (I,3) or the Treatise on Resurrection (I,4), may have been written by Valentinus himself, but this is at best speculation. Another major group of documents has been labeled Sethian, because of the prominence given to Seth, the third son of Adam. These include, among others, the Hypostasis of the Archons (II,4), the Gospel of the Egyptians (III,2), the Apocalypse of Adam (V,5), and the Three Steles of Seth (VII,5). These documents do have a number of features in common, which justifies grouping them together, but the existence of an actual sect of Sethians has been disputed and is by no means certain.

It was noted several years ago that a complete gnostic "New Testament" could be put together from the Christian gnostic texts in the library: the gospel of Thomas or of Philip, the Gospel of Truth, the Acts of Peter and the Twelve Apostles, the Letter of Peter to Philip, two Apocalypses of James, an Apocalypse of Peter, and an Apocalypse of Paul. Despite their titles, however, these texts are not comparable to those in the canonical New Testament: the gospels, for example, do not relate the life and ministry of Jesus, his death and resurrection. The Gospel of Truth is a meditation on the theme of Jesus' message, the gospel of Philip a rather rambling discourse whose continuity seems largely due to catchwords or the association of ideas. The gospel of Thomas is a collection of sayings attributed to Jesus, some parallel to sayings in the canonical Gospels, others completely new, and including all the sayings in the famous Logia papyri found at Oxyrhynchus (*see* Agrapha). The titles in fact are no sure guide to content: the gospel of the Egyptians and the Apocalypse of Adam have been claimed as non-Christian documents, and the former is not a gospel in the accepted sense, while the latter is more a testament than an apocalypse. Moreover, similarity of title does not mean that the documents are the same: the gospel of Thomas is completely different from the apocryphal infancy gospel of Thomas, the gospel of Philip is not the one known to Epiphanius, the gospel of the Egyptians is not the one quoted by Clement of Alexandria. The Nag Hammadi library itself contains two quite different Apocalypses of James. Mention should also be made here of a group of gnostic "gospels" that report revelations given by the risen Jesus to his disciples in the period between his *resurrection and *ascension, which the gnostics extended to eighteen months (in the Pistis Sophia eleven years).

Evaluation of these texts is still in progress, and in some respects they raise as many questions as they answer: the identity of the owners, the purpose of the collection, the reasons for its concealment. The discovery has not solved the problem of gnostic origins, or the vexed question of a pre-Christian gnosticism, but it has enriched our knowledge in several ways. Comparison of different versions of the same document, or different presentations of the same basic system, shows how the gnostics could develop and adapt their ideas, sometimes

using older material for their own purposes. Some texts show signs of the
Christianization of earlier, possibly non-
Christian material, while the Christian
gnostic documents often quote or allude
to both the Hebrew Bible and the New
Testament. The discovery has given fresh
stimulus to theories of a Jewish origin for
the movement, but however that may be
there is no doubt of the significance of
the Jewish contribution. Above all, we
now have for the first time a comprehensive collection of firsthand gnostic
material, from which it is possible to gain
some idea of what gnosticism meant to
a gnostic: it was not merely bizarre and
eccentric but an attempt to deal with the
human predicament, to resolve the problem of evil; not a counsel of despair but
a religion of hope and deliverance.

See also Apocrypha, *article on* Christian Apocrypha.   Robert McL. Wilson

NATURE AND ECOLOGY. Ecol-
ogy, the study of the relations between
people and their environment, has become a topic of interest within biblical
studies as a result of the global environ-
mental crisis. Standing at the beginning
of Western religious, ethical, and philosophical traditions, the Bible has received
considerable attention in the search for
the sources of modern attitudes toward
nature. The results have been paradoxical, some blaming the Bible for a
human-centered ethic that legitimates
the exploitation of nature for human
ends, others praising it for its reverence
for nature and ethic of responsible ste-
wardship of the earth's resources.

The more negative of these assess-
ments of biblical attitudes is based in part
on the traditional treatment of biblical
religion as uniquely historical. While
neighboring religions have been depicted as oriented toward nature, their

adherents viewing nature as the place of
divine revelation and the realm with
which human society had to attune itself
through ritual and daily behavior, biblical religion has been described as valuing
history supremely, its members seeing
human society as the location of divine
activity and the arena of primary concern. The result of this approach has
been to regard the natural world as separate from and subordinate to human
history and to consider nature and human interaction with it of little significance for understanding the genius of
biblical religion.

The Bible is without question preeminently about human existence, and
in this sense it may be described as historical or human centered in outlook.
Yet nature and society are so interdepen-
dent in the Bible that to distinguish them
sharply or subordinate one to the other
misrepresents biblical thought. Biblical
languages, for example, possess no terms
equivalent to the Western conceptions of
nature and history, suggesting that this
familiar modern distinction was not a
part of biblical thought. A more complex relationship between people and
nature is presented in the Bible than either traditional scholarship or recent polemical debates would suggest.

Biblical views of the interrelationship
between people and nature are best understood by exploring them within the
context of the actual environment
within which biblical writers lived and
their attitudes were shaped. For the Hebrew Bible, as the texts themselves and
archaeological evidence from the Iron
Age (1200–587 BCE) both indicate, the
ecological setting is a predominantly rural society in the Mediterranean highlands that subsisted on a mixed agricultural economy, including the cultivation
of grains and fruits and the herding of

sheep and goats. The literature of the Hebrew Bible is the literature of an agricultural society, and this perspective infuses the attitudes toward nature reflected in it.

The essence of the human being and the purpose of human life are both related to agriculture in the Bible's oldest creation story (Gen. 2.4–3.24), in which the first human being (ʾādām) is made out of fertile soil (ʾădāmā) to which it is destined to return at death, and given the primary task of cultivating—literally "serving" (ʿābad)—the soil from which it was made. Life in such an earthly setting, nourished by the agricultural bounty of the fertile soil, was believed to be the highest form of human experience, not a prelude to a better world. As the source of life, the earth and its produce were viewed as God's creation and inherently good. Historians, although interested primarily in political affairs, recognized a productive land as the basis for Israelite life and identity. Prophets saw natural disaster and degradation as punishment for sin and agricultural plenty as the experience of redemption. Psalmists sang of divine activity and sages reflected on human wisdom in such an agricultural environment.

The Israelite sense of dependence on the arable land is reflected in its religious ritual, which originated in the cycle of the agricultural year. In its major communal festivals, Israel celebrated the primary harvests of Mediterranean agriculture: barley and wheat in the spring and fruit in the fall. As an acknowledgment of the divine powers believed to make the land and the flock fertile and as an appeal for fertility and bounty in the future, the worshiper presented to the deity the first, best fruits of the harvest and the first, choicest specimens of the flock. Integrated with these important seasonal celebrations were the commemorations of political events such as the *Exodus from Egypt, which were held to be formative and unifying. (See Feasts and Festivals.)

The natural phenomena on which the lives of Israelite farmers depended took on for them a kind of sacred character. Features of the landscape, believed to provide points of contact between the earth and the divine worlds above and below—springs, rivers, and trees—marked sites of divine appearances and places of worship. Especially important to Israel were mountains, in particular Sinai and Zion, whose ground was considered holy and whose summits were the points of Israel's great revelations. The thunderstorm, the most powerful and essential natural phenomenon for highland farmers dependent on rain-fed agriculture, became one of the most common ways of picturing the presence and activity of the deity in biblical *theophanies.

The traditional village agrarian culture within which Israelite attitudes toward nature were shaped is essentially the setting within which Christianity originated. The life and ministry of Jesus and his first followers was located in the agricultural world of village peasants who made up the bulk of the population in Roman Palestine. In the New Testament Gospels, the stories about Jesus and the *parables he told present human life in terms of the dynamics of planting and harvesting, of herding flocks, and of fishing, an occupation prominent among Jesus' followers because of the Galilean setting of his ministry. Christianity is thus rooted in the land and agrarian culture of its Hebrew scriptures, and its gospel stories reflect modes of thought about nature much like those in these scriptures.

Yet new social and intellectual forces, shared with certain groups within the Judaism of its time, modified in some significant ways the viewpoint of the first Christians toward the natural world. One of these forces was the early urbanization of the Christian movement. Within a decade or two of Jesus' crucifixion, the center of Christianity shifted from the rural villages of Palestine to the great cities of the Roman empire. Paul and his followers were city people and wrote to city churches, and their epistles address issues of religious life in urban settings with little reflection on the world of nature.

A second force was the development in the centuries prior to the birth of Christianity of the notion that humans could hope for a meaningful life in another world. The sources of such thinking were *apocalyptic Judaism that, in its mature form already seen in the book of Daniel, affirmed the transcendence of *death and a life for the righteous in a better world, and Hellenistic dualism, reflected in Neoplatonism and *gnosticism, in which the material world was sharply differentiated from the spiritual world and viewed as alien to authentic human experience. The implication of such thought, more prominent in certain strands of later Christianity than in later Judaism, was that the earthly environment was no longer home for humanity, no longer the setting for true human existence, and was thus dispensable if not downright evil. (*See* Afterlife and Immortality.)

Influenced by both of these movements, early Christians viewed the highest form of human experience as life beyond death in a heavenly realm free from earthly struggles. Yet the New Testament vision of the new world, rooted most deeply within apocalyptic Judaism and its ancient holistic heritage, was modeled closely on the earthly environment. The entire world of nature was to participate in the final *redemption, and the individual would not escape the prison of matter (as Neoplatonism and gnosticism held) but would experience the *resurrection of the body, as had Jesus. Thus, even in its vision of another world, the New Testament is deeply rooted in the conceptions of the interrelatedness between people and their environment found in the Hebrew scriptures.

Theodore Hiebert

NEEDLE'S EYE. The term stands for the smallest imaginable opening in the saying attributed to Jesus (Mark 10.25 par.) which announces that the camel, largest of familiar animals, can pass through the needle's eye more easily than a rich person can enter the *kingdom of God. The shocking image is softened by the comment that with God all things are possible. The whole story draws attention to the difference between human activity and divine *grace. Some patristic interpreters eliminated the mixed metaphor by reading rope (Grk. *kamilos*) rather than camel (Grk. *kamēlos*). Talmudic parallels, however, retain the animal imagery and speak of an elephant passing through a needle's eye as something impossible. Medieval fondness for moral allegory generated the suggestion that "needle's eye" referred to a narrow pedestrian gate that a camel could squeeze through only after its burden and saddle had been removed, but there is no evidence for any gate with this name.

Robert Stoops

NEIGHBOR. The most frequently occurring Hebrew word translated "neighbor," *rēaᶜ*, has a wide range of meanings, from "lover" (Song. of Sol. 5.16; Jer. 3.1) to "friend" (2 Sam. 16.7; Job 2.11) to "neighbor" in the familiar sense of someone living nearby (Exod. 11.2; cf. 3.22; Prov. 27.10); in general, its semantic field encompasses anyone not considered either a "brother" (a kinsman) or an "enemy." In legal contexts, however, "neighbor" has the more specialized meaning of a member of the same social group, but not as close as a blood relative—in other words, a fellow Israelite. A key text is Leviticus 19.16–18, where the neighbor is grouped with one's "people," one's "brother," the "sons of one's people, one's fellow"; the passage concludes with the command "You shall love your neighbor as yourself." This command is repeated with a significant variation later in the chapter: "You shall love the alien as yourself" (Lev. 19.34), which indicates that legally at least the alien was not subsumed under the category of neighbor, who would be the "native-born" (Lev. 19.34; NRSV: "citizen").

This sense of "neighbor" as a fellow member of the covenant-community seems also to apply to the occurrences of the word in the *Ten Commandments, where the Israelites are instructed not to bear false witness against a neighbor nor to plot to expropriate ("covet") a neighbor's property (house, wife, slaves, livestock). It is likely that other commandments dealing with social relations have the same restriction: premeditated murder, adultery, and kidnapping are prohibited when perpetrated by one Israelite against another; the commandments against these crimes are not necessarily universal in scope.

Varying understandings of the extent of the obligations of mutual assistance are found in different legal traditions in the *Pentateuch. Thus, while Deuteronomy 22.1–4 enjoins the Israelites to return lost animals and property to their "brother" (NRSV: "neighbor"), and to assist him when a pack animal has fallen under a heavy load, in Exodus 23.4–5 this philanthropic obligation extends even to the enemy, to "one who hates you."

Given the wide range of meanings for the word "neighbor," it is not surprising that debate about its interpretation existed in Jewish tradition. The lawyer's question to Jesus reported in Luke 10.29 seems to echo that debate: "Who is my neighbor?" Jesus' response to the question is the parable of the Good Samaritan, in which Jesus extends the obligations of Jews toward each other to include those outside the community as well. By choosing as the hero of the parable a Samaritan, a member of another group, Jesus implies a maximalist interpretation of the concept of "neighbor." The same view is expressed in Jesus' saying "Love your enemies, do good to those who hate you" (Luke 56.27; cf. Matt. 6.44), and is generally characteristic of the *ethic demanded of Christians, as derived from Jewish tradition: the command of Leviticus 19.18, "Love your neighbor as yourself," is cited throughout the New Testament as an essential part of, even the very essence of, the *Law.   *Michael D. Coogan*

NUMBER SYMBOLISM. In common with most people in the ancient world, the Israelites attached symbolic significance to numbers. So whenever the biblical writers mention a number, it is likely that they had a symbolic meaning in mind; in many cases the numbers must not be taken in their literal sense at all.

One signifies uniqueness or undivided wholeness or both. "Hear, O Israel: YHWH is our God. YHWH is one" (Deut. 6.4; *see* Shema), means not only that the God of Israel is unique, but also that there is no contradiction within him. The oneness of God therefore calls for the trust and love of his people. As God is one, so, some New Testament writers insist, Christ is one with the Father; therefore his people must be one.

Two the smallest number larger than one, was the minimum number of witnesses required to establish the truth.

Three is widely regarded as a divine number. Many religions have triads of gods. Biblical faith has no room for a triad, and the number three is rarely connected directly with God. But in some cases this number hints that God is involved. When Abraham was visited by three men, this meant that God was calling on him. The Temple was divided into three parts. Three days were the proper time for a work of God, which meant, by the ancient reckoning of time, that it was completed on the third day. This is also true of the *resurrection of Christ. Time is divided into three parts, past, present and future, and God is he who is, who was, and who is to come. According to Paul there are three chief gifts of the Spirit. The expression "Father, Son, and Holy Spirit" is not found in the Bible (1 John 5.7b is found only in very late manuscripts); the closest is Rev. 1.4. Neither is the doctrine of the *Trinity expressed there in so many words.

Three and a half years is a strictly limited period, half the full seven of God's plan. It was regarded as significant that there were three and a half years between the desecration of the Temple and its rededication. The drought under Ahab was believed to have lasted three and a half years.

Four is the number of the created world. There are four corners of the earth, four wind-directions, four seasons, and four kinds of living creatures: humans, domestic animals, wild animals, and creatures of sky and sea. The four horsemen of the Apocalypse were derived from the four winds, but have a different function. The four Gospels were later regarded as signifying the universality of the gospel, and the evangelists were identified with the living creatures of Revelation 4, but this was long after biblical times.

Five is the number of fingers on one hand, and could stand for a handful, that is, a few.

Six is seven minus one. It is the number of incompleteness. The six days of the *creation were not complete until the seventh day of rest had come. In the book of Revelation six seals, trumpets, etc., represent the course of the world before God's final seventh act brings about the eternal *Sabbath. And in spite of its seven heads, the number of the beast is only *six hundred sixty-six.

Seven the sum of three plus four, of heaven and earth, signifies completeness and perfection. There were seven chief heavenly bodies (sun, moon, and the five planets known to the ancients), seven days of the week, seven archangels. The great festivals lasted seven days, and there were seven weeks between the *Passover and the feast of weeks (*Pentecost). Every seventh year was a sabbath year, when the land would rest and lay fallow, and *Hebrew slaves were allowed to go free; and every fiftieth year was a jubilee, when alienated property had to be returned ("jubilee" from Hebr. *yōbēl*, the ram's-horn that heralded its beginning). The seventh day represented God's completed work, and in the book of Revelation the seventh seal, trumpet, bowl, etc., represent the completion of God's plan. The seven spirits of God represent either the seven archangels, or "all spirits," or the Holy Spirit. Seven churches represent the universal church. It is necessary to forgive, not just seven times, but seventy times seven times, that is to say, always.

Outside Israel seven was also known as a significant number, and the monster

Leviathan had seven heads. Later interpreters noted that the Hebrew Bible refers to God by seven different names: *YHWH* ("the Lord"); *ʾădōnāy* (Lord); *ʾēl* and *ʾĕlōhîm* (God); *ʾehyeh ʾăšer ʾehyeh* ("I am who I am"); *šadday* ("the Almighty"); and *ṣĕbāʾôt* ("[Lord God of] Hosts"). Later Christian tradition noted that the Gospels report seven last words of Jesus in all.

Eight was later used for God's new creation, the day of the Resurrection being regarded as the eighth day rather than the first, but this plays no role in the Bible.

Ten is simply a round number, the number of fingers on both hands. Some interpreters have found a special significance in the fact that the *Ten Commandments correspond with a ten-times repeated "and God said" in the creation story (Gen. 1.1–2.4): ten words to create the world were matched by ten measures to keep it in order. Generally, however, ten, a thousand, and ten thousand simply signify small or large numbers, or are used by multiplication to enhance the significance of other numbers.

Twelve like seven, is a number of completeness and perfection. This number in particular must not always be taken literally. Israel always comprised more tribes than the twelve that were actually counted, and the counting of the twelve was not always uniform, but the twelve meant "all Israel." It was regarded as important that there were twelve apostles and that their number should be complete, but the lists do not quite tally. The twenty-four elders clearly represent all Israel and the whole church. The twelve cornerstones and gates of the new Jerusalem not only link the city with the tribes of Israel and the apostles, but also signify its divine perfection, as do its measurements of 12,000 stadia square and its walls of 144 cubits. The 144,000 of Revelation 7 and 14 in each case mean that the number is complete and not one of the elect is lost; in Revelation 7 John hears the 144,000 from Israel (all Israel) being counted, but sees "a great multitude that no one could count, from every nation, from all tribes and peoples and languages" (the redeemed gentiles).

Thirty was the age at which one was believed to reach full maturity.

Forty days was a strictly limited period of time (for six, not seven, weeks?). Forty years was the length of one generation. It was regarded as significant if a king reigned for this number of years.

Seventy meant a comprehensive number, and should not normally be taken literally. Seventy descendants of Jacob moved to Egypt (Gen. 46.8–27; an overliteral scribe added some absurd names to make up the number); seventy elders led the Israelites in the wilderness; the Temple lay in ruins for seventy years; the Greek version of the Hebrew Bible was believed to have been translated by seventy (or seventy-two) men, hence its name, the Septuagint, and its abbreviation, LXX; there were believed to be seventy nations; and the Sanhedrin had seventy members.

In spite of the significance attached by its writers to numbers, the Bible contains no speculation about numbers of the kind found among the Pythagoreans, or later in the Qabbalah.

David H. van Daalen

O

OMEGA. *See* Alpha and Omega.

ORACLE. A communication from a deity on some particular matter. The documentation from the ancient Mediterranean world, both biblical and extrabiblical, preserves many citations of, or allusions to, such oracles. Frequently, oracles are conveyed in the setting of a sanctuary, for example, the temple of Apollo at Delphi in Greece, or the high place of Gibeon where Solomon received a divine message in a dream. In communicating its oracles, the deity may make use of either mechanical devices—for example, the lots known as Urim—or a human intermediary, the "prophet." Oracles may come in response to a human "inquiry" (Jer. 21.2) or at the divine initiative. In either case, however, it is recognized that God remains free either to give or withhold the oracle.

In content, biblical oracles range from one-word responses to yes-or-no questions to the extended discourses mediated by prophets like Jeremiah or Ezekiel. Like extrabiblical oracles, the latter are characterized by an elevated, poetic style, evidencing a certain ambiguity and indeterminacy.

In terms of purpose, the oracles of the prophetic books can be classified generally as either "judgment speeches" or "oracles of salvation." The former have as their intention the announcement of the evil fate awaiting the addressee. They typically consist of an accusation that serves to motivate the following statement of the punishment that God will bring on the guilty individual, group, or nation. This type predominates in the material of the preexilic prophets. The oracle of salvation, which comes to the fore during the *exile (with Second Isaiah) and afterward, announces God's coming positive interventions for those addressed. These may concern both the improvement of their external circumstances (return to the land, restoration of the Davidic line, etc.) as well as their internal purification or revitalization. Oracles of salvation are sometimes conditional on a prior human initiative of *repentance, but more often are grounded solely on God's impenetrable *mercy.   *Christopher T. Begg*

P

PARABLES. A parable is a picturesque figure of language in which an analogy refers to a similar but different reality. In the Hebrew Bible, the word "parable" (Hebr. *māšāl*) can refer to a proverb, taunt, riddle, or allegory. Although story parables are not specifically called parables, we should include them in any definition. It is not surprising that in the New Testament "parable" covers a broad semantic range as well, for the Greek term *parabolē* was used to translate *māšāl* in the Septuagint in all but two instances. In the Gospels it can refer to a proverb, aphorism, metaphor, similitude, story parable, example parable, or allegory. In contrast to Aristotelian tradition, no sharp distinction is drawn in the Bible between simile/allegory and metaphor/parable. This is true also in rabbinic tradition. In view of the broad semantic range of the term, it is impossible to give an exact list of Jesus' parables. Although *parabolē* is used explicitly to designate thirty different sayings of Jesus, when one adds other clear examples in which the term is not used and other likely possibilities, the total number is about eighty. If the instances of the *paroimia* or "figure" of John are added, the number becomes still greater. Moreover, if one includes every simile, proverb, and aphorism that Jesus taught, then almost everything Jesus said falls into the category of parable.

Numerous attempts have been made to classify the parables. These involve the use of specific chronological periods in Jesus' ministry, distinctive subject matter, as well as literary, theological, and existential categories. None of these attempts, however, has been very successful.

Historical and Literary Analysis. In his parables Jesus repeatedly used illustrations from daily life. These often contain a distinctly Palestinian and even Galilean flavor. This was originally intended to make the parables more understandable for Jesus' audience, but today it serves also to authenticate them. It is clear, for example, that the Sower (Mark 4.2–20) reveals a Palestinian method of farming in which sowing preceded plowing. Likewise, the references to a priest, Levite, Samaritan, a road going from Jerusalem to Jericho (Luke 10.19–35), as well as a Pharisee, publican, and Temple (Luke 18.9–14), indicate that such parables originated in Palestine. The portrayal of a fishing environment in the parable of the Great Net (Matt. 13.47–50), where good fish are separated from bad, strongly suggests that this parable originated around the Sea of Galilee. The example of farm laborers being paid at the end of the day (Matt. 20.8) according to biblical law shows the contrast between Palestinian farming, which often employed laborers, and the farming in most of the Mediterranean world, which relied on slaves.

Most scholars agree that in the parables one stands on the bedrock of authentic Jesus tradition.

Although the parables are drawn from daily life, they do not necessarily portray normal, everyday actions. On the contrary, at times one encounters both exaggeration and unexpected behavior. The forgiveness of the enormous sum of a thousand talents (Matt. 18.24–27), the fact that all ten maidens are sleeping (Matt. 25.5), and that all the invited guests refused the banquet invitation (Luke 14.18) suggests the intentional use of exaggeration. In the commendation of the Unjust Steward as well (Luke 16.1–8), the hearer is taken by surprise. These forms of exaggeration, however, are fairly specific; nowhere in the parables of Jesus does one find fables in which animals speak or trees sing.

The artistic character of the parables should be noted. Jesus' portrayal of the Prodigal Son is most memorable: Having squandered his fortune, starving and destitute in a far country, "joined" to a gentile (Luke 15.15), feeding the forbidden pigs, he wishes that he could fill his stomach by sharing the food of the pigs he feeds! And how beautifully the father's love is described. Laying aside his dignity, he runs to embrace his son, refuses to hear out his confession, reclothes him in appropriately filial garments, and joyfully celebrates having regained his lost son. The artistry and descriptive power of the parables often require only a single hearing for them to be forever remembered. Such parables as the Prodigal Son and the Good Samaritan must by any standard be recognized as literary masterpieces.

The primary reason that Jesus taught in parables appears to be self-evident: he used them to illustrate. Can one find a better illustration of the love of God for the outcast than the parable of the Prod-igal Son? Some of Jesus' parables are clearly "example" parables and require no explanation. Yet Mark 4.10–12 gives a different reason why Jesus taught in parables—in order to conceal his message. The reason given for concealing his message is more difficult still: Jesus did so in order that his hearers would not believe lest they repent and be forgiven. Numerous attempts have been made to explain this difficult passage, but none is truly convincing and without problems. The most common explanation is to see the lack of understanding as being the result rather than the cause of the unbelief of those "outside" (*see also* Messianic Secret). That the meaning of certain parables was not in fact self-evident is clear from the various explanations associated with them. Parables served a useful purpose in concealing Jesus' message from those hostile to him: by his parables he could publicly teach about the *kingdom of God, but the representatives of the Roman empire could find nothing in them that was seditious. A third reason Jesus taught in parables was to disarm his listeners and allow the truth of the divine message to penetrate their resistance. Often hearers could be challenged to pass judgment on a story before discovering that in so doing they had in fact condemned themselves. A fourth reason for the use of parables was to aid memory: since Jesus' listeners preserved his teachings by memorizing them, the memorable quality of the parables proved useful.

History of Interpretation. The early church saw in the parables (and in all scripture) three distinct levels of meaning: the literal, the moral, and the spiritual. In the Middle Ages an additional level was added, the heavenly. These deeper levels of meaning were discoverable by allegorical interpretation (*see* Interpretation, History of, *article on*

Early Christian Interpretation). A famous example of this is the parable of the Good Samaritan (Luke 10.30–35), in which each detail was seen as meaningful, so that the man going down to Jericho = Adam; Jerusalem = heaven; Jericho = our mortality; robbers = the devil and his angels; priest = the Law; Levite = the prophets; Good Samaritan = Christ; beast = the body of Christ; inn = the church; two denarii = two commandments of love; innkeeper = the apostle Paul; return of the Good Samaritan = the resurrection or the *second coming; and so on. Of course, such an interpretation lost sight of the original question of what it means to be a neighbor!

Although interpreters of the Reformation sought to end allegorical methods of interpreting scripture, the parables continued to be allegorized. More recently, however, new insight has been gained as to the difference between parables and allegories. An allegory consists of a string of *metaphors that have individual meanings, whereas a parable is essentially a single metaphor possessing a single meaning. The details of parable, then, should not be pressed for meaning; rather, one should seek only its basic point of comparison. Although some parables do contain details that have allegorical significance, this distinction between allegory and parable is useful and provides an important rule for interpretation: seek the main point of the parable and do not seek meaning in details unless it is necessary.

In identifying the main point of a parable, several questions prove helpful: (1) What comes at the end? This rule of end stress recognizes that the main emphasis of a parable, as in most stories, comes at the end. (2) What is spoken in direct discourse? In a parable what is found within quotation marks is espe-

cially important. (3) To what or whom is the most space devoted? Usually the most space is given to the main point of the parable.

A second rule for interpreting the parables is to try to understand their meanings in their original settings. Jesus did not address his parables to modern readers but to a first-century Jewish audience. The parables take on new life and vitality when one tries to understand them as Jesus' original audience would have. In this regard, the following questions prove helpful: (1) What is the general theological framework of Jesus' teachings? Each parable of Jesus should be interpreted in light of the totality of his teachings. (2) To what possible audience did Jesus address this parable? If addressed to Pharisees and scribes, its emphasis might be quite different than if addressed to publicans and sinners. The discovery of the Coptic Gospel of Thomas at *Nag Hammadi has provided additional help for ascertaining the original form and meaning of the parables. Since this collection of 114 sayings and parables of Jesus did not stem from any canonical Gospel, it offers an independent tradition for investigating the original form of numerous parables.

A parable may have a specific meaning not only for its original situation of Jesus but also for that of the evangelist. One example is the parable of the Lost Sheep: in Luke 15.3–7 the parable is addressed to Pharisees and scribes, but in Matthew 18.10–14 it is addressed to the church and the "wandering" within Matthew's community. At times the evangelists added allegorical details to the parables that reveal a particular emphasis. This leads to a third rule of parable interpretation: Seek to understand how the evangelists interpreted Jesus' parables.

Recently, the focus in research on the parables has shifted to literary-aesthetic interpretation. Parables are seen as autonomous works that possess multiple meanings and power in themselves, completely apart from their author. Although it is important to appreciate the aesthetic quality of the parables, the parables of Jesus have been treasured and loved primarily because they are parables of Jesus.   *Robert H. Stein*

PARACLETE. *See* Holy Spirit.

PARADISE. Originally a Persian word meaning "park" or "enclosure," paradise first appears in the Septuagint with reference to the garden of Eden and became associated with a pristine state of perfection free of suffering. In *apocalyptic literature the loss of this original paradise represented the loss of the presence of God in human experience, and therefore redemption was imagined as the recovery of paradise whether it was on earth or in heaven. At the end of the world the righteous would be rewarded by a return to paradise.

Although paradise was initially an earthly garden, New Testament writers lifted it above the evils of this world. Paul says that his visionary flight to the "third heaven" carried him into paradise (2 Cor. 12.1–4), and according to Luke 23.43 Jesus tells the penitent thief that at the moment of death they will be together in paradise. Yet Jesus also is reported to have said that the eschatological paradise described by Isaiah was manifested in his ministry and that the qualities of Eden were revealed in his person. Clearly, early Christian writers believed that the traditions of paradise were fulfilled in Jesus and his ministry.   *Gregory Shaw*

PARAPHRASES. Paraphrase is a restatement of a text or passage in another form or other words, often to clarify meaning. It is generally restricted to a restatement made in the same language, rather than in another language. As applied to Bible translation, it usually means a version that often alters the original cultural and literary setting of the original, sometimes adding or omitting material in order to make the text more intelligible and acceptable to intended readers. What is sometimes called "paraphrase" in Bible translation is actually a legitimate and necessary device to represent the meaning clearly and faithfully in the target language. As C. H. Dodd noted, the line between translation and paraphrase is a fine one: "But if the best commentary is a good translation, it is also true that every intelligent translation is in a sense a paraphrase." And Ronald Knox made the cutting comment, "The word 'paraphrase' is a bogey of the half-educated. . . . It is a paraphrase when you translate *Comment vous portez-vous?* by 'How are you?'" No self-respecting translator would translate that French question by "How are you carrying yourselves?"

The earliest scriptures in English, the oral renditions of Caedmon (seventh century CE) and the written works of Aelfric (ca. 1000), were paraphrases. In the sixteenth century, several paraphrases were produced. Jan van den Campen did a Latin paraphrase of the Psalms in 1532, which was translated into English in 1535 (perhaps by Coverdale). The English version of Erasmus's New Testament Paraphrase appeared in 1549. He begins Romans as follows: "I am Paul, though formerly Saul, that is, I have become peaceful, though formerly restless, until recently subject to the law of Moses, now freed from Moses, I have been made a servant of Jesus Christ." In 1653 Henry Hammond, president of Magdalen College, Oxford, produced a paraphrase of the New Testament, which was printed alongside the King James Version.

Edward Harwood's Bible (1768) was, as he stated, "not a *verbal* translation, but a *liberal* and *diffusive* version of the sacred classics." His rendition of Luke 1.46–47 is typical: "My soul with reverence adores my Creator, and all my faculties with transport join in celebrating the goodness of God my Saviour, who hath in so signal a manner condescended to regard my poor and humble station. Transcendent goodness! Every future age will now conjoin in celebrating my happiness!" Ferrar Fenton's Bible (1903) may be considered a paraphrase, at least in some passages. It begins, "By Periods God created that which produced the Solar System; then that which produced the Earth." However, because of criticism of the rendering "periods," in the fifth edition Fenton replaced it with "ages," which is also paraphrastic.

Most paraphrases are limited to one book and are usually included by their author in the commentary on that book. Such is the case of J. B. Mayor's paraphrases in his commentaries on James (1892) and on Jude and 2 Peter (1907), and W. O. Carver's paraphrase in his commentary on Ephesians (1949).

F. F. Bruce published his paraphrase of Galatians in the *Evangelical Quarterly* (January–March 1957), and of other Pauline letters in subsequent issues. In 1965 they were all published in one volume, *An Expanded Paraphrase of the Epistles of Paul*, together with the text of the Revised Version. In light of current modern language translations, Bruce's work appears quite conservative, hardly qualifying as a paraphrase. Romans 1.16–17 reads, "Believe me, I have no reason to be ashamed of the good news which I proclaim. No indeed; it is God's effective means for the salvation of all who believe, for Jews in the first place

but for the Gentiles too. Why? Because in this good news there is a revelation of God's righteousness—a way of righteousness based on the principle of faith, and offered to all men for acceptance by faith, in accordance with the words of the prophet: 'It is he who is righteous by faith that will live.' "

The most popular English Bible paraphrase of all times is Kenneth N. Taylor's *The Living Bible Paraphrased* (1971). In his preface he explains that, in attempting to be faithful in paraphrasing the text, he has been guided by "the theological lodestar [of] a rigid evangelical position." It must be stated, however, that Taylor's penchant for adding to or deleting from the text, without any justification other than what is dictated by his "rigid evangelical position," effectively removes *The Living Bible* from being regarded as a trustworthy rendering. It is not that every passage in his paraphrase is tainted (in fact, some are very well done); it is that readers who are not acquainted with the biblical text will too often be misled by Taylor's handling of it. From dozens of examples that could be cited, two must suffice here. Whereas the Hebrew of 2 Samuel 24.1 states that Yahweh incited David to take a census of the people, Taylor exonerates Yahweh from any responsibility by editing the passage, "and David was moved to harm them." Contrary to what the synoptic Gospels report, John 12.14 states that Jesus himself found the donkey on which he rode into Jerusalem; Taylor takes care of that problem by eliminating the passage completely!

Paraphrases of biblical texts, responsibly made, are a legitimate and useful way of making the meaning of the text clearer to the reader. When produced by translators who are ruled by rigid tenets of whatever kind, however, they serve only to confirm the truth of the Italian aphorism, "Translators are traitors" *(Traduttori traditori)*.

See also Translations, *article on* English Language. *Robert G. Bratcher*

PAROUSIA. "Arrival" or "presence," a Greek word used both of ordinary persons and of an emperor or a god. The term is used in early Christianity for the anticipated return of Jesus, when he was expected to judge humankind as triumphant *Son of man (see Second Coming of Christ). The word parousia is found with this meaning in the eschatological *parables of Matthew 24, but otherwise chiefly outside the Gospels, as in 1 Corinthians 15.23, 1 Thessalonians 2.19, and the urgently apocalyptic 2 Peter. Paul also uses the term to mean the arrival of an ordinary person.

Philip Sellew

PASSOVER. This festival, observed on the fourteenth day of the month of Nisan (March/April), commemorates the *Exodus of the Hebrews from Egypt. Of the five lists of festivals in the Hebrew Bible, only the last three make reference to Passover, and all of these associate the celebration with the seven-day festival of unleavened bread, which commences on the fifteenth of the month. Exodus 23.14–17 and 34.18–23 mention only the festival of unleavened bread as an early spring celebration. The narrative in Exodus 12.1–36 provides an explanation of the origin of Passover as well as the features involved in its celebration; this narrative also associates Passover with the festival of unleavened bread.

According to Exodus 12.1–13, the following were characteristic of Passover. On the tenth day of the month, the animal to be slaughtered was selected and set aside for safekeeping; according to Exodus 12.5, the animal was an unblemished, one-year-old goat or lamb, although Deuteronomy 16.2 includes calves. The animal was slaughtered on the fourteenth day late in the afternoon. Some *blood of the animal was smeared on the doorposts and lintels of the houses. The animal was roasted whole (see Exod. 12.46 and Num. 9.12; Deut. 16.7 specifies boiling, which would have required dismemberment). The flesh was eaten, along with unleavened bread and bitter herbs, by members of the household or associated households. The meal was eaten in haste, with the participants dressed for flight. Any uneaten meat, should there be any, was to be burned the next morning.

The eating of unleavened bread at the meal is explained by the haste with which the Israelites had to flee, but no biblical explanation is offered for the consumption of bitter herbs. The daubing of the blood on the doorposts, later assumed to have been part of only the original episode, is described as marking the houses of the Israelites so that God would bypass their homes in the slaughter of the firstborn. (Note the similar substitution of a ram for the firstborn in Gen. 22, and the similar use of a red marker to avoid death in Josh. 2.17–21.)

If people were ritually unclean or away on a journey when Passover was observed in Nisan, they could celebrate the festival in the second month in similar fashion. Foreigners and thus non-Jews who had settled among the people were allowed to keep the Passover, provided they were circumcised.

Although Exodus 12 seems to imply that Passover was a home festival and thus could be observed apart from a pilgrimage to a sanctuary, Deuteronomy 16.5–7 requires that the slaughter of the animal and the meal occur at a place (sanctuary) that God would choose. The same pilgrimage requirement seems assumed by Exodus 34.25 and Leviticus 23.4–7.

The Hebrew name of the festival, Pesah, is derived from the verb that means "to protect," "to have compassion," "to pass over," and is used to describe the action of God in the Exodus narrative. The English designation "passover" shows the influence of the Vulgate translation.

Most scholars assume that Passover was originally a spring festival, associated with a shepherding culture, that was secondarily related to the Exodus story (note the reference to a festival in Exod. 5.1 before the Exodus). Such a celebration would have been connected with either the annual spring change of pastures or the sacrifice of the firstborn to insure the continued fertility of the flocks or both. Characteristics pointing to such an origin for the festival in Exodus 12 are the lamb or goat to be slaughtered, cooking by roasting, the time of the year (which coincides with the lambing season and the change of pastures), the absence of priest and altar, the lack of dedicating any part of the edible flesh to God, the family nature of the celebration, and the nocturnal observance at the time of full moon.

The tractate *Pesaḥim* in the Mishnah provides a description of the way that the rabbis (about 200 CE) understood Passover to have been celebrated before the destruction of the Second Temple (70 CE). Many of the features reflected in *Pesaḥim* are thus characteristic of the observance at the time of Jesus (*see* Lord's Supper), and some have continued in Jewish tradition to the present. The following elements in the celebration are noteworthy.

The people brought their Passover animals to the Temple in the late afternoon and, because of the numbers of worshipers, were admitted to the sanctuary in three separate groups. The worshipers slaughtered their animals and the priests caught the blood and tossed it against the altar. The animals were flayed and cleaned in the Temple courtyard, with the required fat and internal portions being burned on the altar. While each group was performing these functions, the Levites sang the Egyptian Hallel psalms (Pss.113–118) and repeated them if time allowed.

The animals were carried from the Temple precincts and cooked for the Passover meal. Cooking was done by roasting so as not to break any bone in the animal.

At the meal, everyone ate at least a portion of the Passover animal. The flesh was eaten along with varied herbs, unleavened bread, a dip (*ḥărôset*) composed of pounded nuts and fruits mixed with vinegar, and four cups of wine. After the second cup, a son asked the father, "Why is this night different from all other nights?" and the father instructed the son on the basis of Deuteronomy 26.5–11. Between the second and third cups, Psalm 113 (or 113–114) was sung. After the fourth cup, the Hallel was concluded. At the conclusion of the meal, the people departed but not to join in revelry.

The people sought to celebrate the meal as if they themselves had come out of Egypt—"out of bondage to freedom, from sorrow to gladness, and from mourning to festival day, and from darkness to great light, and from servitude to redemption" (*Pesaḥ.* 10.5).

See also Feasts and Festivals; Leaven.
                                    John H. Hayes

PEACE. The Hebrew word translated "peace," *šalôm*, occurs more than 250 times in the Bible, and its richness is shown in its many usages. It is used as a courteous greeting, and also to refer to health or to restoration to health, to general well-being such as sound sleep, length of life, a tranquil death, and even to the physical safety of an individual.

Šālôm is also used to describe good relations between peoples and nations. Thus, it has important social dimensions that can also be seen from the association of peace with righteousness, law, judgment, and the actions of public officials.

Šālôm is used, too, to describe quiet tranquility and contentment. It can also be almost synonymous with friendship. The root ideas of the Hebrew word are well-being, wholeness, soundness, completeness.

Šālôm also has theological dimensions. God is described as peace, and its creator and source, who gives it to his people. Peace in its fullest sense thus cannot be had apart from God, a conclusion especially prominent in exilic and postexilic literature.

The usual Greek word for "peace" is *eirēnē*. In classical literature it denoted the opposite of war or conflict; later it came to describe a harmonious state of mind, an imperturbability that could exist irrespective of external circumstances. In the New Testament, *eirēnē* has these overtones as well as meanings derived from *šālôm*.

The distinctive idea about *eirēnē* in the New Testament is its mediation through Jesus Christ. He is described as the peace that ultimately unifies humanity, reconciling humanity with God through his death.   *Gerald F. Hawthorne*

PENTATEUCH.

Form. The first five books of the Bible, known as the Pentateuch (Grk. "five-volumed work"), are essentially in the form of a narrative running from the *creation to the death of Moses just before the entry of the Israelites into the Promised Land. Although these books

contain a great deal of *law, they are not law books in essence. The Hebrew term *Torah, by which the Pentateuch is known, is indeed conventionally translated as "law," but its meaning is better represented as "instruction" or "guidance." Thus, the narratives of the ancestors in Genesis 12–50 are as much "torah" as are the *Ten Commandments of Exodus 20, since they too offer instruction about the nature of Israel's God, the relationship of Israel to him, and the moral behavior appropriate to life in relationship to him. The "guidance" offered by the more legal parts of the Pentateuch is explicitly directive, as in the many social laws, whether in the style of legal maxims or of hypothetical cases. Only in a few instances, though, as in the rules governing *sacrifice or in the instructions for the building of the *tabernacle, is the legislation systematic. In the book of Deuteronomy, chaps. 1–26 being represented as a farewell speech of Moses, there is indeed a distinct hortatory tone in the recollection of the nation's past history (chaps. 1–11) and in the presentation of laws for life in the Promised Land (chaps. 12–26), but the historical setting keeps before the reader the fact that a particular generation in the nation's history is here directly addressed. In the more narrative materials, the "instruction" is indirect and implicit. In some cases the reader is presented with models for imitation (as in the case of Abraham's faithfulness or Joseph's uprightness), but even here, and more especially in the stories like those of Abraham's deceptions or Jacob's trickery, there is little direct moralizing. So the Pentateuch does not present itself as a comprehensive set of rules for life, nor does it develop a cohesive theological system, nor does it typically narrate the past for the sake of illustrating obvious or explicit moral truths.

Authorship. Although the Pentateuch has in most centuries been known as "the five books of Moses," perhaps because he is the major human figure in the narrative, it has long been recognized that he cannot have been the author, and that the Pentateuch is in fact anonymous. The Jewish tradition of referring to everything in the Pentateuch as the work of Moses, which is reflected in the New Testament, proves nothing about its authorship, since it had obviously become customary to refer to these books as "Moses." Within the Pentateuch itself, Moses is indeed credited with the authorship of a relatively small portion of its content: Exodus 21–23, the laws known as the "Book of the Covenant"; Numbers 33, the itinerary of Israel in the wilderness; Deuteronomy 5.6–21, the Ten Commandments. These sections are, as it happens, among the elements generally considered most ancient by historical scholars. Whether or not Moses can be called the author in a literal sense of anything in the Pentateuch, it is reasonable to hold that his work and teaching were the initial stimulus for the creation of the Pentateuch.

Origins and Date. The overwhelming tendency in biblical scholarship has been to explain the origin of the Pentateuch as the outcome of a process of compilation of various documents from different periods in Israelite history. According to the classical Documentary Theory of the Pentateuch, formulated by Julius Wellhausen and others in the nineteenth century (*see* Interpretation, History of, *article on* Modern Biblical Criticism), the oldest written source of the Pentateuch was the document J (so-called from its author, the Jahwist or Yahwist, who used the name Yahweh for God) from the ninth century BCE. The E document (from the Elohist, who employed the Hebrew term ʾĕlōhîm for

God) came from the eighth century, and the J and E sources were combined by an editor in the mid-seventh century. The book of Deuteronomy, a separate source dating from 621 BCE, was added to the JE material in the mid-sixth century. The final major source, the Priestly work (P), was combined with the earlier sources about 400 BCE. The Pentateuch as we know it thus came into existence no earlier than the end of the fifth century BCE.

No item in the foregoing reconstruction remains unchallenged, and indeed the theory as a whole can no longer be called the consensus view; nevertheless, no other theory has gained any wide support, so this one remains the point of departure for all study of the date and origins of the Pentateuch. Among those who still hold that it is essentially correct, there has been a tendency to date the Yahwist's work a century earlier, in the time of the united monarchy, to favor an eighth-century rather than a seventh-century date for the composition of at least the core of Deuteronomy, and to allow that the Priestly work, set down in writing during the *exile in the sixth century rather than after the exile in the fifth, may well preserve much older material. More radical revisions of the theory include the proposal that the Yahwist's work should be seen as the latest, not the earliest contribution to the Pentateuch, and that it rather than the Priestly work gave the definitive shape to the whole.

A valuable development of the theory in recent decades has been the attempt to reconstruct the intentions of the authors of the presumed sources as theologians anxious to convey by their presentation of Israel's traditional history a message to their contemporaries. Thus, the Yahwist's message has come to be seen as an address to the age of Solomon, urging Israel to prove itself to be a blessing to the nations in accord with the command to Abraham of Genesis 12; the Elohist's work is an appeal to ninth-century Israel to live in the "fear" of God in the face of persuasive foreign cults. The Deuteronomist's work is seen as a program for national reform, emphasizing the unity of Israel despite the political reality of the divided kingdom and calling for a unified worship of Yahweh. The Priestly work, then, is addressed to the Babylonian exiles, reiterating the authenticity of Israel's religious and cultic traditions and renewing the divine promise of blessing and superabundance in the land to a generation who had all but given up hope for the future.

Other techniques of analysis beside the detection of sources can sometimes be integrated with the documentary analysis, and sometimes run counter to it. The form-critical approach, by which the literary forms (such as saga, tale, and moral story—sometimes called legend) are analyzed in order to discover the role they played in everyday life, has on the whole proved congenial to the documentary analysis. Its concern has been to press back behind the literary sources of the Pentateuch to reconstruct the original life settings of its diverse materials, and to postulate patterns of growth of the traditions prior to the existence of any written source. Thus, for example, one influential analysis, by Martin Noth, fully accepted the documentary reconstruction but detected behind them five major "themes" or organizing ideas around which the total material of the Pentateuch had gradually gathered: the promise to the ancestors, the *Exodus from Egypt, the guidance in the wilderness, the giving of the Law, the guidance into the land.

On the other hand, studies in the techniques of oral composition and transmission of oral literature have tended to call into question the theory of an essentially or ultimately literary growth of the Pentateuch. It is possible, for example, to see the whole of Genesis as one large oral composition, in which differing influences have left their mark in the form of relatively minor discrepancies and disagreements in representation, but which was intended to be heard as a whole, later elements in the story deliberately reflecting and building on earlier (so, for example, with the so-called ancestress in danger stories of Gen. 12.10–20; 20.1–18; 26.1–16). Other researches on the processes of literary composition as disclosed by the present shape of the Pentateuch have suggested that we should envisage individual authors creating large blocks of its material rather than editors interweaving a number of narrative strands, as the documentary theory supposed.

Themes. The question here is, what is the organizing principle of the Pentateuch as a whole, considered as a literary entity? An initial answer is, of course, that the subject matter of the Pentateuch is sufficiently unified to create the impression of general coherence in the work. The last four books in particular, beginning as they do with the birth of Moses and ending with his death, have a strong narrative connection. But it would be wrong to regard the Pentateuch as primarily a biography of Moses, for then there would be no evident connection between its last four books and Genesis, for Genesis is a narrative of the ancestors of Israel in general and not especially of Moses' forebears.

Some have suggested that certain brief summaries of the Pentateuchal narrative found at Deuteronomy 26.5–10 and 6.20–24, having the character of Israelite confessions of faith in the God who had directed their history, indicate the fundamental story line of the Pentateuch as a whole. The essential elements in this "little creed" (Gerhard von Rad) are the forebears' origins and divine election, their descent into Egypt, and the entry of the people into the promised land. This outline does indeed correspond roughly with the content of the Pentateuch, though it makes the remarkable omission of the events at Sinai, which constitute a major section of the Pentateuchal narrative. We may perhaps seek a more conceptually unified theme in the Pentateuch than a mere summary of its narrative.

The mainspring of the action of the Pentateuch seems to be the divine promise of Genesis 12.1–3 (repeated with varying emphases in 15.4–5, 13–16, 18–21; 17.4–8; 22.16–18; and alluded to in scores of passages throughout the Pentateuch). This promise contains three elements: a posterity ("I will make of you a great nation"), a relationship ("I will bless you"), and a gift of land ("the land I will show you"). It is the fulfillment, and the partial nonfulfillment, of these promises that may be said to be the theme of the Pentateuch.

The theme of the posterity is plainly the theme of Genesis. In the Abraham cycle of stories, the theme appears mostly in the shape of anxious questions: Will there be a son at all? What will become of him? Here lies the significance of the many Genesis narratives of threats to the family's survival: the sterility of matriarchs, the strife between brothers, often with near-fatal consequences, and the repeated famines in the land of promise.

The theme of the divine-human relationship comes most strongly to expression in Exodus and Leviticus. Both at the Exodus and at Sinai it becomes plain what the words of the promise ("I

will bless you," "I will make my covenant between me and you," "I will be your God") meant. The blessing comes in the form of salvation from Egypt and in the gift of the law. The *covenant of Sinai, of which the opening words are "I am Yahweh your God," formalizes the relationship adumbrated by the covenant with the forebears. Leviticus spells out how the relationship now established by Yahweh is to be maintained: the sacrificial system is to exist, not as a human means of access to God, but as the divinely ordered method whereby breaches of the covenant may be repaired and atoned for.

The theme of the land dominates Numbers and Deuteronomy. Numbers begins with preparations for the occupation of the land, and ends with the actual occupation of that part of it lying to the east of Jordan by two and a half of the tribes. Deuteronomy sets before the people laws for their life under God, explicitly "in the land which Yahweh, God of your fathers, is giving to you" (Deut. 4.1).

None of the promises is fully realized within the Pentateuch itself: the posterity as numerous as the sand on the seashore is a promise that has only begun to achieve fulfillment by the time the Pentateuch is over, the relationship of *blessing and of covenant is a continuing and never wholly fulfilled promise, and the land, at the end of the Pentateuch, is a promise that is only partly fulfilled. The whole structure of the Pentateuch, then, is shaped by the promises to Abraham, which are never final but always point beyond themselves to a future yet to be realized.   *David J. A. Clines*

PENTECOST. The word Pentecost (Greek "fiftieth") appears twice in the Septuagint as one of the designations of the "feast of weeks" (Exod. 34.22; Deut.

16.10), which comes between *Passover and Tabernacles (see Feasts and Festivals). In the Hellenistic period, the feast also called for renewal of the *covenant God made with Noah. Later, after the destruction of the Temple in 70 CE, the feast began to lose its agricultural association and became linked with Israel's sacred history by celebrating the giving of the *Torah on Sinai. In synagogue worship, it became customary to read the book of Ruth and Exodus 19–20 (see Lectionaries, article on Jewish Tradition).

Luke gives new significance to the first Pentecost following the *resurrection and *ascension of Jesus. For Luke it is the fulfillment of Jesus' promise that his followers would receive power when the Holy Spirit would come upon them.

The narrative is replete with allusions to biblical traditions, including *creation and the *Flood, the tower of Babel, and various *theophanies, especially that at Sinai. Luke does not tell us where the followers of Jesus were assembled when the Spirit came, but the subsequent scene seems to be in the Temple court. The Spirit's coming was attended by "a sound like the rush of a violent wind" filling the house where they were gathered, and is marked by the appearance of "tongues, as of fire"; then the followers "were filled with the Holy Spirit and began to speak in other languages" (Acts 2.2–4). While the reported charge of drunkenness may suggest the kind of ecstatic speech that Paul describes in 1 Corinthians 12–14 (see Glossolalia), Luke understands these "other tongues" as foreign languages and articulate witness. Within Israel, near and distant neighbors are finding their unity in the gospel. For Luke, what happens at Pentecost is a promise of what will happen among all the nations when the gospel will be preached to the gentiles.

For Christianity, *Easter as the new

Passover and Whitsunday as the new Pentecost became the basis for the liturgical year.   John Frederick Jansen

PERIODIZATION. See Chronology.

PHILO.
Philo of Alexandria (ca. 15 BCE–50 CE), also known as Philo Judaeus, is the most important representative of the Greek-speaking variety of Judaism that flourished in Alexandria from ca. 200 BCE to 100 CE. The historian *Josephus tells us that he was highly respected in the Jewish community and was "not unskilled in philosophy." The only event of his life known to us is his leadership of an embassy of Alexandrian Jews that appeared before the Emperor Gaius Caligula in 40 CE to protest against anti-Jewish mob violence. Vivid descriptions of this event and its background are given in his treatises In Flaccum and Legatio ad Gaium.

By far the majority of his writings concentrate on the interpretation of the *Law of Moses, or *Pentateuch, as found in the Septuagint translation. These treatises can be divided into three lengthy series: the Allegorical Commentary, the Exposition of the Law, and Questions and Answers. In the Allegorical Commentary, Philo gives a very detailed and complex exegesis of Genesis 1–17, interpreting early history and Abraham's wanderings in terms of the moral life and religious quest of the soul. The Exposition of the Law is a more varied work, containing biographies of the patriarchs and an explanation of the *Ten Commandments and the other ordinances of Mosaic law, with emphasis both on literal observance and symbolic interpretation. The third series, imperfectly preserved in an Armenian translation, poses questions and gives answers on the text of Genesis and Exodus; most of the usually short chapters contain literal followed by figurative or allegorical exegeses.

Philo's attention centers on the interpretation of scripture, but in his exegesis he demonstrates his considerable knowledge of Greek philosophy. Through the use of allegorical and symbolic interpretation, Moses is presented as the lawgiver, prophet, and even philosopher par excellence, who is the source of all later philosophy. The apologetic motive is clear: in his Alexandrian context Philo is eager to show that Jewish culture is not inferior to Hellenistic culture. In his doctrine of God, Platonic ideas of transcendence and immanence are prominent. God as Being is distinguished from his powers at work in the cosmos. Highly influential is the doctrine of the *Logos, which builds upon Hellenistic Jewish wisdom speculation. The Logos can be described as that aspect of God which stands in relation to created reality. But Philo often talks about the Logos as if it were an entity with a separate existence from God himself, that is, a divine hypostasis.

Philo's thought and writings were warmly embraced by the early Christian church. His allegorical themes and theological ideas exerted a strong influence on Clement of Alexandria, Origen, and later patristic authors. In Byzantine manuscripts Philo is often called "the Bishop." It was his popularity in Christian circles that caused his writings to be preserved.

See also Judaisms of the First Century CE; Interpretation, History of, *article on* Jewish Interpretation.   *David T. Runia*

PHYLACTERIES. Small receptacles, generally called *tefillin,* attached by leather thongs to the upper left arm (or right, for a left-handed person) and the forehead. Normally rectangular in shape, both *tefillin* contain tiny slips of parchment inscribed with short portions of the Bible. There are usually four interior compartments into which the slips are placed open-side up, tied round with a goat-hair thread.

The custom of praying with phylacteries on a daily basis and not on holidays is based on Exodus 13.9, 16, and Deuteronomy 6.8; 11.18. Because no explicit or detailed injunctions are provided, divergent traditions developed very early in the postexilic period. The four texts that were originally inscribed on the parchment slips are Exodus 20.2–17 (the *Ten Commandments), Deuteronomy 6.4–9 (the *Shema), Deuteronomy 11.13–21 (the second paragraph of the Shema), and Numbers 15.37–41 (the commandment to wear tassels or fringes). The first and last passages were ultimately excluded for fear that unorthodox views would creep into Judaism, and they were replaced by Exodus 13.2–10, 11–16.

According to rabbinic tradition, both *tefillin* and *mezuzot* (small boxes containing scrolls attached to the doorpost of a house or room) could be written from memory. Hence it is not surprising that many of the texts found from Qumran and the Judean wilderness caves contain departures from the *Masoretic Text. In addition, there is great variation in the passages selected from the Bible that were inserted into the compartments.

Some have argued that in antiquity only distinguished persons put on *tefillin,* either daily or occasionally. Even though in rabbinic times it became obligatory to wear them, the practice was ignored in some countries of the Diaspora. One view holds that even women, minors, and slaves should pray with phylacteries.

The extensive archaeological evidence of *tefillin* suggests that their use was already widespread in late Second Temple times. Before prayer capsules were attached to leather thongs, as attested in the archaeological record, phylacteries probably consisted merely of inscribed scrolls attached to the head and arm in order to fulfill the biblical precept: "Keep these words that I am commanding you today in your heart. . . . Bind them as a sign on your hand, fix them as an emblem on your forehead" (Deut. 6.6, 8).

Eric M. Meyers

PLAGUES OF EGYPT. The story of the ten plagues of Egypt (Exod. 7.14–12.36) is based on the ancient Israelite tradition of the "great and awesome signs and wonders against Egypt" (Deut. 6.22) that God accomplished in order to force Pharaoh to allow the Israelites to leave that country. Each plague, except the last, has a basis in natural phenomena or diseases that occur in Egypt, either annually or at intervals, between July and April. They form an orderly series, each related to its successor; and their rapid and cumulative severity mounts to a climax in the death of Egypt's firstborn. In these partly ordinary events, the Israelites saw the hand of God active in their behalf.

All three strands composing the book of Exodus told of plagues, though no single source lists all the plagues; J gives eight (1–2, 4–5, 7–10); E, five (1, 7–10); and P, five (1–3, 6, 10). All agree on the first and the last. Sometimes God is shown as directly effecting the plague; sometimes Aaron, at Moses' command, is the agent; and sometimes Moses himself calls down the plague.

The ten plagues of the final form of the Exodus narrative are as follows:

1. Nile water turns to blood (Exod. 7.14–15). The annual rise of the river normally brings life to Egypt's soil, but on rare occasions putrid waters carrying decaying algae from the vast swamplands of the Sudan join with the waters from Ethiopia's Blue Nile into which volcanoes —active in those days—had spewed sulphuric lava and ash. Thus, once per century or so the water of the Nile would turn red in color and become undrinkable.

2. Frogs (Exod. 7.25–8.14). When the flooding Nile subsided it left heaps of dead frogs over the land, so many that some were even piled in people's homes. The Egyptians may have believed that their magicians could prevent such a disaster from falling upon the common people.

3. Gnats (Exod. 8.16–19). Swarms of "gnats" (whatever noisome insect this name represents) had bred and multiplied in the stagnant pools of water. The magicians confess that "this is the finger of God."

4. Flies (Exod. 8.20–32). The plague of "flies" (the word simply means "insects") appears to be a variant of the preceding plague; note the poetic parallelism in Psalm 105.31. The sign was not just the coming of myriad flies but the isolation of Goshen, so that the Hebrews were not affected.

5. Cattle murrain (Exod. 9.1–7). Anthrax, hoof-and-mouth, or some such disease, resulting from conditions created by former plagues, struck Egypt's farm animals, a principal source of food.

6. Boils (Exod. 9.8–12). Ashes from the kiln were thrown into the air and caused boils breaking out in sores on humans and animals alike. The magicians could not

stand before Moses because of the boils.

7. Hail (Exod. 9.18–35). The scourge of hail (a rare occurrence in Egypt) and thunderstorm destroyed a whole season's crops.

8. Locusts (Exod. 10.3–20). Always a bane of the Middle East, a plague of locusts devoured whatever was left after the storm was over. The Lord "brought" the locusts by an east wind; when Pharaoh confessed his sin God "drove" the locusts by a west wind into the Red Sea.

9. Darkness (Exod. 10.21–23). Thick darkness that could be felt may have been brought on by the wind from the desert, carrying with it much dust and sand; but the Israelites had light. The Lord was clearly confronting Amon-Ra, the sun god, whom the Egyptians worshiped as their divine father.

10. Death of the Egyptian firstborn (Exod. 11.1–8). The announcement of the final plague, the death of the firstborn in Egyptian families, from Pharaoh's down even to those of slave girls, is linked with what took place at the first *Passover ceremony. It was then that the Lord "chose" Israel, which he had "passed over," as his firstborn son (Exod. 4.22–23).

The popular theme of the superiority of the Lord's power over that of pagan gods and magicians has here found expression in one of the most characteristic products of Israelite skill in narrative prose. The account has been the source of poetic summaries in Psalms 78.43–51; 105.28–36; of the homily on them in Wisdom of Solomon 11.1–12.2; and the general references to them elsewhere in the Bible. Several features of the Egyptian plagues reappear in the account of the "seven last plagues" in the book of Revelation (15.1–16.21; 21.9).

See also Exodus, The.

George A. F. Knight

PLANTS. Despite its relatively small size, ancient Israel had a rich and varied flora, a function of its topographic and climatic diversity and the associated variations in soil type and rainfall. The Bible, however, mentions only 110 names of plants, for many of which the identification is unknown or uncertain, notwithstanding the recent advances of archaeologists, botanists, and biblical scholars. Thus, the *tappûaḥ* has been identified as an apricot, quince, and apple, the ambiguity stemming both from the vagueness of the biblical texts and the lack of certainty concerning the dates when these fruits were present in Israel. Similarly, the famed *šôšannâ* of the Song of Solomon has been identified as a white lily, hyacinth, narcissus, crowfoot, chamomile, and rose; one can state with certainty only that it was a showy flower, or group of flowers, of some kind. Furthermore, there is no necessary correlation between the number of times, if any, that a plant is mentioned in the Bible and its importance in the agriculture or ecology of Israel. For example, the foreign cedar of Lebanon, the wood of gods and kings, topics of special interest to biblical authors, appears seventy times, more than twice the number of references to wheat, one of the major cereal crops of ancient Israel and an essential dietary staple. The probably abundant carob tree is not mentioned at all in the Bible. In general, the Bible mentions plants only in passing. It contains no system of plant classification (though such may have existed), and rarely offers descriptions of sufficient detail for identification. It is not always certain whether a plant name refers to an individual species or to a larger category such as thorns and thistles. A study of the plant terminology in such ancient *translations as the Septuagint and the Vulgate and in the commentaries of the rabbis and church fathers often adds to the uncertainty, since translators and commentators frequently identified biblical plant names with local flora with which they were familiar, many of which were not even found in Israel. Over the centuries, many peoples outside the region have given biblically sounding names to flora that are not native to Israel (such as the Joshua tree [*Yucca brevifolia*] of North America), again contributing to the confusion. On the other hand, the botanic data that can be derived from present-day studies, given the absence of significant climatic change in Israel since the Bronze Age, the growing body of evidence from archaeological excavations concerning the dates by which many wild and cultivated plants were present, and comparative data from Egypt and Mesopotamia have all contributed substantially to the current understanding of the biblical flora. Exhaustive compilations of biblical plant names and their possible or probable identifications can be found in a number of Bible dictionaries and encyclopedia articles and in such books as Michael Zohary's *Plants of the Bible* (Cambridge, England, 1982).

Although the biblical authors did not mention specific plants in great number or detail, they vividly portrayed the centrality of plants and their cultivation for ancient Israel, whose well-being depended on the successful harvesting of such cereal crops as wheat, barley, and emmer, as well as varieties of legumes, fruit trees, and vines. Plants are described as the basic food in the first creation account. The well-watered and fruitful garden was understood as the best of all places. This characterization is not surprising: the early Israelite community sought sustenance from land often beset by drought and composed of poor soil, with a topography that necessitated such labor-intensive forms of cultivation as terrace-farming. The challenges and frustrations of the Israelites may be reflected in the punishment meted out by God to the first man at the end of the second creation account: "Cursed is the ground because of you; in toil you shall eat of it all the days of your life; thorns and thistles it shall bring forth for you; and you shall eat the plants of the field" (Gen. 3.17–18). The biblical authors envisioned God's blessings and favor as yielding rainfall and abundant harvests. Thus, Micah 4.4 depicts peace and prosperity as all sitting "under their own vines and under their own fig trees." But when Israel violated her *covenant with God, she experienced drought, blight, and barren fields.

Israelite *law reflected a concern with and some understanding of the ways in which crop production could be well managed. Thus, the Israelite farmer was forbidden to harvest immature fruit trees, and was expected to allow his fields to remain fallow during the sabbatical year. Vegetable and *incense offerings were an essential component of the system of *sacrifice and atonement, a central piece of Israelite religion until the destruction of the Temple by the Roman army in 70 CE. The Bible also abounds with similes, *metaphors, and *parables rooted in the plant world. The images are as diverse as the flora itself. Thus, in addition to fertility, abundance, and continuity, plants are used to represent life's frailty, brevity, and transitory nature. Biblical symbolism draws also on the characteristics of individual plants, such as the great height and longevity of the cedar tree (Ps. 92.12; see similarly the parable of Jotham, Judg. 9.8–15, and the parable of the mustard seed, Matt. 13.31–32). The New Testament is replete with agricultural imagery; see, for example, Mark 4.3–8, 26–29; Matthew 9.37–38; Luke 13.6–9.

Representations of plants adorned the columns and carvings of the Solomonic Temple. Plants appeared also on Hasmonean and Herodian coinage, and on the coins issued by the rebels in the anti-Roman Palestinian Jewish revolts of the first and second centuries CE. To commemorate the defeat of the Jewish rebels in the First Jewish Revolt, the Roman government issued coins, in circulation by 71 CE, with the inscription *"JUDAEA CAPTA"* ("Judea captured"). The coin depicts a palm tree, perhaps in recognition of the importance of the date palm in Israel. On one side of the tree is a Roman legionary, on the other a woman in mourning seated under the palm. The mosaics of the synagogues and churches of Roman and Byzantine Palestine were rich with representations of plants, depicted both realistically and in highly stylized forms.

Barbara Geller Nathanson

POETRY, BIBLICAL HEBREW. Poetry is the elevated style in which songs, hymns, lamentations, proverbs, wisdom, and prophetic speeches are composed. Biblical poems tend to be of short or medium length, ranging from two to about sixty lines. Longer poems exist, such as Psalm 119, but they are rare, and there is no continuous poem of epic proportion. Unlike most epic traditions, the Bible contains few narrative poems: its major narratives are in prose. Nevertheless, close to one-third of the Hebrew Bible is poetry, distributed

in small amounts among the narrative books, in greater amounts in the prophetic books, and predominant in the collections of Psalms, Proverbs, and Lamentations, and in the wisdom books of Job and Ecclesiastes.

Biblical poetry is characterized by a terse, binary form of expression that is eloquent and evocative. The terseness is effected by the juxtaposition of short lines with few specific connectives between them. The connective may be lacking altogether, or may consist of the multipurpose conjunction *wāw,* meaning "and," "but," "or," and so forth. Thus, the exact relationship between lines is often not made explicit. The lines themselves are short, usually three or four words, and their terseness is enhanced by the omission, in many cases, of the definite article, the relative pronoun, and other grammatical particles. Two examples, the first from a narrative poem and the second from a psalm, illustrate the terseness and parataxis of biblical poetry:

> Water he asked:
> Milk she gave:
> In a lordly cup she offered cream.
> [Judg. 5.25]

You give to them, they gather:
You open your hand, they are satisfied well.
[Ps. 104.28]

These two excerpts also illustrate the most prominent feature of biblical poetry, its binary form of expression known as parallelism. Parallelism is the pairing of a line (or part of a line) with one or more lines that are in some way linguistically equivalent. The equivalence is often grammatical—that is, both parts of the parallelism may have the same syntactic structure, as in "Water he asked: Milk she gave." In many cases, however, the grammatical structure is not identical, at least on the surface level. In Judges 5.25, the third line expands and rearranges the syntax of the first two lines. Similarly, in Psalm 104.28 there is partial grammatical equivalence by virtue of the "you-they ‖ you-they" pattern, but the syntax of the lines is different. Grammar has many facets, and any one of these facets may be brought into play in parallelism.

Another common form of equivalence is semantic equivalence; the meaning of the lines is somehow related: perhaps synonymous, perhaps reflecting the converse or reverse, or perhaps extending the meaning in any one of a number of ways. Again, equivalence does not imply identity. The second line of a parallelism rarely expresses exactly the same thought as the first; it is more likely to expand or intensify it. The relationship between "they gather" and "they are satisfied well" in Psalm 104.28 is a progression. The relationship between "water he asked" and "milk she gave" in Judges 5.25 is more than a progression—it sets up an opposition, a conflict, between the request and its fulfillment.

Grammatical and/or semantic equivalence account for most parallelisms, but because there are so many equivalent permutations for any given line, the number of potential parallelisms is enormous if not infinite. Although readers/listeners may learn to anticipate a parallelism, they cannot, except in the most formulaic of expressions, predict exactly what the parallelism will be. Each parallelism is cast to fit its context, and the effect of each must be evaluated individually.

There are, however, several general effects that parallelism has. For one thing, it helps to bind together the otherwise paratactic lines, so that the basic structure of the poem is not a single line but rather sets of lines (often called a couplet or a bicolon). Another byproduct of parallelism is the rhythm or

balance that it creates. Scholars have long sought metric regularity in biblical poetry, but no system—be it syllable counting, stress counting, thought-rhythm, or syntactic constraints—has met with unanimous acceptance. If there is such a metric form, it continues to elude us. It is more likely that the Hebrew poets embraced a looser system—one in which many lines of a poem are more or less the same length and partake of the rhythm of their parallelisms, but without the requirement of precise measurement.

Beyond the level of specific parallel lines it is possible to find a larger structural unit that is often called a strophe or stanza. This is identified by dividing the poem into its major sections, based on contents or on structural or lexical repetitions. Although a longer poem is likely to have more strophes, that is, more subdivisions, the strophe is less well defined than the couplet and seems less basic to the overall poetic structure. The principles whereby couplets are combined into longer segments or entire poems is not well understood, but it is clear that poems have movement and development, and that their lines and couplets cohere as unified compositions. Psalm 104, for example, portrays the creation of the world by means of a description of God's habitat, the sky, and then moves to various natural habitats and the creatures that occupy them. The progression in the poem is obvious even though its strophic divisions may not be.

In addition to their main characteristics, terseness, and parallelism, biblical poems often employ devices such as word repetition, word association, ellipsis, sound play, chiasm (an *A-B B-A* pattern of words, grammatical structures, or lines), inclusio (frame or ring composition), and imagery. Although these devices are not limited to poetry, and are not poetic requirements, they do enhance the poeticality, that is, the sense of elevated style and rhetoric associated with poetry. We draw again on Psalm 104 to illustrate:

> Wrapped in light as (in) a garment:
> Spreading the sky like a curtain.
> [Ps. 104.2]

Through similes, the first elements of creation, light, and the heavens become the personal effects of God, the glory surrounding and enhancing him. There is also a good deal of assonance in the Hebrew in these two lines, as there is elsewhere in the poem. The psalm begins and ends with "Bless the Lord, O my soul," which provides a sense of closure.

The rhetorical impact of biblical poetry is considerable and its aesthetic dimensions manifold. The prophets used it to convince, the wise to instruct, the psalmists to offer praise. In the Bible, language—that is, forms of verbal expression—takes on paramount importance, and it is in poetry that verbal expression reaches its epitome.

Adele Berlin

POLITICS AND THE BIBLE. The Bible is not a purely religious book; its pages are full of kings and empires, armies and wars, cries for justice. Its political implications have had great influence on the way in which it has been interpreted.

The Bible does not, however, present any systematic or unambiguous teaching about political matters. Its books were written over many centuries and under widely differing political systems, from Israelite tribal society to the Roman empire. Many remarks that have political implications are brief hints rather than clearly stated principles. Later tradition, however, has tended to draw from the Bible certain great architectonic images

of political life, and many have taken one such image to be the dominant one, even when the Bible itself furnishes counterindications. This article will sketch some of these classic images.

The Theocratic Image. Perhaps the most influential such image in history has been the theocratic image. God has laid down the way in which society ought to be governed; the essential constitution for human society has been written by God. The Mosaic *law exemplifies this. Basic norms were explicitly laid down by God: how to deal with homicide, which animals might be eaten, what to do if a corpse was found in the fields. Even if such rules could not be exactly followed within the very different world of Christendom, they continued to support a theocratic image. The Middle Ages struggled with the problem of interest upon *loans because "usury" was understood to be directly forbidden by God. And not only the laws, but also the centrality of persons with divine authority—kings, judges, patriarchs—reinforced the theocratic idea. Hence came the establishment of religion, the linkage of church and state, religious sanction for *war, and the divine right of kings. Later, some of these connections were weakened: monarchy was challenged, church and state could be separated, but the force of the theocratic paradigm continued; the belief that direct divine instructions for state and politics exist enshrined in the Bible lingers on. A central text was Romans 13.1: "The powers that be are ordained of God" (KJV).

In fact, the Bible's support for the theocratic image is ambiguous. *Kingship and state were not there from the beginning; when kingship, much later, was proposed, it was regarded in some circles as a rebellion against God—a principle that might have led toward a pious anarchism. Royalty is limited in theory, and in historical event it was often condemned; yet democracy is hardly considered an alternative—if monarchy was revolt against God, it was the people's voice that had demanded it.

The Alien State. The great empires could at times be seen as blessed by God and as serving his purposes, but at the best they were heathen empires and their polity did not derive from the God of Israel. In Judea in the first century CE, Roman rule was often bitterly resented, and the war of 66–70 was approaching.

Thus Jesus, with his talk of the *kingdom of God, and people's belief that he was the son of David, might easily raise political questions. The position he takes up is depicted as a strikingly neutralist one; asked if it is lawful to pay taxes to the emperor, he commands, "Render to Caesar the things that are Caesar's, and to God the things that are God's" (Mark 12.17). He does not define what is Caesar's and what is God's, but at least there is something that is Caesar's; there is a certain dualism in society; not everything is God's, nor can everything be derived from the theocratic idea. When asked to decide about an inheritance, Jesus asked, "Who made me a judge or divider over you?" (Luke 12.14); some things are human business, and Jesus refuses to involve God in people's partisan struggles. He does not encourage nationalist yearnings for revolt against Rome. Some New Testament sources, such as Luke-Acts, seem to give a favorable picture of Rome (e.g., the Roman administration protects Paul against Jewish violence). Roman persecutions of the church, however, pointed in the other direction: is Rome the beast of Revelation 13, the Babylon of Revelation 18?

Some have thought that the historical Jesus was much more involved in the nationalist politics of his time, as indicated

by the superscription "the King of the Jews" on the cross, suggesting that Jesus was put to death for political sedition; the reality of this was then covered up in the Gospels as we have them. The New Testament, seen in this way, is sometimes taken to support involvement in political conflict and violence, contrasting with the neutralist image conveyed by the existing Gospels.

The Prophetic Image. From the nineteenth century onward, the prophets have been seen in the context of their own times as those who demanded social justice and warned of divine judgment if this demand was not met; the heathen empires would serve God in punishing his own people. The "prophetic" task of the church was thus to protest against the evils and injustices of society. Since the New Testament had not done much of this—Paul in Philemon touches upon *slavery but does not attack the institution as such—the example of the Israelite prophets was appealed to all the more.

The prophetic image often clashes with the theocratic: God will not hesitate to overthrow that which has theocratic legitimacy if by its inaction it favors the powerful and leaves the weak to suffer. Much progressive, reformist, politically activist religion has thus relied on the prophetic image. Yet the prophets rarely proposed reform, and after early times they did little to foster political action within the nation; God's action came rather through forces from without.

The Eschatological Image. Allied with the prophetic, and still more evident in the *apocalyptic movement, is the image of the coming of a new world in which war and evil will be no more—and one that may come to pass very soon. Political upheavals and international violence may be birth pangs of this new era. This vision of immediate catastrophe and a new world nourishes two hostile but related tendencies: millenarianism, which almost welcomes catastrophe because it ushers in the end, and sympathy for Marxist revolution.

The Image of Migration. The Hebrew Bible emphasizes the migrations of Abraham, of the Hebrews from Egypt to the Promised Land, of the returning exiles; the New Testament also pictures the church as a pilgrim people. This biblical image of migration and return was the motive power for modern Zionism. Christian nations often saw themselves in the same way: they were Israel, going out to find a land where they could build a life in the pattern ordained by God— the Puritan settlers of New England and the Afrikaners in South Africa are examples.

The Image of Liberation. New Testament passages often emphasize freedom or liberty, and modern scholarly trends have emphasized the *Exodus as the dominant event of the Hebrew Bible. In Egypt, the Hebrews were enslaved and subjected to forced labor; their male population was threatened by infanticide. They looked back on the time in Egypt with horror, and their escape from Egypt was the great event, ever afterward to be celebrated. No biblical theme has received more attention for its political importance in recent years than liberation. This theme was taken up by and on behalf of the exploited and oppressed of Latin America, Asia, and Africa, and made into the keystone of liberation theology. The church must take the side of the poor and oppressed, stand with them in their struggle, join with their cry to God for deliverance, and read the Bible from within that context. Neutrality in relation to this situation is intolerable.

This use of the Exodus theme, powerful as it seems, has also been questioned on the ground that it implies a peculiar selectivity within the biblical traditions and a neglect of contrary aspects. Why did the Hebrews not organize politically to resist oppression? Why is their demand not a call for social justice but a request to leave Egypt in order to worship God in the wilderness? If the Exodus theme is so authoritative, what about its sequel when the liberated Hebrews enter Canaan and destroy or reduce to slavery the entire population of that land? Why should one aspect be more authoritative than the other? Liberation theologians generally answer by an appeal to the context of the interpreter: if the context is right, then it will be obvious which aspects of the biblical materials are relevant.

Conclusion. The Bible is certainly deeply interested in human political, social, and historical existence, and it presents powerful images relevant for understanding it. But all of these images have a somewhat relative character within the Bible and are limited through inner qualifications and through the coexistence of other, different images. It is doubtful therefore whether any clear and unitary political view can be derived from the Bible taken alone and as an entirety. If we appeal to the contextual situation of the interpreter, then the source is not the Bible as a whole but one's contextual selection. Or is it intrinsically mistaken to appeal so directly to the Bible at all? May the biblical images be valid and salutary only insofar as they are taken up into a total religious and philosophical position that includes, but goes beyond, the actual material of the Bible? These are fundamental questions posed by a consideration of politics and the Bible.

James Barr

PONTIFICAL BIBLICAL COM-
MISSION. By his Apostolic Letter *Vi-gilantiae* (30 October 1902), Pope Leo XIII established the Pontifical Biblical Commission to promote biblical studies in the Roman Catholic Church, "that God's words will both be given, everywhere among us, that thorough study that our times demand and be shielded not only from every breath of error but even from every rash opinion." The commission was to study biblical questions in the light of modern trends and recent discoveries and to disseminate for the service of all whatever was useful for biblical interpretation. The first-word title of the Apostolic Letter, "vigilance," however, sounded a note that was to mark the activity of the commission, which sought above all to safeguard the authority of the Bible against the exaggerated criticism of early-twentieth-century Modernism. Although the commission was not strictly a Roman congregation, it was organized, as were Vatican commissions of that period, with five cardinal members and thirty-nine consultors (biblical scholars from many nations).

Pope Pius X (1903–1914) furthered the work of the commission. During his reign it issued thirteen *responsa* (often popularly called "decrees"), and subsequently others (until 1933), with various other declarations about biblical studies in seminaries and requirements for ecclesiastical biblical degrees.

The *responsa* were issued in the form of brief answers (affirmative or negative) to long, intricate, often "loaded" questions. They dealt with such topics as the theory of implicit quotations in the Bible; the theory of apparently historical narratives; the Mosaic authorship of the *Pentateuch; the authorship and historicity of the Fourth Gospel; the author-

ship and character of the book of Isaiah; the historicity of Genesis 1–3; the authorship, date of composition, and character of the Psalms or of Matthew; of the Marcan and Lucan Gospels; the synoptic problem; the authorship, date of composition, and historicity of Acts; the authenticity, integrity, and date of composition of the Pastoral Letters; the authorship and composition of the letter to the Hebrews; the *parousia in Pauline writings; the interpretation of two texts (Ps. 16.10–11 and Matt. 16.26 = Luke 9.25). These *responsa* caused a dark cloud of reactionary conservatism to settle over Roman Catholic biblical scholarship in the first half of the twentieth century.

The commission's *responsa* were never understood to have been infallibly issued. Pius X in his Motuproprio *Praestantia sacrae scripturae* considered them to be "useful for the proper progress and guidance of biblical scholarship along safe lines." But he did require the same submission of Catholics to these *responsa* as to similar papally approved decrees of other Roman congregations.

In 1943, Pope Pius XII issued an encyclical, *Divino afflante spiritu*, on the promotion of biblical studies. Since that time, the Biblical Commission has played a more open-minded role in encouraging such studies. Its *responsa* have given way to "letters" and "instructions," in which it has gradually assumed a more positive stance, though concern is still expressed about some errors or excessive tendencies.

To many people, however, both inside and outside the Roman Catholic Church, the *responsa* have seemed to be still in effect. This, however, is not true. In 1955, a semiofficial explanation of the character of the *responsa* was issued by the secretary and the subsecretary of the commission, distinguishing *responsa* that touched on faith and morals from those that dealt with literary questions, authorship, integrity, date of composition, and so on. The former were to be regarded as still valid, whereas the latter were recognized as time-conditioned, corresponding to a historical context that no longer existed. Both secretaries explained that in matters pertaining to the *responsa* of the second category Catholic interpreters were to pursue their research and interpretation "with full freedom." Significantly, almost all of the above-mentioned *responsa* belong to the second category.

In 1964, the Biblical Commission issued an instruction "On the Historical Truth of the Gospels," in which it dealt concretely and in a positive way with a problem that has vexed modern students of the Gospels both within and without the Roman Catholic Church. Instead of merely reiterating the historical character of the Gospels, it adopted valid aspects of form criticism and distinguished three stages of the gospel tradition: (1) what Jesus of Nazareth did and said; (2) what his disciples preached after his death and resurrection about him, his message, and his deeds; and (3) what the evangelists selected and synthesized from that preaching and explicated for the needs of their churches. Whereas the instruction insinuated a continuum between the first and third stages, it did not in any way (fundamentalistically) identify them. (The essential content of that instruction was briefly repeated in chapter 5 of the dogmatic constitution of Vatican Council II, *Dei verbum*.)

In 1971, Pope Paul VI revamped the commission, making it a counterpart of the International Theological Commission and associating it with the Congregation for the Doctrine of the Faith. The members of the Biblical Commission are no longer cardinals, but twenty biblical

scholars from across the world, appointed for five years, most of them of widely acclaimed competence.

Joseph A. Fitzmyer, S.J.

POPULAR CULTURE AND THE BIBLE. The Bible has been a fixture in American popular culture from the first European settlements to the present. Mentioning only a few random facts is enough to suggest the breadth of the Bible's presence in American civilization. The first English book published in North America was *The Whole Booke of Psalmes Faithfully Translated into English Meter* (1640). The American Bible Society, founded in 1816, has distributed well over four billion copies of the Bible or biblical portions (*see* Bible Societies). Throughout the nineteenth century, American settlers regularly named their communities after biblical places, like Zoar, Ohio, or Mount Tirzah, North Carolina, as well as forty-seven variations on Bethel, sixty-one on Eden, and ninety-five on Salem. When in 1842 the Roman Catholic Bishop of Philadelphia, Francis Patrick Kenrick, petitioned city officials to allow schoolchildren of his faith to hear readings from the Douai-Rheims translation of the Bible instead of the Protestant King James Version, the city's Protestants rioted and tried to burn down Philadelphia's Catholic churches. In 1964, a thought-provoking book was published on the biblical content of a famous comic strip (Robert Short, *The Gospel According to Peanuts*). Two of the most popular rock-operas of the 1970s, *Jesus Christ Superstar* and *Godspell*, were based on the biblical Gospels. During the same decade, the best-selling book of any kind (except the Bible itself) was Hal Lindsey's *The Late Great Planet Earth*, which attempted to show how current events were fulfilling prophetic passages of scripture. In 1990, at least seven thousand different editions of the Bible were available from hundreds of publishers. However difficult it may be to define the impact of the Bible on ordinary people precisely, scripture has always been a vital element in American popular life.

From the first colonists, the Bible provided themes for Americans to define themselves as a people, and then as a nation. Puritans in New England believed they were in *covenant with God just like the ancient Israelites. The first public political campaigns of the 1830s were modeled directly on the organized enthusiasm and passionate rhetoric of the religious revival. In the intense sectional strife leading to the Civil War, the Bible became a weapon put to use by both sides. In the South, passages like Leviticus 25.45 ("the children of the strangers that do sojourn among you . . . they shall be your possession") defined the righteousness of their cause. In the North, favored passages, usually from the New Testament, like Galatians 5.1 ("Stand fast . . . in the liberty wherewith Christ hath made us free"), did the same. (*See* Slavery and the Bible.) Abraham Lincoln, in his Second Inaugural Address, put the Civil War into perspective by quoting Matthew 18.7 and Psalm 19.9, and by noting that "both [sides] read the same Bible." Biblical phrases and conceptions, particularly with politicians from the South like Woodrow Wilson or Jimmy Carter, continued to exert a political force even in the more secular twentieth century.

If anything, the Bible has been more obviously at work in the popular culture of African Americans than among whites. Slaves made a sharp distinction between the Bible their owners preached to them and the Bible they discovered for themselves. Under slavery, stringent regulations often existed against unsupervised preaching, and sometimes even against owning Bibles. But with or without permission, slaves made special efforts to hear black preachers. One slave left this striking testimony: "a yellow [light-complexioned] man preached to us. She [the slave owner] had him preach how we ought to obey our master and missy if we want to go to heaven, but when she wasn't there, he came out with straight preachin' from the Bible."

Blacks sang and preached about Adam and Eve and the *Fall, about "wrestlin' Jacob" who "would not let [God] go," about Moses and the *Exodus from Egypt, about Daniel in the lions' den, about Jonah in the belly of the fish, about the birth of Jesus and his death and future return. The slaves' profound embrace of scripture created a climate for Bible reading and biblical preaching that has continued among African Americans since the Civil War. (*See* African American Traditions and the Bible.)

In the popular media, scripture has been as omnipresent as in politics. Fiction, hymns, and poetry employing biblical themes have always made up a huge proportion of American publishing. Composers William Billings (1746–1800), John Knowles Paine (1839–1906), and many in the twentieth century, such as Charles Ives and Aaron Copland, followed earlier precedents by writing musical settings for the psalms. Among the populace at large, the flood of sheet music, hymnals, chorus books, and gospel songs has never ebbed. In the nineteenth century, one of the most frequently reprinted sheet-music titles was "My Mother's Bible." Its first appearance (1843) evoked an emotional domestic ideal: "My mother's hands this Bible clasped, / She dying gave it me." At another level, millions of Sunday school students have learned songs like "The B-I-B-L-E, / Yes, that's the book for me, /

I stand alone on the word of God, / The B-I-B-L-E." (*See* Music and the Bible.)

American writers of popular fiction have always drawn on biblical materials. Biblical allusions feature prominently in works such as Herman Melville's *Moby-Dick* (which begins, "Call me Ishmael"), William Faulkner's *Absalom, Absalom!* (1936) and *Go Down Moses* (1942), James Baldwin's *Go Tell It on the Mountain* (1953), and Peter Devries's *The Blood of the Lamb* (1961). The American people have never been able to get enough of popular fiction inspired directly by the Bible. The first important novel of this kind was William Ware's *Julian: Or, Scenes in Judea* (1856), which described gospel events through the letters of its fictional protagonist. General Lew Wallace's *Ben Hur* (1880), which climaxed in a breathtaking chariot race, is probably the supreme example of biblical fiction. President Garfield wrote his personal thanks to Wallace from the White House, and it soon became a huge success with the public at large (in part because Sears, Roebuck printed up a million inexpensive copies). *Ben Hur* was also the inspiration for an immensely successful touring drama (complete with surging horses on a treadmill) and two motion pictures. Other similar books have had nearly as much success, including Henryk Sienkiewicz's *Quo Vadis?* (1896), Lloyd Douglas's *The Robe* (1942) and *The Big Fisherman* (1949), Marjorie Holmes's *Two from Galilee* (1972), and several novels of both Taylor Caldwell and Frank G. Slaughter. One of the most unusual examples of this fiction was written first in Yiddish by a Jewish author, Sholem Asch. When published in English in 1939, *The Nazarene* won praise from Christians for its sensitive portrayal of contemporary customs at the time of Jesus. (*See* Literature and the Bible; *article on* North American Literature.)

Many of the blockbuster biblical novels eventually found their way to the screen. Cecil B. de Mille's *The King of Kings* from 1927 (with H. B. Warner as a diffident Jesus) and George Stevens's *The Greatest Story Ever Told* from 1965 (with Max von Sydow as a Jesus who was allowed to show traces of humor) were among the most memorable, but there have been many others.

The Bible as a theme in popular communications is hardly exhausted by songs, poems, stories, and movies. In the visual arts, biblical materials have provided inspiration for German immigrants embellishing needle work with *Fraktur* print, lithographers such as Currier and Ives, countless painters at countless levels of ability, and a few masters acclaimed by both public and critics, such as Edward Hicks, who in the mid-nineteenth century painted several versions of *The Peaceable Kingdom*. (*See* Art and the Bible.) Since the beginning of mass-marketed religious objects about the time of the Civil War, both Catholics and Protestants have purchased immense quantities of pictures, statues, games, children's toys, paperweights, refrigerator magnets, jewelry, T-shirts, greeting cards, calendars, and business cards decorated with biblical motifs.

Allene Stuart Phy, editor of the best book on the subject, once observed that there is often a "ludicrous discrepancy . . . between the ancient wisdom of the scriptures and the vulgarities of American popular culture" (*The Bible and Popular Culture in America*, 1985). But Phy also saw clearly that even these "vulgarities" show the "profound ways in which the holy books of the Jewish and Christian religions relate to [the] lives of Americans."

See also Everyday Expressions from the Bible.   *Mark A. Noll*

POTTERY. *See* Archaeology and the Bible.

PRAYER(S). The Bible both talks about prayer and gives the texts of specific prayers to God. Underlying the biblical story is the conviction, so fundamental that it rarely needs to be voiced explicitly, that it is both possible and desirable for humans to address the Divine and that the Divine both can and will respond. Indeed the God of the Bible is characterized as "you who answer prayer" (Ps. 65.2; cf. 1 Kings 9.3; Matt. 7.11).

Yet the very terminology of "prayer" is much more problematic than might seem at first glance. Sometimes, in modern usage, the term is used to include any form of address to God or even outbursts of praise about God, such as hymnic compositions in which God is not addressed directly but talked about in the third person. Furthermore, communication with God can be expressed not only in words but in acts of *sacrifice, dance, ritual bodily gestures, and other nonverbal modes of communication, and in a broad sense all of these are often included in the category of prayer. Biblical scholars usually define the term more narrowly and precisely, distinguishing between "psalms" as sung poetic compositions in formulaic language that belong to the formal, public *worship in the Temple and "prayers" as prose compositions, usually with some component of petition. Often it is difficult to draw a line between conversation with God and the more formalized style of address and content that should be termed a "prayer."

Both prayer and sacrifice are understood in the Bible as service (Hebr. $^c\bar{a}b\bar{o}d\hat{a}$) rendered to God as king. It is debated whether set words of prayer may have accompanied sacrifice in the Temple; certainly no such texts have been preserved. Sometimes the language of prayer and sacrifice is brought together, and the Temple itself came to be called a "house of prayer" (Isa. 56.7; 1 Kings 8; Luke 18.10). Little is known about origin of the practice of set statutory prayers for the community (particularly for morning and evening), although the process certainly began in the postexilic period. Among the *Dead Sea Scrolls there are, albeit preserved only in an extremely fragmentary state, the actual texts of prayers from perhaps the midthird century BCE, prayers for each day of the week, each month of the year, and for special feasts; in these certain features that came to be standard in subsequent Jewish prayer are already attested (in particular the blessing formulary at beginning and end of each prayer and the practice of petitionary prayer on weekdays and prayer of praise on the *Sabbath).

When we turn to actual texts of prayers given in the Bible, much study has focused on the Psalms and on the *Lord's Prayer; yet these are by no means the only prayers in the Bible. In the Hebrew Bible alone there are over ninety prose prayers in which individuals address God directly in a time of need. These range from a short simple petition (like that of Moses' "O God, please heal her," Num. 12.13), to more lengthy and formal prayers blending elements of praise and petition, to communal confession of sin and lament. Such prayers are presented as spontaneous, unrepeatable, and arising out of the immediate situation, although as Moshe Greenberg (*Biblical Prose Prayer as a Window to the*

Popular Religion of Ancient Israel [Berkeley and Los Angeles, 1983]) has shown, there are links in contact, structure, and vocabulary between these prayers of individuals and the more formal psalms and public prayers. Of special interest are those narratives that portray an individual drawing on a psalm from the cultic realm as a personal prayer in time of need and, from the postexilic period, a special collection of extended prayers of confession of sin and penitence.

The *Apocrypha is especially rich in actual prayer texts, including the prayers of Esther and Mordecai added on to the Greek text of Esther; the prayers of Azariah and the three youths in the fire in Daniel 3; Tobit 3.2–7, 11–15; 8.5–7, 15–17; 13; Judith 9.2–14; 13.4–5; 16.1–17; and many other short prayers. These provide a window into the continuing development of prayer forms in the Persian and Hellenistic periods, such as the increased use of the blessing formulary to begin a prayer, and give evidence of a number of new concepts about prayer that find expression in this period, such as the introduction of an angelic intermediary who presents prayers to God and the possibility of prayers for the dead.

In the New Testament we continue to find both statements about prayer and the text of prayers, especially on the lips of Jesus and Paul. Thus Jesus not only teaches his disciples about prayer and gives them words to pray "like this" (Luke 1.2–4; Matt. 6.5–13) but he himself is portrayed as praying at each of the decisive moments of his life. Much of what the New Testament says about prayer continues and reiterates what is said in earlier sections of the Bible about the necessity and efficacy of prayer and the characteristics of humility and persistence to be brought to prayer. Distinctively Christian is the emphasis that

prayer, though directed to God, is to be "through Jesus Christ" (Rom. 1.8) or in the name of Jesus, and the role of the Spirit in making prayer possible.

See also Lectionaries.   *Eileen Schuller*

PREDESTINATION. The notion of predestination, God's foreknowledge and arrangement of events, has been an important doctrine in certain forms of Christianity, mostly Protestantism, and particularly in forms historically and theologically related to John Calvin, the sixteenth-century reformer from Geneva. In particular this doctrine refers to God's predetermining who is elected and therefore, naturally, who is not. In the ancient world, however, the idea of predestination and foreknowledge had a wider connotation and was common in secular as well as religious writings.

God's providence or forethought was a common feature of ancient Greek writers from the time of Plato and Xenophon, and later in the writings of Diogenes Laertius and Plutarch. It is therefore not surprising to find that foreknowledge (Grk. *pronoia*) figures prominently in such first-century writers as *Josephus and *Philo. Josephus claims that it may have been *pronoia* that somehow allowed him to avoid participating in the mass suicide at Jotopata at the outbreak of the Jewish revolt in 67 CE; while others died or killed each other, Josephus was spared, taken captive by Vespasian, and lived to write his multivolume works *The Jewish War* and *The Antiquities of the Jews*. Philo wrote an entire treatise on *pronoia*. That a person should be able to ascertain God's plan and will or enjoy the predestination of the divine was a claim to one's own influence and position. Such claims were not nearly as fanciful to ancient writers and philosophers as they may seem to many moderns.

In the New Testament the few times

this concept is employed it involves trying to figure out how God's actions embodied in Jesus of Nazareth can be understood in the context of and reconciled with God's plans. The writers who took this point up were deeply steeped in the Hellenistic milieu of the cities of Asia Minor and the Greek East. The speculative and philosophical nature of this discussion accords well with the ethos of these eastern urban Greek centers. Thus, the author of 1 Peter says that the elect were chosen by the foreknowledge of God and also claims that Jesus was foreknown before the foundation of the world. Likewise, Acts 2.23, in a speech attributed to Peter, asserts that Jesus was delivered up "by the predestined plan and foreknowledge of God."

Paul utilized this language to articulate what he believed God had done in Jesus of Nazareth and what this means for Jews, gentiles, and current believers in Jesus. To the church in Rome he says God foreknew and predestined those whom he called to become the image of his son. In both Romans 11.2 and Galatians 3.8 Paul tries to reconcile God's predestiny of Israel with the predestiny of believers who are not Jews. This is a difficult argument. He claims finally that God has both chosen and foreordained Israel, and God predestined non-Jews or gentiles to be included in Israel through his selection of Abraham to be a light to the nations. God was able to foresee that the gentiles would be justified by faith through the gospel preached to Abraham beforehand when he said, "All the nations shall be blessed in you" (Gal. 3.8, quoting Gen. 12.3).

In the New Testament, then, the rather common Greek notions of foreknowledge and predestiny were used by writers comfortable with the Greek philosophical milieu to reconcile the events that had taken place recently in Jesus of Nazareth with the historic events and promises of Israel's past.

Over the centuries the notion of *pronoia* itself was modified and utilized for a host of theological and social conflicts that the Greek and Jewish writers of the first century CE could not have anticipated and probably would never have imagined.   *J. Andrew Overman*

PRINTING AND PUBLISHING.
This entry consists of five articles:

> The Printed Bible
> Production and Manufacturing
> Economics
> Royal Printers' Patent
> Red Letter Bible

The first article surveys the history of the printed Bible. The second and third articles describe the modern processes of production and manufacturing and their cost. The remaining articles deal with particular aspects of the history and composition of printed Bibles. The reproduction of the Bible prior to the invention of printing is treated in Books and Bookmaking in Antiquity. For further discussion of the history of printing and the design of printed Bibles, see Chapter and Verse Divisions; Children's Bibles; Curious Bibles; Family Bible; Gutenberg, Johannes Gensfleisch zum; Illustrated Bibles; and Scofield Reference Bible.

The Printed Bible
The Significance of Printing. The process of printing from movable types was developed in Mainz in the 1450s by a partnership that included Johannes *Gutenberg. Among the first printed books were the forty-two-line Latin Bible (folio, ?Mainz, ?1455) called the "Gutenberg" or "Mazarin," and the thirty-six-line Bible that may have followed it (folio, ?Mainz or Bamberg, ?1457–1461). Both books are in

"gothic" or black-letter types, in two columns, in a single size of type; they are simplifications of contemporary manuscript formats, in that they leave headings and initials for the rubricator to fill in by hand. Printing was at first seen as a means of speedy duplication, making relative cheapness possible. Later, it was understood that printing theoretically permitted a series of editions in which each copy could be identical and each edition could improve upon the previous one, but this ideal could not be fully realized until the nineteenth century. Early printers were under severe constraints: none had enough type to set up a whole Bible, so they followed a rhythm of setting and printing one "sheet" of four or eight pages, dispersing the type, and setting the next sheet. Correction took place as the sheets were printed, so that variant states of each sheet were mixed in infinite permutations through the whole edition. In keeping with the same rhythm, early edition sizes were small— normally between 250 and 1,500 copies, rarely as large as 3,000 or 4,000. A new biblical text (e.g., Erasmus's or Luther's) was disseminated in a rapid succession of small reprints, many of which were unauthorized, since copyright protection was rudimentary; as a result, the text was quickly corrupted. While translators were alive, they could supervise corrected editions; after their death, safeguarding the text of its version of the scriptures gradually became a concern for each church. In such supervision the Vatican (from 1590) and the Lutheran Church (from 1580) were pioneers.

The Fifteenth Century. As printing spread, the international trade for the leading houses was in the Vulgate, the Bible of the European church in the language of the educated, therefore an obvious best-seller. By the end of the century, over a hundred editions had been

printed, in Germany, Switzerland, Venice, and France. Unwieldy formats and the drastically simple design originally imposed by a single size of type and primitive skills gave way to smaller formats (e.g., Froben's first octavo of 1491) and a more complex international page-layout based on the traditional manuscript two-column format, using two or three sizes of type, with marginal notes and ample prefatory matter (the *plenus apparatus*). Books were entirely reproduced from type, so the rubricator was dispensed with. For a national sale, vernacular texts were also printed: between 1466 and 1522, fourteen High German and four Low German editions, some with illustrations; Italian Bibles in Mallermi's Version from 1471; the French *Bible Historiée* from the early 1470s (complete in 1478); a Catalan version in 1478; portions of a Dutch Bible in 1477; and Czech Bibles in 1488 and 1499. These versions all used a national variant of black-letter, considered appropriate to the use of the vernacular; roman type was still associated with classical learning and Latin eloquence, but was also used for Italian Bibles. Printing did not reach England until 1476; since Wycliffe, English translations had been discouraged, so readers in England (essentially scholars) could use only the Vulgate, in imported copies. (*See* Translations.)

Hebrew printing began in Italy before 1475; a Psalter was printed at Bologna in 1477, and a Pentateuch in 1482. The Soncino press in 1488 printed the whole Hebrew Bible with vowel points and accents. Greek-Latin psalters were printed in Milan in 1481 and by Aldus at Venice before 1498.

The Sixteenth Century. Renaissance scholarship and Reformation translation coincided with the great age of scholar-printers. The new movements meant that the Bible, always a steady seller, became available in its new versions in unprecedented numbers, since it was now a burning political-religious issue as well as an article of mass consumption. By the end of the century, literate laypeople of Reformed churches of Calvinist tendency would expect to possess a personal copy of the scriptures in English, French, or Italian: usually a handy octavo in roman type, in double-column for compactness, with numbered verses for easy reference, Calvinist marginal notes, "arguments" to each book, maps, diagrams, and indexes; usually with a metrical psalter bound in, and often a form of common prayer and a catechism. In territories of Lutheran tendency—the North German territories and North America—the old black-letter continued to be used for several centuries, and the Bibles were never so portable or so adapted to study.

At the beginning of the sixteenth century, the black-letter Vulgate was the staple of a popular trade dominated by Parisian printers. Scholarship and reform came mostly from elsewhere, but one Parisian (later Genevan) stands out as the greatest of all Bible printers, Robert Stephanus (Estienne). It was he who took the standard small Vulgate and first printed it in roman type (octavo, 1534); he took the device of verse numbering first used in a whole Bible by Pagnini in 1528, and applied it to the French text of Olivetan in 1553 and to the Vulgate in 1555 (see Chapter and Verse Divisions). His layout for small Bibles, in some ways traditional, was above all economical. Because he moved to Geneva in 1550 as the result of opposition from the Faculty of Paris, he transferred to Calvinist printing a repertory of skills and, basically, the fundamental design of most cheap Bibles in roman type up to recent times. Before he left Paris he had also printed in 1528, 1532, and 1540 a

series of noble folio Vulgates that are among the most beautiful and original ever printed, as well as important contributions to the Latin text.

In Basel in 1516, Froben printed Erasmus's Greek-Latin New Testament using roman for the Latin and Greek types for the first complete Greek New Testament. Aldus printed a complete Greek Bible in Venice in 1518–1519 using the Septuagint and Erasmus's New Testament. Printed before Erasmus but issued later, the Complutensian Polyglot (Alcalá, 6 volumes, 1514–1517, issued 1522) uses Hebrew, Greek, black-letter, and roman types in an exceedingly complicated layout—the greatest achievement of printing thus far. It was not matched until 1569–1572, by Plantin's Royal Polyglot, which uses two sizes of italic and roman, three sizes of Hebrew, and Greek, all with decorated initials, in a demonstration of the repertory of Europe's (by then) leading printer.

Luther's September and December Testaments (Wittenberg, 1522) were in a distinctively large format, in single-column black-letter with a characteristic arrangement of elements, including illustrations, which were at once imitated by followers and opponents. Whereas perhaps eight to ten thousand copies of the old German text had been printed since 1466, and sold at high prices, Luther's official printers at Wittenberg produced a hundred large editions of his complete Bible between 1534 and 1620—perhaps 200,000 copies. Another three hundred editions came from other towns. Such an output required capital; a partnership of booksellers bought the "privilege" (the sole right to sell in a defined area) and administered it until 1626.

Similar problems later affected the English Bible. Tyndale's first English New Testaments (Worms, 1526; Antwerp, 1534) would have struck the contemporary observer as obviously Lutheran because of their typography. By the time Coverdale's Bible was printed (Cologne, 1535), Luther had completed his translation, and his printers, faced with a whole Bible, were forced into a two-column design that looked archaic; Coverdale's followed this pattern, as did "Matthew" in 1537, the first Bible printed in England. The subsequent "Great" and "Bishops' " Bibles were also large, double-column folios in black-letter, reflecting the desire of the authorities to provide only a lectern-sized format, for reading in church. Meanwhile, in France, Stephanus's design in roman type was developed further, and in 1559 Barbier printed in Geneva a French octavo that gives the whole Genevan apparatus, to be repeated in countless editions—Latin, French, Spanish, Italian, and especially English. When Rowland Hall printed his English Geneva Bible (quarto, Geneva, 1560) it reproduced this pattern, and rivaled official English Bibles both with a more radical text and apparatus and also an intrinsically portable, more usable commodity: a layperson's Bible for private reading and devotion, visibly more modern than the competition. The handiness of the format contributed to the popularity of the version, which went on being printed until the 1640s. The King James Version of 1611 was originally a large folio in black-letter on the antique pattern; its commercial success was in doubt until smaller formats in roman type eliminated the disadvantage.

The Seventeenth and Eighteenth Centuries. After the great period of the sixteenth century, Bible printing dwindled into a national concern, though for a while Antwerp remained what Geneva had been—an exporter of Bibles in several languages, including the English Ge-

neva Version. The Protestant countries now supplied themselves with their authorized version in the vernacular; in Catholic countries, the vernacular was not encouraged, and the Vulgate had been overproduced in the previous era. There are few monuments of printing skill: the London Polyglot of Roycroft (folio, 1655–1657, 6 volumes) adds Arabic and Samaritan to Hebrew, Greek, and their Latin versions, and is more impressive editorially than typographically. In England, the success of the 1611 version meant that money was to be made by supplying it, and the peculiar conditions governing Bible printing led to combinations and lawsuits (*see the article in this entry on* Royal Printers' Patent). European wars, especially in Germany, led to economic decline, which affected standards of materials and workmanship. The major economic constraint, that even if printers had had enough type to set a whole Bible, they could not afford to keep the text, once set, for more than one impression, was met head-on by the philanthropist Karl Hildebrand Baron von Canstein, who founded the Cansteinsche Bibelanstalt at Halle in 1710. This was a prototype Bible society, designed to supply very cheap Bibles at no profit or even at a loss (*see* Bible Societies). The types of the New Testament of 1712 and the Bible of 1715 were kept standing, so that subsequent impressions could be corrected. The type was replaced when it wore out, usually after some thirty impressions. By 1803 the society had circulated three million copies of the scriptures, mostly in German. A Canstein Bible was the copy text for the Bible printed by Christoph Saur at Germantown, Pennsylvania, in 1743 in twelve hundred copies—the second American Bible (the first being John Eliot's Algonquin text, printed at Cambridge, Massachusetts, in 1663).

The rise of the missionary movement, especially of the British and Foreign Bible Society (1804) and its daughter societies, meant that for a century or more England became the major manufacturer of Bibles, for a market once again conceived as European-wide, and then worldwide. Effective and economical production on that scale was the consequence of technological development. (*See the article in this entry on Economics.*)

The Nineteenth Century. For four hundred years, printing had changed very little, remaining a handcraft, and permitting limited economies of scale. Mechanization produced a dramatic increase of production and so remarkable cheapness for the first time, just when missionary activity and the spread of literacy opened a vast market. The invention of stereotyping, first applied to the Bible at Cambridge in 1805–1806 in time to supply the British and Foreign Bible Society (BFBS), meant that type need no longer be kept standing: the whole surface of the page of type was molded, and a cast made from the mold. Later, electrotyping gave the cast plate a very hard surface, so that hundreds of thousands of copies could be printed before there were signs of wear.

Presses began to be made of iron before 1800, giving greater pressure over a wider area and more precision of register. But the revolutionary printing machine of König and Bauer and the application of steam power meant that from 1814 it was possible to print over a thousand copies an hour. By 1849 major Bible printers had converted to steam-driven machinery. Paper had been machine-produced since 1815, and by the 1860s wood pulp and esparto-grass had replaced linen rag as the basis of paper. Composition of type was not mechanized until the end of the nineteenth century and was not universal until the twentieth, but since a single setting could now produce millions of copies, composition had become a minor factor. By the 1860s the Oxford University Press, the world's major manufacturer, regularly produced over a million Bibles a year, of which at least half went to the BFBS. Because of the scale of production, unit costs were minimal, and the strange monopoly situation in England was countered by the charitable activity of the BFBS and competition between the privileged presses.

Modern Times. The late nineteenth and early twentieth centuries saw the ultimate development of Gutenberg's process, by which individually cast metal types were set up together to make a page, inked, and impressed onto paper. Molding the surface of the type, wrapping the paper around a reciprocating cylinder, or even running it in a continuous sheet from a roll, were just some of the developments within the process that increased speed and cheapness; mechanical composition and binding changed no basic principle. Since 1945, printing has been revolutionized, abandoning "hot metal" in favor of computerized photocomposition, so that in place of metal type photographic images of letter shapes are used. Reproduction is effected by lithography, which uses chemical reactions to transfer an ink image from a flat surface. Printing takes place on large "web-fed" machines that print both sides of the paper at great speed, many pages at a time, so that whole "book blocks"— the printed and stacked pages—are delivered, folded, and ready for simple "casing" in an uninterrupted process. The data bank in the computer memory and associated programming facilities mean that a text of almost infinite length and complexity can be stored and printed out at will in any format that the program permits. In principle, stability of the text is guaranteed, or rather a correction facility promotes constant improvement. The Bible has ceased to be what it once was, a mountain that few printers could climb. It is now merely a long text with a number of special features. The rapid succession of popular modern versions (especially in the United States) is easily permitted, and the systematic development of a classic or authorized version is greatly facilitated. (*See the article in this entry on* Production and Manufacturing.)

Aesthetics. The great age of Bible printing was the sixteenth century. Froben, Stephanus, De Tournes, Oporinus, Froschauer, Plantin—the scholar-printers—produced typographical treatments of marked originality and beauty. Greatest of them all was Stephanus, whose Latin folio Bibles of 1532 and 1540 are the most original. Paradoxically, his introduction of verse-numbers and roman type fixed Bible design in the classic Genevan format for centuries. Many verses are short and would not fill a whole line in a single-column format. Over the course of an entire Bible, this would waste much space, so for economic reasons double-column became the rule. Bibles therefore looked "like Bibles" from the late sixteenth century to the middle of the twentieth. Distinguished printers like Baskerville (Cambridge, folio, 1763) could use their own type, refine the conventions, and insist on good paper, ink, and presswork, but could not break the classic mold. During the nineteenth century the *family Bible—that mark of respectability—often incorporated engraved illustrations and encyclopedic notes; and the elaborate bindings broke away from the standard black cloth of the early publisher's bindings. The Arts and Crafts movement of the 1890s first went back behind the six-

teenth century to revive the type-designs of early printing and broke away from "Bible" typefaces. The Doves Press Bible (1903) used a mixture of old scribal and early humanist conventions to produce an eclectic result—handsome but not readable. Bruce Roger's folio lectern Bible (Oxford, 1935) modifies the classic design by using Stephanus's headings, and is worthy to stand alongside its original.

New versions proclaim their newness by modifying, even rejecting, the old typography. The Library Edition of the New English Bible achieved an elegant page in a modest format. But it is the lectern bible that offers the possibility of magnificence or monumentality, and since Rogers no printer has challenged the sixteenth century.   *M. H. Black*

Production and Manufacturing

The production and manufacturing of a Bible, though in outline the same as that of any other book, is affected by its length (as much as five times longer than an average novel) and by the extra use it must withstand. These factors have their effect throughout the entire process.

A Bible's production may be conveniently divided into five parts: setting the type; manufacturing the paper; printing the pages; manufacturing the binding materials; and binding the pages into a single volume.

Setting the Type. The text of a full Bible can contain over 800,000 words (for the Hebrew Bible and the New Testament), and close to one million words (if the *Apocrypha are added). In addition are nearly 1,200 chapter numbers and over 31,000 verse numbers; in editions including the Apocrypha, there are almost 2,000 chapters and close to 40,000 verses.

With punctuation included, any typesetting of a Bible translation requires millions of separate keyboard entries, all of which must be checked carefully. For this reason, among others, nearly all Bible translations are now prepared in electronic form. These electronic databases include not only the letters and chapter and verse numbers, but coding to specify capitalization and other special type elements. Once a database is in final form, a given version with a specific type design can be produced relatively quickly by specifying all of the different elements and giving the instructions to the computer typesetting machine. The machine imposes the design elements on the database, sets the type to the specified width of the type column (breaking words at the ends of lines as necessary to fit), and then produces typeset pages. The typesetting for a full Bible can now be done in a few hours.

Once this typesetting is finished, a high-contrast printout of the pages is produced on glossy paper. This reproduction proof, or "repro," is photographed and the film is laid out in "forms" of 32-, 48-, 64-, or 128-page units. From these forms the printing plates are manufactured.

Paper Manufacture. Because Bibles are so long, the paper used for them must be thin; but because Bibles must be able to withstand repeated use, it must be strong as well. Modern paper manufacturing has developed a sheet that is very thin, highly opaque, and strong. The paper begins as a wet pulp mixture that is poured over a moving fine wire mesh, which allows the water to run through but retains the pulp. After most of the water has been shaken free, the matted pulp is fed into a series of heated rollers that dry out the remaining water and smooth the surface of the paper. The paper is produced in a continuous roll and the rolls are shipped to the printing plant.

Printing. Most Bibles today are printed in 64- or 128-page forms, to produce "signatures" of 64 pages. A 64-page signature consists of a large sheet of paper that is printed on both sides and is then folded in half, then in half again, five times in all. This results in a packet of paper that, when fastened through the middle and trimmed around the edges, will become one 64-page section of the finished Bible.

Most full Bibles are longer than one thousand pages, and many of the Bibles with study apparatus included can be longer than two thousand pages. Each Bible, therefore, will contain from 16 to over 30 separate 64-page signatures. These are printed one at a time, usually on a web offset machine, which receives the paper in a continuous roll at one end, prints it on both sides simultaneously, cuts it into individual sheets, and folds it into signatures.

After all the signatures have been printed (for a large printing of a lengthy Bible this can take over a week), they are "gathered," that is, collated in order on a gathering machine. All the gathered signatures for one book are called the "book block." Once the signatures have been gathered, the manufacturing process differs, depending on the kind of binding that will ultimately be done.

Binding Materials. There are three basic types of bindings: paperback, hardcover, and leather. Paperback covers are made of thick, coated paper. Hardcovers are made of "boards" (cardboard), either two or three pieces, that are covered with cloth or textured paper. Leather covers are made of a single piece of leather or leatherlike material. The leather is either the whole skin of an animal (genuine leather), leather fibers held together with a polymer bonding (bonded leather), or plastic textured to look like leather (imitation leather). The leather cover is stamped or cut (clicked) out of a larger piece, the edges are trimmed to allow them to be turned over at the corners, and the title and other designs are stamped (and sometimes outlined with metallic foil) onto the finished cover. At this point the covers are ready to be joined to the finished book blocks in the binding process.

Binding. In paperback and some hardcover Bible bindings, the book block itself is held together with glue. This is done in one of two ways: either the inner edges of the pages are trimmed and glue is applied to that edge ("perfect binding"), or notches are cut in the inner edge and glue is applied to that edge and forced into the notches ("burst binding"). The outer pages of the book block are then glued to the case of a hardcover book; the spine of the paper cover is glued to the spine of the book block.

In other hardcover bindings, and in most leather bindings, the signatures are "sewn"; that is, the pages are held together by thread that is passed through the central fold, and the book block itself is attached to a backing. The book block is then "smashed" (compressed to drive out the air between the pages), "trimmed," and "round cornered." The edges are sanded and burnished, and metallic foil is bonded to the edges by heat. The back of the book block is then "rounded," or curved outward by the application of pressure to the page edges. The book block itself is then attached to the board or leather cover by gluing the endpapers to it. Leatherbound books may be bound in two ways: either "glued-off," as just described, or "lined-to-the-edge." Lined-to-the-edge bindings are different in two respects. The cover is lined by turning the outer edges of the cover material over the lining, with a flap of the lining left at the inner edge, front and back. The flap is glued between a second piece of lining and the white endsheet attached to the book block. Then a hollow tube is glued to the spine of the book block on one side and to the cover on the other, which provides strength and flexibility to the binding. This is the most sturdy kind of binding, since the book block is attached to the leather cover over its entire surface, including the spine.

Books may be reinforced in several ways. Hardcovers and leatherbound books have a piece of woven material called "crash" glued to the spine, with flaps on either side that are glued between the endpaper and the board. Leatherbound books may have the first and last signatures "whipstitched," that is, the signature is stitched along the inner edge, to provide reinforcement at the hinges of the book, which receive the most wear and tear. This stitching is visible in the finished product. Some binders, instead of whipstitching, use eight pages of heavy white endsheet (instead of four pages). A piece of cambric may also be wrapped around the endpapers and first signature.

The entire process, from the beginning of composition to the delivery of finished leatherbound books, can take over a year.

Donald Kraus and Lynn Stanley

Economics

Bibles have always been an expensive commodity. As early as 1641 a London bookseller, Michael Sparke, wrote a tract entitled "Scintilla" in which he maintained that the high cost of Bibles was due to monopolies among Bible publishers (*see the article in this entry on* Royal Printers' Patent). Some of the factors contributing to the costs over three hundred years ago continue to operate today, making the world's most popular book also one of the most difficult and costly to produce.

Bible production presents the manufacturer with some of the most exacting and unusual challenges in the book industry. It also requires of the editorial staff rigorous quality standards that are time-consuming and costly. The following analysis of the specialized process of creating printed Bibles will indicate why the costs remain high.

The Editorial Process. *Translating.* The largest expense can be the work of translating the text. If it is to be highly accurate, this may take from several years to several decades and consume millions of dollars, though an individual occasionally may pursue this task as a hobby and a "labor of love." (Translators have frequently volunteered their time and expertise, for example with the KJV, RSV, and NRSV.)

Typesetting. Computers and databases for typesetting the Bible have certainly reduced the very great amount of time ordinarily needed for composing the Bible text. Typesetting the text in various styles of type and in different sizes of page now requires hours rather than months or years. What once was costly because of the labor involved is now costly in technical equipment. Only a few typesetting companies in the world can meet the high-volume, high-quality demands of Bible composition at a reasonable price. Composing a basic text Bible is in itself a technically exacting task. Even more difficult is the process of composing a complex study-Bible. Combining footnotes, commentary, and a reference system with the text while keeping all pertinent information together on the same page requires either a labor-intensive manual process or a highly sophisticated computerized system. Either way, the expense is high.

Proofreading. Accuracy can be accomplished only through proofreading. The use of a master database for computer typesetting has made the tedious process of word-for-word proofreading optional, yet nothing has been found as reliable as the human eye and mind for guaranteeing an accurate text. Because of the quantity of information contained in a Bible and the accuracy demanded and expected in such a book, the proofreading process takes hundreds of hours and costs thousands of dollars.

Development of new materials. Basic text Bibles will always be popular, but the most popular and bestselling editions contain some or all of the following: reference system, concordance, commentary, maps, charts, articles, dictionary, and pictures. The cost of creating, writing, and editing new materials can range from a few hundred to hundreds of thousands of dollars.

The editorial cost of Bible creation is substantial. In general, however, it is a one-time, fixed-cost investment that may be spread over several printings, several years, or even several products. The editorial expense represents, however, only the first half of the Bible publishing sequence. Once the contents of the book have been determined, the actual books must then be created.

The Production Process. The following costs vary from year to year, and are affected by inflation, labor disputes, and quality requirements. The percentage that each step in the process adds to the total cost of a Bible varies in accord with the style of binding. Each step will be described separately.

Paper. Paper that is strong, thin, lightweight, and opaque is difficult and expensive to make. The high cost of such lightweight paper, coupled with the high page count of Bibles, makes paper one of the largest factors of cost in Bible manufacturing.

Printing. High-speed, high-quality web presses designed to handle lightweight paper are available at only a few specialized printing houses. Printing on lightweight paper is an exacting science and art requiring skilled press operators and finely tuned machines. Such factors mean that the cost of printing a Bible exceeds by a large percentage the usual cost of printing an ordinary book.

Binding. Binding involves both the cover-material used for a Bible and the actual process of putting the book blocks and covers together. Some Bibles have inexpensive paper covers, others cloth or Kivar covers. The deluxe, expensive editions are bound in imitation leather or in real leather, drastically increasing the sales price. Although modern technology has to some extent replaced the skilled artisans who bound Bibles in the past, the cost of creating a beautifully bound leather Bible is still high.

Packaging. Almost every Bible must be wrapped, boxed, slipcased, banded, or jacketed. These packaging items must not only be designed and printed, but some, such as a box, also must be assembled. Each of these items adds to the cost of a Bible.

Cover Style	Paper	Printing	Binding	Packaging
softcover	55%	20%	20%	5%
hardcover	50%	15%	30%	5%
bonded leather	20%	10%	60%	10%
top grain leather	15%	5%	75%	5%

The chart above indicates how the percentages of cost shift according to the nature and style of the cover.

Bruce E. Ryskamp and staff

Royal Printers' Patent

In England, the printing of the Authorized or King James Version of the Bible (KJV) and the Book of Common Prayer (BCP) of 1662 is the monopoly of the Royal Printer, by virtue of a patent first granted to Christopher Barker in 1577. Only the University Presses of Cambridge and Oxford are permitted by royal charter to override this monopoly; one other publisher, originally Scottish, is an accepted interloper.

Originally the office of Royal Printer, instituted in Henry VII's reign, brought with it only the right to print statutes, proclamations, injunctions, and Acts of Parliament. The first officially sanctioned Bibles in English had the normal "privilege," granted to whomever was the printer—the original form of copyright, which protected the printer of a single title from competition, usually in a specific territory, and for a specific term. Since the Great Bible and later the Bishops' Bible were "appointed to be read in the churches," and the Geneva Bible, though officially disapproved, was very popular (*see* Translations, *article on* English Language), printing them became an attractive commercial enterprise; and the right to print them in various formats was shared in the 1560s and 1570s by important members of the Stationers' Company, the guild that regulated the English book trade. But during the reign of Elizabeth I, trading monopolies in various commodities were granted or sold by the Crown to deserving or rich individuals, and certain whole categories of books became the exclusive monopolies of individual printers. In 1577, Christopher Barker became Royal Printer, and the terms of his patent gave him the right to print all Bibles and Testaments whatsoever, and the BCP. This patent, renewed, was left to heirs, so it fell to Barker's son to finance the collation, revision, and printing of the KJV in 1609–1611.

So sweeping a monopoly was contested by other printers, deprived of the market for the best-selling printed book.

The weakness of the royal printers' position was that the capital required to exercise their right was very large; so they were often forced to take partners, or even to lease to the company itself, which ran a cooperative part-charitable venture called the English Stock, later the Bible Stock, which among other titles printed Bibles, by agreement (usually) with the monopolists.

By its royal charter of 1534, the University of Cambridge had acquired the perpetual right to appoint three printers, who could print "all manner of books." The right preexisted Barker's patent, and was taken to cover Bibles, so Cambridge printed a Geneva Bible in 1591 and its first KJV in 1629. Oxford acquired a similar charter in 1636, and in the 1670s printed Bibles. During a large part of the seventeenth century, there were disputes and lawsuits between Royal Printers and Stationers about the patent but the two contestants tended to combine against the interloping universities. All the rights of all the parties were more than once pronounced valid by the courts, and accommodations followed; by the end of the century, the two universities were at times either compensated for not exercising their right, or the right was leased and farmed by the richer London printers who had control of the market. The supreme monopolist of the time was John Baskett, who bought a share of the royal printer's patent in 1710, leased the Oxford Privilege in 1711, and bought a third-share of the similar Scottish royal printer's patent. The Baskett family remained printers until 1769, when they were bought out by Eyre and Strahan, the forebears of the later patent-holders Eyre and Spottiswoode. After the mid-eighteenth century, the position stabilized: the Stationers' Company ceased to trade; the monopoly was accepted, as was the overriding right of the univer-

sities. In Scotland, the royal printer's patent lapsed in 1839, and the right to print Bibles was subject to license by a supervising body. Scottish Bibles were not allowed south of the border until 1858, when William Collins set up an office in London and sold his product. Until then, the only permitted infringements of the monopoly were commentaries on the Bible that included the text, and the polyglots of Bagster. In particular, the British and Foreign Bible Society had had to buy its supplies from the privileged presses—though it also offered serious competition by selling at subsidized prices.

The monopoly had always been resented. It was investigated by a Parliamentary Committee in 1859–1860, when the expected criticisms of principle were made. But the system was found to work well; supplies were ample, and Collins's intervention had forced prices down further. The patent was renewed in 1860, and is not now subject to review. The terms of the original patent were tested in 1961 when the New English Bible (NEB) was published by Cambridge and Oxford, who had previously financed and published the Revised Version without the opposition or participation of the royal printer. The Queen's Printer now attempted to include the NEB within the scope of the old monopoly by printing an unauthorized Gospel of John. The universities brought action for breach of copyright and won their case. The old monopoly is now limited to the KJV and the BCP (1662) and is sometimes defended on the twin grounds that the first is perpetual Crown Copyright and the second, its use in England being required by Act of Parliament, is indeed an Act of State. The two university presses showed that the right could be operated for the public good, since for centuries Bible printing helped to provide them, as charities, with funds to finance learned publications. Moreover, they had, since the eighteenth century, in their own recensions of the KJV text provided standard editions of the national classic, the Bible of 1611. Stability of the text was not required or secured by the monopoly itself. With the demise of Eyre and Spottiswoode in 1990, the patent passed to Cambridge.

See also article on The Printed Bible *in this entry.* M. H. Black

Red Letter Bible

A Bible or New Testament with all the words spoken by Jesus printed in red. This practice has been traced to the journalist Louis Klopsch, publisher of *The Christian Herald* in the late nineteenth century. Klopsch was inspired by the words of Jesus in Luke 22.20: "This cup that is poured out for you is the new testament in my blood." Luxurious Bible manuscripts of the Middle Ages would use specially colored inks to mark chapter headings or prominent words; Codex 16 used crimson, blue, and black inks for the words of different characters. Some Red Letter Bibles print only the words of the earthly Jesus in red, leaving the words of Jesus as heard in visions (as in the books of Acts and Revelation) in black ink. Others use red ink for those sayings of God or angels in the Old Testament that have been interpreted by Christian theology as inspired by the preexistent Christ. A modern effort to determine the authentic words of Jesus on historical-critical grounds (the Jesus Seminar) has led to the production of new Red Letter Gospel editions, beginning with Robert W. Funk, *The Gospel of Mark: Red Letter Edition* (1991).

Philip Sellew

PSEUDEPIGRAPHA.

Definition. The term Pseudepigrapha refers to a body of diverse Jewish or Jewish-Christian writings (there are others also of specifically Christian origin) that (a) are not included in the Hebrew Bible, the New Testament, the *Apocrypha, and rabbinic literature; (b) are associated with biblical books or biblical characters; (c) are more often than not written in the name of some ancient biblical worthy; (d) convey a message from God that is relevant to the time in which the books were written; and (e) were written during the period 250 BCE to 200 CE or, if later than this, preserve Jewish traditions of that period.

The word "pseudepigrapha" is the transliteration of a Greek word meaning "with false subscriptions," referring to books written under an assumed name. Although it is true that many of the writings in question are indeed pseudepigraphical, the word is inappropriate and misleading for at least two reasons: there are also nonpseudepigraphical books in any such list and there are pseudepigraphical books outside it!

It is much less confusing to use the word apocryphal, commonly found in ancient Christian usage, or the rabbinic expression "the outside books" (Hebr. *ḥîṣônîm*, "external"), signifying those books outside the *canon: Certain of these "apocryphal" books that found their way into Greek and Latin manuscripts of the scriptures treasured by the church are known as the Apocrypha (among Protestants) or the Deuterocanonical books (among Roman Catholics and in Eastern Orthodox churches). Those that did not gain entry, together with others subsequently written, were much later designated "pseudepigraphical" (among Protestants) or retained the designation "apocryphal" (among Roman Catholics).

There is no agreed list of such writings if only because there are no agreed criteria by which they should be determined. The situation is all the more complex because there is no agreement concerning the content of the Apocrypha itself. It would seem best to include in the Apocrypha those "extra" books that appear in most Septuagint manuscripts but not those that appear only in the Vulgate.

Genres. The writings of the Pseudepigrapha are varied in both content and literary form. A number of them are apocalypses, which emphasize the revelation of divine secrets relating to the cosmos and "the end of the age" (*see* Apocalyptic Literature). Among these are 1 Enoch, the Apocalypse of Zephaniah, the Apocalypse of Abraham, 2 Enoch, 2 Esdras 3–14 (= 4 Ezra; traditionally included in the Apocrypha in English Bibles), 2 Baruch, and 3 Baruch. Some, like 1 Enoch, are composite in character and range over a period of some centuries.

Others take the form of testaments, purporting to be the words of the ancient worthy in whose name the book was written. Some of these contain apocalyptic sections or elements. The best-known writing of this kind is the Testaments of the Twelve Patriarchs, which, though Christian in its present form, is in the opinion of many scholars a redaction of a Jewish work of the second century BCE. Other writings in this category are the Testaments of Job, Moses, Abraham, Isaac, Jacob, Adam, and Solomon, ranging from the first century BCE to the second or third century CE.

A third category comprises midrashic-type comments on scripture, often in the form of stories picking up but going beyond the Hebrew texts. The most significant of these is the book of Jubilees, which comments on Genesis and part of Exodus. To this can be added the Genesis Apocryphon from Qumran, which comments on the story of Abraham in Genesis 12 and 13, embellishing the biblical text with colorful amplifications. Other books of this type are the Letter of Aristeas, the Apocryphon of Ezekiel, the Martyrdom of Isaiah, the Life of Adam and Eve, Lives of the Prophets, Joseph and Asenath, the Book of Biblical Antiquities, 4 Baruch, Jannes and Jambres, Eldad and Modad, and the Ladder of Jacob.

The tradition of Israelite wisdom literature expresses itself in folklore and in philosophical musings in the story of Ahikar, 3 Maccabees, 4 Maccabees, Pseudo-Phocylides, and Syriac Menander. The religion evidenced here shows the influence of Greek thought.

Hymns and *prayers are also a medium of literary expression. Most important in this connection are the Psalms of Solomon dating from the middle of the first century BCE. To these may be added the moving Prayer of Manasseh, five apocryphal Syriac Psalms, the Prayer of Joseph, and the Prayer of Jacob.

The influence of the surrounding Greco-Roman culture can be seen in many of these writings, not least perhaps in such books as the Sibylline Oracles (from the second century BCE onward) with their prophetlike predictions of gloom, and in the Treatise of Shem (perhaps first century BCE), which describes the characteristics of the year based on the twelve signs of the zodiac.

All these books named as "pseudepigrapha" are only part of a much larger literature produced from the second century BCE onward, including the *Dead Sea Scrolls. It is a continuing point of debate which of the latter, if any, should be considered as belonging to this classification. It may be conceded that the commentaries and other works peculiar to the life and ordering of the Qumran community ought not to be included; but there is good reason to include others that have much in common with the recognized pseudepigraphical writings.

Mention has already been made of the Genesis Apocryphon, to which may well be added the Temple Scroll and the Book of Giants, together with certain other writings with an apocalyptic interest, such as the Book of Mysteries and the Description of the New Jerusalem. It is of significance that among the Dead Sea Scrolls many fragments have been found of 1 Enoch and the book of Jubilees, together with a Testament of Levi and a Testament of Naphtali. But whether or not they are to be classified as pseudepigrapha, it is clear that the scrolls and the known pseudepigraphical writings must be studied together if we are to gain a true picture of Judaism in the centuries immediately preceding and following the beginning of the common era.

Preservation. For the most part, the Pseudepigrapha were preserved within Christianity, which went on to produce its own pseudepigraphical texts based on the model of the New Testament writings. Their preservation within this setting in the course of time created two problems difficult to solve, one linguistic and the other textual. Although written originally in Hebrew, Aramaic, or Greek (in Palestine or in the Dispersion), such was their popularity in Christianity, especially in the east, that many survived only in such languages as Ethiopic, Coptic, Syriac, Georgian, Armenian, and Slavonic. This means that in a number of cases the language in which a book now appears may be once, twice, or even three times removed from the language in which it was composed.

Not a few of them, moreover, are composite in character, containing Christian interpolations or substantial additions, or representing a fundamental redrafting of the entire book. The exact dating of such writings is not always easy to determine; but it must be borne in mind that late additions or even late documents may contain elements that illuminate an earlier period of Jewish history, and so should not be summarily dismissed.

The identification of these books is helped by quotations and other references in the early church fathers and by certain stichometries that emerged in Christianity which help to differentiate between canonical and apocryphal writings. Most of the books referred to are identifiable and already available, though a few remain unknown.

Significance. It is increasingly recognized that the pseudepigraphical writings, taken in conjunction with other literature of the same period, are of considerable importance for a study of the growth of Judaism and the origins of Christianity.

The picture of Judaism presented here of the period 250 BCE to 200 CE is complex, unlike the "normative" Judaism of later years when it came to be deeply influenced by rabbinic teaching. It is thus misleading to speak of heresy or of sects during this time, as if these could be set against an accepted orthodoxy. What we have is a religion in ferment, true to the scriptures and tradition and yet open to winds of change blowing from many quarters. Alongside deep traditional piety we find a cosmopolitan concern that probes the mysteries of God's workings not only in the world but also through the whole cosmos. Indeed, one of the marks of this literature is that of cosmic speculation that reveals a surprising sophistication in religious thought and expression. The picture presented is that of a Judaism far from merely parochial and very much alive. (*See also* Judaisms of the First Century CE.)

Speculative theology is seldom systematic, and with vitality went variety. The Pseudepigrapha, and not least those books among them of an apocalyptic kind, show certain areas of particular concern: the perennial problem of the origin of *evil and its outworking in the life of the world, the consequences of this for the Jews and indeed for the whole universe, the cataclysmic end that will result in the defeat and eradication of evil, and the final triumph of God in the coming of his kingdom and the age to come. Variety, not consistency, remains the hallmark of such speculations.

Christianity grew out of the soil of Judaism, and so the Pseudepigrapha, as expressions of Judaism, are of importance for an understanding of Christian origins also. Their relation to what came to be regarded as the canon of scripture is a particularly intriguing one. The letter of Jude is a case in point. There, in v. 9, allusion is made to an apocryphal story about a dispute between the devil and the archangel Michael over the body of Moses that may have come from a lost Assumption (or Testament) of Moses, and in vv. 5–7 and 14–15 reference is made to 1 Enoch, which is quoted as prophecy. This strongly suggests that, to Jude and no doubt to many other Christians, there was in fact no clear line of demarcation between certain of the Pseudepigrapha, regarded as inspired works, and other books that in the course of time came to be regarded as canonical. This is hardly surprising because, as we know from other sources, the limits of that part of the canon known as the Writings remained somewhat indeterminate for some time in contrast to the other two parts, the Torah and the Prophets.   *D. S. Russell*

PURITY, RITUAL. Throughout the Bible reference is made to a system of ritual purity that had both social and theological significance for the Israelites. While its specific origins are not known, it can be related to practices in other ancient Near Eastern cultures in which cultic functionaries followed similar regulations, involving, for example, ritual washing and food restrictions. What appears to be unparalleled about the biblical system, however, is its extension beyond the priesthood to the general population.

In addition to cultic activity, texts describing ritual purity focus on food and individual status related to specific events. With regard to priestly behavior, those participating in *sacrifice are required to purify themselves beforehand. This purification is achieved through ritual immersion. In Leviticus 11 and Deuteronomy 14, detailed lists are given of *animals that are ritually pure and therefore permitted for consumption, and of those that are ritually impure and therefore prohibited. Leviticus and Numbers also contain regulations concerning the purification of individuals, regardless of cultic status, after childbirth, menstruation, ejaculation, disease, and contact with corpses.

While the regulations concerning ritual purity may be clear, their significance has been variously interpreted. The Hebrew words *ṭāhôr* and *ṭāmēʾ* are commonly translated "clean" and "unclean" respectively, renderings which imply associations with dirt or hygiene not present in the original. Additional confusion results from the fact that while in our culture the difference between the human and the divine is often identified with the difference between the material and the spiritual, that was not the case in early Israel. Ritual purity and impurity could be considered spiritual states, yet they are inextricably linked to physical processes. In turn, physical acts such as sacrifice and sprinkling are used to alter relationships with the divine.

Following the lead of anthropologists such as Mary Douglas, many contemporary biblical scholars consider the status of being *ṭāmēʾ* as one of pollution resulting from a disruption of divine order. Thus, animals prohibited for food are those that cross paradigmatic boundaries of sky, earth, and sea. Shellfish, for example, live in the ocean but crawl like land animals. From this perspective, human ritual impurities are connected with disorder since they involve uncontrolled bodily emissions or death.

Another interpretation of biblical notions of ritual purity focuses on impurity as a state of power rather than pollution. Again using anthropological models, this view examines the relationships between human ritual impurity and liminal states, transitions between one status and another or between life and death. In a biblical context, it is argued, these moments are linked to the nature and power of the divine, a power that contains death and destruction as well as life and creation. They are also tied to actions, such as procreation and care for the dead, which are positive and necessary for social order. Thus, rather than being "unclean" or "impure" in a negative sense, the biblical state of ritual impurity is the result of contact with the sacred. This sense of ritual impurity is evident in the later rabbinic definition of canonical (i.e., sacred) texts as those that "render the hands ritually impure." Biblical rituals of purification may have been the result of a belief that direct contact with divine power could be dangerous if sustained too long. This conception of divinity is supported by passages such as Exodus 33.20, where God warns Moses, "You cannot see my face; for no one shall see me and live." Another possibility is that ritual purifications served as a consistent reminder that the power of life and death is not human but divine.

A third interpretation addresses the social implications of the ritual purity system. The sociologist Nancy Jay has pointed out the priestly control involved in purifications and its retribution of reproductive powers from the individual women who exhibit them in menstruation and childbirth to the male (imaged) deity represented by male priests. Food prohibitions can also be interpreted functionally as a means of social separation.

While it may be argued that legislative texts concerning ritual purity are descriptive and relational in their uses of the terms *ṭāhôr* and *ṭāmēʾ*, other biblical writings imply a more polarized viewpoint. Ezekiel, for example, frequently uses *ṭāmēʾ* in contexts that clearly indicate a notion of defilement not only of persons but also of places, an impurity that is rooted in apostasy. Texts such as Lamentations 1.9 associate negative concepts of defilement with female sexuality as exemplified by menstruation. These different perspectives may be due to historical change, since the legislative materials are generally dated to earlier periods than the historical and prophetic texts.

With the destruction of the First and Second Temples, the cultic basis of the system of ritual purity was first disrupted and then destroyed. Remnants of the system were preserved in rabbinic practices such as ritual immersion for conversion or following menstruation, handwashing, and the separation of implements as well as categories of food in keeping kosher. While Christianity rejected the system as a whole, it retained ritual immersion in *baptism.

See also Social Sciences and the Bible, *article on* Cultural Anthropology and the Hebrew Bible. *Drorah O'Donnell Setel*

Q

QUOTATIONS OF THE JEWISH SCRIPTURES IN THE NEW TESTAMENT.

All the writers of the New Testament regarded the Jewish scriptures as their Bible. They would not have thought of them as an *Old* Testament at all. They sought in them confirmation of their beliefs, and often used them to prove their point in argument. To a large extent, knowledge of how the New Testament writers used the Jewish scriptures enables one to understand their modes of thought.

New Testament writers inherited a long tradition of Jewish exegesis of the Bible (*see* Interpretation, History of, *article on* Jewish Interpretation). Although they differed in some important respects from the principles of this exegesis because they were Christians and not, or not only, Jews, this was their starting point, and they saw no reason to repudiate a great deal in that tradition. Jewish exegetical tradition was in no way monochrome: various schools of exegesis can be distinguished. There were certainly some Jews who were more open toward the gentile world than others; they would put more emphasis on those parts of the Bible that look forward to a time when Israel's God would be made known to the whole world. Again, there was in Alexandria a school of exegesis that used very extensively the allegorical method of interpretation, which had originated in a purely Greek milieu; of these, *Philo is by far the most important representative. And contemporary with the beginning of Christianity there also existed in Palestine the Qumran community, which produced the *Dead Sea Scrolls. This sect believed that they could discover in the scriptures, both in the *Law and in the prophets, hidden prophecies of the history of their own sect. Nor must we forget the influence of the Targums, the Aramaic paraphrases of the Hebrew Bible, used in synagogues for the benefit of worshipers who could not understand Hebrew (*see* Translations, *article on* Targums). These writings aimed above all to make the sacred text relevant to contemporary conditions, and frequently incorporated edifying legends or elaborations of the biblical narrative. We must also bear in mind that most early Christians seem to have read their scriptures in a Greek translation (the Septuagint), which was not always an accurate rendering of the Hebrew.

All the authors of the New Testament shared certain assumptions about the Bible. The scriptures, they held, were entirely true and infallible, internally consistent, with no contradictions. Above all, the scriptures were filled with references to, and prophecies of, Jesus Christ. The primary feature that distinguishes New Testament interpreters of the Jewish scriptures from Jewish exegesis is that the New Testament exegesis was christocentric.

Paul was a master of *typology; he often takes for granted that his readers will know about and believe Jewish traditions of exegesis. For example, in Galatians 4.29, a parallel is drawn between the relations of Isaac and Ishmael, on the one hand, and those of Christians and Jews in Paul's day, on the other. Paul writes, "But just as at that time the child who was born according to the flesh persecuted the child who was born according to the Spirit, so it is now." Paul is referring to Genesis 21.8–14, where Sarah sees Ishmael and Isaac playing. Some Jewish scholars, wishing to justify Sarah's harsh treatment of Ishmael and Hagar, argued that the Hebrew word "playing" in Genesis 21.9 really meant "persecuting"; Paul takes this interpretation for granted. Paul's interpretation of scripture also helps him with the problem of the Law. In Galatians 3 and Romans 4, he appeals to the text of Genesis 15.6 in order to prove that faith came before the Law; Abraham was justified by faith before he underwent *circumcision. Again and again Paul finds in the scriptures texts that, so he believes, identify Christ with the suffering servant of God; see, for example, Romans 15.3, where he sees a verse from Psalm 69.9 as being the utterance of Christ to the Father. Or again, in 1 Corinthians 15.45 he quotes Genesis 2.7 in order to show that Christ was the second Adam. In fact, a great deal of Paul's doctrine about Christ is based on biblical exegesis.

The author of Matthew's gospel uses quotations from the Jewish scriptures freely in order to prove that Jesus was the promised Messiah. He has a set of eleven quotations that he introduces with some such phrase as, "All this was done to fulfill what was spoken by the prophet." This usage strikes the modern reader as rather literalistic. But in a much more general sense, Matthew represents

Jesus as the fulfillment, in certain respects, of Moses: like Moses, he has to be hidden by his parents to escape persecution; like Moses, he is a great teacher; and like Moses, he gives out his teaching on a mountain. Matthew, however, is capable of using scripture in what we would regard as a more sensitive way. Thus, in Matthew 8.17 he quotes Isaiah 53.4 of Jesus, suggesting that Jesus' healing activities were in some sense vicarious, because his healings meant that he bore our diseases.

The Fourth Gospel does not have many explicit biblical quotations, but the text is full of allusions and echoes. As well as the standard texts that all the evangelists quote, John employs several allusions in a unique way. One such is in 3.14, where the episode of the brazen serpent is presented as a foreshadowing of the cross. In several places, John uses biblical allusions to support his contention that the preexistent Christ was present on occasions during Israel's history. Thus, in 8.40, Abraham is described as one who believed a man sent from God to tell him the truth. This alludes no doubt to Genesis 18.1–15, where three men visit Abraham, one of whom he addresses as "my Lord." When in 8.51–58 we read that Abraham saw Jesus' day and that before Abraham was Jesus is, we can have no doubt that John identifies the preexistent Christ with this angel. John's characterization of Jesus as *lamb of God also draws heavily on biblical models, even to the extent of quoting the description of the *Passover lamb in his account of the *crucifixion (19.36).

The usage of the Bible in the book of Revelation is also unique. There are no explicit citations, but the symbols and images employed by John the seer are nearly all taken from the Hebrew Bible, especially from Ezekiel and Daniel, so that John weaves out of these materials a brilliant tapestry proclaiming the events of the new dispensation.

The way in which New Testament writers use the "Old Testament" is very different from the way most Christians understand it today. Where they found prophecies and foreshadowings, and even occasional appearances of the preexistent Christ, Christians today see a developing revelation of God's nature and purpose, a revelation that is complete in the life, teaching, death, and resurrection of Jesus Christ. Much that they believed to be history is held today to be legend or *myth. But myth and legend are vehicles of expression for the faith of Israel, and readers cannot dispense with the evidence of the Jewish scriptures in seeking to understand the meaning of the New.   *Anthony Tyrrell Hanson*

QUR'ĀN AND THE BIBLE, THE.

The belief that God speaks through scripture he has inspired is shared by Jews, Christians, and Muslims. In spite of the considerable differences among them, these three monotheistic communities lay claim to a common distinction that links them as "People of the Book." Each community deems itself to be in possession of a written record of God's will, revealed at moments of crisis in history, recorded for the instruction of future generations, and constantly reinterpreted in acts of individual and corporate remembrance. Each community is founded upon a faithful response to the word it has received, using as its model of obedience to the divine call the example of Abraham.

Origins of the Qur'ān. The Qur'ān (Koran) is the holy book of Islam. Muslims believe that it was revealed by God to the prophet Muhammad, through the agency of the angel Gabriel. These revelations came to Muhammad between 610 CE (the year of his call to be the

messenger of God) and 632, the year of his death. The Qur'ān consists of 114 sūrahs, or chapters. The length of the complete book is about two-thirds that of the New Testament. The Arabic word *qur'ān* most probably means "that which is to be read aloud." The first sūrah to be revealed to Muhammad starts with the command "Read! [aloud] in the name of your Lord who creates." In the Arabic the opening imperative *iqra'* ("Read!") contains the same consonantal elements that form the word Qur'ān.

The sūrahs are named. Some of the names are familiar to readers of the Bible: "Jonah" (10), "Joseph" (12), "Abraham" (14), "Mary" (19), "The Prophets" (21), "The Resurrection" (75). Others are unfamiliar: "The Cow" (2), "The Pilgrimage" (22), "The Pen" (68), "The Dawn" (89). Others are introduced by combinations of letters, the precise significance of which is unknown. In addition to its name, each sūrah is prefaced by an indication of the place where it was revealed, either Mecca or Medina. The language of the Meccan sūrahs is appropriate for summoning an unbelieving people to accept Islam as a matter of immediate and urgent decision. At the last day, unbelievers will be given the reward merited by their unbelief, and cast into *jahannam* (Gehenna), which is graphically described. On the other hand, the reward for believers on the day of reckoning will be the *afterlife in *paradise, a place described with comparable vividness. The Medinan sūrahs are longer, and chiefly concerned with the organization of life in the developing Islamic community.

In 622 CE, Muhammad and his small group of Muslim converts were obliged to leave Mecca because of persecution; this event is called the *hijrah* (hegira). They moved to Yathrib, about 290 mi (465 km) to the northeast. In honor of

Muhammad, the place was renamed *madīnat (al-nabī)*, "City (of the Prophet)." Medina, the name by which it is still known, is the city in which Muhammad lies buried. The year 622 CE divides the Meccan from the Medinan period in the life of the prophet Muhammad, and is the year from which the Islamic community dates the beginning of a new era, whose dates are sometimes given the designation A.H. (Latin *Anno Hejirae*).

Unlike the Bible, which emerged over a period of centuries as the work of many different (and often unnamed) witnesses to God's redemptive activity, the Qur'ān passed from the oral tradition to its written form in just over a decade after the death of Muhammad. The revelations were passed on by Muhammad orally, and those who listened to him wrote them down on whatever materials were to hand, including dried leaves, sun-bleached animal bones, and stones. This written material was finally brought together during the caliphate of ʿUthmān (644–656 CE), the third "Rightly Guided Caliph" (Arabic *khalīfah*, "successor" of the prophet Muhammad), to form the authoritative written text of the Qur'ān. No additions or deletions have ever been permitted by Muslim authorities, though many textual variations in the manuscripts have been collected by western scholars. After the first short sūrah, which is a brief exordium of praise to God, who is both creator and guide, and which is sometimes compared to the *Lord's Prayer, the other sūrahs follow each other in an order of decreasing length. The first sūrah to be revealed is numbered 96 in the final sequence.

Both Jews and Christians were present in parts of Arabia prior to the time of Muhammad. In Mecca and in Medina (as well as in his travels north and south over the ancient caravan routes), Muhammad would have come into contact with some of them. But the internal evidence of the Qur'ān provides little evidence to support the view that Muhammad had any direct knowledge of the Jewish and Christian scriptures. According to Islamic tradition he was, in any case, unable to read or write. That such an unlettered man was able to "read" the revelations has always been accepted by Muslims as a special sign of God's favor.

Biblical Connections. The similarities between the biblical and the Qur'ānic material suggest that, even had there been any direct borrowing from the former to the latter, it was highly selective. Major prophets like Amos and Jeremiah, for example, do not appear in the Qur'ān. And the Qur'ānic interpretation of trinitarian orthodoxy as belief in the Father, the Son, and the Virgin Mary, may owe less to a misunderstanding of the New Testament itself than to a recognition of the role accorded by local Christians to Mary as mother in a special sense.

The use of historical criticism in studying the Qur'ān has been resisted by Muslims. For them, the Qur'ān is the sure guide to right belief, thinking, and action. The guidance it furnishes is complemented by guidance about what constitutes knowledge, and about the way knowledge is to be attained. Knowledge consists of that which God has revealed. The path to knowledge is that of submission *(islām)* to the revealed will of God. There are limits to human speculation, precisely because of what God has revealed. Intellect, will, and reason are all to be schooled by the revelation. To study the Qur'ān according to methods developed in a non-Muslim society is not encouraged in Islam. Discussion about whether or not the Qur'ān is "the Word of God" belongs to a different intellectual tradition.

According to Islamic belief, each sacred "Book" was revealed at the appropriate time and place by God, through the agency of human messengers. The message of all scriptural revelation is essentially the same; it could not be otherwise, since God himself is the author. Thus, any differences between the scriptures of the "People of the Book" are to be attributed to human distortion, and not to divine caprice. To Moses and his people was given the *Tawrah* (the *Torah); to David and his people was given the *Zabūr* (the book of Psalms); to Jesus and his people God gave the *Injīl* (the *gospel); and finally, to Muhammad was revealed the Qur'ān, the restatement of the eternal and unchanging purposes of God, to which all the messengers originally bore witness. Muslims believe that the Qur'ān is God's authoritative final word, with a particular significance for Muhammad's own people, but also a universal message for humankind.

The designation "People of the Book," viewed from outside the Islamic community, is as much a reminder of the differences as of the similarities that exist between Jews, Christians, and Muslims in their understanding of what constitutes scripture. Yet despite this there are still points of contact between the Bible and the Qur'ān, as the references to *monotheism and to Abraham, Moses, David, and Jesus indicate. In the Bible and in the Qur'ān, the themes of God's creative and re-creative activity are taken up. The reader is confronted by the one true God, besides whom there is no other. In these different scriptures are revealed the divine will and plan for humankind, the service required by God of those whom he has created, the nature of sin, the way of salvation, and the penalty for self-imposed separation from God.

Other names and incidents are recorded in both the Bible and the Qur'ān. Two examples can be mentioned to provide a start for further reading. The first is the story of Joseph in Genesis 37–50 compared with the story of Yūsuf ("the fairest of stories" in the Qur'ān, sūrah 12). Common to both accounts is Joseph's rise to power and authority in Egypt after being brutally treated by his brothers, his faithfulness to God through periods of suffering, his careful use of the gifts given to him by God, and his reconciliation with his family following their appeal for food in time of famine. In the Qur'ānic account, Joseph finds favor because of his exemplary acceptance of everything that God willed for him, both in times of adversity and in times of success. His submission to the will of God is held up to succeeding generations of Muslims as an example worthy of imitation.

The second example is that of Mary, the mother of Jesus. Sūrah 19, called *Maryam* (Mary), may be compared with Matthew 1.8–2.23 and Luke 1.5–2.51. To anyone familiar with the New Testament passages in which Mary appears, this holds a twofold interest. The first point of interest is that the Qur'ānic account acknowledges the *virgin birth of the child Jesus (*Īsā*). The second is in the Qur'ānic denial of the implications of trinitarian theology. In the Qur'ān, Jesus is a human being, a messenger of God, but still a creature; he is not God incarnate. In associating the creature with the Creator, Christians are, therefore, guilty of the gravest impropriety. The belief of Muslims is expressed in sūrah 4.171: "O People of the Book! Commit no excesses in your religion: nor say of God (Allāh) aught but truth. Christ Jesus, the son of Mary, was (no more than) an Apostle of Allāh, and his (Allāh's) Word, which he bestowed on

Mary. And (Jesus was) a spirit proceeding from him (Allāh). So believe in Allāh and his apostles. Say not 'Trinity.' Desist, it will be better for you. For Allāh is one (Allāh). Glory be to him. He is far exalted above having a son. To him belong all things in the heavens and on earth."

Edward Hulmes

R

RAINBOW. The meteorological event called the rainbow was of course well known in ancient times, and it is referred to occasionally in the Bible. In Sirach 43.11 it is mentioned in a catalog of God's creative wonders, and elsewhere its multicolored splendor is used metaphorically. The most familiar passage in which the rainbow occurs is the conclusion to the *Flood story in P (Gen. 9.12–16), where it is a sign of the *covenant between God and Noah and all living creatures. The Hebrew word used here and elsewhere is *qešet,* which is also the ordinary word for the weapon called the bow. There is a mythological background to P's use of the rainbow in the Flood narrative. Like other ancient Near Eastern deities, the God of Israel was frequently depicted as a warrior-god, especially in his role as god of the storm; lightning bolts are his arrows, which he shoots from his bow. The rainbow after the Flood is then a sign that the deity of the storm will never again use his most powerful weapon for total destruction. He has put it in the clouds as if for storage; the bow's visible presence in the clouds is a guarantee that it is not being used.   *Michael D. Coogan*

RED COW. Numbers 19 describes an unusual ritual, to be performed in cases of impurity resulting from contact with a corpse, requiring a red cow (Hebr. *pārâ,* whose usual translation "heifer" is probably too precise). Remarkable aspects of the passage include that it specifies not only the sex but the color of the animal, that the whole animal be burned, and that participants in the act of purification are themselves rendered ritually impure (*see* Purity, Ritual). The ashes of the sacrifice are mixed with running (literally, "living") water to produce a substance called *mê niddâ.*

Hyam Maccoby has interpreted these puzzling aspects of the ritual by focusing on the term *mê niddâ.* Usually the phrase is translated "water for cleansing" (NRSV), but it can also be rendered "water of separation." The word *niddâ* is also used for a menstruating woman, "separate" from normal spheres of activity because her physical state demonstrates her participation in the divine process of giving life. Similarly, contact with the equally sacred power of death also separates individuals from the community. The red cow ritual uses "waters of separation" to counteract the effects of such contact. The substance is a symbolic substitute for *blood, the sign of life. The requirement that the sacrifice be both red and female suggests that it represents the blood of potential life, of menstruation or birth. Like the divine, it is inherently powerful, and can therefore have a different effect on those who prepare it and those who receive it.

Other scholars have connected the ritual with a cult of the dead (cf. Homer,

Odyssey 11.23–50; *see* Afterlife and Immortality, *article on* Ancient Israel; Israel, Religion of). The tractate *Para* of the Mishnah is devoted to the ritual described in Leviticus 19.

Drorah O'Donnell Setel

REDEEM. The Hebrew verb generally translated "to redeem" is *gāʾal.* Its basic idea involves doing something on behalf of others because they are unable to do it for themselves. The motivation to redeem someone is most often familial obligation. If no relative steps forward, however, the king or God is expected to take up that person's duty. Whoever the redeemer is, in the act of redemption, he or she is providing for the redeemed as a man would provide for his own immediate family.

The most common situation in which redemption arises is when property or persons have been confiscated to reconcile a debt. A redeemer is one who pays the debt for the debtor, thus buying back what was confiscated. Similarly, a prisoner, perhaps of war, can be redeemed through payment of a ransom. It is not surprising, then, to find the term *pādâ* ("to ransom, buy back") used in the same sense.

The Hebrew idea of redemption, however, extends beyond payment of money. Redemption occurs in levirate marriage. One who seeks revenge for a man who has been murdered is a "redeemer of blood." In fact, redemption is sometimes used to refer to rescue or deliverance in general. In this vein, God is the ultimate redeemer. He redeems persons from Death. He redeems Israel from Egypt and Babylon. He also redeems in a more typical way, helping those in financial distress. He is seen as a good husband and father when he acts as redeemer.

These ideas set the stage for the ways in which New Testament writers use the Greek verb *(apo)lutromai.* Redemption is most often spoken of as a ransom, but the idea entails more than a figurative business transaction. Christ redeems by his death, in that he gives humanity the forgiveness that humanity could not give itself. Moreover, God redeems Christians from slavery to *sin in order to adopt them as his children, thus perpetuating the idea that the redeemer assumes the role of familial protector over the redeemed.   *Timothy M. Willis*

REGENERATION. Regeneration has played a larger role in theology than would be expected from its scant use in the Bible. In the King James Version, it is used at Matthew 19.28 and Titus 3.5 to translate the Greek *paliggenesia,* which occurs only in these two passages and literally means "rebirth." The RSV interprets the first occurrence by translating "new world," and NRSV uses "renewal" for the first and "rebirth" for the second.

The concept of a new creation is found in passages such as Isaiah 65.17; 66.22; Rev. 21.1; and it is this hope to which Matthew 19.28 alludes. Just as after the corruption of the first creation by human sin, God destroyed it and created a new world, so apocalyptic writers looked for a similar renewal following divine judgment.

The language of birth is applied to this renewal in the New Testament, as in Romans 8.22. Elsewhere the image of being born again is related to *baptism by water and by the Spirit.

Douglas R. A. Hare

RELIGION. Narrowly understood, religion means actions, especially cultic or ceremonial, that express reverence for the gods. The usual Greek word for this is *thrēskeia,* which can also have a negative sense when used of deviant or suspect cults. The word is rare in the Septuagint, and is never used to translate a Hebrew original. It is applied to idolatrous worship in Wisdom of Solomon 14.18, 27, but to Jewish worship in 4 Maccabees 5.6, 13 and Acts 26.5, as well as by *Josephus. (A Greek word with similar connotations is used of Judaism in Acts 25.19, and of the Athenian cult of the unknown god in Acts 17.22.) *Thrēskeia* is also rare in the New Testament. In Colossians, the "worship of angels" is condemned (2.18; cf. 2.23), but the letter of James speaks of "pure religion" (1.27), perhaps implying a contrast between the expression of religion in cultic forms and its expression in acts of charity and self-control.

More broadly, religion involves a complex of faith and conduct. For this the common Greek term is *eusebeia*, "piety," that is, reverence for the gods and for the social or moral order, which they uphold. This term is also rare in most of the Septuagint, though in Proverbs 1.7 and Isaiah 11.2 it translates "fear of the Lord." Ben Sira writes of the "godly" (Sir. 11.17 [NRSV: devout]; 37.12), using the adjective *eusebēs,* and the whole word group is frequent in the hellenized 4 Maccabees. In the New Testament, the related words are used in Acts, especially of the "god-fearer" Cornelius and his household (10.2, 7, 22), but elsewhere the language is confined to the Pastoral Letters and 2 Peter. In the Pastorals it is related to correct belief, and in both to a way of life deemed to result from Christian belief. In neither is it directly associated with acts of worship.

Theological conclusions are sometimes drawn from this linguistic evidence. The relative rarity of words for "religion" in the Bible, and the confining of the broader terms to what are generally considered the latest writings of the New Testament, has been used to argue that "religion," with its connotations of outward activity or generalized piety, is inappropriate language to use of ancient Israel or of earliest Christianity. "Faith," as the inner response to God's call, would be more proper. To use the term "religion" of the *Pentateuch is, however, appropriate, since there the correct performance of cultic activity, as well as ethical duty, is essential in Israel's response to God. In the New Testament there is no comparable concern with the correct performance of ritual acts, but it is clear that both Jesus and Paul expected that a new way of living would result from acceptance of their teaching.

Sophie Laws

REMNANT. The various terms used to express the concept of remnant in the Bible represent two closely linked ideas. On the one hand, the word indicates those who are "left over" after some great catastrophe; on the other, those who have "escaped" the disaster and are able to continue the community's life. In a theological sense, the emphasis can fall primarily either on God's judgment on his sinful people or on his *mercy in still preserving a nucleus of them as a hope for the future, and these differing emphases are reflected in various biblical writers.

Perhaps the earliest occurrence of the idea is in the *Flood story, where the stress is on the scale of the judgment, although with the implication that the survivors will constitute a new beginning. But it is with the prophets that the concept of remnant is really developed. In Amos, the remnant is above all the hopeless residue of the nation's utter destruction, although there is a faint hint that repentance may yet avert the fullness of judgment.

It is in the book of Isaiah that the idea

of remnant assumes particular prominence. In the basic message of the prophet, it is a sign of doom, and the name of his son, "a remnant shall return" (Isa. 7.3), originally signified the same. However, in what are probably postexilic supplements, the remnant is the group that returns to God and so embodies hope for the future, where the son's name is reinterpreted. This group consists of the "needy," who trust in God alone, as is most clearly brought out in Zephaniah. Jeremiah and Ezekiel display the same phenomenon as Isaiah, the remnant as evidence of utter destruction but also as a promise of a future hope.

Hence those who survived the *exile identified themselves as the remnant. But, in the postexilic period, dissident groups emerged, such as the Qumran community, who saw themselves as the true remnant to be vindicated at the end. So Paul, in the long argument of Romans 9–11, citing biblical prophecies, concludes that the Jews who follow Christ are the remnant of Israel, "chosen by grace" (Rom. 11.5).   *J. R. Porter*

REPENTANCE. Sincere contrition, involving acknowledgment of wrongdoing in the sense of both admitting guilt and feeling guilty. The sinner might signal repentance through *fasting, weeping, rending garments, and donning sackcloth and ashes. Such emotional and even public acknowledgment of prior wrongdoing is but the first step toward forgiveness: remorse must be accompanied by resolve to cease doing wrong and do what is right. In biblical idiom, the sinner is called on to "circumcise the heart" (Deut. 30.6; Jer. 4.4), "wash the heart" (Jer. 4.14), or become "single-hearted" (Jer. 32.39); to make a new heart (Ezek. 18.31), a heart of flesh, not stone (Ezek. 36.26). These ideas are

summed up in the great prophetic concept *šûb*, "turn" (cf. rabbinic *tĕšûbâ*, "repentance"), meaning both a turning from *sin and a returning to right action, *Torah, and God.

From the earliest biblical narratives through the Roman destruction of Jerusalem in 70 CE, Jewish ideas of repentance were allied to the great system of *sacrifice detailed in the Torah and centered especially in the Temple cult. Rites of communal and national repentance were enacted on the *Day of Atonement; but at any time penitent individuals could make offerings at the Temple to atone for transgressions. Full repentance for voluntary wrongdoing against one's *neighbor required, beyond remorse, restitution (plus, where pertinent, one-fifth more of the value of the thing restored). Only then could one make the Temple offering for remission of sin. Sources stress that these offerings did not effect atonement automatically: the sinner's inner repentance is the necessary precondition of forgiveness.

In the Septuagint, *metanoia* and *metanoeō* (literally, "a change of mind") often express "repentance" and "repent," and both appear frequently in the New Testament. Mark's Jesus begins his ministry with a call for repentance in the face of the coming *kingdom of God (1.14; cf. Matt. 3.2, where the call is transposed to John the Baptist). Luke presents Jesus' mission as particularly a call to sinners to repent in order to receive forgiveness.

Paul scarcely speaks of repentance at all in his letters, but his audiences were for the most part gentiles who, unlike Jews, were under no obligation to live and worship according to the Torah. Hence Paul summons these gentiles to God: they are called not to "repent" as such, that is, to return, but to turn (Grk. *epistrephō*) for the first time. This term appears in prophetic passages both in the Septuagint and in Hellenistic Jewish literature as the anticipated response of the nations once the God of Israel reveals himself in glory at the end of days. In the context of Christianity, the "turning from" idols meant a "turning to" Christ, and so *epistrephō* comes to mean "to convert." (*See* Conversion.)

Christian thinkers eventually expressed an elaborate theology of atonement and expiation for sin centering around the sacrifice of Christ, yet the emphasis on the importance of individual repentance remained. In his commentary on Paul's letter to the Romans, written in 395 CE, Augustine observed that the only sin against the Holy Spirit that could never be forgiven is despair. Despair, he argued, inhibits repentance; if one does not repent, he cannot repudiate his sin and so be forgiven. In taking this position, Augustine came close to the view of the rabbis: "Let the sinner repent, and he will find atonement" (*y. Mak.* 2:7, 31d).   *Paula Fredriksen*

RESURRECTION OF CHRIST.

Biblical Background. In all but the latest parts of the Hebrew Bible, the concept of resurrection was applied not to the life of the individual after death but metaphorically to the renewal of Israel corporately after the return from *exile (see Isa. 26.19; Ezek. 37.1–14, where the resurrection language, especially in v. 13, is clearly metaphorical). In *apocalyptic literature, beginning with Daniel 12.2, resurrection language is applied literally, denoting coming to life again after death through an act of God in a transcendental mode of existence beyond history. This new existence, however, is not conceived in an individualistic fashion; it is the elect people of God who are corporately resur-

rected. The transcendental character of this resurrection life is indicated by such similes as "shine like the brightness of the sky" (Dan. 12.3).

Jesus proclaimed the *kingdom of God, a concept couched in apocalyptic terms and involving a new cosmic order. It was to arrive shortly; God was already at work in Jesus' ministry to bring it about. Jesus' proclamation thus implied impending corporate resurrection of the people of God, or at least of those who responded positively to his message. In the controversy with the Sadducees, Jesus used a simile reminiscent of Daniel 12.3 to describe the transcendental character of the resurrection life; the resurrection will be "like angels in heaven" (Mark 12.25). Critical scholarship regards the predictions by Jesus of his own resurrection as creations of the post-Easter community after the event. Since, however, Jesus' preaching of the kingdom implied resurrection, there can be no question that he foresaw the corporate resurrection of God's people as lying beyond his own death. But there is nothing in his authentic preaching to suggest that he expected an individual resurrection for himself.

The Easter Event. It is in this framework that the *Easter event should be understood. Jesus appeared alive to his disciples after his *crucifixion. The earliest record of these appearances is to be found in 1 Corinthians 15.3–7, a tradition that Paul "received" after his apostolic call, certainly not later than his visit to Jerusalem in 35 CE, when he saw Cephas and James, who, like him, were recipients of appearances. The early community adopted three models to interpret this fact: rapture, resurrection, and exaltation. According to the first model, Jesus was "taken up" (Acts 1.11; Luke 9.51; Mark 16.19) or "received" in heaven (Acts 3.21; *see* Ascension of Christ). According to the second, God "raised Jesus from the dead" (1 Cor. 15.4, where the passive "was raised" is a divine passive denoting an act of God; cf. Acts 2.24). The third model, exaltation, is found by itself, without a preceding reference to the resurrection, in a pre-Pauline hymn (Phil. 2.6–11). The letter to the Hebrews operates almost exclusively with the exaltation model (a reference to the resurrection occurs only in the benediction at Heb. 13.20). In Acts, exaltation occurs in combination with resurrection. In John, the exaltation language is applied both to death and to resurrection. Of these three models, resurrection is the one that proved most persistent; it either absorbed or replaced the others. Its advantage was that it brought out the corporate and cosmic significance of the Easter event. Jesus was raised by God as the first and determinative instance of the resurrection of the elect people of God and the renewal of the whole cosmos. His resurrection will make possible all the other resurrections that will occur at the end.

The resurrection, while a real event according to the unanimous testimony of the New Testament, is not historical in the sense that ordinary events are. It occurs at the point where history ends and God's end-time kingdom begins. And it is not in itself an observable occurrence. No one saw God raise Jesus from the dead. Nor can it be verified. In a sense, it is an inference from the disciples' Easter visions (and to a lesser degree from the empty tomb; see below).

The Easter Traditions. The early community, beyond asserting in its proclamation that God raised Jesus, further organized the appearances in lists. It did not at this stage tell stories of the appearances, probably because the recipients found themselves at a loss to find

language to express the ineffable (as is likely the case with Paul). The word "appeared" denotes a visionary experience, for the same word is used of angelic appearances. On the other hand, the appearances are not to be downgraded as mere subjective experiences or hallucinations. The word "appeared" denotes a disclosure from God in heaven. The most accurate description of the appearances would be "revelatory encounters." They revealed Jesus as alive.

The appearances had several effects. First, they restored the disciples' faith and hope in Jesus (cf. Luke 24.21, which accurately captures the mood of the disciples after Good Friday). Second, this faith was expressed by means of christological titles: God had vindicated Jesus and made him Lord and Messiah. Having deserted Jesus at his arrest, the disciples were now reassembled and welded into a community that soon described itself as the *church, that is, God's end-time people. Third, their Easter faith impelled them to embark on a mission, first to Israel, and ultimately to the gentile world. Fourth, the leaders of the mission became apostles, which is to say, envoys, sent ones.

Alongside the lists of appearances there existed a story of the empty tomb. This story apparently was part of the passion narrative, and functioned as the framework for the angelic proclamation of the resurrection at the conclusion of the reading of the passion during the Christian *passover. Its presence in at least two traditions (Mark/Matthew and John; behind the Lucan account there may lie yet another independent version) indicates that the basic nucleus of the tradition, that certain women discovered Jesus' empty tomb on the Sunday after his death, is very early, despite its absence from Paul. There is also indication that the disciples verified the women's discovery. Probably this followed the disciples' return to Jerusalem, after their visions in Galilee; they must have welcomed the empty tomb as congruous with the Easter faith, which they had already arrived at through the visions. The empty tomb did not create the Easter faith, and in any case it is in itself an ambiguous fact, susceptible of other explanations alluded to in the New Testament itself. The Gospels, however, are at pains to insist that the women took note of the tomb on Good Friday evening, and therefore did not go to the wrong tomb on Easter morning.

Appearance Stories. Mark, generally regarded as the earliest Gospel, originally contained no appearance stories, but merely pointed forward to subsequent appearances in Galilee. Appearance stories seem to have grown up as isolated units (pericopes), like the bulk of the gospel material. Inevitably, what was originally indescribable came to be described in earthly terms. The risen Christ talked, walked, and even ate with the disciples, as he had while on earth. Clearly, the only way the postapostolic community could construct appearance stories was to model them on the stories from the earthly ministry. These stories were more than simple narratives, though. They were expressions of the impact of the appearances, as they were first experienced by the original recipients and as the community subsequently came to understand them. This impact is expressed in the words attributed to the risen one. They include a missionary charge, a command to baptize, a promise of abiding presence or the gift of the Spirit, instruction about the fulfillment of biblical promises in his death and resurrection, the assurance of his presence in the breaking of the bread, and finally the hope of his coming again. The church and its whole faith and life are

seen to have originated in the Easter event.

A particularly acute problem is created by the portrayal of the physical reality of the Lord's risen body in some of the later stories. This seems to run counter to the earlier tradition (see above), to Pauline teaching on the nature of the postresurrectional existence, and to the categorical statement in 1 Corinthians 15.50. We must ask, however, what exactly these narratives are saying. Their purpose is to assert that, in the resurrection, Jesus did not leave his earthly life behind but took it with him. As a result, his whole "being for us," which characterized his earthly ministry and which culminated on the cross, are forever present and available to us. The wounds of the nails and the hole in his side are still there in the risen body. These stories are not to be dismissed merely as later materializations, for they convey important truths about the resurrection. In the risen one, the incarnate, earthly, crucified one, with all the saving benefits that result from his being in the flesh, is present for us.

The Resurrection of Believers. With all the concentration of the later Easter narratives upon the personal fate of Jesus, it must never be forgotten that resurrection is a corporate event. Jesus was raised as the first fruits. Believers share in his resurrection initially through *baptism. Paul is very cautious about this: believers share his death but their resurrection is conditional upon their present obedience and will not be complete until the parousia or *second coming (*see also* Biblical Theology, *article on* New Testament).

The deutero-Pauline Colossians and Ephesians are less cautious. Colossians asserts that we are already risen with Christ through baptism, though this risen state carries with it present moral responsibilities and its full consummation is not realized until the end, while in Ephesians believers are already raised to life and made to sit at Christ's right hand in heavenly places. Ethical obedience is still required in Ephesians, as the exhortation in chaps. 4–6 shows, and there is still a final consummation. Similarly, the Fourth Gospel teaches that resurrection and eternal life are already realized for believers, though here again there is a future consummation to be awaited. The corporate and cosmic dimensions of resurrection are thus never completely lost in the New Testament.

See also Afterlife and Immortality.

Reginald H. Fuller

REVELATION. Revelation has to do with disclosing, uncovering, or unveiling what previously was hidden, making known what had been secret. Sometimes the biblical terms for revelation have common usages. When used theologically, however, revelation refers to God's deliberate manifestation of his plans, his character, and himself.

Ancient Near Eastern Background. The Israelites were not alone in their desire to discern divine mysteries. Other ancient Near Eastern peoples sought to discover the wills of their gods, and many diverse methods were employed to this end. Looking for omens in the universe, astrologers considered the movements of sun, moon, and stars when making predictions. Significance could be found in ordinary positions of heavenly bodies, but extraordinary occurrences such as eclipses were especially noteworthy. Similarly, usual natural phenomena like the movements of birds, animals, or clouds could be interpreted, but so could the unusual, like floods, plagues, or babies born with defects. Animals were cut open so that their entrails might be examined, the livers of sheep

being subject to special scrutiny. Distinguishing features such as the shape of the liver would portend future events. Certain individuals were trained to read and analyze these omens. Others were skilled in the interpretation of visions and *dreams. Sometimes people consulted the deity by casting lots: they threw bones or stones on the ground as dice are thrown today. The way they landed signified certain things. Prophecy also was practiced; gods would give oracles through human messengers, whether cultic functionaries or otherwise. Mediums were consulted to summon spirits from the underworld. Similar practices are attested in the Greco-Roman world. (See Magic and Divination.)

Hebrew Bible. Some of the above were allowed in Israel, while others were not. The God of the Bible is one who hides himself. There is a boundary between God and humanity, and between what God knows and what humans may know. Some things are to remain secret while others are revealed. This line cannot be crossed, nor should humans attempt to cross it. Therefore, certain occult avenues to the transcendent were closed. Witchcraft, necromancy, augury, soothsaying, and sorcery were forbidden to the Israelites. Sometimes God revealed to his messengers secrets that could not be transmitted to others, and sometimes knowledge was given that was to remain sealed until a later time; otherwise, the revelations were transmitted to successive generations in perpetuity.

Knowledge of God may be gained from the natural world. *Creation implies a creator; therefore, something of the existence and power of God can be grasped by observing the universe. But this means of information is limited, and other ways are therefore required.

Sometimes revelation is through

God's actions in history. This might involve direct intervention, as when he delivered his people from Egypt (see Exodus, The), or it might be more indirect, as when he used the Assyrians and Babylonians to punish them. In either case, the history can be ambiguous—hence the need for someone to interpret the ways of God to the people, a need filled in part by prophets. God communicated verbally to his prophets, and, according to Amos 3.7, he would not do anything without first revealing it to his human messengers.

Concerning the content of revelation, God makes known his plans, as when he told Noah he was about to destroy the world in a *flood; or when he disclosed to Abraham that he was about to destroy Sodom and Gomorrah. He gave Daniel and John visions of the end of the world. He also reveals his nature, as when he declared his name to Moses, proclaiming that he is Yahweh, merciful and compassionate, yet holding the guilty responsible; or as when he revealed himself to Isaiah as the Holy One of Israel.

Regarding modes of revelation, sometimes the casting of lots was employed: to choose a king, or to choose a disciple to replace Judas. A special type of lot was the priestly Urim and Thummim. God also communicated through visions, auditions, dreams, the interpretation of dreams, and angels. Sometimes the text simply says that God revealed himself, as when he appeared to Jacob or Samuel. While some passages assert that no one can see God and live, it seems that God appeared in human form to Abraham, and Jacob wrestled with God. One tradition has it that Moses only saw the back parts of God but others aver that God spoke to him "mouth to mouth" (Num. 12.8) or "face to face" (Deut. 34.10). Sometimes one can prepare oneself to receive revelation by waiting in a holy place or by playing *music.

New Testament. In the New Testament revelation centers on Jesus Christ. For Matthew, Jesus controls the knowledge of God absolutely: "No one knows the Father except the Son and anyone to whom the Son chooses to reveal him" (Matt. 11.27). While many opinions abounded about who Jesus was, Simon Peter recognized that Jesus was the Messiah and the *Son of God. In response, Jesus told Peter that this insight did not have a human source; rather it came to him by divine revelation.

Jesus often taught in *parables. This was partly, no doubt, to use common things around him such as plant seed and different types of soil to illustrate the truths of the *kingdom of God. But another reason may have been to conceal those truths from those who were not serious about following him. He offered the parables publicly but explained their meanings privately to his inner circle of disciples. (See Messianic Secret.)

John calls Jesus "the Word" because he is the complete revelation of God (John 1.1; see Logos). The *word of God came to the prophets, especially Moses, but now the Word has become a human being. Only Jesus, the Son of God, the very Word of God, has seen God; now that he has taken on flesh, he has fully explained God to the rest of humanity. To know Jesus is to know God. Likewise, the opening of the letter to the Hebrews acknowledges that God previously revealed himself in various ways, but that history of revelation has culminated in Jesus.

When Jesus departed from the earth, according to John, the *Holy Spirit was sent to the church to continue the revelatory function of the Son. Paul concurs. Things never before known have now been revealed by the Spirit to the church. The Spirit of God, who fully comprehends the depths of the knowledge of God, lives inside the Christian believers so that it may be said that they have the mind of Christ.

Later Developments. In the early church, certain individuals were considered to be endowed with spiritual gifts, such as utterances of knowledge, utterances of wisdom, revelation, and prophecy. When the New Testament *canon was completed, these special charisms became less important. Emphasis shifted to the interpretation of existing revelation. Sporadically throughout the history of Christianity, there have been those who claimed to have personal revelations. The orthodox churches have always tested these by and subordinated them to scripture. The Roman Catholic Church has allowed that new revelation also exists in the form of church tradition and is as binding as scripture, while Protestants consider the Bible to be the sole *authority.

In Judaism there have been similar developments. Toward the end of the biblical period, the Jewish community came to be less interested in new revelation and more interested in studying the books that had already achieved authoritative status. There was a belief that when the messianic age arrived, it would be accompanied by new revelation, but in the meantime prophecies, visions, and dreams were not to be trusted. The oral law in Judaism is somewhat akin to church tradition in Catholicism in that it is a later elaboration of the Bible yet is also a form of revelation and hence authoritative.

See also Inspiration and Inerrancy.

William B. Nelson, Jr.

RIGHTEOUSNESS. The Hebrew word translated "righteous" (*ṣādíq*) and its related nominal and verbal forms has the basic meaning of someone or something proven true, especially in a legal context. It therefore has the meaning "innocent" and is applied in the Bible especially to moral conduct and character. But the scope of righteousness is much wider than judicial procedures and embraces the whole covenanted life of the people under God. The specific meaning depends on circumstances: for a ruler, it means good government and the deliverance of true judgment; for ordinary people, it means treating one's neighbor as a covenant partner, neither oppressing nor being oppressed; and for everyone it means keeping God's will as conveyed in the *Torah. Sometimes human righteousness is seen as a response to or reflection of the divine righteousness or graciousness, and essentially it is the acknowledgment of God in worship of him alone and in living as he wants.

God's righteousness means that he is a just and reliable judge who keeps his side of the *covenant and who thus delivers Israel from her enemies, so that they experience that righteousness as punishment, while Israel experiences it as *salvation and vindication. Indeed in some places God's righteousness and salvation are virtually synonymous, and from the *exile onward we find God's righteousness as an object of hope.

In rabbinic literature of the Tannaitic period, righteousness is often specified to mean generosity in general and almsgiving in particular. There is also development of the biblical tendency for righteous to refer to Israel, or a group within Israel, everyone else being at least relatively unrighteous; this may reflect experience of oppression. In the *Dead Sea Scrolls we find the Qumran sect regarding themselves as the only truly righteous. Righteousness is still, however, essentially conformity to the divine ordinances, that is, covenantal obedience. In the Septuagint there is very high consistency in rendering the derivatives of the Hebrew root *ṣdq* by the Greek *dikaiosunē* and its cognates, whose semantic field overlaps considerably with that of the Hebrew words.

In the New Testament, righteousness occurs with greatest frequency in the gospel of Matthew and in Paul's letters. In the case of Matthew, there is discussion about whether he uses the word for life under God in the Christian community or reserves it for life under God before Christ came and outside the Christian community, and whether righteousness is not only a divine requirement but also a divine gift.

For Paul, the issues are even more widely debated. It is usually agreed that sometimes he uses righteousness in a broadly biblical fashion but in a Christian context for the life of the people of God. It is also usually agreed that "the righteousness of God," whether or not we can speak of a fixed formula, means God's saving activity, characteristically seen in *justification by his *grace through *faith. Indeed one of the reasons why the apostle is often held to be quoting a pre-Pauline formula in the last passage is that in Romans 3.25 God's righteousness can be held to mean God's justice in a strictly judicial sense and not his saving activity. Under the influence

particularly of Galatians 3 and Romans 4 and the terminology of reckoning, there has traditionally been a view that in justification Christ's righteousness is placed to the account of sinners (is "imputed" to them).

The question remains whether in some places righteousness and justification are synonymous in Paul or at least that righteousness can sometimes be a purely forensic or relational word. The best evidence for this is Galatians 2.21, but it is widely held for other passages as well. Nevertheless, it has also been maintained that Paul consistently uses "justify" *(dikaioō)* for the restoration and maintenance of the relationship with God and "righteousness" *(dikaiosunē)* for the consequent life as his people, with both justification and righteousness being by faith. But there is disagreement about the exact meaning of most of the relevant passages. Some scholars find the key to the whole matter in the idea of God's righteousness as a power, with the gift of righteousness being inseparable from God, the giver, so that the believer is drawn into the sphere of his power.

In the New Testament apart from Paul and Matthew, righteousness normally means life as God wants it and in relation to him. It is not surprising that righteousness is sometimes found as a particular predicate of Jesus Christ.

John Ziesler

S

SABBATH. (Hebr. *šabbāt*). The last day of the week; the only day bearing a name, the others being merely numbered. It is considered the absolute day of rest without exceptions. Its observance is probably very old but is attested only since the eighth century BCE. An earlier date is suggested by Israelite legal traditions; the references in the *Ten Commandments may not be older than Deuteronomy itself.

The etymology of *šabbāt* is uncertain. A relation to the verb *šbt*, to which it has naturally been connected, is questionable, since *šbt* is never attested in the intensive form or in connection with the practice of resting from work, while its meaning is "coming/bringing to an end." A connection with the Akkadian *šab/pattu*, the day of the full moon, falling on the fifteenth of the lunar month, or with the seventh, fourteenth, twenty-first, and twenty-eighth days should probably be rejected, as they are unpropitious days, the opposite of what the Sabbath seems to be. Nevertheless, the former connection is so obvious etymologically that one should ask whether the abstention from work on such a day does not lead, eventually, to the Israelite concept of rest. Sometimes the Sabbath is connected with the feast of the new moon; what this means we do not know.

The origins of the Sabbath are also obscure. Biblical tradition (but in late texts) attributes it to Moses; this, however, cannot be verified and, since the practice presupposes a relatively advanced agricultural society, is improbable. In preexilic times its observance cannot have been very strict; 2 Kings 11.5–9 tells us, without any criticism, of the arrest and execution on the Sabbath of the Queen Mother Athaliah, who had been usurping the kingship, something inconceivable in later times.

By postexilic times keeping the Sabbath had become one of the distinctive practices of observant Jews. During this period detailed regulations developed so as to make its observance absolute, a tendency already evident in the explanations in the Ten Commandments. The Sabbath was also a socioeconomic institution and meant feeding humans and animals although they were not working, besides losing profit; thus attempts were made to circumvent the law, and these needed to be countered. In Maccabean times the problem of fighting on the Sabbath arose, the faithful preferring to be killed rather than desecrate the Sabbath.

In the New Testament and in rabbinic Judaism we hear echoes of the debates that developed around the observance of Sabbath until finally a criterion was proposed: "Every case of danger of life allows for the suspension of the Sabbath" (*Yoma* 8.6). According to Rabbi Akiba, one should not desecrate the Sabbath for things that can be done the day before or the day after, but no desecration exists when such a possibility is not offered. Therefore a midwife can function and should be helped on the Sabbath. Rabbinic teaching differs from the New Testament in that healing in the New Testament is considered to fall under the principle of "danger of life," a point that later rabbinic teaching did not accept. The rabbis concluded, "Sabbath has been given to you; you have not been given to the Sabbath" (*Mekilta* to Exod. 31.13; cf. Mark 2.27). Some sectarians thought otherwise; so at Qumran on the Sabbath one was not supposed to help an animal when it was giving birth or involved in an accident.

New Testament discussions about the Sabbath seem therefore to be inner-Jewish discussions. By the end of the first century CE, the first day of the week was celebrated as the day of the Lord, to which Christian observance of the Sabbath was transferred. Some Christian groups, notably the Seventh-day Adventists, following biblical legislation exactly, observe the seventh day of the week, the original (and continuing) Jewish Sabbath.   *J. A. Soggin*

SACRAMENT. The term is not found in the New Testament, though the Vulgate sometimes uses *sacramentum* to render the Greek word for *mystery (mystērion)*, as in Ephesians 1.19. The word may have been suggested by its secular meaning, the oath of allegiance taken by a Roman soldier on enlistment. The Roman governor Pliny (ca. 112 CE) described Christians as those who bound themselves by an oath *(sacramentum)* not to commit crimes.

By the third century CE, the word was being used to describe *baptism and eucharist (see Lord's Supper)* as specific acts of Christian worship, and it was later extended to include other official liturgical acts of the church. In 1564 the Council of Trent defined seven sacraments as instituted by Christ, namely, baptism, confirmation, eucharist, penance, extreme unction, holy orders, and marriage. The Reformers with their biblical emphasis preferred to confine the term to baptism and eucharist, which are generally recognized as the two gospel sacraments.

The development of sacramental theology reflects different views found in the New Testament concerning the relation between God and human beings, where some stress God's *grace and others *faith. The Donatist controversy of the third century led to the use of the phrase *ex opere operato* to indicate that the efficacy and value of the sacrament did not depend on the worthiness of the minister but on the promise of God to the church. Therefore, as long as the church was obedient to its Lord and used the right "matter" (e.g., water in baptism, bread and wine at the eucharist) and the right "form" (the words or prayer expressing the meaning of the action), participants could be assured of God's presence and action in the sacrament. To avoid the mechanical understanding to which this view could easily lead, the Reformers emphasized faith in differing ways. Some, like Ulrich Zwingli, thought of the sacraments as signs of God's action in the past, whereas others regarded them as means of grace assured by the outward sign and the promise of Christ.

Modern theology tends to describe the sacraments as occasions of encounter between God and the believer, where the reality of God's gracious actions needs to be accepted in faith to effect a true meeting. This accords with New Testament teaching, which sees God's grace focused in the person of Jesus and his death and resurrection. This is the "mystery" of Christ (Col. 4.3), in the sense that God's secret purpose has been declared and made known in Christ. The sacraments therefore are means of grace insofar as they are occasions when the gracious act of God is made present to the believer. Paul expresses this understanding with regard to both the eucharist and baptism.

The use of the term "the holy mysteries" (encouraged by 1 Cor. 4.1) to refer to the sacraments, especially in the Eastern Orthodox churches, shows more clearly the connection between the redemptive acts of Christ and their liturgical representation.   *John N. Suggit*

SACRIFICE. The offering of some commodity to God, generally making use of the services of a cultic official, a priest. In the Bible, the various kinds of sacrifices are presented most systematically in Leviticus 1–7. The different sacrifices cited there can be classified in several ways. Most prominent are those utilizing clean animals (cattle, sheep, goats, doves, pigeons). All such animal sacrifices have a number of features in common: killing/dismemberment of the victim, burning of at least some part of it (the fat in particular) on the altar, application of the *blood to the altar by the priest in some manner (sprinkling or smearing).

The burnt offering or *holocaust is particularly distinctive. As the latter name implies, a complete consumption of the victim's remains (except for the skin, which was given to the priest) by fire was involved here. The rite opened with the offerer's laying his hand on the victim's head; this gesture of self-identification signifies that, through the beast, he is offering himself to God. The intended purpose of the holocaust was to effect atonement with Yahweh for the offerer.

Another major animal sacrifice is the peace offering (NRSV: "offering of well-being"; the differently translated Hebrew word is *šĕlāmîm*), described in Leviticus 3.1–17; 7.11–36. In this instance, the designation employed points to the ritual's aim, that is, to (re-)establish "peace," fellowship between the divine and human parties. In line with this end, the victim's remains are divided between God (for whom the fat is burned on the altar), the assisting priest, and the offerer's household. The peace offering can further be specified, in accordance with the motive prompting it, as a thanksgiving, votive, or free-will offering. In the first instance, the victim's flesh must be consumed on the day of the sacrifice itself; in the latter two, the time allotted for this extends through the following day.

Two further animal sacrifices are the sin offering and the guilt offering. The Bible does not clearly distinguish these in terms of either their ritual or the situations that necessitate them. Both are designed to effect atonement in cases of a nondeliberate offense (e.g., bodily discharges, contact with the unclean), and in both it is only the victim's fat that is burned on the altar. The sin offering is, however, the more public of the two, being offered on the major *feasts of the year, while the guilt offering functions as part of a process of reparation undertaken by an individual.

The Bible also prescribes various nonbloody sacrifices; these utilize cereals, frankincense, and *wine. Of these, the last must accompany other sacrifices, whereas the first two may be offered separately. Finally, biblical narratives evidence familiarity with the practice of human sacrifice; this, however, is strongly condemned in the laws of the Pentateuch.

Taken as a whole, the Hebrew Bible manifests a certain ambivalence regarding sacrifice. In the Pentateuch, it is solemnly enjoined as a positive divine requirement, while other passages seem to articulate God's rejection of the practice as a whole. The latter formulations are best seen as hyperbolic reminders of the truth that cultic sacrifice is pleasing to God only when offered by one whose whole life is lived in accordance with God's will.

In the New Testament, particularly in Hebrews, the death of Jesus is described as a sacrifice that definitively secures for the whole of humanity the effects (atonement, fellowship with God) that older sacrifices brought about only temporarily. Likewise in the New Testament, the notion of a spiritual sacrifice comes to the fore. In this conception, every action of a Christian's life has the capacity, when performed in faith, to be an offering acceptable to God.

Christopher T. Begg

SALVATION. The primary meaning of the Hebrew and Greek words translated "salvation" is nonreligious. Thus, the derivatives of the Hebrew root $y\check{s}^c$ are used frequently in military contexts, as of victories by Gideon, Samson, Jonathan, and David; of projected defeats of Aram and of the enemies of Gibeon; and of victory in general. In fact, recent translations often translate nominal derivatives of $y\check{s}^c$ with "victory." An analogous sense is found in Deuteronomy 22.27: a woman who has been raped "in the field" is not guilty, because there would have been no "rescuer" (Hebr. *môšîa^c*) to hear her cry for help. And, in poetry, synonyms used in poetic parallelism for $y\check{s}^c$ often mean "to rescue, to deliver, to help escape, to protect."

This sense of victory or rescue from danger, defeat, or distress is also primary when God is the agent. Thus, in the clearly military metaphors of Psalm 91,

the conclusion sums up the divine promise of protection as follows: "I will satisfy him with length of days, and show him my victory (*yešú^cātî*)"; the NRSV is inconsistent both here and in other places where God is the source of the victory, often using the theologically weighty word "salvation." In fact, when God is the source of "salvation" in the Hebrew Bible the meaning is overwhelmingly physical rather than spiritual, and in this life rather than in some *afterlife. It is difficult to stress this too much, since Christian readers of the Bible especially have understandably read back into the Hebrew Bible the spiritual and eschatological nuances of the concept of salvation found in the New Testament. Despite the fact that in a great majority of the occurrences of the root $y\check{s}^c$ in the Hebrew Bible God is the agent of "salvation," it rarely if ever has an unambiguously spiritual nuance. An eschatological sense is of course present in such passages as Ezekiel 34.22 and throughout Second Isaiah, but the "salvation" prophesied is the restoration of Israel in its land, not some otherworldly bliss. Even in the New Testament salvation can be physical and this-worldly. In the healings of both the woman with the hemorrhage and the blind Bartimaeus, Jesus proclaims that their faith has "saved" them; most recent translations correctly render the Greek verb *sōzō* "has made you well." Likewise, *sōzō* is used by the disciples when they thought they were drowning and (in a compound form) of Paul's escape from shipwreck.

But the majority of occurrences in the New Testament of the Greek verb *sōzō* ("to save") and its derivatives, especially the noun *sōtēria* ("salvation"), have to do with the ultimate salvation of believers in Christ Jesus. The same phrase used in the stories of healing is also used of forgiveness of sin, and in the account of the paralytic forgiveness of sin is a spiritual kind of healing concomitant with the physical restoration of health. For the one forgiven this spiritual healing is thus "salvation," in the sense of admission into the *kingdom of God understood as both a present and a future reality. The salvation of individuals is the principal focus of the earlier New Testament writings. In Paul this salvation is both present and future; the two are closely linked, in part at least because of Paul's expectation of a prompt *second coming. So Paul can speak of those "who are being saved" (1 Cor. 1.18; 15.2; 2 Cor. 2.15), as well as those who will be "saved in the day of the Lord" (1 Cor. 5.5), both Jews and gentiles. This same kind of "realized eschatology" is also found in the synoptic Gospels and in Acts, though in both it is a future salvation that dominates.

In the gospel of John not only is Jesus identified as "savior," an interpretation of his name (see below), but the object of salvation is frequently identified as "the world" (Grk. *kosmos*), the created order now at enmity with God and therefore in need of salvation through Jesus.

A large number of personal names are derived from the Hebrew root *yšʿ*, including those of Moses' successor Joshua, the prophets Hosea, Isaiah, and probably Elisha, the Moabite king Mesha, and Jesus (a Grk. form of Hebr. *yēšûaʿ*); in all of these names God rather than the person with the name is explicitly or implicitly the agent of salvation. The exclamation transliterated "Hosanna" is also from this root.   *Michael D. Coogan*

SCIENCE AND THE BIBLE. The dramatic conflicts between Galileo and the Roman Inquisition and between Darwin and his biblicist opponents have understandably dominated the percep-

tion of the relation between science and religion in the popular imagination. But this perception is distorted because it neglects the indispensable role that religious beliefs played in the Western approach to *nature that led to the rise of modern science. On the other hand, emphasis on the integration of scientific and religious beliefs has often led to facile syntheses, provoking reactions that emphasize the separation of science and religion. Even if this separation were philosophically sound, it provides little basis for understanding the historical interaction, often constructive on both sides, between science and religion.

Augustine. On the relation of science to the Bible, the diversity of views and interpretations is vast, but representatives can usefully serve to indicate the variety of types of reactions found in the Judeo-Christian tradition. In *De Doctrina Christiana (DDC)* and *De Genesi ad Litteram (DGL)*, Augustine (354–430 CE) makes clear the relative insignificance of specialized sciences as compared with understanding scripture, yet Augustine does not suggest that all knowledge can be found in scripture. In *DDC*, Augustine provides general rules for the interpretation of ambiguous terms. It is a mistake to read figurative signs literally (a rule that covers anthropomorphisms) and literal signs figuratively. The method of determining whether a particular expression is literal or figurative is that an expression that does not literally pertain to virtuous behavior or to the truth of faith must be taken figuratively. If the meaning of an expression is absurd when taken verbally, then we must examine its figurative possibilities. It follows from these guidelines that the believer should not read the Bible to learn facts about the natural world unrelated to salvation. In *DGL*, however, Augustine seems to require the certain truth of a new claim about nature in order to revise the apparently plain meaning of the biblical text, but even in *DGL* Augustine reiterates the principle that God did not wish to teach men and women things of no relevance to their salvation. It was clear to Augustine that secular knowledge was indispensable for the correct interpretation of scripture. Although not a license for the autonomy of science, the principle in Augustine's approval of secular disciplines was expanded by later authors into arguments legitimating knowledge of the natural universe as another way of honoring God. Such authors, like William of Conches (1080–1154), presumably did not foresee the developments that would contribute to the autonomy of the sciences, but they were confident that natural science would still perform its proper role when rightly interpreted.

Copernicus. The revival of Aristotle in the medieval Latin West prompted scholars like Thomas Aquinas (1225–1274) to construe theology by analogy with Aristotelian science. Even so, in the context of medieval society, the definitive resolution of anomalies in the understanding of the cosmos was impossible and hence generated a resignation to the limitations of human knowledge. Nicholas Oresme (1320–1382) took seriously the hypothesis of the diurnal rotation of the earth but rejected it because no confirmation seemed possible; he fell back on the Bible in this case as providing persuasive confirmation of the greater probability of the geocentric view.

In *De Revolutionibus* (1543) Copernicus's arguments for the heliocentric theory rely partly on his religious point of view. Copernicus (1473–1543) shared not only the traditional beliefs about the intrinsic rationality and harmonious design of God's creation but also another

traditional belief that God had made the universe for human beings; he then concluded, perhaps originally, that it therefore must be knowable. Copernicus had no reason to believe that the heliocentric theory would ever be empirically confirmed by some neutral test or observation, but he believed that criteria already existed for preferring the heliocentric hypothesis, namely, the ordering of the planets and the spheres that arose from the mathematical coherence between period of planetary orbit and distance from the sun, and the natural relation between hypothesis and some observations. In the preface dedicated to Pope Paul III (d. 1549), Copernicus denigrates those ignorant of astronomy who distort some passage of scripture in order to censure his undertaking. The biblical texts most often cited in later controversies are Joshua 10.12–14, Ecclesiastes 1.5, and Psalms 19.4–6; 93.1; 104.5.

There is evidence of early official Catholic opposition to Copernicus, but plans to censure the theory in the mid-1540s were supposedly frustrated by the death of the master of the Sacred Palace, Bartolomeo Spina, in 1547. Lutheran reactions to the Copernican theory permitted use of the Copernican models even as the system was rejected as a literal truth. One of Tycho Brahe's (1546–1601) reasons for rejecting the Copernican theory was its incompatibility with texts of scripture, but Tycho's other reasons were astronomical and physical. Nevertheless, there is no question that Johannes Kepler (1571–1630) shared Copernicus's beliefs in divine design, the knowability of the universe, and the clues provided by mathematical coherence and commensurability for determining the order of the planets and even the true shape of their orbital paths.

Galileo. Likewise, Galileo (1564–

1642) shared the views of Copernicus and Kepler on mathematical coherence, but he also felt the need to demonstrate the truth of the Copernican theory, and his personal relations with several theologians, cardinals, popes, and political leaders introduced further complications into the story.

The text in which Galileo most directly and fully addresses questions about the Bible and science is the *Letter to the Grand Duchess Christina* (1615). Galileo cites Augustine several times, and he initially adopts the traditional view, emphasizing the principle of accommodation and arguing that it is not the purpose of the Bible to teach science. Where Joshua 10.12–14, then, reports the sun standing still, we are not to read the text as a literal description of the motions of the heavenly bodies.

Almost immediately, however, Galileo apparently accepts the criterion proposed by Cardinal Robert Bellarmine (1542–1621) earlier in 1615 in a letter to Paolo Antonio Foscarini (1580–1616), a theologian who supported the Copernican theory, that only in cases in which a scientific conclusion is demonstrated, and not merely probable, are we authorized to reinterpret the plain meaning of the biblical text. Later in his letter Galileo presses the attack further. If geocentrists insist on the literal interpretation of scripture, the passage from Joshua requires that the motion of the sun be stopped. According to the Ptolemaic theory, however, the proper motion of the sun is its annual motion on the ecliptic. Stopping the sun's annual motion would shorten the day, not lengthen it, argues Galileo. Then Galileo suggests a literal interpretation of the text of Joshua consistent with the Copernican theory. The very idea is astounding; it is hardly surprising that theologians were shocked, and even less surprising that they misinterpreted the point of Galileo's critique.

Although Galileo's intention was to demonstrate the absurd consequence of insisting on using scripture for proof of a scientific hypothesis, it does appear that Galileo got carried away by his telescopic observations, his discovery of the sunspots, the cleverness of his own literal reading of the text of Joshua, and by his conviction that he could demonstrate the truth of Copernican theory. If Galileo intended to forestall official restrictions being placed on the Copernican theory, then his acceptance of Bellarmine's challenge and the introduction of the second reading seems to have provoked the very reaction he was trying to deflect.

In 1616 the Congregation of the Index condemned Foscarini's work supporting the Copernican theory, and it suspended Copernicus's *De Revolutionibus* and Diego de Zuniga's (1536–1597) Copernican interpretation of texts of scripture until they were corrected. The decree followed the decision of the Congregation of the Holy Office, which accepted the arguments propounded by Bellarmine, who in a letter to Foscarini had expanded the Augustinian criterion about faith and morals to include under faith any natural assertion declared by the Holy Spirit. Hence, the text of Joshua had to be interpreted plainly as asserting the geocentric view, and because it was declared by the Holy Spirit, the conclusion had to be accepted as pertaining to faith. Bellarmine's reasoning was faulty, and through adoption by the Holy Office it set a dangerous precedent. Galileo was issued a warning, but one that also confirmed that his views had not been censured.

By the end of 1616, however, the premises for the eventual case against Galileo were in place: the Copernican theory was under censure and it appears that Galileo had been warned against defending it. From a narrow, legal point of view, Galileo's *Two Chief World Systems* (1632), even with the license that he was granted, violated the spirit, if not the letter, of the earlier injunction. Historians tend to excuse the Inquisition's mistake in condemning Galileo in 1633 on the grounds that the Roman Catholic Church felt itself under pressure from some Protestant critics to guard against individual interpretations of scripture, thus abandoning its traditional, sound view for a narrower, literalist interpretation of the biblical text. In spite of Pope John Paul II's public acknowledgments in 1983 of Galileo's mistreatment at the hands of church authorities in 1633, and in 1992 of the correctness of Galileo's views, the Vatican continues to refuse scholars complete access to the Vatican archival records on the Galileo case, fueling further speculation about the case.

The Catholic reaction partly provoked by Protestant literalistic criticisms lent the more open approaches of yet other Protestants an air of free inquiry. Scholars still debate the concreteness of supposed Puritan or Anglican influences on scientific activity, but there seems little question that, in England and Holland, religious ideology played a role in the advancement of empirical science. Francis Bacon's (1561–1626) appeal to the recovery of the garden of Eden in a technological paradise, Robert Boyles's (1627–1691) efforts to Christianize Epicurean atomism, the development of a natural theology supportive of scientific activity, the legitimation of science as a profession, and other similar consequences, however diverse and however loosely connected with any official doctrine, cannot be dismissed as irrelevant. Isaac Newton's (1642–1727) religious

beliefs, even if not orthodox, and his extensive biblical commentaries attest to the importance that he himself attached to the Bible and to the partly religious foundations of his own conception of the universe. The later separation of the legitimation of science from religious motivations does not argue against the importance of religion for science prior to the eighteenth century.

Evolutionary Theory. In the nineteenth century, the controversies provoked by Charles Darwin's (1809–1882) theory of evolution were viewed as the focal point for a much broader perception of conflicting loyalties—to the belief in a universe divinely created with purpose or to the belief that the universe is the result of chance. The notion that the human eye could be the result of millions of years of evolution seems as improbable to those who believe in a special divine *creation as the biblical story of Eve's creation from Adam's rib seems to the paleontologist. The official Roman Catholic response of the late nineteenth century was subordinated to the church's antimodernist reaction, constituting a position between liberal Protestantism and *fundamentalism. In 1950 Pope Pius XII declared the belief in monogenesis as a foundation for the biblical account of original sin and its universal consequences. The a priori proscription of polygenesis on theological grounds has restricted Catholic evolutionists' options. Liberal Protestants have not seen fit to restrict God's options on this question. The impact of the theory of evolution on biblical interpretation is undeniably clear from the further developments in historical-critical method and the emphasis on the social-ethical message of scripture. Literalistic creationists have rightly pointed out problems with the theory of evolution, but to most scientists the theory remains the best available and is strongly supported by evidence from physics and astronomy. Some scientists speak of evolution dogmatically as a fact, but such a dogmatic stance seems partly provoked by the educational threat posed by fundamentalists; efforts in America to legislate the teaching of religious alternatives to the theory of evolution and the effect of such efforts on textbook publishers demonstrate the reality of such threats. Ironically, in the case of Teilhard de Chardin (1881–1955), the French Jesuit paleontologist, the Roman Catholic Church was concerned with tying Christian dogma to scientific theory and hence advocated more circumspect theological discussions of evolution, thus demonstrating the caution it had painfully learned from the Galileo case.

Theoretical Concerns. There is always a theoretical background to empirical research, but the danger for theology lies in the use of science to advance a particular interpretation of the Bible and the danger for science lies in the use of dogma to obstruct scientific theorizing; it does not lie in the use of dogma or the Bible to promote scientific research or to question a specific interpretation of the Bible. The advance of science depends to some extent on skeptical questioning of established views. The recognition of the contingency of nature is consistent with the belief in creation and in the dependence of nature on God's sustaining and controlling presence. Contemporary theologians who advocate the revival of traditional natural theology seem unaware of its earlier fate. The preference of some cosmologists for the anthropic principle requires the theological assumption that human beings are the goal of God's creation in order for the anthropic principle to be regarded as explanatory. But even from a theological point of view, such an account is unsatisfactory for it places a priori limitations on how God could have accomplished the divine purposes. The principles enunciated by Augustine seem susceptible of a broad interpretation with modern amendments: the Bible does not teach natural science; theology makes legitimate knowledge claims; our understanding of the meaning of the Bible has changed with our growth in knowledge of the physical universe; belief in the divine origin of the universe has often motivated and sustained confidence in the ability of humans to penetrate the secrets of the universe; the failures of science and the excesses of human intervention alert us to the relevance of values for decisions in science and technology; historical experience enjoins us to admit the possibly ultimate futility of human achievements; biblical homage to the sacredness of nature and human responsibility is harmonious with the awe and wonder expressed by cosmologists and environmentalists; and the search for meaning in human existence supports the limited aim of consonance between theological and scientific interpretations of the cosmos.   *Andre L. Goddu*

SCOFIELD REFERENCE BIBLE. A popular and influential reference Bible published by Oxford University Press early in the twentieth century. The editor, C. I. Scofield (1843–1921), was a successful lawyer, but after his religious conversion in 1879 he devoted himself to Bible study and Christian service, eventually becoming an ordained Congregational minister of some prominence. In 1909 he published *The Scofield Reference Bible,* with a second, revised edition in 1917. By 1930, total sales of the two editions had exceeded one million copies.

Utilizing the King James Version with

Scofield's notes and comments in the margins, *The Scofield Reference Bible* featured the so-called dispensational system of biblical interpretation. Dispensationalists claim that God's dealings with humankind have varied throughout the different eras or "dispensations" of biblical history. They emphasize their "literal" interpretation of the Bible, suggesting, for example, that some of the prophecies concerning the land of Israel are yet to be fulfilled. A controversial feature of this system is the nearly total separation of God's relationship with Israel and the Jewish people from that of the Christian church. Dispensationalism has been and remains a significant force in Protestant Christianity in North America.

In 1967, Oxford University Press published *The New Scofield Reference Bible* under the editorial direction of E. Schuyler English; this edition was also based on the King James Version and retained the dispensational flavor of Scofield's notes. More recently, editions based on the New International Version and the New American Standard Bible have also been published.

See also Fundamentalism.

William H. Barnes

SECOND COMING OF CHRIST.

"He will come again to judge the living and the dead": in this way, the Apostles' Creed summarizes the Christian hope that God will complete his purpose for the world in a final, triumphant coming of Christ. The parallel terms "first coming" and "second coming" (suggested in Heb. 9.26–28) highlight the theological connection between these two chief moments of Christ's work.

The prophets had declared that God's purpose in history would reach its goal in a future period of blessing under God's rule, a rule that would be righteous, peaceful, universal, and permanent. Often God was said to exercise his rule through an earthly king descended from David.

Jesus taught that this longed-for time of salvation had dawned, the *kingdom of God had drawn near. The promises were now being fulfilled in him, and his possession of God's spirit, his *miracles and *exorcisms were evidence of this. Yet God's kingdom had not fully arrived. For although through his ministry the blessings of God were experienced with a new immediacy, still death and suffering and the ambiguities of life remained for his followers. The complete realization of the kingdom was in the future. Thus he taught his disciples to pray, "Your kingdom come" (Luke 11.2; *see* Lord's Prayer), and proclaimed that the coming of the *Son of man would mark the dividing line between the present course of history and the full realization of God's kingdom.

The so-called apocalyptic discourse of Mark 13 (and the related passages in Matt. 24; Luke 17.22–37; 21) warns of the sufferings and conflicts that Jesus' followers should expect before his final coming as Son of man. Both here and elsewhere the nearness of Christ's coming is stressed. But there is also an expectation that certain events must take place before the end comes, and an insistence that the date cannot be predicted. So the statements about nearness are best understood as vivid assertions of the certainty that God's purpose, begun in Christ's first coming, will be completed in his second coming.

Similarly, the New Testament writers are more concerned with the purpose of Christ's coming than with its manner, which is variously described. Christ will come to complete the work of rescuing humankind, which began with his first coming. He will come to pass judgment on the whole human race, to welcome into his presence those who have lived by trust in him, while those who have rejected him will find themselves shut out. Thus his coming will mark his final conquest over evil, and the realization of his kingdom of peace, righteousness, and love. This is described as "new heavens and a new earth, where righteousness is at home" (2 Pet. 3.13; cf. Rev. 21.3–4).

Not all interpreters take the New Testament's message of the second coming at face value. Some argue that Jesus' sayings about the coming of the Son of man are not authentic to him, or that he intended them as symbols of God's triumph rather than as promises of an actual future coming; in that case, the hope of the early Christians would be based on a misunderstanding of Jesus' teaching. Others argue that since the expectation of Christ's coming within a generation of his lifetime did not materialize, it must be interpreted symbolically to mean that Christ "comes to me" in my decision for him and his rule. In contrast, some understand all references to the second coming quite literally, and believe the passages about "the signs of the times" (e.g., Mark 13) enable its timing to be calculated precisely. In any case, it is possible to affirm the basic structure of Christian hope, with its emphasis on the second coming as the goal and fulfillment of God's past work in Christ, without committing oneself to any precise view about its nature or when it will be.

See also Biblical Theology, *article on* New Testament; Parousia.

Stephen H. Travis

SERMON ON THE MOUNT. In popular thought the Sermon on the Mount epitomizes Jesus' ethical teaching; it is the first of five discourses by Jesus in Matthew's gospel and is found in Matthew 5–7. Augustine first called this discourse the "Sermon on the Mount"

because of its setting in Matthew 5.1. Matthew describes it as a speech or teaching given by Jesus while seated, the typical Jewish position for teaching.

Literary History. The sermon shares a striking structural and material parallel with Luke 6.20–49, often called the "Sermon on the Plain" because of its setting. Each opens with a series of beatitudes followed by a series of demands for conduct and concludes with a series of alternatives, the last being a parable of two builders. Although some have attributed these similarities to Jesus' use of the same "sermon" on more than one occasion, most explain them as the evangelists' use of a common tradition that had already taken its basic shape.

Why then the extensive differences between the two accounts, such as length (Matthew has over a hundred verses, Luke thirty)? Careful examination of the material indicates that some of the differences arose in the development of the tradition used by each evangelist respectively, and some, especially in wording, arose from the evangelists' adaptation of the tradition for their purposes. Much of Matthew's additional material, however, appears elsewhere in Luke's gospel and suggests that Matthew thematically combined other parts of the tradition common to Matthew and Luke (Q) to expand the "sermon" tradition. And if Matthew has drawn from the larger, common tradition with Luke, it is likely that he also drew from other traditions to fill out this discourse. Consequently Matthew's Sermon on the Mount represents an underlying "sermon" tradition expanded by the use of other traditions.

Does then the Sermon on the Mount come from Jesus? If one precisely defines the Sermon as the discourse found in Matthew 5–7, the answer is no. Matthew 5–7 as it now stands is the evangelist's final product of an oral/literary process involving several traditions. Yet analysis of the traditions found in the Sermon indicates their strong claim to being rooted in Jesus' own ministry, and to represent his teaching faithfully.

Some have drawn a parallel between Matthew's structure with five discourses and the five books of Moses (the *Torah). Consequently, the mountain setting and the apparently ethical content of the Sermon have naturally led to interpreting the Sermon as a new law or the messianic Torah given by Jesus, the new Moses. This view, however, fails to do justice to Matthew's gospel as a whole by relegating the infancy, baptism, and temptation narratives to the status of a preamble and the passion narrative to that of an epilogue. It suffers from the lack of evidence that Jesus' role either in the Sermon or in the gospel was that of a new Moses.

Others have found the clue to Matthew's structure in the transitional statement, "From that time on, Jesus began . . ." (4.17; 16.21), which divides Matthew's portrait of Jesus into three parts, the first focused on the person of Jesus Messiah, the second on the presentation of Jesus Messiah, and the third on the passion of Jesus Messiah. In this schema, the Sermon comes as part of Jesus' presentation of himself and his summons to the Kingdom in 4.17–16.20. This reading concurs with Matthew's immediate setting for the Sermon. The discourse in 5–7 and the miraculous deeds in 8–9 are enclosed by the identical programmatic summary in 4.23 and transitional summary in 9.35. These summaries point to Jesus as the promised Messiah presenting the message of the Kingdom and effecting its work.

Audience. The audience of the Sermon is the disciples, a group that for Matthew has a dual significance. In the context of Jesus' ministry the disciples always refers to the twelve. But the disciples also represent a model or paradigm of the followers of Jesus in general. They are the community of the Messiah, who have responded to Jesus' message of the Kingdom, and in whose lives the Kingdom is at work. Therefore, the Sermon is also a statement about the identity of the new people of God and their conduct in relationship to each other and to God.

Content. The beatitudes (Matt. 5.3–12) bear witness to Jesus and identify the people of the Kingdom. Although Matthew appears to have spiritualized or ethicized the beatitudes to the poor, the hungry, and the weeping, his first four beatitudes reflect a deliberate alignment in wording and order with Isaiah 61 to show Jesus to be the fulfillment of Isaiah's promised messenger anointed by the Spirit to proclaim the good news of God's deliverance.

At the same time the beatitudes identify the people of the Kingdom as those who stand before God empty-handed, vulnerable, seeking a right relationship with him and others, open to receive and express his *mercy and *forgiveness with integrity, ready to experience and to establish peace. These are the people of the Kingdom who find themselves at odds with this world. Yet they are the "salt of the earth" (5.13) and the "light of the world" (5.14–15) whose "good works" bring glory to God (5.16).

The demands of the Sermon set forth the "greater righteousness" (5.20) of the followers of Jesus. But Matthew prefaces these demands by noting again that Jesus' coming meant the fulfillment of biblical promises, "the law and the prophets" (5.17).

The first set of demands (5.21–48), often referred to as the "antitheses," assumes a new relationship between individuals that issues in conduct that supersedes the Law. These six demands, like much biblical *law as well as other teachings of Jesus, are more illustrative than comprehensive.

The second set of demands (6.1–7.11) reflects a right relationship with God. These demands fall into two groups, the first of which has three illustrations of traditional Jewish piety. The second group consists of a series of apparently miscellaneous exhortations. The connecting link between these two groups of demands may lie in the petitions of the *Lord's Prayer, which was inserted into the first group as an example of how to pray. Each exhortation corresponds to a petition of the Lord's Prayer, and the series concludes with a promise for answered prayer.

Matthew rounds off the demands of the Sermon with the *Golden Rule (7.12). Drawn most likely from the context of love for one's enemy, this demand, now located after the second set of demands pertaining to one's relationship with God, resumes the first set of demands regarding one's relationship with others. Therefore, the heart of the Sermon defines the life of the Kingdom in terms of horizontal and vertical relationships.

The Sermon concludes with three sets of alternatives—two ways, two trees, and two builders. One alternative offers life, the other death or destruction. Jesus' way, followed by few, is the more difficult but is productive and capable of weathering the storm of judgment.

Theological Significance. But can one really "hear" and "do" Jesus' words as the Sermon suggests? Apart from the beatitudes that appear to bless conduct contrary to what it takes to survive in the real world, can one today love the enemy and live with anger, evil thoughts, the guarantee of one's word,

the recourse to legal justice, or even *divorce? To understand the Sermon, one must read it in its biblical context woven into the fabric of Matthew's gospel as a statement, above all, about who Jesus is. In this initial discourse, one "hears" Jesus whose words support his preaching about the presence of the Kingdom and point to his person in whom God is acting in keeping with the promise of Isaiah 61. With these words, Jesus declares that a new day has dawned in human relationships because God is offering new relationships with those who are willing to let God be sovereign in their lives. Thus the Sermon is the message of the "good news," the "gospel of the kingdom," that declares "blessed" those who have nothing to claim or cling to before God.

At the same time, the Sermon does offer, in a sense, the ethic of the Kingdom. It sets forth how the people of the Kingdom live in relationship with God and others. When accepting Jesus' words of God's gracious acceptance in the beatitudes, one does not "perform" to achieve God's reward, but, placing one's life in God's hands, one responds to God out of gratitude and love. Furthermore, in light of the recognition of God's rule, one is free to leave one's best interest in God's hands and to respond to others out of love rather than self-interest. Only then does the prohibition of anger, lust, and use of legal justice and divorce, or the demand for total honesty and love for the enemy avoid being utopian.

Robert A. Guelich

SEX. An appreciation of the biblical concern with the establishment of a holy people—the "children of Abraham," variously understood—reveals the relationship between sexuality and such related issues as virginity, pre- and extramarital sexual behavior, *marriage, polygyny, concubinage, *adultery, and *homosexuality.

Sexual Behavior in the Hebrew Bible. The paradigmatic biblical statement on sexuality and sexual behavior is found in Genesis 1.26–28, the creation of human beings in God's image as male and female with the duty to "be fruitful and multiply," and it reflects the vigorous pronatalist worldview that characterized most of the period of the composition of the Hebrew Bible. From the call of Abraham in Genesis 12 to the death of Joseph in Genesis 50, the combined promises of land, heir, and many descendants provide the scaffolding by which the history of earliest Israel is erected. Israel shared this desire for offspring with its ancient Near Eastern neighbors, as evidenced in the fourteenth-century BCE *Ugaritic epic of Kirta. The threat of the extinction of one's biological line is a commonplace in ancient Near Eastern treaty curses, and was appropriated directly by biblical writers.

All sexual behavior that did not produce legitimate Israelite offspring to the holy commonwealth was, in varying degrees, censured or controlled, and there was a concomitant double standard with regard to sexual behavior. Premarital virginity, for example, was incumbent only upon females; there is no indication that males were expected to be virgins at marriage, and there is no provision in the Hebrew Bible for lifelong virginity. If a husband accused his wife of not having been a virgin at the time of her marriage, and if his charges were substantiated, the woman was stoned. If, on the other hand, the man's charges were refuted, he was merely flogged and fined.

Marriage was regarded as the normal estate of adults by the biblical writers, although in actuality the closing of the Israelite frontier and concomitant laws granting patrimony to the firstborn son

would almost certainly have deprived some sons and daughters of the economic resources necessary to establish families of their own. Such unmarried sons were shunted into military, bureaucratic, or clerical careers (e.g., the landless Levites). Some unmarried women may have found a social role among the temple functionaries termed *qādēš/qĕdēšâ* (literally, "set apart," but usually translated "sacred prostitute" on the basis of such passages as Gen. 38.21–22 and Deut. 23.18). There is no direct evidence, however, that the wages of such persons were derived from sexual activity.

The function of marriage in the Hebrew Bible was (a) social (the regulation of sexual behavior, especially of women); (b) psychological and emotional (to provide companionship for the partners); (c) economic (through family agrarian and artisan enterprises); (d) religious (since the majority of festivals centered on household participation); and, most important, (e) theological (through the procreation, legitimation, and socialization of children, the basis of the people of God). In the majority of biblical writings, children were the supreme example of divine favor, and childlessness was understood to be a curse.

Endogamy was prescribed, but intermarriage was routine in actuality, especially by kings. The Samson cycle (Judg. 13–16) vividly illustrated the perceived danger of exogamy. Ezra and Nehemiah attempted to restore ethnic endogamy after the *exile, but by Hellenistic times intermarriage was again recorded as a practice among diaspora Jews.

The conviction that procreation is an unqualified good is also reflected in three well-known institutions regulating sexual behavior: polygyny, concubinage, and levirate marriage.

Polygyny seems to have been practiced since the earliest periods of Israelite history, but was probably never statistically prevalent due to the relative affluence necessary to support more than one wife; note Jacob's fourteen-year indenture for his two wives and two concubines. Both David and Solomon practiced polygyny on a grand scale, although the Deuteronomic theologians admonished even royalty to refrain from the practice because of its religiously adulterating possibilities.

Although concubines did not enjoy the same rights as a wife, they were socially and legally recognized in ancient Israel. A concubine's children did not share the rights of a wife's children, unless, like Hagar, sexual contact with the concubine was for the explicit purpose of producing heirs, in which case the children became the wife's children. Wives and concubines of a deposed or conquered king were considered war booty. Thus, Absalom's public intercourse with David's concubines during the latter's flight from Jerusalem was considered treasonous, and Adonijah's request for the concubine Abishag amounted to insurrection.

Although the legislation concerning levirate marriage specifies the brother of the deceased as bearer of the responsibility to marry his widowed sister-in-law, the story of Judah and Tamar in Genesis 38 indicates that the responsibility to the widow rested with the dead man's family, not merely with his brother (v. 26). Further, "to preserve the name" refers to the dead man's property, not merely to his nominal existence, as is clear from the account in Ruth 4. *Josephus is probably correct, then, in seeing the purpose of levirate marriage to be threefold: to continue a lineage, to prevent the alienation of family property, and to provide for the social and economic welfare of widows. Levirate marriage was at least known (if not actually practiced) into the Hellenistic period.

All sexual behavior that did not contribute to the biblical notion of "the children of Israel" was proscribed. Homosexuality, bestiality, contraception, and masturbation were all prohibited, directly or by inference. Adultery—sexual activity between a married woman and a man of any marital status—is consistently condemned in the biblical writings. Sexual activity by an unmarried woman, whether for hire or not, was termed prostitution (the same Hebrew words, zānâ and its derivatives, are also translated as "to fornicate," "to be a harlot, a whore") and the response ranged from toleration (in the case of Rahab) to burning (in the case of a priest's daughter). Harlotry as a metaphor for spiritual unfaithfulness was used by the prophets to denounce Israel's apostasy.

A conspicuous exception to the dominant sexual ideology of the Bible is the Song of Solomon. The Song's frank erotic imagery, its indifference to social proprieties such as marriage and reproduction, and its lack of overtly religious sentiments have forced generations of exegetes to allegorize its sensuality to bring it into harmony with the social control of sexuality sought by most biblical authors.

Sexual Behavior in the Greco-Roman Period. Beginning in the later books of the Hebrew Bible and continuing through the New Testament, there is a general decline in the value of sexuality and a tendency toward exaggerating its sinfulness. This shift in attitude resulted less from the influence of apocalyptic religious thought than from the Greco-Roman cultural hegemony of the third century BCE to the second century CE. *Philo (ca. 20 BCE–ca. 50 CE) interpreted the Septuagint's reordering of the *Ten Commandments to place adultery at the top of the list of sins against one's neighbor, before murder and theft, to indicate that adultery was the most serious of all sins. Philo also condemned any expression of sexuality, even within marriage, that was not for the purpose of procreation.

The Essenes at Qumran, who believed that they were living on the eve of the final eschatological battle between "the children of light and the children of darkness," considered themselves especially susceptible to pollution from sexual contact, and so some of them, according to statements of Philo, Josephus, and other ancient sources, renounced marriage and reproduction. The paucity of juvenile and female skeletons in the Qumran cemetery lends credence to these statements.

Early Christian attitudes toward sexuality arose from this background of Hellenistic asceticism, Jewish apocalypticism, and *ethics inherited from the Hebrew Bible. Adultery and homosexuality are forbidden, for example, and other sexual activities are proscribed, such as fornication by males as well as females. We find in the synoptic Gospels antimarital and antifamilial sentiments attributed to Jesus, and Paul unambiguously counseled the Corinthian Christians that marriage represented a compromise of the spiritual life, the highest degree of which was attainable only by celibates like Paul.

New Testament endorsement of marital sexuality and *family life is clearest in the deutero-Pauline and pastoral letters, where the patriarchal household current in the Mediterranean world of the first century CE (with such modifications as premarital chastity for males) was assumed as the Christian norm. The tension between sexual renunciation and full participation in married life was not decisively resolved in early Christianity, however, as both apocryphal and patristic writings attest.

See also Know.   *Gene McAfee*

SHEMA. The first word of Deuteronomy 6.4 in Hebrew, "Shema" is used as the name of the verse as a whole ("Hear, O Israel, YHWH is our God, YHWH alone / is one"). While acknowledging that the Shema was a central confessional statement of ancient Israel, modern scholars do not agree on its interpretation. If it is connected with the centralization of the cult in Jerusalem during the reforms of Josiah in the late sixth century BCE, then it could mean that there is only one acceptable manifestation of YHWH, namely in Jerusalem. The Shema could also imply that among all gods Israel is to worship only YHWH (henotheism), or that YHWH is the only God (*monotheism). It is in this latter sense that the Shema has become the central Jewish declaration of faith in one God. The Shema in its expanded form includes Deuteronomy 6.5–9 (love of God); 11.13–21 (rewards and punishments for observance); and Numbers 15.37–41 (duty of remembrance). It is recited by observant Jews as part of the morning and evening prayers, as well as before going to sleep. Deuteronomy 6.4–9 and 11.13–21, written on parchment, are also to be found in *phylacteries and on doorposts (mězûzôt). Following the lead of Rabbi Akiba (died ca. 135 CE), the Shema is to be recited before death, especially in cases of martyrdom. The early and great importance of the Shema is underlined by Jesus' reference to it as the greatest commandment.   *Carl S. Ehrlich*

SHEOL. *See* Hell.

SHIBBOLETH. ("flowing stream" or "ear of grain"). In Judges 12.1–4, troops from Ephraim crossed the Jordan, angry with the east-bank Gileadites for not including them in the Ammonite war reported in Judges 11 (ca. 1100 BCE). The Gileadites fought the Ephraimites, defeated them, and secured the fords by which the surviving Ephraimites would cross back to their own land. Ephraimites who wanted to escape would simply claim not to be Ephraimites; the Gileadites discovered these impostors by having them pronounce the word written in the Hebrew text as *šibbolet*. The Ephraimites could not pronounce the word properly; the Hebrew text represents their pronunciation as *sibbolet*. The two dialects had different pronunciations for the same word, and the story might mean that the Ephraimites simply slipped and used their own pronunciation. The text implies, however, that the Ephraimites were not able to pronounce a consonant that existed in the Gileadite dialect (the initial sibilant of the word in question).

Jo Ann Hackett

SIN. Sin is basically an offense against God. Although by sinning people cannot do God any actual harm, they do act against God by despising him and his commandments, and by injuring others (or themselves), since the person injured is also an object of divine providence and protection. The principal Hebrew words for sin express these basic notions. The verb *ḥāṭāʾ* and the nouns related to it, such as its Greek translation *hamartanō* and its derivatives, originally means to miss a target or to fail to reach it; with the connotation "to sin," it is used most frequently in relation to God, as a violation of his law. The verb *pāšaʿ* and the noun *pešaʿ* mean rebellion, either against a human being, such as a king, or against God. Both of the words just discussed are used together in Isaiah 43.27 and Job 34.37. A third main word for sin in He-

brew is *ʿāwōn*, which can mean an offense, the guilt resulting from it, or the punishment that follows.

In the *Dead Sea Scrolls and other postbiblical Jewish literature, there is a tendency to speak of sin less as an individual deed than as a power that governs men and women and inspires their conduct. This is particularly the case with the nouns *ʿāwel* and *ʿawlâ*, meaning "wickedness." Correspondingly, the role of the opposite force, the "holy spirit," is stressed in these writings. Depending on such passages as Isaiah 11.1–9; Jeremiah 31.33–34; and Ezekiel 36.26–27, several passages speak of this "holy spirit" as repairing the broken relationship between God and human beings.

The New Testament vocabulary for sin is largely that of the Septuagint, where the word *hamartanō* and its derivatives can translate all three Hebrew terms discussed above. Another important word is *anomia*, literally meaning lawlessness, which mainly translates *ʿāwōn* but can also be used for *pešaʿ* and *rāšāʿ*, "wicked." Also used to translate *pešaʿ* are *asebeia*, meaning impiety, and its derivatives.

In the Gospels, sin is often understood as a kind of debt. This metaphor is found in Jewish tradition and is developed in the *Lord's Prayer, whose fifth petition links divine forgiveness of human sins to a corresponding human forgiveness of others. The synoptic Gospels speak of sins to be forgiven in the plural, but this plural form is found only three times in the gospel of John, probably in dependence on earlier traditions. More often *hamartia*, in the singular, means not just a particular sinful deed, but a state or even a power that separates a person and the world as a whole from God. This power is personified as the devil, or Satan, who is the adversary of God's Son and his followers.

In Romans 5–7, Paul elaborates the view that sin, like death, originated with Adam; long dormant, its power emerged simultaneously with the giving of the *Law. Christ's death was the expiatory sacrifice that liberated human beings from their enslavement to the power of sin.

See also Fall, The; Temptation.
Leopold Sabourin, S.J.

SIX HUNDRED SIXTY-SIX. This number, mentioned in Revelation 13.18, is not, as is sometimes thought, a conundrum to be solved by readers in order to discover the identity of the beast described in that chapter. The identity of the beast is clear: it is the absolutist state as personified in the Roman Emperor Nero. The emperors claimed divine authority and their power seemed invincible. John wanted his readers to understand that the state and its rulers were neither divine nor invincible. They were human and carried the seed of their own destruction: their number is only 666, and does not reach the completion of seven (*see* Number Symbolism). The number was arrived at by presenting Nero's Greek name *Kaisar Nerōn* in Hebrew letters, which also function as numbers: *qsr nrwn; q* = 60, *s* = 100, *r* = 200, *n* = 50, *w* = 6, so *qsr nrwn* adds up to 666. (Some western manuscripts read "six hundred sixteen"; the scribes possibly did not understand John's usage of Hebrew numbers, and thought in terms of the Greek *kaisar theos,* the "god-emperor," which would add up to 616 using the Greek letters as numerals; but it is more likely that they simply dropped the final *n*: *qsr nrw* for *Kaisar Nerō,* making 616.)　David H. van Daalen

SLAVERY AND THE BIBLE. Slavery in the New World produced one of the great biblical controversies of early modern times. Especially in sixteenth-century Spain and in the United States between 1730 and 1860, biblical texts were used on both sides of the protracted debates over the institution of slavery. The Spanish controversy was largely about *encomienda,* a form of labor slavery imposed on the native peoples of New Spain by the Laws of Burgos (1513). Court spokesmen cited the conquest of Canaan, the destruction of Sodom, and Jesus' parable of the wedding feast to advocate *encomienda* as part of a just Christian war against New World "barbarians." Reform-minded missionaries led by Bartolomé de Las Casas, a Dominican friar and the bishop of Chiapas in Mexico, condemned *encomienda* as unjust and rejected its biblical defense. In his treatise *In Defense of the Indians* (1550), Las Casas insisted that all three texts were historically conditioned commands superseded by Jesus' teaching of love to neighbors and enemies.

Meanwhile, a new kind of slavery—the importation and ownership of Africans as property—spread quickly in the seventeenth century to Portuguese, Dutch, French, and British colonies in the New World. The Church of England was the legally established religion in the British colonies of Virginia, Barbados, and the Carolinas, but planter elites there guaranteed that Anglican priests neither opposed slavery nor missionized the slaves. Instead, the church used biblical authority to depict Africans as bearers of the mark of Cain and as children of Ham, cursed by Noah to be the "servants of servants" (Gen. 9.25, AV; NRSV: "lowest of slaves"). Anglican support for slavery went largely unquestioned until the 1730s, when Evangelicals in Britain and America launched a new biblical critique of slavery. John Wesley and George Whitefield, founders of Methodism, condemned slaveholding as a grave sin inconsistent with their theology of spiritual rebirth, sanctification, and evangelism. Truly born-again Christians, they taught, will know through the Spirit to free their slaves and evangelize them.

During the Revolutionary era, the major evangelical Calvinist denominations in America—Congregationalists, Presbyterians, and Baptists—joined the antislavery cause. These churches added the argument that slavery violated America's covenant with God as the new chosen people. In his *Dialogue Concerning the Slavery of the Africans* (1776), the Congregationalist Samuel Hopkins established the scriptural ground for this contention by invoking the prophets' vision of justice and mercy, and judgment. At the same time, the Society of Friends in America also undertook a powerful witness against slavery led by the preaching and writing of John Woolman, especially in his *Considerations on the Keeping of Negroes* (1754, 1762) and his *Journal* (1774). Warning that slaveholding was disobedience to the characteristic Quaker doctrines of plainness and peace, Woolman cited Jesus' warnings against materialistic greed and violence toward poor strangers as his principal biblical evidence.

By 1825, however, thriving cotton plantations had revived American slavery, and southern evangelicals, both Methodist and Calvinist, began to construct new biblical arguments justifying Christian slaveholding. A classic example is *A Scriptural View of Slavery* (1856), a sermon by Thornton Stringfellow, a Virginia Baptist, who held that God had sanctioned slavery through Noah, Abraham, and Joseph, that slavery was "incorporated" in the Mosaic law, and that Jesus and the apostles recognized slavery as a "lawful institution among men."

Evangelical abolitionists answered these proslavery arguments in writings like Angelina Grimke's *Appeal to the Christian Women of the South* (1836). Grimke claimed that Hebrew slavery differed in nature and kind from American slavery and therefore could not justify it. In Mosaic law she found six warrants for Hebrew slavery, all more limited than America's chattel slave system, along with substantial legal protections for slaves lacking in American law. Other abolitionists contrasted Greco-Roman and American slavery to obviate the Pauline instruction that slaves obey their masters.

Slaves and free blacks in the antebellum period created their own radical vision of evangelical Christianity, understanding their condition as analogous to Israel in Egypt. African American preachers ceaselessly proclaimed the victorious Exodus as the slaves' destiny here on earth. This oral tradition inspired some leaders, including Gabriel Prosser, Denmark Vesey, and Nat Turner—all Methodists—to lead slave rebellions in the name of God. African American protest found its classic literary voice in David Walker, whose *Appeal to the Coloured Citizens of the World* (1829) arraigned hypocritical evangelical slaveholders for not observing the Christian mandate of peace, calling down on them the judgment of the returning Christ.

Britain abolished slavery peacefully in 1833, but in the United States these disputes over slavery brought Presbyterians, Methodists, and Baptists to schism by 1845, and encouraged the fratricidal Civil War that finally resolved the crisis. One of the chief ironies of the conflict over slavery was the confrontation of America's largest Protestant denominations with the hitherto unthinkable idea that the Bible could be divided against itself. But divided it had been by intractable theological, political, and economic forces. Never again would the Bible completely recover its traditional authority in American culture.

See also African American Traditions and the Bible; Exodus, The.

Stephen A. Marini

SOCIAL SCIENCES AND THE BIBLE. This entry deals with the application of anthropology and sociology to the Bible, and consists of two articles, the first on Cultural Anthropology and the Hebrew Bible, and the second on Sociology of the New Testament.

Cultural Anthropology and the Hebrew Bible

Cultural anthropology as understood in the United States, and its British counterpart social anthropology, is the study of the material culture and the beliefs and social organization of preindustrial societies. Although it did not obtain the status of a distinct discipline until the nineteenth century and did not establish methodological precision until the twentieth, it has a long prehistory, some of which deeply affected the study of the Bible.

Travelers to Palestine, Egypt, and Mesopotamia over many centuries recorded their observations of life and customs in those lands, and these were often used to help interpret biblical texts. Further, the Hebrew Bible contains material that invites speculation of an anthropological nature. How were Israelite tribes organized? How did *sacrifices achieve their desired ends? In the second half of the nineteenth century, when general theories of the evolution of culture and religion were propounded, the Bible was fitted into the resultant schemes. Israelite religion, it was thought, had evolved from animism (belief in spirits) through polytheism to *monotheism, and there had been both a progressive elaboration

of the sacrificial cult, and a spiritualization of that religion in terms of social justice.

These evolutionary schemes were largely abandoned after World War II, but until around 1970 it was commonplace to regard the people of ancient Israel as quasi primitives who knew little about scientific causality, and who thus lived in a mystical and magical world in which any event was potentially a miracle. A variation on this view was that the Canaanites, among whom the Israelites lived, had an essentially magical worldview, whereas Israel had broken with this outlook thanks to God's revelation to them through historical events.

Since 1970 there has been a renewal of interest in social anthropology among biblical scholars, and the work done has been based upon thorough and up-to-date knowledge of anthropological literature. Special attention has been focused on the following areas, each of which will be discussed in turn: Israel's origins and social organization, Israel's classification of the world and its sacrificial system, and the social dimensions of prophecy.

Israel's Origins and Social Organization. Visitors to Arabia and Palestine in the sixteenth through nineteenth centuries were able to observe tribes of bedouin who were predominantly camel nomads. It was understandable that such visitors thought they were seeing people living the same kind of life as Abraham, and many comparisons were made between the bedouin and the people of biblical times. With the rise of theories about the evolution of culture, the early Israelites were described as seminomads, people some way along the road from "pure" nomadism to being fully settled. In the 1930s, it was suggested that the Israelite occupation of Canaan was in fact a largely peaceful process of sedentarization in which Israelite seminomads ceased to move from winter to summer pasturages and settled down in one area.

Recent studies have shown that "pure" nomadism is a late phenomenon in the ancient Near East, and that seminomadism is not a staging post along an evolutionary road from nomadism to being permanently settled. Indeed, settled peoples can become seminomads by being expelled from their lands, or because of small changes in the climate. There is, however, growing agreement that the Israelites were, from the mid-thirteenth century BCE, settled farmers living in villages in the central highlands of Canaan remote from the main cities and loosely associated in an acephalous society, that is, one without a central political organization.

Exactly how Israel came into being in this form is a hotly debated issue. Norman Gottwald has argued that Israelite society was the result of a retribalization process that enabled groups oppressed by the Canaanite city-states to form an alternative, liberated, and egalitarian society. He has focused attention upon the nature of Israelite tribes and of their political organization. Niels Lemche disagrees with Gottwald on anthropological grounds, arguing against the retribalization view and pointing out that acephalous societies are not necessarily egalitarian.

From the viewpoint of the evidence of the Bible, Lemche is probably correct. The lists of "minor judges" in Judges 10.1–5; 12.8–15 indicate that these "judges" (probably the heads of dominant families who arbitrated disputes) had considerable wealth and prestige in return for the responsibilities that they bore. This evidence also militates against another theory, that early Israel was a segmentary lineage society, that is, a society in which power was distributed horizontally among equally ranked segments. This theory has been adopted from the influential book by Christian Sigrist (*Regulierte Anarchie,* 1967), and has been used to explain why opposition to monarchy continued for long after that institution became established in Israel. However, segmentary lineage societies as described by Sigrist have features that can hardly have existed in early Israel, such as indifference to murder within the family groups and avoidance of the inheritance rights of the eldest son. The persistence of opposition to monarchy can best be explained in terms of Jürgen Habermas's theory of conflict between belief systems and social mechanisms of integration. Israelite tribes could well have been simple chiefdoms, ruled by dominant families. Economic and external political pressure combined to make these chiefdoms accept a form of monarchy at the close of the eleventh century BCE, but Israel's belief systems remained critical of the institution for many generations. (*See also* Kingship and Monarchy.)

Israel's Classification of the World and Its Sacrificial System. One of the largest changes in perception of the ancient Israelites brought about by social anthropology has been in relation to "the Hebrew mind." Studies in the early part of the twentieth century suggested that the Israelites were like contemporary "primitives," unable to distinguish clearly the limits of a group or of individuals, and attributing many natural events to supernatural causes. Attempts to explain the logic of sacrifice concentrated upon the psychology of individual Israelites: how did they think that sacrifices achieved their aims? As a result of the structural-functional study of preindustrial peoples, given classical expression in the work of E. E. Evans-Pritchard, a different picture of "primitives" emerged. They were seen to be no less rational than people in industrial societies, provided their overall framework of understanding was appreciated. This framework was articulated in sacred traditions and worked out in social networks and corporate activities.

The application of such an approach to the Hebrew Bible has drawn attention to Israel's classification of reality as detailed in Genesis 1, in the prohibitions of clean and unclean animals (see Purity, Ritual), and in the regulations for dealing with the violation of sacred boundaries in Leviticus generally. It has emerged that, for Israel as for other ancient peoples, *creation meant order: the dividing of reality into distinct spheres such as sky/earth/sea, clean/unclean, life/death, Israel/other nations, holy/profane. To violate these distinctions was to run the risk of offending God, who would withhold his blessing by not sending the rains necessary for producing food. Thus, far from living in a chaotic universe where distinctions familiar to us were not made, the Israelites made distinctions and organized them into a particular worldview. Their difference from us lies not in their supposed inability to divide reality into categories but rather in the organization of the categories. They regarded holy places and objects as the property of the deity, to be approached only by properly designated people. They had a sense that *blood was the property of the deity, that it was not to be eaten, and that it should be carefully handled. This "danger" also inhered in corpses, which no longer strictly belonged to human society, and contact with which required washing with water medicated with special ashes.

Sacrifice has come to be interpreted by scholars not from the viewpoint of the psychology of individual worshipers, but as communal, symbolic action set within the framework of a strongly delineated world. Sacrifices enabled boundaries to be crossed: by priests moving from the ordinary to the sacred and by "lepers" moving from exclusion to acceptance in the community. They removed the defilement believed to infect the sanctuary when offenses occurred for which a sin or guilt offering was required. On the *Day of Atonement, all types of moral uncleanness and social disharmony were identified with a goat, whose journey through the community and out into the desert symbolized and effected the removal of these factors from the society. The view just outlined was not, however, necessarily true for all Israelites in all periods. It is clear that in the premonarchic period there was no priesthood in Israel with exclusive rights, and that the predominant sacrifice was the burnt offering, given as a communal activity on occasions such as preparing to fight a battle. The view of reality and order implied in Genesis 1 and in Leviticus is that of the postexilic community, which was a Temple-based community living in close proximity to Jerusalem. Although the details of sacrifices no doubt contain elements much older than the postexilic community, in their present form they take their meaning from the story of God's deliverance of Israel from slavery in Egypt. Thus, social anthropology can shed light on many details of these rituals, but cannot supply the religious ideology of the traditions in their final form.

The Social Dimension of Prophecy. We often think of prophets as individuals with an abnormal or unusual psychology, despite the evidence that Elijah, Elisha, and Samuel were the heads of prophetic guilds; that Isaiah had a group of disciples; and that Jeremiah was supported by the family of Shaphan. Research into the roles of prophets in many cultures has indicated the importance of support groups and of the expectations that such support groups, as well as the societies in which prophets function, held. David Petersen has suggested two main types of prophets: peripheral prophets and central morality prophets. The former operate on the margins of society, and whose conduct in calling down fire on those who sought to capture him was certainly amoral. Such a description fits well with Elijah, who was a marginal figure at the head of groups of prophets withdrawn from society, and whose conduct in calling down fire on those who sought to capture him was certainly amoral. A good example of a central morality prophet would be Isaiah, who moved in royal circles and who, though critical of the king, also provided support for the state when it was attacked by the Assyrians in 701 BCE. Researches of this kind illustrate the shift that has been noted above—from the study of the psychology of individual prophets to a study of the corporate functioning of social groups and activities. Whereas earlier studies were concerned with the psychology of prophecy, recent study concentrates on its social dimensions. While this is valuable, drawing upon models taken from general observations of social phenomena, it must be noted that such studies illuminate only the outer aspects of the phenomena. As with sacrifice, it is the task of theology to illuminate the distinctive beliefs that formed the basis for the social actions of prophets.

J. W. Rogerson

Sociology of the New Testament

Although it is possible to trace earlier roots, the sociological perspective became embedded in the soil of New Testament studies in the 1970s. Sociology is the disciplined study of social relationships and the changes that occur in them over time. It will be readily seen how the application of the techniques and perspectives of sociology to the New Testament holds much promise for our understanding of it. The disciples of Jesus originated from the rural hinterland of Galilee and served as a renewal sect within Judaism before spreading throughout the Roman world and becoming most successful in the urban environment of Greek civilization.

Sociological explanations should not supplant a theological explanation of the New Testament. Rather, they should complement it, enriching the theological understanding of the text by bringing the real social content and the actual social relationships to the fore. Theological explanations alone too easily become abstract and academic. For example, the tensions in the church at Corinth are usually attributed by theologians either to the presence of incipient *gnosticism or to overrealized *eschatology. Without rejecting the value of such insights, one can also appreciate how the diversity of the social classes that rubbed closely together in a church—unusual for clubs and guilds in Roman society—illuminates the divisions that are mentioned in 1 Corinthians. The "strong" were the socially powerful who would act as hosts at the Lord's table and would see no difficulty in eating meat offered to idols, whereas the "weak" were the poor (1 Cor. 8.1–13; see also Meals).

The application of sociology to the New Testament is not without difficulty. There is danger that the birth and growth of Christianity might be reduced purely to explanation in social terms, and theology might not be given sufficient weight as an independent factor in explanation. Sociology tends to compress unique historical events and processes into general models and recurring patterns. The data with which the sociologist must work are limited and not selected originally for the benefit of the sociologist. Given the limited data, it is tempting to draw parallels between the social behavior of early churches and other contemporary social institutions where such parallels may not be legitimate. Nonetheless, for all the caution that needs to be exercised, a sociological perspective has much value for New Testament studies.

Social Contexts. Several major areas of interest may be identified, though they cannot be distinguished neatly from each other. One is the description of the social context in which the disciples of Jesus came together and developed into a worldwide movement. This is most akin to social history but can never be divorced completely from sociological interpretation. The Roman occupation of Palestine had major political and economic implications for the Jews of that region, many of which are evident in the Gospels (e.g., references to "a house divided against itself"; the existence of beggars, robbers, and absentee landlords; and paying taxes to Caesar). But the presence of Rome also posed major questions for the Jews' self-understanding as the covenant people of God who had a unique destiny in the world. Several movements had offered solutions to that cultural crisis, including the Herodians, the Pharisees, the Essenes, and the Zealots; Jesus offered another that was to meet with a tremendous response.

Contributions have been made to our understanding of specific aspects of Pauline Christianity by describing such features as city life, mobility, the place of women, and the nature of urban Judaism. There is a growing consensus that early Christianity was not a proletarian movement but was very mixed in its social composition. Its members main-

tained their strength and purity through their leadership, through procedures for handling conflicts, rituals of initiation (*baptism) and of solidarity (communion), common beliefs, and common life.

Social Institutions. A second major area of study has been contemporary social institutions. An understanding of the nature and functioning of the household is vital to the interpretation of the leadership, organization, mission, training, place of women, and ethical teaching of early Christianity. The household was a large inclusive unit in which freedmen, slaves, and other dependent families grouped around a principal family. Often these people were economically dependent on the principal family and expressed their solidarity by adopting a common religion. The household structure had an impact even on the entire Roman empire, which saw itself as one vast household. In addition to the household, there were many unofficial associations, guilds, and cults through which people found personal identity and fellowship in the empire.

Social Organization. An extension of that area is the investigation of Christianity as a social organization. The primary understanding of Jesus, in this regard, is to see him as the founder of a millenarian movement. Such movements, frequently found among disinherited people, cater to a desire for change, offer a radically new interpretation of life, and center in a prophet whose role is to bring heaven into being on earth and to vindicate his followers. Although this model when applied to the mission of Jesus has its difficulties, it largely fits and has the merit of rooting the ministry of Jesus in the real social world of his time.

After the death of the charismatic founder, the movement is usually seen in terms of a sect, that is, a small voluntary religious institution with an exclusive membership, clearly separated from the world as well as world-rejecting in outlook. This provides us with a framework for understanding not only the early church in Jerusalem but also some of the developments in structure and theology that took place as it spread and eventually became acceptable to more people.

A number of secondary issues are raised by the study of social organization. In relation to Jesus, these concern the relationship between those who leave everything to follow him and those, such as Mary and Martha, who remain settled in their homes, as well as the structure of the band of twelve disciples. In the study of early Christianity, much has been done to explore the nature of apostolic authority and to set wandering preachers and prophets in the broader context of wandering philosophers of whose style of teaching and means of support we know. The relationship of the Pauline mission, originating in Antioch, to the church of Jerusalem, and this, in turn, to the authority of the original apostles is of special interest here.

Corollary Insights. The sociological insights mentioned so far aid the task of exegesis. But in addition to illuminating particular aspects of the text there is a growing body of literature concerned with sociological redaction. An excellent example is Philip Eschler's work on Luke/Acts, where he demonstrates the way in which the material has been shaped to answer questions posed by the mixed sociological situation of its readers (Jew/gentile, rich/poor, and so on).

A further major area is the tentative offering of sociological explanations for events described in the New Testament. The above-mentioned concept of the millenarian movement, when applied to Jesus is not just a description but ventures toward an explanation as well. John

Gager has also proposed an explanation as to why the dispirited apostles turned into zealous missionaries after the day of *Pentecost. According to the theory of cognitive dissonance, when a specific belief that many hold has been proved wrong (in the case of the early disciples, that Jesus would usher in his kingdom on earth), rather than giving up the belief people lessen their unease (dissonance) by converting others to their way of thinking. The addition of new members suggests to them that they could not have been wrong! Such an explanation is debatable. Less controversial, but still debatable, is the explanation that many joined the Christian movement because of status inconsistency. To be a woman of wealth, or a wealthy Jew in a gentile environment, or a skilled freedman stigmatized by one's origin, involved status contradictions. These could be resolved by joining a church, for there the sufferer would find a welcoming home that would provide an emotional buttress against the loneliness of a status-ridden world. Much is also made of the process of institutionalization and its effect on the development of early Christianity. Such explanations vary in effectiveness but can prove illuminating, provided one does not resort to the view that the growth of Christianity was due to nothing but the operation of such social forces.

A final area may be identified as the sociology of knowledge. Everyone inherits as pregiven an interpretation of the world. But one's experience may raise questions, leading to modification or sometimes even to radical replacement. One's interpretation of life is formed in response to one's social location. Potentially, this is the most enriching perspective: already it has led to a deeper understanding of the way in which the gospel writers variously express the same life of Jesus, to a fuller understanding of the title "*Son of man," and to a fresh understanding of *miracles. The perspective has also been used to relate the "ascent/descent" motif in John's gospel to the social location of John's readers; the idea of homelessness in 1 Peter to those who were literally displaced persons; and the cosmic conflicts of Revelation to the persecuted Christians.

Others have expressed interest in the social functions of literature and in the insights of anthropology. The sociology of the New Testament is a diverse discipline and is still in a youthful stage of development. Some theologians remain skeptical of its value, preferring to tread the well-worn paths of more traditional approaches, but many have welcomed its perspective. As a youthful discipline, it will doubtless make many mistakes, not the least of which will be the mistake of thinking the traffic should all be one-way, from sociology to the New Testament, rather than two-way, enabling our understanding of the New Testament to enrich sociology in general and sociology of religion in particular. But the perspective these approaches offer will be ignored only at great cost to New Testament studies. It cannot be overstressed that the formation of earliest Christianity took place in a real social context and was inhabited by real flesh-and-blood people, not by abstract theologizers.

Derek J. Tidball

SOCIOLOGY AND THE BIBLE.
See Social Sciences and the Bible.

SON OF GOD.
The Hebrew *ben* and Aramaic *bar*, "son," designate not only a male descendant but also a relationship to a community, a country, a species (e.g., animals), etc. "Son of God" can thus mean both a mythological figure of divine origin, a being belonging to the divine sphere (such as an angel), or a human being having a special relationship to a god. In antiquity, son of god was used predicatively of kings begotten by a god (in Egypt) or endowed with divine power (in Mesopotamia). In the Roman period, it also was used in the East as a title for the emperor.

In the Hebrew Bible, sons of God occur in Genesis 6.1–4, where they marry human women and became fathers of the giants (KJV) or Nephilim (NRSV); in Job 1.6; 2.1 (NRSV: "heavenly beings"), where they make up the court of God; and also in Deuteronomy 32.8 (NRSV: "gods") and Psalms 29.1 and 89.6 (NRSV: "heavenly beings"; cf. Psalm 82.6 "sons of the Most High" [NRSV: "children of the Most High"]). Elsewhere, the designation son of God is used especially of the king. Thus, in the primary passage of the Israelite ideology of divine *kingship, it is said of Solomon, "I will be his father, and he will be my son" (2 Sam. 7.14; cf. 1 Chron. 17.13). Neither in 2 Samuel 7.12–14 nor in Psalm 89.26–29 does the designation son of God express anything more than a special relationship; there is no question of deification. This also applies to Psalm 2.7, where God says to the king, "You are my son; today I have begotten you"; "today" rules out a mythological interpretation. The title son of God indicates that the king has his kingdom from God, and the saying belongs to the coronation day or its anniversary.

This manner of speaking of God as a father and the correlative usage, son or sons of God, has also been extended to cover the people of God. In Exodus 4.22 and Jeremiah 31.9, God calls Israel his firstborn son; in Exodus 4.23 and Hosea 11.1 his "son." Correspondingly, in Deuteronomy 32.6, 18 and Jeremiah 3.4, God is called the people's "father," and in Deuteronomy 14.1; 32.5, 19 the Israelites appear as "sons" (and "daughters") of God. Finally, the plural form may designate a special group, like the pious or the priests.

In postbiblical literature, "son of God" designates either the pious or the suffering righteous, while the plural denotes the elect people. Obviously, son of God was not a common messianic title in Judaism before Roman times. Passages like 2 Esd. 7.28–29; 13.32, 37, 52; 14.9, which speak of "my son [the Messiah]," and 1 Enoch 105.2, do not alter this, since both are influenced by the "servant of the Lord" in Second Isaiah. Messianic usage of the expression outside the New Testament from this period does occur in the *Dead Sea Scrolls, as in a fragment of a Daniel Apocryphon from Qumran and in 4Q246, another fragment, which has a close parallel in Luke 1.32, 35. But the fact that the title was used for the king makes it understandable that it could also be applied to the Messiah.

In the New Testament, Son of God (and its abbreviated form, "the Son") is a title often used in christological confessions. From the beginning it seems to have been used in connection with the belief in the *resurrection and exaltation of Jesus. The confessional fragment in Romans 1.3–4 speaks of the gospel "concerning his Son, who was descended from David according to the flesh and was declared to be Son of God with power according to the spirit of holiness by resurrection from the dead." The originally exchangeable expressions Son of David and Son of God are here conferred on the earthly Jesus and the risen Lord, it being presupposed that before his death Jesus was Messiah-designate, and that the resurrection implied a new position. The authors of Acts 13.33 and Hebrews 1.5; 5.5 also

quote Psalm 2.7 in this connection. Yet it is still possible to speak of a special "Son of God" christology insofar as the designation expresses Jesus' unique relationship to God. From an early stage, this belief included the idea of a preexistence and the sending of Jesus to the world. The title seems to have attracted to it ideas connected with wisdom as well.

In the synoptic Gospels we may observe how the title Son of God has penetrated into the traditions about the life of Jesus. In Mark, it is used only by God and the demons; the one time it is used by a human (15.39), the past tense ("was") suggests a distinction between the confession of the centurion to the deceased Jesus, and later on, to the risen Lord. In Matthew we also find it in the confessions of the disciples, in the story of the *temptation, and the story of the mocking at the cross. In Luke, it is mostly found in traditional material; the idea of a *virgin birth probably does not belong here. In John, the Son of God, together with the title the Son, plays a central role in depicting Jesus as being one with the Father.

The origin of the title seems, in the first place, to be Jesus' unique addressing of God as father (see especially Mark 14.36, where the Aramaic *abba is preserved), and second, its connection with kingship ideology in view of the conviction that Jesus was the anticipated son of David. Yet characteristically in the New Testament it stands beside the usage of the phrase sons of God, referring to those whom Jesus has brought to salvation. In the apostolic fathers, the designation describes the divine nature of Jesus as apart from his human nature.

To summarize the evidence in the New Testament, it might be said that the title Son of God primarily expresses Jesus' unique relation to God, while the Lord, the christological title preferred by Paul, emphasizes his position in the church and in the world.

Mogens Muller

SON OF MAN. The self-designation most often used by Jesus in the Gospels. It occurs seventy-two times in the synoptics; two passages are, however, textually uncertain, and if parallels are not counted, the number of different Son of man sayings is forty-three. To these may be added thirteen in the Fourth Gospel. John 12.34, like Luke 24.7, is only an apparent exception to the rule that the expression is always uttered by Jesus himself, the only genuine exception being Acts 7.56. Apart from John 5.27, the designation in all these passages is literally "the son of the man." In the New Testament the undetermined form, "a son of man," is found in Hebrews 2.6 (quoting Ps. 8.5) and in Revelation 1.13 (the exalted Christ) and 14.14 (an angel).

The Son of man sayings in the synoptics fall into two groups, those about the Son of man's mission and his fate on earth together with the passion predictions, and those concerning the position and role of the risen and exalted Son of man and his *parousia. All Son of man sayings are christologically significant. Nevertheless, in the synoptics there are many passages without the expression where textually and linguistically there could be no objection to it, and such passages sometimes have synoptic parallels containing the expression. In the synoptics, there seems to be an increasing monopolization of the expression in sayings of Jesus about his mission, his fate, and his position beyond the resurrection. In the Fourth Gospel the situation is different: here Son of man sayings compete with the "I am" sayings and the

self-designation "the Son." The distinction in usage is always significant; "Son of man" is always used in major statements.

Being central in the Gospel tradition, then, it is no wonder that Son of man is one of the most debated expressions in the New Testament. Its seemingly enigmatic character can be measured by the endless attempts to find an acceptable solution as to its meaning, and despite tendencies apparent in more recent research, it is not accurate to speak of a growing consensus. It is possible, however, to distinguish between two main views: (1) The expression was current and, under certain circumstances, understandable as a messianic title at the time of Jesus. (2) Such usage must be excluded on linguistic grounds alone. There is also the question whether the expression as it now stands in the Gospels is to be understood as a messianic title or not. And in the case of the former, are we to presume a development in meaning from Jesus to the Gospel tradition?

The New Testament itself does not give us the slightest hint as to the meaning of the expression, and there is no evidence for the double-determined form ("the Son of the man") before it appears in the New Testament. In the *Greek of the Septuagint it appears only in the undetermined form, which, similar to the *Hebrew original *ben ʾādām*, conveys a generic meaning synonymous with "man," that is, human being. In the Hebrew Bible, the expression occurs 108 times, 93 of which are in Ezekiel as God's way of addressing the prophet. The *Aramaic equivalent, *bar ʾĕnāš*, occurs only once, in Daniel 7.13, which speaks of "one like a (son of) man." This saying has had a decisive impact on the understanding of Son of man in the New

Testament, and it is quoted or alluded to many times. The imagery of Daniel 7.13–14 may be the foundation of the Son of man sayings relating to the status of the exalted Christ.

Now, "one like a man" in Daniel 7.13 is by no means a messianic figure, but a symbol of the victorious Israel, the kingdom of the saints of the Most High, which succeeded the four world empires. Thus, when we find in 1 Enoch 46–71 and 4 Ezra 13 similar imageries of a son of man or simply a man, these cannot be independent witnesses of a special concept, but uses of the imagery of Daniel to describe a messianic figure. The comprehensive attempt to verify the existence of a special son of man conception, sometimes assumed to be a variant of the ancient Near Eastern myth of the primeval man, universal and transcendent in its outlook (in contrast to the nationalistic and earthly expectation of a Davidic messiah), has obviously failed.

Another question is whether the expression in the Gospels and Acts 7.56 is to be understood as a title. With the exception of Matthew 16.13 and John 9.35, this is possible. On the other hand, the title never occurs in confessions (e.g., Jesus is the Son of man), nor is it used predicatively (Jesus, the Son of man). The determined form must not be taken as a reference to the expression "like a son of man" in Daniel 7.13.

There is, however, yet another possibility. Granted that the Greek form of the expression originates in Aramaic, it may be explained as a direct extension of the idiomatic use of the expression *bar* ʾĕnāš. It is now almost universally agreed that at Jesus' time this expression was in general usage in Galilean Aramaic both as a noun (meaning "a human being") and as a substitute for the indefinite pronoun and as a periphrasis for "I," the actual meaning depending on the context.

The double entendre may express a generalization, meaning "one," "a human," or it may be a self-reference provoked by awe, modesty, or humility, in accord with the content of the actual saying. In that case, the double entendre is deceptive, a near parallel being Paul's way of speaking of himself in 2 Corinthians 12.2–3. It is possible to understand the Gospel Son of man sayings in accordance with this Aramaic idiom. But the double entendre has been done away with by the Greek rendering with its awkward literalness ("the son of the man"), which substitutes an explicit indication of the identity of the subject speaking. This does not mean, however, that the expression has become a title. In the Gospels it is, at the same time, Jesus' periphrasis for "I" and a way to emphasize who is speaking. In other words, it is not the expression "son of man" that tells us who Jesus is, but on the contrary, it is Jesus who tells us who the Son of man is.

It is thus reasonable to suppose that the usage of the expression in the Gospels originates in the way in which Jesus spoke of himself. The question of the genuineness of the individual Son of man sayings must therefore depend on their content: are they understandable in the mouth of the historical Jesus or not? Naturally, the answer will depend upon the individual interpreter's idea of what Jesus believed and preached about himself, and what may be referred to the early community. It seems probable that the sayings about the risen and exalted Son of man and his parousia, depending on Daniel 7.13–14 for their imagery, were created in the process of interpreting the faith in the *resurrection of Jesus, and that they were shaped in analogy to other sayings of Jesus about himself. As indicated by 1 Thessalonians 4.15–17, this interpretation is early and reflects the same tradition expressed later in Mark 13.26 and especially Matthew 24.30–31.

The uncomplicated way in which the expression is used in the Gospels indicates an early foothold in the Greek gospel tradition, which is confirmed by its occurrence also in the Fourth Gospel. In this gospel, one can perceive a beginning of reflection upon its wording, which transcends the purely idiomatic meaning it had in Aramaic. In the apostolic fathers, it is understood as a statement of Christ's human nature and corresponds to the title *Son of God. Later, it is seen as a reference to the figure in Daniel 7.13 and is read as a messianic prophecy. Not until the nineteenth century do we find an attempt to see a specific conception behind the expression.   *Mogens Muller*

SORTES BIBLICAE. In the ancient world, a method of fortune-telling called sortilege was performed by randomly choosing one of several slips on which were written verses of a poet, such as Homer or Virgil *(sortes Homericae* or *sortes Vergilianae).* Another soothsaying system involved randomly opening a copy of Homer's *Iliad* or Virgil's *Aeneid* and interpreting as prophetic the first line upon which the eye settled. Even though Christianity denounced augury and the related practice of sortilege, many continued to use such practices in the early church. A specific type of soothsaying *(sortes biblicae)* pursued by Christians involved using the Bible to divine their destiny by "sacred lots." After randomly opening the Bible and selecting the first line their eyes fell upon, early Christians considered the passage a divine message to be applied to the problem that had caused them to employ such means of divination. The widespread use of *sortes biblicae* is confirmed by its repeated condemnation. For example, in France, the Gallican synods of Vannes (465 CE),

Agde (506), Orléans (511), and Auxerre (570–590) passed ordinances vowing to excommunicate any Christian who "should be detected in the practice of this art, either as consulting or teaching it."

Along with gleaning messages from randomly chosen texts of scripture, early Christians also sometimes consulted specially prepared copies of the Bible, especially the Gospels, to learn their fortunes. In the lower margin of successive manuscript pages there occasionally appear brief comments, before each of which the Greek word *hermēneia* ("interpretation") is written. And so early Christians opened the Bible at random, or even cast dice to determine page numbers, in order to divine their fortunes. Such "interpretations" are found, for example, on eight Greek manuscript copies of John's gospel from the third or fourth century to the eighth century. Similarly, the fifth-century Codex Bezae bears such comments written in the lower margins of the gospel of Mark. Dating perhaps from the ninth or tenth century, these sixty-nine successive short statements include "You will be saved from danger," "Expect a great miracle," "You will receive joy from God," "Seek something else," "After ten days it will happen," and "What you seek will be found." An Old Latin codex of the Gospels of the eighth century is also inscribed along the margins of the gospel of John with a similar collection of sayings.

Sortilege was the influencing factor of St. Augustine's conversion; Augustine himself, however, credits a providential calling. His account *(Confessions* 8.12) reveals that, upon hearing a child's voice urging *Tolle, lege; tolle, lege* ("Take up, read; take up, read"), he opened up a copy of the scriptures and his eyes were drawn to Romans 13.13–14, a passage that caused him to repudiate his former life. Later Augustine looked unfavorably on using the scriptures for divination: "As to those who read futurity by taking at random a text from the pages of the Gospels, it is better that they should do this than go to consult spirits of divination; nevertheless I am displeased with this custom, which turns the divine oracles, which were intended to teach us concerning the higher life, to the business of the world and the vanities of the present life" (*Epistle* 55.20.37).

Undoubtedly, the use of the lot to select Matthias as the twelfth apostle after Judas' suicide, along with the verse "The lot is cast into the lap, but the decision is wholly from the Lord" (Prov. 16:33), stimulated the practice of biblical sortilege. John Wesley and early Methodists were known to take seriously this method of consulting the scriptures, and it is still practiced from time to time in various places.

See also Magic and Divination.
                                 Bruce M. Metzger

SPIRIT, FLESH AND. *See* Flesh and Spirit.

SPIRIT, HOLY. *See* Holy Spirit.

STRUCTURALISM.

Characteristics. Structuralism is interdisciplinary, involving a variety of methods. It is not concerned with the intent of the author, the observable phenomena, or the organization of the text (rhetorical criticism), but with constraints and cultural codes that impose themselves on any speaker or author (deep structures). It studies structure as a totality in which the whole and the parts are integrally related; the fundamental structures are those "below" the surface of the empirical manifestation.

The dichotomy expression/content (signifier/signified) is basic. Structuralism emphasizes the synchronic dimension (the timeless aspect of a text), as opposed to the diachronic aspect, which focuses on its historical development; modern biblical studies have traditionally emphasized the diachronic dimension. The syntagmatic and paradigmatic features of a text are also important. The syntagmatic order, the chainlike manifestation of what precedes and what follows, primarily reflects the intention of the author. A paradigmatic reading presupposes various systems, but manifests only a certain section of these systems or paradigms. Further essential features are the emphasis on fundamental binary oppositions, as well as the challenge to penetrate through the surface structure of spoken discourse *(la parole)* in order to reach the basic laws of language *(la langue)*.

Background and Proponents. The roots of structuralism go back to the linguistic theories of Ferdinand de Saussure (1915) and the influence of the Russian formalists, with their emphasis on linguistics and the poetics of the text, how it is made. Roman Jakobson was influential in the shift in European criticism from Russian formalism to structuralism; he placed the study of poetics within the context of linguistics by describing six basic external factors and corresponding internal functions.

The roots of structuralism can further be traced to anthropology, especially to the pioneering work of Claude Lévi-Strauss. The influence of de Saussure (culture as a generalized version of language-as-system model) and Jakobson (binary opposition) can be detected in his work. He claims that literature gives evidence of the unconscious structuring patterns of society. In myths, the binary oppositions of life are mediated and transformed. So, for example, the opposition between life and death is mediated by the concept of hunting (to kill in order to live). Myth consists of both *langue* (reversible time, the synchronic element) as well as *parole* (nonreversible time, the diachronic element). The meaning of myth is to be found not in the intrinsic content of the actions but rather in the combination of the synchronic and diachronic elements.

Structuralism is also related to three different streams of literary studies: Russian (Vladimir Propp), French (Roland Barthes and A. J. Greimas), and American. Barthes was one of the most important proponents of structuralism, though he later abandoned this approach. For him there is no antithesis between history and structure: the structure of the sentence serves as a model for the structure of discourse. Barthes abandons the inductive model and opts for a deductive approach, seeing a text as a homogeneous unit. He proceeds with a sequential analysis (division of the text into basic units), as well as a structural analysis of sequences. Barthes distinguishes three levels of narrative structure: functions (Propp), actions (Greimas), and narration (Tzvetan Todorov). He concentrates on a specific text, underlining its plurality of meanings, rather than inferring common structures from a number of texts.

Greimas, with his deductive and scientific methodology, is concerned not with the meaning of the text as such but rather with the semantic structures underlying the narrative. Three levels of text are to be distinguished. The level of manifestation concentrates on performance, the competence of the author as it is realized in the empirical text. The level of narrative structure deals with functions (Propp) and actants, as well as the axes of communication, volition, and power. On the discursive or thematic level, isotopies as levels of coherence constructed from classemes allow the reader to discern the interaction of various levels of meaning. Paradigmatic meaning is related not in a syntagmatic manner to the context of the rest of the sentence but rather, in a binary or ternary fashion, to oppositions of meaning.

Structuralism and Biblical Studies. In 1961 Edmund Leach was the first to apply the approach of Lévi-Strauss to the text of Genesis 1–3, explicating myths that are the product of universal structures of human thought, involving binary oppositions and their reconciliation. Lévi-Strauss himself did not consider this exercise to be successful. In a comparison made by Leach of Jesus and John the Baptist, he points out various parallel and opposite features. Beneath the surface structure of the text, which seems to deal with Jesus, the geological substratum of universal structure deals with humankind.

Roland Barthes addressed the account of Jacob's struggle with the angel (Gen. 32.22–32). He emphasizes the element of ambiguity and paradox in the Genesis account, and shows how imagining a countertext can illuminate the narrative. He also uses the actantial model of Greimas: Barthes takes this narrative to be typical of a common Russian folk-narrative in which a hostile spirit guards a difficult passage over a ford.

Jean Calloud applied the methodology of Greimas to Matthew 4.1–11. First, a syntactic or narrative analysis is given of the lexies of the text, as well as its functional and actantial schemes. Jesus is the Receiver of a mandate given by the Spirit. The devil as Sender then sends tests to Jesus. The Word as Helper gives assistance to Jesus. In the glorifying test Jesus proves to be the Hero. The consequent semantic analysis deals with the paradigmatic aspect of the text. The functioning of the semantic contents, skillfully woven around the two main actors Jesus and Satan, is then interrelated with the analysis of the narrative structure.

Robert C. Culley is more interested in the "syntagmatic" narrative structures, the linear and rhetorical tradition, the repetition of patterns in seven miracle stories from the Hebrew Bible. Jean Starobinski's analysis of Mark 5.1–20 is also an example of a purely synchronous reading of the text from a literary point of view. He demonstrates the oppositions in the text between the unchanging singularity of Jesus and the pluralization of the demoniac.

The approach of Erhardt Güttgemanns is called generative poetics or linguistic theology. He sees a particular text as the result of grammatical rather than historical forces. Generative poetics is a deductive method, which aims to free theology from its traditional confinement by means of a scientific and interdisciplinary approach. The narrative analysis is interested not in the performance text but in the deep text, the underlying semantic content of the narrative. This is arrived at by way of two separate analyses, a motifemic and an actantial analysis.

Daniel Patte, applying the methodology of Lévi-Strauss to biblical texts, aims to study the symbolic and connotative dimension of language, which should be distinguished from the informational dimension of language. By describing the system of convictions and symbolic values of the authors of biblical texts, structural exegesis aims to open up hermeneutic possibilities.

In his analysis of Galatians 1.1–10, Patte shows that mythical structures can be discovered in nonmythical texts. In Galatia there is a conflict between two mythical structures—the gospel of Paul

and the antigospel of his opponents. By a syntagmatic reading, the text is tentatively deconstructed into elements of a mythical system. By a subsequent paradigmatic reading, the structure that governs these mythical elements is discerned: through the mediating of the oppositions of this mythical structure, it becomes clear that Christ is the mediation of the fundamental opposition between the divine and the human.

In his structural introduction to the letter, Patte deals with Paul's faith as a system of convictions. Faith and theology are to be distinguished in the light of semiotic and structural research. In order to describe Paul's faith, attention is given to the convictional pattern that underlies and validates his arguments, as well as to the motivating factors presupposed.

Discourse Analysis. Besides analyzing the universal "deep" structures of a text (as described above), more attention should be given to the "surface" structure, and to the function of a text's stylistic, organizational, and rhetorical features. This implies an awareness of the importance of different discourse patterns in the text as a whole. The text must therefore be mapped in a way that will allow us to discern the syntactic, semantic, and pragmatic relationships of the various constituent parts. This approach includes attention to the inter- and extratextual dimensions of the text.

Building on the metatheory of structural semiotics of Greimas, Patte has recently proposed a six-step method incorporating the main features of different structural exegetical methods. Through a multiplicity of underlying structures, the reader is guided to a close reading of the surface structure of the text. In this way, the specific features of a discourse unit as well as the basic convictions of the author are conveyed.

Evaluation. On the negative side, one can point to the lack of unity and clarity among proponents, their neologisms, and the methodological complexity. Although the universal dimensions and internal relations of a text are emphasized, the more specific forms of a given culture or of the biblical text are often played down. The message becomes only a quotation of the underlying code, and specific saving acts of God are reduced to general truths. The methodology of Propp, devised for the description of Russian folktales, cannot simply be applied to the Bible, for the folktales do not have universal validity. Lévi-Strauss himself had reservations about applying his approach to the Bible. Without detracting anything from the grammaticality and literality of the text, the specific context of the Bible should also be taken into account.

On the positive side, structuralism can be an aid to biblical exegesis and *hermeneutics within the context of semiotics. A text and its structural analysis collectively form a sign-system. Codes should not be deemed more important than the message itself; therefore adequate emphasis should be given to the surface structure of the text. Attention to deep structures underlines the depth of meaning and the coherence of different books. The synchronic approach serves as a corrective to the one-sided emphasis of the genetic (diachronic) paradigm. The integrity of the text as object is emphasized.

The critic/reader acquires a new role in the process of reading the text. Structuralism and hermeneutics can be complementary when the text is seen again as message, *parole.* While structuralism reveals the multiplicity of readings, it also controls them by means of a structural analysis of the text. Hermeneutics limits the possibilities by confronting the ver-

tical aspect of meaning (diachronic) with the synchronic coexistence of meanings.

See also Interpretation, History of, *article on* Modern Biblical Criticism.

H. J. Bernard Combrink

SUFFERING. Like prosperity, suffering introduces a test into human lives, both disclosing and forming character. For religious people, suffering comes as a special trial, particularly its unjust distribution. Belief in the goodness and power of God implies a just distribution of misery. When good persons experience undeserved suffering, it becomes difficult to maintain the conviction that God controls a universe that operates on a principle of reward and retribution. One biblical response to this dilemma was daring: chosen individuals voluntarily take upon themselves the suffering of the guilty. Less bold, but also significant, is the view that suffering offers an opportunity to learn something worthwhile, especially patience.

The world of suffering is special, causing everyone to think that the experience of pain is unique and consequently focusing the ego inward, which heightens self-centeredness. Suffering takes place in solitude, isolating one from the community and generating a sense of alienation. At the same time, suffering strives toward the building of community, for its power extends from the greatest to the least. Genuine sympathy is possible precisely because others have felt pain and isolation. Hence the language of suffering is readily comprehended by all who are searching for meaning in a hostile world.

In ancient literature suffering was often expressed in lyrical poetry. Emotion-laden speech tends to exaggerate, but even such hyperbole fails to evoke the full range of feelings in suffering. Personal pronouns abound in laments, focusing remembered joy and present pain, individualizing both in a powerful manner. Simile and *metaphor call attention to language's poverty in describing the misery resulting from invasion from outside by hostile forces.

Drawing on ancient insights from Mesopotamia to some degree, biblical attempts to explain suffering throw considerable light on the problem, although failing to clarify the mystery altogether. An early explanation seized the partial truth (well articulated much later by Paul in Rom. 7.15) that most individuals do *evil even when willing good, and hence suffering is in a very real sense punishment for sin. The book of Proverbs regularly insists on this retributive understanding of evil, and the same view is shared by the Deuteronomic history and by Israel's prophets. When reportedly offered an opportunity to endorse this view of suffering, Jesus refused to do so (John 9.3). Job's friends appealed to parental discipline of children, assuming by analogy that God punishes those who enjoy divine favor. The profound story about the divine test of Abraham (see Aqedah) and the prologue to the book of Job suggest that adversity may indicate a divine test to which God's "favorites" are submitted.

Confidence in God's integrity and character resulted in an *eschatological hope that deliverance would come in the end, setting all things right. *Apocalyptic literature found this view compatible because of the extreme suffering of the periods in which it arose. Injustice could elicit the daring hope in survival beyond earthly existence (see Afterlife and Immortality). In some circles suffering was seen as redemptive, both for self and for others. Doxologies of judgment dared to praise God in the face of execution, and the "servant poems" in Second Isaiah envisioned the death of their leader as

vicarious, a view that Christians shared in reflecting on Jesus' passion.

In some instances biblical writers thought of suffering as transitory, resulting from an illusion that resembles a dream, while others believed that God's revelatory presence in suffering compensated adequately for any amount of misery. The astonishing conclusion to the dialogue in the book of Job acknowledges a seeing of God that corrects hearsay information and leaves the sufferer speechless but content. At the same time, the poet admits that an adequate answer to Job's suffering cannot be offered, and hence the mystery remains. A wholly different response occurs in Ecclesiastes, in which the author accuses the distant, divine despot of indifference to the human suffering that distresses him, a mere human being.

Both Judaism and Christianity find the problem of suffering especially acute because of their elevated view of God as ethical, that is, their belief in theodicy. These religions further suggest that suffering is not merely a human phenomenon, for God also suffers because of rebellion on the part of men and women. The prophets emphasized divine pathos, and Christianity adopted this understanding of God. The suffering of Christ manifests the divine response to evil, culminating in victorious *resurrection. Christians are called on to enter into the suffering of Christ for the sake of the Kingdom.

Suffering, therefore, is rooted in divine mystery, and at the same time it is profoundly human. God's redemption of the world employs suffering in its numerous forms to enable persons to recognize their own humanity and to acknowledge their true selves. As a result of this divine pedagogy, suffering offers potential for enriching faith and life itself. Nevertheless, some suffering, by its very intensity, lacks this positive dimension, introducing destructive powers that ultimately triumph over its victim. In the face of this kind of suffering, believers find their faith tested to the limit. Neither Judaism nor Christianity has denied the existence of such suffering, nor did they trivialize it by offering simple answers. Instead, moving beyond tragedy, they insisted that evil is under the dominion of God.   *James L. Crenshaw*

SUMER. Shumer (conventionally: Sumer) is the name given to the lower Mesopotamian plain by its Akkadian neighbors; in its own Sumerian language, the land was called Kengir. It occupied the area between the city of Nippur in the northwest and the shoreline of the Persian (or Arabian) Gulf in the southeast; upstream from Nippur lay the land of Akkad. Together, Sumer and Akkad occupied all the land between the rivers Euphrates and Tigris below their nearest convergence around modern Baghdad. In this relatively constricted area (the later Babylonia), there arose not only the world's first civilization but also one of its great ancient cultures, destined to influence all Near Eastern cultures, including Israel, and to bequeath a lasting legacy to civilization as a whole.

The origin of the Sumerians is uncertain. They themselves looked to Dilmun, that is, the islands and Arabian shore of the Persian Gulf, as a kind of paradise, and may have originated from there, or even further east. They regarded Eridu, then on the northern edge of the Gulf, as their first city, and perhaps this was indeed their first foothold in Mesopotamia. Traces of this tradition survive in Genesis 4.17b, which may be understood thus: "And he [Enoch] became the [first] builder of a city, and he named it after his son [i.e., Irad], did Enoch."

The basic ingredients of civilization as it emerged in Sumer at the end of the fourth millennium BCE included cities, *writing, and the formation of capital. Building on the earlier agricultural revolution and its domestication of plants and animals (symbolized in the biblical account by Cain and Abel respectively), the urban revolution in Sumer soon brought in its train such secondary developments as craft specialization, metallurgy, and the emergence of *kingship. A rich documentation in cuneiform preserves the records of these achievements as well as the Sumerians' own interpretation of them in literary texts. Long after Sumerian itself had ceased to be spoken, these literary texts continued to be studied and translated in the scribal schools of Babylonia and the rest of the Near East. Some of them are thus echoed in the Bible, whose primeval history is situated in Sumer.

The centerpiece of Sumerian historiography is the "Sumerian King List," perhaps better described as a Sumerian city list, which records the eleven cities that exercised hegemony over all of Sumer and Akkad, together with the names of their kings, their length of rule, and occasional biographical notes. It begins in legendary times, when kingship "descended from heaven," and ends with the destruction of the city of Isin in 1794 BCE, one year before the accession of King Hammurapi of Babylon. Its antediluvian rulers, in most recensions eight in number, and the wise counselors associated with them (in other sources), bear an undeniable resemblance to the lines of Seth and Cain in Genesis 5 and 4 respectively.

The Sumerian story of the *flood is preserved in a single fragmentary tablet that, via various Akkadian intermediaries, no doubt helped shape the biblical version in Genesis 6–8. After the flood, kingship was believed to have come down from heaven again, first to the city of Kish and then to Uruk, the Erech of the "table of nations" (Gen. 10.10). Its fourth ruler, Dumuzi, is celebrated in poems about his sacred marriage with the goddess Inanna, and passed into Akkadian—and Hebrew—as the deified Tammuz. The epic of "Enmerkar and the lord of Aratta" includes a passage reminiscent of the biblical tale of the confusion of tongues that, in Genesis 11, is linked to the building of "a city and a tower" clearly modeled on the ziggurat (stepped temple tower) characteristic of Sumerian cities. The end of the "Early Dynastic Period" in Sumer (ca. 2900–2300 BCE) is marked by the conflict of two other city-states (Lagash and Umma) over the *edin,* a fertile area lying between them that may have inspired the biblical tale of the garden of Eden.

There followed an interval of subjugation to the Semitic-speaking Akkadians (ca. 2300–2150 BCE), so named after the city of Akkad whose greatest rulers, Sargon and especially his grandson Naram-Sin, may conceivably have provided the model for Nimrod and Akkad in Genesis 10.8–12. Then the Sumerians reasserted themselves under local rulers such as Gudea of Lagash, who left a magnificent legacy of both literary and sculptural remains, and under the hegemony of Ur, which reunited all of Sumer and Akkad for a century (ca. 2100–2000 BCE) under the city recalled in the Bible as the birthplace of Abraham.

After the fall of Ur (ca. 2000 BCE), Sumerian traditions were preserved intact by the dynasty of Isin (ca. 2000–1800 BCE) and thereafter by the schools and temples of Babylonia and Assyria. Among the Sumerian innovations thus passed on to later ages are the sexagesimal system of counting and computation (using the base 60), irrigation agriculture, and a variety of literary genres.

The Akkadian language, and the civilization of the Babylonians and Assyrians who inherited and preserved Sumerian culture, transmitted the Sumerian legacy, or portions of it, to posterity. Among the heirs of this legacy was biblical Israel. While the name of Sumer itself is no longer thought to lurk behind the biblical Shinar, other Hebrew words and names can be traced to Sumerian, such as *hêkāl* ("palace, temple"), *tipsār* ("scribe"), *mallāh* ("sailor"), and numerous names of spices, plants, minerals, and other commodities whose names traveled with the products they identified. Many ideas too can be traced from their biblical formulation back to Sumerian origins, for example the casuistic (conditional) formulation of precedent *law. When the Bible placed the origins of (civilized) humankind, and of Israelite prehistory, in the lower valley of the Tigris and Euphrates, it was anticipating the modern rediscovery of the Sumerians and their formative contributions to civilization.   *William W. Hallo*

T

TABERNACLE. The portable sanctuary constructed by Moses at Sinai and primarily associated with the people's wilderness wandering. Various expressions are used in referring to this sanctuary—"tent," "tent of meeting," "tabernacle," "tabernacle of the testimony [NRSV: covenant]." Conceived as a movable shrine, the tabernacle was constructed so that it could be assembled, dismantled, and reassembled as the people moved from one place to another.

The account of the construction of the tabernacle is found in the book of Exodus: in chaps. 25–31, God provides instructions to Moses for its construction, and chaps. 35–40 report how these were carried out. Included in these texts are directions for the construction of the cultic furniture used in conjunction with the tabernacle. These include the *ark, the table of showbread, the lampstand or *menorah, the altar of burnt offering, the altar of *incense, and the bronze basin. In addition, directions are given for preparing priestly garments, for ordaining Aaron and his sons as priests, for collecting the sanctuary tax, for mixing the anointing oil and incense, and for other matters associated with the ritual of the tabernacle.

The tabernacle and its furnishings were made of materials and with labor contributed voluntarily by members of the community under the supervision of Bezalel of the tribe of Judah and Oholiab

of the tribe of Dan. The tabernacle complex was rectangular in shape, measuring 100 by 50 cubits. The exact dimensions expressed in modern equivalents are uncertain, since the length of the ancient cubit (the distance from the point of the elbow to the end of the middle finger) remains in doubt; estimates range from 17.5 to 20.4 in (45 to 52 cm). The approximate dimensions of the sanctuary were 105 × 75 ft (32 × 23 m). The complex was oriented so that the short sides faced east and west with a 20-cubit entrance on the east protected by the embroidered screen.

The tabernacle was divided into three distinct zones of increasing *holiness: the courtyard, the holy place, and the holy of holies. The courtyard was divisible into two 50-cubit squares. The eastern square contained the altar of burnt offering where *sacrifices and offerings were burned (5 × 5 × 3 cubits), located at its center, and the basin, to the west of the altar, which held water for the priests to wash their hands and feet before officiating. The western square contained the tent of meeting or tabernacle proper. This was a separate enclosure measuring 30 × 30 × 10 cubits subdivided into the holy place (20 × 10 × 10 cubits) and the holy of holies (10 × 10 × 10 cubits).

Located within the holy place were the table of showbread (2 × 1 × 1.5 cubits) situated on the north side, the menorah on the south side, and the altar of incense or golden altar (1 × 1 × 2 cubits) located between the table and lampstand immediately in front of the veil to the holy of holies. Every *Sabbath twelve freshly baked loaves were placed on the table, arranged in two rows. The lamps on the menorah were lit each evening by the high priest and allowed to burn all night. Every morning and evening, at the time when the lamps of the menorah were tended, the high priest burned incense on the golden altar.

The holy of holies, separated from the holy place by an embroidered curtain, housed only the ark (2.5 × 1.5 × 1.5 cubits) containing the "testimony" (Exod. 25.21; 40.20), assumed to be the tablets of the *Law. A special lid or "mercy seat" covered the top of the ark and was ornamented with two cherubim whose outspread wings overarched the cover and touched one another. The covering of the ark was the place where God promised to meet and communicate with the representative of the community. Only the high priest was to enter the holy of holies.

The entire courtyard of the enclosure with its perimeter of 300 cubits, with the exception of the entryway, was surrounded by hangings of twisted linen, 5 cubits high, hung on upright posts placed at intervals of 5 cubits. The inner rectangle, the tabernacle proper, was enclosed, except on the eastern end, by forty-eight wooden frames. The assembled frames were overlaid first by a covering of sheets of linen and then by a covering of goats' hair curtains, which was overlaid by a covering of tanned ram skins.

Gradations of holiness are reflected in the layout, building materials, and use of the tabernacle enclosure. The less holy area, the outer courtyard, was open to the laity, and the metal associated with its construction was bronze. Only priests and Levites were admitted to the holy place in which the items were overlaid with gold (except for the menorah, which was of pure gold). The contents of the holy of holies were gold-plated outside and inside (the ark) or else were of pure gold (the mercy seat). The sacredness of the entire precinct is evident from the command that the priests and Levites should camp between the tabernacle and the tents of the tribes on their journeys in the wilderness.

The tabernacle was the place where God was present among his people, where he met with them and communicated with them. The symmetry and wholeness of the tabernacle were reflective of the unity and perfection of God and of the divine relationship to *creation. Note the association of the construction of the tabernacle with the Sabbath and the presence of six formulas of divine address to Moses dividing the material into six units, thus paralleling the six days in the account of creation in Genesis 1.1–2.3.

Questions have been raised about whether an edifice as elaborate as the tabernacle existed in the wilderness. Scholars have pointed to a number of difficulties. Could the Israelites, newly out of slavery in Egypt, have possessed the necessary artistic skills to produce such a structure when later Solomon had to hire the Phoenicians to build the Jerusalem Temple? Would they have had sufficient precious metals, gems, and fabrics to make the cultic furniture and priestly garments? (Estimates indicate the need for at least 1 ton [1,000 kg] of gold, 3 tons [3,000 kg] of silver, and 2.5 tons [2,500 kg] of bronze.) Could such a massive and heavy structure have been dismantled and reassembled with any practicability? Why is there no mention of carrying the tabernacle across the Jordan in the account of the entry into the Promised Land and such infrequent reference to the structure in the narratives after the entry? How is the tabernacle, situated in the center of the tribal camp and guarded by thousands of Levites, related to the wilderness tent that was pitched outside the camp, guarded by a single individual, and used to communicate with the deity? Such questions have led to the theory that the tabernacle was an idealized version of the Jerusalem Temple projected back into the wilderness and that the portable shrine was much simpler.

In support of the historicity of the tabernacle or at least some modified version of it, scholars have pointed to the use of portable shrines among other cultures, especially Arab Bedouin cultures; to the fact that Egyptian armies camped encircling the sacred tent and artifacts associated with the Pharaoh; and to the "despoiling of the Egyptians" as a source of the wealth required for the tabernacle.
John H. Hayes

TARGUMS. *See* Translations, *article on* Targums.

TAXATION. *See* Tribute and Taxation.

TEMPTATION. In biblical traditions, temptation is generally a test or trial to which the tempter subjects another person, often by confusing what is good with what is evil. Along with strength of will, the capacity to discern good is being tested, and the tester is usually the God of Israel or occasionally the adversary, Satan. Less frequent is the understanding of temptation as the conscious desire of individuals to do what they know to be wrong, though this does occur.

In the Hebrew Bible, the most fa-

mous example of God setting a specific trial for an individual is the testing of Abraham (*see* Aqedah). Another is God's permission to Satan to put Job to the test. In the New Testament, God is likewise the ultimate initiator of the temptation of Jesus (*see* Temptation of Christ) for it is the Spirit that drove Jesus into the wilderness, where Satan's offers would serve as a maximum test of Jesus' discernment and courage. Similarly, God is pictured as setting tests for Jesus' followers.

The Bible also speaks of putting God to the test. Israel presumes that because God has delivered it from earlier crises, he will do so again. Evildoers challenge God to punish them, but they escape unscathed. The same language is used in the New Testament, where Jesus refuses to test God; Christians may test him by their improper conduct.

A larger role is assigned to Satan in the New Testament than in the Hebrew Bible. God uses Satan to tempt people; Satan uses them to tempt God. The afflictions believers suffered because of their faith were often understood as an opportunity for the tempter. This provides a background for interpreting the climactic petitions designed by Jesus for his followers as they faced persecutions. These petitions can be understood as asking, "Father . . . do not bring us to the time of trial by the Evil One, but rescue us from his power" (*see* Lord's Prayer). It was because Jesus had also been tempted that he was able to help those struggling against the same foe.
Paul S. Minear

TEMPTATION OF CHRIST. Each of the synoptic Gospels gives an account of the temptation of Christ, and all three place the temptation within the same sequence, following Jesus' *baptism by John, and preceding the first statement of Jesus' preaching of the *kingdom of God. Luke has interrupted the sequence with the insertion of Jesus' *genealogy, but the common themes of Spirit and Sonship together with the geographical reference establish the close connection between Luke's baptism story and his account of the temptation.

This agreement in sequence should not hide the fact that we have two very different types of narrative in Mark, on the one hand, and in Matthew and Luke, on the other. Mark includes the temptation in a single sentence that is more a cryptogram than a narrative, while Matthew and Luke write of three scenes in which a minimum of action provides the setting for three verbal exchanges between Jesus and Satan, all of which center in quotations from Deuteronomy 6 and 8 (from the Septuagint). The quotations are the climax of each scene so that the narrative as a whole resembles a midrash. The stories cannot be derived one from the other; they represent the literary result of two different traditions about Jesus' temptation, and efforts to interpret them should refrain from harmonizing one version with the other.

Both narratives combine topics that had grown through centuries of Israelite and early Jewish tradition. They had, therefore, become so rich in associations with traditional themes that the expositor is faced with a wide array of interpretive possibilities, and no single governing theme can do justice to them.

Mark includes the temptation in a single, terse statement (1.13): "He was in the wilderness forty days, tempted by Satan; and he was with the wild beasts; and the angels waited on him." There is no narrative or dialogue; no fasting is mentioned; but Jesus is placed in the presence of wild beasts, which goes beyond the record of Matthew and Luke. The forms of the four verbs are suffi-

ciently ambiguous to leave unclear whether they comprise a sequence of episodes or are simultaneous aspects of one event. There are two major interpretations of Mark's cryptic sentence: Jesus as the second Adam who restores *paradise, and Jesus as the protagonist in God's struggle against Satan. Both rely on Jewish adaptations of biblical themes.

According to the first, the temptation is only one motif alongside others, which renders it doubtful whether Mark 1.13 is exclusively a temptation story. The picture of a peaceful coexistence of humans with wild animals is a well-attested eschatological theme, and the idea of service of angels to Adam and Eve in paradise is found in Jewish tradition. According to the principle that the world to come would restore the conditions of the original creation, ideas about creation and about the end time became interchangeable. The introduction of the wilderness and the temptation by Satan does not necessarily provide a discordant note to the image of paradise restored, because satanic temptation is an element of the story of Adam and Eve (Gen. 3; the identification of the serpent with Satan had already been made), and the wilderness is a place not only of horror and judgment but also of ultimate restoration. The coordination of three (or four?) equal motifs therefore provides a reading of Mark 1.13 that sees Jesus, in consequence of his declaration as God's Son in his baptism and prior to the beginning of his public activity, as the new Adam who triumphs over Satan (in contrast to the first Adam) and thereby inaugurates a promised new condition in which wild animals are no longer a threat and the angels render service.

The alternate understanding of Mark 1.13 relies more on a similarity to the accounts of the temptation in Matthew and Luke: the forty days are part of a *typology alluding to Israel's forty years in the desert, the wilderness is the haunt of demons and terrifying animals, and the service of the angels is regarded as the resolution of the conflict after the devil's departure. This assumes that the motifs of the wild animals and the angels are subordinate to that of the wilderness, which represents the time and the place controlled by powers hostile to God. Mark 1.13 thus presents Christ as the protagonist of God's fight against satanic forces, who invades the stronghold of the enemy and thus overcomes him.

Matthew and Luke differ in the order of the second and third temptations and in some details, but generally the content of their three temptation scenes is the same, so that a common tradition behind them (Q?) must be assumed. Since the vocabulary in Luke, where he differs from Matthew, shows clear traces of Lucan style, and since Luke's sequence of the scenes can be explained by his tendency to emphasize the crucial role of Jerusalem, it is probable that Matthew preserves the more original order and wording. The following comments are therefore based on the Matthean order. Matthew's scenes shift from the wilderness to the Temple and finally to a very high mountain, each culminating in Jesus quoting Deuteronomy (8.3, 6.16, and 6.13, respectively, all close in content and position to the *Shema, whose first part contains Deut. 6.4–9).

Attempts have been made to understand the whole temptation story in Matthew as a logically constructed unit with one organizing idea. This has been variously described as the demand of Deuteronomy 6.5 to love God with one's whole heart, soul, and might, so that the tripartite division of human faculties is explicated in the three episodes of Jesus' temptation, describing him as

one who lives in total dedication to the one God of Israel; or the fullness of the messianic office, which combines a prophetic messiah (Moses in the wilderness, the prophet par excellence according to Deut. 18.18), a priestly messiah (the Temple as center of the priestly office), and a political messiah (world dominion offered on the mountain), each episode containing a strong antithesis to popular conceptions of these messianic offices; or a thoroughgoing Israel-typology that coordinates the climactic quotation in each scene of the temptation with an analogous situation in Israel's wilderness sojourn, patterned after the textual sequence in the Exodus story (Deut. 8.3–Manna–Exod. 16; Deut. 6.16–provocation of God at Massah–Exod. 17; Deut. 6.13–promise of land, warning against idolatry–Exod. 23.20–33; 34.11–14), portraying Jesus as the true Israelite who did not yield to temptation precisely at the point of Israel's failure.

Each of these unifying interpretations draws on a wealth of pertinent evidence in Jewish tradition, but none is conclusive. A variety of complex motifs coalesce, forming a confessional narrative in which four intentions merge. First, the title *Son of God binds together baptism and temptation; the baptism of Jesus culminates in his being declared Son of God, the temptation describes the cost of this Sonship. Second, in the temptation narrative Jesus is presented as the authentic interpreter and doer of God's will in scripture. Third, the dominance of the title Son of God marks the temptation as a christologically and soteriologically oriented narrative. Finally, factually, and perhaps intentionally, the story implies a radical criticism of popular conceptions about the eschatological agent of God. The true Son of God does not abuse his status for self-preservation, he refrains from using his power for protection against death, and he refuses to exercise world dominion in any form other than that bestowed on him by God in consequence of his death and resurrection.   *Ulrich W. Mauser*

TEN COMMANDMENTS.

Also called the Decalogue ("the ten words"; see Exod. 34.28), the Ten Commandments comprise a short list of religious and ethical demands laid by the Deity on the people of ancient Israel and are of continuing authority for the religious Jewish community and the Christian community. They appear in two places in the Bible (Exod. 20.1–17 and Deut. 5.6–21) and are alluded to or quoted in part in several places in the Hebrew Bible and the New Testament.

The commandments prohibit the worship of any God other than Israel's God, held to be the true God of the other nations as well (*see* Monotheism). They rule out the making of images of the Deity in any plastic form (*see* Graven Image; Idols, Idolatry); the misuse of the divine Name and the power associated with it; and they require observance of the *Sabbath day and the honoring of one's parents (especially in view are the elderly parents of adults, not the parents of young children). They also prohibit *murder, *adultery, stealing, false testimony (not primarily the telling of untruths in general), and the coveting of the life and goods of others.

The enumeration of the commandments varies among the religious communities. Worshiping other Gods and making images of the Deity are placed together in a number of religious communities (Jewish, Roman Catholic, Lutheran), while Reformed and Orthodox Christian communities treat these as the first two commandments. For the Jewish community, the first commandment is "I am the Lord your God who brought you out of the land of Egypt, out of the house of bondage," while the ninth and tenth commandments for Roman Catholic and Lutheran communions are the two prohibitions of coveting: the household (commandment 9) and the remainder of the list in Exod. 20.17 (commandment 10). The contents of the Ten Commandments are, however, the same for all of the religious communities, despite the differences in their enumeration. The differences between the contents of Exodus 20 and Deuteronomy 5 are quite small, reflecting changes over time in the way in which the commandments were understood and applied.

The commandments are of enormous value and influence—on the community of Israel, within the Christian community, and throughout the entire world today. The commandments fall into four groups. The first three, the commandments demanding the worship of God alone, against image-making, and against the use of God's name to do harm, are commandments stressing God's exclusive claim over the lives of the people. God will brook no rivalry; as Israel's savior, God demands a commitment that preserves the people from divided loyalties, protects them from supposing that anything in the whole of creation could adequately represent the Deity, the Creator of all, and also protects persons from the religious community's misuse of divine power to serve its own ends.

The next two commandments, calling for observing every seventh day as a day of rest and for honoring parents even when they might no longer be of significant economic value within the community, are special institutions for the protection of basic realities in society—human need for rest from labor as well as for labor and the preservation of human dignity against any kind of exploitation.

The next three commandments focus especially on the life of the individual or the family in the larger community. They insist on the sanctity of human life, the sanctity of marriage and of sexual life, and the necessity to maintain a community in which the extension of the self into one's property is recognized and respected.

The last two commandments are more social and public, calling for speaking the truth before the courts or the community's elders and for living a life not distorted or corrupted by the lust for other persons' goods or lives.

Moses is identified as the great lawgiver in ancient Israel. The Ten Commandments are understood by the community to have been handed down from God through Moses. It is clear, however, that the legal materials of the Hebrew Bible have developed over centuries, reflected changes in religious understanding and practice, and incorporated those changed perspectives into the legal heritage assigned to Moses and to Moses' God.

The substance of the Ten Commandments probably does originate in the work and discernments of Moses. The unique understanding of idolatry reflected in the Ten Commandments, and the requirement that one day in seven be characterized by an absolute break with the other days—by cessation from normal pursuits for a full day—these are without precedent in the ancient Near Eastern world. Other commandments are not unique, but this tenfold collection of short, primarily negative, statements is unique. It stems from a person of extraordinary religious discernment—and Moses was such a person.

The Ten Commandments probably had a place in family life, as a means by which the young were introduced to the fundamental requirements of the covenant between God and people. They also had a place in public religious life and in the great festivals when the bond between people and God was regularly reaffirmed and confirmed (see Feasts and Festivals).

The Ten Commandments were of great value as summations of the demands of God, easily remembered by reference to the ten fingers of the hand. As negative statements, they helped shape the community's recognition of those kinds of conduct that simply ruined life in community and so could not be allowed. They were not intended to be legalistic in character or in effect; they were to ward off conduct from the community that could be its ruin. Positive law must develop in association with these pithy, negatively put demands. Rather than such "dos and don'ts" encouraging oppressive control of a society by its leaders, they are a summons to a life freed to enjoy existence in community.

See also Neighbor. *Walter Harrelson*

TETRAGRAMMATON. A Greek word meaning "four letters," used to designate the consonants of the divine name Yahweh. This name of God is so sacred that Jews traditionally do not pronounce it but use a substitute, and the vowels of Adonai (*ʾădōnāy*), "my Lord," are written in the Hebrew Bible (with "e" as the first vowel instead of "a") with the four letters *yhwh* (whence "Jehovah"), though they are not pronounced with those consonants.

Outside the Bible, *yhwh* is first found in the Moabite Stone (ca. 830 BCE) and in inscriptions from Khirbet el-Qom and

Kuntillet ʿAjrud (late ninth or early eighth century BCE). In the Bible, we also find the related form *yāh,* and the elements *yĕhô-, yô-,-yāhû,* and *-yâ* in personal names. Jews in Egypt in the fifth century BCE wrote *yhw (yāhû)* and *yhh (yāhōh).*

It is probable that the first part of *yhwh* was pronounced *yah-* (cf. the "a" vowel in related forms and in Greek transcriptions in Christian times), and the second *-eh* (cf. the assonance with *ʾehyeh* ["I AM" in the NRSV] in Exod. 3.14), hence *yahweh.* If *yahweh* is shortened by the omission of *-eh,* the natural result in Hebrew is *yāhû,* whereas the former cannot easily be derived from the latter. The name *yahweh* looks like the third-person singular of the verb *hāwâ,* a rare alternative to the usual *hāyâ,* "to be." The "a" vowel suggests the causative theme of the verb ("he causes" or "will cause to be"), but that theme is not used with this verb in the Bible. If, however, the name is archaic or of non-Israelite origin, then another meaning is possible, and some have sought a meaning found in Aramaic ("to fall" [cf. Job 37.6] as well as "to be") or in Arabic ("to fall, blow," etc.), but firm evidence is lacking.

Some have suggested a connection with the element *ya* in cuneiform personal names at *Ebla and in Mesopotamian texts, but this interpretation is disputed, and a connection with *yw* in a *Ugaritic name is also questionable. More plausible—though still uncertain—is a connection with *yhw* (perhaps *yahweh*) in Egyptian texts from ca. 1400–1200 BCE, which may be a place (the site of a shrine?) associated with pastoral nomads in or near the Sinai peninsula. What is important, however, is not the origin of the name but the nature of the God who bore it in the Bible.

J. A. Emerton

TEXTUAL CRITICISM. Because at times the word "criticism" can mean "finding fault with," it is important to note that when it is used here it means "evaluation," the analysis of something with the intent of determining its value. The wording of the manuscripts of the Hebrew Bible and of the Greek New Testament varies here and there to a greater or lesser degree. It is necessary, therefore, to employ the criteria of textual criticism in order to evaluate the various readings so as to determine, if possible, the original author's text prior to the modifications that appear in extant manuscripts—for the original autographs were lost long ago. There are three classes of sources that scholars use in textual criticism of biblical texts: the Hebrew or Greek manuscripts; ancient *translations in other languages; and quotations made by rabbis and church fathers.

The first step in the determination of the original text involves a scrupulous comparison of all the witnesses (or, at least, the important witnesses) in these three classes of texts, and then producing a compilation of the differing readings. Such a compilation is known as a critical apparatus. At times this process sheds light on how and why a scribe introduced a textual variation. The majority of differing readings occurred because of unintentional error; in other instances, the text may have been intentionally altered. Accidental variations can result from one letter being mistaken for another; from the reversal of the sequence of two letters (metathesis); from exchanging letters and words that sound similar; from confusing two successive lines that begin with the same letters or words (homoeoarchton) or that end with the same letters or word (homoeoteleuton), by allowing the eye to skip from the first to the second line (parablepsis), thus omitting the intermediate text (haplography); and from the eye accidently processing the same word or groups of words twice so that the scribe writes for a second time a text that was meant to be read only once (dittography).

Oddly enough, scribes who thought about the text were more likely to make emendations than those who simply wanted to produce an accurate copy. Deliberate changes include correcting spelling and grammar; conforming a reading to a parallel passage; expanding or polishing the text by adding a familiar word or phrase where one seemed to be called for; combining similar phrases; clarifying historical and geographical problems; substituting synonymous words or expressions; and modifying or deleting expressions considered objectionable by the scribe.

The textual critic's fundamental considerations when assessing variant readings involve both external and internal evidence. External evidence relates to the date of the witnesses, the geographical distribution of the witnesses that agree, and the family relationship (if determinable) of manuscripts and groups of witnesses. Internal evidence is concerned with transcriptional probabilities, which require analysis of paleographical details and the scribe's habits, and intrinsic probabilities, which necessitate examination of the author's style and vocabulary throughout the book.

The differing conclusions of textual critics can usually be traced to one's judgment as to which criteria are deemed most significant. For example, for the Hebrew Bible most scholars use the *Masoretic text as a point of departure for textual criticism because it is a complete, established text that was scrupulously transcribed. In some cases, however, readings in the Qumran Hebrew manuscripts are considered superior to the Masoretic text by virtue of

their agreement with ancient translations. The Qumran manuscripts, however, are not complete, and some were negligently copied.

As a general rule, the more difficult reading is usually to be preferred, as is also the less smooth or unassimilated reading—since in both instances scribes resisted the urge to produce a more polished, harmonious text. The shorter reading is also favored by the majority of textual scholars (unless specific omissions can be traced to homoeoteleuton, or unless the shorter reading does not conform to the character, style, or scope of the author), since scribes tended to supplement the text with explanations or material from parallel passages rather than to abridge it. Simply stated, the reading that best explains the origin of the other readings should be preferred as the original.   *Bruce M. Metzger*

THEOLOGY. *See* Biblical Theology.

THEOPHANY. A deity's physical manifestation that is seen by human beings. The appearance of gods and their involvement with humans are common motifs in ancient Near Eastern and classical mythology. That similar phenomena are found in the Bible seems problematic at first, for a persistent tradition in the Hebrew Bible affirmed that death comes to any human who sees God. In most of these contexts, however, the narration undermines this sentiment by depicting the pleasant surprise of those who survive. The text presents this perspective as a misperception to which human beings subscribe, for no humans in the Bible ever die simply because they have seen God. On the contrary, throughout the Bible God wants to communicate intimately with humans. The problem of how God can adequately show himself to humankind without harm is a conundrum that is never really resolved in the Bible.

The ease and frequency with which God visits and talks with humans in the early biblical narratives underscore how comfortable ancient Israelites were in depicting God's confrontation with humanity. Such theophanies are unspectacular, for God appears in form as an undistinguished human being who walks and stands. Humans speak freely of seeing God's face, and it is possible that the phrase used to describe a pilgrimage to the Temple ("to appear in the presence of Yahweh") has been modified by later tradition from an original vocalization that should be translated as "to see the face of Yahweh" (e.g., Exod. 23.15; 34.23; Deut. 16.16; 31.11; 1 Sam. 1.22; Ps. 42.2). In the scores of cases where the text simply reads, "God said," it is not clear if a theophany is to be presumed. Only when the narrative clarifies that "God appeared" is a theophany explicit (Gen. 12.7; 17.1; 26.24; 35.9; 48.3). Occasionally, God is described as descending when the theophany begins and/or ascending when it ends.

Although God may reveal himself whenever and to whomever he wishes, it is only to select individuals and in isolated places that God repeatedly appears. Moses, for example, is depicted as having a unique relationship with God, who knew and spoke with Moses face to face. The most common types of places where theophanies occur are near trees and mountains.

Because God characteristically reveals himself at such places, they become places of pilgrimage for humans seeking divine guidance or assistance. Shrines and temples, along with their sacred objects (such as the *ark), are built to formalize, protect, and regulate the approach to the divine presence. Those who enter such sacred precincts may ex-

perience a dramatic revelation of God's presence, particularly those who spend the night. God's presence in this institutionalized framework can be confirmed by the theophanic cloud inside the shrine. Here it is common to find people dying not because they have seen God but because they have not followed the rules in approaching him.

As in other ancient Near Eastern traditions, one of the common forms in which God is depicted as appearing is as a warrior, garbed with battle armor and weapons, smiting his foes and saving his people. He may go into battle alone or he may be accompanied by an army or entourage as he rides upon horses and chariot. He returns from battle drenched in the enemy's blood. When God makes such a dramatic appearance, characteristic visible phenomena that accompany his presence include clouds, lightning, earthquakes, and fire. Particularly when God marches into battle, he rocks creation with convulsions that shatter rocks and mountains, creating an upheaval and diminution of sun, moon, stars, and heavens (*see* War).

The book of Kings explains why earlier manifestations of God were dramatic in contrast to the more subdued revelation of the later writing prophets. In 1 Kings 19.8–13, the ninth-century BCE prophet Elijah returns to Mount Horeb and witnesses the typical convulsions of nature that accompany a theophany (storm, earthquake, fire), but this time God is in none of them. Instead, it is only a subdued, calm voice that testifies to God's presence. This narrative accounts for the gradual cessation of the classical theophanies and a rise in importance of the prophetic word as the medium of God's self-revelation. It is in the following century that the first of the known so-called writing prophets, Amos, appears in Israel.

The New Testament affirms that Jesus is the only adequate manifestation of God. Jesus' transfiguration and *ascension correspond to theophanies of the Hebrew Bible (on a mountain, voice from a cloud, radiance) in order to stress the continuity of God's self-revelation.

Samuel A. Meier

TIME, UNITS OF. The universal division of time into past, present, and future is expressed in Hebrew (as in other Semitic languages) by a spatial metaphor. Contrary to Western usage, the past is what lies ahead (Hebr. *qedem*) and is therefore known; the future is unknown and is behind (Hebr. ʾāḥôr, ʾaḥărôn).

There is no clear evidence for division of the day into smaller, equal parts in ancient Israel, though such systems were known elsewhere in the ancient Near East. By the Roman period, a system of twelve hours of daylight was in use. Generally in the Bible the term "hour" is used in a nonspecific sense. The day was either the period of sunlight, contrasted with the night, or the whole period of twenty-four hours, though not defined as such in the Bible. In earlier traditions a day apparently began at sunrise, but later its beginning was at sunset and its end at the following sunset. Thus, in Genesis 1, the six days of *creation are each described as follows: "there was evening, and there was morning." It should be stressed that this clear description makes impossible any understanding of the days of creation in Genesis 1 as longer periods, such as geological eras. This system became normative and is still observed in Jewish tradition, where, for example, the *Sabbath begins on Friday evening at sunset and ends Saturday at sunset. The word "day" can also be used metaphorically, referring to a critical time, such as the day of birth or death, the *day of the Lord, and the

day of Christ. The plural form can be used in a looser sense, equivalent to the general notion of time, as in phrases like "in those days" and "days of old."

The night was apparently divided into watches, three of which are implied in Judges 7.19 and four apparently named in Mark 13.35.

The week consisted of seven days, the last of which was the Sabbath, the only one to be named. The first six days are designated by ordinal numbers.

The two Hebrew words for month (*yeraḥ* and *ḥodeš*) are both related to the moon and its cycle (cf. *yārēaḥ* "moon" and *ḥādāš* "new"). Different names are used for the months in different periods, as follows (those in parentheses are not attested in the Bible but are found in other ancient sources):

CANAANITE NAME	BABYLONIAN NAME	MODERN EQUIVALENT
Abib	Nisan	March/April
Ziv	(Iyyar)	April/May
	Siwan	May/June
	(Tammuz)	June/July
	(Ab)	July/August
	Elul	August/September
Ethanim	(Tishri)	September/October
Bul	(Marheshvan)	October/November
	Chislev	November/December
	Tebeth	December/January
	Shebat	January/February
	Adar	February/March

Four of the months have Canaanite names: Abib, used only in connection with the *Exodus and its commemoration in the festival of unleavened bread or *Passover, and the remaining three in the account of the dedication of the Temple in 1 Kings. The Babylonian names are used in texts dating from the sixth century BCE on. Often months are simply indicated by their ordinal number, with Abib/Nisan being the first, at the time of the vernal equinox. But this also seems to be a relatively late innovation, patterned after the Babylonian system; earlier traditions imply that the new year was celebrated in the fall, at the autumnal equinox, apparently in agreement with Canaanite practice. A tenth-century BCE calendar from Gezer lists the agricultural activities characteristic of twelve months, beginning with the fall harvest.

The year was apparently based on the lunar cycle and consisted of twelve months, apparently of twenty-nine or thirty days each. The use of an intercalary month is disputed but may have occurred. It is possible that there was also use of a true solar year, although the evidence is fragmentary.

No absolute system of *chronology is used in the Bible, most systems referring either to the regnal years of various rulers or to key events, although the figures given in various sources are frequently inconsistent. Contrary to modern practice, in totaling units both the first and the last were usually counted.

                              Michael D. Coogan

TITHE. Attested in ancient Near Eastern sources apart from the Bible, in Israel the development of the practice of tithing (Hebr. *ma'ăśēr*, meaning a tenth) is unknown and not all the particulars are mutually reconcilable. According to Genesis, tithes were voluntarily offered by Abraham to Melchizedek and accepted by him on God's behalf, long before the Temple (Gen. 14.20). This was confirmed as an obligation by Jacob in his vow (Gen. 28.22): "Of all that you give me, I will surely give one tenth to you," God being the universal donor. In other traditions, the chief purpose of tithe was to maintain priests and Levites, who had not been allotted a share in realty in Canaan. Tithe was assessed on the fruits of the land of Israel and herds and flocks there, such tithes not being redeemable for money. The Levites at one time received tithes and passed on a

tenth to the priests or for the use of the Temple; but by the first century CE priests collected for themselves. It is not unknown for some priests to forestall others forcibly. The king no longer collected tithes, if he ever did.

Particularity about tithing, as required in the Mishnah, was not inconsistent with neglect of other commandments not so easily quantified. Priests obtained income from other sources, but failure to pay tithes was a spiritual offense, so as to excite God's anger. A perfect Israel would proudly contribute to the cult with its tithes, and Pharisees could boast of their reliability. But there was a discrepancy between such observances and spirituality. What accretions and what gains, natural and otherwise, must be submitted to Pentateuchal tithe could be argued, but the Mishnah declares all cultivated and edible growths liable. Pharisees regarded food that might not have been tithed as unfit for consumption by the righteous.

Another tithe of produce is required at Deuteronomy 14.22–23 to be realized by its owners and spent in Jerusalem to subsidize the city, its Temple, and the Levites. This may refer to the first fruits or the money received from their sale, which the producers had to take to Jerusalem, but this is doubtful. It is important that that "second tithe" was to be spent on servants, orphans, widows, and aliens as well as Levites. A regular collection for the poor was known by the second century BCE, and the Mishnah speaks of a tithe for the poor even though payment of it was voluntary. On the other hand it rules that the animals of Leviticus 27.30–33 are subject to the "second tithe."

Luke 11.41–42 suggests the probability that, in at least some churches, the Pentateuchal precepts were applied by analogy for the benefit of the Christian poor. Matthew 23.23 suggests that the custom of tithing was preserved somehow. The New Testament nowhere explicitly requires tithing to maintain a ministry or a place of assembly.

J. Duncan M. Derrett

TONGUES, SPEAKING IN. *See* Glossolalia.

TORAH. One of the basic concepts of biblical religion and rabbinic literature. The meaning of "torah" (Hebr. *tôrâ*) is "instruction, teaching." "Torah" is often rendered "law," as consistently in the Septuagint, although Greek *nomos* had broader meaning than simply "law." This rendering has been deplored, but it has validity. For example, Exodus 12.49 reads, "There shall be one torah for the native and for the resident alien." Clearly the translator must render "torah" here as "law." "Law" is an extension of the basic meaning of "torah," for divine instruction assumes the force of law. In Leviticus and Numbers particularly, the individual divine laws are referred to as "torahs" (Hebr. *tôrôt*). Underlying the biblical concept of Torah is another concept, one of there being a way of God that had to be followed, a concept that finds its fullest expression in the prophets and the Psalms.

If the divinity is the promulgator of Torah as law, Torah in its broadest sense may be promulgated by kings, priests, wise men, and even wise women. Most significant historically is the promulgation of Torah through Moses, an idea found already in the *Pentateuch, as in Deuteronomy 4.44: "This is the torah that Moses set before the Israelites." The tractate of the Mishnah known as "the Ethics of the Fathers" (*Pirqe *Abot*) begins with the statement "Moses received the Torah at Mount Sinai," one of the fundamental precepts of rabbinic Judaism. Not only were the *Ten Commandments given at Sinai, but, as we shall see, the Torah in a wider sense.

The development of the concept of Torah proceeded as follows: (1) the promulgation of individual divinely directed *tôrôt;* (2) the Torah of the divinely inspired figure of Moses; (3) a definite idea of Torah as the book of the Torah, which by the days of Ezra and Nehemiah meant the Pentateuch in an early form; (4) in the rabbinic period, the Torah as Pentateuch, in a form not unlike the Pentateuch of the present day (*see* Canon). Rabbinic usage of the term was quite broad. It could refer to the five books of Moses or to the totality of divine revelation. It included two basic types of materials: legal (halakic) and literary (aggadic), with the latter including everything from stories to poetry to nonlegal interpretation of biblical texts and more. The rabbis extended Torah to include another dichotomy: the written Torah and the oral Torah, the latter consisting of traditions that were transmitted orally until they were given written expression in the Mishnah, the basis of the Talmud (cf. the "Temple Scroll" from Qumran, which may have functioned as an additional book of Torah). Both Torahs were considered to have descended from heaven; there was even a rabbinic tradition that the Torah preexisted *creation, and another that through it God effected creation. Rabbinic Judaism stressed the joy of fulfilling the Torah's commandments; Torah observance ensured salvation. It is difficult to overstate the importance of Torah in early Judaism, an emphasis that has continued to the present.

In biblical tradition the role of the king in relation to Torah is specified in Deuteronomy 17.18: "When he [the king] is seated on his royal throne, he shall have written for himself a copy of this torah on a book before the levitical priests." No king of Israel or Judah is known to have followed this law, with the partial exception of Josiah, who read the book without actually having it written out. The king's role in relation to Torah is hinted at in the lament of Lamentations 2.9: "Her king and her princes are among the nations; there is no torah." Priests as well are upholders of God's Torah and its interpreters as part of their everyday functions. The prophets too were greatly concerned with Torah, especially when the people failed to follow the divine way. Malachi 4.4 is the only prophetic reference to the Torah of Moses, showing that the early conception of Torah as direct divine teaching had precedence for the prophets over the concept of the Mosaic Torah.

The earliest Christian attitudes toward Torah were ambivalent. One view is found in Jesus' saying in Matthew 5.17: "Do not think that I have come to abolish the law or the prophets; I have come not to abolish but to fulfill. For truly I tell you, until heaven and earth pass away, not one letter, not one stroke of a letter, will pass from the law until all is accomplished." But this clear-cut and positive view is not that of the entire New Testament. Paul, though expressing the belief that the law may be fulfilled through love, also asserts that "a person is justified not by the works of the law but through faith in Jesus Christ" (Gal. 2.16) and that "the power of sin is the law" (1 Cor. 15.56; *see* Justification). With these radical doctrines, Paul was able to sever the Judaic umbilical cord and to set Christianity on its present track.

See also Interpretation, History of, *article on* Jewish Interpretation; Law; Lectionaries, *article on* Jewish Tradition.

Philip Stern

TRANSLATIONS. *This entry deals with translations, or "versions," of the Bible from the original* *Hebrew, *Aramaic, and *Greek, *and consists of ten articles:*

> Theory and Practice
> Ancient Languages
> Targums
> Medieval Versions
> English Language
> Modern European Languages
> African Languages
> Asiatic Languages
> Australian Aboriginal Languages
> Native American Languages

The first article deals with general theories and problems of translation. The second article discusses all ancient versions, except for the Targums, which are the subject of the third article. The remaining articles survey medieval versions and translations into other languages, first English, then groups of languages ordered by continent. Related discussion is found in Circulation of the Bible; Paraphrases; *and* Wycliffe Bible Translators.

Theory and Practice

The theory and practice of scripture translation represent three different traditions with distinctive but largely complementary sets of principles. These three primary approaches to translating may be designated as philological, linguistic, and communicative.

The Philological Approach focuses on such features as the author's background, distinctive features of style, literary genres, the history of text transmission, literary criticism, and the manner in which a text has been interpreted through the years. The first Bible translator to deal overtly with these issues was Jerome, who in accordance with the best classical tradition realized that the sense must have priority over the words. This represented a radical departure from the Old Latin practice.

Luther's translation of the Bible into German also broke with tradition and the dominance of the Vulgate by translating directly from Greek and Hebrew and by using the ordinary words of common people. In the English language, Tyndale likewise insisted that the message of the scriptures should be understood by everyone, and with this intent he produced what later proved to be a major contribution to the King James Version.

The committee that produced the King James Version was especially concerned for the stylistic quality of a text for public reading, and they were surprisingly successful in producing a translation that not only dominated the use of scriptures in English for almost two centuries but greatly influenced the production of early translations by missionaries in Asia, Africa, and the Americas.

The latter part of the nineteenth century and the beginning of the twentieth century were marked by intense interest in archaeological finds and the discovery of many ancient manuscripts, which inevitably led to new insights in interpretation of many biblical passages. The English Revised Version (1885) and the corresponding American Standard Version (1901) represented the best in nineteenth-century biblical scholarship, but the many awkward literalisms in these translations greatly limited their acceptability for English-speaking people.

During this same period certain individual translators produced versions that were stylistically more in line with present-day usage in English, such as Weymouth's *New Testament in Modern Speech* (1902), Moffatt's *The Bible: A New Translation* (1928), and Goodspeed's *The New Testament: An American Translation*

(1923). Such translations inevitably influenced the demand for more standard texts that would have a wider range of acceptance, including the Revised Standard Version (1946, 1952), the New English Bible (1970), and the New American Bible (1970). Similar developments occurred in a number of other major languages, for example, La Bible de Jérusalem (1956), Die Einheitsübersetzung (1974), and Nueva Biblia Española (1975).

The Linguistic Approach became an important factor after 1945, when there was a rapid expansion of missionary work in hundreds of minor languages without any written literary tradition or even system of writing. Most missionary translators had little to guide them in formulating alphabets, analyzing complex grammars, determining the meanings of words in quite different cultures, and learning to appreciate some of the remarkable stylistic features of oral literatures.

To determine what could and should be done, the Netherlands Bible Society organized for the United Bible Societies the first international conference of Bible translators held in Woudschoten, Netherlands, in 1946. The journal *The Bible Translator* began publication the next year, and this was followed by a number of books: *Bible Translating* (1947), *Toward a Science of Translating* (1964), *The Theory and Practice of Translation* (1969), and *From One Language to Another* (1986), as well as a series of *Translators' Handbooks* providing detailed information on exegetical and cultural problems. The Summer Institute of Linguistics, also known as the *Wycliffe Bible Translators, has also published a number of helps for Bible translators.

A major problem in producing revisions or new translations in languages having a long biblical tradition is the change of meaning that has often taken place in words and idioms. For example, most English speakers understand the terms "justify" and "justification" as meaning "using questionable means for making something seem right or correct, even when it is not." Accordingly, some English translations now use expressions such as "to be put right with" or "to make acceptable to." Some of the most creative attempts to express the meaning of the scriptures in present-day language are *The New Testament in Modern English* (J. B. Phillips, 1960), *La Version Popular* in Spanish (1979), *Today's English Version* (1976), *Gute Nachricht* in German (1982), *La Bonne Nouvelle d'Aujourd'hui* in French (1982), and *The Contemporary English Version* (New Testament, 1991).

The linguistic approach to translating may be viewed as a four-phase process: analysis (determining the meaning of the biblical text on the most explicit level), transfer (shifting from the source to the target language on this explicit level), restructuring (reproducing the message on the appropriate language level for the intended audience), and testing (to determine the accuracy and degree of natural equivalence based on readers' responses).

The Communicative Approach to translating (based in large measure on communication theory) has been a natural outgrowth of the linguistic orientation. The key factors in communication are source (for the Bible, both divine and human), message (form and content), receptors (addressees and the wider audience), noise (anything altering the text in the process of transmission, e.g., copyist errors), feedback (how people have reacted to the message), and setting (the original, as well as present-day circumstances of communication). Such an approach to Bible translation depends

heavily on insights from cultural anthropology.

The concept of closest natural equivalence has sometimes been discussed in terms of "dynamic equivalence," but unfortunately some have assumed that any dynamic expression can be an equivalence. Accordingly, it is better to speak of "functional equivalence" in order to specify more clearly the relation between an original text and its translation into another language. Interlingual equivalence can never be an absolute or mathematical equivalence. There can, however, be a communicative equivalence, something that is effective in obtaining an appropriate response.

A definition of translation on a maximal level of communicative equivalence may be stated as follows: "The readers of a translation should understand and appreciate the text in essentially the same way as the original audience understood and appreciated it." But since no two cultures or languages are ever identical, a maximal level is unattainable, even though it can be a helpful theoretical goal. The more practical minimal definition of equivalence would be the following: "The readers or hearers of a translation should be able to comprehend how the original readers or hearers of a text must have understood and appreciated it." Bible translating should fall somewhere between these maximal and minimal levels.

The practical implications of these complementary philological, linguistic, and communicative approaches to scripture translation can be readily seen on the three levels of language: words, grammar, and discourse. Translation problems are more conspicuous on the lexical level, because the boundaries of meaning of words and idioms are almost always uncertain and fuzzy. For most speakers of English the term "grace" represents pleasing form or movement, the name of a girl, or a period of time before a bill must be paid. Accordingly, some translations of the Bible employ "kindness" or "goodness" in order to more accurately represent the meaning of the Hebrew and Greek terms traditionally rendered by "*grace."

In some languages relative clauses always precede rather than follow, and many languages have two forms of "we," inclusive and exclusive of the audience, while a number of languages do not specify a subject when it is evident from the context. All such grammatical features require extensive formal adjustments in translating, as is also evident in most present-day renderings of Ephesians 1.3–14, which in Greek is one sentence but in an English translation must normally be broken up into six to ten different sentences.

On the level of discourse some languages require the order of clauses and sentences to follow the historical sequence. This requires considerable restructuring of Mark 6.16–18. A literal rendering of Hebrew poetic parallelism is regarded in some languages as an insult to hearers because it suggests that the people are not intelligent enough to understand the first expression, but in other languages the lack of parallelism is regarded as a serious mistake. Some languages require rhetorical questions to be changed into emphatic statements and indirect discourse to be altered into direct discourse.

Because Bible translations serve quite distinct purposes for different audiences under varying circumstances, most major languages with marked social-class dialects require at least three different kinds of scripture texts: a traditional type of translation to meet the needs of those whose religious experience has been deeply influenced by a particular kind of "holy language"; a common-language translation (a modern koine) representing a relatively narrow overlapping of literary and colloquial usage; and a translation that fully exploits the total resources of a language and in this way does justice to the literary diversities of the Greek and Hebrew texts.

See also Circulation of the Bible.

Eugene A. Nida

Ancient Languages

The Hebrew Bible. In antiquity, the Hebrew Bible was translated into Greek (Septuagint [= LXX]), Syriac, Jewish Aramaic (the Targums), and Latin (Vulgate). The earliest of these was into Greek, where no precedent existed for any large-scale translation of a Near Eastern religious text. These ancient versions were to exert an enormous and enduring cultural and linguistic influence, above all in Christianity (though two, and perhaps three, of them began as Jewish undertakings). From them a large number of daughter versions were produced. Since the Septuagint in particular dates from a time prior to the stabilization of the Hebrew text (late first century CE), it serves as an important witness, alongside the biblical manuscripts from Qumran (*see* Dead Sea Scrolls), to early textual forms of the Hebrew Bible.

After an initial period of experimentation, "word for word" translation soon came to be regarded as the ideal for biblical texts (whereas literary translations from Greek into Latin were "sense for sense"). This norm, formulated by Jerome, influenced all subsequent translation until the end of the Middle Ages; a different approach only came in during the Reformation, partly as a result of the invention of printing (*see* Printing and Publishing, *article on* The Printed Bible).

Greek: The Septuagint. According to tradition, recorded first in the Letter of Aristeas to Philocrates (late second century BCE) the translation of the Pentateuch into Greek was commissioned by Ptolemy II (282–246); for this purpose an accurate Hebrew manuscript was sent from Jerusalem to Alexandria where the work was undertaken by seventy-two elders from the twelve tribes (rounded off to seventy, whence the term LXX, later extended to cover the entire Greek translation of the Hebrew Bible). Although a direct connection with Ptolemy II is implausible, it is likely that the first group of books to be translated was the *Pentateuch, and that this took place in the early third century BCE in Egypt, probably as a result of the liturgical and educational needs of the large Jewish community there. The translation of other books was carried out piecemeal over the next two centuries and included books of the *Apocrypha whose Hebrew original has been either lost, or recovered in part only in modern times (e.g., Sirach). The style of translation varies from book to book, and some books (notably 1 Samuel and Jeremiah) were translated from editions of the Hebrew text that differ from those surviving in the *Masoretic text.

Two attitudes developed among Hellenistic Jews with regard to the Greek translation once it had come into existence. Some (probably mainly in Palestine), considering the original translations to be too free, undertook to correct and revise them, bringing them into closer line with the current Hebrew text (itself developing); the culmination of this approach was the ultraliteral version by Aquila (early second century CE). Others (notably *Philo) held that the Greek translators were themselves inspired, and so for them the LXX shared equal authority with the Hebrew (thus obviating any need for correction).

Early Christianity inherited from Hellenistic Judaism both the LXX and Philo's attitude to it; Greek-speaking Jews as a result abandoned the LXX in favor of various revised versions, above all that of Aquila. The resulting differences between Jewish and Christian texts of the Greek Old Testament led Origen to undertake a massive revision of the LXX, bringing it into line with the Hebrew and Jewish Greek versions, and producing the Hexapla. Although Origen probably intended his revised LXX only for scholarly use, it came to exercise an extensive influence, thanks to its propagation by Eusebius and Pamphilus. Other Christian recensions of the fourth century, attributed to Lucian and Hesychius, were primarily stylistic in character.

The LXX remains to this day the authoritative biblical text of the Greek Orthodox church (*see* Eastern Orthodoxy and the Bible).

As regards manuscripts of the Septuagint, the earliest fragments, on papyrus, date from the second century BCE. Manuscripts normally contain groups of books, rather than the whole Bible; notable exceptions are three fourth- and fifth-century CE codices, Vaticanus, Alexandrinus, and Sinaiticus (Old Testament and New Testament, all nearly complete, each with slightly different contents). The order of books differs from that of the Hebrew Bible (*see* Canon).

Syriac: The Peshitta. The origins of the Syriac version are shrouded in uncertainty. As was the case with the LXX, different books were translated at different times (probably first and second centuries CE), and perhaps at different places (Edessa, Nisibis, and Adiabene have been suggested). At least some books were translated by Jews, and there are links with the Targum tradition especially in the Pentateuch; the Targum of Proverbs actually derives from the Peshitta. Although the translators worked basically from the Hebrew, in some books they evidently occasionally consulted the LXX. Apart from some stylistic improvement, there appear to have been no subsequent revisions of the Peshitta text, which is remarkably stable (unlike the LXX where there are many variations between manuscripts). With the exception of Sirach, based on Hebrew, the books of the Apocrypha were translated from Greek.

The Peshitta remains the authoritative biblical text of the Syrian churches (Syrian Orthodox, Church of the East, Maronite). The oldest manuscripts are of the fifth and sixth centuries CE; these normally contain groups of books, and only five complete Bibles earlier than the seventeenth century are known, the earliest being Codex Ambrosianus of the sixth/seventh century. The term "Peshitta," meaning "simple," distinguishes this version (made from Hebrew) from the Syrohexapla (made from Greek; see below).

Latin: The Vulgate. Jerome's earliest biblical translations were made from Origen's revision of the LXX (a few books, notably the Gallican Psalter, survive), but in ca. 393 he boldly turned to the Hebrew original as a better source, and in the course of a dozen years he produced a Latin version that quickly became the standard version of the Western church (hence the term *Vulgata*), replacing the Old Latin, translated from the LXX. Jerome's undertaking was both remarkable and revolutionary: remarkable in that he achieved a knowledge of Hebrew unique for a Christian at that period (it went well beyond Origen's), revolution-

ary in that he successfully overthrew the authority of the LXX within the Latin church. Of the many Vulgate manuscripts, the Codex Amiatinus, a complete Bible of the early eighth century, is one of the most important.

Daughter translations. Since LXX, Peshitta, and Vulgate became the official Old Testament texts for the Greek-, Syriac-, and Latin-speaking churches, they became the bases for subsequent translations into many other languages for the use of daughter churches. The most important are

1. From the Septuagint (in approximate chronological order): Old Latin, Coptic, Ethiopic, Armenian, Georgian, Christian Palestinian Aramaic, Syriac (the Syrohexapla, translated ca. 616 from Origen's revised LXX text), Arabic, and Slavonic. Not all of these are preserved complete.
2. From the Peshitta: Persian and Sogdian (mostly lost), and Arabic.
3. From the Vulgate: the medieval western vernacular translations and some of the earlier Reformation translations (*see article below on* Medieval Versions).

The New Testament. The most important translations of the Greek New Testament are the Latin and the Syriac, both of which go back to the second century CE.

Old Latin. The earliest translations that constitute the Old Latin were probably made in the second half of the second century CE, and perhaps in North Africa rather than Rome. They are of considerable textual interest. The extant manuscripts (mostly fragmentary and some going back to the fourth century) exhibit many variations among themselves, and the version was subject to constant sporadic revision from the

Greek. Jerome's revision of the Old Latin New Testament, known as the Vulgate, was completed ca. 384; the gospel text was the most revised. The oldest Vulgate gospel manuscript may belong to the fifth century.

Syriac. The oldest Syriac version is probably the Diatessaron (Gospel Harmony), made by Tatian ca. 160. In Syriac (which may even be its original language), the Diatessaron at first enjoyed wide popularity, but as a result of its suppression in the early fifth century only quotations survive. The subsequent translation of the four Gospels (late second–early third centuries), known as the Old Syriac, survives in two early manuscripts, the Curetonianus and Sinaiticus; the translation was made from an early Greek text form with many "western" features (*see* Textual Criticism). In due course, the rather free translation of the Old Syriac was revised on the basis of an early form of the Koine, or Byzantine, Greek text; this revision, eventually called the Peshitta (to distinguish it from the Harclean), emerged ca. 400 to become the standard New Testament text of the Syriac churches. The Peshitta covers the whole New Testament, apart from 2–3 John, 2 Peter, Jude, and Revelation (none of which formed part of the early Syriac canon). It is preserved in many manuscripts (some of the fifth century), and the text is very stable.

A further revision of the Syriac New Testament was sponsored by Philoxenus of Mabbug in 507/508, but of this only quotations survive (a sixth-century translation of the minor Catholic Epistles and Revelation may also belong). The Philoxenian was itself revised in 616 by Thomas of Harkel, who produced a mirror version of the Greek. Surprisingly, this version, known as the Harclean, was often used for *lectionary purposes. The oldest manuscripts of the Harclean Gospels date to the eighth or even the seventh century.

Other versions. Other ancient versions of the New Testament include translations into Coptic, Gothic, Ethiopic, Armenian, Georgian, Arabic, and Slavonic.

Coptic. The translations into various Coptic dialects were first made in the third or fourth century CE and subsequently revised. Several gospel manuscripts of the fourth century survive.

Gothic. This was made by Ulfilas (fourth century), and the earliest manuscripts date from the sixth century.

Ethiopic. The version probably goes back to the fifth century, but the earliest manuscripts date to about the fourteenth century.

Armenian. The translation is traditionally associated with the patriarchs Mesrop and Sahak (early fifth century); though it was made from Greek, some use may have been made of an earlier translation from Syriac, now lost. The oldest dated manuscripts are of the ninth century.

Georgian. It is not certain whether the original translation, which may go back to the fifth century, was made from Greek, Armenian, or Syriac; subsequently, it was thoroughly revised on the basis of the Greek. The oldest dated manuscripts are of the ninth and tenth centuries, though earlier fragments exist.

Arabic. The earliest translations probably date from the eighth century (some were made from Syriac or Coptic, rather than Greek). The oldest manuscripts are of the ninth century.

Slavonic. The translation goes back to Cyril and Methodius (ninth century). The oldest manuscripts (written in Glagolitic rather than Cyrillic script) are of late tenth/eleventh century.

Several of these translations continue in liturgical use.   S. P. Brock

Targums

The Targums are interpretive renderings of the books of the Hebrew Bible into *Aramaic; the Aramaic word *targûm* means "translation" or "interpretation." The origin of Targum as an institution can be traced to the Second Temple period, when Jews living in Palestine and elsewhere in the Near East were no longer familiar with their ancestral tongue, having adopted Aramaic, the official language of the Persian administration. The Targums cover the whole of the Hebrew Bible, with the exception of the books of Ezra, Nehemiah, and Daniel. In general, their place of origin is Palestine, though in the form in which we have them, Targums Onqelos to the Pentateuch and Jonathan to the Prophets bear signs of substantial revision in Babylonia, where by the second or third century CE they were recognized as "official" Targums. During the same period, the Targum tradition continued to flourish in Palestine, so that there are extant two complete Palestinian Targums to the Pentateuch (Neofiti and Pseudo-Jonathan) and a substantial number of fragments representing other Palestinian Pentateuchal Targums (or, as some would have it, other versions of the one Palestinian Targum). In addition to the "Babylonianized" Targum to the Prophets, there are in later writings many references to and quotations from a "Jerusalem" Targum to the Prophets, but whether these point to the existence at one time of a complete Palestinian version is debatable. The *Dead Sea Scrolls include substantial fragments of a Targum to the book of Job, in a version significantly different from that already known. There are also small fragments of a Targum to Leviticus.

Talmudic tradition traces the institution of Targum to the occasion described in Nehemiah 8.8 when the law of Moses was read "with interpretation" so that the assembled congregation might understand. Whether or not translation into Aramaic was involved, the need for such a provision in synagogues would have become apparent at an early stage. The Mishnah (ca. 200 CE) lays down rules in connection with the reading and translation of scripture in the synagogue; these include a ban on written Targum texts, evidently lest the authority of the original be compromised. Thus, the developing Targum corpus owed much to synagogal traditions of interpretation, but depended for its literary crystallization and transmission on other means of support. Some evidence points to the Jewish schools, which often shared buildings and personnel with the synagogue, as the preservers of this written Targum tradition.

All translations of the Bible are necessarily interpretive to a degree, but the Targums differ in that they are interpretive as a matter of policy, and often to an extent that far exceeds the bounds of "translation" or even "paraphrase." Even the "Babylonian" Targums, which over long stretches give the appearance of being fairly literal, often compress in a word or short phrase an allusion to a tradition of interpretation represented elsewhere in rabbinic (usually Talmudic or Midrashic) literature. At those points in the Pentateuch and the historical books where prose gives way to poetry the Targums tend to be more expansive and more pronouncedly "targumic" in the doctrines and views they superimpose upon the biblical text. Basically, the Targums set themselves to inculcate reverence for God (witness the frequent introduction of the *mêmrâ* ["Word"] of God to avoid any derogation of the truth of divine transcendence); to resolve discrepancies in the sacred text; to contemporize in matters of geography, law, or theology; and to promote teachings beloved of rabbinic authorities but not necessarily present in the biblical text or not as prominent as was wished (e.g., *prayer, meritorious deeds, messianism, resurrection). The tone is often moralistic and the intention obviously pedagogical, as would befit either a synagogal or school constituency. Another feature characteristic of the Targums perhaps more than of any other Bible translation ancient or modern is their reliance upon a number of stock words and expressions that are especially likely to occur where the underlying Hebrew text is obscure. Words like "strong," "strength," "destroy," and "plunder" are very common and often have been the basis of reconstructed readings of the Hebrew text where no such variant readings actually existed. Recurrent expressions like "the rich in possessions" or "cause the Shekinah to dwell" may likewise be translational ciphers, as well as having sociological or theological significance in inner Targumic terms.

There is an extensive literature on the contribution of the Targums to the understanding of the New Testament. The extent of such influence can easily be exaggerated, and the theory has depended to a considerable extent upon the assumption of an early (not later than the first century CE) date of origin for the Palestinian Targum(s) to the Pentateuch in particular. It is not possible, however, to date the Targums with any such degree of precision; the extant texts are probably best viewed as the product of several centuries of development. Thus the grounds for distinguishing between the Targums and other types of rabbinic literature as potential sources of light on the New Testament are questionable. There are nevertheless occasional points of contact, such as Mark 4.12 where "and be forgiven" interprets the refer-

ence to healing in Isaiah 6.10 exactly as does the Targum. Similarly, the exposition of Psalm 68.18 in Ephesians 4.8 reflects an interpretation that is represented in Targum but is scarcely deducible from the standard Hebrew text.

See also Interpretation, History of, *article on* Jewish Interpretation.

Robert P. Gordon

Medieval Versions

Latin was the universal language of learning in the West during the Middle Ages, and the principal version of the Bible was the Latin Vulgate. Yet the common people of the period were not limited to the art and drama of the church, or to homilies and mystery plays, for a knowledge of the Bible in their vernaculars. Educational and devotional needs both of monastic schools and of the laity were served by the glossing of Latin texts. The first books to be glossed or translated were usually the Psalter, the Gospels, and some Old Testament narratives. Before the fourteenth century, complete Testaments were rare, but by the middle of the fifteenth century, when the art of printing from movable type was developed, vernacular versions of the Bible were no longer uncommon. These were generally not translations of the Bible in the modern critical sense, but were either extremely literal or free renderings, frequently paraphrased or expanded with explanations for the reader. The stages of this development in several major European languages are reviewed in the following paragraphs in alphabetical order.

Dutch. The earliest surviving fragment of the scriptures in a Dutch vernacular version is of a paraphrase of the Psalms that dates from the early part of the tenth century. In the twelfth century, the religious revival of the Beguines and the Beghards in the Netherlands and

Belgium, which subsequently spread to Germany and France, led to other biblical translations. The Liège Diatessaron, a vernacular translation of Tatian's harmony, was one of the earliest biblical translations in Dutch. It has been compared with Luther's German version for its vigorous idiomatic quality. Other Dutch translations include the book of Revelation in West Flemish (ca. 1280), a Southern Dutch Psalter, and by 1300 the New Testament Gospels and Epistles. In 1271 the poet Jacob van Maerlant published his *Rijmbijbel*, a free translation that was based on Comestor's *Historia scholastica* and enjoyed considerable popularity. While paraphrases and adaptations continued to appear, the fourteenth and fifteenth centuries showed an increasing demand for more precise biblical versions, with comments and additions clearly distinguished from the biblical text.

English. The earliest surviving examples of Old English literature are the poetic paraphrases attributed by tradition to Caedmon, the seventh-century cowherd, who sang of the creation of the world, the wanderings of the Israelites, and the gospel stories he learned from the monks of Whitby. This school of poetry survived to the tenth century. King Alfred's (849–899) educational policies and monastic reforms undoubtedly did much to promote the status of the vernacular as well as the level of learning among the clergy. The ninth-century *Vespasian Psalter,* the earliest known English gloss on a biblical text, was followed by the continuous gloss by Aldred in the *Lindisfarne Gospels* (ca. 950). The Rushworth Gloss (ca. 975), based in part on the Lindisfarne gloss, is in a continuous prose form and is probably the earliest surviving example of English biblical translation. Although Aelfric (955–1020), the most important English bib-

lical writer before Wycliffe, wrote homilies, *Lives of the Saints,* and a free rendering of the Heptateuch, he remained a biblical expositor and not a translator. An anonymous contemporary produced the West-Saxon Gospels, a literal but readable translation of the four Gospels.

With the Norman conquest, a new Anglo-Norman vernacular developed with a more sophisticated literature. From the twelfth and thirteenth centuries, several versions of the Psalter and a number of passion narratives are known. The medieval Latin Psalter had three forms: the Vulgate, or Old Latin text based on the Greek Septuagint; the Roman revision of it by Jerome; and Jerome's fresh translation made from the Hebrew. The *Eadwine Psalter* (ca. 1160) contained all three, accompanying the Vulgate with the *glossa ordinaria,* the Roman with an interlinear Old English gloss, and the Hebrew with an interlinear Old French gloss. But the homily cycles and biblical versifications of the period (especially the *Cursor mundi*) reflect a general withdrawal from direct biblical study and an increased dependence on scholastic theology, especially the *Glossa ordinaria* and the theological schemes of Peter Comestor's *Historia scholastica,* a digest of biblical history.

In the fourteenth century, when the Franciscan emphasis on spiritual activity gave rise to a demand among lay contemplatives for vernacular scriptures as a guide and ground for private mystical experience, the *English Psalter* of Richard Rolle (1300–1349) proved the vernacular an adequate medium of religious expression. Several decades later (about 1382), the Lollard John Wycliffe (1329–1384) and his colleagues at Oxford began work on the first complete translation of the Bible from the Latin Vulgate into English. The first form of the translation was a quite literal rendering of the Latin

Vulgate, and it was soon revised to conform more nearly to idiomatic English usage. In 1407, Archbishop Arundel issued a "constitution" against Lollardy, condemning the private translation of scripture "into English or any other language," and specifically forbidding the use of any translation associated with Wycliffe under pain of excommunication. The popularity of the version, however, may be gauged from the fact that nearly two hundred copies of it have survived.

French. In the twelfth century, the Psalter was widely known in a very literal French vernacular gloss; it is found in a continuous form in the *Montebourg Psalter* and the *Arundel Psalter,* among others. Not until the *Metz Psalter* (ca. 1300) and the Psalter of Raoul de Presles (ca. 1380) does the gloss become more idiomatic in its syntax and vocabulary. In contrast, there was a late-twelfth-century prose version of Samuel and Kings in an excellent style, though quite free and with considerable commentary added to the biblical text. In Provence, the followers of Peter Waldo (d. 1217), who claimed the scriptures as their sole rule of life and faith, translated the Psalms and other books of the Old Testament and the complete New Testament into Provençal by the early thirteenth century. Pope Innocent III attempted to suppress the movement, but their influence was felt not only in France but also in the Netherlands and Germany and in Italy. Vernacular translations of Judges and other books were being made, and by the mid-thirteenth century, compilations of these were assembled and illuminated for wealthy patrons and royalty—examples are the *Acre Bible* of Saint Louis (1250–1254), which contained over a dozen Old Testament books (including the earliest vernacular version of Job in a European language), and the *De Thou*

Bible (ca. 1280), with a different selection of Old Testament books and parts of the New Testament (Gospels, Acts, and Catholic Epistles). The complete thirteenth-century French vernacular of the whole Bible survives in very few copies. It was a compilation, uneven in its glossing, its style, and its quality; but the translation movement it inaugurated climaxed in the *Biblia historiale* (1291–1295) of Guyart des Moulins. This expanded translation of Comestor's *Historia scholastica* incorporated versions of many biblical books and developed into a veritable medieval biblical encyclopedia. It appeared in many editions, and was both abridged and revised. The Renaissance scholar Jacques Lefèvre d'Étaples, who published the first printed French Bible in 1530, made use of the text of the *Biblia historiale,* revising it literally and eliminating its medieval glosses.

German. Apart from fragments of a Gothic version of the scriptures, translated by Ulfilas in the second half of the fourth century and probably revised under Latin influences during the next two centuries, Germanic theological literature dates from the Carolingian Renaissance. Fragments of the gospel of Matthew written in the Bavarian dialect and surviving in an eighth-century manuscript written at the monastery of Monsee, near Salzburg, have been associated with Charlemagne's reputed concern that Latin works be translated into the German vernacular. In the reign of his successor, Louis the Pious, an East Frankish dialect version of Tatian's *Diatessaron* was made at Fulda about 830, written together with its Latin base in parallel columns, but it was so literal a translation as to be nearly interlinear in character. The contemporary versified Old Saxon epic *Heliand* ("Savior") of about six thousand alliterative lines was also based on the *Diatessaron,* freely combined with material from commentaries, apocrypha, and legend. The *Liber evangeliorum* of Otfrid of Weissenberg in Alsace was based on gospel lessons from a *lectionary and written in South Rhine Frankish; it expanded the lectionary lessons liberally, adding whole chapters of commentary to them. Notker Labeo (950–1022), one of the founders of German vernacular literature, translated the *Psalter,* adding the Latin text, a German translation, and a German commentary in sequential rather than interlinear arrangement. The paraphrase of the Vulgate *Song of Songs* by Williram of Ebersburg (ca. 1060), arranged in parallel columns of Latin hexameters and a German prose rendering mixed with Latin, was remarkably popular and was copied and emulated through the fifteenth century.

By the end of the fourteenth century, German possessed a complete vernacular New Testament (1350, "Augsburg Bible") and Old Testament (ca. 1389–1400, "Wenzel Bible"). The *Codex Teplensis* (ca. 1400), a New Testament written in Bohemia, may reflect Waldensian associations. Opposition to the vernacular scriptures was not altogether lacking. In 1369, Charles IV issued an edict prohibiting the translation of religious books, and a papal rescript in 1375 forbade vernacular scriptures in Germany. Although the tide of scripture circulation could not be stemmed, creative efforts were discouraged, and the first printed German Bible, published by Mentel in 1466, still reflected the language and translation techniques of the early fourteenth century.

Italian. In Italy, vernacular translations of the Gospels and the Psalter may have existed by the mid-thirteenth century if not earlier, and of the entire Bible in the fourteenth century, though the earliest biblical manuscripts are from the fourteenth century, and the earliest surviving complete Bible is from the fifteenth century. Almost invariably these versions were in the Tuscan dialect, made from Latin, usually from the Vulgate text. The Gospels were mostly harmonies based on the Latin translation of Tatian's *Diatessaron* found in the Codex Fuldensis, but a freely glossed Venetian version of the Gospels has survived based on an earlier form of the Latin *Diatessaron.* A Venetian version of the *Psalter* is also known. There is evidence of a thirteenth-century Jewish-Italian version of substantial parts of the Hebrew Bible preserved in manuscripts of the fifteenth or sixteenth century written in Hebrew characters. Vernacular biblical translations otherwise show dependence on the Latin Vulgate text current in southern France in the twelfth and thirteenth centuries and traces of contact with French and Provençal translations. Although they may originally have been the work of Waldensians, they were adopted by the Dominicans and Franciscans and freely glossed for doctrinal instruction. It is interesting that Dante (1265–1321), when referring to the scripture versions, never mentions any in Italian, and that when he cites the scriptures he makes his own translation from the Vulgate. The first printed Italian Bible, attributed to the Venetian monk Nicolo Malermi, was essentially a compilation of fourteenth-century Tuscan texts adapted to Venetian usage.

Spanish. The existence of Spanish vernacular texts in the early thirteenth century need not be inferred from the edict issued by Juan I of Aragon at the Council of Tarragona in 1233 forbidding the possession of a vernacular Bible by anyone, cleric or lay: this edict simply repeats a similar decree of the Council of Toulouse in 1229 directed against the Albigensians. Alfonso X of Castille

(1221–1284) is said to have authorized a vernacular translation of the Bible in the 1270s as part of a *Grande e general estoria*, designed as an expanded and monumental *Bible historiale*. In its execution some portions were literal translations of the Vulgate while others were freely paraphrased, with commentary drawn from both Christian and non-Christian sources. The fourteen extant biblical manuscripts, mostly from the fourteenth and fifteenth centuries, reflect a varied and complex tradition of translation. The *Osuna Bible* is patterned after the French *Bibles moralisées illustrées*. Many translations of the Hebrew Bible were based not on the Latin Vulgate but on the Hebrew *Masoretic Text, observing the Hebrew *canonical arrangement of the Law, followed by the Former and Latter Prophets, yet preserving reminiscences of the Vulgate. The Alba Bible, commissioned in 1422 by Luis de Guzman and completed in 1433, included a fresh version of the Hebrew Bible made from the Hebrew by Rabbi Moses Arragel, and is remarkable for combining Jewish and Christian exegetical lore in its commentary. Scripture versions in Catalan are known from references in the thirteenth and fourteenth centuries, but the earliest surviving copies are from the fifteenth century.   *Erroll F. Rhodes*

English Language

Beginnings. As was the case with other languages, the translation of the scriptures into English was at first an oral process. The Venerable Bede tells how Caedmon (seventh century CE) retold Bible stories in alliterative verses in Anglo-Saxon: "He sang of the world's creation, the origin of the human race, and all the story of Genesis; he sang of Israel's Exodus from Egypt and entry into the promised land, of very many other stories from Holy Writ, of our

Lord's incarnation, passion, resurrection, and ascension into heaven, of the coming of the Holy Spirit and the apostles' teaching."

Bede himself (d. 735) is said to have translated the gospel of John into Anglo-Saxon, which may be the earliest written translation in English of any portion of the Bible. Alfred the Great (reigned 871–901) is credited with having translated part of the *Ten Commandments and other passages from Exodus 21–23. The *Lindisfarne Gospels* are interlinear glosses written in the Northumbrian dialect around 950 on a seventh-century Latin manuscript. The *Wessex Gospels,* a tenth-century translation into West Saxon, is the earliest extant Old English version of the Gospels.

The first complete translation of the Bible into English (1382; New Testament, 1380) is credited to John Wycliffe (Wyclif) (ca. 1330–1384). His translation work was part of his larger task of reforming the church, for which he earned the title "Morning Star of the Reformation." It was his contention that the church could be reformed only if everyone knew God's law, and this required that the Bible be translated into the language of the people. Said Wycliffe, "No man was so rude a scholar but that he might learn the Gospel according to its simplicity." There are two Wycliffite versions, the second of which appeared after Wycliffe's death. It is uncertain how much of either version is the work of Wycliffe himself and how much is the work of his colleagues, John Purvey and Nicholas of Hereford. Although the later version is more idiomatic than the earlier one, the Wycliffe Bible is almost a word-for-word equivalent of the Vulgate. For 150 years this was the only Bible in English, and some 107 manuscript copies have survived. In 1415 the Wycliffe Bible was condemned and burned. Purvey and Nicholas were jailed and forced to recant their Lollard principles; and in 1428 Wycliffe's body was exhumed and burned. The earliest printed edition of Wycliffe's New Testament was published in 160 copies at London in 1731; the first printed edition of the complete Wycliffite version was issued at Oxford in 1850.

Tyndale and His Successors. William Tyndale, "the Father of the English Bible," was born (1494?) in Gloucestershire and educated at Oxford (B.A. 1512, M.A. 1515), and at Cambridge, where he may have studied Greek. As chaplain and tutor in the household of Sir John Walsh, he got into debates with various clergy and other "learned men," and was soon accused of espousing heretical ideas. His opponent in one dispute argued that Christians were better off without God's law (the scriptures) than without the Pope's laws (Canon Law), to which Tyndale replied, "If God spare my life, ere many yeares I wyl cause a boye that dryveth the plough shall know more of the scripture than thou doest!"

Unable to get authorization in England to produce his translation, Tyndale went to the Continent (April or May 1524), staying in Wittenberg for almost a year, after which he moved to Hamburg and finally to Cologne (August 1525). There he gave his translation to Peter Quentel, a printer, but the city senate forbade the printing. Tyndale got the printed sheets, went up the Rhine to Worms, and toward the end of February 1526 the complete New Testament was published. About a month later copies began to appear in England.

Tyndale's translation was the first printed New Testament in English and was also the first English New Testament translated from the original Greek. About eighteen thousand copies of the original 1526 edition and the revisions of 1534 and 1535 were printed, of which only two are known to survive. Cuthbert Tunstall, Bishop of London, bought copies in great numbers and burned them publicly, and Sir Thomas More, the Lord High Chancellor, published a *Dialogue* in which he denounced Tyndale's translation as "not worthy to be called Christ's testament, but either Tyndale's own testament or the testament of his master Antichrist."

Tyndale next began the work of translating the Hebrew Bible: the Pentateuch was published in 1530, and Jonah in 1531. During this time he was living in Antwerp, and many attempts were made to lure him back to England. He was betrayed on 21 May 1535, arrested by agents of Emperor Charles V, and taken to Vilvorde, six miles north of Brussels, where he was imprisoned in a fortress. In August 1536 he was tried, found guilty of heresy, and turned over to the secular power for execution. On 6 October 1536, he was strangled and burned at the stake. According to John Foxe his last words were, "Lord, open the King of England's eyes!"

Before Tyndale's death a complete English Bible, dedicated to Henry VIII, was edited by Miles Coverdale and published on the continent in 1535. The New Testament was essentially a revision of Tyndale's New Testament, and his translation of portions of the Old Testament was used. The first authorized Bible was published in 1537, the so-called Thomas Matthew Bible, edited by John Rogers, a friend of Tyndale. The New Testament and Pentateuch were Tyndale's, and his manuscripts of Joshua through 2 Chronicles were used. In 1539 Richard Taverner, a lawyer, published a revision of the Matthew Bible, the first to be completely printed in England. Coverdale's revision of the Matthew Bible, known as the Great Bible (its pages measured 9 × 15 in [23 × 38 cm]), was printed in Paris in 1539 and was enthusiastically received by Tunstall, now bishop of Durham.

In the reign of Queen Mary (1553–1558) all printing of English Bibles in England was stopped, and the English Bible could not be used in church services. Many Protestant leaders sought refuge on the Continent. William Whittingham, pastor of the English Church in Geneva, translated the New Testament (published 1557) and served as editor of the Old Testament translation; the Geneva Bible of 1560 was dedicated to Queen Elizabeth (whose reign began in 1558). It was printed in roman type, bound in small octavo size, and was the first English Bible to have verse numbers. It became immensely popular: it was the Bible of Shakespeare and Bunyan, of the pilgrims to the New World and the Mayflower Compact, of Oliver Cromwell and his army. It was the first Bible published in Scotland (1579) and was dedicated to James VI, King of Scotland. Over 150 editions were published, and it remained popular for nearly a hundred years. Its extremely Protestant notes were offensive to the bishops, and in 1568 a revision of the Great Bible was published, which became known as the Bishops' Bible, owing to the great number of bishops on the committee. In 1570 the Convocation of Canterbury ordered it to be placed in all cathedrals, and so it became the second Authorized Version. It ran through twenty editions before 1606, but did not replace the Geneva Bible in popular esteem.

The King James Version (KJV) and Its Revisions. When James VI of Scotland ascended to the throne of England in 1603 as James I, there were two competing Bibles: the Bishops' Bible,

preferred by the church authorities, and the Geneva Bible, the favorite of the people.

At a conference of theologians and churchmen at Hampton Court in January 1604, called by King James "for the hearing, and for the determining, things pretended to be amiss in the Church," the Puritan leader John Reynolds proposed that a new translation be made, which would replace the two Bibles. The king approved of the plan and on 10 February he ordered that "a translation be made of the whole Bible, as consonant as can be to the original Hebrew and Greek, and this is to be set out and printed without any marginal notes and only to be used in all Churches of England in time of Divine Service." Fifty-four "learned men" were divided into six panels: three for the Old Testament, two for the New Testament, and one for the Apocrypha. They began their work in 1606, meeting at Oxford, Cambridge, and Westminster Abbey. A list of fifteen rules to guide the translation was drawn up, the first of which was, "The ordinary Bible read in the Church, commonly called the Bishops' Bible, to be followed, and as little altered as the truth of the original will permit." Rule fourteen listed the translations that could be followed "when they agree better with the Text than the Bishops' Bible": Tyndale, Matthew, Coverdale, Whitchurch [that is, the Great Bible], and Geneva.

The translation was published in 1611 and rapidly went through several editions, nearly all of which had changes in the text. The edition of 1614, for example, differs from the original in over four hundred places. The most careful and comprehensive revision was made in 1769 by Dr. Benjamin Blayney of Oxford, who worked for nearly four years on the task. Although never formally authorized by King or Parliament, it became known as "the Authorized Version."

It took some forty years before the 1611 Bible replaced the Geneva Bible in the affection of the people. But once established it became *the* Bible of the English-speaking people. In its various forms and editions it continues to be one of the most widely read Bibles in English.

In 1870, the Church of England authorized a revision of the King James Bible. The work was entrusted to fifty scholars, most of whom were Anglicans, but it included Baptists, Congregationalists, Methodists, Presbyterians, and one Unitarian. They were divided into two companies for the revision of the two Testaments. Of the eight rules drawn up to guide their work, the first specified that changes were to be made only if required by the need to be faithful to the original text. American scholars were invited to participate, by correspondence, with the proviso that an American edition not be published until fourteen years after the publication of the British edition.

The work was done carefully, and in the New Testament alone about thirty thousand changes were made, over five thousand of them on the basis of a better Greek text. The New Testament was published in May 1881 and was enthusiastically received. In the first year three million copies of the New Testament were sold in Great Britain and the United States. In 1885 the complete Revised Version appeared, with an appendix that listed the changes preferred by the American scholars. The Apocrypha appeared in 1895. In 1901 the Americans published their edition, the American Standard Edition of the Revised Version, popularly known as the Amer-

ican Standard Version. It removed many archaisms, replaced a large number of obsolescent words, and substituted American English terminology for words and expressions peculiarly British.

Rheims–Douai Bible. While not conceding the right of the laity to read the Bible in the vernacular without ecclesiastical sanction, Roman Catholic authorities felt the need for an officially approved English version for Catholics. In 1565, William Allen, a fellow of Oriel College, Oxford, like many other Roman Catholics, was forced to leave England. In Douai, Flanders, he founded a college for the purpose of training priests who would eventually go to England, and it was there that the translation of the Bible from the Latin Vulgate was begun. In 1578, the college moved to Rheims, where the New Testament was completed in 1582; eventually the college returned to Douai, and the Old Testament was published there in 1609–1610. In 1738 Bishop Challoner of London assisted in a thorough revision of the New Testament and made extensive revisions of the whole Bible in his 1749–1752 editions. The Challoner revision of the Rheims–Douai Bible was authorized for use in the United States in 1810.

Translations Independent of the KJV. Many Bibles and more than 250 translations of the New Testament in English have appeared since 1611. Robert Young, an Edinburgh bookseller who is famous for his *Analytical Concordance* to the Bible, in 1862 published a literal translation of the Bible, which is practically a word-for-word equivalent of the original. In the United States Charles Thomson, Secretary of the Continental Congress, translated the Greek Septuagint and the New Testament after retiring at the age of sixty from politics and business. After almost twenty years' work his translation was published in 1808. Thomson holds the distinction of having made the first English translation of the Septuagint and of having produced the first English New Testament to be translated and published in America. Ferrar Fenton, an English businessman, published his translation of the Bible in 1903 (New Testament, 1895). He claimed it was the most accurate translation ever made, "not only in words, but in editing, spirit, and sense." It enjoyed considerable success, and as late as 1944 a new edition was published. In 1876 Julia E. Smith, an American, produced a translation of the whole Bible, in which she attempted to use one and the same English word or phrase for every Hebrew and Greek word. One odd principle she followed was that of rendering the imperfect tense of the Hebrew verbs by the future tense in English, even in the account of creation. Genesis 1.3 reads, "And God will say there shall be light, and there will be light." In 1885 Helen Spurrel, of London, translated the Hebrew Bible. She began her study of Hebrew after turning fifty, and in her translation she kept to the unpointed consonantal text, disregarding the vowel points of the Masoretic text.

Modern Translations. The modern era of Bible translation into English began with the *Twentieth Century New Testament,* which was first issued as a tentative edition in separate parts in 1898–1901 and appeared in its definitive form in 1904. The translators, mostly laywomen and laymen, included Anglicans, Methodists, Congregationalists, Presbyterians, and Baptists. The project was begun through the efforts of Mary K. Higgs, the wife of a Congregational minister, and Ernest Malan, a signal and telegraph engineer, both of whom were

troubled by the fact that the language of the KJV was so difficult for young people to understand. One of their advisors was Richard Francis Weymouth, a classical scholar, fellow of University College, London; his *New Testament in Modern Speech* was published posthumously in 1902. His purpose was to produce a translation that lay people could understand. "Alas, the great majority of even 'new translations,' so called, are in reality only Tyndale's immortal work a little— and often very little—modernized!" He intended his translation to be used for private reading, not for public worship.

The translation that made the greatest impact upon the Bible-reading public, though, was that of the Scottish scholar James Moffatt. He began with a rendering included in his textbook, *The Historical New Testament* (1901), and in 1913 published *The New Testament: A New Translation.* His translation of the Old Testament appeared in 1924 and the whole Bible was revised in 1935. He spent the last years of his life as Professor of Church History at Union Theological Seminary, New York, and at the time of his death (1944) he was working on a translation of the Apocrypha.

Edgar J. Goodspeed, of the University of Chicago, answered the long-felt need for a New Testament in American English. "For American readers . . . who have had to depend so long upon versions made in Great Britain," he wrote, "there is room for a New Testament free from expressions which . . . are strange to American ears." His *New Testament, An American Translation* appeared in 1923. In 1927 a group of scholars headed by J. M. Powis Smith produced a translation of the Old Testament, which in 1935 was published with Goodspeed's New Testament as *The Bible, An American Translation.* In 1938 Goodspeed translated the Apocrypha, and *The Complete Bible: An American Translation* appeared in 1939.

Two important translations of the New Testament in the twentieth century are those of J. B. Phillips and William Barclay. As rector of a church in London, Phillips first translated Paul's epistles into modern English under the title *Letters to Young Churches* (1947). Eventually, his complete New Testament appeared, *The New Testament in Modern English* (1958). In 1972, Phillips brought out a thoroughly revised second edition. All translators of the Bible into modern English owe an incalculable debt to Phillips. For clarity of thought, vividness of language, and imaginative use of figures, he is rarely equaled and never surpassed. Barclay's *The New Testament: A New Translation* (2 vols., 1968, 1969) is more traditional in language, but embodies a wealth of scholarship from which all readers can profit. Mention should also be made of Hugh J. Schonfield's *Authentic New Testament* (1955), which was reissued, with very few changes in the text, in 1985 under the title *Original New Testament*. Schonfield's translation claims to be the first one made into English by a Jew. The footnotes, with a wealth of information for the careful reader, are the best feature of his work.

In 1961, the Jehovah's Witnesses (Watch Tower Bible and Tract Society) published a translation of the Bible under the title *New World Translation of the Holy Scriptures,* which reflects the unitarian bias of the Witnesses, most vividly displayed in John 1.1, "and the Word was a god." In 1972, the Watch Tower Bible and Tract Society posthumously published a translation by Steven T. Byington, mainly, it appears, because Byington used Jehovah as the proper name of God. An attempt to make the English text

accessible to all who speak or read English was made in *The New Testament in Basic English* (1941). The term "basic" is an acronym for "British American Scientific International Commercial" (English), which consists of a vocabulary of 850 words compiled by the linguist C. K. Ogden as an international auxiliary language and as an aid in learning English. A committee chaired by S. H. Hooke, of the University of London, used this vocabulary with the addition of another hundred words, plus fifty special Bible words. The complete Bible appeared in 1949.

The latest Bible in the Tyndale–King James tradition is the *Revised Standard Version*. In 1937, the International Council of Religious Education authorized a revision of the American Standard Version, stating that it should "embody the best results of modern scholarship as to the meaning of the scriptures, and express this meaning in English diction which is designed for use in public and private worship and preserves those qualities which have given to the King James Version a supreme place in English literature." The work was done by thirty scholars, headed by Luther A. Weigle. The New Testament appeared in 1946, the Old Testament in 1952, and the Apocrypha in 1957. In 1977 an "Expanded Edition" appeared, which included not only the Roman Catholic deuterocanonical books, but also 3 and 4 Maccabees and Psalm 151, thus making it acceptable to Eastern Orthodox churches. The *New Revised Standard Version* (NRSV), published in 1990, is a model of what a revision of an existing translation should be. In matters of text, exegesis, and language it goes a long way toward becoming *the* Bible of English-speaking readers for generations to come. It has dropped archaic terms and obsolete language, including the pronouns and verb forms used in addressing God. With notable success it has tackled the difficult task of making the English text inclusive where the original is not exclusive. The revisers did their work remarkably well; at times, however, one wishes that in the application of their guiding maxim "as literal as possible, as free as necessary," they had more often favored freedom over literalism.

The *New King James Bible* (1982), falsely claiming to be "the first major revision of the KJV since 1867," aims to maintain the supremacy of the KJV as the Bible of conservative Protestants.

What may justly be called a landmark in Bible translation was achieved with the publication, in 1970, of the *New English Bible* (NEB; New Testament, 1961). Representing nearly all major Christian denominations in Great Britain and Ireland, this translation broke away completely from the Tyndale–King James tradition. As explained by the chairman, C. H. Dodd, in the introduction to the New Testament, "We have conceived our task to be that of understanding the original as precisely as we could (using all available aids), and then saying again in our own native idiom what we believed the author to be saying in his." Using all resources of the English language, the translators produced an English Bible whose language is fresh and natural, but not slangy or undignified. Passage after passage may be read with pleasure and profit. At times the vocabulary is a bit too British for Americans, and many of its textual decisions, especially in the Hebrew Bible, have been criticized as idiosyncratic. The *Revised English Bible* (REB) was published in 1989 with the aim of providing a translation that would be even more faithful and understandable. In textual matters the revision is considerably more con-

servative than the original NEB, especially in the Old Testament. The same conservative restraint is detectable in exegetical and linguistic decisions. The NEB rendering of Genesis 1.1 was fresh and vivid; the REB rendering is hardly distinguishable from that of the King James Version. The delicate and frustrating task of trying to make the English text inclusive seems not to have ranked as high with the revisers as it did with the revisers of the NRSV. In comparison with the stunning achievement of the NEB in 1970, the 1989 revision is a disappointment.

In 1966 *Good News for Modern Man* (The New Testament in Today's English) was published by the American Bible Society. Its main features were the use of "common language," easily accessible to all who read English, whether as their own tongue or as an acquired language, and the systematic application of the principles of "dynamic equivalence" (as opposed to "formal equivalence") translation. The translator, Robert G. Bratcher, was assisted in his task by a panel of specialists. One novel feature of this translation was the imaginative linedrawings by the Swiss artist, Annie Vallotton. A committee of seven translated the Hebrew Bible, and the *Good News Bible* was published in 1976. The deuterocanonical books (Apocrypha) were added in 1979.

When the Revised Standard Version was published in 1952, it was received not only with appreciation and gratitude but also with bitter criticism and condemnation, especially from conservative Protestants. Because of its sponsorship by the National Council of Churches, this Bible was seen by some as tainted by liberal, if not heretical, beliefs. It was even said that the translation committee included communist sympathizers. Conservatives felt a strong need for a modern translation that they could trust. Several appeared, among them *The Amplified Bible* (1965) and *The Modern Language Bible* (The New Berkeley Version) in 1969 (New Testament, 1945). In 1971 the *New American Standard Bible* was offered (New Testament, 1963), intending to preserve and perpetuate the American Standard Version as the most faithful Bible translation in English. All were well received, but none achieved the status of *the* Bible acceptable to a majority of conservative Protestants, most of whom were still using the KJV. (For *The Living Bible*, see Paraphrases.) Finally in 1978 the *New International Version* was published (New Testament, 1973), the culmination of a process that had begun in 1956–1957. The intense advertisement campaign focused on the trustworthiness of the translators, all of whom, it was claimed, had "a high view of Scripture," believing that the Bible, in its entirety, "is the Word of God written and is therefore inerrant in the autographs." In its various editions this Bible is now widely used, and bids fair to become *the* Bible for those who still view the RSV (and other modern translations) with suspicion.

Roman Catholic Translations. Roman Catholics have produced their share of modern translations. In 1955 Monsignor Ronald Knox of Great Britain published a translation of the Bible from the Latin Vulgate, "in the light of the Hebrew and Greek originals." It was a remarkable tour de force and may possibly be the last translation of the Bible into English made by one individual. In 1966, the English version of *La Bible de Jérusalem* (one-volume edition) was published under the title *The Jerusalem Bible;* a revised edition, *The New Jerusalem Bible,* based on the 1973 revised French edition, appeared in 1985. American Roman Catholics began a fresh transla-

tion of the Vulgate in 1937, and in 1941 the New Testament was printed. Work was being done on the Old Testament, but with the publication in 1942 of the encyclical *Divino afflante spiritu,* authorizing vernacular translations made directly from the original Hebrew, Aramaic, and Greek texts, the translation was begun anew, and in 1970 *The New American Bible* was published, the first English Bible translated directly from the original texts by American Catholic scholars. The first step for producing a revision of this translation was taken in 1987 with the publication of the revised edition of the New Testament. One of its main purposes was to eliminate exclusive language in passages that are not exclusive in the original text. Somewhat ingenuously, however, the revisers claim that "brother," which is retained, still has its inclusive sense. Of greater significance is the deliberate return to the principle of formal equivalence in translation, in place of dynamic equivalence. So now Jesus says "Amen, amen, I say to you" (John 3.3) and the obsolete "behold" is found. After the bold step forward in 1970, this revision represents a timorous step backward.

Jewish Translations. One of the earliest Jewish translations of the Pentateuch into English (1785) was the work of Alexander Alexander, of Great Britain. In 1861, Abraham Benisch published a translation of the Hebrew Bible that was called the *Jewish School and Family Bible,* and in 1881 the translation by Michael Friedlander, also of England, was published. In the United States the earliest translation of the Hebrew Bible was done by Isaac Leeser (1854), which became the accepted version in all synagogues in the United States; a revised edition was published in London in 1865. Under the sponsorship of the Jewish Publication Society of America, a group of Jewish scholars headed by Marcus Jastrow produced a new translation, which became known as the *Jewish Publication Society Bible* (1917). This translation became the standard Bible of the American Jewish community until the appearance of what is known as the *New Jewish Version*, which was published in stages. A committee headed by Harry M. Orlinsky translated the *Torah* (1962); the final volume, *The Writings*, appeared in 1981. The complete translation, under the title *Tanakh*, was published in one volume in 1985.

At no other time in history have English-speaking people had such a variety of good translations of the Jewish and Christian scriptures, and those who care to read them will be able clearly to see "the process, order, and meaning of the text," in fulfillment of Tyndale's fervent desire.   *Robert G. Bratcher*

Modern European Languages

Modern versions of the Bible date from the Renaissance and the Reformation, when humanistic studies brought a fresh appreciation of the Greek and Hebrew languages to biblical scholarship. By 1500, the Bible had been printed in four languages besides Latin and Hebrew: German, Italian, Catalan, and Czech. As national languages developed, Bibles were translated and revised. From the sixteenth to the twentieth centuries, discoveries of biblical manuscripts led to new critical editions of the biblical texts with new generations of translations and revisions. In the twentieth century, rapid cultural change prompted "common language" translations, using a range of vocabulary and style common to all speakers of a language, regardless of their social class or formal education, while the pace of linguistic change now requires that standard versions be reviewed every thirty-five years. Interconfessional

versions also witness to growing ecumenical cooperation in Bible translating.

Today the complete Bible is read in more than forty European languages other than English, as listed in the table on p. 515 in the chronological order of their first published Bibles. The following paragraphs sketch this history by the major language groups represented.

Germanic. German. The first fourteen editions of the German Bible (1466–1518) printed a version based on the Latin Vulgate that had circulated in manuscripts since the fourteenth century. Martin Luther's translation of the New Testament in September 1522 marked the beginning of a new era characterized by a commitment to translating from the original languages of the scriptures. Relying on the Greek New Testament edited by Desiderius Erasmus (second edition, 1519), the Soncino edition of the Hebrew Bible (Brescia, 1495), and the linguistic counsel of his scholarly colleagues Philipp Melanchthon and Matthäus Aurogallus, in twelve years Luther translated the entire Bible into a vigorous popular German. Revised eleven times during his lifetime, Luther's Bible established the Reformation, created literary German, and became the model for translations in many other languages. With significant revisions in 1581, 1695, 1883, 1912, and 1956–1984, it remains the standard Bible of German Protestant churches.

Independent Protestant versions were few. The Zwingli Bible (Zürich, 1524–1529) adapted Luther's version to Swiss usage, supplementing it with an independent version of the Prophets; in successive revisions it deviated increasingly from Luther. Johann Piscator's Bible (1602–1606) was based on the Latin Vulgate and was replete with Latinisms. J. Friedrich Haug's pietistic eight-volume Bible (Berlenberg, 1726–1748) drew on

Luther, but included New Testament apocrypha and other postapostolic books. Twentieth-century Protestant Bibles include versions by Franz Eugen Schlachter (1905), Hermann Menge (1926, revised 1949), Hans Bruns (1962, revised 1969), and the common language translation *Die gute Nachricht* (1982, revised 1997).

Roman Catholic versions have been numerous. Hieronymus Emser's New Testament (1527) altered Luther's text only slightly. Johann Dietenberger (1534) relied heavily on Emser's New Testament and Luther's Old Testament, modifying them according to the Vulgate. Johann Eck (1537) used Emser's New Testament and the pre-Luther Old Testament, with unfortunate results. Caspar Ulenberg's revision of Dietenberger (Cologne, 1630), further revised in Mainz (1662), became known as the "Catholic Bible of Mainz." A version begun by Heinrich Braun (1788–1807) and revised by J. F. Allioli (1830–1837) became the standard Catholic version; its New Testament was further revised by

B. Weinhart (1865). This and a New Testament by J. H. Kistemacher (1825) were widely circulated by the British and Foreign Bible Society. Twentieth-century Catholic versions include Bibles by Konstantin Rösch and Eugen Henne (1934), Pius Parsch (1934), the Herder Bible (1966), and the Bishops' Bible "Einheitsübersetzung" (1980).

The first Jewish biblical translation into German was Moses Mendelssohn's Pentateuch (1783). This was opposed at first by Orthodox Jews, but Mendelssohn's colleagues completed the Hebrew Bible in Moses Israel Landau's edition of 1833–1837. Further versions were produced by Leopold Zunz (1837) and Ludwig Philippson (1854). Significant twentieth-century versions include those of Martin Buber and Franz Rosenzweig (1925–1929) and Harry Torczyner (Tur-Sinai, 1935–1958).

Dutch and Frisian. The "Delft Bible" published by Jacob Jacobzoen and Maurits Yemantszoen (1477) contained a fourteenth-century version of the Dutch Old Testament lacking the Psalms. The

1466	German	1584	Slovenian	1739	Estonian	1875	Russian
1471	Italian	1588	Welsh	1751	Portuguese	1889	Tréguier Breton
1478	Catalan	1590	Hungarian	1796	Lower Sorbian	1895	Norwegian Saami
1488	Czech	1642	Finnish	1801	Gaelic	1903	Ukrainian
1526	Dutch	1679	Ladin Sut Romansch	1804	Serbo-Croatian	1921	Nynorsk
1530	French	1685	Irish	1811	Swedish Saami	1943	Frisian
1541	Swedish	1688	Romanian	1832	Slovak	1948	Faroese
1550	Danish	1689	Latvian	1834	Norwegian	1958	Guipuzcoan Basque
1553	Spanish	1718	Sursilvan Romansch	1840	Modern Greek	1973	Byelorussian
1561	Polish	1728	Upper Sorbian	1865	Labourdin Basque	1990	Macedonian
1581	Slavonic	1733	Manx	1866	Léon Breton		
1584	Icelandic	1735	Lithuanian	1871	Bulgarian		

first printed Dutch New Testament (1522) was based on the Latin Vulgate. Anonymous translations of Luther's German New Testament appeared the following year, and in 1526 the first complete Dutch Bible was published by J. van Liesveldt, based on what had been published of Luther's German version, supplementing it at first with a translation of the Prophets from the Vulgate. Revised by Nicholas Biestkins van Diest (1558), Adolf Visscher (1648), Nicholas Haas (1750), and J. T. Plüschke (1823), it remained the Bible of Dutch Lutherans until the Netherlands Bible Society version of 1951.

The Bible edited by J. Gheylliaert in 1556, based on the German Zürich version, was popular in the Dutch Reformed Church, but Govaert van Wingen's version of 1561–1562 ("Deux Aes Bible") became the Bible of the Reformed Church until 1637. The States-General version of 1637 commissioned by the Synod of Dort (1618–1619) is still in use today, most recently revised in 1977 by a committee under the direction of W. L. Tukker and P. den Butter.

Nicholas van Winghe and his colleagues at Louvain found M. Vorsterman's (1528) adaptation of the Liesveldt Bible inadequate, and prepared a revision of the 1477 Delft Bible in 1548 for the use of Roman Catholics. Revised in 1599 to accord with the 1592 Clementine Vulgate text, the Louvain Bible served Dutch Catholics for centuries. The Peter Canisius Society version by B. Alfrink, R. Jansen, J. Cook, and others (1939) enjoyed several printings; the 1939 Bible by Laetus Himmelreich and Crispinus Smits was less successful. The present standard text for Dutch Catholics is a fresh translation in modern Dutch published at Boxtel in 1961–1973, revised in 1995, with notes patterned after the French Jerusalem Bible. A joint Catholic-Protestant publication of the complete Bible in a common language version (1983, revised 1996), edited by A. W. G. Jaakke and a committee, should also be noted.

The earliest modern scripture portion in Frisian was a metrical Psalter begun by Gijsbert Japiks (1668) and completed by Simon and Jan Althuysen (1755). In the twentieth century, a Protestant translation of the Bible by G. A. Wumkes and E. B. Folkertsma was published in 1943, and a common language version jointly by Catholics and Protestants in 1978.

Scandinavian: Swedish, Danish, Norwegian, Faroese, Icelandic. The first Swedish Bible ("Gustavus Vasa's"), translated by Laurentius Petri, archbishop of Uppsala, assisted by his brother Olaus and others (1541), was based primarily on Luther's German Bible. Official revisions commissioned by Gustavus Adolphus (1618) and Charles XII (1703) achieved only minor changes in format and orthography, with few other alterations. The Charles XII Bible remained the standard text until 1917 when the Royal Commission of Gustavus V, working from critical editions of the Hebrew and Greek texts, produced a completely new version that was approved as the Swedish Church Bible. A new official version of the New Testament was translated by David Hedegard in 1965 (revised 1971).

The earliest Danish New Testament (1524), commissioned by King Christian II, was translated by Hans Mikkelsen and Christiern Vinter from the Vulgate and Luther's German in a mixture of Danish and Swedish. Christiern Pedersen, the "Father of Danish literature," produced the first truly Danish New Testament (1529), based on the Latin Vulgate, and also a draft of the entire Bible (1543). Pedersen's work probably underlay the Reformation Bible (1550), which was commissioned by Christian III with instructions to follow Luther's text as closely as possible. Revised in 1589 (Frederick II Bible), and in 1633 (Christian IV Bible), with further editions into the nineteenth century, this remained the standard Bible of the Danish church. Meanwhile Hans Poulsen Resen, bishop of Zealand, prepared a Danish version of the Bible (1607) based on Hebrew and Greek texts; revised by Hans Svane (later archbishop) in 1647, the Svaning-Resen Bible was a "scholarly" Bible, with further revisions in 1712 and 1732 (Orphan House "Mission Bible"), 1824, and 1829. The 1907 Danish Bible Society revision of the Svaning-Resen New Testament served as the standard church text until 1948, when it was superseded by the Danish Bible Society 1931 Old Testament and 1948 New Testament. This was then replaced in 1992 by a new Danish Bible Society translation authorized by Queen Margarethe II. The religious revival of the nineteenth century produced a number of individual translations, such as the Bible by J. C. Lindberg (1837–1856), and the annotated New Testament by Bishop Skat Rørdam (1885). Roman Catholic New Testaments include versions by J. V. L. Hansen (1893) and Peter Schindler (1953).

When Norway became independent of Denmark in 1814, there were two Norwegian languages: the Riksmål or Bokmål of the majority, a kind of "Danish-Norwegian" spoken in urban areas and the southeast, and the Landsmål or Nynorsk (New Norwegian) of the rural regions in central and western Norway. The first Riksmål Bible was a revision of the Danish Svaning-Resen version by S. B. Hersleb (New Testment, 1819) and W. A. Wexels (Bible, 1834), published by the Norwegian Bible Society with revised editions (Old Testament, 1869, 1887, 1891; New Testament, 1873, 1904; Bible, 1903), followed by the New Authorized Version in 1978. A Roman Catholic version of the Bible in Riksmål was published in 1902 (revised 1938 from the original texts).

The first New Testament in New Norwegian (1889) was translated by J. Belsheim, E. Blix, and M. Skard; the complete Bible followed in 1921. In 1938 the Bible was revised, corrected by R. Indrebø to the 1930 Riksmål revision. The present standard Bibles in both Riksmål and New Norwegian were both prepared for the Norwegian Bible Society by committees headed by Magne Saebø and Sverre Aalen, and were published simultaneously (New Testament, 1975; Old Testament, 1978).

The first scripture publication in Faroese was a diglot gospel of Matthew with Danish (1823), prepared by J. H. Schroeter, a Faroese pastor. Jacob Dahl undertook a translation of the Bible from the original languages, but finished only the New Testament (1937) and several books of the Old Testament. His work was completed by a group of pastors and published by the Danish Bible Society in 1961. Meanwhile, Victor Danielsen aided by a committee prepared a Faroese Bible based on a number of modern European versions (1948).

The first Icelandic New Testament (1540) was translated by Oddur Gottskalksson from the Vulgate and Luther's German. Parts of the Old Testament were translated by Gissur Einarsson (1580). These were revised and the Old Testament completed by Gudbrandur Thorlaksson to produce the Reformation Bible (1584), an outstanding example of Icelandic literary and book production. The Gudbrand Bible was replaced by Thorlakur Skulason's revision (1644), which was based on the Danish Svaning-Resen version and became popular through the eighteenth century. The Icelandic Bible Society revision by Geri Vidalin and others (1841) was further revised by Petur Petursson (1866), and further again by Haraldur Nielsson and others (1912) from the original languages. The present Church Bible of Iceland was prepared by Thorir Thordarsson, Jon Sveinnjørnsson, and others (1981).

Romance. *Italian*. The first printed Italian Bible (Venice, 1471) was translated from the Latin Vulgate by Nicolo Malermi (or Malerbi). Antonio Brucioli, a Catholic layman with Protestant tendencies, published a Bible (Venice, 1532) based on the original languages that was widely influential and often reprinted. In Geneva in 1562, Filippo Rustici revised the Brucioli Old Testament and the Massimo Teofilo New Testament (1551, translated from Greek) for the first Italian Protestant Bible. In 1564 Pope Pius IV prohibited the use of vernacular scriptures, effectively discouraging further translations until 1757, when Pope Benedict XIV gave them a qualified approval and prompted Antonio Martini to prepare a vernacular translation (1769–1781). The Martini version became the standard Catholic Bible, an Italian classic. Meanwhile in Geneva, the scholar Giovanni Diodati published a Bible (1607, revised 1641) that gained immediate popularity and through many revisions (M. d'Erberg, 1711; G. Muller, 1744; G. Rolandi, 1819; T. P. Rosetti, 1850; B. Corsani and others, 1994) has remained the standard Italian Protestant Bible.

Twentieth-century Catholic versions were issued by the Cardinal Ferrari Society (1929), the Pontifical Biblical Institute (Old Testament, 1958; New Testament, 1965), and the Italian Episcopal Conference (1971), and there are individual translations by Marco Sales (1931) and Eusebio Tintori (1931); Protestant versions include a revision of Diodati by the Waldensian scholar Giovanni Luzzi and others (1924, revised 1994; Luzzi published his own version independently in 1930); ecumenical versions include the Italian Bible Society's Bibbia Concordata (1968), translated by a committee of Catholic, Orthodox, Protestant, and Jewish scholars, and a common language Bible (1985; New Testament revised 2000) produced by Catholic and Protestant scholars.

***Romansch*.** The first scripture publication in Romansch was a New Testament translated by J. Bifrum from the Latin Vulgate (1560) in Ladin Sura of the Upper Engadine Valley. Later translations were made from the Greek text by J. L. Griti (1640) and J. Menni (1861). The first complete Romansch Bible, translated into Ladin Sut of the Lower Engadine Valley by Jacob Dorta and J. A. Vulpius (1679), was later revised by J. Andreer and N. Vital (1870). A new version of the Bible by J. U. Gaudenz and R. Filli appeared in 1953. The Sursilvan Romansch Bible comprising the New Testament by L. Gabriel (1648, revised 1856) and the Old Testament of P. Saluz (1718), was revised by J. M. Darms and L. Candrian for the British and Foreign Bible Society in 1870.

***French*.** The first printed French Bible (Antwerp, 1530), a literalistic version by Jacques Lefèvre d'Étaples based on the *Biblia historiale,* was printed abroad because of suspicions of a Protestant bias aroused by his earlier New Testament (Paris, 1523). The first Protestant French Bible (Geneva, 1535) was translated by Pierre Robert Olivétan. The 1553 edition was the first modern version to incorporate *chapter and verse numbers throughout. Constantly revised by the Geneva pastors, the definitive Geneva Bible was edited by Theodore Beza (1588). Revisions were made in the seventeenth century by Jean Diodati (1644) and Samuel de Marets (1669), more significantly in the eighteenth by David Martin (Amsterdam, 1707) and J.-F. Ostervald (Amsterdam, 1744). The Synodal version (Paris, 1910) of the Synod of Reformed Churches is a revision of Ostervald, while the widely popular version of Louis Segond (Geneva; Old Testament, 1874; New Testament, 1880) was based on Martin and Ostervald, and was further revised in 1910, 1975, and 1978.

The first French Catholic Bible (Louvain, 1550), which was edited by Nicholas de Leuze and François de Larben and which reproduced the text of Lefèvre slightly revised with some borrowings from Olivétan, was often revised and reprinted. The Port-Royal version (1667–1695), prepared by Antoine and his brother Louis Isaac Lemaistre (de Sacy, pseudonym), was a masterpiece of French literary classicism, achieving popularity among both Catholics and Protestants. Richard Simon's translation of the New Testament (1702) from the Vulgate deserves mention for its nonsectarian scholarship. Among twentieth-century Catholic Bibles should be noted those of Abbé Crampon (1894–1904), revised by J. Touzard and E. Levesque in 1939 and by J. Bonsirven and A. Tricot in 1952; the Pieuse Société Saint Paul (1932); Paul George Passelecq and the monks of Maredsous (1950, revised 1968); A. Liénart (Ligue Catholique de l'Évangile, 1951); and especially that by the École Biblique of Jerusalem (Paris, 1954, revised 1973; the *Bible de Jérusalem* ["Jerusalem Bible"]), whose concise scholarly and exegetical notes have inspired similar editions in many other languages. Other versions of interest include the scholarly Pléiade version (Old Testament, 1859; New Testament, 1971), the *Traduction oecuménique* (1975, revised 1988) of A. Bea and M. Boegner,

and the common language *Français Courant* (Paris, 1982) by Jean-Claude Margot.

A Jewish version of the Hebrew scriptures was produced by Samuel Cahen (1831–1851), which was superseded by *La Bible du rabbinat français* (1899–1906, revised 1966). An independent version of both Testaments was published by André Chouraqui (Paris, 1975–1977).

Spanish; Catalan. Although the Spanish Inquisition allowed biblical themes in the classical Spanish theater of the sixteenth and seventeenth centuries, it acted as an effective check on the spread of vernacular Bibles in Spain. Yet the influence of the Reformation was felt. The first Spanish New Testament (1543), translated in Wittenberg by Francisco Enzinas from Erasmus's Greek text, was published in Antwerp; the second (1556) by Juan Perez de Pineda, a refugee monk from Seville, was published in Geneva. Meanwhile, in 1553 a literal translation of the Hebrew Bible into Spanish, which Protestant and Catholic translators found useful, was printed by a Jewish press at Ferrara, translated by Abraham Usque and published by Yomtob Atias under ducal patronage.

The first complete Spanish Bible (Basel, 1569, the "Bear Bible") was translated by Cassiodoro de Reina. Revised by Cipriano de Valera (Amsterdam, 1602), this text has been frequently revised (in 1960 and 1995 by the Bible Societies) and is still the standard Protestant Bible today. Other Protestant versions include translations by J. G. Tolsa and others (1969) based on the Italian Garofalo version, by Juan Rojas (1979) based on the English Living Bible, the Editorial Vida Bible (1999) based on the English New International Version, and the Lockman Biblia de las Américas New Testament (1973) based on the English New American Standard Version. The first complete Bible printed in Spain was translated from the Latin Vulgate by Felipe Scio de San Miguel (Valencia, 1793). Another Catholic version (Madrid, 1825) was translated by Felix Torres Amat, who probably revised an unpublished translation by the Jesuit J. M. Petisco. Twentieth-century Catholic versions of the complete Bible include revisions of the Amat text (by Severiano del Paramo in 1928 and by Serafin de Ausejo in 1965), and new versions by E. Nacar Fusta and A. Colunga (Madrid, 1944), José Maria Bover and F. Cantera Burgos (Madrid, 1947, revised 1966), Juan Straubinger (Buenos Aires, 1951), E. Martin Nieto (Madrid, 1961), Pedro Franquesa and Jose M. Sole (Barcelona, 1966), Jose Angel Ubieta on the basis of the French Jerusalem Bible (Brussels, 1967), Ramon Ricciardi (Madrid, 1971), Luís Alonso Schökel and others (1975), and A. M. Mendez (1978).

Mention is also due an ecumenical version (Barcelona, 1975) prepared by S. de Ausejo and F. de Fuenterrabia and revised by Catholic and Protestant scholars, and, *Dios habla hoy* (1979, revised 1994), a Bible society common language version.

The first printed Bible in Catalan, the dialect of northeastern Spain and the official language of Andorra, was translated by Bonifacio Ferrer from the Latin Vulgate (1478); it was so thoroughly destroyed by the Spanish Inquisition that only the last page of one copy has survived. The next scripture publication was the New Testament (London, 1832) translated by J. Prat, which enjoyed several reprints. In the twentieth century three complete Bibles appeared: two by Benedictines of Montserrat (Barcelona, 1926–1966, with commentary; and Andorra, 1970), one by the Catalan Biblical Foundation (Barcelona, 1968), and an interconfessional translation by G. M. Camnps and others for the United Bible Societies (Barcelona, 1993).

Portuguese. The first printed Portuguese New Testament (1681) was translated by João Ferreira d'Almeida in the East Indies and published in Amsterdam; his translation of the Old Testament remained unpublished until it was revised by Danish missionaries at Tranquebar (1751). It was repeatedly revised (1753–1773 by J. M. Mohr, 1847 by G. Bush, 1875 by Manoel Soares), and remains a popular Protestant version today, especially in Brazil, where it was revised in 1917 (based on the 1901 American Standard Version), 1958, and again in 1995. The earliest Portuguese Bible published in Portugal (Lisbon, 1781), translated by Anton Pereira de Figueiredo from the Latin Vulgate, has also been frequently revised and widely circulated. In the twentieth century, the Bible Society of Brazil published a common language Bible in 1988, and Roman Catholic versions of the complete Bible have been produced by Matos Soares (Porto, 1930–1934) based on the Latin Vulgate and revised by Manuel Madureira (1956), the Catholic Biblical Center of São Paolo (1959) based on the French Maredsous version, and M. Hoepers and L. Garmus (Petropolis, 1983) influenced in part by the New American Bible.

Romanian. The first printed book in Romania was a catechism (1541?) containing scripture selections; the second was the Gospels (1561), translated by Coresi, a Wallachian deacon. The first New Testament (1648) was begun by the monk Silvestru and completed by others. The complete Bible (1688) by Nicolae Milescu is considered the supreme achievement of seventeenth-century Romanian literature. Revised by Samuil Micu Clain (1795), it was reprinted even into the nineteenth century. Further translations of the complete Bible, sponsored by the British and Foreign Bible Society, were made by Ion Eliade Radulescu (1858), N. Balasescu and others (1867–1873), and D. Cornilescu (1921). A new version by Vasile Radu and Grigorie Pisculescu (Gala Galaction) was published by the Romanian Orthodox church in 1936, and further revised in 1968 and 1974. Romanian was written in the Cyrillic alphabet until 1860, when the Roman alphabet was adopted. In 1984, however, the Cornilescu version was printed also in Cyrillic for use in Moldavia.

Slavonic. The first printed (Old Church) Slavonic Bible (1581) was prepared for Prince Konstantin of Ostrog from a manuscript Bible dated 1499 and attributed to Archbishop Gennadius of Novgorod. Revised successively in 1633, in 1712 for Peter the Great, and in 1751 for the Tsarina Elizabeth, this remains the standard Slavonic Bible of the Russian Orthodox church.

East Slavic: Byelorussian, Ukrainian, Russian. The earliest scripture printed in East Slavic was an incomplete Bible in Byelorussian (Prague, 1517–1525) translated from Slavonic, Latin, and Czech sources by Franciscus Skoryna to supply the laity with a vernacular version. The next Byelorussian scripture publications to appear were the New Testament and Psalms of L. Dziekuć-Malej and A. M. Luckiewič (Helsinki, 1931), the complete Bible by Moses Gitlin and J. Stankievič (New York, 1970–1973), and a New Testament and Psalms by Vasil Sjomukha (Minsk, 1995).

Ukrainian versions of the Bible were first based on the Russian Synodal text of 1751 (Pochayev, 1798; Peremyshl, 1859). Modern versions of the complete Bible have been translated by P. A. Kulisch and D. I. Puluj (1903), Yaroslav Levitsky (1930), and from the original

languages by Ivan Ohienko (1962) and Ivan Khomenko (1963), and New Testaments by Alexander Bachinsky (1903), James Hominuke (a revision of the Kulisch version, 1971), George Derkatch (a common language version, 1993), and R. Turkoniak and F. Raphael (1997).

The earliest scripture portion in modern Russian was Archbishop Mefodiy's translation of Romans (Moscow, 1792). The New Testament was published in 1821 and the Old Testament through Ruth in 1825 by the Russian Bible Society (founded 1814, dissolved 1826), translated by a committee appointed by the Holy Synod at the request of Tsar Alexander I. The complete Bible was published by the Holy Synod in 1875, translated by E. I. Lovyagin, D. A. Khvolson, and others; this remains the standard Bible of the church in Russia. Also notable are a colloquial version of the Bible by K. Logachev (1993), and an ecumenical version of the New Testament by Bishop Cassian, A. P. Wassilieff, and others (1970). Jewish versions of the Pentateuch were published by Leon I. Mandelstamm (Vilna, 1862), J. Herstein and J. L. Gordon (1875), J. Steinberg (Vilna, 1899), and Z. Levin and others (Jerusalem, 1990), and the complete Hebrew Bible by D. Yosippon (Jerusalem, 1978).

West Slavic: Czech, Slovak, Polish. The first printed Czech New Testament (1475) was based on a Hussite revision of the Church Slavonic text by the Latin Vulgate, as was also the first complete Bible (Prague, 1488; revised in Venice, 1506). The Moravian bishop Jan Blahoslav translated the New Testament (1564) from Greek with concern for both scholarly accuracy and practical clarity; the complete Bible produced by his successors (Kralice, 1579–1594) became the standard Protestant Bible, and a definitive influence in the history of the Czech language. Through successive revisions it has remained the standard Czech Bible. The Wenceslaus Bible (1677–1715) of the Counter-Reformation, prepared by Jesuits J. Barner, J. Constantius, and M. V. Steyer, was based on the 1506 Venice revision and the Latin Vulgate but influenced also by the Kralice text. Modern versions that should be noted include a Catholic Bible (1917–1925) translated by Jan Hejč and Jan Sýkora from the Vulgate (New Testament revised by R. Col, 1947, 1970), a Catholic Old Testament (1955–1958) based on the Hebrew by J. Heger, a Catholic New Testament (1948) based on the Greek by Pavel Škrábal, an ecumenical Bible (1979) prepared by M. Bič and J. B. Souček of the Czech Brethren Evangelical church, and a literary Jewish translation of the Hebrew Bible (1947–1951) by Vladimír Šrámek.

The earliest Bible printed in Slovak (1829–1832) was translated by Jiří Palkovič, Catholic canon of Gran, from the Latin Vulgate. This was superseded by a new translation from the Vulgate made by Jan Donoval (1926). Modern Protestant versions of the complete Bible include a translation from the original languages by Josef Rohaček (1936) and the Tranoscius version (1978), based on the Czech Kralice text.

The first printed New Testament in Polish (1553) was translated from Greek by Jan Seklucjan, a Lutheran pastor, but the first complete Bible (1561) was attributed to the Roman Catholic theologian Jan Leopolita (of Lwów) and ostensibly based on the Latin Vulgate. A scholarly Protestant Bible (1563) translated from Hebrew and Greek by Jan Laski, F. Stankarus, and others under the patronage of Nicolas Radziwill was criticized for Socinianism in its notes, but revised by Daniel Mikolajewski and Jan Turnowski (Danzig, 1632) it became the standard Bible of Polish Protestants. Meanwhile, a Bible translated by Jakub Wujek from the Vulgate (1599) was accepted by the Synod of Piotrkow in 1607 as the official Polish Catholic version. Modern editions include revisions of the Wujek version (1935 by S. Styś and J. Rostworowski; 1962 by S. Styś and W. Lohn); three new Catholic versions by A. Jankowski (the "Millennium Bible," now the official Catholic text, 1965; partly revised 1971), by M. Peter and M. Molniewicz (1975), and by Kazimierz Romaniuk (1997); and an ecumenical "Millennium Bible" (1975) prepared by scholars of the Lutheran, Reformed, Orthodox, Old Catholic, and Protestant Free churches.

South Slavic: Bulgarian, Serbo-Croatian, Slovenian. The first biblical portion in modern Bulgarian was the Russian Bible Society edition of Matthew (St. Petersburg, 1823) from the New Testament translated by Archimandrite Theodosius from Old Church Slavonic; the project was discontinued when the Russian Bible Society was suppressed. The first printed New Testament based on the Slavonic (Smyrna, 1840) by Neophyt Rilski and revised from the Greek (1849), as well as the first complete Bible (Istanbul, 1871), were sponsored by the British and Foreign Bible Society, with revisions prepared by Robert Thomson (1923) and Gavrail Tsetanov (1940). The Bulgarian Synod version (1925) had begun in 1891 and was the work of five successive translation committees.

Although Serbo-Croatian is linguistically homogeneous, the Serbs are mainly Eastern Orthodox and use the Cyrillic script, while the majority of the Croats are Roman Catholic and use the Roman alphabet. However, the first New Testament in Serbo-Croatian (1563), translated by Antun Dalmatin and Stipan K. Istrianin from Erasmus's Latin version and Luther's German, was printed in Glagolitic characters. A second printing (1563) was in Cyrillic, and the Prophets (1564) was printed in Roman letters. The translator of the first complete Bible in Serbian (Budapest, 1804) is unknown; the first Bible in Croatian (Budapest, 1831) was a literal translation made from the Latin Vulgate by M. P. Katančić. The linguistic reformer Vuk S. Karadžić sought to promote a common literary language with his Serbian translation of the New Testament (1847); although not approved by the Serbian church, it was later issued together with an Old Testament prepared by his colleague G. Daničić (1868) simultaneously in both Serbian and Croatian. The Vuk-Daničić Bible remains popular in both scripts. Other significant Bibles were issued by Lujo Bakotić (Belgrade, 1933), I. E. Šarić (Sarajevo, 1942, New Testament revised by an ecumenical committee in 1969), and the Stvarnost edition (Zagreb, 1968) based on the French Jerusalem Bible.

The first Slovenian Bible (Wittenberg, 1584) combined the New Testament of the Reformed preacher Primus Truber (Tübingen, 1582) with the Old Testament of the Lutheran Juri Dalmatin, both translated from the original languages with close reference to Luther's German version. The first Roman Catholic Bible (Ljubljana, 1784–1802) was translated from the Vulgate by Juri Japel, Blaz Kumerdey, and others; a second Catholic version (1859) was based on the German Allioli version. Renewed interest in the Slovenian language in the early twentieth century led to a revision of the Truber-Dalmatin version by Anton Chraska (Bible, 1914; Kutna Hora, revised New Testament, 1946), and a new Catholic version of the Bible (New Testament, 1929; Old Testament, 1961),

which was revised by Lutheran and Roman Catholic scholars and as an ecumenical Bible in 1974, then further revised as the Slovenian Standard version in 1996.

The earliest scripture publication in Macedonian was reportedly the Gospels (Saloniki, 1852) translated by the monk Bojigrobskog and published by Trajkov in Greek characters. The first New Testament (Skopje, 1967), however, was translated by Georgi Milošev, Peter Ilievski, and Boris Boškoski of the Macedonian Orthodox Church. This was revised in consultation with Protestants and Roman Catholics in 1976, and combined with the Old Testament translated by Archbishop Gavril assisted by a committee as the first complete Macedonian Bible (London, 1990). The New Testament has also been translated by Dushko Konstantinov (Orthodox, 1997) and Ivan Grozdanov (Baptist, 1999).

Others. Greek. The first modern Greek New Testament (Geneva, 1638) was translated by a monk from Gallipoli, edited by Cyril Lucar, Patriarch of Constantinople, and published at the expense of the Dutch States General. It has been revised and reprinted often: by Seraphim of Mitylene (London, 1703), Anastasius Michael (Halle, 1710), Demetrius Schinas (1827), and others. The Bible translated by N. Bambas (London; Old Testament, 1840; New Testament, 1844) has become the standard Protestant Modern Greek Bible. A vernacular version of the Gospels by Alexander Pallis from the fourth century Codex Vaticanus (Liverpool, 1902) provoked legislation prohibiting all modern versions (repealed in 1924). Modern editions include Bibles translated by Athanasios Chastoupis and Nikolaos Louvaris (Athens, 1955; a paraphrase), and S. Agourides, J. Karavidopoulos, and others (Athens, 1997; an interconfessional version), and a New Testament by B. Vellas (Athens, 1967).

Uralic: Hungarian, Estonian, Finnish, Saami. The first printed Hungarian New Testament (Új Sziget, 1541) was translated by Janos Erdösi (Sylvester), a pupil of Melanchthon. The first complete Bible (Vizsoly, 1590), translated by Cáspár Károli, Reformed pastor at Göncz, played a decisive role in the national life and literature of Hungary comparable to that of Luther's Bible in Germany. Through successive revisions, most recently by Kálmán Kállay and Jozsef Póngracz for the Joint Bible Commission of Lutheran and Reformed Churches (Budapest, 1975 and 1991), it has remained the standard Protestant Bible of Hungary. The first Catholic Bible (Vienna, 1626) was an excellent rendering of the Vulgate by György Káldi, revised by Bela Jozsef Tarkanyi (1865), and again to conform to the Nova Vulgata (1997). Modern Hungarian translations of the complete Bible were made by the Reformed scholar Sandor Czgledy (1938), and the Roman Catholic scholars A. Szöreny, Ferenc Gal, and Istvan Kosztolanyi (1976), translated from the original languages and based on the Jerusalem Bible.

The first Estonian New Testament (Riga, 1686) was in the southern dialect of Tartu (Dorpat), begun by Johann Gutsleff and completed by N. von Hardungen, Adrian Virginius, and Marco Schütz. Revisions were made by Ferdinand Meyer (1836) and Uku Masing (1896). The first Estonian Bible (Tallinn, 1739) was in the northern dialect of Tallinn (Reval), translated by Anton Thor Helle, Heinrich Gutsleff, and others, and later revised by C. Malm (1878) and Uku Masing and John V. Veski (1938). After World War II, a new version of the Old Testament and a further revision of the New Testament (London, 1968) was

sponsored by the Swedish church, prepared by Endel Köpp and Toomas Pöld for Estonian refugees in Sweden.

The first Finnish New Testament (Stockholm, 1548) was translated by Michael Agricola on the basis of Luther's German text. The complete Bible (Stockholm, 1642) was published under the patronage of Queen Christina of Sweden, translated from the original languages by M. Martin Stodius, Gregory Matthaei, and Heinrich J. Hoffman. Frequently revised (by Henrik Florinus, the "War Bible," 1685; by Anders Lizelius, 1776; by E. Stenij, J. Schwartzberg, and others, 1932–1938; by Aimo T. Nikolainen and Aarne Toivanen, an interconfessional version, 1992), this remains the standard Finnish Bible. The earliest scripture portion in Saami (Stockholm, 1648) was an edition of Psalms, Proverbs, Ecclesiastes, and Ecclesiasticus (Sirach), translated in Swedish Saami by J. J. Tornaeus. The first New Testament (Stockholm, 1755) was translated by Pehr Fjellström, and the first complete Bible (Hernösand, 1811) by S. Öhrling, E. J. Grönlund, E. Öhrling, and N. Fjellström. The first New Testament in Norwegian Saami (Christiania, 1840) was the work of N. J. C. V. Stockfleth, which was revised for the first complete Bible (Christiania, 1895), prepared by L. J. Haetta, J. A. Friis, and J. K. Qvigstad.

Baltic: Latvian, Lithuanian. The first Latvian Bible (Riga, 1689) was translated by the Lutheran scholars Ernst Glück and C. B. Witten. Revised often (Königsberg, 1739; Mitau, 1877 and 1898; Riga, New Testament, 1960; London, 1965), it remains the standard Bible of the Latvian church. In 1937, a New Testament was published in Latgalian, the Eastern dialect of Latvian, translated from the Latin Vulgate by Aloizijs Broks.

The earliest biblical publication in

Lithuanian was a Psalter (Königsberg, 1625), revised by J. Rhesa from an unpublished 1590 version of the Bible by J. Bretken, which was based on Luther's German. Samuel B. Chyliński's version of Genesis to Job (London, 1662) was based on the Polish Danzig version; his translation of the New Testament was discovered in 1934 and published by C. Kudzinowski in 1958. The first complete Bible (Königsberg, 1735; revised 1755) was translated by J. J. Quandt and P. Ruhig; it was successively revised by L. J. Rhesa (1816, 1824), Friedrich Kurschat (1869), and A. Velius based on Stuttgart critical editions (1988). A Roman Catholic version of the New Testament by J. A. Goedraitis (Vilna, 1816) based on the Polish Wujek version was popular for more than a century. Bishop Juozapas Skvireckas's translation of the Bible (1913–1916) from the original languages was revised by P. M. Juras (1947–1958). An ecumenical version of the New Testament by Ceslovas Kavaliauskas and others (1972) with the Old Testament by (Catholic) Anthony L. Rubsys (1998) were combined as an interconfessional Bible by the Bible Society of Lithuania (1999).

Celtic: Breton. The first Breton New Testament (Angoulême, 1827) was translated from the Latin Vulgate in the Léon dialect by Jean François Le Gonidec, who later completed the Bible (St. Brieuc, 1866). A revision of this New Testament (1847) by J. Jenkins, who corrected it from the Greek, was often revised and reprinted (1866, 1870, 1885, 1897). More recently, a new Catholic New Testament (1971) was translated by Maodez Glanndour. Meanwhile a New Testament (1853) appeared in the Tréguier dialect under the patronage of the Catholic bishop of St. Brieuc, and a Bible (1889) was translated by G. Le Coat, the Protestant pastor at Tremel.

Basque. One of the earliest publications in Basque was the New Testament in Labourdin Basque (La Rochelle, 1571), translated by Jean Leiçarraga under the patronage of Jeanne d'Albret, the Protestant Queen of Navarre (reprinted by the Trinitarian Bible Society, 1908). A Roman Catholic New Testament was translated from the Vulgate by Jean Haraneder, but only the Gospels were published (Bayonne, 1855), edited by Abbé Maurice Harriet of Halsou. The complete Bible (London, 1865) was translated by Captain Duvoisin for Louis-Lucien Bonaparte. In Guipuzcoan Basque, the gospel of Luke (Madrid, 1838) was translated by Oteiza, a physician, and edited by George Barrow; the first New Testament (Bilbao, 1931) and Bible (Bilbao, 1958) were translated by Raimondo Olabide and José F. Echeverria. In 1983 an interconfessional Bible in Standard, or Batua, Basque, was translated by Amundarain and a committee for the United Bible Societies.   *Erroll F. Rhodes*

African Languages

African translations of the Bible are used in the most complex ethnic, linguistic, and culturally diverse human mosaic on earth. About 2,000 languages are spoken in over 50 different countries by nearly 800 million people. According to the United Bible Societies, scripture versions (of which well over a hundred are complete Bibles) in more than six hundred languages are available to the seven thousand denominations on the African continent. Arabic scriptures are available in some five different script forms. The Tuareq people of Niger Republic speak the language they themselves call Tayrt, but it is part of the Tamahaq language of nomads in the Sahara; several portions of scriptures in at least three alphabetic systems are available in this complex language. In about eight hundred places on the continent, linguistic groups are separated by political boundaries. This creates special challenges for translators; for example, portions of the scriptures for the Borana people living in Kenya are written in Roman characters while the same version for the Boranas living in Ethiopia requires Amharic characters.

By the end of the eighteenth century the complete Bible was available in two African languages, namely Ge^{c}ez (Ethiopic) and Arabic, while a New Testament was available in Coptic. During the nineteenth century, growing Christian missionary activity generated a steady stream of versions of the Bible, or parts thereof, in the indigenous languages of Africa. Pioneering missionaries used available European versions to reach unevangelized Africans. For example, a Dutch New Testament (printed in the Netherlands in 1692) provided the foundation for the work of the Lutheran church in Southern Africa. Georg Schmidt left this Testament in the early eighteenth century with five converts in a valley some 80 miles (130 km) from the Cape of Good Hope. The Khoisan speaking community used it for nearly fifty years without any missionaries present, because Schmidt had to go back to Europe. The only complete Bible available in a Khoisan language, namely Nama—still the living language of some fifty thousand people in Namibia—was published in 1966. It took more than 140 years to complete this translation.

By 2000 the complete Bible (66 books) was available in 144 indigenous versions in Africa, amounting to 38 percent of complete Bible versions available around the globe. Many of these versions also contain the expanded *canon used by the Roman Catholic and other churches. The first Bible in Africa published by Bible Societies that was accepted in unaltered form and sanctioned for use by Roman Catholics was the Afrikaans version, in 1965, with the chiChewa version approved shortly afterward.

At least seventeen indigenous languages in Africa (and offshore islands) are spoken by five million people or more. These languages (in alphabetical order) are Afrikaans, Amharic, Arabic, chiShona, Fulfulde, Hausa, isiXhosa, isiZulu, kinyaRwanda, kiRundi, kiSwahili (Central), kiSwahili (Zaire), liNgala, Malagasy, Oromo (Western), Somali, and Yoruba. Complete Bibles are available in all these languages. Because of language development and refinement of translation techniques, retranslations continue to be made in most of these languages, mostly by indigenous speakers.

A noteworthy trend in linguistic development in Africa has been the merging of languages used in Bible versions into the "Union Versions." For example, in the Xhosa version elements of some seven dialects are merged. By the middle of the twentieth century, there were at least fourteen union language versions available, namely in chiChewa, chiShona, chiTonga, ichiMambwe, Igbo, Kalenjin, kiSwahili (Ngwana-Zaire), loMongo, Nuer, oluLuyia, Omyene, runyaNkore, isiXhosa, and seTswana. In kiSwahili—the lingua franca of East Africa—a complete Bible was published in 1914.

The first complete Bible version translated and printed by movable type on the continent of Africa itself was the seTswana Bible, published in 1857 at Kuruman, Southern Africa. Space allows more extended discussion of only a few versions.

Arabic. Although various complete Bible versions in this language already existed, the translation by Eli Smith and Cornelius van Dyck attained the status of a standard edition after its publication in 1865. The complex dialectal, orthographical, and denominational needs within Arabic-speaking communities provide an ongoing challenge for the various geographical areas. The spread of Islam south of the Sahara, especially in the twentieth century, with its emphasis on its scripture, the *Qur²ān, has stimulated the program for Bible versions in Arabic.

Hausa. The Hausa Bible is available in both Arabic and roman script. This version had a complex translation history from 1857 to 1932, when the complete Bible was published. Missionaries of Sudan Interior Mission, with the help of Hausa-speaking Christians under the guidance of the British and Foreign Bible Society (BFBS), produced a version that has maintained record levels of distribution over the years.

Malagasy. The Malagasy Bible, published by the BFBS in 1835, was the first version of the Bible for an African country that was printed by movable type—although in England.

Tiv. Although the Tiv people (of Northern Nigeria) numbered only about two million, the publication of the New Testament in this language in 1936 provided a stimulus for this language group to convert from Islam to Christianity; in 1940, less than 1 percent of the people were Christian, but by 1972, 95 percent were Christian.

Amharic. Amharic is the official language of Ethiopia and has been in existence as a literary language since the fourteenth century. Parts of the Bible have been published since 1824 in a diglot version together with the ancient language of Ethiopia, Geᶜez. An official version of the Bible was published in 1961 through the work of a joint committee appointed by Emperor Haile Selassie and the BFBS.

seTswana. In 1830 the gospel of Luke in seTswana was published. Through the perseverance of Robert Moffat and his Batswana helpers during the early part of the nineteenth century, the translation was completed and ten thousand copies of the Old Testament printed on a hand press at Kuruman in 1857. These copies of the Old Testament were attached to available printed New Testament sections. The press used by Moffat was carted by ox wagon over more than 800 miles (1,300 km) of the most difficult terrain from the Cape of Good Hope into the interior.

isiZulu. The complete Bible was published in 1883 by the American Bible Society. The people speaking the related Nguni languages of siSwati and Ndebele (both Southern and Northern) have used this version for many years. Translation into these related languages of various individual books of the Bible is still in progress. The complete Bible in Ndebele (Northern) was published in 1978, while versions of the New Testament and Psalms in siSwati and Ndebele (Southern) were published in 1986. The complete Bible in isiZulu was retranslated and published in 1959. In 1986, a new version of the New Testament and Psalms in isiZulu was published. This edition is unique because the type was set in such a way that hyphenation was eliminated and lines were carefully segmented into meaningful sentences and word clusters.

Afrikaans. This Indo-Germanic language came into being on the African continent over the last three centuries and has generated an extensive literature. The complete Bible was published in 1933, and some six million copies were distributed in fifty years. It is the only African version in which the translation directly from the original Hebrew and Greek was done exclusively by native speakers. In 1983, a new translation was published, of which one million copies were distributed within a period of three years.   *Gerrit E. van der Merwe*

Asiatic Languages

In addition to the Syriac, Armenian, Georgian, and Arabic versions *(see the article on* Ancient Languages *earlier in this entry),* there are also other, less well known, early versions of the Bible in Asia, some still extant. For example, in China a version of the Gospels, prepared by Nestorian missionaries for Emperor Taizong of the Tang Dynasty, is known to have existed as early as 640 CE. When the Jesuit missionary Francis Xavier arrived in Japan in 1549, he reportedly brought with him a translation of Matthew prepared by a Japanese convert in India. The Dutch traders were instrumental in translating several early versions: examples include the gospel of Matthew in High Malay (1629), which was the first translation in a non-European language made expressly for the purpose of evangelism; the gospels of Matthew and John (1661) in the now extinct Sinkang dialect of Taiwan; and the Gospels in Sinhalese (1739). Ziegenbalg, the first missionary sent to India by the Danish-Halle Mission, published the Tamil New Testament in 1715, and, assisted by B. Schultz, the Bible in 1727.

A flurry of Bible translation followed on the heels of the great missionary movement inspired by Pietism and the Great Awakening. Starting from the Middle East, the Arabic "Smith–Van Dyck Version" (New Testament, 1860; Bible, 1865), which has gone through successive revisions, is still in use today. Franz Delitzsch's New Testament in Hebrew (1877) has appeared in several revised editions. The first complete Turkish Bible (New Testament, 1819; Bible, 1827), known as the "Ali Bey Version,"

was originally translated in the mid-seventeenth century. Ali Bey, a Pole sold at Constantinople as a slave, was requested by the Dutch ambassador to Constantinople to translate the Bible because of his exceptional linguistic skills. Henry Martyn translated the most influential Persian version; his New Testament (1815), translated in Calcutta, has remained the basis of subsequent revisions. The common-language Persian New Testament appeared in 1973. Martyn also translated the first New Testament into Urdu (1814), the state language of Pakistan. The first Urdu Bible, translated by the Benares Committee, appeared in 1843. Pashto, one of the official languages of Afghanistan, had its first New Testament in 1818, and a full Bible in 1895. Dari, the other official language of Afghanistan, had its first New Testament published in 1982.

India has the Bible or a portion of it in 142 of its languages and dialects. William Carey is reported to have translated the Bible into six languages, and parts of it into twenty-nine more. The Serampore Press, which he established, has published scriptures in no fewer than forty-five languages, of which thirty-five are languages of India. The first Bengali New Testament, which he translated, appeared in 1801, and the complete Bible in 1809. It was due largely to his work and influence that most of the major languages in India got their first Bible in the early nineteenth century—for example, Oriya (1815), Marathi (1821), Sanskrit (1822), Gujarati (1823), Kannada (1831), Assamese (1833), Hindi (1835), Malayalam (1841), Urdu (1843), and Telugu (1854). Although Panjabi had the first New Testament in 1815, the Bible did not appear until 1959. Common-language Bibles include Hindi (1978), Panjabi (1985), Sema Haga (1985), Marathi (1987), Rongmei Naga (1989),

Boro (1991), and Gangte (1991). Nepali, a language used both in Nepal and India, had its first New Testament in 1821 and Old Testament in 1914. The common-language New Testament was published in 1981, and the complete Bible is in preparation. A notable version from Bangladesh is the common language New Testament (1980) in Musalmani Bengali, a form of language spoken by its Muslim population.

Adoniram Judson translated the first Burmese New Testament in 1832 and the Bible in 1835. Due to Burmese hostility to Europeans, he spent twenty-one months in prison while translating the New Testament. The first Hwa Lisu New Testament (1938), by J. O. Fraser in the syllabic script that he developed, is an example of the Bible translator as an inaugurator of vernacular literature. The new common-language Lisu Bible appeared in 1987. In Thailand, the gospel of Luke (1834), translated by Karl Gutzlaff, was the first scripture published in Thai. The first New Testament appeared in 1843, then the Bible in one volume (1891–1896), and finally an interconfessional common-language Bible in 1981. In Laos, the first Lao New Testament was released in 1926, the Bible in 1932, and the common-language New Testament in 1975 and Shorter Old Testament in 1980. In Kampuchea, the first Khmer scripture was the gospel of Luke (1899), translated by a king's interpreter, and the next publication, Luke-Acts (1900), by a Buddhist monk. The first New Testament appeared in 1929, and the Bible in 1954. The first Vietnamese Bible (1913–1916) was translated from the Latin Vulgate by a Catholic priest. A Protestant version followed, the New Testament in 1923, and the Old Testament in 1925; the New Testament, revised in 1954, is still in circulation. In Malaysia, the first complete Malay Bible

(1733), translated by Melchior Leidekker, was the basis for several subsequent revisions. Another version, consisting of the 1879 Old Testament and 1938 New Testament, is still in use today. The common-language New Testament was published in 1976, and the Bible in 1987.

In Indonesia, the Bible or a portion of it has been translated into seventy-two languages and dialects. The first language of Indonesia to have the complete Bible was Javanese (1854). Another version by P. Jansz (New Testament, 1890; Old Testament, 1893) has undergone several revisions and appeared in Javanese, Arabic, and Roman scripts. Indonesian, the national language, had its first New Testament only in 1968, and the Bible in 1974; the common-language New Testament followed in 1977, and the Bible in 1985. Other major language versions include Bugis and Makassar (New Testament, 1888; Old Testament, 1891–1901), Sundanese (New Testament, 1877; Bible, 1891), and Toba (New Testament, 1878; Old Testament, 1894). In addition to Indonesian, other common-language Bibles published include Batak Koro (1987), Batak Toba (1989), Bali (1990), Batak Angkola (1991), and Sunda (1991).

In the Philippines, the Bible or a portion of it has been translated into eighty-three languages and dialects. The Pangasinan Luke (1887) was the first portion to appear. Pilipino, or Tagalog, the national language, had its first New Testament in 1902 and Old Testament in 1905. Most of the major languages had their first Bible in the first half of the twentieth century: Bikol (1914), Cebuano (1917), Hiligaynon (1912), Ilokano (1909), Pampango (1917), Pangasinan (1915), and Samarenyo (1937). Being a dominantly Roman Catholic country, it is very active in interconfessional translations. Interconfessional Bibles in common language have appeared in Tagalog, Bikol, Cebuano, Hiligaynon, Ilokano, Pangasinan, and Samarenyo.

In China, the Bible or a portion of it has been translated into fifty-eight languages and dialects. Marshman and Lassar produced the first Chinese literary Wenli Bible in 1822; however, the 1823 Bible by Morrison and Milne made a greater impact. W. H. Medhurst, Karl Guszlaff, and Elijah Bridgman also exerted considerable influence when they produced the 1838 Bible; they left their mark on several subsequent versions, some of which bear their names. The 1855 Delegates' Version is still in circulation. Among the Easy Wenli versions, the 1902 Bible by Joseph Schereschewsky deserves special mention. Stricken with paralysis in 1881 and unable to hold a pen, he continued to work on the translation of the entire Bible, typing with one finger of each hand. Hence this Bible is known as the "Two-finger Edition." Important Mandarin versions include the 1878 Bible (Old Testament by Schereschewsky and New Testament by Peking Committee) and the 1919 Union Version, which continues to be the standard Bible today. The Today's Chinese Version in common language, translated entirely by Chinese scholars, appeared in 1985. The Bible (Old Testament, 1946–1952; New Testament, 1957–1959), translated by Franciscan Fathers, is widely used by Roman Catholics. Schereschewsky was also involved in producing the first Bible portion (Matthew, 1872) in Khalka Mongolian (the official language of the People's Republic of Mongolia), based on the literary Mongolian New Testament published in 1846. The common-language New Testament, in Cyrillic script, appeared in 1990. In Taiwan, the

Amoy Bible (1882–1884), revised by Thomas Barclay in 1933, remains the standard Bible for Taiwanese speakers in Taiwan. Common-language translation is in progress in Taiwanese and Hakka. For the tribal people, the common-language Old Testament with a shorter New Testament has appeared in Amis (1981) and Taroko (1988), and the New Testament in Bunun (1973), Paiwan (1973), and Tayal (1974).

In Korea, the first portion (Luke and John) appeared in 1882, the New Testament in 1887. This translation, in Hankul characters, was done by John Ross in Manchuria. The 1911 Bible, revised in 1938 and 1956, is still in use today. Korea is also the first country in the world to have published the common-language and interconfessional Bible (1977). In Japan, Karl Gutzlaff, an influential figure in the history of Chinese and Thai Bible translation, in 1837 translated the first ever portions (John and 1–3 John). J. C. Hepburn, the originator of the Hepburnian system of romanization, translated the first New Testament (1880), which formed the basis of the Standard Version Bible (1887). In 1917 a revised New Testament was released. The Colloquial Version Bible (1955), translated entirely by Japanese scholars, is still the standard Bible. However, the circulation of the New Interconfessional Translation Bible (1987) has passed one million copies.

In Micronesia, Hildegard Thiem and Harold Hanlin made an outstanding contribution. The former translated the Palauan New Testament (1964), Shorter Old Testament (1985), and the Yapese Shorter Bible (1981); the latter, the Trukese New Testament (1957) as well as the Ponapean New Testament (1972) and Shorter Old Testament (1977). Hanlin also helped in the preparation of the

Marshallese Shorter Bible (1983). In Papua New Guinea, the Bible or a portion of it has been translated into more than two hundred languages and dialects. The first Bible in the national language (Tok Pisin) was published in 1989. Translation in Pijin, the lingua franca of the Solomon Islands, is in progress. In the rest of the Pacific Islands, most of the major areas had their first Bible by the mid-nineteenth century—for example, Tahitian (1838), Hawaiian (1839), Rarotongan (1851), Samoan (1855), and Maori (1858). Bislama, the national language of the new Republic of Vanuatu, had its first New Testament in 1980. Because of their expertise, the translators were called upon to help translate the Constitution of the new republic.

According to a report compiled by the United Bible Societies, as of the end of 2000, complete Bibles, New Testaments, and portions of the Bible have been published in over nine hundred different languages and dialects from Asia and the Pacific Islands.   *I-Jin Loh*

Australian Aboriginal Languages

At the time of the arrival of the Europeans in Australia at the end of the eighteenth century, there were at least 300,000 aborigines speaking more than 500 languages and dialects; the present aboriginal population (tribal and other, including many with European blood) is about half that, or 1 percent of the total population of Australia. Portions of the Bible have been translated over the last century into approximately thirty Australian languages. Most translations cover only small parts of scripture. This selective approach is because the number of speakers of most aboriginal languages is lower than one thousand, often far less.

One reason for the activity of Bible translators is, of course, their desire to evangelize. Among churches and missionary organizations, however, a much greater appreciation of aboriginal culture has replaced earlier attitudes that were intent on eradicating tribal customs and traditions. The aborigines themselves are aware of their non-European position in relation to scripture. Although most tribal aborigines have received a traditional Christian education from white ministers and teachers at aboriginal mission stations, as aboriginal people become more assertive they discover the similarity between their own position and that of the people of God in the Bible. The stories of *creation, of the ancestors, of the oppression under Pharaoh, of the *Exodus, the conquest, the *exile, and the return have a special appeal. In their struggle for land rights they discover that the biblical concept of land as a gift from God and as something with which humanity is inseparably united is much more closely related to their own aboriginal understanding than to the European understanding of land as a commodity to be bought and sold. Similarly, the concept of *covenant, with its strong emphasis on community and on corporate life, appeals to them much more than the individualistic thinking of Europeans.

Djiniyini Gondarra, a prominent aboriginal United Church Minister, the first aboriginal theologian, and vice president of the United and Islander Christian Congress, provides a good illustration of the new assertiveness of aboriginal Christians. Two important addresses given by him in 1983 and 1985 were entitled, respectively, "Let my people go" and "Overcoming the captivities of the western church context" (the latter being based on Galatians 5.1). Djiniyini, as a black theologian, sees God as black, and he is most conscious of the

European wrapping in which the aborigines have received Christianity and the Bible. He is therefore a strong supporter of the movement to translate the biblical message to aboriginal cultural forms.

It would be incorrect to assume that all aboriginal Christians are critical of the Western wrapping in which the biblical message is received. Many aborigines still receive the biblical message as it was presented fifty and even a hundred years ago. Until very recently, the destruction of all aboriginal culture was propagated, and in some cases this may still occur. Nevertheless, the new developments may be the sign of a new era in biblical interpretation: they will influence not only aborigines, as they try to understand Christianity in their own cultural setting, but also European traditional understandings. The latter may be noted in two particular points.

First, the biblical and theological interpretation of land has stimulated aboriginal Christians to new understandings. Is it valid, some ask, to use the Hebrew Bible in the current debate on land rights? Does this not impose the life and thought of an ancient culture upon modern times? Should the Old Testament not be interpreted in the light of the New Testament, and if this cannot be done (because the New Testament does not offer any thought on the matter in discussion), should we then not abandon all attempts to make connections between the Old Testament and our present world? Others argue that the Old Testament is not subservient to the New Testament, that the difference in culture does not necessarily mean a difference in ethos, and that it is this ethos with which the church has to wrestle when it interprets the biblical message.

Second, a significant outcome of the new developments in aboriginal biblical understandings for the Europeans is that they are forced to reconsider some of their own assumptions. The thought that there is only one way of understanding scripture is challenged, and the question is raised whether Western biblical interpretations are not more influenced by prejudices related to Western civilization and culture than has often been thought. The newer aboriginal understandings challenge and stimulate those whose prerogative it has been for many centuries to interpret scripture.

                              Hendrik C. Spykerboer

Native American Languages

At the end of 2000, over four hundred native American languages (Indian, Eskimo, and Aleut) had at least one book of the scriptures in published form. Over 250 of these languages have complete New Testaments, and 27 have complete Bibles. Out of a total population of approximately 20 million, some 98 percent have at least something of the Bible in a form meaningful to them, provided they can read. In addition to these strictly native American languages, there are publications in 7 creole languages, including an entire Bible in Haitian Creole, based on French and spoken by more than 6 million people; a New Testament in Sranan, an English-based creole spoken by some 300,000 people in Surinam; and a New Testament in Papiamento, a Portuguese-based creole with heavy Spanish borrowings spoken in the Netherlands West Indies by more than 250,000 people.

Evaluating this important development in the translation of the scriptures is extremely difficult in view of a number of crucial factors: (1) in many instances lack of adequate field surveys for determining the degrees of mutual intelligibility between languages and dialects; (2) extreme differences in population sizes (e.g., in Ecuador, Peru, and

Bolivia 6 million Quechuas are divided into some 20 different dialects, while in Brazil 77 languages out of 136 have fewer than 200 speakers); (3) extent of literacy (e.g., 600,000 literate Aymaras out of a total population of 1.7 million in contrast with 90 percent illiteracy in some other language areas); (4) 92 percent bilingualism in the Mexican Indian population and less than 40 percent in a number of the Quechua dialects of Peru; and (5) significant differences in the quality of translations depending on the linguistic training of missionaries and the theological training of indigenous translators.

The majority of translations published in the languages of North America took place prior to 1900, while in Latin America and the Caribbean only 13 out of 391 translations were published by that date, and most of the translations have appeared in print since World War II.

The first Bible to be translated and published in the Western Hemisphere was in the Massachusetts Indian language, spoken by a tribe of Indians settled along the Atlantic Coast north of Boston. John Eliot, a Roxbury minister originally from England, spent fifteen years learning the Indian language before beginning to translate. Genesis and Matthew were published in 1655 and the entire Bible in 1663. Eliot's decision to translate the Bible for the Indians living nearby was without precedent in modern times. Not since the eighth century CE had anyone undertaken to translate the entire Bible primarily for missionary purposes. Unfortunately, there are no Indians who still speak this language. But in Mohawk, an Iroquoian language, the gospel of Mark was first published in 1787, and later in the nineteenth century the rest of the New Testament appeared. These scriptures continue to be used by Mohawk Indians, many of whom live in New York City.

A fascinating story of biblical translation in North America concerns the Cherokee language and an orthography designed to represent the many distinctive sounds. Although an Indian named Sequoya could not read or write in English, he was deeply impressed by the power of written words. "If I could make things fast on paper, it would be like catching a wild animal and taming it," he said. Finally, he devised a remarkably accurate syllabary, completed in 1821 and subsequently used by missionaries to translate the New Testament in a version still widely used and cherished by Cherokees, who constitute the second largest tribe in the United States.

In Latin America and the Caribbean the translation of the scriptures has been carried out by Christian missionaries representing a number of denominations as well as several so-called Faith Missions, such as the South American Indian Mission, New Tribes Mission, and the *Wycliffe Bible Translators, also known as the Summer Institute of Linguistics. The Wycliffe Bible Translators have been responsible for the production of New Testaments in 180 languages and have plans to undertake translations of the New Testament in 20 more languages and to complete work in 35 other languages in which work was begun but not completed.

Because of the limited educational opportunities for most native people in the Americas, Bible translating has generally been carried out by missionaries, but in some cases translation committees consist entirely of indigenous people. An example is the manuscript of the New Testament in the Inuktitut dialect of Eskimo (Eastern Arctic), published in 1992; the Old Testament is preparation for some 20,000 Inuktitut speakers, of whom 90 percent are members of the Anglican church.

The languages of the Americas are remarkably diverse and in many instances structurally very complex. Linguists have classified these languages into more than thirty families, each with distinctive structural features and different vocabularies. A number of languages in southern Mexico have even more tones than Cantonese Chinese and must employ a complex system of tone marks to indicate crucial differences of meaning. Some languages, like Eskimo and Quechua, have exceptionally long words, consisting of as many as a dozen syllables. Verbs in Quechua begin with a root and may be followed by a number of different suffixes and clitics in as many as eight positions in some dialects, with the result that many verbs have more than ten thousand forms.

Because of the linguistic problems faced by translators working in languages not previously reduced to writing, missionary translators have generally invested a great deal of time and effort in the development of scientific alphabets, the analysis of unusual grammatical constructions, and the study of oral literature. The Summer Institute of Linguistics has been particularly active and creative in this area of research.

Because of the linguistic and cultural differences between the biblical text and the indigenous ways of life, some people have seriously doubted the possibility of effective functional equivalence in translating, but the resources of language and culture are generally adequate. In fact, in one language there are two expressions for the ambiguous English expression "love of God." God's love for people is expressed as "God hides them in his heart" and people's love for God is "their hearts go away with God."

But for a full understanding of the biblical message there are serious cultural differences. Many Indians in South America see no reason "to fear God." He is generally regarded as being too far away to be of any real concern for people. What they fear are the malicious spirits of the forests, streams, and caves, which must be placated with gifts.

A traditional syncretistic Christopaganism also poses real problems for communication. In many areas a name such as *Tata Dios,* literally, "Father God," is really a name for the sun, and *Mama Dios,* literally "Mother God," is in some places a triple reference to the moon, the earth, and the Virgin Mary.

For a variety of reasons the publication of the scriptures in some Indian languages has not been a success, but where there have been missionaries or leaders of national churches who have encouraged literacy, instructed people in the meaning and relevance of the Bible message, and trained local leadership, the response has been remarkable.

The production of the scriptures in indigenous languages of the Americas has produced three important byproducts: literacy by believers anxious to learn to read the scriptures; concern for further education in their own language as well as in the dominant language of the area (Spanish, Portuguese, English, or French); and a sense of ethnic pride, so important for socially and economically exploited people. As one Totonac Indian said when he first purchased a New Testament in his own language, "Now we are a people because we have a book."

Eugene A. Nida

TRIBUTE AND TAXATION. *This entry deals with payments exacted upon subject populations by imperial powers, and consists of two articles, the first on the* Ancient Near East, *and the second on the* Roman Empire.

Ancient Near East

Tribute and taxation encompass all obligations in precious metals, other goods, or service imposed by a central government on its own people, on visiting traders, or on regions that submitted to it. Tribute generally refers to payments made by one state to another dominant state to prevent attack or in ongoing submission. Taxation would then describe obligations within a state, including payments by visiting merchants. In the empires conquered by Assyria (ninth to seventh centuries BCE), Babylon (605–539 BCE), and Persia (539 to the late fourth century BCE), payments by distant territories incorporated into the realm as provinces might still be called tribute, but with sovereignty lost this simply represented the highest stage in a pyramid of taxation required to support the central authority.

In the biblical portrayal of Israel's conquest of the Promised Land, the defeated peoples are annihilated when possible in holy *war, without negotiation. This extreme policy only applied where the goal was to occupy the land. When the Canaanites managed a negotiated settlement, the obligation was not tribute but forced labor. In the period of the judges, Israel repeatedly suffered defeat and is once said to have paid tribute, to Eglon of Moab.

By contrast, David (ca. 1000–961 BCE) carved out a small empire that brought a flow of booty and tribute to the new capital at Jerusalem, from Moab, Aram, and Hamath. This income continued under Solomon, supplemented by gifts and taxes received from foreign trade. David's new dynasty not only brought Israel great wealth but building projects, a standing army, and a palace bureaucracy, all of which required support by internal taxation along with the foreign revenue. There is no mention of

civil taxation before the monarchy, although legal traditions provide for support of the religious institutions by payments such as offerings of first fruits and *tithes.

The institution of *kingship in Israel is remembered by this negative side of success, and the Bible acknowledges painful new taxation while boasting of Solomon's wealth. Solomon divided Israel into twelve (nontribal) districts to supply the monthly needs of the palace and appointed high-ranking administrators. He made the Israelites contribute forced labor for building the palace. 1 Samuel 8.11–17 lists further demands of royal taxation, including military conscription to support a chariot army and forced service as craftsmen, palace workers, and farmers. The burden of taxation is remembered as the principal cause of the separation by the northern tribes after Solomon, under Jeroboam I (922–901). Even under David, a census for possible conscription of fighting men is treated as a crime.

After the split into two kingdoms, there is little mention of internal taxation, although the kings surely continued the system at some level, in order to sustain palace and army. The Bible's depiction of the divided monarchy focuses once more on tribute, this time paid by Israel and Judah to hold off foreign attack. In the ninth century this consisted of one-time payments to the Aramean kingdom centered at Damascus by Asa (913–873) and Joash (837–800) of Judah, and Ahab (869–850) of Israel. Aram gave way to the more distant but more serious threat from Assyria. Menahem (745–737) of Israel paid "Pul" (Tiglath-pileser III, 745–727) to withdraw, and one-time payments are recorded for Ahaz (735–715) and Hezekiah (715–687) of Judah to Tiglath-pileser and Sennacherib (704–681). Assyrian royal annals also claim

such tribute from Jehu (843–815) of Israel to Shalmaneser III (858–824) and
from Israel to Adad-nirari III (809–782).

Traumatic as it was, one-time payment represented the least of obligations
in a hierarchy that proceeded to annual
tribute and finally incorporation as a
province of the empire. The first biblical
indication of annual tribute occurs just
before the fall of the north, when
Hoshea (732–724) pays Shalmaneser V
(726–722). Before their revolts, Jo-
haiakim (609–598) and Zedekiah (597–
587) of Judah probably paid annual tribute in becoming vassals of Babylon.

Detailed records from Assyria show
us the system into which Israel and Judah
were drawn. The Assyrian king received
payments from foreign rulers as "tribute"
(Akkadian *maddattu*) and *namurtu*, originally a gift brought for a royal audience.
Payments from territories annexed to the
empire were no longer called *maddattu*,
but obligations increased, including various taxes on agricultural produce, animals, and other materials, along with the
ilku, or personal service to the state. The
ilku might involve military service or
forced labor for public projects (canals,
building repair, etc.), and it could be
avoided by paying and supplying a
replacement.

The provincial administration of the
Assyrian empire was taken over by Nebuchadrezzar (605–562) of Babylon,
who could not otherwise have consoli-
dated his new realm. Innovation was left
to the Persians, who further expanded
the empire. Darius I (522–486) set up
twenty satrapies, which combined existing provinces into larger units, including
"Across-the-(Euphrates) River," or
Syria-Palestine (Herodotus 3.89). Each
satrapy then made a fixed payment according to its productive capacity, which
actually protected the populace from local officials who might curry favor by

promising higher revenue. Persian regulation of taxation was designed to produce stable submission, and complemented the measured local autonomy
allowed in matters of religion and administration. Within each satrapy, however, enforcement of obligations for payments or service was handled mainly by
local lords.

The sum of tax obligations in the district of Yehud (Judea) is described as
"tribute, custom, and toll" in the complaint to the king by those who opposed
reconstruction of Jerusalem, with the
claim that a revolt would stop payment
(Ezra 4.13, 20). The one concern of the
empire was that its authority be recognized by an uninterrupted flow of revenue. There was ample opportunity for
oppressive local taxation, as Nehemiah
acknowledged when he refused the standard governor's levy for maintaining his
household.

Persian rule was brought to an abrupt
end with Alexander's sweep across the
empire, but he simply took over the existing administrative systems. The dynas-
ties of his generals, the Ptolemies in
Egypt and the Seleucids in Mesopotamia
and Syria, competed for control of Palestine, and eventual Seleucid domination
in the second century BCE brought increased taxation, with collection rights
sold to whomever promised the highest
revenue. Standard taxes are described in
1 Maccabees 10.29–30 as tribute, salt
tax, crown levy, one-third of grain, and
one-half of fruit.   *Daniel E. Fleming*

Roman Empire

Rome acquired its first province (part of
Sicily) in the middle of the third century
BCE after defeating the Carthaginians,
and took over the system of taxation
they had instituted there. Similarly, as
more provinces were added during the
next two centuries, local systems were

for the most part taken over without any attempt to introduce uniformity. A new general tax was instituted only where there had been no previous control or systematic taxation by any power. The chief purpose of direct taxation was to pay the costs of the wars of conquest and of continuing control. Thus, the tax in Spain was called *stipendium*, that is, "soldiers' pay." Although government monopolies and indirect taxes, farmed out to publicans, were often profitable, and although a great deal of wealth flowed in various ways from the provinces both to Roman individuals and to the state, no major profit seems to have been derived from direct taxation before the annexation of the kingdom of Pergamum.

The gradual annexation of the kingdoms around the eastern Mediterranean, from Pergamum (133 BCE) to Egypt (30 BCE), produced a major change. Most of them had been thoroughly organized by their Hellenistic monarchs for their own profit, and Rome inherited both the organization and the profits, often simplifying collection by using the experienced *publicani*. In the 60s BCE, Pompey annexed some of these territories and reorganized others, greatly increasing public revenues. He also initiated the practice of imposing tribute on minor client rulers, thus increasing public profit without assuming any direct administration of intractable populations.

The result, by the end of the Republic, was an aggregate of provinces in which direct taxes were levied at different rates and collected in different ways (either by officials or by *publicani*), and each province was a mosaic of political entities of varying degrees of administrative and fiscal subjection. Extortion and dissatisfaction increased as the state proved unable to control either its administrators (members of its governing body, the Senate) or the powerful corporations of *publicani*, and the civil wars of the 40s and 30s BCE greatly increased the financial burdens of the provinces while disrupting their administration and economy.

Augustus tried to tighten control and begin some systematization. Censuses of people were taken in new and in some old provinces (thus the famous one of Sulpicius Quirinius in Syria and Judea: see Luke 2.1–4, with some chronological confusion, and cf. Acts 5.37; *see also* Chronology, *article on* Early Christian Chronology); and, following a limited example set by Caesar, he continued the removal of *publicani* from the collection of direct taxes and had them collected instead by officials in new provinces. His immediate successors completed these measures, but the large variety of local statuses and the farming of the numerous indirect taxes (see below) by *publicani* were only very slowly reduced. On the whole these changes benefited the government and not the taxpayers.

In Palestine, Herod paid a fixed tribute to Rome and could collect his own taxes as he saw fit. We know little about how he did so, and the protests to Augustus after his death about his administration do not dwell on fiscal oppression. His sons inherited his obligations and his privilege, and although we are told the total of their revenues, we do not know much about their method of collection. In outline, though, their system did not differ much from that introduced by Augustus into Judea after its annexation (6 CE) or from that of Roman Syria, since both were descended from Hellenistic models.

In Judea there were two regular direct taxes: a tax on agricultural produce, still levied in kind, but during the early empire converted into a fixed amount of money as in all other provinces; and a poll tax, about which we know little in detail. Perhaps paid only by those not liable to the produce tax, it consisted of a flat-rate personal tax on all men from age fourteen and women from age twelve to age sixty-five and was levied at least at the rate of one denarius (about a day's wage) per year (see the tribute money of the Gospels: Matt. 22.15–22 par.). Later (we do not know when) it was combined with a percentage tax on property. These were paid to Roman officials, but we do not know who collected them from the taxpayers. (Income taxes were unknown in antiquity.) By 17 CE they were so burdensome that a joint deputation from Syria and Judea asked Tiberius for relief. We casually hear of other taxes, for example, a house tax in Jerusalem, and we must assume the impositions known from other provinces: the notorious *aurum coronarium*, originally a contribution to a governor's Roman triumph, but later demanded by emperors on various occasions; lavish free hospitality for governors and their staffs and friends; perhaps quartering of soldiers; and—an item subject to unsuccessful regulation ever since Augustus—responsibility for the transport of official parties by communities along the roads. The incidence of the total of direct taxation was thus uneven and unpredictable.

Indirect taxes were probably worse. Government monopolies (such as salt, the produce of lakes and rivers, and the famed Judean balm) were farmed out to *publicani*, as were the Roman customs duties and road tolls at provincial boundaries (and perhaps elsewhere) and harbor dues. On top of these, cities were free to impose charges for their own revenues. The result was great disparity in the cost of the same products between communities, as well as the usual bribery at the point of collection, and the highest cost of living in the Near East. The poor naturally suffered most, and this social and economic component merged with religious and nationalist feelings in the revolts against Rome. Each failed revolt resulted in harsher exactions and an increase in distress and dissatisfaction.

E. Badian

TRINITY. Because the Trinity is such an important part of later Christian doctrine, it is striking that the term does not appear in the New Testament. Likewise, the developed concept of three coequal partners in the Godhead found in later creedal formulations cannot be clearly detected within the confines of the *canon.

Later believers systematized the diverse references to God, Jesus, and the Spirit found in the New Testament in order to fight against heretical tendencies of how the three are related. Elaboration on the concept of a Trinity also serves to defend the church against charges of di- or tritheism. Since the Christians have come to worship Jesus as a god, how can they claim to be continuing the *monotheistic tradition of the God of Israel? Various answers are suggested, debated, and rejected as heretical, but the idea of a Trinity—one God existing in three persons and one substance—ultimately prevails.

While the New Testament writers say a great deal about God, Jesus, and the Spirit of each, no New Testament writer expounds on the relationship among the three in the detail that later Christian writers do.

The earliest New Testament evidence for a tripartite formula comes in 2 Corinthians 13.13, where Paul wishes that "the grace of the Lord Jesus, the love of God, and the communion of the Holy Spirit" be with the people of Corinth. It is possible that this three-part formula derives from later liturgical usage and was added to the text of 2 Corinthians as it was copied. In support of the authenticity of the passage, however, it must be said that the phrasing is much closer to Paul's understandings of God, Jesus, and the *Holy Spirit than to a more fully developed concept of the Trinity. Jesus, referred to not as Son but as Lord and Christ, is mentioned first and is connected with the central Pauline theme of *grace. God is referred to as a source of love, not as father, and the Spirit promotes sharing within the community. The word "holy" does not appear before "spirit" in the earliest manuscript evidence for this passage.

A more familiar formulation is found in Matthew 28.19, where Jesus commands the disciples to go out and baptize "in the name of the Father and of the Son and of the Holy Spirit." The phrasing probably reflects baptismal practice in churches at Matthew's time or later if the line is interpolated. Elsewhere Matthew records a special connection between God the Father and Jesus the Son, but he falls short of claiming that Jesus is equal with God.

It is John's gospel that suggests the idea of equality between Jesus and God ("I and the Father are one"; 10.30). The Gospel starts with the affirmation that in the beginning Jesus as Word (see Logos) "was with God and . . . was God" (1.1), and ends (chap. 21 is most likely a later addition) with Thomas's confession of faith to Jesus, "My Lord and my God!" (20.28). The Fourth Gospel also elaborates on the role of the Holy Spirit as the Paraclete sent to be an advocate for the believers.

For the community of John's gospel, these passages provide assurance of the presence and power of God both in the ministry of Jesus and in the ongoing life of the community. Beyond this immediate context, however, such references raise the question of how Father, Son, and Spirit can be distinct and yet the same. This issue is debated over the following centuries and is only resolved by agreement and exclusion during the christological disputes and creedal councils of the fourth century and beyond.

While there are other New Testament texts where God, Jesus, and the Spirit are referred to in the same passage, it is important to avoid reading the Trinity into places where it does not appear. An example is 1 Peter 1.1–2, in which the salutation is addressed to those who have been chosen "according to the foreknowledge of God the Father in holiness of spirit." This reference may be to the holiness of spirit of the believers, but translators consistently take it as the Holy Spirit in order to complete the assumed trinitarian character of the verse: "who have been chosen and destined by God the Father and sanctified by the Spirit" (NRSV). This translation not only imposes later trinitarian perspectives on the text but also diminishes the important use of the spirit of human beings elsewhere in 1 Peter.

Daniel N. Schowalter

TYPOLOGY. The practice in the New Testament and the early church whereby a person or a series of events occurring in the Old Testament is interpreted as a type or foreshadowing of some person (almost invariably Christ) or feature in the Christian dispensation. For example, in 1 Peter 3.19–21 the story of Noah's *ark is taken as a type of *baptism, and in Hebrews 11.17–19 Abraham's willingness to sacrifice his son Isaac (see Aqedah) is understood as a type of Christ's *resurrection. These two examples also show that the word "type" need not be used for a typological comparison to be made.

The very possibility of such typology depends on the Christian assumption that the Bible recounts the course of salvation history. By this is meant the Bible as a record of the long development by which God, with a redemptive purpose always in mind, called Israel into being out of Egypt, led her through the wilderness, made a *covenant with her, brought her into Canaan, guided and admonished her through her troubled history (including the traumatic experience of the Babylonian *exile), and consummated his relationship by sending his Son in Jesus Christ—thereby effecting an eternal salvation by establishing a people of God whose membership is open to all. What justifies understanding the Bible typologically (if it can be justified) is the conviction that God is always the same. If he is fully known in Jesus Christ, then when he revealed himself under the old dispensation, he must in some sense have been known as the God of Jesus Christ. It is, therefore, justifiable to seek in his revelation of himself under the old dispensation some similarity with his revelation under the new. In fact, a sort of typology can be found in the Hebrew Bible itself: see, for example, Isaiah 43.1–19; 51.9–11, where God's action of old in creation and redemption from Egypt are treated as types of the new deliverance from exile about to occur (*see* Exodus, The).

Clear examples of typology occur in 1 Corinthians 10.1–11, where the events of the crossing of the Red Sea, the giving of the *manna, and the water issuing miraculously from the rock are taken as types of baptism and of the bread and wine in the Eucharist. What is more, the presence of the preexistent Christ with Israel in the wilderness is implied.

If used excessively or indiscriminately, typology can pass over into allegory. Allegory means using any person, event, or object in the Old Testament arbitrarily to signify a corresponding event or thing in the New Testament. The difference lies in the authenticity of the analogy. Allegory does sometimes appear in the New Testament; in Galatians 4.21–30, for example, Paul launches into an elaborate comparison of Ishmael and Isaac, on the one hand, with Judaism and Christianity, on the other. But he brings in so many terms of comparison that the meaning merges into an unconvincing allegory. Again, in 1 Corinthians 9.9–10 Paul argues that apostles have a right to be supported because, according to the Law, an ox is allowed to eat the grain as it treads it out. The comparison fails to carry much conviction, however, because oxen are not apostles.

Some modern Roman Catholic scholars have used the medieval concept of *sensus plenior* to justify a modern use of typology. This was the idea that the words of inspired writers in the Old Testament might bear a deeper or fuller sense than they were aware of, and that this deeper sense can be perceived in the New Testament. This can be a helpful and illuminating way of reading the Bible as long as it is kept within reasonable bounds. For example, in Psalm 119.105 the psalmist exclaims, "Your word is a lamp to my feet." A Christian, who knows of the Word made flesh, may reasonably and profitably apply this to Christ, as long as one does not claim that the psalmist knew about Christ in writing the words.

See also Interpretation, History of, *article on* Early Christian Interpretation.

Anthony Tyrrell Hanson

U

UGARITIC. In 1928 a Syrian farmer accidentally uncovered ancient tombs on the Mediterranean coast, directly opposite the northeastern tip of Cyprus. This led to the excavation of the main city at nearby Ras Shamra, which yielded one of the most sensational archaeological finds of the twentieth century: the political and religious texts of archives of the ancient kingdom of Ugarit. The French excavators uncovered numerous cuneiform tablets, many of which were written in a hitherto unknown alphabetic script. On decipherment of that alphabet, it was seen that the language of Ugarit belongs, with *Hebrew and *Aramaic, to the family of Northwest Semitic languages. Dating roughly from the fifteenth to the thirteenth centuries BCE, these tablets now include a large collection of various kinds of texts: literary, religious, epistolary, administrative, and economic. Together they form the single most important archaeological contribution in the twentieth century to our knowledge of the language and symbol world of ancient Israel.

In the first place, the discovery of the Ugaritic tablets has greatly enhanced, and at times corrected, our understanding of biblical Hebrew. Many Hebrew words whose meanings had been unknown or merely conjectured have been clarified by Ugaritic cognates. The close relationship of Hebrew with Ugaritic, moreover, allows one to reconstruct still more accurately the early history of the Hebrew language and to discern some early linguistic features in (and hence the relative dates of) parts of the Hebrew Bible. The identification of certain grammatical elements in Northwest Semitic languages has greatly facilitated the task of translating the Hebrew Bible; texts that were hitherto grammatically awkward, if not impossible, can now be explained. On the basis of Ugaritic literature too, scholars have been able to make advances in the study of Hebrew prosody, for the two languages apparently share the same poetic structures and utilize the same stylistic devices (*see* Poetry, Biblical Hebrew).

Beyond the details of language and prosody, the tablets also contribute to our knowledge of Canaanite religion. The Ugaritic pantheon includes many of the gods already known to us from the Hebrew Bible as Canaanite deities against whom the prophets inveighed. Much more is now known, for example, about Baal and Asherah (Athirat in Ugaritic) and the fertility cult with which they are associated. Thus, in Elijah's encounter with the prophets of Baal, the failure of the latter to bring rain demonstrates the impotence of Baal even in what was thought to be his domain; instead, it is Yahweh who controls nature. But the value of the Ugaritic texts goes beyond the horizons of Canaanite faith. The evidence suggests that Israelite theology was not as radically discontinuous with Canaanite religions as was once thought. Yahweh was imbued with characteristics associated with El and Baal. Like El, the chief deity of the Ugaritic pantheon, Israel's God is regarded as the Most High who presides over the divine council and judges other gods. The Ugaritic descriptions of El's abode (a tent) in "the far north" and "at the source of the two-rivers" correspond to the biblical depiction of the divine abode, which, according to Judean theology, was on Mount Zion. Like the storm-god Baal, Yahweh is portrayed as a divine warrior who sets out to fight the cosmic forces of *chaos most commonly depicted as the flood(s) and "mighty waters," as sea and river (corresponding to the Ugaritic synonymous parallelism Prince Sea/Judge River), and as sea monsters, including Leviathan (Ugaritic *ltn*). Accordingly, the manifestation of divine presence is often couched in the language of a storm *theophany. Indeed, the language and content of Psalm 29 are so reminiscent of Ugaritic that scholars are generally agreed that it was originally a Canaanite hymn to Baal adapted for Yahwistic worship. As in the Ugaritic myths and hymns, the divine warrior in the Bible is enthroned in the sanctuary as a consequence of the victory over enemies. It has also become clear that Isaiah's metaphor of the fallen "Day Star" (Isa. 14.12–15) is to be located in the Ugaritic myth of the fallen astral deities, notably Athtar, who presumed to usurp the throne of Baal; the persistence of this theme is seen in the later development of traditions about Satan.

From the Ugaritic tablets, much can also be learned about the social institutions and structure of the region. The legends and administrative texts provide insights into the Israelite understanding of divine and human *kingship. Among other things, it was the king's task to "decide the case of the widow" and to "judge the suit of the orphan"; failure to do so was tantamount to surrender of royal prerogative. Besides the king, one learns about various cultic functionaries, military personnel, and people of various social strata. Among the military elite and powerful nobility are people designated "bulls," "gazelles," "boars," and the like. In the Ugaritic texts, one encounters a respected group known as the *nqdm,* a class or guild to which Mesha the king of Moab and Amos belong, calling into question the traditional translation of *nqd* as "shepherd" (Amos 1.1).

In minute details of the Hebrew language as well as in our understanding of broad themes and literary forms in the Bible, Ugaritic has had an impact. Several commentaries and numerous reference works have been written with the explicit purpose of elucidating the biblical text through the advances made possible by the discoveries at Ras Shamra. Although the correspondences between the Ugaritic texts and the Bible have at times been exaggerated in scholarly works, the study of Ugaritic is an indispensable discipline in biblical scholarship.

See also Israel, Religion of; Myth.

C. L. Seow

V

VENGEANCE. In biblical thought, God's vengeance is an expression of his *holiness. Rendering vengeance to his adversaries is essentially a response to evil. Vengeance is punishment in retribution for injury and so is often linked with the wrath of God. Vengeance was understood as God's way of redressing wrongs, and the word seldom has a connotation of vindictiveness. Cries to Yahweh for vengeance are cries for healing and redemption—even though a restoration may call for retributive justice. God's vengeance is balanced by his *mercy. Vengeance, then, is very much a part of God's character and does not contradict his love.

God's vengeance is directed at those who oppose him and who refuse to acknowledge his commands. These include his enemies, who are often other nations, or a single nation that has done evil, especially toward Israel, God's people. When, however, Israel becomes unfaithful to Yahweh and breaks *covenant, God's vengeance exacts punishment also on Israel. In the absence of justice in the land, God puts on his "garments of vengeance" (Isa. 59.17), ready to punish Israel, ready to display his wrath. Vengeance, then, is a sign of God's working in history, fulfilling his purposes. Although vengeance belongs to him alone, God can authorize people to act as agents of his vengeance.

Since wrongs are not always righted in the present and God's vengeance is delayed because of his patience, later prophets look forward to a "day of vengeance" in the future—an apocalyptic day that will mark the beginning of a new age (*see* Day of the Lord).

Although the Hebrew Bible has little to say about life after death (*see* Afterlife and Immortality), the hope that sin will be punished and faithfulness be rewarded in the life to come is stated in Daniel 12.2, 3. In the New Testament divine vengeance is closely tied to the *day of judgment at the end of the age, when Christ will return in glory (*see* Second Coming of Christ). For the wicked he appears "in flaming fire, inflicting vengeance" (2 Thess. 1.8; Jude 7), but innocent sufferers who wonder why God does not act on their behalf have the assurance that in the end he will vindicate his servants.

Vengeance as a principle of *law was well established in ancient Israel: "life for life, eye for eye, tooth for tooth" (Exod. 21.23–24; cf. Deut. 19.21); this is known as the *lex talionis* (the law of equivalent retribution). On its face it seems brutal, but it was an advance in legal thinking. It shut the door to unlimited revenge and kept the punishment from exceeding the crime. It established the principle of equity in punishment and allowed for no favoritism. The law functioned under the jurisdiction of judges.

The New Testament upholds the right of the governing authorities to avenge wrongs, acting as God's servants for the well-being of the community. As in ancient Israel, personal vengeance was forbidden; indeed, doing an enemy good was considered to be a part of wisdom. Jesus not only taught nonretaliation, exhorting his followers to suffer loss rather than resort to personal vindictiveness, but he also modeled it.   *David Ewert*

VERSE DIVISION. See Chapter and Verse Divisions.

VERSIONS. See Translations.

VINE AND VINEYARD. The "Song of the Vineyard" (Isa. 5.1–7) describes the different steps that were required to plant a vineyard and successfully harvest its grapes. First the soil had to be cleared of stones before planting the vine stocks in it. The stones could be used to build a wall to keep out animals such as boars and foxes. A watchtower might also be constructed to ensure the safety of the crop, especially at harvest time. The vinedresser would prune away the new small shoots so that the main fruit-bearing stems would obtain greater nourishment. A wine press would be constructed (usually hewn of rock), for the main purpose of raising grapes in ancient times was for the making of *wine.

The symbolic use of the vine occurs throughout the Bible. In Psalm 80.8 Israel is identified as a vine: "You brought a vine out of Egypt; you drove out the nations and planted it." While this imagery is used positively to indicate how Israel will bear fruit as a vine, more commonly Israel is described as an unproductive vine, a vine that is plucked up and left to wither away, a choice vine that has become wild. Closely related to

this imagery is the portrayal of Israel as a vineyard, as in Isaiah 5.1–7. Here Israel, whom Yahweh planted looking for choice grapes, has yielded wild grapes. Many have understood John's image of Jesus as "the true vine" (John 15.1) as a deliberate contrast to the portrayal of Israel as a vine/vineyard that has not proved fruitful.

In the Gospels, Jesus is quoted as using the vineyard in two *parables: the parable of the laborers in the vineyard who were hired at different hours of the day, and the parable of the wicked vinedressers; the description in the latter of the work done in the vineyard is derived from Isaiah 5.1–7.   *Edgar W. Conrad*

VIRGIN BIRTH OF CHRIST. As a major tenet of Roman Catholic teaching and a foundation for fundamentalist belief, the virgin birth remains an essential doctrine for many Christians. Since the advent of modern historical criticism, however, others have been skeptical about the virgin birth. Ultimately, the issue will be decided by a person's faith stance and view of scripture.

Belief in the virgin birth of Christ is based on the stories of Jesus' birth found in the gospels of Matthew and Luke. In Luke 1.5–38, shortly after Elizabeth miraculously conceives in her old age, the angel Gabriel appears to Mary who is specifically described as a virgin (Grk. *parthenos*). He tells Mary that she will conceive and bear a son who will inherit the throne of David. Mary, surprised by this news, asks, "How can this be, since I do not know a man?" Gabriel reassures her that she will be impregnated by the Holy Spirit and cites as proof the fact that Elizabeth is now with child. There is no confusion possible in Luke's account. The author wants it to be clear that this is a miraculous impregnation of a woman who had not had sexual relations. The detailed nature of this dialogue between Mary and Gabriel suggests that the author of Luke was responding to specific questions about the virgin birth of Christ. Luke also alludes to the virgin birth in his *genealogy of Jesus when he says that Jesus was "the son (as was supposed) of Joseph" (Luke 3.23).

Matthew 1.18–25 takes the tradition about Jesus' miraculous conception and develops it in a slightly different way. The angel, who is not named, appears not to Mary but to Joseph, who has discovered that Mary is pregnant. Although Joseph plans to break off his engagement, the angel commands him to go through with the marriage since the child is from the Holy Spirit. As in Luke, Matthew wishes to make it clear that Mary and Joseph had not had sexual relations prior to this announcement. In fact, the author stresses that Joseph "did not know her until she had borne a son" (Matt. 1.25).

The author of Matthew often attempts to prove that Jesus is the Messiah by showing how the details of his life fulfill the Hebrew scriptures. In this case, Matthew presents a passage from Isaiah 7 in which the prophet is speaking to Ahaz, king of Judah. Ahaz faces attack from the forces of Syria and Israel (734 BCE), and so he is contemplating an alliance with the king of Assyria. God makes it clear to Ahaz that such an alliance should not take place. Isaiah declares that the Lord will provide a sign that will make known the Lord's will in spite of Ahaz's recalcitrance. A young woman who is pregnant will bear a son, and before that child is old enough to tell the difference between good and evil, the powers that threaten Judah will be defeated. Ahaz refuses to believe the sign and sends tribute to the Assyrian king who destroys Damascus and kills the king of Syria. The other threatening

force, Israel, is conquered by Assyria twelve years after the occasion of this sign at about the time that the child mentioned in the sign would have reached the age of maturity.

Isaiah's intent in discussing this child is clearly to set a time frame for the destruction of Israel. There is nothing miraculous about the mother or the conception process. The Hebrew word used, ᶜalmâ, means simply "young woman," without any implication of virginity. The Greek word *parthenos* used to translate ᶜalmâ can mean either a young woman or a virgin. Matthew used a Greek Bible, so he naturally reinterpreted Isaiah 7.14 as a prophecy referring to the virgin birth of Jesus. For the evangelist, Isaiah's original meaning was superseded by the identification of Jesus as Immanuel (Grk. *Emmanouēl*).

One of the most frequently raised objections to the virgin birth is that, with the exception of Matthew and Luke, New Testament authors do not make explicit mention of it. Other alleged references are at best vague allusions. Such an argument from silence cannot be determinative, but it is an important consideration for people who see the virgin birth as a feature created within the early traditions about Jesus rather than a historical occurrence.

Those who doubt the historicity of the virgin birth argue that it was created by the early church as a way of honoring the coming of Jesus as the *Son of God or of explaining the idea of God becoming flesh. Miraculous human birth stories are common in biblical tradition, going back to Abraham and Sarah, and numerous references to deities impregnating women are found within the Greco-Roman tradition. The mother of Heracles, for instance, was said to have been impregnated by Zeus.

Affirmation of the virgin birth by the

apostolic father Ignatius confirms that the concept was an early and strongly held belief. As Christian doctrine developed, the virgin birth became a preeminent statement of faith and the ultimate test of belief in biblical inerrancy. It was also expanded in several directions. The veneration of Mary is related to the virgin birth, as is the tradition that Mary was ever virgin. Belief in this latter concept requires that the brothers and sisters of Jesus mentioned in the New Testament must have been stepbrothers and stepsisters or cousins. Mary's virginity also becomes an important factor in ascetic Christianity and in the promotion of a life of celibacy.

Daniel N. Schowalter

W

WAR. In the Hebrew Bible war almost always refers to armed struggle between nations; in the New Testament the word more often refers to spiritual or cosmic conflict against evil.

Hebrew Bible. It is important to recognize that Israel was both a nation and a people of Yahweh its God. As a nation, it lived among other nations and was subject to the struggles—military, economic, social, and political—that are common to all nations. As a people of God, the Israelites were constantly being reminded that they were to put their trust in the Lord.

Since God had chosen them to be his "treasured possession" (Deut. 14.2) and had entered into *covenant with them, he fought their battles and drove out the enemy before them. Yahweh is called a warrior, and the expression "the Lord of hosts" (1 Sam. 17.45; Isa. 1.24; "God of hosts," Amos 5.27) is sometimes interpreted to mean that he leads an army or wages a war; another interpretation conveys the idea of heavenly hosts, either the sun, moon, and stars or the heavenly beings. For theological or sentimental reasons, this concept is repulsive to many moderns. Yet, according to treaties from the ancient Near East, the ruler who made such a covenant with a people was obligated to protect and defend them. On another line of reasoning, the only way Yahweh could preserve the identity of this small nation against the more

powerful nations surrounding them was by fighting their battles for them.

Particularly objectionable to many are the wars in which the Israelites were commanded by Yahweh to exterminate (or "devote") a people, "men and women, young and old, oxen, sheep, and donkeys" (Josh. 6.21) with the sword; this command is explained in Deuteronomy 20.16–18 as a safeguard against idolatry. It must also be noted that Yahweh punished his people similarly for their transgressions against him. Accordingly, Amos grouped the rebellions of Judah and Israel with those of other nations (1.3–2.16).

War, both in Israel and in the ancient Near East, was in some respects a religious act. God was to be consulted before going to war. Perhaps this was the reason for God's anger when David held a census, the method of mustering an army for war, without first seeking God's will. The leader was possessed of "the spirit of the Lord" (Judg. 6.34), and when the spirit departed, the leader was powerless before the enemy. Sacrifice was offered before the conflict began. War was "sanctified" (Hebr. *qiddaš;* NRSV "prepare"). The camp was a holy place where God himself was present, therefore there was to be nothing unclean (e.g., a nocturnal emission or human excrement). The warrior refrained from sexual intercourse, which is why Uriah refused to comply with David's devious request (2 Sam. 11.6–12). The priest gave counsel and encouragement, and those who could not devote themselves fully to the conflict were sent back home. Terms of peace were to be offered, but if rejected, then the Israelite army was to carry out the Lord's judgment.

After the return from *exile, Israel was no longer an independent nation—although there was a tolerated independence resulting from the wars of the Maccabees for about a century. The idea of war became more eschatological: it represented freedom from the oppressor. Two ways to this freedom were envisaged; the one was by the Messiah, the son of David, who would lead the armies to victory; the other was by divine intervention, a heavenly "*son of man" and his angels (Dan. 7.13; Enoch 37–71). The *Apocrypha and *Pseudepigrapha furnish many and varied details of this hope for deliverance.

A remarkable picture is drawn in the War of the Sons of Light with the Sons of Darkness (the "War Scroll," 1QM), one of the *Dead Sea Scrolls. In this document, dating from the first century BCE, there are detailed plans for the final battle, including the location of the tribes in the camp, the standards, and many other points. The son-of-man concept is apparently not found in the Qumran documents, but the final battle is suddenly ended by the appearance of the archangel Michael (1QM 17.6).

New Testament. Contrary to a widely held view, the position of the New Testament is not total pacifism: that was the product of church fathers, principally Tertullian, Origen, and Cyprian. According to Matthew, Jesus stated that "wars and rumors of wars" are part of the present world order (Matt. 24.6–7) and said bluntly that he had not come to "bring peace to the earth, but a sword"

(Matt. 10.34). According to Luke, John the Baptist did not forbid the soldiers to participate in war. When Jesus' disciples were about to face the hostile world, he advised them to sell their robes to buy a sword. Paul recognized that the governing authorities maintain order with the sword and urged his readers to be subject to such authorities.

At the same time, Jesus is not reported to have commanded his followers to use warfare as a means of conquest (contrary to the method of the emperor Constantine). He apparently rejected the implication that he lead a messianic war; he rebuked the disciple who used the sword against those who had come to arrest him; he pointedly told Pilate that, if his kingdom "were from this world," his soldiers would be fighting to defend him (John 18.36).

Like ancient Israel, the church is composed of the people of God and is under attack from enemy forces. Unlike Israel, the church is not one of the nations of the world; rather it is transnational, composed of peoples from all nations. Its warfare was not against "enemies of blood and flesh" but rather against demonic forces intent on destroying God's redemptive work (Eph. 6.12); hence its defense must be spiritual. The author of 1 Peter urged his readers to "abstain from the desires of the flesh that wage war against the soul"; yet at the same time they were told to submit "for the Lord's sake" to "every human institution," whether emperor or governor (1 Pet. 2.11–14).

According to the apocalyptic view of the book of Daniel, the kingdoms of this world—each more terrible than the preceding—would be defeated by the action of God himself. The book of Revelation likewise proclaims that the final triumph will be brought about by One who is called Faithful and True, who comes with the armies of heaven to smite the nations. At last the dreams of the prophets of old will come true: "they shall beat their swords into plowshares, and their spears into pruning hooks; nation shall not lift up sword against nation, neither shall they learn war any more" (Isa. 2.4; Mic. 4.3).

William Sanford LaSor

WATER. Compared to the alluvial plains of Egypt and Mesopotamia, hilly Syria-Palestine relies more upon ground- and rainwater for its fertility. Its peoples venerated storm gods, among them Yahweh, often accompanied by the tempest. Water is God's gift par excellence, which he may withhold in punishment. Running water is called "living" in Hebrew; in the New Testament this image becomes "water of life" (John 4.7–15; 7.37–38; Rev. 21.6; 22.17).

In the Israelite conception, boundless water was the original constituent of the universe, perhaps coeval with God himself (Gen. 1.1, by one interpretation); compare Egyptian Nun, Sumerian Nammu, Babylonian Apsu and Tiamat, all personifying primordial waters. God's first act of *creation was to suffuse a diurnally pulsating light through the aqueous void. Next he restricted the waters, creating a bubble bounded by water below and the firmament above. The lower waters were restricted, and the flat earth emerged, surrounded by seas and floating upon the deep. The dry land and the crystalline firmament were semipermeable, penetrated by springs and precipitation.

Water has four primary connotations in the Bible: birth, fertility, danger, and cleansing. More than one aspect can operate in any given passage.

Birth imagery is dimly present in Genesis 1, with the world emerging from the grammatically feminine "Deep." Moses is drawn from water by his foster mother. The Israelite nation is "born" in the Red Sea. After crossing the Jordan, the Israelites circumcise themselves, a rite that is associated with birth. (*See* Circumcision.)

The fertility motif is clear in Genesis 2.6, 10–14, where Yahweh moistens the earth with ground water and rivers. Similarly, a fertilizing river will one day flow from Jerusalem, granting Israel prosperity comparable to that of Egypt and Mesopotamia; compare the Temple's bronze sea (1 Kings 7.23–26), and also the Canaanite image of El's dwelling "at the source of the two rivers, in the midst of the channels of the two deeps." Yahweh's gift of drinking water in the desert seems also to symbolize fructification.

The waters treated so far are passive or benign, but other texts describe a hostile Sea or aquatic monster that God kills, tramples, or confines and will one day defeat anew. This story has antecedents in Mesopotamian and Canaanite *myths of creation, wherein a storm god defeats the Sea. The image of Jesus mastering the wind and treading upon the sea may echo these motifs.

We see the danger of water in the *Flood, likewise a popular Near Eastern myth. Israelite fear of the water is also reflected in awestruck descriptions of the sea and navigation.

Water cleanses actually and symbolically, as when Pilate washes his hands. Water is a key ingredient in purification and healing rites in both the Bible and the *Dead Sea Scrolls; some writers refer metaphorically to spiritual cleansing.

Purification imagery combines readily with (re)birth imagery. Naaman immerses himself and his leprous skin becomes "like that of a small child" (2 Kings 5.10, 14). *Baptism, like the Jewish conversion rite of immersion, signifies spiritual rebirth; note the reference to "water and blood" in 1 John 5.6, 8. And the images of birth and cleansing are combined with danger when God rescues a sufferer from metaphorical drowning.   *William H. Propp*

WAY, THE. As a word having literal, metaphorical, and theological connotations, "way" is used in the Bible with a variety of meanings. The specific term "the Way," though, can be attributed to Luke, who used it in Acts to designate the early Christian movement; according to Luke it was known in both Palestine and Ephesus and also to the Roman procurator, Felix. The theology of the Way is further developed by Luke in the form of a travel narrative in two stages, first from Galilee to Jerusalem, and from Jerusalem to the ends of the earth.

The specific use of the Way as another name for Christianity seems to have its background in various sources, including the Qumran community. In the document known as the Manual of Discipline, the Essene way of life is referred to as "the Way," and it consists in the strict observance of the *law. The inspiration for this comes from Isaiah 40.3, with its invitation to prepare the way of the Lord in the wilderness, used also by the synoptic Gospels as the starting point of the New Testament preaching by John the Baptist. Later John identifies Jesus as the way, the truth, and the life.

Joseph Pathrapankal, C.M.I.

WINE. The cultivation of the grape *vine and the fermentation of grape juice into wine seem to have occurred in prehistoric times in Eurasia; the Semitic words related to the word "wine" are apparently loanwords from ancient *Greek or its predecessors. Cultivated (rather than wild) grapes are found in deposits from the fourth millennium BCE onward throughout the Near East, and

there is archaeological evidence for wine making by the third millennium. In biblical times, the production and consumption of wine were familiar aspects of everyday life, to which the Bible refers repeatedly and, for the most part, positively.

To produce wine, harvested grapes were placed in a wine vat, often carved out of bedrock for that purpose, where the juice was squeezed from the grapes by foot. From this first vat the juice was drained into a lower vat, where the pulpy liquid could be pressed again, often with a stone weight. The juice was then placed in skins or in large storage jars; the latter may have a capacity of 10 gallons (40 liters) or more and are often inscribed with the name of the place of origin. A well-preserved winery with most of these features was excavated at Gibeon (el-Jib). Stamped jar handles attest to wine production (and standard royal measurement) in the kingdom of Judah and to the import of wine from Rhodes and other Greek islands, beginning in the Persian period; wine jars from Italy have been found in a late first-century BCE house in Jerusalem.

Wine is metaphorically called "the blood of grapes/the grape" (Gen. 49.11; Deut. 32.14; Sir. 39.26; 50.15), and so the trampling of grapes can be a figure for destructive divine fury (Isa. 63.1–6; Rev. 19.15; cf. Julia Ward Howe's biblicizing phrasing, "He is trampling out the vintage where the grapes of wrath are stored").

Wine was a staple of life, as the formula "grain, wine, and oil" shows (Deut. 11.14; Joel 1.10). It was a source of pleasure for both humans and the gods and was thus a regular component of ritual. Wine was a divine gift and would be provided abundantly in the end time.

Overindulgence in wine is condemned in the Bible by both precept and example (*see* Drunkenness). Total abstinence, however, is not advanced as a general ideal, although it was practiced, either for a time, by nazirite vow, or as a lifelong commitment, as by the Rechabites.

The generally positive attitude of biblical writers toward moderate consumption of wine posed a problem for modern advocates of total abstinence ("temperance") as both a personal and a social ideal. How could those who accepted the Bible as supreme authority reject its teaching that wine was good, a teaching exemplified by the practice of Jesus and others? Was the use of wine at the Christian Eucharist defensible? Some made a distinction between naturally fermented wines and distilled spirits, including fortified wines, although biblical support for such a distinction was questionable. Others argued that social changes since biblical times made the legal prohibition of any alcoholic beverage necessary, citing not only general biblical norms but also such passages as Romans 14.21.

One curious influence of the Bible on the use of wine is in the names given to ascending sizes of bottles used for champagne. After a magnum (the equivalent of two bottles [1.5 liters]), the sizes are as follows: Jeroboam (four bottles), named for the first king of the northern kingdom of Israel; Rehoboam (six bottles), Solomon's son and successor as king of Judah; Methuselah (eight bottles); and the three largest for kings of Assyria and Babylon: Salmanazar (Shalmaneser, twelve bottles), Balthazar (Belshazzar, sixteen bottles), and Nebuchadnezzar (Nebuchadrezzar; twenty bottles), who destroyed Jerusalem.

Along with wine, "strong drink" (Hebr. *šēkār,* probably beer or ale made from barley and other grains) is mentioned in the Bible and is well attested in both archaeological and literary sources throughout the Near East.

Michael D. Coogan

WITNESS. As a juridical term, a witness is one who has direct knowledge about certain facts and can declare before a court of law what he or she has seen or heard. In the Bible, witnesses are used to attest contracts and to certify proceedings. Sometimes, inanimate objects provide the evidence that an agreement has been concluded. The tables of the law in the *ark are described as the "tables of testimony," for they are inscribed with God's commandments; sometimes the ark itself is termed "the testimony" (Exod. 25.16; 31.18; Num. 17.4).

False or malicious witness was prohibited, and sanctions were imposed against it. False witnesses are mentioned in the New Testament in the trials of Jesus and Stephen.

Israelite law required the evidence of several witnesses to convict a person of a capital offense. This principle is alluded to in the New Testament, and was apparently honored in questions of church discipline.

An important use of this terminology is its application to the role of Israel and of Jesus and his followers as God's witnesses before the world. Israel's mission is to bear witness to God as his chosen servant: "You are my witnesses," Yahweh emphatically declares (Isa. 43.10, 12; 44.8). Israel is to take God's side and bear witness to him as the lord of history, the only true God, and her redeemer and savior. Here the controversy language comes alive with freshness and power.

In the New Testament the witness theme is central in the gospel of John, Acts, and Revelation. In John's gospel, God in Christ has a controversy with the world. A cosmic lawsuit is under way, and each side presents its evidence and argues its case. The different witnesses to Jesus present their testimony to refute the hostile charges of his enemies. Jesus himself bears witness to the truth, as will the *Holy Spirit as the "Advocate" (15.26).

In Acts the witness of the apostles is of prime importance, as is that of Paul. The center of their witness is the resurrection.

In the book of Revelation, witness is set against the background of persecution. The seer of Patmos presents Jesus as the model witness, whose example Christians must follow. "The testimony of Jesus" probably refers not to the testimony concerning him but to the testimony borne by him (Rev. 1.9; 12.17). Jesus is "the faithful and true witness" (1.5; 3.14), and loyalty to him may mean martyrdom. Here one traces the first steps of the process by which the Greek word for witness *(martys)* developed into the later sense of "martyr."

Allison A. Trites

WORD. *See* Logos.

WORD OF GOD. "The Word of God" is a common expression for *revelation. In biblical tradition, the term is first applied to prophecy and later comes to describe the *Law as communication from God; in the New Testament, it is used for scripture and also for the gospel and the person of Jesus Christ. In Christian tradition, the expression occurs in a loose, popular sense that implies the *inspiration of the Bible, and in a stricter way, particularly in modern Protestant *hermeneutics (see below).

In preexilic Israel, the phrase "the word of Yahweh" denotes the source of prophetic inspiration, not necessarily its character as verbal or rational. The word may be received in visionary form by a prophet whose own mental processes are temporarily suspended. In the exilic prophets and exilic redaction of earlier traditions, however, the transcendence of the divine self-disclosure comes into sharper focus. Thus, Jeremiah can speak of his struggle with God's word, and Second Isaiah contrasts its effective purpose with the transience of human nature. While for Jeremiah the prophetic word and the Law remain distinct, in Deuteronomy they are brought into closer conjunction. In the postexilic period, the word of God becomes an overarching concept comprising revelation through abidingly valid legal commandments, through prophetic interpretation of historical experience, and through creation. The latter two understandings are especially prominent in *apocalyptic literature and in Hellenistic Judaism, respectively.

In the New Testament, the word of God, along with equivalents like "God says," "it was spoken," and so on, is used in connection with biblical *quotations (e.g., John 10.35; Rom. 15.10; and Mark 7.13, where the phrase implies the idea that written law is superior to the oral tradition of the scribes). Echoing prophetic language, in the prologue to Luke's gospel, the motif of a new era of active prophecy is evoked by the coming of the word of God to Simeon and John the Baptist. Moreover, the word of God, or variants such as "the word of the Lord" or "the Word," is applied especially in Luke-Acts (but frequently elsewhere as well) to the gospel message of salvation through Jesus. Because of this it is occasionally difficult to decide whether the word refers to Jewish scripture or to the gospel. The word in the sense of the gospel message is closely paralleled with the person of Christ as the content of preaching. It is therefore but a small step to identify Jesus himself as the divine Word or *Logos incarnate.

Throughout postbiblical tradition, the word of God is regularly found as a pious periphrasis for the Bible. At the Reformation, however, the phrase acquired a new, controversial emphasis, and often carries the implication of the supremacy of scripture over both tradition and the sacraments in the theology and practice of the church. Whereas Luther, following Augustine, still maintained a distinction between the transcendent Word of God and the biblical text, holding the preaching of the gospel to be its essential mediation, other reformers tended to identify the two more closely and saw revelation as conveyed inwardly to the individual through the text itself. As a result, in the following centuries, the word of God came to be understood in terms of a propositional view of revelation and the verbal inspiration of scripture. In the twentieth century, this understanding was challenged by dialectical theology, which is sometimes known as "the Theology of the Word of God," associated especially with Karl Barth and Rudolf Bultmann. They emphasized the contrast between God's Word as sovereign address and human response to it in faith. While Barth attempted a complex system of interrelation between the Word of God in three senses, Jesus Christ, the witness of scripture, and preaching, Bultmann's existentialist philosophy led him to stress preaching as the occasion for actualizing the divine word. Recent developments have tended in different directions, emphasizing variously the historical and eschatological or the linguistic and symbolic aspects of revelation, so that it is no longer possible to speak of a coherent concept of the word of God in Protestant thought.

John Muddiman

WORSHIP. In teaching that "man's chief end is to glorify God and to enjoy him forever," the Westminster Catechism of 1647 faithfully captured the developed biblical vision. As creator and redeemer, God calls for worship on the part of humankind. Human salvation consists in communion with the beneficent God. The first commandment is to worship the Lord God alone. The content of that worship, according to the *Shema, is total devotion: "You shall love the Lord your God with all your heart, soul, and might" (Deut. 6.5; Mark 12.30 par.). The idolatry of the *golden calf epitomizes the perennial human tendency to turn from the creator and worship the creature. Nevertheless, God visits and redeems his people. The prophets picture the future time of salvation as a flocking of the nations to the Temple, a banquet on God's holy mountain when death will have been destroyed. According to the book of Revelation, salvation will be marked by worship in the heavenly city where there is no temple apart from the Lord God Almighty and the Lamb.

When the Lord called on Pharaoh to let his people go, it was so that they might "worship" or "serve" him (Exod. 3.13). The Lord who commissioned Moses to lead Israel out of Egypt was the God who had appeared to the ancestors as God Almighty and had been worshiped by them. Safely delivered through the Red Sea, Israel worshiped the Lord on Mount Sinai and there received the terms of the Lord's *covenant with them, including their sole obligation to Yahweh, their "jealous" God (Exod. 19–31). The deliverance was to be commemorated each year in the *Passover rite, and the covenant would be renewed regularly as under Joshua at Shechem (if Gerhard von Rad is correct in his interpretation of Josh. 24; cf. Deut. 31.10–13). In the Promised Land, agricultural festivals would be related to the events of Israel's history, for example, the feast of weeks to the whole ancestral story as far as the entry into the land flowing with milk and honey, and the feast of booths or tabernacles (sukkôt) to the dwelling in tents in the wilderness (see Feasts and Festivals). Nevertheless, the gods of the land remained a permanent temptation to Israel; the conflict between Elijah and the prophets of Baal is emblematic. The book of Deuteronomy records an attempt to reform, purify, and control Israel's worship by centering it in one place, presumably the Jerusalem Temple, which had been built under Solomon as a focus of the Lord's presence amid the nation. Prophets kept reminding the nation of the unacceptability of worship that was not matched by the performance of God's will in daily living.

The Babylonian *exile, itself seen as divine punishment for infidelity, affected the worship of Israel in various ways. The nation's experience led it to recognize Yahweh as the one, universal God. The older *sacrifices had been the whole burnt offering (ʿōlâ or kālîl), symbolizing total consecration, and the communion sacrifice (zebaḥ šēlāmîm), in which the meal was shared by God and the worshipers with the intention of either thanksgiving or a vow or freewill offering. To these were added, in the rebuilt Temple, the sin offering (ḥaṭṭāʾt) and the guilt offering (ʾāšām). The *Day of Atonement is also postexilic. The Psalter has been called "the hymnbook of the second Temple." Doubtless much of its material is older, and the Psalms have continued in liturgical use among Jews and Christians: the praises, thanksgivings, confessions, complaints, and prayers are suited to recurrent events and situations in the life of a people and of individuals.

From its earliest days, Christianity interpreted the Psalms christologically, see-

ing in them messianic prophecies and prayers that could be addressed either to Christ or, with Christ, to the God he addressed as "*Abba, Father." The dispute between Jews and Christians as to whether Jesus was the Messiah is at heart a dispute about worship, since it concerns the identity of God. Christians believed that the God of Israel, the one true God, had acted decisively in Jesus, and indeed in such a personal way that Jesus was not only the mediator of salvation but did himself, as "the Word made flesh" (John 1.14), call forth worship ("My Lord and my God!" John 20.28). "Worship in spirit and in truth" (John 4.19–26) would no longer take place in the Temple in Jerusalem (itself destroyed in 70 CE), but the temple was now Christ's body, into which believers were incorporated and themselves became temples of the Holy Spirit. The letter to the Hebrews argues that Jesus' death fulfilled the sacrifices of the old covenant by achieving what its foreshadowings were not able to deliver. After Jesus' self-offering, believers now approach "the throne of grace" through him as their great high priest in the heavens (Heb. 4.14–16; cf. Eph. 2.18). In several hymnic passages of the New Testament, Jesus is included in the worship rendered to God.

The earliest Christians in Jerusalem continued to worship in the Temple. Fairly soon, however, Christian worship took on a clearly independent character, marked particularly by the fact that Christians assembled "in the name of Jesus" (cf. Matt. 18.20). When Christians gathered together as a church, the most characteristic thing they did was to celebrate the *Lord's Supper, the rite that Paul and the synoptic Gospels describe Jesus as instituting at the Last Supper. It is debated whether or not the Last Supper was a Passover meal, but it seems clear from the narratives that the Christian meal was intended to commemorate the "*exodus" and the new "covenant" inaugurated by the death of Jesus; the word "exodus" is used of Jesus' death at Luke 9.31, and the Gospels speak of his covenant blood poured out for the many. At their liturgical assemblies, the early Christians hailed the presence of the risen Jesus and called for his return: "Maranatha" (1 Cor. 16.22; cf. Rev. 22.20; 1 Cor. 11.26).

The earliest deliberate description we have of Christian worship dates from the second century. Justin Martyr in his *First Apology* (66.1–3) describes Christians as gathering from town and country on "the first day of the week," the day of Christ's resurrection and so the beginning of a new creation. They would listen to "the writings of the prophets" and "the memoirs of the apostles." The president of the assembly interpreted these scriptures (the sermon). Prayers were said for church and world. Bread and a cup of mixed wine were brought to the president, who gave thanks to God over them for creation and redemption. The bread and the wine, signs of the body and the blood of Christ, were distributed and consumed. Deacons took them to the absent. In light of this description, it may be possible to see already the reflections of such a "service of word and sacrament" in such passages as Luke 24.13–32, where the risen Jesus expounds the scriptures to the two travelers on the road to Emmaus and is made "known to them in the breaking of the bread," and Acts 20.7–12, where the Christians of Troas gather on the first of the week and Paul preaches all night to them before they break bread.

In fact, little is known about the "service of the word" in New Testament times. Later evidence suggests influence from the synagogue, in the form of readings and prayers. Christians sang "hymns, psalms, and spiritual songs" (Eph. 5.18; Col. 3.16), and 1 Corinthians 14 includes some ecstatic elements among "prophecy," "revelations," "speaking in tongues," "interpretations," and "teaching."

Since for Paul the greatest spiritual gift was love, like the prophets he implied an ethical test for true worship. He used cultic language to exhort Christians to appropriate conduct: "I appeal to you . . . to present your bodies as a living sacrifice, holy and acceptable to God, which is your spiritual worship" (Rom. 12.1; cf. 1 Cor. 6.18–20; 2 Cor. 6.6–7.1). Paul also spoke of his apostolic labors in liturgical terms.

Recent scholarship has rediscovered how much material in the Bible arose from and was shaped by the worship practiced by the Israelite, Jewish, and Christian communities. It is the continuing use of the Bible in worship that preserves it as a sacred and "living" book.

See also Lectionaries; Prayer(s).

Geoffrey Wainwright

WRITING IN ANTIQUITY. The invention of writing in the strict sense of the word was preceded by a series of earlier developments that gradually led up to it. Soon after the invention of pottery in the Neolithic period (ca. 8000 BCE) in the Near East, excavations reveal the existence of a system of clay counters and tokens that, in their earliest form, appear to have served to identify the number and kinds of goods traded, entrusted to second parties, or otherwise dealt with. By the fourth millennium BCE, such counters were being enclosed in hollow clay envelopes (bullae) which, after drying, constituted a sealed physical record of the transaction; but until and unless the envelope was broken open, this record could not be verified or retrieved. Before long it was realized that, like the seals, the counters could be impressed on the surface of the bulla before it dried, thus providing an ever-present record of the counters enclosed in it; only if their number and character needed to be verified was it necessary actually to break the bulla open. Next it must have been seen that the counters could be dispensed with altogether, and thereafter it became logical to abandon the hollow bulla format as well, in favor of a more or less flat clay tablet with an only slightly rounded writing surface. Finally, the counters themselves were abandoned and their approximate shapes reproduced instead by means of a stylus made of reed. This final development seems to have occurred first in *Sumer, where clay and reeds were both abundant; it signaled the emergence of writing in its full sense and may probably be dated about 3100 BCE.

Within a century or so, the system expanded from the depiction of concrete objects by means of pictograms to the expression of sounds or syllables by means of syllabograms, a first application of the rebus principle. An example is the name ᵈEn-lil-ti, "the god Enlil lives (or gives life)," in which the first three signs may be described as logograms (word signs) but the last is a picture of an arrow whose pronunciation in Sumerian is ti, as is (more or less) the pronunciation of the Sumerian word for "life, live" (actually til).

No further significant innovations in the inner structure of the cuneiform script were needed beyond this point, nor indeed were they forthcoming. All subsequent changes involved only phonetic adjustments to the needs of other dialects and languages, or the external forms of the signs, whose total number was stabilized at about six hundred.

From their pictographic origins, they rapidly evolved into stylized linear representations. Gradually, these were replaced in turn by the wedge-shaped characters that result from the impression of a split reed (shaped like a prism) into wet clay and that justify the modern designation "cuneiform" first applied to them by Thomas Hyde in 1700 CE.

The newly invented cuneiform script remained in use in the Near East for three millennia (until ca. 100 CE), undergoing considerable changes in external appearance as it spread rapidly from its Sumerian base. In Elam (southwestern Persia) to the east and Egypt to the west, it stimulated native writing systems ("proto-Elamite" and hieroglyphics respectively) that owed no more than their basic inspiration to the original invention. Elsewhere, the borrowing was more direct. The syllabic values of the cuneiform script were taken over in their entirety for writing Akkadian by Babylonians and Assyrians; the Sumerian logograms were given their Akkadian equivalents; some new syllabic values were assigned to existing cuneiform signs on the basis of such equivalents, others by convention to render sounds not found in the Sumerian phonemic roster. A little later in the third millennium BCE, the Elamites also adopted the Sumerian system.

In Anatolia (central Turkey) the first attested writing, early in the second millennium BCE, consists of Old Assyrian texts and a few native inscriptions modeled on them. But the conquest of the area by the Hittites about 1700 BCE led to the adoption of a Babylonian version of cuneiform, probably from *Mari, and its adaptation to the special requirements of their Indo-European language. A distinct script was developed by Luvian, a language (closely related to Hittite) that survived the fall of the Hittite empire about 1200 BCE, especially in northern Syria. This script is pictographic in form and essentially syllabic in structure. It is conventionally designated as Hieroglyphic Hittite, though it has nothing to do with Egyptian hieroglyphics (see below) and is not, strictly speaking, used for Hittite. Mesopotamian cuneiform also provided the vehicle for Urartian, the language of eastern Anatolia from ca. 1300–600 BCE.

While the Elamite, Hittite, and Urartian adaptations retained the essential forms and functions of Mesopotamian writing, a wholly new cuneiform script was devised about 520 BCE to record Old Persian. Its individual characters were wedge-shaped, but beyond that they owed nothing to Mesopotamian cuneiform; they were nearly all syllabograms of the form consonant-plus-vowel (or simply vowel) and numbered no more than forty; only four of them were logograms. And while Persia thus continually experimented with new scripts inspired by Mesopotamian models, native factors predominated in the further development of writing in Egypt. From its origins before the end of the fourth millennium BCE, it quickly evolved into the elaborate logo-syllabic system known by its Greek designation as hieroglyphics (literally "sacred carvings"). Its syllabograms were indifferent as to vowels; they distinguished only the consonants and must therefore be transliterated without vowels (or with the vowel e conventionally inserted between the consonants). Extensive use was made of logograms and (to a greater extent than in cuneiform) of determinatives or "semantic indicators," that is, signs not pronounced in speech but alerting the reader to the meaning class of the ensuing word.

Like Mesopotamian cuneiform, Egyptian hieroglyphics survived for over three millennia, their last use dating from the Roman period. On monumental texts, the hieroglyphic signs retained their essentially pictographic character, and even elaborated on it secondarily by adding color or direction to the individual signs. But before the end of the third millennium BCE, a cursive adaptation of hieroglyphic, the hieratic script, began to evolve for use on papyrus and ostraca (potsherds). Early in the first millennium BCE, the Demotic dialect of Egyptian developed its own cursive script, while, at the end of the millennium, twenty-three hieroglyphic signs and their Demotic equivalents were adopted for the unrelated Meroitic language of Nubia, south of Egypt. The various Coptic dialects of Egyptian were written in a modified Greek alphabet.

The internal development of hieroglyphic also continued. By the side of the traditional logo-syllabic script, there developed in the second millennium a so-called syllabic orthography, particularly for foreign names, which attempted to indicate vowel quality by means of semiconsonants. It is this form of syllabic hieroglyphic writing that is generally thought to have inspired the first attempts at the written recording of Northwest Semitic speech, beginning in the Sinai peninsula, where speakers of Canaanite (or proto-Canaanite) came in contact with Egyptian culture in the middle of the second millennium BCE. At the Sinaitic site of Serabit el-Khadim, where Canaanite laborers (or slaves) worked copper and turquoise mines under Egyptian overseers, graffiti and other inscriptions in the "proto-Sinaitic" script employed clearly pictographic characters (which in some cases may have been conventionalized replicas of hieroglyphic signs) to represent the Northwest Semitic roster of phonemes. According to the acrophonic theory advocated by many scholars, the Canaanite word represented by the sign provided its name, and the first syllable of that word became the pronunciation of the sign. This principle works better for some signs than for others; it may therefore be best to regard the decipherment of proto-Sinaitic as provisional and the assignment of letter names as a later development.

Meantime Northwest Semitic also came into contact with the cuneiform tradition of writing, knowledge of which had spread through the Near East in the Late Bronze Age (ca. 1550–1200 BCE), at least among scribes trained at scribal schools on the Babylonian model that are known from El-*Amarna in Egypt to Hattusha in Anatolia and along the entire Levantine littoral in between, especially at Ugarit on the north Syrian coast. Here, some time after 1400 BCE, thirty cuneiform signs were newly devised to represent the consonantal phonemes of *Ugaritic (which represents another early form of Canaanite), its three basic vowels (when preceded by the glottal stop) and a Hurrian phoneme for words and names in that non-Semitic language. Outside Ugarit itself, scattered examples of the new script have been found as far away as Israel. The spread of the invention was helped by the mnemonic device of arranging the signs in a conventional sequence and inscribing them in this sequence on practice tablets today referred to (like their later Latin counterparts) as abecedaries (from a-b-c-d-arium); allowing for the intervening reduction in the number of signs, this sequence already equals that of the subsequent *Hebrew and *Greek alphabet (from the latter's first two letters, alpha, beta), the former attested in the alphabetic acrostic-poems of the Bible.

Both Ugaritic and proto-Sinaitic served as prototypes and possibly as inspirations of the earliest forms of what is loosely called Phoenician script, the an-cestor of all later alphabets. This script was not, however, a true alphabet, but more properly a syllabary, which continued to ignore vocalic quality in favor of syllables of the type consonant-plus-(any or no)-vowel. It was adopted without essential modifications for the writing of such Northwest Semitic languages as Hebrew and *Aramaic as well as Phoenician, the last probably responsible for spreading its knowledge westward as early as the beginning of the first millennium BCE to Greece and beyond, as Greek sources state. The Greek world had evolved an earlier system of writing in the Late Bronze Age, the Linear B known from archival texts found on Crete and the Greek mainland. These texts were written on clay and thus may represent a response to a Mesopotamian, or at least a cuneiform, stimulus. (The contemporary Linear A and the Phaistos Disc have not yet been satisfactorily deciphered.) But the greater simplicity of the new script recommended itself to the Greeks as it had to the Phoenicians.

The Greeks, moreover, turned the new invention into a true alphabet by employing some of the otiose consonantal phonemes into signs for vowels; they also took advantage of the fixed order of the letters to assign them numerical values. Both of these ideas were subsequently adopted, with modifications, for the original Northwest Semitic signs, notably in Hebrew. But the vowel signs (*matres lectionis,* or mothers of reading) never fully succeeded in distinguishing vowel quality, so that later Hebrew, Aramaic, and, eventually, Arabic developed a system of (optional) diacritics for this purpose.

Via the Greeks, the alphabet was transmitted to the Romans and to the rest of the European world. Meantime the Aramaic version of the Northwest Semitic script inspired the Indic writing

Wycliffe Bible Translators 559

of Asoka and, indirectly, Sanskrit and other scripts of Asia to the east, and North Arabic, South Arabic, and Ethiopic to the south. The alphabet was thus truly ready to conquer the world, with the notable exception of China and Japan. But in antiquity, the older scripts of Mesopotamia and Egypt continued side by side with it. The last datable cuneiform text is an astronomical tablet for 75 CE. The last Egyptian texts are rock inscriptions from the island of Elephantine (Philae), below the Aswan Dam, and are dated 394 and 425 CE for hieroglyphic and hieratic respectively.

See also Books and Bookmaking in Antiquity; Literacy in Ancient Israel.

William W. Hallo

WYCLIFFE BIBLE TRANSLATORS. A nondenominational missionary agency devoted to the *translation of the Bible for those peoples who lack it in their own native languages. Founded by William Cameron Townsend in 1934,

Wycliffe Bible Translators (WBT) takes its name from the famous fourteenth-century British reformer John Wycliffe, who was responsible for the first complete English translation of the Bible. Wycliffe Bible Translators was incorporated in 1942 along with its sister organization, the Summer Institute of Linguistics (SIL). Although closely aligned with WBT (members of SIL must belong to WBT and vice versa), SIL presents itself as a secular linguistics institute, thus enabling it to enter countries otherwise restricted to missionary activity. This strategy, pioneered by Townsend in Mexico in the 1930s, has engendered some controversy in missiological circles in recent years. Nevertheless WBT/SIL has long been recognized as the world's largest organization for the translation of the scriptures, with over five thousand members currently working with more than a thousand different language groups all over the world.

William H. Barnes

Y

YOM KIPPUR. *See* Day of Atonement.

BIBLIOGRAPHY

To assist readers, the editors have prepared this bibliography of some important and useful books available in English about the Bible.

Critical Introductions. These provide summaries of modern scholarly research on the formation of the Bible from the smallest literary units to the final canonical arrangement, as well as a bibliographic starting point.

Childs, Brevard S. *Introduction to the Old Testament as Scripture*. Philadelphia: Fortress, 1979.

———. *The New Testament as Canon: An Introduction*. Philadelphia: Fortress, 1985.

Collins, Raymond F. *Introduction to the New Testament*. Garden City, N.Y.: Doubleday, 1983.

Hayes, John H. *An Introduction to Old Testament Study*. Nashville, Tenn.: Abingdon, 1979.

Koester, Helmut. *Introduction to the New Testament*, vol. 2: *History and Literature of Early Christianity*. 2d ed. New York: de Gruyter, 2000.

Kümmel, Werner G. *Introduction to the New Testament*. Rev. and enl. ed. Nashville, Tenn.: Abingdon, 1996.

Popular Introductions. These are frequently used as texts in undergraduate courses, and provide readable surveys of the development of the Bible and of the history of the biblical world.

Alter, Robert, and Frank Kermode. *The Literary Guide to the Bible*. Cambridge, Mass.: Belknap, 1987.

Anderson, Bernard W. *Understanding the Old Testament*. Abr. 4th ed. Englewood Cliffs, N.J.: Prentice-Hall, 1998.

Barr, David L. *New Testament Story: An Introduction*. 2d ed. Belmont, Calif.: Wadsworth, 1995.

Court, John M., and Kathleen M. Court. *The New Testament World*. Englewood Cliffs, N.J.: Prentice-Hall, 1990.

Crenshaw, James L. *Old Testament Story and Faith: A Literary and Theological Introduction*. Peabody, Mass.: Hendrickson, 1992 (repr. of 1986 ed.).

Duling, Dennis C., and Norman Perrin. *The New Testament: Proclamation and Parenesis, Myth and History*. 3d ed. Fort Worth, Tex.: Harcourt Brace, 1994.

Ehrman, Bart D. *The New Testament: A Historical Introduction to the Early Christian Writings*. 2d ed. New York: Oxford University Press, 1999.

Freed, Edwin D. *The New Testament: A Critical Introduction*. 3d ed. Belmont, Calif.: Wadsworth, 2000.

Gottwald, Norman K. *The Hebrew Bible: A Socio-Literary Introduction*. Philadelphia: Fortress, 1985.

Harrington, Daniel J. *Interpreting the New Testament: A Practical Guide*. Collegeville, Minn.: Liturgical, 1990.

Harris, Stephen L. *The New Testament: A Student's Introduction*. 3d ed. Mountain View, Calif.: Mayfield, 1998.

Johnson, Luke T. *The Writings of the New Testament: An Interpretation*. Rev. ed. Minneapolis, Minn.: Fortress, 1999.

Kee, Howard C. *Understanding the New Testament*. 5th ed. Englewood Cliffs, N.J.: Prentice-Hall, 1993.

Metzger, Bruce M. *The New Testament: Its Background, Growth, and Content.* 2d. ed., enlarged. Nashville, Tenn.: Abingdon, 1983.

Rendtorff, Rolf. *The Old Testament: An Introduction.* Philadelphia: Fortress, 1986.

Rogerson, John W., and Philip Davies. *The Old Testament World.* Englewood Cliffs, N.J.: Prentice-Hall, 1989.

Sandmel, Samuel. *The Hebrew Scriptures: An Introduction to their Literature and Religious Ideas.* New York: Oxford University, 1978.

History

Bickerman, Elias J. *The Jews in the Greek Age.* Cambridge, Mass.: Harvard University, 1988.

Bright, John. *A History of Israel.* 4th ed. Louisville, Ky: Westminster John Knox, 2000.

Cohen, Shaye J. D. *From the Maccabees to the Mishnah.* Philadelphia: Westminster, 1987.

Coogan, Michael D., ed. *The Oxford History of the Biblical World.* New York: Oxford University, 1998.

Edwards, I. E. S., ed. *The Cambridge Ancient History.* 3d ed. London: Cambridge University, 1970– .

Herrmann, Siegfried. *A History of Israel in Old Testament Times.* 2d ed. Philadelphia: Fortress, 1981.

Jagersma, Henk. *A History of Israel in the Old Testament Period.* Philadelphia: Trinity, 1983.

———. *A History of Israel from Alexander the Great to Bar Kochba.* Philadelphia: Fortress, 1986.

Koester, Helmut. *Introduction to the New Testament*, vol. 1: *History, Culture, and Religion of the Hellenistic Age.* 2d ed. New York: de Gruyter, 1995.

Miller, J. Maxwell, and John H. Hayes. *A History of Ancient Israel and Judah.* Philadelphia: Westminster, 1986.

Safrai, Shmuel, and Menahem Stern, eds. *The Jewish People in the First Century: Historical Geography, Political History, Social, Cultural and Religious Life and Institutions.* 2 vols. Philadelphia: Fortress, 1974, 1976.

Schürer, Emil. *The History of the Jewish People in the Age of Jesus Christ.* 4 vols. Rev. and ed. by Geza Vermes and Fergus Millar. Edinburgh: T. and T. Clark, 1973–87.

Shanks, Hershel, ed. *Ancient Israel: A Short History from Abraham to the Roman Destruction of the Temple.* Rev. ed. Washington, D.C.: Biblical Archaeology Society, 1999.

———, ed. *Christianity and Rabbinic Judaism: A Parallel History of Their Origins and Early Development.* Washington, D.C.: Biblical Archaeology Society, 1992.

Soggin, J. Alberto. *An Introduction to the History of Israel and Judah.* 2d ed. Valley Forge, Penn.: Trinity, 1993.

de Vaux, Roland. *The Early History of Israel.* Philadelphia: Westminster, 1978.

Nonbiblical Texts. These standard anthologies and surveys provide introductions to the literatures of the ancient Near Eastern and Greco-Roman neighbors of ancient Israel and earliest Christianity, as well as to early Jewish and early Christian writings not included in the canon.

Barrett, C. K., ed. *The New Testament Background: Selected Documents.* Rev. ed. San Francisco: Harper and Row, 1989.

Cameron, Ron, ed. *The Other Gospels: Non-Canonical Gospel Texts.* Philadelphia: Westminster, 1982.

Charlesworth, James H., ed. *The Old Testament Pseudepigrapha.* 2 vols. Garden City, N.Y.: Doubleday, 1983, 1985.

Coogan, Michael D. *Stories from Ancient Canaan.* Philadelphia: Westminster, 1978.

Hallo, William W., and K. Lawson Younger, eds. *The Context of Scripture.* 3 vols. Leiden, Neth.: Brill, 1997, 1999, 2001.

Miller, Robert J., ed. *The Complete Gospels: Annotated Scholars Version,* Rev. ed. Sonoma, Calif.: Polebridge, 1995.

Nickelsburg, George W. E. *Jewish Literature between the Bible and the Mishnah: A Historical and Literary Introduction.* Philadelphia: Fortress, 1981.

Pritchard, James B., ed. *Ancient Near Eastern Texts Relating to the Old Testament*

[ANET]; The Ancient Near East in Pictures Relating to the Old Testament [ANEP]. Rev. ed. Princeton: Princeton University, 1969. (There is an abridged version of both: The Ancient Near East: An Anthology of Texts and Pictures [ANETP], 2 vols., 1958, 1975.)

Robinson, James M., ed. The Nag Hammadi Library in English. Rev. ed. San Francisco: HarperCollins, 1988.

Schneemelcher, Wilhelm, ed. New Testament Apocrypha. Ed. Robert McL. Wilson. 2 vols. Nashville: Westminster/John Knox, 1991 (1965).

Sparks, H. F. D., ed. The Apocryphal Old Testament. Oxford: Clarendon, 1984.

Stone, Michael E., ed. Jewish Writings of the Second Temple Period: Apocrypha, Pseudepigrapha, Qumran, Sectarian Writings, Philo, Josephus. Philadelphia: Fortress, 1984.

Vermes, Geza. The Complete Dead Sea Scrolls in English. New York: Allen Lane, 1997.

Archaeology

Aharoni, Yohanan. The Archaeology of the Land of Israel. Philadelphia: Westminster, 1982.

Ben-Tor, Amnon, ed. The Archaeology of Ancient Israel. New Haven: Yale University, 1991.

Kenyon, Kathleen M. The Bible and Recent Archaeology. Rev. ed. by P. R. S. Moorey. Atlanta: John Knox, 1987.

Mazar, Amihai. Archaeology of the Land of the Bible: 10,000–586 B.C.E. New York: Doubleday, 1990.

Meyers, Eric M., ed. The Oxford Encyclopedia of Archaeology in the Near East. 5 vols. New York: Oxford University, 1997.

Stern, Ephraim, ed. The New Encyclopedia of Archaeological Excavations in the Holy Land. 4 vols. New York: Simon and Schuster, 1993.

Stillwell, Richard et al., eds. The Princeton Encyclopedia of Classical Sites. Princeton: Princeton University, 1976.

Wilkinson, John. The Jerusalem Jesus Knew: An Archaeological Guide to the Gospels. New York: Thomas Nelson, 1983.

Geography

Aharoni, Yohanan. The Land of the Bible: A Historical Geography. Rev. ed. Philadelphia: Westminster, 1979.

Aharoni, Yohanan, and Michael Avi-Yonah. The Macmillan Bible Atlas. 3d ed. New York: Macmillan, 1992.

Baly, Denis. The Geography of the Bible. Rev. ed. New York: Harper and Row, 1974.

May, Herbert G. Oxford Bible Atlas. 3rd ed. rev. by John Day. New York: Oxford University, 1984.

Orni, Ephraim, and E. Ephrat. Geography of Israel. 4th ed. Jerusalem: Israel Universities, 1980.

Pritchard, James B. The Harper Atlas of the Bible. New York: Harper and Row, 1987.

Religion and Society. All of the following are major contributions to the study of Israelite, early Jewish, and early Christian religion, literature, and culture. While the discussion is frequently technical, they will repay serious reading.

Albertz, Rainer. A History of Israelite Religion in the Old Testament Period. 2 vols. Louisville: Westminster John Knox, 1994.

Cross, Frank Moore. Canaanite Myth and Hebrew Epic: Essays in the History of the Religion of Israel. Cambridge, Mass.: Harvard University, 1973.

Kaufmann, Yehezkel. The Religion of Israel from Its Beginnings to the Babylonian Exile. Chicago: University of Chicago, 1960.

Kraemer, Ross Shepard. Her Share of the Blessings: Women's Religions among Pagans, Jews, and Christians in the Greco-Roman World. New York: Oxford University, 1992.

Kraus, Hans-Joachim. Worship in Israel: A Cultic History of the Old Testament. Richmond, Va.: John Knox, 1966.

Miller, Patrick D. The Religion of Ancient Israel. Louisville, Ky.: Westminster John Knox, 2000.

Noth, Martin. A History of Pentateuchal Traditions. Trans. Bernhard W. Anderson. Englewood Cliffs, N.J.: Prentice-Hall, 1972.

Sandmel, Samuel. *Judaism and Christian Beginnings.* New York: Oxford University, 1978.

Segal, Alan F. *Rebecca's Children: Judaism and Christianity in the Roman World.* Cambridge, Mass.: Harvard University, 1986.

Schiffman, Lawrence H. *From Text to Tradition: A History of Second Temple and Rabbinic Judaism.* Hoboken, N.J.: Ktav, 1991.

Stambaugh, John E., and David L. Balch. *The New Testament In Its Social Environment.* Philadelphia: Westminster, 1986.

de Vaux, Roland. *Ancient Israel: Its Life and Institutions.* New York: McGraw-Hill, 1965.

Weber, Max. *Ancient Judaism.* New York: Free Press, 1952.

Biblical Theology

Botterweck, G. Johannes, and Helmer Ringgren, eds. *Theological Dictionary of the Old Testament.* Grand Rapids, Mich.: Eerdmans, 1977–.

Bultmann, Rudolf. *Theology of the New Testament.* New York: Scribner's, 1955.

Childs, Brevard S. *Biblical Theology of the Old and the New Testaments: Theological Reflection on the Christian Bible.* Minneapolis: Fortress, 1993.

Conzelmann, Hans. *An Outline of the Theology of the New Testament.* New York: Harper and Row, 1969.

Eichrodt, Walther. *Theology of the Old Testament.* 2 vols. Philadelphia: Westminster, 1961–1967.

Fredriksen, Paula. *From Jesus to Christ: The Origins of New Testament Images of Jesus.* New Haven: Yale University, 1988.

Fuller, Reginald H. *The Foundations of New Testament Christology.* New York: Scribner's, 1965.

Hanson, Paul D. *The People Called: The Growth of Community in the Bible.* San Francisco: Harper and Row, 1986.

Kittel, Gerhard, and Gerhard Friedrich, eds. *Theological Dictionary of the New Testament.* Grand Rapids, Mich.: Eerdmans, 1985.

Levenson, Jon D. *The Hebrew Bible, the Old Testament, and Historical Criticism.* Louisville, Ky.: Westminster/John Knox, 1993.

von Rad, Gerhard. *Old Testament Theology.* 2 vols. New York: Harper and Row, 1962–1965.

Wright, G. Ernest. *God Who Acts: Biblical Theology as Recital.* Chicago, Ill.: Regnery, 1952.

Methodology. A series of useful "Guides to Biblical Scholarship" is published by Fortress Press (Minneapolis). More detailed surveys are found in three volumes on "The Bible and Its Modern Interpreters," published by the Society of Biblical Literature and Scholars Press (Atlanta); they are:

Knight, Douglas A., and Gene M. Tucker, eds. *The Hebrew Bible and Its Modern Interpreters.* 1985.

Kraft, Robert A., and George W. E. Nickelsburg, eds. *Early Judaism and Its Modern Interpreters.* 1986.

Epp, Eldon Jay, and George W. MacRae, eds. *The New Testament and Its Modern Interpreters.* 1989.

Textual Criticism

Aland, Kurt, and Barbara Aland. *The Text of the New Testament: An Introduction to the Critical Editions and to the Theory and Practice of Modern Textual Criticism.* 2d ed. Grand Rapids, Mich.: Eerdmans, 1989.

Metzger, Bruce M. *The Text of the New Testament: Its Transmission, Corruption, and Restoration.* 3d ed. New York: Oxford University, 1992.

Tov, Emanuel. *Textual Criticism of the Hebrew Bible.* 2d ed. Minneapolis: Fortress, 2001.

History of Interpretation. In addition to articles in *ABD* and *IDB* and *IDBSup* (see next heading), good starting points are:

Baird, William. *History of New Testament Research,* vol. 1: *From Deism to Tübingen.* Minneapolis: Fortress, 1992.

Coggins, R. J., and J. L. Houlden. *A Dictionary of Biblical Interpretation.* Philadelphia: Trinity, 1990.

Greenslade, S. L., et al. *The Cambridge History of the Bible.* 3 vols. Cambridge University, 1963–1970.

Hayes, John H. *Dictionary of Biblical Interpretation.* 2 vols. Nashville, Tenn.: Abingdon, 1999.

Kümmel, Werner Georg. *The New Testament: The History of the Investigation of Its Problems.* Nashville: Abingdon, 1972.

Kugel, James L., and Rowan A. Greer. *Early Biblical Interpretation.* Philadelphia: Westminster, 1986.

Morgan, Robert, and John Barton. *Biblical Interpretation.* New York: Oxford University, 1988.

Neill, Stephen, and N. T. Wright. *The Interpretation of the New Testament, 1861–1986.* 2d ed. New York: Oxford University, 1988.

Orlinsky, Harry M., and Robert G. Bratcher. *A History of Bible Translation and the North American Contribution.* Atlanta: Scholars, 1991.

Reference
Encyclopedic Dictionaries.
Of the many Bible dictionaries available, these are some of the better and most recent. All provide extensive bibliography for further reading.

Achtemeier, Paul J., ed. *The HarperCollins Bible Dictionary.* San Francisco: HarperSanFrancisco, 1996.

Buttrick, George A., ed. *The Interpreter's Dictionary of the Bible [IDB],* 4 vols., with *Supplementary Volume [IDBSup]* (ed. K. Crim). Nashville: Abingdon, 1963, 1976.

Freedman, David Noel et al., eds. *The Anchor Bible Dictionary [ABD].* New York: Doubleday, 1992.

———, ed. *Eerdmans Dictionary of the Bible.* Grand Rapids, Mich.: Eerdmans, 2000.

Metzger, Bruce M., and Michael D. Coogan, eds. *The Oxford Companion to the Bible.* New York: Oxford University, 1993.

Mills, Watson E., ed. *Mercer Dictionary of the Bible.* Macon, Ga.: Mercer University, 1990.

Concise Commentaries

Anderson, Bernhard W., ed. *The Books of the Bible.* 2 vols. New York: Scribner's, 1989.

Brown, Raymond E., et al., eds. *The New Jerome Biblical Commentary.* Englewood Cliffs, N.J.: Prentice Hall, 1990.

Laymon, Charles M., ed. *The Interpreter's One Volume Commentary on the Bible.* Nashville: Abingdon, 1971.

Mays, James L., ed. *The HarperCollins Bible Commentary.* San Francisco: HarperSanFrancisco, 2000.

Newsom, Carol A., and Sharon H. Ringe, eds. *The Women's Bible Commentary.* Exp. ed. Louisville: Westminster John Knox, 1998.

Other Useful Reference Works.
These more general encyclopedias have a large number of articles on the Bible and related topics.

Eliade, Mircea et al., eds. *The Encyclopedia of Religion.* New York: Macmillan, 1987.

Roth, Cecil, ed. *Encyclopaedia Judaica.* New York: Macmillan, 1972.

Bibliographies

Fitzmyer, Joseph A. *An Introductory Bibliography for the Study of Scripture.* 3d ed. Rome: Pontifical Biblical Institute, 1990.

Harrington, Daniel J. *The New Testament: A Bibliography.* Wilmington, Del.: Michael Glazier, 1985.

Stuart, Douglas. *Old Testament Exegesis: A Primer for Students and Pastors.* 2d ed. Philadelphia: Westminster, 1984.

Zannoni, Arthur E. *The Old Testament: A Bibliography.* Collegeville, Minn.: Liturgical, 1992.

INDEX